CREATIVE DAOISM

Daoism series

CREATIVE DAOISM

Monica Esposito

UNIVERSITYMEDIA
2016

Copyright © 2016 UniversityMedia, Wil / Paris
www.universitymedia.org
All rights reserved.

Printed on acid-free and lignin-free paper

Library of Congress Cataloging-in-Publication Data
Esposito, Monica 1962–2011
    Creative Daoism. / Monica Esposito
    p. cm. — (UniversityMedia, Daoism Series)
    Includes bibliographical references and index
    ISBN 978-3-906000-05-3 (acid-free paper)
    1. China—Religion—17th century—18th century—19th century.
    2. Daoism—Taoism—Quanzhen—Longmen—History.
    3. Qing Dynasty—Society—Intellectual life.
    4. Religion—Daoism—Buddhism.
    5. History—China—17th century—18th century—19th century.
I. Title.

ISBN 978-3-906000-04-6 (hardcover, 2013)
ISBN 978-3-906000-05-3 (paperback, 2016)

Dr. Monica Esposito (1962–2011)

Contents

ABBREVIATIONS IV
LIST OF FIGURES VI
LIST OF TABLES VIII
EDITOR'S PREFACE IX
INTRODUCTION: Min Yide and the Daoist Vatican 1

PART ONE: CREATION OF LINEAGE

I.1: Longmen Daoism's Apostle Peter: Zhao Daojian 17
     Zhao Daojian according to the *Jingai xinden* (19th century) 20
     Zhao Daojian according to the *Baiyun xianbiao* (late 19th century) 23
     Zhao Daojian according to 13th-century Quanzhen hagiographers 26
I.2: Longmen's Seven Patriarchs and the invention of precepts transmission 37
     First Patriarch Zhao Daojian and the Longmen generational poem 39
     Second Patriarch Zhang Dechun (14th century) and his orthodoxy 43
     Third Patriarch Chen Tongwei (14th c.) and early Ming Longmen 48
     Fourth Patriarch Zhou Xuanpu (15th c.) and the split into two transmission lineages 50
     Fifth Patriarch Zhang Jingding (15th century) 54
     Sixth Patriarch Zhao Zhensong (d. 1628) 57
     Seventh Patriarch Wang Changyue (d. 1680) and his reform 60
I.3: The two faces of Eighth Patriarch Tan Shoucheng (d. 1689?) 71
I.4: The mystery of Ninth Patriarch Zhan Tailin (d. 1712) 79
     Conclusion: The myth of Longmen revival 87

PART TWO: CREATION OF ORDINATION

II.1: The invention of the Quanzhen Ur-Vinaya tradition 91
II.2: The Three Stages of Precepts 107
      Chuzhen jielü and the Initial Refuges and Precepts 121
      Zhongji jie and the 300 Intermediate Precepts 126
II.3: The search for the 10 Perfect Precepts 131
      The *Tianxian dajie* set of Ultimate Precepts 132
II.4: The Manufacture of Quanzhen Ordination 155
      Conclusion 171

PART THREE: CREATION OF CANON

III.1: The *Daozang jiyao*'s invented and true editors 177
  Three main theories about the history of the Canon 179
  The wrong attribution to Peng Dingqiu or Peng Wenqin 182
  The discovery of Jiang Yuanting's Canon in Jiangnan 187
  Ding Fubao and his Index to Jiang Yuanting's *Daozang jiyao* 193
  Two kinds of extant editions of Jiang Yuanting's *Daozang jiyao* 196
III.2: Editor Jiang Yuanting's work and inspiration 201
  The editor Jiang Yuanting alias Jiang Yupu 205
  Jiang Yuanting's spirit writing altar: beliefs and aspirations 207
  The central role of Lü Dongbin and his revelation 211
  A new Canon, quintessence of the genuine path of inner alchemy 215
III.3: The Qing Canon's two main editions 219
  The early 19th-century Jiaqing edition ("Old" *Daozang jiyao*) 221
  The early 20th-century Chongkan edition ("New" *Daozang jiyao*) ... 225
III.4: The Three Teachings in the new *Daozang jiyao* Canon 231
  New Scriptures in the Chongkan and the Three Teachings 241
III.5: Legitimacy and Canonization 249

PART FOUR: CREATION OF SALVATION

IV.1: The *Secret of the Golden Flower* 263
  Content of the *Golden Flower* 267
  Major editions of the *Golden Flower* 272
  Version 1: Shao Zhilin's edition and the Taiyi lineage 274
  Version 2: Chen Mou's edition and the Jinhua lineage 280
  Versions 3 & 4. Jiang Yuanting's edition and the Tianxian lineage 284
IV.2: The *Golden Flower*'s Longmen transplant 293
  The Altar of Mount Jingai lineage and its tradition 297
  The Lineage for Healing the World 299
IV.3: The *Golden Flower* in the twentieth century 305
  The *Golden Flower* in the West 309
  Short annotated *Golden Flower* bibliography 313

BIBLIOGRAPHY OF PRIMARY SOURCES 317
BIBLIOGRAPHY OF SECONDARY SOURCES 329
LIST OF PUBLICATIONS BY MONICA ESPOSITO 350
INDEX 359

Abbreviations

BYGZ *Baiyun guan zhi (Hakuunkan shi)* 白雲觀志 (A Gazetteer of the Abbey of White Clouds) by Oyanagi Shigeta 小柳司氣太. Tokyo: Tōhō bunka gakuin Tōkyō kenkyūjo, 1934.

BYXB *Baiyun xianbiao* 白雲仙表 or *Chart of the Immortals of the White Clouds*, 1847. Reprint in vol. 31:373ff. of the *Zangwai daoshu* 藏外道書 (Daoist Texts not included in the Daoist Canon) edited by Hu Daojing 胡道靜 et al. Chengdu: Bashu shushe, 1992. Also referred to as *Immortals' Chart*.

CK *Chongkan Daozang jiyao* 重刊道藏輯要, 25 vols. Taipei: Kaozheng, 1971.

DJYL *Changchun daojiao yuanliu* 長春道教源流 (Origins and Development of the Daoist Teachings of [Qiu] Changchun), 1879, by Chen Minggui 陳銘珪 (1824–1881). Reprint in ZWDS 31:1–157.

DTYL *Daotong yuanliu zhi* 道統源流志 (Gazetteer on the Origins and Development of Orthodox Daoism) by Yan Liuqian 嚴六謙 (*hao*: Zhuangyan jushi 莊嚴居士). Wuxi: Zhonghua yinshuju, 1929. Also referred to as *Gazetteer of Daoist Origins*.

DZ *Daozang* 道藏 (the numbers are given according to Kristofer Schipper and Franciscus Verellen eds., *The Taoist Canon*. Chicago: Chicago University Press, 2004.

DZJHL *Daozang jinghua lu* 道藏精華錄 (Record of Quintessence of the Daoist Canon) by Ding Fubao 丁福保 (*zi*: Shouyi zi 守一子, 1874–1952). Reprint in 2 vols. (*shang* /*xia*). Zhejiang guji chubanshe, 1989.

DZJY *Chongkan Daozang jiyao* 重刊道藏輯要 (Reedited Epitome of the Daoist Canon) by Yan Yonghe 閻永和, Peng Hanran 彭瀚然 and He Longxiang 賀龍驤. Chengdu: Erxian an 二仙庵, 1906. Reprint in 25 vols. Taipei: Xinwenfeng, 1977.

DZXB *Daozang xubian* 道藏續編 (Supplementary Collection of the Daoist Canon), 4 vols., by Min Yide 閔一得(1758–1836). Wuxing: Jingai cangban, 1834. Photolithographic edition by Ding Fubao 丁福保 (*zi*: Shou yi zi 守一子, 1874–1952). Shanghai: Yixue shuju. Reprint Beijing: Haiyang 1989.

JGXD   (*Chongkan*) *Jingai xindeng* 金蓋心燈 ([Re-edition of the] Transmission of the Mind-Lamp of Mt. Jingai), 10 vols., by Min Yide (1758–1836). Wuxing: Yunchao, Gu Shuyinlou cangban, 1876 (1st ed. 1821). Reprint in ZWDS 31. Also referred to as *Mind-Lamp*.

JYDT   *Longmen zhengzong Jueyun benzhi daotong xinchuan* 龍門正宗覺雲本支道統薪傳, compiled by Lu Yongzhi 陸永銘 in 1927. Reprint in ZWDS 3: 464–65. Also referred to as *Jueyun benzhi daotong*.

SKQS   *Wenyuan ge Siku quanshu* 文淵閣四庫全書 (Complete Texts in Four Repositories, 1773–1782), 1500 vols. by Yong Rong 永瑢 et al. Edited by Zhu Jianmin 朱建民. Taipei: Shangwu yinshuguan, 1986.

T   *Taishō shinshū daizōkyō* 大正新修大藏經, 85 vols., edited by J. Takakusu and K. Watanabe. Tokyo: Taishō issaikyō kankōkai, 1924–32. Also referred to as *Taishō*.

TSLM   *Taishang lümai Longmen zhengzong* 太上律脈龍門正宗 (1919, hand-scroll manuscript conserved at Baiyun guan, also known as *Longmen chuanjie puxi* 龍門傳戒譜系). Also referred to as *Taishang lümai*.

YLCS   *Gu Shuyinlou cangshu* 古書隱樓藏書 (Collection from the Ancient Hidden Pavilion of Books), 14 vols., by Min Yide (1758–1836). Wuxing: Jingai Chunyang gong cangban, 1904. Reprint in ZWDS 10:150–721.

ZHDZ   *Zhonghua Daozang* 中華道藏, 49 vols. Beijing: Huaxia, 2004.

ZWDS   *Zangwai daoshu* 藏外道書 (Daoist Texts not included in the Daoist Canon) edited by Hu Daojing 胡道靜 et al. Chengdu: Bashu shushe, 1992 (vol: 1–20); 1994 (vol. 21–36).

ZZ   *Shinsan Dai Nihon Zokuzōkyō* 新纂大日本續藏經 90 vols. (Tokyo: Kokusho Kankōkai, 1975–1989). Also referred to as *Zokuzōkyō*.

List of Figures

Fig. 1: Portrait of Min Yide from the *Gu shuyinlou zangshu*.................XII
Fig. 2: Entrance gate to the Baiyun guan compound in Beijing................4
Fig. 3: Laolütang (Old Vinaya Hall) at Baiyun guan..................................7
Fig. 4: Qiu Chuji on wall of Founder's Hall, Baiyun guan.......................9
Fig. 5: Lineage Chart of Early Daoist Longmen Traditions....................16
Fig. 6: Zhao Daojian and Qiu Chuji in *Xuanfeng qinghui tu* 32
Fig. 7: Table of Contents of j. 5 of *Xuanfeng qinghui tu* 33
Fig. 8: Title page of Min Yide's *Mind-Lamp of Mount Jingai* 36
Fig. 9: Chan's "Second Patriarch" Huike and Bodhidharma..................45
Fig. 10: Wang Changyue Portrait in Baiyun guan 68
Fig. 11: Sanctuary and hermitage on Mt. Wudang...................................74
Fig. 11: Intermediate Precepts *Zhongji jie* (Hackmann 1931)..................95
Fig. 12: Three-tiered altar, *Shishi yuanliu yinghua shiji* (1486) 118
Fig. 13: Ordination certificate from Beijing's Baiyun guan (1931) 130
Fig. 14: Invocation of the Wondrous Spirit of the Northern Dipper ... 142
Fig. 15: Qiuzu dian (Hall of Patriarch Qiu Chuji) at Baiyun guan........ 148
Fig. 16: Ordination Platform at Baiyun guan 153
Fig. 17: Precinct of Qingyanggong temple (Chengdu)........................... 178
Fig. 18: *Daozang jiyao* original printing blocks, Qingyanggong........... 178
Fig. 19: *Chongkan Daozang jiyao* printing blocks at Qingyanggong..... 192
Fig. 20: *Daozang jiyao* Table of Contents, Jinbun version 197
Fig. 21: *Daozang jiyao* Table of Contents, Pelliot version 197
Fig. 22: Old *Daozang jiyao* at Taiwan National Library, Taipei 199
Fig. 23: Lü Dongbin in the old *Daozang jiyao* 200
Fig. 24: Two major *Daozang jiyao* editions juxtaposed........................... 203
Fig. 25: Dragon-headed tip of a spirit writing instrument 208

Fig. 26: Spirit writing altar (1884) 213
Fig. 27: "Flying Dragon" spirit writing instrument on altar board 214
Fig. 28: Author and editor of this book with spirit writing team 214
Fig. 29: Lü Dongbin who ordered the compilation of *Daozang jiyao* .. 218
Fig. 30: *Hezhetu* in old *Daozang jiyao* (Sichuan Provincial Library) 220
Fig. 31: Yan Yanfeng's *Daozang jiyao* (Sichuan Provincial Library) 223
Fig. 32: Printing bureau of the *Chongkan Daozang jiyao* (Chengdu) 229
Fig. 33: Newly printed fascicles of the *Chongkan Daozang jiyao* 229
Fig. 34: The *Chongkan Daozang jiyao* conventions 233
Fig. 35: Yongzheng edict in the *Chongkan Daozang jiyao* 234
Fig. 36: Recorded Sayings of Emperor Yongzheng 236
Fig. 37: Recorded Sayings of Zhang Boduan 236
Fig. 38: Recorded Sayings of Zhuhong 236
Fig. 39: Dharma assembly in Yongzheng's Preface 237
Fig. 40: Confucians, Buddhists, Daoists in Yongzheng's Preface 237
Fig. 41: Three Teachings in He Longxiang's Postface 239
Fig. 42: Opening pages of *Chongkan Daozang jiyao* (Hong Kong) 240
Fig. 43: Sample of new and old *Daozang jiyao* prints 240
Fig. 44: Frontispiece of *Daozang jiyao* with the "Three Pure Ones" 248
Fig. 45: Frontispiece of the *Chongkan Daozang jiyao* 249
Fig. 46: Canonization modalities in *Daozang* and *Daozang jiyao* 251
Fig. 47: Canonization modality in *Chongkan Daozang jiyao* 256
Fig. 48: Lü Dongbin image in *Lüzu quanshu* 262
Fig. 49: Jiang Yuanting's edition of the "Golden Flower" 266
Fig. 50: Min Yide's *Daozang xubian* 296
Fig. 51: The Daoist temple complex on Mt. Jingai 297
Fig. 52: Overview of the textual history of the *Golden Flower* 304

List of Tables

Table 1: List of Longmen "orthodox" Vinaya Patriarchs from the 7th to the 17th generation..................86

Table 2: Main categories and subcategories of the old *Daozang jiyao*..... 224

Table 3: Main categories and subcategories of *Chongkan* and reprints... 228

Table 4: Main categories and subcategories of scriptures added in the *Chongkan Daozang jiyao* and the Three Teachings...................... 243

Table 5: Contents and arrangement of the first four versions of the *Secret of the Golden Flower* text.................................290-291

Table 6: Changes in the first four *Secret of the Golden Flower* versions (1775 to 1852) 292

Editor's Preface

Ever since my wife Monica Esposito—after having published two books in Italian (1995, 1997) and her Ph.D. thesis (1993) in French— had begun to publish in the English language in 1998, I assisted her as copy editor. But editing the present book was a different and more difficult task. Monica had always handed me articles she considered more or less ready for publication; and my job consisted in spotting errors, polishing her English style, providing suggestions for improvement, and making sure that all citations were duly referenced in footnotes and bibliography. In short, my role was that of a copy editor whose corrections and suggestions could be accepted or rejected by the author who then incorporated the changes as she deemed appropriate.

When Monica succumbed on March 10 of 2011, one day prior to the terrible Tōhoku earthquake, to pulmonary emboly at the young age of 48, she was just inputting the last revisions to the second part of this book into her computer. It was her habit to present first drafts of papers at conferences, to publish revised versions (often in Japanese or Chinese) in journals read by specialists, and to keep improving such published versions, as her research progressed, for later use in books.

When she began to write this book in 2008, she first reworked parts of her French Ph.D. thesis (1993) and of subsequent articles (2001, 2004a) and incorporated this in Part One.

A first draft of Part Two was presented at a Daoism conference in China and published in Chinese (2011b), whereupon Monica produced a much enlarged English version that she planned to first publish in a scientific journal and subsequently revise it for use in Part Two of the book she had entitled *Creative Daoism*. This part was, as mentioned above, finished just before death struck, as was the Introduction.

The first three chapters of Part Three were first drafted as Chinese conference papers (2009a, 2010a, 2010b) and took more ample form in an article Monica published in Japanese as well as Chinese (2007b, 2010b). As basis for the fourth and fifth chapter of this part she used her revised English version of another article published in Japanese (2011a). She intended to also integrate arguments from an article whose revisions she finished a few months before her passing: "The Invention of a Quanzhen Canon: The Wondrous Fate of the Daozang jiyao." This article has in the meantime appeared in *Quanzhen Daoism in Modern Chinese History and Society* (edited by Xun Liu and Vincent Goossaert. Berkeley: Institute of East Asian Studies, 2014: 44–77) and should be read in conjunction with Part Three.

Part Four contains the most recent revision of the English text of an article Monica had first published in Japanese (2004b, 2007a) along with summaries and tables that she had produced for her model entry on the *Secret of the Golden Flower* 金華宗旨 distributed in 2010 to over sixty Chinese, Japanese and Western collaborators in her International Daozang jiyao Project. Her summaries stemming from these guidelines are included in grey boxes.

The author's habit of correcting printouts of published and unpublished versions of her work burdened the editor with the complicated task of dealing not only with computer files but also with handwritten revisions on printouts whose dating was at times unclear. Moreover, the author's sudden death had prevented her from revising the Introduction, adding a survey of recent research on Qing Daoism, including a section on Lü Dongbin, unifying and streamlining bibliographic references, and welding the different parts and arguments more tightly together along the thematic line indicated in her Introduction.

Since sections of this book still had the form of articles with bibliographic references suited to that format, full references are frequently repeated in the footnotes of the book's four parts. I decided that it did not make sense to eliminate such repetitions since each part can also be studied independently and because it is common academic practice to assign chapters or parts rather than entire books for study. Furthermore, removing detailed references would have forced readers, as is common, to keep searching for information in the bibliography. The footnotes were thus left in "journal format," as the author had written them. However, as editor I added (in curly brackets) chapter and page information to this book's companion volume, *Facets of Qing Daoism*, which contains five of Monica's major articles. Since the author was so eager to present her work not only to Western scholars but especially also to specialists and students of Daoism in China, Japan, and Korea, she consistently included the original Chinese text along with her English translations. Furthermore, she usually included Chinese characters for names of persons, places, and titles of texts. When she occsionally failed to do so, or when she omitted Pinyin transliterations, Chinese characters or

Pinyin readings were added by the editor. Eventual mistakes of this kind are thus to be blamed on the editor rather than the author.

The author had prepared a folder with numerous illustrations for this book and sent some to the graphic artist in charge of cover design, but she had not yet inserted some of them into the text. It fell to me as editor to appropriately place such illustrations and tables and to supply references or cross-references to them in the text. In formatting and layout, the aim was to produce a book that lives up to the author's often-stated preferences: a book with footnotes rather than endnotes, with Chinese texts as well as their English translation, with Chinese characters for all important names and terms, with explicit and precise literature references, and with an index that facilitates locating not merely names of places and persons but also themes, titles of Chinese texts, and Chinese technical terms. Needless to say, shortcomings in these endeavors are due to the editor rather than the author.

Readers who did not have the chance to meet the author in person, and also those who did, are welcome to enjoy her wonderful smile and a few minutes of her Taiji practice that I happened to film on Riederalp in the Swiss Alps in the summer of 2001, set to symphonic music by Bruckner (search for "Monica Esposito Universitymedia" on youtube.com).

Her sudden death prevented Monica from expressing her profound gratitude to many people in a preface to this book. She would certainly not have failed to thank her father Dr. Carlo Esposito, her mother Iris Barzaghi, her beloved sister Adriana, her late teacher Prof. Isabelle Robinet, Professors Kunio Mugitani and Christian Wittern of Kyoto University and Monica's assistants at that university's Institute of Humanistic Studies, Alexander Huwyler whom she put in charge of cover design, the five dozen collaborators who agreed to join her International Daozang jiyao Project, Prof. Lai Chi-tim of the Chinese University of Hong Kong who now directs this research project, and to a probably page-long list of friends and colleagues in China, Japan, Taiwan, and the West.

This paperback edition of 2016 is substantially identical to the hardcover edition of 2013; apart from a few corrections, the only major change is the inclusion of a comprehensive bibliography of Monica Esposito's publications.

Paris, March 10, 2016   The editor, Urs App

Fig. 1: Portrait of Min Yide from the *Gu shuyinlou zangshu*

Introduction

Min Yide and Modern Daoism's Vatican

When we mention Min Yide 閔一得 (1748/58–1836), a Daoist master of the Qing dynasty, we cannot but think of his association with the so-called *Longmen pai* 龍門派 or "School of the Dragon Gate."[1] This Daoist school, commonly classified as a branch of Daoism's Quanzhen 全真 order, has a relatively short history. In recent times its popularity has been enhanced thanks to the interest shown by newly converted adepts, Chinese religious officials, and scholars in East and West for the "older Quanzhen tradition" to which the Longmen pai allegedly belongs. The beginning of Longmen's modern popularity can be traced back to the 1980s when, with the re-opening of Daoist monasteries in China's Southern Jiangnan region, Longmen appeared to be the dominant Daoist lineage.

At the time of my pilgrimages to the most famous Daoist Mountains in the 1980s I was able to watch Longmen's sunrise. Every Daoist temple that was reopening its doors claimed, in the words of its religious officials (who were still dressed in Mao-style) to belong to "Longmen." Helped by Deng Xiaoping's "reform and opening" 改革開放, a more tolerant attitude towards religious life and local culture gradually took root. Under the Long-

---

[1] The correct dates of Min Yide are still subject to investigation. See Xie Zhengqiang 謝正強, "Min Yide xiaogao erze" 閔一得小考二則 in *Zhongguo daojiao* 中國道教 2004/1, pp. 46–47); Wang Zongyao 王宗耀, "Min Yide shengnian kaoyi" 閔一得生年考疑 in *Zhongguo daojiao* 中國道教 2005 (6), pp. 39–40; Wu Yakui 吳亞魁, *Jiangnan Quanzhen daojiao* 江南全真道教; and Monica Esposito, *La Porte du Dragon—L'école Longmen du Mont Jin'gai et ses pratiques alchimiques d'après le Daozang xubian*, Ph.D. diss. Paris VII, 1993 / PDF 2012. For a short analysis of the different biographies on Min Yide, see Monica Esposito, "Shindai dōkyō to mikkyō: Ryūmon seijiku shinshū 清代道教と密教—龍門西竺心宗. In *Sankyō kōhō rongyō* 三教交涉論叢, edited by K. Mugitani (Kyoto: Kyōto Daigaku Jinbun Kagaku Kenkyūjo 京都大学人文科学研究所): 287–338 {revised English version in Chapter 5 of Esposito, *Facets of Qing Daoism*}.

men label, Daoist temples were allowed to recuperate their lost memory and to restore their tradition. Even when I asked the new officials of Suzhou's Xuanmiaoguan 玄妙觀—a famous temple associated with the Celestial Masters of Daoism's Zhengyi 正一 (Orthodox Unity) tradition—to which tradition they belonged, they promptly answered to me "Longmen."

During my first stay in China I became intrigued by this phenomenon, which is why I embarked on my research on Longmen history: visiting sites connected with it, copying stone inscriptions, interviewing priests, studying texts, and eventually submitting my doctoral thesis in 1993. The phenomenon of "Longmen fashion" or "Longmen indoctrination" was taking root in the China of the 1980s and 1990s side by side with what came to be known as "Qigong fever" 氣功熱.[2] While "Longmen" was employed as a kind of generic label for orthodox Daoist temples, "Qigong" was used for denoting and legitimizing all kinds of practices that had previously been banned as superstitious. Hypnosis or trance-like techniques, meditative exercises inspired by Buddhist, Daoist or Confucian traditions, gymnastics or yoga-like techniques, martial arts ... everything now was baptized "Qigong." What I used to call *taijiquan* (T'ai-chi), *wushu* (martial arts), or *yoga* appeared in a brand-new package named "Taiji qigong" 太極氣功, "Qigong wushu" 氣功武術, or "Quiet qigong" 靜氣功. The Longmen and Qigong trends even seemed to merge since I recall hearing the expression "Longmen qigong" — another package with an interesting label![3]

Religious scriptures, classics of inner alchemy, Tibetan Buddhist manuals of practice, and all kinds of esoteric texts whose circulation had been strictly prohibited during Mao and post-Mao years were filling, under the label and cover of Qigong, the bookshop shelves of the People's Republic of China. Qigong gathered a great deal of attention in the Chinese official press. Communist cadres converted to Qigong, pro-Qigong Chinese intellectuals and scientists gave interviews, Qigong schools and Qigong associations proliferated, and everywhere Qigong practitioners seemed to sprout like mushrooms. Scholarly studies and books on Qigong traced its origins back to the remote past. Continuity with old traditions was increasingly asserted and justified by the discovery of occurrences of "Qigong"-like terms

---

[2] For a study on this phenomenon and its different phases see David Palmer, *Qigong Fever: Body, Science, and Utopia in China* (New York: Columbia University Press, 2007).

[3] Monica Esposito, *Il Qigong, la nuova scuola taoista delle cinque respirazioni* (Padova: Muzzio, 1995).

in early sources including stone inscriptions.⁴ On this seemingly solid basis, modern Qigong masters erected wonderful genealogies. Some traced their inherited tradition to famous patriarchs and saints like Bodhidharma, Lü Dongbin, Zhang Sanfeng, or Qiu Chuji, while others claimed to be in direct contact with gods or entire assemblies of Bodhisattvas.

Today, scholars see Qigong as the product of a well-defined period in modern Chinese history. Historians tend to analyze it in terms of its religious creativity, but some also show interest in political issues including persecution, secret societies, etc.⁵ However, as we turn our gaze to older traditions, we are inclined to apportion more authority and to assume solid historicity. The more ancient the traditions, the more reliable they tend to appear to us—even more so, of course, when sources are literally written in stone.

From a broader perspective, "qigong-like phenomena" are part of the history of world religions and of all peoples' search for the origins of their culture and identity. They show us that claims of orthodoxy are often motivated by a need to establish historical continuity with an idealized past and with some glorious school or tradition of antiquity featuring famous masters, practices, techniques, etc. Such traditions tend to equip newly invented phenomena with genealogies that reach back to eminent ancestors or movements by reenacting a set of norms of behavior that supposedly have ancient origins.⁶

---

4   I refer to the jade inscription *Xingqi yupei ming* 行氣玉佩銘. For a study on Qigong as related to ancient techniques of longevity see for instance Catherine Despeux, *La moelle du phénix rouge: santé et longue vie dans la Chine du XVIe siècle* (Paris: Guy Trédaniel, 1988), p. 9. In her study Despeux emphasizes that the first reference to the term "qigong" was already found in the work of the Jingming Patriarch Xu Xun 許遜. Miura Kunio 三浦邦夫 found a very early occurrence in Sima Chengzhen 司馬承禎's *Fuqi jingyi lun* 服氣精義論 used in the sense of "applications of *qi* 氣 之為功." Miura underlines that the combination of the characters *qi* and *gong* as a technical compound "cannot be dated to before the Ming dynasty. It occurs in the *Jingming zongjiao lu* 淨明宗教錄 attributed to Xu Xun." Miura Kunio, "The Revival of Qi: Qigong in Contemporary China," in *Taoist Meditation and Longevity Techniques*, ed. Livia Kohn (Ann Arbor: The University of Michigan, 1989): 331–362, in particular p. 341. See also the recent work by Livia Kohn, *Chinese Healing Exercises. The Tradition of Daoyin* (Honolulu: University of Hawai'i Press, 2008).

5   See the web pages of Barend ter Haar on "Qigong movements" (http://website.leidenuniv.nl/~haarbjter/chinPRCbib.html), and "Falun Gong" (http://website.leidenuniv.nl/~haarbjter/falun.htm); consulted in spring of 2010.

6   See Eric Hobsbawn, "Introduction: Inventing Traditions," in *The Invention of Tradition*, ed. Eric Hobsbawn and Terence Ranger (Cambridge: Cambridge University

As we will see, the history of Min Yide and his work show a surprisingly similar pattern. Min Yide invented and attempted to establish continuity with a suitable historical past in order to bolster the authority of his own local tradition, thus presenting it in conformity with dignified protocol as part of well-established and time-honored Daoist orthodoxy. This Daoist orthodoxy was to obtain the name of "Longmen" (龍門, "Dragon Gate"), and its headquarters were to be established at the famous Baiyun guan 白雲觀: the White Cloud Temple in Beijing, modern Daoism's Vatican.[7]

Fig. 2: Entrance gate to the Baiyun guan compound in Beijing (1983)

Press, 1983): 1–14, and articles in that book discussing various inventions in European culture. See also John Henderson, *The Construction of Orthodoxy and Heresy: Neo-Confucian, Islamic, Jewish, and Early Christian Patterns* (New York: University of State Press, 1998).

[7] I use the term "Daoist Vatican" for the Baiyun guan to highlight its status as *locus* of a central religious authority and institution. Baiyun guan was in fact described in relatively recent sources as the center of ordination for all Daoists, including the Zhengyi 正一 orthodoxy of the Celestial Masters (*tianshi* 天師). See Oyanagi Shigeta 小柳司氣太, *Hakuunkan shi* 白雲觀志 (Tokyo: Tōhō bunka gakuin Tōkyō kenkyūsho, 1934): fascicle 2, pp. 70–89 and fascicle 3, pp. 91–121. See also the descriptions of the Baiyun guan furnished by Vincent Goossaert, *The Taoists of Peking, 1800–1949* (Cambridge: Harvard University Press, 2007): 134–168.

Every "Vatican" is in need of the equivalent of "apostolic" legitimacy involving a history of certified transmission of a founder's "original, genuine" teaching, and this is exactly what Min Yide supplied in the form of his Daoist Lamp History: the *Mind-Lamp of Mount Jingai* (*Jingai xindeng* 金蓋心燈; from now on abbreviated as JGXD or *Mind-Lamp*). Inspired by Chan Buddhism's Lamp Histories,[8] Min Yide's *Mind-Lamp* of 1821 is the first extant work to narrate in explicit genealogical terms the origin and development of Longmen as a Daoist lineage (*zong* 宗, in the ancient Chinese sense of "ancestor line" or "clan") and mapping out its "family tree."[9] Starting with the Ancestor of the Dao 道祖 (Laozi) and the Lineage Master of the Dao 道宗 (Lü Dongbin 呂洞賓), this pedigree conveyed a distinctive identity to Longmen Daoism and still has this function today. Moreover, Min Yide presents in his *Mind-Lamp* a sequence of detailed biographies of Longmen masters active in Jiangnan. They are a remarkable source for investigating the Daoism of the Ming and Qing dynasties.[10]

Min Yide is said to have published the *Mind-Lamp* in eight fascicles (*juan*) for the first time in 1821 in the *Gu Shuyinlou cangshu* 古書隱樓藏書 at Mt. Jingai 金蓋山 (Huzhou 湖州, Zhejiang). Because the woodblocks were later destroyed, Shen Bingcheng 沈秉成 (1823–1895), a second-generation disciple of Min Yide, reprinted Min's book in 1873.[11] The

---

[8] For the evolution and role of Chan Buddhist "lamp histories" that evidently served Min Yide as a model, see numerous pioneering articles in the Collected Works of the eminent Chan historian Yanagida Seizan 柳田聖山 (2000, 2001).

[9] As in the case of Chan 禪, an interesting question is to know how and when Longmen became a *zong* 宗. On the term *zong* in Chinese Buddhism see Stanley Weinstein, "The Schools of Chinese Buddhism," in Joseph M. Kitagawa, ed., *Buddhism and Asian History* (New York: Macmillan, 1989): 257–267. For the specific context of Chan see T. Griffith Foulk, "The Ch'an Tsung in Medieval China: School, Lineage, or What?" *The Pacific World*, New Series 8 (1992):18–31. See also note 93.

[10] For more details see Monica Esposito, "The Longmen School and its Controversial History during the Qing Dynasty," in John Lagerwey, *Religion and Chinese Society*, vol. 2, 621–698, especially 622–625 {Chapter 2 of Esposito, *Facets of Qing Daoism*}.

[11] Shen Bingcheng 沈秉成, preface entitled "Chongkan Jingai xindeng xu" 重刊金蓋心燈序 to the *Jingai xindeng* 金蓋心燈; reprint in *Zangwai daoshu* 藏外道書 vol. 31, p. 158. Shen is also the author of one of Min Yide's biographies plagiarized from the one compiled by Yang Weikun 揚維崑. See Monica Esposito, "Shindai dōkyō to mikkyō," pp. 304–306 {revised English version in Chapter 5 of Esposito, *Facets of Qing Daoism*, here pp. 265–8}. See also Wang Zongyu 王宗昱, "Historical Materials for the Quanzhen Daoism in the Wuxing Area." In *Scriptures, Schools and Forms of Practices in Daoism: A Berlin Symposium*, ed. by P. Andersen and F. Reiter (Wiesbaden: Harrassowitz, 2005): 215–232.

biographies of the *Mind-Lamp* include commentaries by the well-known scholars Bao Tingbo 鮑廷博 (1728–1814) and Bao Kun 鮑錕 (fl. 1814). For his comments, Bao Tingbo is said to have consulted no less than fifty-two works which he listed at the beginning of the *Mind-Lamp* under the title *Jingai xindeng zhengkao wenxian lu* 金蓋心燈徵考文獻錄.

In addition to the biographies of Jiangnan masters, the *Mind-Lamp* is also the fundamental source for the presentation of the first seven generations of patriarchs that are recognized as representatives of the Longmen orthodox lineage (Longmen zhengzong 龍門正宗) at Beijing's Baiyun guan, at its affiliated monasteries, and in subsequent Longmen branches and sub-branches.[12] Indeed, this lineage is also reproduced in more recent Daoist lamp histories like the 1927 *Longmen zhengzong Jueyun benzhi daotong xinchuan* 龍門正宗覺雲本支道統薪傳; in Daoist biographical records such as the 1848 *Baiyun xianbiao* 白雲仙表, or the 1919 hand-scroll *Taishang lümai Longmen zhengzong* 太上律脈龍門正宗 (also known as *Longmen chuanjie puxi* 龍門傳戒譜系); in ordination materials like the 1874 manuscript *Xuandu lütan weiyi jieke quanbu* 玄都律壇威儀戒科全部 or the 1929 *Daotong yuanliu zhi* 道統源流志; and in monographs such as the *Baiyun guan zhi* (*Hakuunkan shi*) 白雲觀志 compiled in classical Chinese by Oyanagi Shigeta 小柳司気太 (1870–1940), or the *Dōkyō sōrin taiseikyū shi* 道教叢林太清宮志 by Igarashi Kenryū 五十嵐賢隆 (1906–1985).

From the Qing dynasty onward, the list of the first seven Longmen patriarchs (as publicized in the *Mind-Lamp*) came to represent for all ordained Daoist priests the orthodox lineage of Longmen abbots of the Baiyun guan, a lineage that was gradually adopted by other Daoist public monasteries. This list also represents the orthodox ancestry of the Longmen sub-branches in Jiangnan that had allegedly spread throughout China after the advent of the seventh patriarch Wang Changyue 王常月 alias Wang Kunyang 王崑陽 (?–1680). Similar to Chan Buddhism's "Lamp Histories," the *Mind-Lamp* was given the vital task of conveying an official genealogy. The creation of its own ancestry was designed to confirm not only the noble pedigree of the institutionalized Longmen order at the capital, but even more to legitimize its local lineage of Jingaishan and the various Jiangnan Longmen

---

[12] See below. For earlier studies of the biographies of these seven legendary Longmen patriarchs see Monica Esposito, *La Porte du Dragon*, and "The Longmen School and its controversial History during the Qing Dynasty": 625–654 {Chapter 2 of Esposito, *Facets of Qing Daoism*}.

branches. For that purpose a majestic genealogical edifice was construed in the early nineteenth century with the help of Confucian scholars and Longmen disciples under the guidance of Min Yide.

Portrayed as a retired Confucian scholar who converted to Longmen Daoism at an early age, Min Yide is the key figure in the creation of the self-image of an "orthodox" Longmen in Jiangnan. He depicted Longmen not only as an institutionalized order at the capital with a standardized ordination system (known later as *santan dajie* 三壇大戒) and with established monastic rules, codes of behavior, and liturgy (see Part Two here below), but also as an intellectual and doctrinal tradition capable of producing specific inner alchemical theories on cosmology, self-cultivation, and ethics (see especially Part Four).

Fig. 3: Laolütang 老律堂 (Old Vinaya Hall) at Baiyun guan enshrining the Quanzhen patriarchs (1983)

When we peek behind the façade of this majestic edifice as presented in Min Yide's *Mind-Lamp* and explore its structure and interior, we can discover the original plan of its architects and the models they aspired to. Like chambers that ultimately converge in a single central hall, the biographies of the first seven Longmen patriarchs appear to have been construed in order to apportion the guest of honor from the seventeenth century, Wang Changyue, his central place. Although, judging by the façade, the edifice seems solid, a closer look soon reveals cracks, and on further inspection the walls crumble one by one until only a construction plan is left that reflects the intention of the architects. The seven patriarchs, as portrayed in Min Yide's *Mind-Lamp*, form the pillars of the main edifice that even today houses official Daoism—the government-controlled National Daoist Association—represented by the Baiyun guan in Beijing. Whereas the Vatican in Rome, with very flimsy evidence, is said to have been built on the grave of Saint Peter, the Daoist Vatican or Baiyun guan prides itself to be the grave site of the purported "Longmen founder" Qiu Chuji 邱處機 (1148–1227) and the headquarters of his Quanzhen orthodoxy.[13]

Like the Seven Perfected for Quanzhen, the seven Longmen pillars support an ancestral hall built for the purpose of commemorating the establishment of the Longmen lineage at Baiyun guan.[14] If the Vatican in Rome became the capital of Catholicism based on a mythical "apostolic" transmission, a contrived link of two major founding figures (St. Peter and St. Paul) with the city of Rome, and an invented lineage of early "bishops," Beijing's Baiyun guan turned into the "Daoist Vatican" based on the myth of Longmen foundation via the secret transmission of the "Mind-Lamp" 心燈 from the founding ancestor Qiu Chuji to his first heir Zhao Xujing 趙虛靜 (Zhao Daojian), and through the myth of Longmen Quanzhen restoration via the legendary transmission of public ordinations in the Hall of the Bowl (Botang 缽堂) by its first abbot Wang Changyue 王常月 (d. 1680).[15]

The term "Longmen" refers to a place, namely, the Longmen mountains 龍門山 in Longzhou Prefecture 隴州 (Western Shaanxi) where Qiu Chuji

---

[13] Headquarters of new religious traditions are often erected on the gravesite of their founders. In Japan, the gravesite of Hōnen 法然 (1133–1212) at Kyoto's Chion-in 知恩院 became the center of the Jōdoshū 淨土宗, while the gravesite of Shinran 親鸞 (1173–1263) at Honganji 本願寺 functioned as center for the new establishment of the Jōdo Shinshū 淨土眞宗. See William M. Bodiford, "Remembering Dōgen: Eiheiji and Dōgen Hagiography," *Journal of Japanese Studies* 32.1 (2006): 1–21, especially 8.

[14] On the Baiyun guan Ancestral Hall see Oyanagi Shigeta, *Baiyunguan zhi*, j. 2 (Tokyo: Tōhō bunka gakuin Tokyo kenkyūjo, 1934), pp. 31–48.

[15] A preliminary study of the biographies of Zhao Xujing and Wang Changyue in the *Mind-Lamp* (JGXD) was presented in my PhD thesis, parts of which were later published in "The Longmen School and its Controversial History during the Qing Dynasty," 647–654 {Chapter 2 of Esposito, *Facets of Qing Daoism*, pp. 67–70}. Very recently, the historicity of the transmission of precepts by Wang Changyue at the Baiyun guan has at last also begun to be questioned by Chinese scholars; see for instance the studies by Yin Zhihua 尹志華 in the bibliography.

underwent his ascetic training. Founder Qiu is the most famous among the "Seven Perfected" of the Quanzhen school.[16] Because of his important relationship with the imperial house he was even granted a biography in the official history of the Yuan dynasty (*Yuanshi* j. 202). Since the thirteenth century, Qiu was particularly celebrated for his long and arduous journey to Central Asia to meet Chinggis Khan,[17] an event that today's tourists find depicted in very graphic detail on both lateral walls of the Hall of Founder Qiu in Beijing's Baiyun guan (Fig. 4).

Fig. 4: Qiu Chuji traveling to Central Asia; wall of Founder's Hall, Baiyun guan

Following this meeting, the Quanzhen school of Daoism entered its Golden Age by obtaining an imperial edict granting it exemption from

---

[16] According to most recent sources, each of the Seven Perfected of Quanzhen founded his own school; see Judith M. Boltz, *A Survey of Taoist Literature* (Berkeley: Institute of East Asian Studies University of California, 1987): 279–280, note 172, .

[17] This journey was reported in the *Changchun zhenren xiyouji* (DZ 1429 fasc. 1056) by Li Zhizhang, one of the eighteen disciples who took part in it; see the translation by Arthur Waley: *Travels of an Alchemist: The Journey of the Taoist Ch'ang-ch'un to the Hindukush at the Summons of Chingiz Khan* (London: George Routledge & Sons, Ltd, 1931); see also J. Boltz, *A Survey of Taoist Literature*, 66–68 and 157–59.

taxes and labor. Thus Qiu rose to the position of leader of all native religions and reportedly took charge of all "who leave their families."[18] After his return to Beijing in 1224, Qiu took control of the capital's Tianchang guan 天常觀 (Abbey of Celestial Endurance). Soon afterwards, this abbey received in Qiu's honor the name of Changchun gong 長春宮 (Palace of Perennial Spring). After Qiu's death in 1227 his corpse was buried in a patch of land adjacent to this abbey.[19] An annex was then built in its vicinity by Yin Zhiping 尹志平 (1169–1251), one of Qiu's main disciples, and it was this annex that eventually received the name of Baiyun guan or "White Cloud Abbey."[20]

During the Yuan dynasty (1260–1368) the Baiyun guan became the headquarters of the Quanzhen school, and the Changchun gong assumed the role of center of Qiu Chuji's teachings. However, with the advent of the Ming dynasty only the Baiyun guan survived and a great change took place in this temple: it now fell under the supervision of the Celestial Masters of the Zhengyi order of Daoism. After its destruction at the end of the Yuan era, the Baiyun guan was rebuilt toward the end of the fourteenth century by the Masters of the Zhengyi order. At that time the Zhengyi wielded more influence at the Ming court than the Quanzhen order which appears to have lost its identity and power.[21] However, since the temple had been conceived as a memorial shrine built over Qiu Chuji's grave, the Baiyun abbey's prestigious tradition survived independently of its original Quanzhen affiliation. Due to the presence of Qiu Chuji's tomb, the temple continued to enjoy strong devotion by the people and support by the imperial authorities.

According to Hu Ying 胡濙's stele of 1444, restoration work at the temple began in 1394 following a visit to Qiu Chuji's tomb by the crown prince on the occasion of Qiu's birthday (the 19th day of the first lunar month). Influential masters linked to the Zhengyi order were successively in charge

---

[18] Yao Tao-chung, "Quanzhen: Complete Perfection," in Livia Kohn, ed., *Daoism Handbook* (Leiden: Brill, 2000) 572.

[19] J. Boltz, *A Survey of Taoist Literature*, 66–68 and 127–28 and P. Marsone "Le Baiyun guan de Pékin: épigraphie et histoire," *Sanjiao wenxian* 3, 1999: 79–80.

[20] BYGZ 12–13. As Pierre Marsone ("Le Baiyun guan", 80) notes, the name Baiyun guan in that period referred only to an annex built by Yin Zhiping.

[21] Ishida Kenji 石田憲司, "Mingdai Dōkyō shijō no Zenshin to Seii" 明代道教史上の全真と正一, in Sakai Tadao 酒井忠夫 ed., *Taiwan no shūkyō to Chūgoku bunka* 台湾の宗教と中国文化 (Tokyo: Fukyūsha, 1992):145–185.

of supervising the extensive construction work.²² Once completed, the Baiyun guan became the spiritual training and ordination center of Daoism. Hence, paradoxically, the Quanzhen monastic tradition at the Baiyun guan was at that time rehabilitated thanks to Zhengyi Celestial masters who gradually integrated all kinds of Daoist schools into their order. Under a Zhengyi-approved reorganization, the important Qingwei 清微 master and patriarch of the Jingming zhongxiao dao 淨明忠孝道, Liu Yuanran 劉淵然 (1351–1432), received the Daoist name of Changchun 長春 in honor of the Perfected Qiu Chuji and celebrated the beginning of a new era for the "Zhengyi Qingwei-Quanzhen."²³

Toward the end of the Ming dynasty the Quanzhen order made its reappearance at the Baiyun guan. However, it was only in the late seventeenth century under the official guidance of Wang Changyue 王常月 that this Daoist order gained independence as the new "Longmen lineage."²⁴ In his role as abbot of the Baiyun guan, Wang was recognized as belonging to the seventh Longmen patriarchal generation affiliated with the Quanzhen Northern tradition.

Although many inconsistencies surround Wang Changyue and his work, he is often portrayed as the great "Longmen restorer" who promoted the "Quanzhen renaissance" by reestablishing at the Baiyun guan the Quan-

---

22 "Baiyun guan chongxiu ji" 白雲觀重修記 (1444) by Hu Ying 胡濙 (BYGZ 4.124–28).

23 I call this a new era for the "Zhengyi Qingwei-Quanzhen" since one can regard Liu Yuanran 劉淵然 as a founding patriarch. Indeed, Liu Yuanran received from Emperor Renzong the honorary name of "Changchun zhenren" 長春真人 and was elevated to a second-rank position equalling that of the Zhengyi zhenren 正一真人. He transmitted his Daoist methods to the 43rd Celestial Master Zhang Yuchu 張宇初 (*Mingshi*, j. 299, 7654/12–13 and 7656/9–12) and is known as disciple of Zhao Yizhen 趙宜真 (d. 1382; see K. Schipper, "Master Chao I-chen and the Ch'ing-wei School of Taoism," in Akizuki Kan'ei 秋月觀暎 ed., *Dōkyō to shūkyō bunka* 道教と宗教文化, 715–734, Tokyo: Hirakawa, 1987) from whom he received the heritage of the Golden Elixir of the Northern Lineage (北派金丹之傳). See Ishida Kenji, "Mingdai Dōkyō shijō no Zenshin to Seii," 157; P. Marsone, "Le Baiyun guan," 85 and 98; and Akizuki Kan'ei, *Chūgoku kinsei*, 150–160. Akizuki explains that Liu Yuanran, known as a patriarch of the Jingming zhongxiao dao in the early Ming, was during the reign of Taizu (1368–1398) and Chengzu (1403–1424) also head of the Daolu si, the highest agency in the central government in charge of Daoist affairs. Liu also held the title of *zhenren* (perfect master) that put him on equal footing with the Celestial Master upon whom this title was also conferred by the Ming court (quoted by Richard Shek, "Daoism and orthodoxy", 2004, p. 152).

24 See BYGZ: 24, 141–42, 162–63; JGXD (I, 1.15a–16b, in ZWDS 31:183–84).

zhen monastic liturgy purportedly transmitted without interruption from Quanzhen's founding patriarch Qiu Chuji to Wang. He is associated with the Quanzhen collective ordination procedure of the three altars (*santan dajie* 三壇大戒) that will be discussed in detail in Part Two: the Initial Precepts for Perfection (*chuzhen jie* 初真戒), the Intermediate Precepts for Perfection (*zhongji jie* 中極戒), and the Precepts for Celestial Immortality (*tianxian jie* 天仙戒). This "Quanzhen collective ordination" was allegedly staged by Wang for the first time in 1656 at the Quanzhen public monastery Baiyun guan. Recognized as the Seventh Longmen Patriarch in an invented genealogy, Wang Changyue became the central figure in the foundation myth of the Longmen and served to legitimize various new Daoist local lineages that came to recognize this Quanzhen patriarchal lineage. Thanks to this invention, first set in stone by Min Yide's "Daoist Lamp History" *Jingai xindeng* 金蓋心燈, Wang today occupies the abbot's throne at the Baiyun guan and is seen as the exponent of a glorious Quanzhen past as well as the guarantor of a supposedly continuous "Quanzhen identity."[25]

It is thus evident that Wang Changyue played a pivotal role in the history both of the Baiyun guan and the Longmen tradition. Indeed, the foundation stone on which Baiyun guan's memorial service rests is the *Bojian* 缽鑑 or *Examination of the Bowl*, a work allegedly authored by Wang Changyue that is also referred to as *Bojian lu* 缽鑑錄. Though—to my knowledge—no ordinary mortal has ever laid eyes on this text, its reliability was accepted based on quotations in Min Yide's *Mind-Lamp* and in the *Yilin* 逸林 (a work attributed to Yang Shen'an 楊慎菴), and on revisions and comments by eminent Qing scholars such as the above-mentioned Bao Tingbo and Bao Kun.

On this extremely tenuous basis, Beijing's Baiyun guan was from the Qing onward recognized as the celebrated headquarters of the so-called "orthodox Longmen lineage" and the clerical heart of the older Quanzhen legacy. How did all of this come about? To address this question and related issues, I will in Part One of this book examine Min Yide's creation of a line of "apostolic" transmission, a product of the early nineteenth century. As with the Roman Catholic church, doctrinal and institutional legitimacy tends to be intimately linked not only to a pedigree reaching back to a founder

---

[25] See my article "The Invention of a Quanzhen Canon: The Wondrous Fate of the *Daozang jiyao*." In: Goossaert, Vincent, and Xun Liu (eds.). *Quanzhen Daoism in Modern Chinese History and Society*. Berkeley: Institute of East Asian Studies, 2014: 44–77.

figure, but also to an unbroken line of transmission of the founder's genuine teachings coupled with a system of ordination designed to guarantee institutional and doctrinal orthodoxy, continuity, and central control. Indeed, one of the striking similarities to the Catholic church is Longmen's retro-projection of an elaborate, relatively recent ordination system onto the early history of the movement.

In Part Two of this book I will describe the creation of such a system, namely, the "three-fold ordination" of the so-called "orthodox Longmen tradition" (Longmen zhengzong 龍門正宗).

Part Three describes the creation of a collection of more than three hundred sacred scriptures, the *Daozang jiyao* 道藏輯要 (Essence of the Daoist Canon), that—due to Saint Lü Dongbin's 呂洞賓 inspiration and miraculous involvement—was presented as Daoism's ultimate canon.

Part Four is dedicated to the creation of Longmen doctrine using the example of the most famous text of the *Daozang jiyao* canon: the *Jinhua zongzhi* 金華宗旨 which is known in the West as *The Secret of the Golden Flower*.

Part One

CREATION OF LINEAGE

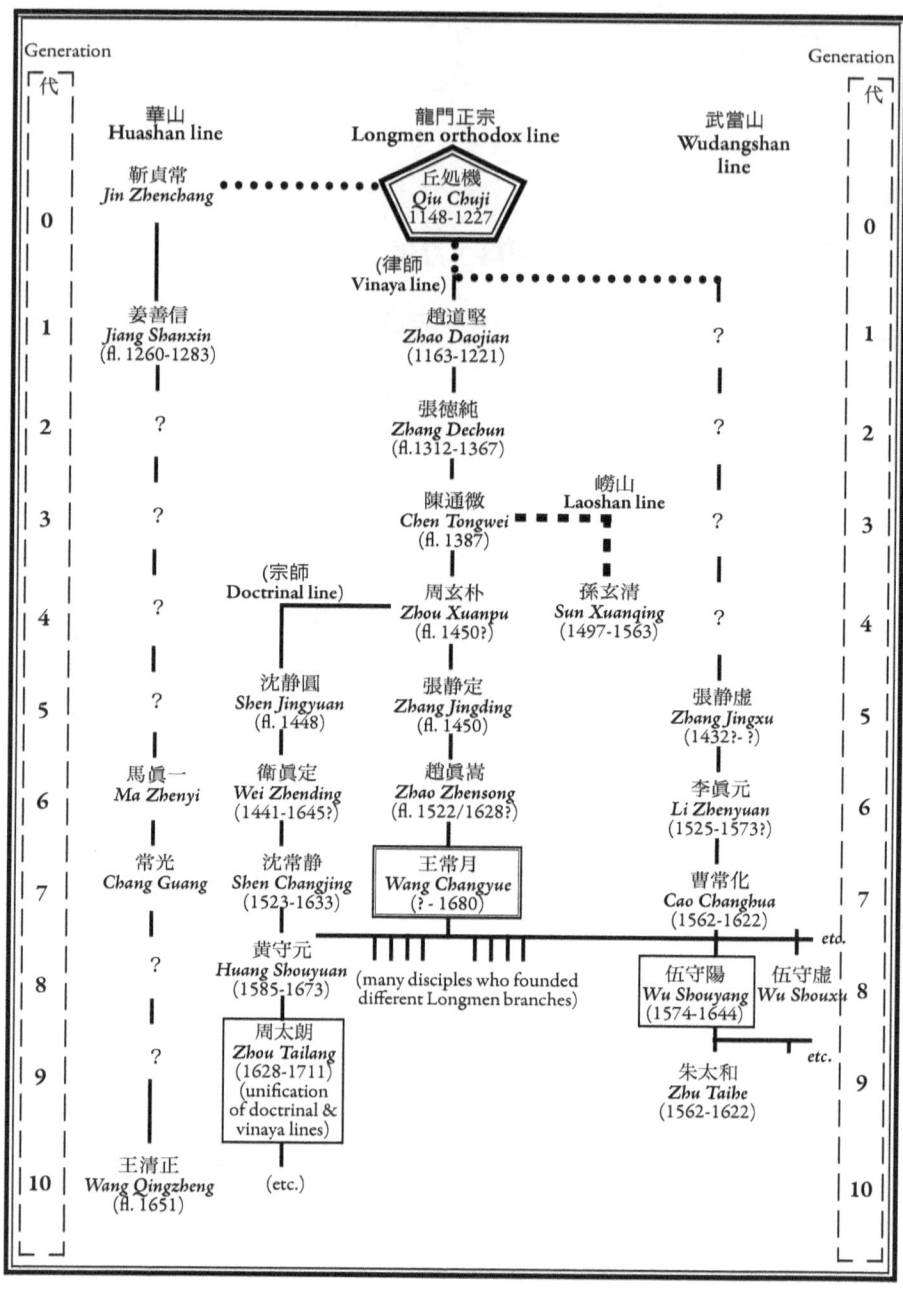

Fig. 5: Lineage Chart of Early Daoist Longmen Traditions

Chapter 1

Longmen Daoism's Apostle Peter: Zhao Daojian 趙道堅

According to Min Yide's *Mind-Lamp of Mount Jingai* (*Jingai xindeng* 金蓋心燈; abbr. JGXD), the "Longmen orthodox lineage" (Longmen zhengzong 龍門正宗) was born in the thirteenth century with the transmission of the "lamp of mind" (*xindeng* 心燈) from Qiu Chuji to Qiu's disciple Zhao Daojian. Min's text commemorates this event by staging a fateful meeting between Zhao Daojian and founder Qiu Chuji who greets Zhao as "pillar of the teaching of mysteries [i.e., Daoism] and guide of celestial immortals 此元門柱石、天仙領袖也."[26] This greeting has a parallel in Jesus's equally legendary and anachronistic election of a humble Galilean fisherman, Peter, as the "rock upon which my church will be built."

Qiu's words became a stereotyped phrase for the foundation of the Longmen orthodox lineage that is also found in the more recent biography of Zhao Daojian published in the 1848 *Baiyun xianbiao* 白雲仙表 or *Chart of the Immortals of Baiyun guan* (from now on abbreviated as BYXB or *Immortals' Chart*). The text of this chart includes a preface by Wanyan Chongshi 完顏崇實 (1820–1876) dated 1847 that is preceded by a frontispiece dated 1848. This text's woodblocks were originally stored at the Baiyun guan.[27]

---

[26] "Zhao Xujing lüshi zhuan 趙虛靜律師傳" (JGXD 1.1b). Here the expression *yuanmen* 元門 stands for *xuanmen* 玄門 because *xuan* 玄 was a taboo character since it formed part of the name of the Kangxi emperor (r. 1662–1722), Xuanye 玄燁. The same sentence also occurs in the *Longmen zhengzong Jueyun daotong xinchuan* 龍門正宗覺雲道統薪傳 (1927, from now on JYDT; reprinted in ZWDS 31: 462) and in *Longmen chuanjie puxi* 龍門傳戒譜系 (manuscript of 1919 stored at Baiyun guan); but in these later sources the Kangxi taboo was no longer observed.

[27] I use the date 1848 given in the frontispiece, which indicates the date of its carving. This text has been reprinted in ZWDS 31: 373–45, here 392. On Zhao's biography, see below.

Its late nineteenth-century authors—the Baiyun guan prior Meng Yongcai 孟永才 (d. 1881) and the Manchu elite official Wanyan Chongshi 完顏崇實[28]—considered it necessary to explicitly link the rather blurred Zhao (the first pillar of the Longmen lineage as described in Min Yide's *Mind-Lamp*) with a better-known Zhao, namely, the leader of eighteen disciples who accompanied Qiu Chuji on his famous journey to the West. Why did they feel this need? Who was Zhao Daojian? What kind of relationship did he have with the founding father Qiu Chuji, and how did Zhao acquire his status as the first Longmen Vinaya Patriarch?

In order to better understand Zhao and his role as first "Vinaya Patriarch" of the Longmen orthodox lineage, I will in the following subsections of this chapter briefly analyze the three main biographies devoted to him:

1. "Zhao Xujing lüshi zhuan 趙虛靜律師傳 (Biography of the Vinaya Patriarch Zhao Xujing) compiled by Min Yide (1748/58–1836) in 1821 (reprint 1873/1876 JGXD 1.1a–2b) with the commentaries by Bao Tingbo 鮑廷博 (1728–1814) and Bao Kun 鮑錕 (fl. 1814) based on:
    a) *Daopu* 道譜 (whose parts are found in the opening scroll of the *Mind-Lamp* under the name of "Daopu yuanliu tu 道譜源流圖," a commented lineage chart compiled by Lü Yunyin 呂雲隱, fl. 1710);
    b) *Yilin* 逸林 by Yang Shen'an 楊慎菴;
    c) *Bojian lu* 缽鑑錄 (apparently referring to the *Bojian*, a work attributed to Wang Changyue 王常月 alias Wang Kunyang 王崑陽, quotations of which are said to have been included in the *Yilin*).[29]

---

[28] On the role of Meng Yongcai in promoting Baiyun guan's prestige see Yin Zhihua 2008. Wanyan Chongshi was a Manchu official who received the *jinshi* degree in 1840 and was granted an official biography in the *Qingshi gao* 清史稿. See Arthur Hummel (ed.), *Eminent Chinese of the Ch'ing Period (1644–1912)*, 2 vols. (Washington, DC: U.S. Government Printing Office, 1943–44): 1: 211–12. He is also the author of *Ti'an nianpu* 惕盦年譜 (one fascicle, 1877). More on Wanyan Chongshi's ties with Daoism and his patronage of the Baiyun guan in Xun Liu, "Visualizing Perfection: Daoist Paintings of Our Lady, Court Patronage, and Elite Female Piety in the Late Qing." *Harvard Journal of Asiatic Studies* 64.1 (2004): 57–115, in particular 77–84.

[29] See the list of bibliographical works revised by Bao Tingbo under the title "Jingai xindeng zhengkao wenxian lu," JGXD 1a–2b.

Annotations to these biographies are based on even later sources from the late nineteenth and early twentieth centuries that are, by and large, based on the *Mind-Lamp*, such as:
  (i) *Taishang lümai Longmen zhengzong* 太上律脈龍門正宗 (1919, hand-scroll manuscript conserved at Baiyun guan, also known as *Longmen chuanjie puxi* 龍門傳戒譜系), abbreviated as TSLM or *Taishang lümai*;[30]
  (ii) *Longmen zhengzong Jueyun benzhi daotong xinchuan* 龍門正宗覺雲本支道統薪傳 compiled by Lu Yongzhi 陸永銘 in 1927, abbreviated as JYDT or *Jueyun benzhi daotong* (reprinted in ZWDS 3: 464–65);
  (iii) *Daotong yuanliu zhi* 道統源流志 compiled in 1929 by Yan Liuqian 嚴六謙 (*hao* Zhuangyan jushi 莊嚴居士, lineage name: Heyi 合怡), abbreviated as *Gazetteer of Daoist Origins* or DTYL, xia 2.
2. "Baoyuan Zhao zongshi 抱元趙宗師" (The Patriarch Zhao Baoyuan) in Meng Yongcai 孟永才 (d. 1881) and Wanyan Chongshi 完顏崇實 (1820–1876), *Baiyun xianbiao* 白雲仙表, abbr. *Immortals' Chart* or BYXB, 35a–b (ZWDS 31:392);
3. "Zhao Jiugu 趙九古," in Li Daoqian 李道謙 (1219–1296), *Zhongnan shan Zuting xianzhen neizhuan* 終南山祖庭仙真內傳 (Inner biographies of the immortals and perfected of the Ancestral Court in the Zhongnan Mountains, DZ 955) along with some passages found in Li Zhichang 李志常 (1193–1256), *Changchun zhenren xiyou ji* 長春真人西遊記 (Record of the Journey to the West by the Perfected Changchun, DZ 1429). On the basis of these two works, Chen Minggui 陳明珪 (1823–1881) compiled in 1879 a biographical account of this patriarch in his *Changchun daojiao yuanliu* 長春道教源流 (abbreviated as DJYL; ZWDS 31:1–157). The few variations of this late nineteenth-century account will be signaled only in the notes.

---

30 Some parts of this text (from the biography of the sixth patriarch onward) have also been published in *Zhongguo daojiao xiehui yanjiushi* 中國道教協會研究室 ed., *Daojiao shi ziliao* 道教史資料 (Shanghai: Guji chubanshe, 1991). For a preliminary study on the TSLM see Yin Zhihua 尹志華, "Beijing Baiyun guan zang Longmen chuanjie puxi chutan 北京白雲觀藏 龍門傳戒譜系 初探," *Shijie zongjiao yanjiu* 世界宗教研究 (2009.2): 72–82. I am indebted to Dr. Yin Zhihua for having procured me a copy of this manuscript.

1. Zhao Daojian 趙道堅 according to the *Mind-Lamp of Mount Jingai* 金蓋心燈 (early 19th century)

>Date of birth: no mention
>Date of death: 1312 (?)
>Lineage name (*ming* 名): Daojian 道堅[31]
>Daoist name (*hao* 號): Xujing 虛靜[32]
>Granted title: Baoyuan (xuan?) Zhao Da zongshi 抱元(玄)趙大宗師[33]
>Birthplace: Nanyang, Xinye 南陽新野 (Henan)

According to the "Biography of the Vinaya Patriarch Zhao Xujing" (Zhao Xujing lüshi zhuan 趙虛靜律師傳) in Min Yide's *Mind-Lamp* 金蓋心燈 of 1821, Zhao was a native of Xinye 新野 (Nanyang 南陽 county, Henan). From an early age he exhibited signs of genuine learning, a rare gift of sages and saints. He was endowed with a nature so sincere and pure, cautious and taciturn that his fellow villagers named him "man from antiquity" (Guren 古人).[34] He enjoyed studying Daoist classics, in particular *Zhuangzi* and *Laozi*. As soon as he heard about the diffusion of Daoist teachings by the Quanzhen Seven Perfected he left, carrying only his gourd and bamboo grass hat 攜瓢笠 in the image of a wandering monk, and visited Qiu Chuji. Founder Qiu immediately recognized him as the genuine recipient of "the lamp of mind" and heir of the precept doctrine (*jiefa* 戒

---

[31] In *Longmen zhengzong Jueyun daotong xinchuan* 龍門正宗覺雲道統薪傳 (JYDT) 18a (ZWDS 31: 462) it is clearly given as "*paiming* 派名." The *Taishang lümai Longmen zhengzong* 太上律脈龍門正宗 (TSLM) wrongly writes his name as Daojian 道監. In the *Jingudong zhi / Jinggu dongzhi* j. 6 (a work of the Jiaqing period, ZWDS 20: 277) one finds for Zhao the title "Baoyuan zongshi."

[32] The TSLM wrongly records this *hao* as Xuqing 虛清. His Daoist name is also wrongly written as Xujing 虛靖 in the commentary by Min Yide to the *Xiuzhen biannan* 棲雲山悟元子修眞辯難前編參證 (DZXB vol. 4, 20b).

[33] A poem offered to a certain Zhao Baoxuan, "Zeng Zhao Baoxuan 贈趙抱玄," is found in the *Danyang shenguang can* 丹陽神光燦 (DZ 1150, ZHDZ 26: 482c). This might be our Zhao since, as we shall see, Zhao was also linked with Ma Danyang. The title "Baoyuan 抱元" given in JGXD probably stands for "Baoxuan 抱玄" (Kangxi taboo?). The "Daopu yuanliu tu 道譜源流圖" (JGXD, 4b–5a) mentions another title, "Hunyuan zongshi 混元宗師," also given as "Hunyuan Da zongshi" in JYDT; but none of these are attested in sources from the *Daozang* or *Daozang jiyao*.

[34] This might allude to Zhao's posthumous name Jiugu 九古 as recorded in the earlier biography of Li Daoqian. See here below.

法). Here the marginalia of *Mind-Lamp* remind us that the title of Min Yide's book, the *Mind-Lamp of Mount Jingai*, stems from this very "lamp of mind" transmission that Qiu Chuji was on the verge of conveying to Zhao Daojian.

Zhao is then said to have followed Patriarch Qiu in his travels to Yan (i.e., Beijing) in order to spread the teaching (*chanjiao* 闡教). He engaged in voluntary silence, and "whatever he did, even without a word being uttered, accorded naturally (with the Way) 凡有作為不言自合."[35] Thus Founder Qiu transmitted "the secret of pure emptiness and natural spontaneity 清虛自然" to him, upon which Zhao withdrew to Mount Longmen for many years.[36]

According to the commentary in the *Yilin* 逸林 (which allegedly is based on the *Bojian lu*), Zhao remained on Mt. Longmen for seventeen years, which is longer than the period spent by Qiu Chuji on the same mountain.[37] However, according to another commentary based on the *Daopu yuanliu tu* 道譜源流圖, Zhao was sent to the northwestern regions for seven years. There he persuaded more than two thousand Han refugees (*liumin* 流民) to peacefully submit to China's new rulers.[38] After his return, Zhao is said to have attended to Patriarch Qiu at Beijing's Baiyun guan, and "on the

---

[35] The TSLM does not mention the passage on Zhao's voluntary silence but records a slight modification in the passage: 凡有作為皆不言而同. See also below for the version recorded in the BYXB.

[36] The last sentence is also copied in JYDT 18a (ZWDS 31: 462) and in the *Longmen chuanjie puxi* 龍門傳戒譜系, though with the substitution of "*qingxu ziran* 清虛自然" by "*qingjing ziran* 清靜自然" (the secret of pure quietude and natural spontaneity; as in the BYXB discussed below).

[37] Although the commentary in the JGXD (1.1b/2) does not specify the length of Qiu Chuji's retreat on Mount Longmen, the majority of hagiographic and epigraphic materials devoted to Qiu Chuji have him spend about six years in Panxi 磻溪 (Shaanxi) and seven additional years in Longmen.

[38] JGXD 1.2a (p. 75). This commentary is not found in the "Daopu yuanliu tu" (JGXD 4b-5a, p. 26-27). The glosses to "Changchun dijun" (i.e., Qiu Chuji) in the "Daopu yuanliu tu" (4b-5a) and the comments on Qiu Chuji in Zhao's biography (1.1b) manifest parallels between Zhao's travels to the northwestern regions and the travels of Qiu and his eighteen disciples for "pacifying the entire country." In fact, JYDT 18a (ZWDS 31: 462) features the commentary of the JGXD based on the *Yilin* as integral part of Zhao's biography. Zhao is said to have withdrawn to Longmen for many years before traveling in northwestern regions with Founder Qiu. In contrast to the JGXD, the JYDT does not specify how many years Zhao traveled but still refers to Zhao's actions of saving twenty thousand people (using the term *ren* 人 and no longer *liumin* 流民).

fifteenth day of the first lunar month of the *gengchen* year of the Zhiyuan era 至元庚辰正月望日" (1280) he reportedly received the Initial Precepts of Perfection (*chuzhen jie* 初真戒) and the Intermediate Precepts or Precepts of the Medium Ultimate (*zhongji jie* 中極戒). At last he obtained directly from Qiu the final investiture: the "seal of mind" (*xinyin* 心印) along with the robe and bowl (*fu yibo* 付衣鉢).[39] Through this "direct transmission," Zhao obtained the last and highest set of precepts, the Cestial Immortal Precepts (*tianxian jie* 天仙戒), along with the famous Longmen poem in twenty characters confirming him as the first Vinaya Patriarch (*lüshi* 律師) of the Longmen lineage. I will return below to the content of this set of precepts and the importance of this poem in establishing Longmen identity. According to the commentary based on the *Yilin* 逸林, this transmission poem was granted by Emperor Shizu 世祖 (Khubilai Khan, r. 1260–1294) as imperial legitimization of the foundation of the Longmen lineage.[40]

In 1312, thirty-three years after the above-mentioned "direct transmission" by Qiu Chuji had purportedly taken place at Baiyun guan, Zhao is said to have conferred the "secret oral transmission of precepts" (*jiefa koujue* 戒法口訣) onto the second Vinaya Patriarch Zhang Dechun 張德純.

Whereas the text of the *Mind-Lamp* does not provide many hints about Zhao's identity, the genealogical chart *Daopu yuanliu tu* 道譜源流圖 identifies Zhao as the first of eighteen disciples accompanying Qiu Chuji on his travels to the West (see above, Fig. 4). This epic journey of Qiu Chuji to Central Asia in order to meet the Mongol Emperor Chinggis Khan (Taizu, r. 1206–27) was the most famous "political" event of Qiu Chuji's life.[41] It was the object of a detailed narration by Li Zhichang 李志常 (1193–1256) in his 1228 *Changchun zhenren xiyou ji* 長春真人西遊記 or *Record of the*

---

[39] The expression "conferring robe and bowl" (*fu yibo* 付衣鉢), the symbol of Chan "mind-to-mind" transmission from one patriarch to another, is not attested in Daoist texts included in the *Daozang* or *Daozang jiyao*. However, a few occurrences of a "transmission of robe and bowl" (*chuan yibo*) are found in the *Daozang* and *Daozang jiyao*. See for instance "Luo zushi zuowang 駱祖師坐亡" in *Lushan Taiping xingguo gong Caifang zhenjun shishi* 廬山太平興國宮訪真君事實, preface 1154, DZ 1286, j. 5 (Schipper and Verellen eds., *The Taoist Canon*, vol. 2: 877–78). There are also other occurrences in the *Daozang*.

[40] This is also recorded in the late *Daotong yuanliu*, xia 1a/2.1a. This source, compiled by the disciples of Min Yide, also refers (like the JGXD) to the 1280 transmission at Baiyun guan of the three precepts from Qiu Chuji to Zhao Daojian. See also JYDT (ZWDS 31: 419).

[41] Yao Tao Chung, "Ch'iu Ch'u-chi and Gingis Khan," *Harvard Journal of Asiatic Studies* 46 (1986): 201–19.

Journey to the West by the Perfected Changchun (DZ 1429).⁴² References to this journey are of course found in many works and epigraphic materials related to Quanzhen, for example those by the foremost historiographer of the earlier Quanzhen, Li Daoqian 李道謙 (1219–1296) who also authored a short biography of Zhao Daojian. On the basis of this biography —compiled in the 1284 *Zhongnan shan Zuting xianzhen neizhuan* 終南山祖庭仙真內傳 (Inner biographies of the immortals and perfected of the Ancestral Court in the Zhongnan Mountains, DZ 955)—Meng and Wanyan published in 1848 a new biography that prominently lists Zhao among the immortals of Baiyun guan.⁴³

2. Zhao Daojian 趙道堅 according to the *Baiyun Immortals' Chart* 白雲仙表 (late 19th century)

> Date of birth: 1163
> Date of death: no mention
> Posthumous name (*hui* 諱): Daojian 道堅⁴⁴
> Daoist name (*daohao* 道號): Xujing zi 虛靜子
> Granted titles: Baoyuan (xuan) zongshi 抱元（玄）宗師,
>   Zhongzhen yijiao zhuying zhenren 中貞翊教主應真人⁴⁵
> Birthplace: Tanzhou 檀州 (Miyun xian 密雲縣, today's Beijing)

---

⁴² This text, included in the Ming Daoist Canon (DZ 1429, see Schipper and Verellen eds., *The Taoist Canon*, vol. 2:1141–42) was widely reedited outside the *Daozang* during the Qing and is also included in the *Daozang jiyao* canon (discussed below in Part Three). Around the middle of the Qing dynasty, thanks to a growing interest in Central Asian geography, this text was discovered and studied by Qing scholars such as Qian Daxin 錢大昕 (1728–1804) before being translated into European languages. For a short presentation of this text and its partial Western translations see Emil Bretschneider, "Si Yu Ki: Travels to the West of K'iu Ch'ang Ch'un," in *Medieval Researches from Eastern Asiatic Sources* (London: Kegan Paul, Trench, Trubner & Co Ltd, 1888, 35–108; reprinted by Routledge 2000) and Arthur Waley, *The Travels* (1931). More information about Chinese translations and studies is found in Zhang Guangbao, "Quanzhen Daoist Studies in China (1879–2007)," in Xun Liu & Vincent Goossaert, eds., *Quanzhen Daoism in Modern Chinese History and Society*. Berkeley: Institute of East Asian Studies (2014).

⁴³ Some passages from Li Daoqian and Li Zhichang are reproduced and translated here below.

⁴⁴ As far as I know, Daojian appears as posthumous name only in this biography. As we shall see, Daojian is the religious name given to Zhao by Qiu Chuji.

⁴⁵ While the first title is mentioned in the "Longmen zhengzong liuchuan zhipai tu 龍門正宗流傳支派圖" (JGXD 1a and *Jingudong zhi* 金鼓洞志 6.17a, ZWDS 20:

While the renowned Quanzhen chronicler Li Daoqian 李道謙 (1219–1296) had entitled his biography "Zhao Jiugu 趙九古" using Zhao's real name (*hui* 諱),[46] Meng and Wanyan compiled their late 19th-century biography under the title *Baoyuan Zhao zongshi* 抱元趙宗師, which refers to a title of Zhao that is also recorded in the *Mind-Lamp*.[47] However, in contrast to the *Mind-Lamp* version, the *Immortals' Chart* authors rely on Li Daoqian's work to the point of copying almost all passages from it. In tune with Li Daoqian's text, they record that Zhao was born in 1163 in Tanzhou 檀州, the modern district of Miyun in today's Beijing. Zhao is described as having a nature so exceptionally serene that his "bones of an immortal" were already divined at an early age. In 1177, against the will of his mother who wanted him to marry, Zhao converted to Daoism under the guidance of master Cui Yangtou 崔羊頭. After having tried Zhao's patience severely for three years, master Cui sent him to Ma Danyang 馬丹陽 (1123–1184) in Huating 華亭 (today's Gansu). In 1180 Ma, who was about to return to the ancestral sanctuary erected on the grave of his master Wang Chongyang 王重陽 (1113–1170) in Zhongnan, ordered Zhao to join his fellow Qiu Chuji in Longmen.[48] It was there that Qiu conferred upon Zhao the religious name Daojian 道堅.

---

277), the second—"Zhongzhen yijiao zhuying zhenren 中貞翊教主應真人"—is recorded in the *Jinlian zhengzong xianyuan xiangzhuan* 金蓮正宗仙源像傳 (DZ 174, ZHDZ 47: 57c) as title bestowed on Zhao in 1310. In Li Daoqian's biography (j. *zhong*, ZHDZ 47: 91a) one also finds "Zhongzhen yijiao xuanying zhenren 中貞翊教玄應真人" as title reportedly granted in 1250. More on this below.

[46] The mention of Jiugu 九古 as Zhao's posthumous name is only found in Li Daoqian's biography. Meng and Wanyan mention instead Daojian 道堅 as posthumous name. In Li Zhichang's record Zhao is often called Xujing xiansheng Zhao Jiugu 虛靜先生趙九古 or simply Xujing xiansheng 虛靜先生. One also finds, though more rarely, the name Zhao Xujing 趙虛靜 (*Jinlian zhengzong xianyuan xiangzhuan* 金蓮正宗仙源像傳, DZ 174, fasc. 76; ZHDZ 47: 65b).

[47] See above note 33.

[48] Ding Peiren 丁培仁 ("*Jingai xindeng* juan yi zhiyi 金蓋心燈卷一質疑" [Questions on the first *juan* of the *Jingai xindeng*], *Daojia wenhua yanjiu* 道家文化研究 23 (2008): 411–29, in particular 413–14) emphasizes how perfectly the dates given in Li Daoqian's biography match Quanzhen chronicles and stelae. But Hachiya Kunio 蜂屋邦夫 (*Kindai dōkyō no kenkyū: Ō Chōyō to Ba Tanyō* 金代道教の研究—王重陽と馬丹陽 [Studies on Daoism in the Jin dynasty: Wang Chongyang and Ma Danyang], Tokyo: Kyūko shoin 1992, 286–87), on the basis of Li Daoqian's chronicle *Qizhen nianpu* 七真年譜 (DZ 175), expresses doubts about such dates and the exact period when Zhao went to visit Qiu in Longmen.

Zhao then attended to other close disciples of Wang Chongyang such as Li Lingyang 李靈陽 and Liu Changsheng 劉長生 (1147–1203)[49] before joining Qiu Chuji in Qixia 棲霞 (Shandong) in order to assume Daoist official charges.[50] In 1219, at the summons of the Mongol Khan, Qiu is said to have finally designated Zhao as the leading disciple in his embassy to Samarkand.[51] It is in the context of Zhao leaving for this epic journey as leader of the eighteen disciples allegedly selected by Qiu Chuji that the 19th-century authors add the following sentences inspired by the previous *Mind-Lamp* biography:

> Zhao followed the Perfected Lord [Qiu][52] in establishing meritorious acts by spreading the teachings, and whatever he did, even without uttering a word, accorded so naturally [with the Way] that the

---

[49] While Li Lingyang is regarded by some scholars more as Wang Chongyang's companion than his disciple, Liu Changsheng was one of the four close disciples of Wang. In his records Qiu often mentions his fellow companions Ma, Liu and Tan; see for instance Li Zhichang's *Xiyou ji* 西游記, j. *shang* (DZ 1429, fasc. 1056; ZHDZ 47: 11c), *Xuanfeng qinggui lu* 玄風慶會錄 (ZHDZ 47: 26b) or *Jinlian zhengzong xianyuan xiangzhuan* 金蓮正宗仙源像傳 (ZHDZ 47: 65a). For an introduction to these figures and previous studies on early Quanzhen masters see Stephen Eskildsen, *The Teachings and Practices of the Early Quanzhen Taoist Masters* (Albany: State University of New York Press, 2004).

[50] *Wenshi* 文侍.

[51] According to the stela by Yi Gou 弋轂 "Qinghe miaodao guanghua guanghua zhenren Yin zongshi beiming 清和妙道廣化真人尹宗師碑銘" (1264) devoted to Yin Zhiping in *Ganshui xianyuan lu* 甘水仙源錄 j. 3 (ZHDZ 47:136a), Yin was the leading disciple among the eighteen who allegedly accompanied Qiu Chuji on his journey to the West. See also the stela by Li Zhiquan and Wang E (quoted by Ding Peiren [2008]: 415, note 2). This contradicts Li Daoqian's biography where Zhao is instead given the leading role among Qiu's eighteen escorts.

[52] The late 19th-century biographies of Zhao by Meng and Wanyan use for Qiu the title "zhenjun 真君." According to them the title "Changchun quande shenhua mingying zhenjun 長春全德神化明應真君" was conferred upon Qiu during the Zhida 至大 era (BYXB 11b in ZWDS 31: 380). By contrast, the JGXD credits emperor Shizu 世祖 with the conferral of this title (JGXD j. 1.1b). According to the *Jinlian zhengzong xianyuan xiangzhuan*, the title "Changchun yandao zhujiao zhenren Qiu Chuji 長春演道主教真人丘處機"—originally bestowed by the emperor Shizu—was altered in 1310 (至大 3) by emperor Wuzong into "Changchun quande shenhua minying *zhenjun* 長春全德神化明應真君". The same work states that emperor Wuzong bestowed titles on Quanzhen ancestors and patriarchs that go beyond those of the earlier 1269 decree, calling them "Dijun" and "Zhenjun." Similarly, Qiu Chuji's eighteen disciples were promoted from "Dashi 大師" (great teachers) to "Zhenren 真人" (true accomplished men).

Perfected Lord greeted him with admiration, saying: "Here is the pillar of the teaching of mysteries (i.e., Daoism), the guide of the celestial immortals." After having obtained the "secret of pure quiescence and natural spontaneity," Zhao transmitted it to the Henan Daoist Zhang Bizhi [i.e., Zhang Dechun] who thus became the first-generation Vinaya master of the Longmen orthodox lineage.

遂從真君闡教立功、凡有作為不言而喻、真君與語奇之曰：「此元（玄）門柱石、天仙領袖也。」既得清靜自然之秘、傳河南道士張碧芝、為龍門正宗第一代律師。

Having briefly examined the nineteenth-century hagiographies in the *Mind-Lamp* and *Immortals' Chart*, we now turn to Zhao's image in Quanzhen hagiographies that precede them by six centuries.

3. Zhao Daojian 趙道堅 according to 13th-century Quanzhen hagiographers

>Date of birth: 1163
>Date of death: 1221
>Posthumous name (*hui* 諱): Jiugu 九古[53]
>Daoist name (*daohao* 道號): Xujing zi 虛靜子
>Religious name from Qiu Chuji: Daojian 道堅
>Granted titles: Zhongzhen yijiao xuanying zhenren 中貞翊教玄應真人[54]
>Birthplace: Tanzhou 檀州 (Miyun xian 密雲縣, today's Beijing)

According to the record by Li Zhichang 李志常 (1193–1256) of Qiu Chuji's journey that is also confirmed in the work of Li Daoqian 李道謙 (1219–1296), Zhao Daojian died on the fifth day of the eleventh lunar month (November 20th) of 1221 in Sairam (Sailan 塞藍). A few days prior to his death he confided his fears to Yin Zhiping 尹志平 (1169–1251), the

---

[53] The explicit reference to the posthumous name Jiugu is only found in Li Daoqian's biography (ZHDZ 47: 90b). Li Zhichang often mentions Zhao in his record as Xujing xiansheng Zhao Jiugu 虛靜先生趙九古 (*Changchun zhenren xiyou ji*, j. *shang* in ZHDZ 47: 6c, 9b), or Xujing xiansheng Zhao/Xujing xiansheng (j. *xia*, ZHDZ 47: 15b, 16a). Li Zhichang uses Jiugu only once in the context of his burial (j. *shang*, ZHDZ 47: 9b).

[54] This title was reportedly granted in 1250 by Zhenchang zhenren 真常真人 (i.e., Li Zhichang). See also note 45..

future successor of Qiu Chuji in the Quanzhen patriarchy.⁵⁵ Since his time in Xuande 宣德 (today's Xuanhua 宣化縣 in Hebei) with Master Qiu, Zhao had the premonition that he was destined to never return.⁵⁶ Although he was worn out by the journey, he tried every day to recall what the Master had taught him about life and death and how he should face it without letting joy or sorrow catch hold of him. "What comes along must be faced. For me it is time to depart. I hope the rest of you will serve the Father and Master with all your might."⁵⁷ Then, according to Qiu Chuji's request, Zhao was buried in the plain to the east of the town of Sairam.

Li Zhichang and Li Daoqian both mention in their respective works that on the way back from their visit to the Khan, Qiu Chuji's disciples performed rites at Zhao's tomb. They were intent on taking his remains back with them, but Master Qiu uttered the following verses:

A temporary compound of Four Elements,
The body at last must suffer decay.
The soul, composed of one spiritual essence,
Is free to move wherever it will.

This settled the discussion and the following day they journeyed on, leaving behind Zhao's mortal remains.⁵⁸

---

⁵⁵ Interestingly, precisely at the place where the 13th-century hagiographer Li Daoqian 李道謙 launches his narration of the imminent death of Zhao on his way to Samarkand, the nineteenth-century hagiographers Meng and Wanyan inserted the investiture by Qiu and Zhao's recognition as the first Longmen Vinaya Patriarch.

⁵⁶ Xuande is the place where Qiu Chuji assured his Daoist friends that he would return from his journey within three years. See Li Zhichang, *Xiyou ji* 西游記 j. *shang* (ZHDZ 47: 4c) and Waley, *The Travels*, 61–62. One can compare the certainty of Patriarch Qiu in prognosticating his return within three years with Zhao's premonition that he would never return from that journey.

⁵⁷ Arthur Waley, *The Travels*, 90. See also the translation by Emil Bretschneider, "Si Yu Ki: Travels to the West of K'iu Ch'ang Ch'un," *Medieval Researches from Eastern Asiatic Sources* (London: Kegan Paul, Trench, Trubner & Co Ltd, 1888; reprinted by Routledge, 2000): vol. 1, 35–108, here 74.

⁵⁸ Li Zhichang's *Xiyou ji* 西游記 j. *xia* (ZHDZ 47: 15b) and Waley, *The Travels*, 120. This is also recorded in Li Daoqian, *Zhongnan shan zuting xianzhen neizhuan* 終南山祖庭仙真內傳 (ZHDZ 47: 90c) and in Chen Minggui's *Daotong yuanliu zhi* 道統源流志.

These thirteenth-century portrayals are food for thought and raise a number of questions with regard to their use by hagiographers who lived six centuries later. Is it conceivable that the first Patriarch of the Longmen orthodox lineage had died before Founder Qiu Chuji? Why would Qiu Chuji, who was known for the accuracy of his predictions, have chosen a disciple who died before him to guarantee the continuity of the "lamp of mind"?[59] And how could Zhao's mortal remains have been abandoned in China's Far West instead of receiving a resting place adequate for a "First Patriarch" of a lineage?[60]

Like Min Yide, Meng and Wanyan do not address such questions. Min simply attributes a new date of death to Zhao in his *Mind-Lamp*, and Meng and Wanyan erase Zhao's date of death along with related passages from Li Daoqian's biography. Furthermore, because Zhao in the *Mind-Lamp* also received a new birthplace—the Nanyang instead of the Beijing region—along with fresh biographical anecdotes, modern scholars have rightly wondered whether we are dealing with two Zhaos who at some point had been conflated into one.[61] It is surely no coincidence that Meng and Wanyan compiled a new biography in which, while omitting delicate passages from the older biography by Li Daoqian, merged one Zhao (whom Li portrays as the leader of the eighteen disciples) with the *Mind-Lamp*'s Zhao. The latter was, as we have seen, hailed in the *Mind-Lamp* as the first Vinaya Patriarch of Longmen and conveyor of Qiu's transmission to his Henan disciple Zhang Dechun, Longmen's second patriarch.

---

[59] Apart from the famous prediction made by Qiu about his return from the western journey after three years (whose accuracy was also emphasized in the Preface by Sun Xi 孫錫 to Li Zhichang's *Xiyou ji* 西游記 ZHDZ 47: 1a, and Waley, *The Travels*, 44; see also note 56 above), Li Zhichang's work as well as hagiographical materials on Qiu often refer to Qiu's miracles and divinatory skills. One wonders whether the reference in Li Zhichang about the intention of Qiu to choose nineteen disciples (ZWDS 47: 2b) instead of the eighteen usual ones—eighteen being the number in the official biography on Qiu Chuji included in *Yuanshi* 元史 or History of the Yuan—should be seen from that "predictive" angle. The majority of scholars suggest that such varying numbers of Qiu's disciples might indicate that this topic was not yet settled at that time. Some sources also speak of fifteen disciples of Qiu under the leadership of Yin Zhiping. See note 42 above.

[60] As if conscious of this problem, Li Daoqian concludes his biography by offering a more adequate resting place for Zhao. See here below.

[61] Wang Zhizhong 王志忠, *Ming-Qing Quanzhen daojiao lungao* 明清全真道教論稿 (Chengdu: Bashu shushe, 2000): 70, note 1.

For today's scholars who have at their disposal many sources and epigraphic materials, it seems relatively easy to trace a more "historical" portrait of Zhao than the one furnished in the thirteenth century by Li Daoqian and to find many contradictions in the nineteenth-century *Mind-Lamp* biography that purportedly deals with the same figure. For them, reliance on Li Daoqian appears to be more opportune in view of the effort he devoted to building a "true history" of the Quanzhen movement. As a matter of fact, Li's chronicles are still praised today for closely matching information that is preserved in numerous Quanzhen stone inscriptions.⁶² One cannot but be puzzled by the historical incongruence of the *Mind-Lamp* and the commentaries authored by eminent Qing scholars such as Bao Tingbo and Bao Kun. Of course, Qiu Chuji's journey to the West was of great renown; yet all references given in the *Mind-Lamp* show that the 19th-century hagiographers and their commentators postdated this event to the later reign of Khubilai Khan (Shizu 世祖, r. 1260–1294). But this is not a peculiarity of the *Mind-Lamp*; a local gazetteer of the Qing also refers to a certain Qiu Changchun who allegedly founded a Quanzhen monastery under Khubilai's reign (1263–1294) and did so precisely in the Nanyang region of our Zhao Daojian.⁶³ This incongruence appears to be widespread

---

62 For Li's historiography and his struggles against perceived distorted views regarding Quanzhen history see Miura Shūichi 三浦秀一, "Gendai shisō kenkyū josetsu: Zenshin dōshi Ri Dōken no dōkō o shujiku ni 元代思想研究序説—全真道士李道謙の動向を主軸に" [A preliminary study of Yuan thought, based on the stance of the Quanzhen master Li Daoqian], *Shūkan tōyōgaku* 集刊東洋學 67 (1992): 66–84. See also the article by Ding Peiren (2008) cited above where he emphasizes on the basis of epigraphic materials how Li Daoqian's biography matches historical facts.

63 The 1876 *Zhenping xianzhi* 鎮平縣志 (Gazetteer of Zhenping county) compiled by Wu Lianyuan 吳聯元 and revised by Li Qinggao 李慶翱 et al. in 6 *juan*, j. 5.61 states that "during the Zhiyuan era Qiu Changchun built the Taijiguan where he cultivated perfection and attained the Dao, thus becoming one of the seven patriarchs [of Quanzhen]. During the Zhizheng reign he was summoned to the capital but declined." 邱長春至元間創建太極觀、修真成道為七祖之一。至正間特詔詣京師不赴." More information is found in the study of Xun Liu, "General Zhang buries the bones: early Qing reconstruction and Quanzhen Daoist collaboration in mid-seventeenth century Nanyang," *Late Imperial China* 27.2 (Dec. 2006): 67–98, here 80, note 30. It seems that the temple-building activities of Qiu under Khubilai were part of current legends that were also recorded by the eighteenth Baiyun guan abbot in 1814. The 1811 *Baiyun guan juanchan beiji* 白雲觀捐產碑記 by Cai Yongqing 蔡永清, pp. 145–147 (also mentioned in Marsone 1999:27) states: The first year of Shizu 世祖 of the Yuan (1260), an imperial decree ordered the

during the Qing and was subsequently perpetuated by renowned literati such as Zhu Yicun 朱彝尊 (1629–1709), the author of a poem that is still extant at Beijing's Baiyun guan.[64]

Dates familiar to earlier Quanzhen chroniclers such as the "first month of the *gengchen* year 庚辰正月" (1220)—when Qiu Chuji allegedly selected his eighteen disciples and began his journey from Laizhou 萊州 (present-day Yexian 掖縣, Shandong) to Yan (Beijing)—were postdated in the *Mind-Lamp* to "the fifteenth day of the first lunar month of the *gengchen* year of the Zhiyuan era 至元庚辰正月望日" (1280), which is when Longmen's first patriarch Zhao allegedly received the precepts at Baiyun guan. According to Quanzhen chronicles, however, it is clear that Qiu arrived in Yan (Beijing) in the second month of 1220 and that two months later he performed at the request of high officials the Offering (*jiao*) rituals at the Tianchang guan 天常觀, the future Baiyun guan, where "ascending the Baoxuan hall 寶玄堂 he transmitted the precepts (*chuanjie* 傳戒)."[65]

The *Mind-Lamp*'s nineteenth-century tale of Qiu's transmission to Zhao at Beijing's Baiyun guan appears to have employed such thirteenth-century sources in order to give a veneer of "historical reality" to its construction of the Longmen ancestral hall. But if one takes the *Mind-Lamp*'s date of 1280 at face value, this ideal genealogical edifice crumbles. Was 1280 not the year when emperor Khubilai transmitted to Qi Zhicheng 祁志誠 (1219–93)

---

construction of the Baiyun guan as the altar-temple and dwelling of the Perfected. Daoist teaching being clearly in expansion, it became known as the Ancestral Sanctuary of the empire (元世祖初年、勅建白雲觀、以為棲真壇宇、道風昭廓、遂稱天下祖庭). The *Jinggu dongzhi* (ZWDS 20:278), which is another gazetteer on which the JGXD relies, also explains in a note based on the *Ganshui xianyuan lu* (j. 2 stela in ZHDZ 47:127 B): "Shizu ordered that Qionghuadao, where Qiu Chuji had lived, be changed into Wanyangong and that the name Changchun be used for the previous Tianchangguan. During the Jin it was called Taijigong and today Baiyun guan."

64 This poem is quoted by Yin Zhihua ("Beijing Baiyun guan zang...," 2009, p. 73): "世祖興元日、真人獨召丘。...."

65 Li Zhichang's *Xiyou ji* 西游記, *shang* (ZHDZ 47: 2b-3b; Waley, *The Travels*, 55–56). In Li Daoqian's *Qizhen nianpu* 七真年譜 (ZHDZ 47: 75a), Tianchan guan is mentioned under the name of Taiji gong 太極宮 (momentarily used during the Jin dynasty). (庚辰長春眞人年七十三、正月自萊州北行。二月至燕都。四月官僚請作醮於太極宮。五月至德興府寓龍陽觀。八月至宣德州寓朝元觀). Taiji gong is also used in Li Daoqian's stela of 1281 "Quanzhen diwu dai zongshi Changchun yandao zhujiao zhenren neizhuan 全真第五代宗師長春演道主教真人內傳" (*Daojia jinshi lüe*, 634–37) where the first month of the *gengchen* year 庚辰正月 is given as date when Qiu Chuji selected the eighteen disciples for his journey.

the order to burn the entire Daoist canon except for the *Daodejing*?[66] The date of 1280 may even appear macabre if we consider that it would turn the *Mind-Lamp*'s crucial first transmission into a decidedly posthumous event since Qiu had passed away in 1227 and his purported successor Zhao in 1221!

However, from the perspective of 19th-century hagiographers such as Min Yide or Meng and Wanyan, Zhao was as much a "figure of memory," chosen to establish the orthodox Longmen lineage, as a "figure of history." Correcting history to serve memory and their particular sectarian agenda, Zhao was portrayed as the only disciple in the group of eighteen to become closely associated with Longmen. This wishful association appears to have been an important reason for the nineteenth-century conflation of two Zhaos. According to Li Daoqian's biography from the thirteenth century, Zhao received his religious name precisely in Longmen and directly from Qiu Chuji. As a matter of fact, Zhao even makes an appearance in the 1305 *Xuanfeng qinghui tu* 玄風慶會圖 or *Felicitous Meetings with the Mysterious School, with Illustrations* where he is depicted serving his Master Qiu who sits in meditation at the Longmen cave where he attained enlightenment[67] (see Fig. 6).

---

[66] See *Yuanshi* j. 11 ("Benji 11, recorded in *Daojiao shizi liao*, p. 329). While for some scholars Khubilai's order (known as the 1281 edict) caused such losses that reconstructing the history of Daoism became difficult, others saw a less severe impact. It is in this context that the works of Li Daoqian and other Quanzhen chroniclers should be read as a transparent attempt to preserve Quanzhen history and its glory for posterity. See also Goossaert 1997:97–102

[67] *Xuanfeng qinghui tu* (Nara: Tenri Library, 1981; reprint of the Hanfenlou edition, 1925): 269–274. Zhao Jiugu is said to have served Qiu at Longmen along with Yu Shanqing 于善慶 (1166–1250), also known as Dongzhen zhenren 洞真真人, as well as Bi Zhichang 畢知常 (?–1231). The hagiographies of these two masters are included in Li Daoqian, *Zhongnan shan zuting xianzhen neizhuan* 終南山祖庭仙真內傳 (ZHDZ 47: 94–95 and 99–102). According to the stela devoted to Yu Shanqing ("終南山重陽萬壽宮洞真于真人道行碑," in *Ganshui xianyuan lu*, ZHDZ 47: 140) he received the religious name Zhidao from Qiu Chuji in 1206 via Bi Zhichang. Like Zhao Jiugu, Yu Shanqing and Bi Zhizhang were at the outset disciples of Ma Danyang; see Hachiya Kunio, *Kindai dōkyō no kenkyū*, 269–70 and 300. Yu Shanqing (Zhidao) was also known as the master of Li Daoqian.

Fig. 6: Attended by Zhao Daojian (lower left), Qiu Chuji attains enlightenment in Longmen ("Longmen quanzhen 龍門全真", detail from *Xuanfeng qinghui tu* 玄風慶會圖, j. 1).

Li Daoqian's 李道謙 work emphasized that despite his premature death, Zhao was the person most closely associated with Master Qiu. Qiu allegedly entrusted Zhao with important charges culminating in his election as leader of the group of eighteen disciples.[68] The preeminent place of Zhao also found further expression in the late thirteenth-century *Xuanfeng qinghui tu* 玄風慶會圖 where Zhao's biography (using his name Xujing 虛靜) follows immediately after that of his Master Qiu (see Fig. 7).

Unfortunately, this biography in the *Xuanfeng qinghui* chart's fifth *juan* under the title "Xujing xiansheng neizhuan 虛靜先生內傳" (Inner Biography of Master Zhao Xujing; ZWDS vol. 31) is today lost. Of the sixty-four illustrated accounts of this text that describe Qiu Chuji's life, only the first *juan* with sixteen illustrated accounts is extant. This text appears to have been popular; after having been published for the first time in 1274

---

[68] As recorded in the late 19th-century biography of Zhang by Meng and Wanyan (which, as was explained above, heavily relies on Li Daoqian's 13th-century work), the conferral of official charges from Qiu shows his determination to choose Zhao as his main disciple. On this see also Ding Peiren, "*Jingai xindeng* juan 1...," 415.

by Shi Zhijing 史志經 (1205–?)—one of Qiu's second generation disciples linked with thirteenth-century hagiographer Li Daoqian—it was reprinted in 1305 in Hangzhou thanks to donations by later generations of disciples affiliated with Beijing's Baiyun guan as well as by southern believers (mainly from Hangzhou).[69]

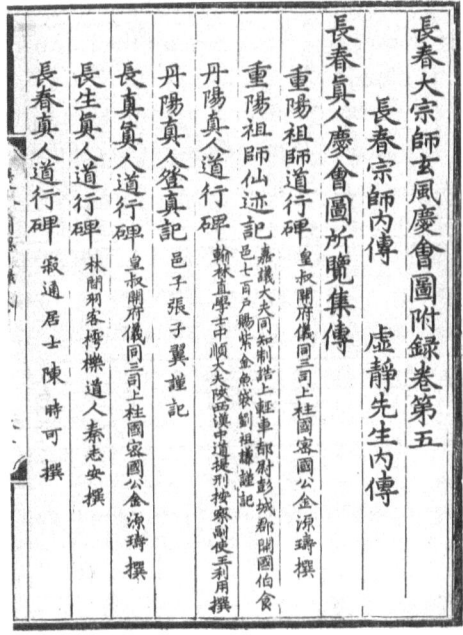

Fig. 7: Table of Contents of j. 5 of *Xuanfeng qinghui tu* 玄風慶會圖

Since Zhao is said to have been inspired by the ascetic training of Qiu Chuji, it comes as no surprise that in the *Mind-Lamp* the figure of Zhao was credited with withdrawing to the same Longmen cave even longer than his Master Qiu even though—according to the records of Li Daoqian and Li Zhichang—Zhao was able to manifest freely in different places and appear to different disciples even after his death because "his soul was free to roam wherever it wished."[70] Although Zhao's mortal remains had been aban-

---

[69] For a presentation of this text see Paul Katz, "Writing History, Creating Identity: A Case Study of *Xuanfeng qinghui tu*," *Journal of Chinese Religions* 29 (2001): 161–189.

[70] See the description of the manifestations of Zhao in Li Zhichang's *Xiyou ji* 西游記

doned in China's Far West, as Li Daoqian emphasizes at the end of his biography, Zhao's head-gear and sandals were later entombed in Wuhuashan 五華山 to ensure that he could finally receive proper offerings on an annual basis.[71] Interestingly, this was the exact burial place later allegedly chosen by Yin Zhiping 尹志平 (1169–1251), the successor to Qiu Changchun's patriarchy at the Baiyun guan. This strengthens the link between Zhao Daojian and Yin Zhiping who thus competed not only for the first place in Qiu Chuji's escort to Samarkand but even for their own grave. At any rate, apart from their mention in Li Daoqian's biography, Zhao's "Daoist relics" do not appear to have elicited much interest in the spiritual market of the time since apparently no temple or monastery was built to honor them. Instead, the far more potent relics of Zhao as a "figure of memory" were some centuries later enshrined in texts.

Regardless of the historical inconsistencies in the *Mind-Lamp* account, and although the title "Vinaya Master" (*lüshi* 律師) is not attested in Qiu's time,[72] the fact that Zhao in the nineteenth century was given the status of

---

(Waley, *The Travels*, 125, 131), also recorded in the last part of the biography compiled by Chen Minggui in his DTYL. See also Li Daoqian's biography, *Zhongnan shan* ... (ZHDZ 47: 90c—91a).

[71] In *Zhongnan shan Zuting xianzhen neizhuan* 終南山祖庭仙真內傳 (ZHDZ 47: 91a), Li Daoqian concludes the biography by telling us that in 1250 Li Zhichang conferred on him the title of "Zhongzhen yijiao xuanying zhenren 中貞翊教玄應真人" and that his hat-crown and shoes were buried in Wuhuashan so that he could receive offerings on an annual basis 庚戌歲真常真人奉命褒美道門師德、贈先生中貞翊教玄應真人號、葬冠履於五華山以奉歲祀焉。 This is not recorded in Li Zhichang's *Xiyou ji* 西游記 or in Chen's DTYL. In epigraphic materials we find the name of Wuhuashan (located in the Western periphery 西郊 of today's Beijing behind the Wofo si 臥佛寺, the monastery of the Reclining Buddha) mentioned as the place where in 1243 Yin Zhiping began executing his plan to build his own grave ("Shouzang 壽藏"); see Wang Zongyu 王宗昱, "Quanzhen jiao de rujiao chengfen 全真教的儒教成份," *Wenshi zhishi* 文史知識 12 (2006). See also the stela by Yi Gou "Qinghe miaodao guanghua..." (1264) in *Ganshui xianyuan lu* j. 3 (ZHDZ 47:136a). Although we still lack studies on the cult of Daoist relics, we know on the basis of Quanzhen epigraphic materials and other sources that Quanzhen Daoists apportioned an important place to their cult; see for instance Zhang Guangbao, "Jinyuan shiji Quanzhen jiaozu ting yanjiu" [The Quanzhen Patriarchal Halls during the Jin-Yuan period], in Chen Guying, ed., *Daojia wenhua yanjiu* 23 (2008): 52–143, in particular, 54. On the cult of Buddhist saints' relics see Reginald Ray, *Buddhist Saints in India: A study in Buddhist Values & Orientations* (Oxford NY: Oxford University Press, 1994): 326–32 and 342.

[72] The term *lüshi* 律師 is attested during the Tang dynasty as one of the three official titles of Daoists (along with *fashi* 法師 and *weiyishi* 威儀師). See the section

first Longmen Vinaya Patriarch, allegedly designated by Qiu Chuji shows the iron will of the inventors of the Longmen "orthodox lineage" to be affiliated with Baiyun guan and with the place where Qiu had engaged in ascetic training: Mount Longmen. This obstinacy may point to a controversy among different early nineteenth-century groups concerning the most appropriate sanctuary for the nascent Longmen lineage. But before we turn to this topic it is important to understand the logic of the nineteenth-century architects who designed and erected the ideal Baiyun guan ancestral hall on the foundation of seven Longmen pillars and decided to give to Zhao his very prominent place among Baiyun guan immortals.

"Shangshu Libu, Cibu Langzhong yuan Wailang 尚書禮部祠部郎中員外郎" in *Tang liudian* 唐六典. But this term was apparently no more in use during the Yuan.

Fig. 8: Title page of Min Yide's *Mind-Lamp of Mount Jingai* 金蓋心燈

Chapter 2

Longmen's Seven Patriarchs and the Gradual Revelation of the Longmen Method of Precepts

The secret of "pure emptiness and natural spontaneity" (*qingxu ziran* 清虛自然)—later also recast as the more stereotyped secret of "pure quiescence and natural spontaneity" (*qingjing ziran* 清靜自然)[73]—is said to have been transmitted from one patriarch to the next, only to be finally revealed by the seventh Longmen patriarch in form of the "Most High's Vinaya treasure of pure quiescence" (*Taishang qingjing lübao* 太上清靜律寶).[74] Each Longmen patriarch was required to transmit it to a successor to guarantee an unbroken transmission line from the Most High Lord Lao. Once Zhao Daojian had conveyed this secret in form of "the oral transmission of the method of precepts" (*jiefa koujue* 戒法口訣) to second patriarch Zhang Dechun, Zhao's mission was fulfilled and he could leave the stage to his successor. This act of transmission is repeated in *Mind-Lamp* 金蓋心燈 biographies from the second to the seventh of Longmen patriarch. The date of each transmission by a Vinaya Patriarch and the time lapse from the previous transmission are recorded with astounding precision: The first patriarch performed the transmission to his successor "on the

---

[73] The expression *qingxu ziran* 清虛自然 is also used in the Preface of Min Yide's *Mind-Lamp of Mount Jingai* 金蓋心燈 (JGXD). The late hagiographers Meng and Wanyan changed it into the more common expression *qingjing ziran* 清靜自然 (BYXB). The expression *jingxu wuwei* 清虛無為 is used in the biography of Li Zhichang, the Daoist fellow who shared the Longmen cave with Zhao Daoqian and Yu Shanqing. See the biography of Li Daoqian, *Zhongnan shan zuting xianzhen neizhuan* 終南山祖庭仙真內傳 (ZWDS 47: 94b) and note 49 above.

[74] In the *Longmen chuanjie puxi* this is referred to as *Taishang qingjing lübao* 太上清靜玉律寶 and is already mentioned in the transmission from the first Vinaya Patriarch to the second. See below. In the Preface to the *Chuzhen jielü* 初真戒律 attributed to Wang Changyue one also finds the expression "Taishang qingdu lüzong."

fifteenth day 望日 of the tenth lunar month" of 1312, exactly "thirty-three years" after Qiu's initial transmission at Baiyun guan that had taken place on "the fifteenth day of the first lunar month" of 1280. In turn, the second patriarch transmitted the secret to the third "on the fifteenth day of the seventh lunar month" of 1367 "after fifty-six years;" the third to the fourth "twenty-two years later, on the fifteenth day of the first lunar month" of 1387, and so on.[75]

Through the exemplary life of these earlier Longmen patriarchs, key moments in Daoist history are highlighted as if they were turnings of the Vinaya Dharma wheel. The entire transmission narrative culminates "on the fifteenth day of the third lunar month" of 1656 in the public transmission of the precepts at Baiyun guan by the seventh patriarch Wang Changyue 王常月 alias Wang Kunyang 王崑陽. While the biographies of the first and seventh Longmen Vinaya Patriarchs are also found in other sources, the biographies of the second to the sixth patriarchs stem exclusively from Min Yide's *Mind-Lamp of Mount Jingai* 金蓋心燈 (JGXD). This work is therefore the fundamental source for the earlier history of Longmen. It canonizes an ideal and romantic view of Longmen origins for posterity. Later works by Min Yide's disciples—such as the *Daotong yuanliu zhi* 道統源流志 (abbr. *Gazetteer of Daoist Origins*) by Yan Liuqian 嚴六謙 and the *Longmen zhengzong Jueyun benzhi daotong xinchuan* 龍門正宗覺雲本支道統薪傳 (abbr. JYDT) compiled by Lu Yongzhi 陸永銘—or by Baiyun guan-affiliated masters, such as the *Taishang lümai Longmen zhengzong* 太上律脈龍門正宗 (abbr. TSLM), also relied on Min Yide's *Mind-Lamp of Mount Jingai* 金蓋心燈, as did Republican-era abridgments and digests of Longmen hagiographies of the first seven Longmen patriarchs.[76]

---

[75] It is interesting to note that for the biographies of the first seven patriarchs, the transmission always takes place on the 15th day in months that are noted for the transmission of precepts. As *Chuzhen jielü* 初真戒律 (CK 24: 10476 in the section on "the three masters" [40a–b] of "Rujie yaogui" 入戒要規 [38a–46b]) states: "Each year, on the fifteenth day [full moon] of the first lunar month, the fifteenth day of the seventh lunar month, and the fifteenth day of the tenth lunar month, the master convenes the four ranks of the assembly [i.e., monks, nuns, laymen, and lay women], opens the altar, and transmits the precepts. After the precepts are received, they must be practiced and observed in the Bowl [Hall] for one hundred days." 每於正月十五、七月十五、十月十五日、會集四眾、開壇傳戒、戒後行持演鉢一百日。

[76] For a chart of the succession of Longmen patriarchs and a discussion of the Longmen orthodox line in a larger sectarian context see my "Longmen School and its Controversial History" {*Facets of Qing Daoism*, chapter 2} and here above Fig. 5.

1. First Patriarch Zhao Daojian 趙道堅 and the transmission of the Longmen generational poem

Returning now to Longmen's "first patriarch" Zhao Daojian, whom I have called Longmen Daoism's "Apostle Peter," one notes that the further clarification of his role in the propagation of the Longmen orthodox lineage was a task of the *Longmen zhengzong Jueyun benzhi daotong xinchuan* 龍門正宗覺雲本支道統薪傳 (JYDT). In its Preface of 1927 by Cha Fugong 查復功—the fourteenth Longmen patriarch in the line of Min Yide's third-generation disciples—the foundation of the Longmen tradition is presented as the achievement of the unique blood-line (*yimai* 一脉) of Quanzhen that, thanks to the support of emperor Taizu, had been propagated in the North from the time of Qiu Chuji who by imperial decree had been granted the title of "Changchun yandao zhujiao zhenren" 長春演道主教真人 (Perfected Eternal Spring, Bishop who spreads the Way) and was charged with presiding over the Quanzhen Longmen lineage.

The establishment of the Longmen orthodox ancestral line was portrayed in the context of the pacification of the entire country. As the disciple of Qiu, Vinaya Patriarch Zhao is said to have succeeded in pacifying the country and to have received from emperor Shizu 世祖 the title of "Hunyuan dazong shi 混元大宗師" (Great Patriarch of Chaotic Origin). According to the *Jueyun benzhi daotong xinchuan* (JYDT) it was Zhao who was charged with "transmitting the Longmen line along with the imperially bestowed twenty-character generational poem in order to widely propagate the method of precepts and broadly spreading the sublime teaching [of Daoism] 命傳龍門派、御賜二十字輩、廣行戒法、大闡玄風." This important passage of 1927 merits to be quoted in full:

> Great is the purport of the Dao! Its orthodoxy should be worshiped and respected, and what runs deep has its origins in antiquity. The unique line (*yimai*) of Quanzhen was founded as early as the time when Emperor Taizu sent a dispatch to solicit Patriarch Qiu to propagate it in the North, and this was done in perfect agreement with imperial will. Thus Emperor Taizu granted Qiu the title of Changchun yandao zhujiao zhenren 長春演道主教真人 (Perfected Eternal Spring, Bishop who spreads the Way) and charged him with presiding over the Longmen branch of Quanzhen (*Quanzhen Longmen fapai* 全真龍門法派). The Longmen orthodox lineage (*Longmen zhengzong* 龍門正宗) was established around this time. Since then the entire world has

been converted, and the wind (of the doctrine) in conformity with the Dao has spread to every corner of the empire. Subsequently, Emperor Shizu of Yuan praised the Vinaya Patriarch Zhao Xujing—the disciple of Qiu—for his meritorious actions in pacifying the country by granting him the title Hunyuan dazong shi 混元大宗師 (Great Patriarch of Chaotic Origin) and charged him with transmitting the Longmen line along with the imperially bestowed twenty-character lineage poem in order to widely promulgate the method of precepts and broadly spread the sublime spirit of Daoism. The miraculous feat of offering it to one or two masters opened the way of the teachings for centuries and millennia, enabling the ascent to immortality, the achievement of perfection, and the attainment of Dao.

道之旨大矣哉。崇其正而宗之、則蓄之深者發自遠。全真一脉、溯自元太祖聖武皇帝遣使徵聘邱祖、應宣北面、以召對稱旨、褒贈長春演道主教真人、命主全真龍門法派。龍門正宗實肇造於此、縣是天下向化、而風同道合、有無往弗屆者。逮元世祖皇帝嘉邱祖門下趙虛靜律師招撫有功、敕封混元大宗師、命傳龍門派、御賜二十字輩、廣行戒法、大闡玄風。奉一二師之神功、啟千百年之宏教而登仙、而成真、而得道。

This passage reflects the twentieth-century orthodox Longmen view that its line constitutes a movement within Quanzhen inaugurated in the thirteenth century by Patriarch Qiu under the auspices of emperor Taizu with the aim of pacifying the entire country. Nineteenth-century hagiographers also emphasize that the Longmen line was established under emperor Taizu by Qiu, whose meritorious services in pacifying the country were successfully continued by his heir Zhao who is also portrayed as an imperially sanctioned transmitter of the Longmen line and its twenty-character lineage poem.

In contrast to the custom of the Yuan-period Quanzhen order of sharing just a few common characters in the religious names of its affiliates, the reinvented Quanzhen of the Qing adopted generational poems for its new affiliates. In the Qing, each "orthodox" sect ideally affiliated with Quanzhen came to have a poem between twenty to one hundred characters in length. The most famous example is of course the poem of the Longmen lineage. Although this poem was supposedly granted by the first Yuan emperor Shizu 世祖 (1260–1294), it is in reality only found in relatively recent sources.[77]

---

[77] Yoshioka Yoshitoyo, "Taoist Monastic Life," 231. In *Jingai xindeng*, 1.1a–2a (accord-

In the *Mind-Lamp,* this Longmen lineage poem forms a crucial element of Founder Qiu's transmission narrative:

> Subsequently, Zhao followed the Patriarch [Qiu] to Yan [Beijing] in order to spread the teaching. He acted in the world in spontaneous harmony and in silence. At times he attended [Qiu] throughout the night without uttering a single word. The Patriarch thus transmitted to him the secret of pure emptiness and natural spontaneity, upon which Zhao withdrew to Mount Longmen for many years. After having come out [from this retreat], he [Zhao] served Patriarch [Qiu] at the Baiyun guan and gathered a great number [of disciples]. The fifteenth day of the first month of the *bingchen* year of the Zhiyuan era (1280), Zhao received the Initial Precepts of Perfection (*chuzhen jie* 初真戒) as well as the Intermediate Precepts (*zhongji jie* 中極戒).[78]
>
> 遂侍祖遊燕闡教。凡有作為不言自合。或侍終夜不發一語。祖乃傳以清虛自然之秘。棲隱龍門者多載。復出侍祖於白雲觀。統大眾。師於至元庚辰。正月望日。受初真戒、中極戒。

It is here that the nineteenth-century narrative of Qiu's transmission to Zhao arrives at its culminating point where Chan-inspired elements (conferral of the "mind-seal" along with robe and bowl) are linked to Longmen Daoism's ultimate precepts and its transmission poem:

> After [Qiu] had practiced in accordance with the rules without losing his sublime virtue, the Patriarch personally transmitted the "seal of mind" (*xinyin* 心印) to him [Zhao] and entrusted him with robe and bowl. Zhao received the Precepts of Celestial Immortals along with

---

ing to its quoted source *Yilin* 逸林 "*Quanzhen lu* 全真錄") the Longmen poem, which originally featured twenty characters, was allegedly legitimized by the edict of first Yuan emperor Shizu (re. 1260–1294). This poem in twenty characters is also listed in Wu Shouyang's work and in Liu Xianting's *Guangyang zaji* (with the substitution in its last verse of the character *yuan* 圓 for *zhen* 真). A one hundred character version is listed in the *Daotong yuanliu, zhong,* 5–6, Oyanagi Shigeta, *Hakuunkan shi,* etc. See Esposito, "La Porte du Dragon," vol. 1, 103, note 40, and "The Longmen School and its Controversial History," 629–30 {*Facets of Qing Daoism,* pp. 68–69}. Recently some Chinese scholars have come around to agree that this poem is not found in Yuan sources and did not yet exist as generational Quanzhen-Longmen poem during the Yuan period. See for instance, Ding Peiren, "*Jingai xindeng* juan 1 zhiyi," 424, 428, and Zhang Guangbao, "Mingdai Quanzhenjiao de zongxi fenhua." (2011).

[78] These precepts are discussed in Part Two.

a four-verse *gatha* amounting to twenty characters that forms the Longmen branch's poem: *Dao de tong yuan jing, zhen chang shou tai qing, yi yang lai fu ben, he jiao yong yuan ming.*

如法行持。無漏妙德。祖乃親傳心印。付衣缽。受天仙戒。贈偈四句。以為龍門派計二十字。道德通元靜。真常守太清。一陽來復本。合教永圓明。[79]

As is well known, the characters of this Longmen transmission poem (*Dao de tong xuan jing* 道德通玄靜...) were used for naming and distinguishing each generation of Longmen masters. For instance, a master with the lineage name *Dao-X* (*Dao* 道 representing the first generation) would name his disciple *De-X* (*De* 德 indicating the second generation), and so on (*Tong* 通 for the third generation, *Xuan* 玄 for the fourth generation, *Jing* 靜 for the fifth generation, etc.).

This method of apportioning names based on a transmission poem that permits identification of the lineage generation stands in stark contrast with the naming habits of Quanzhen during the Yuan. Disciples affiliated with Quanzhen had as the first character of their religious names one of the three characters *zhi* 志, *dao* 道, or *de* 德. The choice of these three characters was independent of the lineage position of their masters. Such use of the "three-character system," which was regarded as central to the identity of the Quanzhen order during the Yuan since it allegedly gave "all Quanzhen clerics a concrete sense of belonging to the same timeless and universal community,"[80] was no more in use during the Qing. By adopting the generational principle, the new multi-branched "Quanzhen" local sects of the Ming and Qing came to be inscribed into a fragmented time and space as they split into a variety of branches and sub-branches, each of which had its own particular lineage poem.

---

[79] "Zhao Xujing lüshi zhuan" (JGXD I, 1.1a–2b); see M. Esposito "La Porte du Dragon," 103. The fourth character of the poem is here *yuan* 元, but this was a substitution for the Kangxi era (1662–1722) taboo character *xuan* 玄.

[80] Goossaert, "The Invention of an Order," 131–2. About the phenomenon of fragmentation in the reinvented Quanzhen of the Qing, see Esposito, "The Longmen School and its Controversial History," 629–30 {*Facets of Qing Daoism*, chapter 2, pp. 68–69}.

2. Second Patriarch Zhang Dechun 張德純 (fl. 1312–1367) and the Orthodox Lineage of the Most High

>Date of birth: no mention
>Date of death: no mention
>Original name (*benming* 本名): Heng 珩
>Lineage name (*ming* 名): **Dechun** 德純 (Pure Virtue)
>Daoist name (*hao* 號): **Bizhi** 碧芝 (Magical Mushroom of Jade)
>Birthplace: Kaifeng 開封 or Luoyang 洛陽 (Henan)

According to the "Biography of the Vinaya Patriarch Zhang Bizhi" ("Zhang Bizhi lüshi zhuan 張碧芝律師傳," JGXD 1.3a–b), Zhang Dechun was born in Henan province into a wealthy family from Kaifeng or Luoyang.[81] Instead of taking care of his family he preferred to visit alchemists and experts of occult techniques. Only after having squandered his entire fortune, ruined his family, and succumbed to diseases did he realize the futility of his original pursuits and became a Daoist priest. For more than thirty years he then fully devoted himself to this religious path in order to eradicate his past habits. After having heard that the "Longmen robe and bowl 龍門衣鉢" had been transmitted to Patriarch Zhao Daojian, he served him for more than eighteen years. Although he did not receive any teachings, Zhang never lost his faith and respect for Patriarch Zhao.

Among the many Chinese narratives of teachers reluctant to impart their teachings, Patriarch Zhao's reticence reminds us of the tale of Bodhidharma who, according to legend, sat for nine years silently facing a wall and drove his eventual successor Huike to such desperation that Huike finally sliced off his own arm and presented it to Bodhidharma in order to prove his absolute determination to obtain the silent monk's instruction (see Fig. 9).

Similar to the Bodhidharma of Chan legend who is said to have finally relented and imparted his teachings to his successor Huike, Patriarch Zhao ended up recognizing that Zhang was indeed "a vessel of the Dao" (*daoqi* 道器) and, foreseeing his own imminent death, called him to his side and said:

>In bygone days, my master Qiu widely spread the subtle spirit of Daoism; he extensively put it in action and converted the people. How could it be that those who at that time obtained the Dao and took charge of the lineage remained so few? At any rate, it was only

---

[81] The *Taishang lümai Longmen zhengzong* 太上律脈龍門正宗 (TSLM) mentions instead only Luoyang.

to me that he transmitted the supreme Dao, and since then already thirty years have passed.[82] In order to prevent the *'orthodox lineage of the Most High'* from being disgraced I never dared to transmit it to incapable men. Having obtained you as successor, my task is now achieved. Take care of it and preserve it.

昔我子邱子大闡元（玄）風、廣行教化。其間得道承宗者、豈為鮮少。乃獨以無上之道、傳付於我。今又三十年矣。不敢輕授匪人、以辱太上正宗。得子以承、我事畢矣。汝其珍重以持。

Zhang subsequently withdrew to Huashan (Shaanxi), "shouldering the Vinaya teachings for years" (*jianhe lüjiao younian* 肩荷律教有年).[83] In 1367—"the last year of the Yuan dynasty, fifty-six years after 1312" when Zhang had at last received the transmission from his master Zhao—Zhang went on to transmit it to his heir, third patriarch Chen Tongwei, before disappearing.

This 19th-century narrative in Min Yide's *Mind-Lamp of Mount Jingai* 金蓋心燈 (*Mind-Lamp*) is unsupported by earlier sources. Although we find the name of Zhang Dechun on a stela erected in 1320 where he is described as one of the disciples of Zhang Zhide 張志德—the supervisor (*tidian* 提點) of the Shengshou gong 聖壽宮 of Jizhou 濟州—he does not appear to be related to Qiu Chuji and his disciples, and regrettably remains only a name for us.[84] As in the case of early catholic "popes" and early Chan "pa-

---

[82] Because, according to the dates given in JGXD biography, "thirty-three years" had already passed since the last transmission, the *Taishang lümai Longmen zhengzong* 太上律脈龍門正宗 (TSLM) amends this passage by augmenting the number of years: "In bygone days my master, the Perfected Changchun, had widely spread the subtle spirit of Daoism by extensively putting it in action and bringing enlightenment to people by educating them so that those who obtained the Dao were not few. At any rate, it was only to me that he transmitted the supreme and solely genuine Dao. More than thirty years have already passed since I respectfully received the teachings and sincerely spread the 'Treasure of the Jade Code of Pure Tranquility from the Most High.' In order to prevent the true lineage of the Most High from being disgraced I did not dare to transmit it to others. Having today conferred it to you, my task is achieved." 昔吾師長春真人大闡玄風、廣行教化、得道之士亦為不少。獨以無上真一之道、傳付於我。敬謹受教、誠演太上清靜玉律寶經。今三十餘年、不敢輕付於人、以辱太上真脈。今付於子、吾事畢矣。

[83] The TSLM revises this to "shouldering the doctrine and Vinaya 肩荷教律."

[84] "Zhang tidian shouzang ji 張提點壽藏記" stela by Cao Yuanyong 曹元用 (?–1329) erected in 1320, in Chen Yuan, *Daojia jinshi lüe*, 754. See also Ding Peiren 2008:424–25.

triarchs" including Bodhidharma's successor Huike (Fig. 9), such historical blankness lent itself to the later construction of "figures of memory" perfectly suited to their ideal role.

Fig. 9: Chan's "Second Patriarch" Huike presenting his severed arm to Bodhidharma. Detail from the painting by Sesshū Tōyō (1420–1506). (Brinker & Kanazawa 1996:233)

Forced to limit ourselves to Min Yide's portrayal of Longmen's "Second Patriarch" in his *Mind-Lamp of Mount Jingai* 金蓋心燈, we can only note that the hagiographers seem to make use of Zhang Dechun's previous life as an example of being on guard against the vain research of alchemical techniques and ingestion of immortality drugs, and that his devotion to his silent master presents a model of extreme religious determination. It is only through his absolute devotion to Daoism's quintessential teachings that Zhang is finally judged to be a "vessel" worthy of receiving the "supreme Dao" fit for transmitting the "orthodox lineage of the Most High" (Taishang zhengzong 太上正宗).[85] In evoking the direct transmission of the "Longmen robe and bowl" from the idealized founder Qiu Chuji to its first Vinaya Patriarch, the hagiographers emphasize the secrecy of this empowerment rite. In contrast to the wide diffusion of Quanzhen teachings during the Jin and Yuan dynasties, the Longmen lineage is portrayed as the unique vehicle of the Supreme Dao embodying the "orthodox lineage of the Most High" that was secretly transmitted from one patriarch to the next. This is the main idea that is continuously repeated up to the point where its genuine content, rooted in Vinaya teachings,[86] was ripe to be divulged to the world. If in the case of Chan Buddhism such an occasion had arisen with the Sixth Patriarch's *Platform Sutra* and its "formless precepts,"[87] the crucial role of divulging formerly secret teachings to a broader public belonged in the Longmen tradition to its seventh patriarch Wang Changyue 王常月 (d. 1680; see Part Two). In the present context it is interesting to note that the expression "orthodox lineage of the Most High" (Taishang zhengzong 太上正宗) as the embodiment of the Daoist Vinaya tradition appears precisely in a passage about the precept-scripture—the *Chuzhen jielü* 初真戒律 (CK vol. 24, 10473)—that is attributed to the said seventh patriarch:

> When first entering the Dharma-gate of the *"orthodox lineage of the Most High,"* regardless of whether you come from Daoist clerical or lay

---

[85] The *Taishang lümai Longmen zhengzong* 太上律脈龍門正宗 (TSLM) uses instead the expression "Genuine lineage of the Most High" (Taishang zhenmai 太上真脈). See note 82 above.

[86] The TSLM calls it *Taishang qingjing yulü bao* 太上清靜玉律寶 or "Treasure of Jade Statutes of Pure Quiescence from the Most High." The expression "Treasure of Jade Statutes of pure quiescence from the Most High" also occurs in other biographies of Wang Changyue, but JGXD calls it "Taishang qingjing lübao 太上清靜律寶."

[87] See several contributions in Fo Kuang shan (ed.), *The Sixth Patriarch Platform Sūtra in Religious and Cultural Perspective*. Taichong: Fo Kuang shan, 1988.

background, you must honor and obey the golden rules and jade statutes of the Most High (Lord Lao) as well as the various precept-texts of the Three Caverns (i.e., the Daoist Canon). You must also present offerings to the statues of the worthies of the great Dao and send a formal petition to Wang Tianjun, the disciplinary supervisor of the various heavens,[88] requesting to become a member of the community. Then you must take the precepts of the Three Refuges.

凡初入太上正宗法門,不問道俗,必先遵依太上金科玉律、三洞戒文,供養大道尊像。表通都天糾察王天君,請祈盟證,受三皈依戒。

The "orthodox lineage of the Most High," after a period of secret incubation from the first to the sixth patriarch, was to be finally revealed in form of the public transmission of the Daoist Vinaya.[89] Allegedly supported by the Qing emperors, it was to be conveyed by the seventh patriarch, Wang Changyue 王常月, during a legendary public ordination ceremony at the capital's Baiyun guan (see Part Two). Interestingly, the same expression (related again to the seventh patriarch) was later employed in Min Yide's effort to legitimize the "Longmen esoteric Vinaya transmission" conveyed at its private altars. But before bearing such fruit, this unique transmission first had to pass through several additional waystations involving the third, fourth, fifth, and sixth Longmen patriarchs. We will now return to the discussion of the construction of this lineage.

---

[88] Wang Tianjun, also called Wang jiucha, is better known as Wang lingguan (Numinous Officer Wang 王靈官) or Marshal Wang (Wang Yuanshuai 王元帥), protector of all Daoist monasteries and equivalent of Weituo 韋馱 (jap. Ida), the guardian deity of Buddhist monasteries whose statue even today graces and protects the kitchen building of every Zen monastery in Japan. For his image see for instance Yoshioka Yoshitoyo (1979, 250–5), quoted by Katz 2008: "In the proclamation scriptures he has the appellation Dutian jiucha, Daling guan. For that reason he is named Wang jiucha. 其誥文有都天糾察大靈官之號、故稱王糾察." See the commentary to the biography of Huang Chongyang, JGXD 2.31b.

[89] Min Yide also refers to it as "Taishang lüzong 太上律宗" (Vinaya tradition of the Most High). See Min Yide's commentary to the *Huangji zhengdao jing*, and here below.

3. Third Patriarch Chen Tongwei 陳通微 (fl. 1387) and the Southern accommodation of Longmen at the beginning of the Ming

> Date of birth: no mention
> Date of death: no mention
> Original name (*yuanming* 原名): Zhizhong 致中
> Lineage name (*ming* 名): **Tong**wei 通微 (Penetrating the Subtle)
> Daoist name (*hao* 號): Chongyi zi 沖夷子 (Master Filled with the Invisible)
> Birthplace: Dongchang 東昌 (Shandong)

The "Biography of the Vinaya Patriarch Chen Chongyi" ("Chen Chongyi lüshi zhuan 陳沖夷律師傳," JGXD 1.4a–b) presents Chen as inaugurator of a new phase of Longmen history at the beginning of the Ming dynasty. This development is apparent in Chen's successful study of the so-called "Zhengyi rites of prayers and exorcism" (Zhengyi quxie qidao zhi fa 正一驅邪祈禱之法). As is known, Zhengyi was the Daoist tradition promoted by the founder of the Ming dynasty who in 1368 had charged the forty-second Celestial Master with supervising Daoism throughout the empire.[90]

Chen's *Mind-Lamp* biography opens with a description of the extraordinary abilities he acquired in Zhengyi rites. He was so good at them that people competed to have him as teacher. However, as one would expect of a future Longmen heir, Chen suffered from such distractions and fled to Mt. Hua 華山 (Huashan, Shaanxi) in order to escape from such unsolicited attention. As he passed by the hermitage of Zhang Dechun he discovered the old man completely absorbed in the recitation of the *Daodejing*. Impressed by his calm and composed allure he knelt down and begged him for instruction. Though the master did not react, Chen decided to serve him and cultivate the humility required of a worthy disciple. Only after persevering for many years did he receive the lineage name **Tong**wei 通微 along with the transmission of the full set of three precepts. In accordance with the marvelous virtue of the Way he devoted all his efforts to its practice and wide propagation in the Shaanxi and Shanxi regions. Wishing to convert his fellow Daoists, he kept traveling for years but did not encounter a single

---

[90] Wang Jianchuan 王見川, "Longhu shan Zhang Tianshi yu Huangdi 龍虎山張天師與皇帝," *Daotong zhi mei* 道統之美 3 (2005/11): 84–109, here 93.

disciple worthy of his instruction.[91] Finally in 1387, after having retired to Mount Qingcheng in Sichuan, he transmitted the method of precepts to Zhou **Xuan**pu 周玄朴.

According to this *Mind-Lamp* biography, Chen was at first seen as a wonder-worker inside the Zhengyi tradition. Although he enjoyed great success and popularity on account of his extraordinary powers in performing Zhengyi rites, he abandoned such distracting pursuits in favor of a purist ideal of self-cultivation embodied in the peaceful and sober allure of the second Longmen patriarch reciting the *Daodejing*. By recording these passages, the nineteenth-century hagiographers (Min Yide, Bao Tingbo, and Bao Kun) appear to suggest a certain superiority of Longmen methods and ideals. This is also apparent in Chen's failure to convert his Zhengyi Daoist companions. The time to re-inaugurate massive conversions to Daoism, as in Yuan-dynasty Quanzhen, had not yet arrived, and Chen first had to transcend the liturgical prowess and success of the Zhengyi during the new Ming dynasty. His biography shows that he tried to face this new reality, and in this context it is worthy of note that the *Gazetteer of Daoist Origins* (*Daotong yuanliu zhi* 道統源流志)—probably in reference to Chen's liturgical legacy—have Chen's disciple Zhou Xuanpu also transmit the Lingbao lineage 靈寶派.

Whereas the *Mind-Lamp* biography has Chen wander in the northern regions without finding a single worthy disciple, the *Gazetteer of Daoist Origins* specify that before leaving for Sichuan he conferred his transmission on Sun Xuanqing 孫玄清 (1497–1569), a man who later came to be recognized as a Longmen patriarch of the fourth generation and founder of the Laoshan lineage (see Fig. 5). With such claims we are once more fac-

---

[91] The JGXD passage reads: "He had trouble to devote his mind to the mysterious teaching (Daoism) and to spread it in many places between Shanxi and Shaanxi. Wishing to convert "feathered vagabonds" he wandered here and there for many years without success until he withdrew to Qingcheng 苦志元（玄）功、秦晉之間多所闡揚、愛度羽流、周遊有年、不得遇、乃入青城." The TSLM does not include the passage on Chen's incapacity of finding disciples but emphasizes instead Chen's wide propagation of teachings in the regions of Shanxi and Shaanxi with the aim of converting the "feathered vagabonds" (*yuliu* 羽流): "He had trouble to devote his mind to meritorious actions and to spread the teachings in many places from Shanxi to Shaanxi in order to save 'feathered vagabonds.' Wandering here and there for years, he at last lived in seclusion on Mount Qingcheng 苦志立功、秦晉之間多所闡揚、普度羽流、周遊有年、後入青城隱居." The term *yuliu* "feathered vagabonds" is also used at the beginning of Chen's biography in reference to the group of Daoist priests with whom he previously performed Zhengyi rites.

ing the kind of historical incongruence characterizing the construction of the "Longmen orthodox lineage." If the first patriarch Zhao Daojian had died before the mythical Longmen founder Qiu Chuji, the third patriarch Chen is said to have left his legacy in the North to the fourth-generation disciple Sun Xuanqing, a man who according to earlier sources lived about one century later. The failure of the *Mind-Lamp* to address this issue may signal a silent frustration of Chen and his disciple Zhou, or rather of their nineteenth-century hagiographers. Though they were natives of Northern China, the third and fourth patriarchs had to flee to Sichuan—the original sanctuary of the Celestial Masters and of southern legacies—in order to preserve their "Longmen orthodox lineage."

This is echoed in a view shared by some modern scholars and also expressed in Chen Minggui's *Changchun daojiao yuanliu* 長春道教源流 (vol. 2, p. 464). It holds that during the Ming, Quanzhen was spreading in the South while disappearing in the North. However, on the basis of newly discovered epigraphic materials, recent scholarship tends to contradict this view and instead emphasizes a continuity of Quanzhen activities in the North from the Yuan until the present. In tune with recent studies, later sources also stress the continuity of the Longmen legacy in Northern China and mention Sun Xuanqing as one of the important Longmen masters of the end of the Ming. It appears that the authors of such later sources felt the need to link the "orthodox Longmen lineage" to that of Sun Xuanqing in his role as the Ming-era founder of another important Quanzhen lineage at Laoshan (Shandong).

4. Fourth Patriarch Zhou Xuanpu 周玄朴 (?–1450?) and the split into two lines of transmission

    Date of birth: no mention
    Date of death: no mention
    Original name (*yuanming* 原名): Zhisheng 知生
    Lineage name (*ming* 名): **Xuan**pu 玄朴 (Mysterious Simplicity)
    Daoist name (*hao* 號): Dazhuo 大拙 (Great Ignorant)
    Birthplace: Xi'an 西安 (Shaanxi)

In the "Biography of the Vinaya Patriarch Zhou Dazhuo" ("Zhou Dazhuo lüshi zhuan 周大拙律師傳," JGXD 1.5a–b) Zhou is portrayed as a man out of the ordinary. While immersing himself in Daoist teachings, he was content even working as a peasant. But his simple and joyful life style came to an abrupt end when, close to the end of the Yuan dynasty, his native region became engulfed in such anarchy and turmoil that nobody was spared. Zhou decided to withdraw to the Zhongnan Mountains (Shaanxi), but even there he was bothered by brigands. Thus he decided to leave his family and take refuge in Sichuan on Mount Qingcheng where he became a disciple of Chen Tongwei, the master who is said to have "shouldered the responsibility for the precept doctrine 擔荷戒法."

Our nineteenth-century hagiographers (Min Yide, Bao Tingbo, and Bao Kun) point out that the majority of Daoist masters during this transitional period preferred to live secluded in the mountains and refrained from involvement in society to such an extent that the propagation of Daoism was endangered:

> At that time, the Mysterious Teaching [i.e., Daoism] was in shambles. Men of good will all wanted to save their necks and avoid blame. Zhou hid on Mount Qingcheng, and for more than fifty years he did not set foot in the dust of the world. He faced the wall practicing introspection in order to avoid bothering his mind by doctrines and worldly matters. His disciples were numerous, but all of them refrained from devoting themselves to the propagation of the teachings. The Vinaya-gate was facing extinction.
>
> 是時元(玄)門零落。有志之士皆全身避咎。師隱青城、不履塵市、五十餘年。面壁內觀、不以教相有為之事累心。弟子數人、皆不以闡教為事。律門幾致湮歿。

The early twentieth-century *Taishang lümai Longmen zhengzong* 太上律脈龍門正宗 (TSLM) offers instead a decidedly less catastrophic picture. In the corresponding passage it states that while Zhao faced the wall and practiced introspection, "his ordained disciples occupied themselves with the propagation of the teachings so that the Vinaya-gate would not meet with extinction."[92] Only toward the end of Zhou's life, at the age of 150 years (!), he is said to have finally managed to find two disciples capable of taking care of his lineage, which thus split into two branches: the Vinaya line represented by Zhang Jingding 張靜定 (fl. 1450) and the Ancestral

---

[92] The TSLM passage in question reads: "[The master] faced the wall practicing introspection. At that time his ordained disciples occupied themselves with the propagation of the teachings so that the Vinaya-gate would not meet with extinction 面壁內觀、時戒弟子以闡教為功、律門庶不致湮歿."

line represented by Shen Jingyuan 沈靜圓 (fl.1448). The *Daotong yuanliu zhi* 道統源流志 (*xia* 1) of 1929 adds that Zhou also "transmitted the Lingbao lineage 傳靈寶派" (see Fig. 5, p. 16). Once his task was accomplished, Zhou took leave in 1450, whereupon his trace is lost.

Zhou's biography embodies a crucial moment for the Longmen lineage. In it, the upheaval and economic hardship of the late Yuan dynasty is linked to the loss of spiritual integrity and influence of the Vinaya transmission of the early Ming dynasty. In order to ensure the lineage's continuity, the "transmission of the Lamp" now had to be divided into two lines. The first is the Vinaya line (*lüzong* 律宗) apportioned to Zhang Jingding 張靜定. Zhang was entrusted with the task of ensuring the transmission of precepts (*chuanjie* 傳戒) to future generations until the advent of Baiyun guan abbot Wang Changyue 王常月, the man credited with reunifying both lines. The second is the Ancestral line (*zuzong* 祖宗) that, via Shen Jingyuan 沈靜圓, had to transmit the doctrinal heritage (*chuanzong* 傳宗) of Daoist traditions (*zongpai* 宗派)[93] until its eventual broad and proper diffusion through Min Yide 閔一得 (1748/58–1836).

In the following I will concentrate on the Vinaya line (see Fig. 5) and postpone the discussion of the Ancestral line. The Vinaya tradition that represents the driving force of the idealized "Longmen orthodox lineage," from its purported founder Qiu Chuji to the fourth Vinaya Patriarch Zhou is, in Zhou's biography, portrayed as almost extinguished. Nonetheless, in contrast to previous Longmen patriarchs, the hagiographers equip Zhou with many disciples. As mentioned above, while using this information, the *Taishang lümai Longmen zhengzong* 太上律脈龍門正宗 draws a less catastrophic picture of that period and asserts that the Vinaya-gate continued to be transmitted thanks to the efforts of Zhao's ordained disciples.

Whereas the earlier Longmen Vinaya Patriarchs resemble Chan patriarchs in search of vessels worthy of being heirs to a unilinear tradition, the new generation was now in need of genuine masters as founts of multilin-

---

[93] As is known, *zong* 宗 has different meanings: essence or truth, but also ancestral lineage or tradition. The term can refer to a "line" of transmission of an ancestral temple but also to the transmission of traditional doctrine. Like the English word "tradition" it connotes both an active transmission via proper conduit or *lineage*, and the *content* of a transmitted idea or doctrine. In this double sense the word *zong* applies both to the Vinaya lineage and the Doctrinal lineage; both are necessary for the proper, uninterrupted transmission and preservation of "original," "genuine," "traditional" teachings. See also note 9 above (p. 5).

ear or multi-branched transmissions.[94] Inspired by the model of Confucian recluses, such masters are the protagonists of a new phase of Longmen creativity: they were "men of good will" who, though momentarily refusing to collaborate with the government, embraced the ideal of scholar-priests and were animated by the Confucian virtue of filial piety. As we shall see in the following biographies, this core Confucian virtue was progressively introduced into the Longmen scheme of precepts. It promised peace and prosperity in the world and offered a significant role to future rulers.[95]

Echoing the words of the aging Ming Taizu emperor (r. 1368–1394) about people's bad custom, in his time, of "changing names" (that is, adopting religious names) "in order to avoid trouble and save their necks,"[96] the hagiographers appear to suggest that such withdrawal and apparent loss of power turned out to be beneficial for the future of the Longmen lineage. As we shall see, the Vinaya transmission—the Qing-era invention of an uninterrupted continuation of Qiu Chuji's Northern Quanzhen tradition—was to embody the state-approved Daoist orthodoxy at the public monastery Baiyun guan through the figure of its reformer and abbot Wang Changyue. But before it fully manifested in form of the abbots' orthodox transmission of ordination procedures involving the reinterpretation of rituals and precepts, the Longmen Vinaya line had to pass through two more waystations: the fifth and the sixth generations of masters.

---

[94] It is interesting to note that in Chan Buddhism, too, the Fourth Patriarch marks the point where different branches originated. See John Jorgensen, *Inventing Huineng, the Sixth Patriarch. Hagiography and Biography in Early Ch'an* (Leiden / Boston: Brill, 2005): 122.

[95] This "Confucian line" of Daoist Vinaya will be also emphasized in the works of Peng Dingqiu while writing an epitaph for one of Wang Changyue's disciples (see here below).

[96] This refers in particular to the 1394 Hongwu edict that criticizes about Buddhism and its immoral clergy. See Timothy Brook, "At the Margin of Public Authority: The Ming State and Buddhism," in *Culture & State in Chinese History*, ed. Theodore Huters, Bin R. Wong and Pauline Yu (Stanford, CA: Stanford University Press, 1997): 161–81, here 161 and 175.

5. Fifth Patriarch Zhang Jingding 張靜定 (fl. 1450) and the Unique Lineage of Former Saints

Date of birth: no mention
Date of death: no mention
Original name (*yuanming* 原名): Zongren 宗仁
Lineage name (*ming* 名): **Jing**ding 靜定 (Serene Concentration)
Daoist name (*hao* 號): Wuwo 無我 (Egoless)
Birthplace: Yuhang 餘杭 (modern Hangzhou, Zhejiang)

According to the "Biography of the Vinaya Patriarch Zhang Wuwo" ("Zhang Wuwo lüshi zhuan" 張無我律師傳, JGXD 1.6a–7a, ZWDS 31.178–9), Zhang hailed from a family of officials and excelled in Confucian studies. During the Yongle era (1403–1424) he was admitted to the civil examinations but did not earn any degree and became a private instructor in his native region of Zhejiang at Tiaoxi 苕溪.[97] After the death of his parents he fell into such despair that he felt the need to leave all worldly affairs. Having fulfilled his filial obligations he left to roam about, visiting famous mountains in search of eminent and accomplished men. Had he had the chance of meeting a patriarch like Chen Chongyi, he used to say, he would not have hesitated to revere him as his master. He was glad to finally arrive at Tiantai (Zhejiang) and find a group of three or four Daoists to serve and with whom he could chant and perform liturgy. Initiated into the classics of Daoism and alchemical formulae, he understood them at first glance. According to the commentary reportedly based on the *Dongyuan yulu* 東原

---

[97] According to the commentary based on the *Bojian*, the period corresponds to the reign of Chengzu 成祖 (Yongle 永樂, r. 1403–1424), but according to the *Dongyuan yulu* 東園語錄—a work attributed to Lü Quanyang 呂全陽—this took place in the Chenghua 成化 period (1465–1487). Bao Tingbo adds that *hua* 化 (in Chenghua 成化) is probably a mistake. However, the Chenghua period is also referred to in the TSLM: "During the Chenghua period he took the civil examinations, but he did not fill any official post and was a private instructor at Tiaoxi 成化間舉明經不仕、講學於苕溪." One may wonder if later sources preferred referring to the examinations under emperor Xianzong 憲宗, which were less controversial than the ones reestablished by Chengzu whom Ming loyalists regarded as an usurper. Chengzu was known for having executed Huidi 惠帝 (Jianwen 建文, r. 1399–1402) along with his entire family and progeny as well as many officials. See Benjamin A. Elman, "The Formation of 'Dao Learning' as Imperial Ideology During the Early Ming Dynasty," in *Culture & State in Chinese History*, ed. Theodore Huters, Bin R. Wong and Pauline Yu (Stanford, CA: Stanford University Press, 1997): 58–82.

語錄, he wrote many books that were all destroyed. He remained in the Tiantai mountains for more than ten years, reaching the state of Yanzi 顔子 (Yan Hui 顔回) in "sitting and forgetting self 坐忘" and the realization of Ziqi 子綦 in "losing the other 喪耦."[98] Thus he changed his name to Wuwo 無我 (Egoless). Although the number of his disciples increased, he was still looking for a true master. One day, following the advice of a Daoist beggar who encouraged him to leave Tiantai for Mount Qingcheng, he set out on a long journey to Sichuan. After many hazards he finally reached Mount Qingcheng and met the master he was looking for: Fourth patriarch Zhou Xuanpu (Zhou Dazhuo). Zhou confirmed his understanding and entrusted him with the "important matter" (*dashi* 大事):

> Holding up the fly-whisk, Vinaya regulations, and [registers of] the masters' lineage, he [master Zhou] handed them over and said: "Though the present age obliges us to hide our traces, the unique lineage of the former sages cannot but continue. In the future, you must choose the most capable disciple and confer it upon him, and he in turn must transmit it and put it in action."[99]

> 乃舉如意、戒律、師派、授之曰：雖時當晦蹟、先聖一脈、不可不續。後當擇一至士授之、再傳而行矣。

As recorded in the *Mind-Lamp*'s marginalia, the future recipient who will put "the unique line of the former sages" in action was to be Wang Changyue. After having returned to Zhejiang and retired again to Tiantai,[100] he gave

---

[98] This refers to two figures appearing in *Zhuangzi*: Yan Hui as described in chapter 6 ("Dazong shi 大宗師" or The Great and Venerable Teacher), and Ziqi as presented in chapter 2 ("Qiwu lun 齊物論" or Discussion on Making all Things Equal); see the translation by Burton Watson, *The Complete Works of Chuang Tzu* (New York: Columbia University Press, 1968), pp. 90 and 36–37. A presentation of these two figures and their experience of absorption is also found in Jean François Billeter, *Leçons sur le Tchouang-tseu* (Paris: Allia, 2004): 59–102 and in the same author's *Études sur Tchouang-tseu* (Paris: Allia, 2004).

[99] The TSLM omits the reference to the fly-whisk along with the words allegedly pronounced by the master, and simply states: "Then, upholding the Vinaya regulations and the [registers] of lineages, [Master Zhou] transmitted them to him (Zhang), whereupon he (Zhang) withdrew again to Tiantai 乃舉戒律、宗派授之、仍還隱於天台."

[100] According to the *Daopu yuanliu tu*, Zhang Wuwo (Jingding) had been living in Tiantai for more than sixty years before going to Mt. Qingcheng and meeting his master Zhou. After having received the precepts he went back to Tiantai in the first year of the Jingtai era 景泰 (1450).

the transmission to Zhang **Zhen**song 張真嵩 "on the fifteenth day of the seventh lunar month" of 1522.

In contrast to the previous biographies one notes a fundamental change. The hagiographers not only refer to the great despair that the loss of parents may provoke in life (a despair leading the fifth patriarch, and later the sixth, to their religious quest) but also to the new ideal of the Confucian recluse. The fifth patriarch, hailing from a family of elite officials, refused official posts in favor of becoming a private instructor. He chose self-cultivation only after having fulfilled his social duties and filial obligations, and his attainments are said to have matched those of Daoist exemplary figures from Zhuangzi's classical stories.

While living in a small community of Daoist fellow seekers,[101] he looked forward to meeting a genuine master in order to bring to completion his Vinaya mission. In this context the hagiographers refer for the first time to the conferral of the regalia. They do not do so from the point of view of a secret initiation based on the Chan model of the transmission of robe and bowl, but rather from the perspective of the Daoist Vinaya Patriarch who passes his own ritual paraphernalia—fly-whisk, vinaya regulations, and lineage registers—to his successor, thus enabling him to ascend the public ordination platform. The power of the Longmen as the Daoist lineage responsible for performing court-approved public ordinations is thus raising its head; and although its time has not yet quite come, the "unique line of the former sages 先聖一脈"[102] is (according to the text's marginalia) well on the way toward its culmination in the figure of abbot Wang Changyue 王常月. It was Wang who was to fully embody the line of the former sages and represent the ideal of the sage able to exercise his religious activity while assisting an enlightened emperor.

---

[101] The JGXD calls them *huangguan jia* 黃冠家, Family of Yellow-crowned Daoist priests, whereas the TSLM talks of *huangguan zhi bilu* 黃冠之敝廬, a shabby hut of yellow-crowned Daoist priests.

[102] In Daoist classics like the *Daodejing* and *Zhuangzi*, the way of former saints often refers to saints able to transmit *xianjiao* or exoteric teachings.

6. Sixth Patriarch Zhao Zhensong 趙真嵩 (fl. 1522–1628), an Exemplary Daoist Cleric of the Unique Line of the Most High

> Date of birth: no mention
> Date of death: no mention
> Original name (*yuanming* 原名): Deyuan 得源[103]
> Lineage name (*ming* 名): **Zhen**song 真嵩 (Genuine Peak)
> Daoist name (*hao* 號): Fuyang zi 復陽子 (Master Returning to Yang)
> Birthplace: Langya 瑯玡 (Shandong)

According to the "Biography of the Vinaya Patriarch Zhao Fuyang" ("Zhao Fuyang lüshi zhuan 趙復陽律師傳," JGXD 1.11a–12b), Zhao was born under the protection of the Dipper to which his parents prayed in order to receive a descendant. Since his youth Zhao showed aversion to fame and celebrity; yet at the age of twenty he was already renowned as specialist of the classics and history as well as Buddhism and Daoism. Both of his parents died when he was twenty-five, and their loss opened up an abyss of suffering in his heart which was filled with the desire to repay in filial gratitude all they had given to him.[104] He thus journeyed to Mount Wudang (Hubei) before going to Maoshan (Jiangsu). There he went into seclusion to devote himself to the study of Daoist scriptures. Subsequently he traversed southern Jiangsu and northern Zhejiang in the hope of finally encountering a genuine master. But this hope was not fulfilled until, four years later, he arrived at Mount Tongbai (Tiantai, Zhejiang) where he met Zhang Jingding.[105] After having noticed Zhao's abilities to perceive the permanence of Dao in everything, master Zhang conferred the lineage name Zhensong on him. But he made Zhao wait for several more years before secretly transmitting the "quintessence of the Vinaya" (*jiezhi* 戒旨)[106] to him, saying:

> I will go to a different place and you should not remain here for long either, for only by saving yourself first can you save others. The unique lineage of the Most High is now in your hands. The Wangwu

---

[103] The *Taishang lümai Longmen zhengzong* 太上律脈龍門正宗 (TSLM) has instead Deyuan 德源.

[104] The TSLM states in the corresponding passage: "He went traveling with the intention of realizing the fruit of immortality in order to repay to the utmost of his abilities the hard work and kindness of his parents who had taken care of him 遊意証仙果以酬父母劬勞極之恩也."

[105] The TSLM mentions that he stayed at Gelu 葛廬 (the hut of Ge Hong?) in Tiantai.

[106] The TSLM also records this passage but uses the term *jiefa* 戒法.

Mountain is a grotto-heaven of pure emptiness, and you may go there to await the right time.

我將他適、汝毋久居、自度度人。太上一脈惟汝能任。王屋山清虛洞天也、往居以俟時。[107]

Complying with his master's injunction, Zhao went into ascetic retreat at the "grotto-heaven of Pure Emptiness" situated in the heart of the Wangwu Mountains in Henan,[108] and though "a white monkey offered him fruit," he persisted in his wall-gazing meditation with such persistence that "a sparrow was able to build its nest in his top-knot." But only when he one day heard voices resembling those of his parents were his eyes opened. Appropriately this happened precisely at the end of the traditional three-year period of ascetic training. Thus, at the end of this retreat, he experienced the satisfaction of having fulfilled his filial obligations toward his parents who appeared to him and confirmed this.[109] The *Mind-Lamp* also reports that he had developed the six extraordinary spiritual powers (*liutong* 六通).[110]

---

[107] This is also recorded in the TSLM but in different words: "I know you are the best person to be in charge of saving yourself and others in order to continue the unique lineage of the Most High. It is no more suitable for you to stay here any longer. You must reach the grotto-heaven of Pure Emptiness (Qingxu tiandong) in the Wangwu Mountains and bring this great affair to completion 知子甚任此責自度度人、以繼太上一脈。子不宜久居於此、須往王屋山清虛洞天了一大事."

[108] Chinese scholars, when presenting the biography of Zhao Zhensong or Wang Changyue, have often located the Wangwu Mountains in Shanxi (see for instance, Qing Xitai ed., *Zhongguo daojiao shi*, vol. 4, 79 and Wang Zhizhong, *Ming-Qing Quanzhen jiao lungao*, 74). One also finds a reference to Zhejiang (see for instance Liu Houhu 劉厚祜, "Baiyun guan yu daojiao 白雲觀与道教," *Dao xiehui kan* 道協會刊 6 (1980.11): 16–41). However, it seems clear that when the hagiographers mention the famous celestial grotto of Wangwu they refer to the Henan sanctuary quoted in many texts of the *Daozang*. See also the references to the Wangwu Mountains in Wang Changyue's biography below.

[109] As the extensive commentaries of the JGXD show, this passage describing Zhao's retreat was purportedly included, with interesting variations, in the *Bojian* and *Yilin*. The latter records that the three-year retreat took place in Sichuan on Mount Qingcheng. By contrast, the TSLM makes no mention of Zhao's ascesis but simply ends with Zhao reaching the Wangwu mountains where he later conferred the transmission upon Wang Changyue.

[110] In the biographies of eminent Buddhist monks, the six magic powers (*shentong* 神通) play a major role and even form a specific category of biographies (see Kieschnick 1997). In the works attributed to Wang Changyue (*Longmen xinfa* and *Biyuan tanjing*) they are defined as "the abilities to transpierce heaven and earth, spirits and demons, people and objects 通天通地、通神通鬼、通人通物、謂之神通."

In 1628 he passed the transmission on to Wang Changyue before returning to Tiantai. Afterwards he withdrew again into Wangwu Mountains until his death.[111]

At first sight we cannot but note that the biography of the sixth patriarch is incredibly rich in detail and contains fabulous hagiographic elements familiar from such sources as the renowned *Gaoseng zhuan* 高僧傳 (*Biographies of the Eminent Monks*). The image of the scholar-priest who from an early age renounces celebrity and fame in favor of ascetic ideals is now in full bloom. More than previous patriarchs and even the fifth patriarch, the sixth appears to be fixated on repaying his filial debt to his parents. It is the force of filial piety that drove him to undertake ascetic training or, as the *Taishang lümai* puts it, to attain immortality. This training is for the first time quantified as a three-year retreat, which happens to be exactly the required duration of Confucian mourning. It is described by stereotyped images such as monkeys providing food or birds building nests in the folds of monastic robes (or, in a more Daoist key, in Zhao's top-knot): images that are clearly inspired by traditional Buddhist hagiography.[112] These references suggest the dominant role that a Confucian elite—well versed in the Three Teachings and eager to infuse monasticism with social engagement—was playing in the elaboration of this kind of biography. Such elements seem particularly appropriate for the biography of the master bound to transmit

---

[111] In contrast to the previously adduced biographies, it is worth noting that in the JGXD there is no mention of the day and month when this transmission took place. The TSLM fills this apparent gap by specifying that it occurred on "the fifteenth day of the first month." The date of 1628 is also recorded in the Preface to the *Chuzhen jielü* 初真戒律 attributed to Wang Changyue, but there the meeting is said to have taken place in the Jiugong Mountains in Hubei rather than the Wangwu mountains. See below.

[112] Similar literary metaphors are, for example, also found in the biography of the noted Buddhist master Yongming Yanshou (904–975) who performed a ninety-day meditation at Mount Tiantai during which birds purportedly built nests in the folds of his robes, or in earlier lives of eminent monks who were sustained by monkeys' offerings of food. See Albert Welter, "The Contextual Study of Chinese Buddhist Biographies: the Example of Yung-Ming Yen-Shou (904–975)," in *Monks and Magicians: Religious Biographies in Asia*, ed. Phyllis Granoff and Kōichi Shinohara (Oakville: Mosaic Press, 1988): 247–68 and Kōichi Shinohara, "Passages and Transmission in Tianhuang Daowu's Biographies," in *Other Selves: Autobiography and Biography in Cross-Cultural Perspective*, ed. Phyllis Granoff and Kōichi Shinohara (Oakville: Mosaic Press, 1994): 132–49, here 140. For recent studies and translations of the *Gaoseng zhuan* see Kieschnick 1997 and Funayama 2009–10.

the scepter to the seventh patriarch, the very figure for whom the architects erected their Longmen hagiographical edifice.

7. The Birth of a Unifying Reformer: Biography of the Seventh Vinaya Patriarch Wang Changyue 王常月

> Date of birth: 1522 or 1594
> Date of death: 1680
> Original name (*yuanming* 原名): Ping 平
> Lineage name (*ming* 名): Changyue 常月
> Daoist name (*hao* 號): Kunyang 崑陽
> Birthplace: Lu'an 潞安 (Shanxi)

In contrast to the previous biographies, the life of the seventh patriarch is recorded in two additional sources (2–3), and its *Mind-Lamp* version is reportedly based on additional works (1 a,c,d). In chronological order we have:

1. "Wang Kunyang lüshi zhuan 王崑陽律師傳," compiled by Min Yide (1748/58–1836) in 1821 (reprint 1873/1876?) JGXD 1.15a–17b with comments by Bao Tingbo and Bao Kun, reportedly based on:
    a) a biography on Wang Changyue (Wang Kunyang) compiled by Lü Yunyin 呂雲隱 (fl. 1710);
    b) Fan Taiqing's 范太清 (1606?–1748) *Bojian xu* 缽鑑續;
    c) Tao Shi'an's 陶石庵 (?–1692) *Jingai yunjian* 金蓋雲箋 (revised by Xu Ziyuan 徐紫垣, 1630–1719);
    d) Zhao Zhensong's 趙真嵩 (fl. 1522–1628) *Fuyang dedao ji* 復陽得道記 (included in the *Bojian* attributed to Wang Changyue);[113]
2. "Kunyang Wang zhenren 崑陽王真人," compiled by Wanyan Chongshi (1820–1876) in 1847 (BYXB 52a–53b in ZWDS 31: 400–1) and engraved on a stele titled "Kunyang Wang zhenren daoxing bei 崑陽王真人道行碑" (Stele on the virtuous behavior of the Perfect-

---

[113] The authorship of all these sources (which are, to my knowledge, no longer available today) is given in the bibliographical list revised by Bao Tingbo and included in JGXD under the title "Jingai xindeng zhengkao wenxian lu." In the biography of Xu Qingcheng 徐清澄 (alias Xu Ziyuan), the *Jingai yunjian* is presented as a twelve-*juan* journal compiled by Tao Jing'an 陶靖菴 (1616–1673) and Tao Shi'an 陶石庵 (?–1692), initiated in 1644 and completed in 1691.

ed Kunyang), erected by Liu Chengyin 劉誠印 (?–1894) in 1886 on the east side of the Baiyuan guan, facing the Memorial Hall (Citang 祠堂) (BYGZ, p. 162);[114]

3. Chen Minggui 陳明珪 (hao Youshan 友珊 and Jiaoyou 教友, 1823–1881), *Changchun daojiao yuanliu* 長春道教源流 (abbr. DJYL 7.31b), compiled in 1879 (reprint ZWDS 31:134);
4. *Taishang lümai Longmen zhengzong* 太上律脈龍門正宗 (1919 hand-written scroll stored at Baiyun guan) abbr. TSLM;
5. "Diqi dai Wang da lüshi zhuan 第七代王大律師傳," in *Longmen zhengzong Jueyun benzhi daotong xinchuan* 龍門正宗覺雲本支道統薪傳, abbr. JYDT, compiled by Lu Yongming 陸永銘 in 1927 (reprint ZWDS 3: 464–65);
6. Yan Liuqian 嚴六謙 (hao Zhuangyan jushi 莊嚴居士, lineage name: Heyi 合怡), *Daotong yuanliu* 道統源流 compiled in 1929, abbr. *Gazetteer of Daoist Origins* or DTYL, xia 2.

Although sources 4 to 6 are here listed in chronological order, they do not present new material. Mostly based on the *Mind-Lamp* version, they were already used in the previous patriarchal biographies and especially in their annotations. References to the seventh patriarch's life can also be gathered from Min Yide's works; from the Preface attributed to Wang Changyue to the *Chuzhen jielü* 初真戒律 (1656); and from the record of his 1663 Nanjing transmission of precepts that was published by his disciples in form of the *Longmen xinfa* 龍門心法 and the *Biyuan tanjing* 碧苑壇經 (a version revised by Min Yide and included in his *Gu Shuyinlou cangshu* 古書隱樓藏書).

Wang Changyue's main biography stems from the *Mind-Lamp*, on which I will base my discussion while emphasizing differences with the above-mentioned other sources. In the *Mind-Lamp* two different birth dates are mentioned for Wang. According to the biography by Lü Yunyin 呂雲隱 (fl. 1710) Wang was born in 1594, but Fan Taiqing's 范太清 (1606?–1748) *Bojian xu* 缽鑑續 places his birth in 1522. These sources agree with respect to his birthplace; but whereas the *Mind-Lamp* (followed by the derivative *Jueyun benzhi daotong* and *Gazetteer of Daoist Origins*) mentions Lu'an 潞安 in Shanxi, the *Immortals' Chart* (BYXB) and *Taishang lümai* specify that he came from Changzhi county 長治縣 of Lu'an prefecture 潞

---

[114] A presentation of this stela and its reverse side (*beiyin*) is found in Pierre Marsone, "Le Baiyun guan de Pékin," 87–8 and 103.

安府.¹¹⁵ Furthermore, in his preface to the *Chuzhen jielü* Wang uses for his birthplace the ancient name of Shangdang 上黨 which stands for Changzhi prefecture.¹¹⁶ However, only the *Mind-Lamp* biography (along with its derivative *Jueyun benzhi daotong*) begins with a prophecy. Wang is said to have received in his childhood a visit from a Daoist who recognized him as the rebirth of a certain Qiaoyang 樵陽. This event is further elaborated in Min Yide's commentary to the *Huangji hepi xianjing* 皇極闔闢仙經 (j. *xia*, chap. 10):

> Qiaoyang is the surname of an ancient Perfected whose family name was Wang. No one knows when he lived. At the exact moment when the Vinaya Patriarch Wang Kunyang of Luzhou was born, an immortal passing by his house said: "Qiaoyang is reborn! From now on the *Vinaya tradition of the Most High* will prosper again."¹¹⁷

> 樵陽者、古真人之號、姓王、不知何代人。王崑陽律祖、潞洲人、相傳生時、有仙人過其門曰："樵陽再生矣！太上律宗、從此復振矣。"

The *Mind-Lamp* marginalia identify the author of this prophecy as Zhang Mayi 張麻衣, a Daoist venerated in Wang's family who is presented as the source of Wang Changyue's conversion.¹¹⁸ While "his father and elder brothers all believed in Daoism and studied under Zhang Mayi, Wang at the beginning was not interested in anything." But after Zhang Mayi had displayed his extraordinary powers by healing him of a grave illness, Wang left home in order to visit him and devote himself to the religious quest.¹¹⁹

---

¹¹⁵ The DYJL is the only source that fails to mention a birthplace for Wang, but Min Yide's work also refers to Luzhou 潞洲. See below.

¹¹⁶ Preface attributed to Wang Changyue, "Chuzhen jielü xu" (DZJY, vol. 24, 10469), where he signs as "the Daoist priest from Xijin Shangdang who transmits the precepts 西晉上黨傳戒道士." The same birthplace is also given in the above-mentioned biography of the sixth Longmen patriarch Zhao Zhensong (JGXD 1.12b) who "transmitted to Wang Ping [i.e., Wang Changyue] of Shangdang."

¹¹⁷ DZXB 1:5b, also YLCS, ZWDS. This passage is said to stem from the *Sanshan guan lu* 三山館錄, a text allegedly attributed to Han Jichou 韓箕疇 who, according to the *Liaoyang dian wenda bian* (chap. 1, 5a), was a literatus known for his essays and moral integrity, a friend and relative of Tao Shi'an (韓乃康熙間名士有文行者、石庵氏為其戚友、非廬語也).

¹¹⁸ The identification as Zhang Mayi is recorded in JGXD marginalia.

¹¹⁹ 然初無好尚、父兄皆留心元門、尊師張麻衣。麻衣為師治危疾、大顯神力而去。師棄家訪之。The JYDT (based on JGXD) reports the same with the only omission of the passage about Wang's initial lack of interest.

By contrast, the *Baiyun xianbiao* 白雲仙表 or *Chart of the Immortals of the White Clouds* (BYXB) skips all references to Zhang Mayi and his prognostication and instead presents Wang's conversion as the product of the uncertainty and chaos of Wang's times at the end of the Ming dynasty. However, it agrees with the *Mind-Lamp*, *Jueyun benzhi daotong*, and *Taishang lümai* about the period of Wang's religious calling, namely, "the age of his capping" (*ruoguan* 弱冠) that marks for a boy the beginning of adulthood. Having received this call, Wang set out to visit famous mountains, faced many dangers, and endured the hot seasons' heat and the cold seasons' wind and frost.

Whereas, on the basis of Fan's *Baojian xu* version, the *Mind-Lamp* (as well as the *Jueyun benzhi daotong*) state that he journeyed for more than eighty years before reaching Mount Wangwu and meeting his destined master, the *Taishang lümai* fails to mention such a long period of pilgrimage.[120] The *Immortals' Chart* records instead that in his middle age Wang met the sixth Longmen Vinaya Patriarch Zhao Zhensong at Wangwu Mountain. But the four sources are unanimous in recording the scene of Wang imploring Zhao to instruct him and his failure to receive an answer for many months. Without losing faith, Wang persisted and remained at Zhao's side while "nourishing himself from pine branches and pure springs."

The *Mind-Lamp* biography is the only source that at this stage reintroduces the figure of Zhang Mayi and has him intervene in support of Wang's request for instruction. It is thanks to Zhang's mediation[121] that Wang obtains from his master Zhao the lineage name Changyue (Months of Perseverance) along with "the transmission of the precepts in two volumes" 授以二冊.[122]

Neither the *Immortals' Chart* nor the *Taishang lümai* mention Zhang Mayi's intervention and the transmission of the two volumes of precept

---

[120] As the commentary in the JGXD specifies, its information about Wang's travels and their eighty-year duration stems from the *Bojian xu*; it is not mentioned in the biography by Lü Yunyin.

[121] The gloss specifies that "Though Zhang Mayi was close neither to Wang Kunyang nor to Zhao Fuyang, he indeed is the greatest helper of the Longmen orthodox lineage" (麻衣非厚於崑陽亦非厚於復陽、實為龍門正宗一大助教也). The previous marginalia state that the Daoist [who guarded over Wang Kunyang] was perhaps either Zhang Mayi or Zhao Fuyang (Zhao Fuyang zhi liu 此道士殆亦張麻衣趙復陽之流).

[122] According to the commentary to the JGXD, the special intervention of Zhang Mayi along with the reception of the two precept-texts stem from the *Bojian xu*.

texts. Instead, they suggest that a rite of transmission took place and that Zhao, when realizing the sincerity of Wang's request, "secretly brought him to the Grotto of the Queen Mother at the Celestial Altar,[123] announced the covenant with Heaven and Earth, and conferred upon Wang the precepts and codes" 密於天壇王母洞、告盟天地、授以戒律.[124]

As in the previous biographies of Longmen patriarchs, the *Mind-Lamp* does not fail to record the words allegedly pronounced by the master at the key moment of transmitting the precepts to his disciple. The *Immortals' Chart* and *Taishang lümai* also record this pronouncement, albeit in a simplified and abridged form.[125] Following the main *Mind-Lamp* version, Zhao said to Wang:

> Achieving the Way is extremely easy yet extremely difficult. Regarding the necessity of ascetic practices as prerequisite, the various external affairs must be gotten rid of once and for all. Adhere to the rules and observe them with care while immersing yourself in the study of the classics. Realize the original hidden intent of the *Daodejing*'s "self-so" and search for the true knack of the *Nanhua jing*'s "vitality," and you will be stable. You are a "great vessel that will be completed only in the evening [i.e., late in life]."[126]

---

[123] One finds the mention of Wangmu dong 王母洞 in Wangwu shan (Henan) in "Wangwu shan ji 王屋山記" by Li Lian 李濂, in *Tianxia mingshan ji*, section Henan 軫集 4, 52b/2 (CK vol. 25, 11220), as well as in the "Qiyan sanshi yun 七言三十韻" by Tongzhen daoren 通真道人 in *Tiantan Wangwu shan shengji ji* 天壇王屋山聖迹記 DZ 969, 13a/7 (ZHDZ 48: 554b). It is in this place that a rite appears to have taken place.

[124] BYXB, TSLM. Both of these texts suggest here the performance of a kind of ceremony of Daoist transmission and investiture. On this see also Richard G. Wang, "Ming Princes and Daoist Ritual," *T'oung Pao* 95 (2009): 51–119, here 83–4.

[125] Whereas the BYXB records the content of the first three sentences from the JGXD with its own variation ("Great is the Way, and achieving it is not easy; what is easy are the severe ascetic practices that must precede this achievement 大哉之道、成之非易；易也、必以苦行為先"), the TSLM has a version closer to the JGXD and quotes its last sentence inspired by the *Daodejing* ("Achieving the Way is extremely easy yet also extremely difficult. Regarding the ascetic practices that must precede it, there is a dictum that says: 'A great vessel will be completed only in the evening.' So make an effort and be cautious 成道甚易、而亦甚難。然必以苦行為先語云："大器晚成"勉之、慎之"). See also the subsequent note.

[126] This last sentence stems from chapter 41 of the *Daodejing*.

成道甚易、然亦甚難。必以苦行為先、種種外務、切須掃
除。依律精持、潛心教典、體 道德 自然之元奧、探 南華
活潑之真機、方為穩當。汝大器當晚成。

After this meeting, the *Mind-Lamp* biography has Wang continue his round of the mountains, tasting all kinds of sweetness and bitterness while perusing without interruption the classics of all Three Teachings. "He came by an old monastery and, finding countless Daoist scriptures, went on to examine them day and night. Whenever his lamp was on the verge of going out, he lighted it anew with incense and read in its radiance for eight or nine years."[127]

Like the *Mind-Lamp*, both *Immortals' Chart* and *Taishang lümai* refer to Wang's visits of "more than twenty places" and claim that he "received the seal of approval from more than fifty masters"[128]—a requisite that was part of the training of Quanzhen Daoists, as explained in the rules set by founder Wang Chongyang.[129] While surrounded by political turmoil and ravages, Wang heard that Jiugong Mountain 九宮山 was still a sanctuary inhabited by "many extraordinary men" (*duo yiren* 多異人) or, as the *Immortals' Chart* and *Taishang lümai* put it, by "a recluse" (*you yinshi* 有隱士).[130] Thus Wang journeyed there and, to his great surprise, met in the deep forests once more his own master Zhao, majestically sitting all alone.[131]

The *Gazetteer of Daoist Origins* datea this encounter to 1628. The same date also appears in Wang's preface to the *Chuzhen jielü* 初真戒律 where he recalls this event as follows:

---

[127] 過一古觀中、道籍頗多、晝夜檢閱。每乏燈以香續火、光照而讀、八九年間. According to the commentary to the JGXD (1.15a), this passage along with its continuation stem from the *Bojian xu*.

[128] 參師二十餘處、印證五十餘人. JGXD 1.15a, BYXB, and TSLM.

[129] See the *Lijiao shiwu lun* (DZ 1233), in particular the second section about "Wandering like the clouds *yunyou*" in order to visit enlightened masters. See the abstract on this text by Florian Reiter in Schipper and Verellen eds., *The Taoist Canon*, vol. 2, 1170. Qing monastic manuals were to elaborate about the importance of "wandering" for genuine Quanzhen disciples. See for instance Min Yide, *Qinggui xuanmiao* 清規玄妙, 1b–2a, in YLCS, vol. 12 (ZWDS 10: 598). See also Vincent Goossaert, "The Quanzhen clergy 1700–1950," 732–34.

[130] While the BYXB does not refer to the ravages of the war, the TSLM follows more closely the JGXD version but like the BYXB it substitutes the reference to "many extraordinary men," with "a recluse."

[131] The BYXB and TSLM also record this encounter with a few variations.

In 1628 I followed the cloud traces to Chu (Hubei) in order to visit the Perfected Zhao Fuyang of Jiugong Mountain. There I received the method of precepts and obtained guidance concerning what is essential.[132]

余因崇禎初歲雲蹟於楚、謁九宮山復陽趙真人、親授戒法、得其領要。

Zhao asked Wang about his spiritual achievements during those years of separation and Wang instructed him about the decline of Daoism, the rise of heterodoxy, and the intolerable levels of shared hardships of wartime.[133] In response Zhao encouraged him to get rid of such preoccupations and told him:

> When the gentleman (*junzi*) thoroughly examines the Way, "thorough examination" signifies penetrating to the Way. "Penetrating to the Way" is called "breaking through."[134] But since one is by nature equipped with the Way, why should one worry about examining it and penetrating to it? If one acts against one's time, one acts erroneously. How could one then avoid the injustices of the world and the envy of the mob? I entrust you with the matter which in three hundred years I alone was in charge of. Treasure it and keep it secret, and when the time is ripe it will flourish. Then it will be upon you to propagate the Arcane Spirit of the teaching.

君子窮於道、謂窮通於道。謂通道備我身、何憂窮通。若違時妄行、安能免世俗之謗議、匪類之妒忌哉。吾有三百年來、獨任之事、當付於子、寶而秘之、時至而。大闡元（玄）風、是在子矣。

Then Zhao conferred upon Wang the Precepts of the Celestial Immortals and added:

> Formerly, during the years of Emperor Shizu of the Yuan dynasty, Perfected Lord Changchun [Qiu Chuji] widely promoted the teachings of precepts. He propagated *the treasure of the pure and serene rules of the Most High*. As [his disciples] approved of each other from mind to mind and transmitted from patriarch to patriarch while maintaining pure silence and refraining from action,

---

[132] "Chuzhen jielü xu," 25a (DZJY/CK vol. 24, 10469).

[133] The marginalia referring to Wang's spiritual achievements say: "Thus a great master should serve as a maker of great enterprise" 自是宗匠行事業.

[134] This passage uses the Neoconfucian expression *qiong*, which is often translated as the practice of "going to the limits" or "examining thoroughly."

the singular transmission was conferred in secret and could not be widely promulgated. For this reason the "feathered vagabonds and companions of the Way" (i.e., Daoists) rarely observed the rules of comportment and were thus hardly in a position to know that the arcane doctrine has its precepts. Now the chance has presented itself to entrust you with this important matter. If not you, who else could it be?

昔我長春真君於元世祖時、廣行戒法、流演太上清靜律寶、心心相印、祖祖相傳、皆守靜默而厭有為、單傳秘授、不能廣行。是以羽流道侶、鮮覩威儀、幾不知元門有戒矣。今因緣將到、任大事者、非子而誰。

Having said this, Zhao ascended the platform, transmitted the precepts,[135] and conferred upon Wang the robe and bowl. When Wang declined, pretending to be not worthy of this, Master Zhao added:

Finding a person and transmitting is not something to be achieved by studious effort. When twenty years from now you will travel to Beijing and visit [the grave of] Patriarch Qiu at the Baiyun guan, the time will be ripe to put the Way into action.

得人而傳、非勉強也。子于二十年後、遊燕京、謁邱祖於白雲觀、是道行之時也。

After this, Wang is said to have left for another round of the mountains.[136] According to the *Immortals' Chart*, he withdrew to Huashan where he received a similar prediction, this time not from his Master Zhao but from

---

[135] In the *Mind-Lamp* commentary (JGXD 1.16b/3–4), a reference to the platform and the transmission of precepts was added. It wants to show that such transmission was already part of a genuine ritual on the ordination platform where the Vinaya Patriarch, by reenacting the original transmission by Qiu Chuji, empowers his heir to shoulder the Vinaya transmission and become also a Vinaya Patriarch. The gloss has a sentence that includes a misprint: "In his instruction to Wang, Master Zhao made special mention of the Perfected Lord Changchun [to show his high expectations of Wang]. Ever since the Yuan period, it is only with the appearance of [Wang] Changyue and his promulgation of Vinaya texts in the *bingshen* year [1656] that the correct teaching [of Lord Changchun] flourished anew and came to be transmitted" 此番授受特舉長春真君以告之、蓋自元以來、及崑陽始復盛傳正寓丙申說戒張本. This scenario is also reproduced under the name of Wang in the works attributed to him.

[136] Like the JGXD, the BYXB and TSLM also record this encounter, but they reduce the words of Zhao's secret transmission of the Celestial Immortal Precepts to the simple metaphor of the *junzi* 君子.

Doumu, the Dipper Mother. "One day while he was rendering homage to the Dipper, he saw her descending from the heavens. She said to him: 'Your destiny is in the North, you should no longer stay here.'" Obeying the Dipper Mother's injunction, Wang then left for the capital. By contrast, the *Taishang lümai* does not mention any injunction of this kind. It only states that, after having received in secret the Celestial Immortal precepts and the master's approval, Wang continued his journeys to famous mountains, sojourning here and there.[137]

Fig. 10: Wang Changyue. Portrait in Baiyun guan (Esposito 1993:86)

---

[137] The TSLM says: "Subsequently, Zhao secretly conferred the Celestial Immortal precepts and mind-seal on Wang, and time and again he urged him (to keep them in mind). Afterwards Wang went visiting famous mountains, though not much is recorded about his pilgrimages" 遂以天仙戒心印密傳、囑之再三。余自受授以來、朝謁名山、棲遲雲水、茲不多記。

It is worthy of note that the *Mind-Lamp*'s commentary relates, based on the *Bojian xu*, that in 1640 Wang was in the Wangwu Mountains where he transmitted "the manuscript of the Great Precepts in three volumes 手錄大戒三冊" to Wu Shouyang 伍守陽 (1574–1644?). Aside from other inconsistencies that shall be examined shortly, the *Mind-Lamp* hagiographers appear intent on linking Wang's Vinaya transmission—which now consists of three volumes instead of the above-mentioned two—with Wu Shouyang, a well-recognized Longmen master of the late Ming. As we shall see in Part Two, posterity was to attribute to Wang the system of the three-stage ordination related to three precept-texts.

Finally, all the biographical sources except for the *Changchun daojiao yuanliu* 長春道教源流 (DJYL) end with Wang reaching the capital and registering at the Lingyougong.[138] While the *Mind-Lamp*, *Jueyun benzhi daotong*, and *Taishang lümai* record Wang's arrival in Beijing "in the autumn of the year *yiwei* of the Shunzhi era" (1655),[139] the *Immortals' Chart* interestingly moves it back to 1644, the year of the enthronement of Emperor Shunzhi 順治 that marks the beginning of the Qing dynasty.[140] According to the *Bojian xu*, Wang was at that time 154 years old even though he looked like a fifty-year old man. In the biography by Lü Yunyin (source 1a), however, he is said instead to have been in his sixties. But all sources agree that it was "on the fifteenth day of the third month of the year *bingshen*" (1656) that Wang conveyed the precepts at the Baiyun guan. As the *Mind-Lamp* emphasizes, "the opportunity to protect the teaching had fallen into place naturally, all in accord with the words of the Perfected (Zhao)."[141]

Although in all biographies of the *Mind-Lamp* this ordination ceremony appears to be central for the correct transmission of Wang to his direct heirs, one does not find any record of it apart from Daoist internal materials, by and large connected with the *Mind-Lamp* version. From Wang onward new

---

[138] According to the study by Yang Haiying 楊海英 ("Qing qianqi de daojiao yu gongting 清前期的道教與宮廷," *Daojia wenhua yanjiu* 道家文化研究 23 [2008]: 365–410), the Lingyougong 靈祐宮 was originally a "Shifang daoyuan." In 1655 it became the place of residence assigned by the Qing court to the 53rd Celestial Master Zhang Hongren 張洪任. More on this on p. 376 of the same article.

[139] 1655 appears also in the biography of Zhan Yiyang 詹怡陽 who specifies that Wang came from Wangwu and registered at Lingyougong. (JGXD 2.4a).

[140] According to a stela, Guo Shouzhen 郭守真 (1606–1708), an important Longmen master from Shenyang Taiqing gong, could then visit him at the Baiyun guan.

[141] The TSLM records the same but, having made no reference to predictions, omits the last sentence.

Longmen branches were allegedly established all over China and many of Wang's direct disciples founded temples and promoted Wang's Vinaya transmission in Jiangnan.

Here I shall focus on the direct heirs of Wang who purportedly continued the unilinear branch of the "Longmen zhengzong" (orthodox Longmen lineage) at the Baiyun guan. In contrast to the multiple lineages in the *Jingai xindeng* chart, the Baiyun guan tradition, which was incorporated in the ancestral hall dedicated to its Longmen patriarchs, has for the eighth generation only retained Tan Shoucheng 譚守誠 and for the ninth generation Tan's disciple Zhan Tailin 詹太林.[142] By contrast, if one consults the *Mind-Lamp*, in comparison with other masters of the same generation Tan Shoucheng does not appear to have had a special or closer relation with Wang Changyue. He is nevertheless one of the few who, according to the *Mind-Lamp*, "have resided for some years" at the Baiyun guan at the time of Wang Changyue. Interestingly enough, the relationship of Tan with Baiyun guan, which is recorded in the *Mind-Lamp*, is not mentioned in other biographies. Instead of Baiyun guan, these biographies make mention of Wudangshan or Nanjing Yinxian'an. Finally, while no disciples of Tan are listed in the *Mind-Lamp* and its lineage chart, other sources mention thousands of disciples yet offer just a single name: Zhan Tailin.

I shall thus in the following present the biographies of these two masters. They have been little studied until now[143] but deserve a closer look since they have the potential to reveal yet another facet of the history of the "orthodox Longmen lineage" at the Baiyun guan ancestral hall.

---

[142] BYGZ 32. Oyanagi points out that the family name Tan was wrongly recorded as Cheng 程 in his spirit tablet conserved at the Baiyun guan ancestral hall.

[143] An exception is the recent study by Yin Zhihua (2009).

Chapter 3

THE TWO FACES OF THE EIGHTH VINAYA PATRIARCH: TAN SHOUCHENG 譚守誠 (?–1689?)

According to the *Mind-Lamp* (2.33a–34b), Tan Shoucheng (Daoist sobriquet: Xinyue 心月) was a native of Huguang Wuling 湖廣武陵 (today's Changde 常德 in Hunan province). After having eulogized his rectitude and seriousness in speech and manner since his tender age（性篤實、不苟言笑、童時已然）the *Mind-Lamp* relates how, under the influence of a certain Huang Chongyang 黃沖陽 from Jiangxia 江夏 (today's Wuchang 武昌 in Hubei province), the adult Tan received the vocation to transcend the dust of the world（既長、讀書黃鶴樓、飄飄有出塵志）. Huang Chongyang was the son of a Ming vice garrison commander (副總兵任) in Zhejiang province during the Chongzhen era 崇禎 (1628–1644) who, distraught by the destruction of his country and the loss of his entire family, had converted to Daoism.[144] It is on Huang's traces that Tan set out for North China. After having wandered between Yunnan (Dian 滇) and Guizhou (Qian 黔) for more than thirty years, he was in a dream instructed by Huang, who appeared to him in the feathered robe of an Immortal, to go to the capital Beijing. After his arrival in the capital, Tan heard that the Patriarch Wang Changyue "had grandly opened the Bowl-Hall" at the Baiyun guan in order to promulgate the precepts (大開演缽堂於白雲觀). Thereupon Tan visited Wang and succeeded in obtaining "the great precepts" (*dajie* 大戒). To his joy he learned that Huang Chongyang had been at the Baiyun guan since 1660 and had received the entire set of three precepts along with the lineage name Shouzhong 守中.[145] Tan settled at

---

[144] Biography of Huang Chongyang, JGXD 2.30a–32b.

[145] As we shall see, this master has the same lineage name as another extraordinary mas-

the Baiyun guan for some years until, "completely purified, he accompanied Huang Chongyang to Zhejiang" 道既純淯、偕沖陽至浙.

According to the biographies of other disciples of Wang including Huang Chongyang, Tan and Huang were part of a group of Wang Changyue's disciples accompanying the seventh patriarch on his journeys to Jiangnan to spread Vinaya teachings.[146] During their tours they visited the community of Tao Jing'an in Jingaishan, Huang Yinzhen in Hangzhou's Dadeguan, Huang Xutang in Huguan 滸關, and Lü Yunyin in Guanshan 冠山. As members of the same family, they were asked to take advantage of learning from each other and to kindly pass along their knowledge to the next generation while transmitting the heritage of "their lineage's teachings" (*zongjiao*) everywhere (往來於⋯之間、師皆親如骨肉。嗣是益互琢磨、惠諸後學、逸承宗教、四方咸向之).

After that visit to Jingaishan, Tan resided in Guanshan (Suzhou) for "some years" or, as Bao Tingbo specifies in his commentary, for "about fourteen years." In 1687 (Kangxi 26), his trace was suddenly lost, as had happened to his master and fellow practitioner Huang Chongyang twelve years earlier. Some oral accounts state that he was seen "in 1744 (Qianlong *jiazi*) in Yunnan at the Taihegong 太和宮 as he gave his handwritten notes on precepts (*shoulu jielü* 手錄戒律) to a certain Tao 陶 from Guanshan."[147] This creative oral account forms part of the conglomerate of legends circulating in Jingaishan networks and is closely related to the esoteric transmission of precept texts via Min Yide.

In contrast to this *Mind-Lamp* biography—which was also used by Oyanagi Shigeta 小柳司氣太 in his *Hakuunkan shi* 白雲觀志 in presenting Tan as the eighth Longmen patriarch at the Baiyun guan—the *Daotong*

---

ter linked with Min Yide: Jizu daozhe, lineage name Huang Shouzhong.

[146] Among the disciples who, after having received the mythical ordination at Baiyun guan, accompanied him in 1663 to the South in order to spread Wang's teachings, we also find Zhan Shouchun 詹守椿 and Shao Shoushan 邵守善 (who allegedly recorded the *Biyuan tanjing*; see Qing Xitai ed., vol. 4, 80). According to the JGXD, Huang Chongyang and Tan Shoucheng were also present. In 1663 a group of masters including Tan and Huang came to Mt. Jingai and stayed for one month. Subsequently Chongyang returned to Tianmu Fahua, while Tan and Lü Yunyin went to reside at Guanshan 冠山 where Lü opened the Vinaya institute Lüyuan 律院 in order to spread Vinaya teachings (see the gloss to the biography of Huang Xutang, JGXD 2.6a).

[147] JGXD 2.34a. On this basis, the DTYL (xia 4) also records that "in 1744 Tan was seen in Yunnan Taihegong."

yuanliu zhi 道統源流志 (Gazetteer on the Origins and Development of Orthodox Daoism) by Yan Liuqian 嚴六謙 offers a brand-new portrait of him (DTYL 7.31ab–32a). It is based on Chen Ting's 陳鼎 (1650–?) "Xinyue daoren zhuan 心月道人傳" (Biography of the Daoist priest [Tan] Xinyue) which forms part of juan 17 of his *Liuxi waizhuan* 留溪外傳 (Unofficial Biographies from Liuxi).[148] Chen Ting's version also forms the basis of a later biography of Tan contained in the *Taishang lümai Longmen zhengzong* 太上律脈龍門正宗. It is of interest to note that from this biography onward, the *Taishang lümai* does not rely any more on the *Mind-Lamp*.[149]

In Tan's biography by Chen Ting, Tan is said to be a native of Ling County 酃縣 of Hunan (today's Yanling County 炎陵縣) even though his lineage name and Daoist sobriquet coincide with those given in the *Mind-Lamp*.

Like the seventh patriarch Wang, Tan as a child received a prophecy from a mysterious figure. While playing in the courtyard, a Daoist who passed by said: "This child has such extraordinary backbone and energy that one day he will be able to shoulder our Great Dao 此子骨氣異常、他日可肩吾大道." Having uttered these words, the mysterious Daoist disappeared from the stunned gaze of Tan's entire family.[150]

Around the end of the Ming, Tan became a Daoist priest and, while making the rounds of famous mountains in search of eminent sages, visited

---

[148] *Liuxi waizhuan* 17.32a–33a in SKQS 四庫全書存目叢書, Shibu 史部 vol. 122: 797–98. The same date is also recorded in Igarashi, *Taiseikyū shi*, 67

[149] Whereas for the above-mentioned biography of Wang, the TSLM still stands midway between the JGXD and the BYXB versions, the parts following this biography show no more parallels with the JGXD. After the 9th patriarch, the JGXD lists no further names of Longmen heirs at the Baiyun guan hall.

[150] In Chen Ting's biography the mysterious Daoist is identified as "the red-faced and yellow-crowned guest" (or Zhuyan the yellow-crowned guest?) 朱顏黃冠客 from Ganfa 紺髮, but the TSLM calls him Zhuyan laoren 朱顏老人 from Qianfa 鉗髮. See respectively DTYL 7.31b (based on Chen Ting's biography included in his *Liuxi waizhuan* 17.32a–33a) and the manuscript version of the TSLM also printed in Zhongguo daojiao xiehui yanjiushi 中國道教協會研究室 ed., *Daojiao shi ziliao* 道教史資料, 393. Unlike the manuscript version, this printed version just has the character Bin 鬢 instead of Ganfa or Qianfa. The TSLM features a slightly different version: "This child has a constitution out of the ordinary, and one day he will be able to be in charge of the Great Affair 此子骨相不凡、他日可任大事." The ancient idea of predestined immortal backbones forms the background of this prophecy.

many well-known literati of his time.¹⁵¹ Encountering one day the Perfected Wang Changyue, he felt "as if he had met an old friend" and that "they were in perfect agreement." After accompanying Tan to Mt. Wudang 武當山 (Fig. 11), "Wang transmitted to him the secret quintessence" (相見如故、遂契合、偕往武當山中、傳秘密精義). Just like the Perfected Wang after his alleged encounter with enlightened master Zhao, Tan then devoted himself to self-cultivation and put in practice the quintessential teachings without interruption "for more than twenty years" 操修二十余年、無暑刻少懈.¹⁵² Aware of Tan's attainments, Wang Changyue transmitted the "Longmen mind-seal" 龍門心印 to him and urged him to convert people since "causing even one person to realize the Way results in the accumulation of countless merits" (度一人證道、即積無量功德也).

Fig. 11: Sanctuary and hermitages tucked in the rock faces of Mt. Wudang (1987)

Subsequently, Tan journeyed all over the country in order to save and rescue people using every means to convert them while admonishing them

---

¹⁵¹ There are some differences between Tan's biography by Chen Ting and the one found in the TSLM. The TSLM states that after having lost his parents at an early age he became a Daoist priest.

¹⁵² The same span of time is also recorded in Igarashi, *Taiseikyū shi*, 67.

to follow the supreme Way without falling into heterodox paths. Having reached Jiangsu and met many talented persons ready to devote themselves to the religious path, he decided to settle west of Jiangning (today's Nanjing) and established his teaching center at the Yinxian'an 隱仙菴, the Hermitage of the Recluse Immortal on Mt. Huju 虎踞山. He instructed his followers whose number amounted to several thousand "to regard filial piety and loyalty as basis, and sincerity and serenity as practice." In 1689, on the very day he had predicted for his death, he took a bath, changed his clothes and uttered his last verses after having offered his homage to the Lord on High (Shangdi):

> As one-mind reaches the utmost calm, everything disappears
> Revealing but the true face of the moon on high.
> Free, inaudible, and invisible, quietude deepens
> The Longmen Vinaya Dharma will be taken over by Bolin.
> 一心靜极萬緣消、獨露眞容月正高。
> 自在希夷堪湛寂、龍門法律柏林操。

Having designated Bolin—i.e., Zhan Tailin 詹太林 (style name: Jinbo 晉柏, Daoist sobriquet: Weiyang 維陽)—as his heir, Tan passed away in sitting posture. The *Taishang lümai* records instead that one year later, on the "twenty-eighth day of the eleventh lunar month" of 1690, Tan "secretly transmitted his Daoist lineage (*daomai* 道脈) to Zhan Weiyang from Hubei."[153]

We do not find any mention of Zhan Tailin as Tan's heir in the *Mind-Lamp*; and most strikingly, Tan gets a different birthplace, and his encounter with Patriarch Wang as well as his teaching activities are connected with different places. According to the *Mind-Lamp*, under the oneiric influence of Huang Chongyang, Tan met the patriarch Wang at Beijing's Baiyun guan where he received the Longmen ordination in form of the full transmission of the "great precepts." By contrast, Chen Ting's biography has him meet Wang in Wudangshan. For Chen Ting, it is thus at Wudangshan rather than Baiyun guan that Tan received the "secret quintessence" which, according to the *Taishang lümai*, consisted of Wang's gradual transmission of two sets of precepts: the Initial Precepts of Perfection and the Intermediary

---

[153] See the printed version of this TSLM biography in *Zhongguo daojiao xiehui yanjiushi* 中國道教協會研究室 (ed.), *Daojiao shizi liao* 道教史資料 (Shanghai: Guji chubanshe, 1991) and note 30 above.

Precepts.[154] It is also at Wudangshan that, according the biography by Chen Ting, Tan received the "Longmen mind-seal" from Wang.

According to the *Mind-Lamp* biographical records, Wang visited Wudangshan between 1668 and 1674. These dates appear to match other records. One of them is an essay written by Wang Yun that has Tan meet Wang Changyue in Wudangshan in 1673. Another source is a Preface to the *Chuzhen jielü* 初真戒律 authored by Long Qiqian 龍起潛 which asserts that in 1674 Wang transmitted the precepts in Wudangshan at the Yuxugong. Provided that one relies on these accounts, the encounter between Wang and Tan took place during the 1670s.

Returning now to the comparison of the *Mind-Lamp*'s and Chen Ting's biographies of Tan: After the conferral of Wang's transmission the *Mind-Lamp* describes Tan's journey in company of Huang Chongyang to Zhejiang and their encounters with other disciples of Wang, followed by Tan's long sojourn in Guanshan (Suzhou). By contrast, Chen Ting has Tan travel all over the country in order to preach and convert as many people as possible until the establishment of his own teaching center at Nanjing Yinxian'an. In this context it is worth recalling that, according to the *Gazetteer of Daoist Origins*, Yinxian'an was primarily associated with Wang and was his resting place, and that Chen Ting's biography has Tan pass away at the same spot in 1689.

Yinxian'an is also mentioned in the *Chuzhen jielü* attributed to Wang. The author of its preface dated Kangxi 康熙 13 (1674), Long Qiqian 龍起潛, informs us that he had known master Wang in Jiangnan's Yinxian'an 隱仙庵. Though wanting to get rid of his selfishness, he was at that time not yet ready to devote himself to Wang's religious path. Only later, in 1674), he had during his visit to Mt. Wudang the fortune to encounter Wang who performed ordinations at the Yuxugong. It was then that Long decided to take refuge and receive the precepts from Wang. (昔余識師於江南之隱仙菴、私心巳尸祝之矣。因狂心未歇。難遽投拜。今朝謁武當。幸遇師傳戒於玉盧宮中。遂發心皈命而受持戒律). In the postface of this text, the calligrapher and painter Da Chongguang 笪重光 (hao 蟾光, 1623–1692)[155] mentions the important role of Wang Changyue in making Daoist priests (huangguan 黃冠) aware of Vinaya teachings ("Qingdu yulu 清都玉律") and states that Wang withdrew to

---

[154] See this TSLM biography in *Daojiao shizi liao*.

[155] Apart from his works on painting, Da Chongguang is known as the compiler of the *Maoshan zhi* 茅山志 (Preface 1669, repr. 1878, ZWDS 19).

Nanjing's Yinxian'an and was invited to expound and propagate these essential teachings everywhere (先生攝靜於金陵之隱仙庵,受四方迎請為闡揚斯義).

The fact that Yinxian'an is called "ancestral hall" (*zuting* 祖庭) in the introductory essay "Chuzhen jieshuo 初真戒說" by Wu Taiyi 吳太一 of 1686 also suggests that Yinxian'an at that time played a role similar to the one attributed by posterity to Beijing's Baiyun guan, namely, as "ancestral hall" of the Longmen Vinaya transmission.[156] We shall see here below that Zhan Tailin's biography contains an additional reference linking Wang with Nanjing.

Finally, whereas Tan's spirit tablet in the Baiyun guan ancestral hall features the inscription "Eighth Vinaya Patriarch of the Baiyun hall" 白雲堂上第八代律師,[157] the 1874 manuscript *Xuandu lütan weiyi* 玄都律壇威儀戒[158] (in full agreement with the "Longmen orthodox tradition's Dharma scrolls" 龍門正宗法卷) lists him as the eighth patriarch of the Taihe Hall 第八代太和堂.[159] According to Chen Ting's biography and the *Taishang lümai*, the name Taihetang 太和堂 refers to a Wudang sanctuary (Taihegong 太和宮 or Taiheshan 太和山?) where Tan had reportedly encountered Wang and received his transmission.[160] However, Tan's biography in the *Mind-Lamp* could point to the Taihegong 太和宮 of Yunnan where Tan was seen "conferring his manuscript notes on precepts to a certain Tao from Guanshan."

In his role as direct disciple of Wang Changyue, Tan came to be equipped with some of the biographical traits of his master. Like master Wang, Tan at an early age was the recipient of a prophecy by a mysterious Daoist to the effect that he was destined to play an important role. Like Wang, Tan is said to have practiced the essence of the teachings of his master "for more than

---

[156] At the end of this Preface there is the signature of Wu Taiyi, who is said to have written this introduction to the *Chuzhen jielü* 初真戒律 in 1686 at the "Zuting" Yinxian'an of Jinling (Nanjing) on Qingliangshan (康熙丙寅蒲月上澣之吉楚郢吳太一震陽氏書於金陵清涼山祖庭隱仙庵), DZJY 24:10473. On this see also Yin Zhihua, "Qingdai Quanzhendao chuanjie chutan." Paper presented at the International Quanzhen Conference 探古監今－全真道的昨天,今天與明天. Hong Kong, January 6–8, 2010.

[157] BYGZ 32, but Oyanagi records this with the wrong family name Cheng. See also above.

[158] In Wang Ka and Wang Guiping (eds.), *Sandong*, 11: 51.

[159] Igarashi's *Taiseikyū shi*, 64–65.

[160] However, Chen Ting's biography and the TSLM refer only to Wudang.

twenty years." Again like his teacher, Tan is portrayed as an eminent master capable of converting thousands upon thousands of disciples and spreading the teachings throughout the empire. Finally, Tan is associated like Wang to an "ancestral hall" or *zuting* 祖庭. At the image of Beijing's Baiyun guan, Nanjing's Yinxian'an has the double role of transmission center for Longmen orthodox teachings and of grave site. Nanjing was presented as the home not only of the Yinxian'an but also of Wang's legendary ordination of 1663. Appropriately, the content of this ordination—recorded for posterity under the name of *Longmen xinfa* 龍門心法 (Core Teachings of the Longmen) or, in Min Yide's tradition, as *Biyuan tanjing* 碧苑壇經 (Platform Sūtra of the Jade Garden)—is connected with Tan's heir: Zhan Tailin 詹太林, the Ninth Vinaya Patriarch.

Chapter 4

The Mystery of the Ninth Vinaya Patriarch: Zhan Tailin 詹太林 (1625–1712) and the Invented Continuity at the Baiyun guan Hall

Although the *Mind-Lamp* does not mention Zhan Tailin or any other heirs of the eighth patriarch Tan Shoucheng, the spirit-tablets of Zhan and his official and sole heir were still displayed in the Baiyun guan ancestral hall when Oyanagi visited this monastery. In an epitaph written in Zhan Tailin's honor by Peng Dingqiu 彭定求 (1645–1719), Zhan is presented as the scion of a Confucian family in Macheng County (Hubei province).[161] He is said to have repeatedly taken official examinations, but because of several ailments he finally decided to devote himself to the study of the Mysterious teaching (Daoism). At the age of forty-nine he became a Daoist priest in Nanchang (Jiangxi) at the Tiezhugong 鐵柱宮. Later on he received the precepts at the Quanzhen Vinaya altar (Quanzhen *lütan*) of Wumen (Suzhou).

He venerated Maoshan as the secret abode of the tradition of Immortals and often went to the Qianyuanguan of Yugang where he examined the canonical texts for roughly three years.[162] Once

---

[161] Peng Dingqiu, "Zhan Weiyang lüshi taming" 詹維陽律師塔銘 10.15a, contained in his twelve-juan *Nanyun wengao* 南畇文稿 (Preface 1726) in *Siku quanshu cunmu congshu*, 集部, vol. 246: 775–76, here 775. This is also confirmed by the TSLM. In the JGXD, Zhan Shouchun (= Zhan Tailin) is said to hail from a Nanjing family of salt traders with an ancestral home in Anhui. As Qing Xitai notes (1994: 4.99), Zhan was connected with the ordination platform of Nanjing, his mother was a relative of the Emperor, and he was linked with Nanjing literary celebrities. Because he refused to offer his surrender to Ruan Dacheng 阮大鋮 (1587–1646), his wife and concubines were imprisoned and executed, after which he became a priest and entered Quanzhen 皇帝國戚、本人系金陵名士、他由於拒絕阮大鋮的招降、妻妾被拘死節、乃憤世出家加入了全真道。

[162] The TSLM has him study the *Daozang* (the Ming Daoist Canon). See *Daojiaoshi*

while collecting medicinal plants, he passed by the grotto-heaven of Liangchang[163] and saw the *Longmen xinfa* (Core Teachings of the Longmen) scripture in a secret opening inside a stone case. He then devoted all his energy to studying it as he regarded it as a divine revelation. Tan Xinyue (Shoucheng), the disciple of Wang Kunyang (Changyue) regarded Zhan as the most capable disciple ever since his teacher had practiced the Way in Jinling (Nanjing), and he conferred on him the ninth transmission of the Longmen lineage.

慕茅山為仙宗奧府、往寓郁岡之乾元觀。檢閱藏經凡三載。嘗採藥過良常洞天、見石函中秘扃 龍門心法 一帙、精思而勤習之、若有神授。時當昆陽王律師金陵行道之後、其嗣心月譚律師以先生為入室高弟、付龍門派第九傳。

As mentioned above, according to the *Taishang lümai* the conferral of the Longmen lineage to Zhan took place in 1690. However, Zhan's biography by Chen Ting places this event in 1689 on the day of Tan's death at Nanjing's Yinxian'an. After his stay at Maoshan, Zhan went to the capital and continued his journey further north to Lulongsai 盧龍塞 (today's Xifengkou 喜峰口 in Hebei province) in order to spread Vinaya teachings. Meanwhile, "Daoist priests who had heard about this flocked to the imperial capital. Princes, dukes, and high-ranking officials extended their stay and even repeatedly followed on Zhan's heels. His practice of the Way was so respectful and sincere that it made people gladly accept him at first sight" (自是北游京師、直至盧龍塞上、闡揚教律、羽流聞風駢集輦下。王公卿士延訪、亦復接踵。蓋其道行愨誠、使人一見而悅服也).

Now it appears, according to a Preface by Zhan included in the *Guangcheng yizhi* 廣成儀制 collection, that he performed in 1696 an ordination ceremony at Beijing's Lingyougong which is known for having been since 1655 the official residence of the fifty-third Celestial Master at the capital.[164]

---

ziliao, 394. In 1599 the Qiaoyuan guan had obtained the *Daozang* as a present from Emperor Shenzong.

[163] Lianchang was a renowned place in Jurongxian 句容縣 (Jiangsu, Maoshan region) that is for example mentioned in fascicle 11 of the *Zhengao* 真誥.

[164] See the study by Yang Haiying 楊海英 ("Qing qianqi de daojiao yu gongting 清前期的道教與宮廷," *Daojia wenhua yanjiu* 道家文化研究 23 (2008): 365–410). The Lingyougong was originally a "Shifang daoyuan." In 1655 it became the place of residence assigned by the Qing court to the 53rd Celestial Master Zhang Hongren 張洪任. See also p. 376 of the same article.

Subsequently Zhan returned to the South, and on his way back from Tianjin he traversed Yetai (today's Hebei Handan 邯鄲) until Botu, "preaching in all of these places the dharma and explaining the scriptures so that the unique style of his Daoist sect be widely propagated and recognized as the continuous tradition of the Golden Lotus of the Perfected Changchun—a tradition that none but him could shoulder" (演法談經、宗風遐暢、僉謂長春真人金蓮一線、非先生弗克負荷矣).

On reaching Jiangnan he was warmly welcomed as honored guest in Juqu 句曲 (today's Jurong 句容,Jiangsu province) and invited to assume the abbotship of Maoshan's Qianyuanguan 乾元觀.[165] Zhan wished to restore the pure rules of Daoist public monasteries but met with no success. Finally "on the eighteenth day of the twelfth lunar month of 1712," after having met his heir Tang Chuyang 唐初陽 (lineage name: Qingshan 清善) at the Daoist cloister of Jingkou 京口 (today's Zhenjiang 鎮江 in Jiangsu province), Zhan died at the age of eighty-eight years leaving his final gatha. According to the *Taishang lümai* he had already transmitted "on the thirteenth day of the second lunar month of 1709" the Longmen lineage to Mu Qingfeng 穆清風 who became his direct and unique heir at the Baiyun guan ancestral hall.[166]

As we can gather from this biography by Peng Dingqiu, Zhan Tailin converted to Daoism late in life. At the age of forty-nine he joined the "Yellow-crowned fellows" (huangguan lu 黃冠侶) at the Tiezhugong 鐵柱宮 or Iron Pillar Palace, the main Jingming monastery in Nanchang. His initial association with Jingming is further emphasized in the *Taishang lümai* biography that mentions Yulong 玉隆 and Longsha 龍沙 which both are famous sanctuaries devoted to Xu Xun 許遜, the legendary founder and deity of Jingming Daoism.[167] After his ordination at the so-called Quanzhen Vinaya altar of Suzhou, he associated himself with Maoshan and more particularly with the Qianyuanguan 乾元觀 of Yugang 鬱岡.[168] According to Peng, Zhan's "aim was to restore this monastery and revive the pure rules of

---

[165] Peng Dingqiu's biography mentions the names of masters linked with this monastery, starting with a recluse Tao (Tao Hongjing?).

[166] This is also mentioned in Igarashi (1938:67). According to the TSLM, Mu was later known for having performed the ordinations in Sichuan in 1714.

[167] *Daojiaoshi ziliao* 道教史資料 (Shanghai: Guji chubanshe, 1991): 394.

[168] For a short description of the Qianyuanguan tradition in Maoshan during the Qing era see Qing Xitai 卿希泰, *Zhongguo daojiao shi* 中國道教史 (Chengdu: Sichuan renmin, 1996): 100.

the public monasteries so that people from the entire country could come and take refuge by changing, in accordance with these teachings, their bad habits of seeking private gain. With this aim in mind he worked hard, and though suffering for years of hunger and slurping a single bowl of wheat-gruel per day, he continued sitting in meditation day after day without interruption. At the end of his life, conscious that the difficulties of the time prevented him from achieving his aims, he lamented in deep sorrow the loss of Daoist sanctuaries as well as his incapacity to take care of them and to fulfill his mission."

Peng Dingqiu records the aftermath of Zhan's meeting with this master in Maoshan as follows: "Although the Daoist school had Vinaya teachings that are very close to Confucianism and are characterized externally by strict etiquette and internally by intensive study of Life and Destiny (*xingming*), because of continual disagreement among participants such teachings were destined to be interrupted." Peng ends his commemoration of this exemplary master on this note of regret: because of the dire circumstances of his time, Zhan could not achieve what was expected of him.

It is difficult to understand today why an eminent master such as Zhan Tailin is not mentioned in the *Mind-Lamp* even though he reportedly spread Vinaya teachings both in North and South China and was unanimously elected in Jiangnan to assume the abbotship of Maoshan's renowned Qianyuanguan 乾元觀. According to the *Mind-Lamp* this monastery was taken over by the eighth Longmen patriarch (*zongshi*) Sun Yuyang 孫玉陽, a disciple of Shen Taihe (heir of the lineage of Zhao Fuyang). From the ninth generation onward it was seen as part of the Maoshan lineage 茅山法派 and is no longer listed among the Longmen orthodox lineages.[169] Whatever the reason or reasons, one cannot deny that Zhan was not only noted as a preacher representative of "the continuity of the Golden Lotus tradition of Qiu Chuji" but also as a prolific writer. Apart from his wondrous link with the *Longmen xinfa* 龍門心法 (Core Teachings of the Longmen), Peng also mentions in Zhan's biography that he wrote commentaries on numerous Daoist alchemical classics such as the *Cantongqi* 參同契, *Qingjing jing* 清靜經, and *Xinyin jing* 心印經. He also left to posterity the *Dianying ji* 顛影集, and in his old age he compiled the *Yugang xiaozhi* 鬱岡小志.[170]

---

[169] "Daopu yuanliu tu" 道譜源流圖, JGXD 7a. See also the JGXD biography of Sun Yuyang 孫玉陽. On the division of Longmen into two lines see above.

[170] Peng Dingqiu, *Nandou wengao*, 11. 16a (SKQS congmu 246: 776).

Ironically, in spite of all his achievements, his name ended up being not only confused with another Zhan but even erased from the very scripture that was so marvellously related to him. It is probably due to the inexplicable oblivion of this master in *Mind-Lamp* biographies that first Oyanagi and then Li Yangzheng fell into error. Oyanagi informs us that while copying the names of the Longmen patriarchs inscribed on the spirit-tablets of the Baiyun guan ancestral hall, he emended the name of Zhan Tailin—originally written Weiyang 維陽 according to his Daoist sobriquet—to read Yiyang 怡陽.[171] His rationale was that Yiyang is the sobriquet of another Zhan (lineage name: Shouchun 守椿) who is known as a direct disciple of Wang Changyue in Jiangnan and has a biography in the *Mind-Lamp* (2.3a–4b). For the above-mentioned eighth Longmen Vinaya Patriarch Tan Shoucheng and now also for the "double Zhan," Oyanagi strongly relied on the *Mind-Lamp*, the unique source for the biographies of the previous seven Longmen Vinaya Patriarchs at the Baiyun guan ancestral hall.[172]

However, the comparison of the two biographies of "Zhan" (Zhan Tailin's by Peng and Zhan Yiyang's in the *Mind-Lamp*) clearly shows that we are dealing with two different persons. This is also confirmed by consulting the *Longmen xinfa* 龍門心法, the scripture that was allegedly discovered by Zhan Tailin in the heaven-grotto of Liangchang. In this scripture the name of Zhan Tailin as revisor appears along with the name of Zhan Yiyang as one of the recorders of the 1663 Nanjing ordination of Wang Changyue. Interestingly enough, while this text mentions the names of Zhan Tailin and his disciple Tang Qingshan in their role as main editors, the revised version (published by Min Yide under the title *Biyuan tanjing*) eliminates these two names and substitutes them by the name of a brand-new compiler. As we shall see in Part Two, however, Min Yide's revised text still mentions the name of Zhan Yiyang 詹怡陽 (the doppelgänger of Zhan Tailin) as one of the recorders of the Nanjing ordination. This probably contributed to the confusion about and conflation of the two Zhans.

Returning now to our ninth Vinaya patriarch Zhan Tailin, we note that much like his master Tan, Zhan shares interesting biographical traits with the seventh patriarch Wang Changyue. Like Wang, Zhan is related to Beijing's Lingyougong. Like the seventh patriarch, Zhan received high honors and was much appreciated by elite officials, princes, and dukes at the Qing

---

[171] BYGZ, 36. The same holds true for Li Yangzheng who also thought that Zhan Tailin and Zhan Yiyang were the same person.

[172] Oyanagi, BYGZ, 34–36.

court who "followed on his heels." His fame reached such a degree that tradition even attributed to him the discovery of the *Longmen xinfa* 龍門心法, the scripture that purportedly contains the discourses held by Wang Changyue in 1663 in Nanjing on the occasion of his legendary Longmen platform-ordination.

At the same time it is of interest to note that, while Zhan is honored in the North, once back in Jiangnan he had to struggle in order to protect his beloved Maoshan sanctuary from local and powerful clans. Peng's biography of Zhan reveals that the conditions, at least in Jiangnan, were not favorable for the restoration of public monasteries and the performance of large-scale public ordinations. Zhan's first Jiangnan disciple Tang Chuyang (lineage name: Qingshan), with whom he reportedly edited the *Longmen xinfa*, is not at all remembered by posterity. In Min Yide's work one also finds echoes of the interruption, three generations after Wang Changyue, of Vinaya transmissions. This appears to match Tang Chuyang's times.[173] At the end of Zhan's biography by Peng Dingqiu, other Jiangnan disciples of the tenth and eleventh generations are mentioned (for example Zou Qingru 鄒清如, Sheng Qingxin 盛清新, Shen Yicheng 沈一誠, and Jiang Yihe 蔣一鶴); yet none of these are listed in the *Mind-Lamp* or represented in the Baiyun guan ancestral hall.[174] According to Peng, these disciples buried their master seven days after Zhan's death in the southern foothills of Maoshan and erected in his honor a stupa in front of which Peng recited the text of his epitaph.[175]

The Longmen "orthodox tradition" at the Baiyun guan ancestral hall also retained a sole but different heir: Mu Qingfeng 穆清風 who is revered as the tenth Longmen Vinaya Patriarch. This patriarch is no longer linked with Jiangnan. According to Mu's biography in the *Taishang lümai*, after having met Zhan Tailin at Maoshan Qianyuanguan and received from him the Longmen heritage in 1709, Mu performed the ordination ceremony in Sichuan in 1714 at Chengdu's Zitonggong 梓潼宮 with which he is now associated (see Table 1). This is also confirmed by the Longmen dharma scrolls transcribed by Igarashi in the 1930s and the 1874 manuscript

---

[173] Commentary by Min Yide to the *Huangji zhengdao jing*.

[174] These disciples are quoted according to the Longmen lineage names corresponding to the 10th and 11th generation (Qing 清 and Yi 一).

[175] Erecting a stupa is connected with ancestral worship (see Jorgensen 2005:121). This shows that Zhan's lineage was regarded as established at the Qianyuanguan, the place of Zhan's ancestral cult by his disciples.

Xuandu lütan weiyi 玄都律壇威儀戒[176] that were transcribed by the Beijing Quanzhen Daoist Fang Yongqian in 1874.

The examiniation of these documents shows that, whereas the previous list associated, in harmony with Baiyun guan lore, the first Vinaya Patriarch Zhao Daojian 趙道堅 with the seventh Vinaya Patriarch Wang Changyue 王常月 alias Wang Kunyang 王崑陽, the list of Longmen "orthodox" Vinaya patriarchs presented in Table 1[177] features from the eighth to the fifteenth generation not a single Longmen Vinaya Patriarch related to the Baiyun guan.

This indicates that, compared to the first seven patriarchs of Longmen, even more revolutions of the Dharma Vinaya wheel were needed until it came to be firmly lodged in the soil of the Baiyun guan. But the new episodes of the Longmen saga no longer shared the romantic view established by the *Mind-Lamp* for its first Seven Pillars. The story of the Longmen Vinaya Patriarchs from the tenth to the sixteenth generation was now taken over and monopolized by the *Taishang lümai Longmen zhengzong* 太上律脈龍門正宗. The patriarchs of the new saga, following the pattern of reformer Wang Changyue's exemplary life, are associated with the hall where they supposedly transmitted the ordinations. The eighth and ninth Vinaya Pariarchs are the only ones to be listed in association with the halls where they reportedly received the precepts and obtained the Longmen mind-seal.

Furthermore, as Table 1 shows, it is only from the sixteenth generation that the ordination ceremony was again performed at the Baiyun guan. Thanks to the restoration activities of the new Jiaqing era abbots such as Zhang Langran 張朗然 (?–1807?) and Zhang Huisheng 張慧生 (?–1840), the Baiyun guan could proudly display a veneer of antique prestige: the Quanzhen Patriarchal Hall where ordination ceremonies were now regularly performed until the end of the Republican era.

---

[176] Wang, Ka 王卡 and Wang Guiping 汪桂平 (eds.). *Sandong shiyi* 三洞拾遺. 20 vols. Vol. 11 (Hefei: Huangshan shushe 黃山書社, 2005):51–52.

[177] The location of the Halls given in parentheses in Table 1 stem from the *Taishang lümai Longmen zhengzong* 太上律脈龍門正宗 (1919).

Generation/Place of affiliation	Lineage Name	Name
7th / Baiyuntang 白雲堂 (Beijing Baiyun guan)	Changyue 常月	Wang Kunyang (?–1680)
8th / Taihetang 太和堂 (Wudangshan, Hubei)	Shoucheng 守城	Tan Xinyue 譚心月 (?–1689?)
9th / Yinxiantang 隱仙堂 (Nanjing Yinxian'an, Jiangsu)	Tailin 太林	Zhan Weiyang 詹維陽 (1625–1712)
10th / Zitongtang 梓潼堂 (Chengdu Zitonggong 梓潼宮, Sichuan)	Qingfeng 清風	Mu Yufang 穆玉房 (fl. 1709)
11th / Zitongtang 梓潼堂 (Chengdu Zitonggong 梓潼宮, Sichuan)	Yihe 一和	Zhu Ziming 朱自明 (fl. 1714)
12th / Yunxitang 雲溪堂 (Jingfushan 景福山, Shaanxi)	Yangju 陽舉	Yuan Jiuyang 袁九陽 (fl. 1728)
13th / Tainingtang 太寧堂 (嵯峨山雲門宮?) Shaanxi)	Laihuan 來還	Wang Quechen 王卻塵 (fl. 1728–30)
14th / Tongzhentang 通真堂?, Shaanxi)	Fuli 复禮	Bai Huizhi 白慧直 (d. 1740)
15th / Ziyuntang 紫雲堂 (Xiangshan 象山 Ziyunguan 紫雲觀, Shaanxi)	Benhuan 本焕	Cheng Xiangyan 程香岩 (fl. 1737–68)
16th / Baiyuntang 白雲堂 (Beijing Baiyun guan)	Hehao 合皓	Zhang Langran 張朗然 (?–1807?)
17th / Baiyuntang 白雲堂 (Beijing Baiyun guan)	Jiaozhi 教智	Zhang Huisheng 張慧生 (?–1840)

Table 1: List of Longmen "orthodox" Vinaya Patriarchs from the 7th to the 17th generation

The Myth of the Longmen Revival

After this rather detailed presentation of the biographies of the Longmen Vinaya Patriarchs who represent the unilinear "Longmen orthodox lineage" at the Baiyun guan Ancestral hall, it is clear that we are dealing with the construction of a mythical history. It is evident that these Longmen Vinaya Patriarchs are the protagonists of a commemorative saga manufactured centuries after the mythical foundation of the Longmen at the Baiyun guan. It is the saga of the Jiaqing-era reformers who wanted to portray the Baiyun guan as a memorial sanctuary representing the ancient and original Quanzhen tradition. One of their primary aims was to present the Baiyun guan as the Longmen Ancestral hall, the hall where public ordinations are said to have been performed for the first time by the legendary founder patriarch Qiu Chuji as early as the Yuan era. These ordinations were purportedly continued without interruption by founder Qiu's Longmen heirs. It was a myth worthy of being set in stone and celebrated in texts and rituals.

Even though the Baiyun guan did not have the effective authority and knowledge to transmit public ordinations before the Jiaqing era, it thus gained them in the eyes of posterity. After all, it was here that the ancestral hall of the Longmen Vinaya Patriarchs was erected in order to commemorate the continuity of the very lineage that the Longmen historians had invented. As the religious equivalent of an imperial lineage which received its mandate from Heaven, the Longmen tradition obtained its mandate directly from the Most High Laozi. By way of its heavenly messenger Lü Dongbin 呂洞賓 it was equipped with a centralized hierarchy recognized by competing Daoist lines worshiping the same seven patriarchs as the unique representatives of the "correct" lineage. In the image of the imperial lineage, the Longmen "orthodox lineage" thus came to be conceived and presented as an uninterrupted "apostolic" lineage stretching from the Yuan era to the present—a lineage whose patriarchs are firmly connected by direct transmission to the founder figure. This continuous lineage, celebrated at the Baiyun guan Ancestral hall, was so much in need of a history that it had to be manufactured.

This is a phenomenon that can be observed in religious movements all over the world. Just as the historians of the Vatican, when that need arose after some centuries, produced a tailor-made "apostolic" transmission line, starting with Saint Peter whom Jewish reformer Jesus had supposedly called "the rock upon which my church will be built," and invented a succession of early popes (bishops of Rome) reaching back to the first century when neither bishops nor popes nor a "church" existed, the Longmen tradition's historians manufactured, streamlined, and celebrated their own pedigree. Their aim was to establish Wang Changyue as the Seventh Patriarch by whom the "orthodox" Daoist Vinaya of Qiu Chuji could be spread throughout China. This was achieved by linking him to various local lineages; by the establishment of an ordination system that will be described in Part Two; and by the creation of the Daoist "Vatican" Baiyun guan where—at the image of feudal lords paying their respect to the Emperor during the annual enfeoffement rite or of bishops visiting the Roman pope—the representatives of new Longmen branches were required to pay respect and pledge allegiance before obtaining their new mandate.

Like Chan Buddhism and other reform movements in need of legitimizing their new doctrines, rituals, etc., modern Daoism can boast of historians who laboriously invented and fashioned a golden ancient past, excellent founding "patriarchs," an "apostolic" transmission line guaranteeing continuity and purity of genuine ancient doctrine, and other appropriate means for legitimizing their reform movement as the sole true heir of an age-old, divinely sanctioned tradition. The Catholic church in Rome, late heiress of a Jewish reform movement, accomplished this feat by aligning its new doctrines and canonical texts (the "New Testament") with the Jewish past (now the "Old Testament") and by inventing a lineage of early popes who safeguarded "original purity" via an elaborate system of ordination. As we will see in Part Two, ordination plays an equally central role in the Longmen church and its Vatican, the Baiyun guan in Beijing; and Part Three will describe the formation of Daoism's own "New Testament," the ultimate Daoist canon of the Qing era.

Part Two

CREATION OF ORDINATION

Chapter 1

The Invention of the Quanzhen Ur-Vinaya Tradition

After the chaos at the end of the Ming, Daoism allegedly experienced a revival at the beginning of the Qing. Tradition asserts that "Seventh Patriarch" Wang Changyue 王常月 (?–1680) alias Wang Kunyang 王崑陽 was the key figure of this revival. Portrayed as the great "Longmen restorer" 龍門中興, Wang is hailed as the promoter of the Quanzhen Daoist Vinaya renaissance of the Qing.[175] The episode marking the beginning of this "new" Quanzhen era is Wang Changyue's self-proclaimed establishment in 1656 of the precept-altar (*jietan* 戒壇) at Beijing's Baiyun guan 白雲觀.[176] Through this important ritual act, Wang Changyue supposedly reestablished the Quanzhen monastic liturgy that is said to have been transmitted to him in "an uninterrupted way" for more than four centuries from the Quanzhen patriarch Qiu Chuji 邱處機 (1148–1227).[177]

---

[175] Chen Bing 陳兵, "Qingdai Quanzhen dao Longmen pai de zhongxing 清代全真道龍門派的中興," *Shijie zongjiao yanjiu* 世界宗教研究 2, 1988, pp. 84–96. Wang Changyue (also called Wang Kunyang 王崑陽) is portrayed as the "Longmen restorer of the seventh generation" 龍門第七代家風 by his purported disciples. See for instance *Biyuan tanjing* 碧苑壇經, 2a in *Gu Shuyinlou cangshu* 古書隱樓藏書 compiled by Min Yide 閔一得 (1748/58?–1836), reprinted in *Zangwai daoshu*, vol. 10, p. 159. See also the two stelae of 1828 and 1886 in Oyanagi Shigeta 小柳司氣太, *Hakuunkan shi* 白雲觀志 (Tokyo: Tōhō bunka gakuin Tōkyō kenkyūjo, 1934), pp. 148–9 and 162–3.

[176] Preface attributed to Wang to the *Chuzhen jielü* 初真戒律, 25b (*Chongkan Daozang jiyao*, Taiwan Kaozheng reprint, 1971), CK vol. 24, p. 10469. For my analysis of this preface see p. 98 ff.

[177] On the claim of an "uninterrupted transmission" of the Quanzhen precepts from Qiu Chuji to Wang Changyue see Wang Changyue's Biography in Min Yide's *Mind-Lamp of Mount Jingai* 金蓋心燈. On the various inconsistencies surrounding Wang Changyue's biography and his work as well as his legendary performance of

After that important episode at Baiyun guan, Wang purportedly traveled South in order to transmit the precepts on a larger scale. In 1663 he allegedly held the ordination sermons in Jinling (Nanjing) that were later recorded in the *Longmen xinfa* 龍門心法.[178] In 1664 he is said to have been in Hangzhou visiting various monasteries around Zhejiang and Jiangsu until his last transmission of precepts in Wudangshan 武當山 around 1674.[179] Wang's "Vinaya-tours" had the effect of bringing wider recognition to his new tradition: the Longmen Vinaya lineage 龍門律宗.[180] As one would expect, his lineage was subsequently equipped with genealogical registers, precept-

---

the Quanzhen ordination ceremony at Baiyun guan, see Esposito 1993 / 2012 and "The Longmen School and its Controversial History during the Qing Dynasty," in John Lagerwey, ed., *Religion and Chinese Society* (Hong Kong and Paris: Chinese University Press and EFEO, 2004) {chapter 2 of Esposito, *Facets of Qing Daoism*}. On the acceptance of a "continuity view" of the precepts-transmission from Qiu Chuji to Wang Changyue see for instance the works by Min Zhiting 閔智亭, *Daojiao yifan* 道教儀範 (Beijing: Zhongguo daojiao xueyuan, 1990); Li Yangzheng 李養正, *Xinbian Beijing Baiyun guan zhi* 新編北京白雲觀志 (Beijing: Zongjiao wenhua chubanshe, 2003), pp. 241–9; and the recent book by Ren Zongquan 任宗權, *Daojiao jielü xue* 道教戒律學, 2 vols. (Beijing: Zongjiao wenhua chubanshe, 2008). Recently, the first Chinese scholar has also begun expressing doubts about the historicity of Wang Changyue's transmission of Quanzhen ordination at the Baiyun guan: Yin Zhihua, "Wang Changyue chuanjie de xushu lishi 王常月傳戒的敘述歷史" *Daojiao wenhua yanjiu zhongxin tongxun* 道教文化研究中心通訊 8, 2007, pp. 1–2; "Wang Changyue chuanjie," "Qing tongzhi shiernian Beijing Baiyun guan chuanjie kaoshu (shang) 清同治十二年北京白雲觀傳戒考述(上)," *Sanqin daojiao* 三秦道教 46, 2008, pp. 31–4 and "xia 下," *Sanqin daojiao* 47, 2008, pp. 34–37; and "Qingdai Quanzhendao chuanjie chutan 清代全真道傳戒初探," Paper presented at the International Quanzhen conference 探古監今 – 全真道的昨天,今天與明天, Hong Kong, January 6–8, 2010.

[178] Monica Esposito, "Longmen Taoism in Qing China: Doctrinal Ideal and Local Reality," *Journal of Chinese Religions* 29 (2001), pp. 192–231 {chapter 3 of Esposito, *Facets of Qing Daoism*}.

[179] See the biographies of the various disciples of Wang Changyue in the JGXD as well as the Preface to the *Chuzhen jielü* 初真戒律 attributed to Long Qiqian and dated 1674 (Jiaxing 康熙 13). It is not clear if the mention in this Preface of "today" (referring to the time when Long Qiqian reportedly met Wang Changyue in Wudangshan) corresponds to 1674 or earlier. Chinese scholars think that this meeting ought to have taken place in 1673. See for instance Yin Zhihua 2010.

[180] As documented in Igarashi Kenryū 五十嵐賢隆, *Taiseikyū shi* 太清宮志 (Tokyo: Kokusho kankōkai 国書刊行会, 1938, pp. 62 – 75), "Longmen lüzong 龍門律宗" can be well explained as an expression of the Taishang lümai Longmen zhengzong 太上律脈龍門正宗 related to the abbots' transmission of the Longmen orthodox dharma scrolls 龍門正宗法卷.

texts, and its own "Longmen patriarchal garden," Longmen zuting 龍門祖庭. Established at Baiyun guan, this Longmen zuting was located directly on top of the sanctuary housing the grave of the Quanzhen patriarch Qiu Chuji (1148–1227), the Jin-Yuan era Daoist leader and legendary founder of the Longmen. Recognized as the Seventh Longmen Vinaya Patriarch 龍門第七律師 in a manufactured genealogy whose genesis was discussed in Part One, Wang was worshiped at Baiyun guan's Memorial Hall (citang 祠堂) and became the key figure in the foundation myth of the Quanzhen Longmen orthodox lineage 全真教龍門正宗. The affiliation with this master was subsequently used to legitimate a variety of new Daoist Longmen local branches and sub-branches.[181]

As discussed in this book's Introduction and Part One, this late invention of a universal Longmen orthodox history was first presented and divulged through Min Yide's compilation of a "Daoist Lamp History" 道家燈史, the *Jingai xindeng* 金蓋心燈. Today, the statue of Wang Changyue sits on his abbot's throne at the Baiyun guan as the illustrious exponent of a glorious and ideal Quanzhen Vinaya past and guarantor of a supposedly continuous "Quanzhen universal clerical identity."[182] The ordination that Wang purportedly performed from his abbot's throne at the Baiyun guan came to be known as the Quanzhen collective ordination procedure of the

---

[181] Esposito, "La Porte du Dragon" (1993); "The Longmen School and its Controversial History during the Qing Dynasty;" Shindai ni okeru Kingaisan Ryūmonha no seiritsu to *Kinka shūshi* 清代における金蓋山龍門派の成立と金華宗旨," in Kyōto Daigaku Jinbun Kagaku Kenkyūjo, ed., *Chūgoku shūkyō bunken kenkyū* 中国宗教文献研究 (Kyoto: Rinsen shoten, 2007, pp. 252–3, 255–61; revised English version here below in Part Four); and "Qingdai Quanzhen jiao zhi chonggou: Min Yide ji qi jianli Longmen zhengtong de yiyuan 清代全真教之重構：閔一得及其建立龍門正統得意願," Paper presented at the International Quanzhen conference 探古監今 – 全真道的昨天, 今天與明天, Hong Kong, January 6–8, 2010. On the relation of the so-called Quanzhen ordination of the three altars with Chan 禪 and Lingbao, see also Esposito, "Shindai dōkyō to mikkyō: Ryūmon seijiku shinshū 清代道教と密教—龍門西竺心宗," in Mugitani Kunio 麥谷邦夫, ed., *Sankyō kōshō ronsō* 三教交渉論叢 (Kyoto: Jinbun Kagaku Kenkyūjo, 2005), pp. 289–338, here pp. 292–3, 315–8, 321–322 note 12 {revised English version in chapter 5 of *Facets of Qing Daoism*, here pp. 242–246 and 287–290}).

[182] For a presentation of Min Yide's *Jingai xindeng* as the first "Lamp History" in Daoism representing Longmen's "will to orthodoxy," see Esposito, "La Porte du Dragon" (1993);" "The Longmen School and its Controversial History during the Qing Dynasty" (2004a {revised English version in chapter 2 of *Facets of Qing Daoism*}); and "Qingdai Quanzhen jiao zhi chonggou 清代全真教之重構" (2010a).

three altars (*santan dajie* 三壇大戒). It plays a central role in the myth of Quanzhen continuity and consists of three series of precepts:

(1) Initial Precepts for Perfection (*chuzhen jie* 初真戒)
(2) Intermediate Precepts for Perfection (*zhongji jie* 中極戒)
(3) Precepts for Celestial Immortality (*tianxian jie* 天仙戒)

These three series of precepts represent in the Daoist world a newly reformed ordination system associated with Quanzhen.

In contrast to my "innovation" narrative that assumes discontinuity and creative action, Daoist internal sources emphasize continuity and conservation.[183] In such sources, the three series of precepts are portrayed not as the fruit of Wang's activity but rather as the product of an uninterrupted transmission within the Quanzhen legacy starting with Qiu Chuji 邱處機 (1148–1227). As the mythical founder of the Longmen pai 龍門派, Qiu Chuji is regarded as the principal propagator of this system of precepts during the Yuan. Because of unfavorable conditions, so these sources assert, Qiu's successors were obliged to keep this transmission secret. This is supposed to explain why Daoists ended up being unaware of Daoist precepts and Vinaya regulations until Wang's entry into the Baiyun guan and his alleged "re-establishment" of supposedly time-honored precepts under the auspices of the Qing court.[184]

Whether one believes this "conservation" narrative or not, it is a fact that Wang became so strongly associated with the transmission of precepts during the Qing that, in the opinion of modern Daoists and scholars, he is even credited with the three precept-texts known as *Chuzhen jielü* 初真戒律 (or simply *Chuzhen jie* 初真戒), *Zhongji jie* 中極戒, and *Tianxian dajie* 天仙

---

[183] I have published several articles outlining this "innovation" narrative which stands in opposition to the widely accepted "conservation" narrative: see for instance Esposito, "Longmen Taoism in Qing China" {revised ed. in chapter 1 of *Facets of Qing Daoism*}; "The Longmen School and its Controversial History during the Qing Dynasty" {chapter 2 of *Facets of Qing Daoism*}; *Shindai ni okeru Kingaisan Ryūmonha no seiritsu to Kinka shūshi* 清代における金蓋山龍門派の成立と金華宗旨 {revised English version here below, Part Four}; "Yibu Quanzhen Daozang de faming: Daozang jiyao ji Qingdai Quanzhen rentong 一部全真道藏的發明：道藏輯要及清代全真認同," in Zhao Weidong 赵卫东 ed., *Wendao Kunyushan* 问道昆嵛山 (Jinan: Qilu shushe, 2009): 303–43; and "Qingdai Quanzhen jiao zhi chonggou 清代全真教之重構" {revised English edition in Goossaert and Liu, eds., 2014b}.

[184] Biography of Zhang Dechun 張德純 and Wang Changyue in *Jingai xindeng*. See Esposito, "The Longmen School and its Controversial History during the Qing Dynasty" {*Facets of Qing Daoism*, chapter 2}.

大戒. About two centuries after Wang's death, copies of these three texts began to be distributed to the ordinands on the occasion of Quanzhen ordinations performed at Quanzhen public monasteries. These three precept-texts are still used today in the Quanzhen ordination ceremonies that were re-inaugurated at Baiyun guan in 1989 and successively performed in 1995 at Sichuan's Qingcheng shan 青城山 and in 2002 at Liaoning's Qianshan Wulonggong 千山五龍宮.[185]

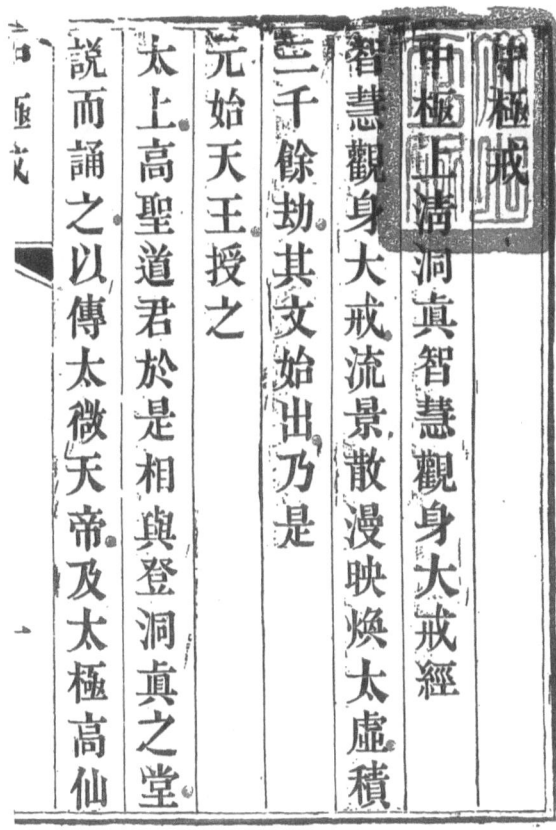

Fig. 11: Beginning of the Intermediate Precepts *Zhongji jie* 中極戒, part of twentieth-century Baiyun guan ordination certificates (Hackmann 1931)

---

[185] For the description of the 1989 Baiyun guan ordination see for instance *Zhongguo daojiao* 中國道教 3 (1989): 5. For the 1995 ordination at Qingcheng shan see *Zhongguo daojiao* 1 (1996): 7–11 and Li Yangzheng, ed. 李养正, *Dangdai daojiao* 當代道教 (北京：東方出版社, 2000), p. 123, as well as Lai Chi-tim, "Daoism in China Today, 1980–2002," *The China Quarterly* 174 (2003): 413–427, here 420.

A presentation of these three precept-texts was provided by the recently deceased Baiyun guan abbot Min Zhiting 閔智亭 (1924–2004).¹⁸⁶ But copies of these three texts with related ordination certificates have also been found at the beginning of the twentieth century by Hackmann in Laoshan.¹⁸⁷ In the words of Livia Kohn, these three precept-texts "were first compiled by Wang Changyue in 1656."¹⁸⁸ Two of them, the *Chuzhen jielü* 初真戒律 and the *Zhongji jie*, were translated into German by Hackmann who published them in 1920 after his return from China. In the Introduction to her book which includes a partial English translation of the *Chuzhen jielü* 初真戒律 based on Hackmann's German translation, Kohn explains that the Quanzhen monastic ordination and precept systems were created in the mid-seventeenth century under the guidance of Wang Changyue and are still in place today. Kohn states that the "three texts [i.e., *Chuzhen jie, Zhongji jie,* and *Tianxian dajie*] are attributed to him matching three levels of ordination and outlining behavioral patterns for beginners, intermediate practitioners, and celestial immortals."¹⁸⁹

Among Western scholars, Goossaert in his recent book *The Taoists of Peking* also presents these three texts as part of the Quanzhen ordination ceremonies performed during the Qing dynasty and in the twentieth century, and he asserts that they were "authored by Wang Changyue and other Longmen leaders who restored Quanzhen consecrations [受戒] beginning in 1656." Goossaert adds that these three texts are included in the Erxian'an 二仙菴 edition of the *Daozang jiyao* under the title "Santan dajie 三壇大戒," which according to him is "a general title to the continuously paginated but separately titled three parts in this edition: *Chuzhen jie* 初真戒, *Zhongji jie* 中極戒, and *Tianxian dajie* 天仙大戒."¹⁹⁰

---

¹⁸⁶ Min Zhiting 閔智亭, *Daojiao yifan* 道教儀範 (1990), pp. 65–89.

¹⁸⁷ Heinrich Hackmann, "Die Mönchsregeln des Klostertaoismus," *Ostasiatische Zeitschrift* 8 (1920): 141–70, here 146–47, and of the same author *Die dreihundert Mönchsgebote des chinesischen Taoismus* (Amsterdam: Koninklijke Akademie van Wetenshapen, 1931): 6–7.

¹⁸⁸ Livia Kohn, "Monastic Rules in Quanzhen Daoism: As Collected by Heinrich Hackmann," *Monumenta Serica* 51 (2003): 367–97.

¹⁸⁹ Livia Kohn, *Cosmos and Community* (Cambridge, MA: Three Pines Press, 2004), p. 12. The partial translation of the *Chuzhen jielü* is included on pp. 253–263. See also her translation of the *Zhongji jie* based on Hackmann's work in the *Supplement to Cosmos and Community* (electronic publication, 2004).

¹⁹⁰ *Chuzhen jie* 初真戒, *Zhongji jie* 中極戒, and *Tianxian dajie* 天仙大戒. Vincent Goossaert, *The Taoists of Peking, 1800–1949* (Cambridge, Mass: Harvard Univer-

However, the Erxian'an edition of the *Daozang jiyao* (i.e., the *Chongkan Daozang jiyao*) shows no trace of the title mentioned by Goossaert; "Santan dajie" as a title is found neither in this collection nor its different catalogs.[191] Furthermore, the attribution of these three precept-texts to Wang Changyue appears problematic. As far as we know they were published for the first time during the Jiaqing 嘉慶 era (1796–1820) in the old edition of the *Daozang jiyao* before being reprinted in the above-mentioned Erxian'an edition of 1906, the *Chongkan Daozang jiyao*. In both of these editions the titles of the three precept-texts and their attribution are given as follows:

1) *Santan yuanman tianxian dajie lüeshuo* 三壇圓滿天仙大戒略說 (abbreviated in the fish-tail 魚尾 as *Tianxian dajie* 天仙大戒) "compiled by Liu Shouyuan... 開玄闡秘宏教真君柳守元撰" (張集7, 1a–24b; CK vol. 24, pp. 10457–10468);
2) *Chuzhen jielü* 初真戒律 (abbreviated in the fish-tail 魚尾 as *Chuzhen jie* 初真戒) "written by Wang Changyue 崑陽子王常月著" (張集 7, 25a–61b; CK vol. 24, pp. 10469–10487); and
3) *Zhongji jie* 中極戒, without any attribution (張集7, 62a–79b; CK vol. 24, pp. 10487–10496).

This forms the background of the questions that I will now pose and attempt to answer. Based on the analysis of the three above-mentioned precept-texts originally included in the *Daozang jiyao* of the Jiaqing era at the beginning of the nineteenth century: is it proper to assume (like the above-mentioned scholars) that Wang Changyue 王常月 alias Wang Kunyang 王崑陽 authored them in the seventeenth century? Is Wang Changyue the founding father of what came to be known as the Quanzhen "ordination of the three altars 三壇大戒"? Assuming this to be the case: what could be the content of Wang Changyue's transmission of precepts, and what did he convey in these three precept-texts? Since when, and why, were the three series of precepts regarded as representative of a full-fledged "Quanzhen

---

sity Press, 2007), pp. 150–151 and 362–363.
[191] "Chongkan Daozang jiyao zongmu" 重刊道藏輯要總目, 56a (CK, 1: 32) and "Chongkan Daozang jiyao zimu chubian" 重刊道藏輯要子目初扁, j. 4. 58b–60a (CK 1: 188–189).

ordination"? Are there any traces of a continuous "Quanzhen identity" in these three precept-texts?

In the following I shall try to answer these questions by presenting and analyzing relevant passages from the above-mentioned three precept-texts and related literature. My aim is to describe and analyze these materials from a perspective that is free, as much as possible, from inherited and preconceived ideas of what Quanzhen ought to be. This might help us to better discern the intentions of the authors, editors, and other persons involved in the genesis of these three precept-texts.

The quintessential episode marking the foundation of the Quanzhen "Ur-Vinaya tradition" is recorded in the Preface to the *Chuzhen jielü* 初真戒律. This preface was allegedly authored by Wang Changyue 王常月 alias Wang Kunyang 王崑陽 and bears the date of 1656. Apart from this Preface and other materials attributed to Wang that will be examined in this part, we do not have any tangible evidence for the grand ordination that Wang claims to have inaugurated in 1656 at Baiyun guan. While waiting for such evidence to be furnished by Chinese scholars, my research has so far not produced any. This lack of evidence, along with other factors described below, led me to regard this event as the commemorative founding act of what I call the Quanzhen Ur-Vinaya tradition, that is, the *Longmen lüzong* 龍門律宗. This act is the outcome of a series of genetic stages echoed in the Preface to the *Chuzhen jielü* that allegedly stems from Wang's pen.

The author opens this Preface by describing the time when the Daoist Vinaya—namely, the *qingdu yülü* 清都玉律 described as the Great Way of the Lord of the Dao, Sovereign of Emptiness (Xuhuang dadao 虛皇大道)—was originally transmitted in the Heavens and "highly cherished and venerated by myriad sages and gods" 萬聖寶重萬靈佩奉. At that time, only the elected "equipped with golden bones and names of jade" 金骨玉名者 could receive it. Subsequently Xuhuang Daojun, the Lord of the Dao and Sovereign of Emptiness 虛皇道君, "was greatly moved by compassion" 大啟慈悲 and decided to transmit it on earth in order to "assist and rescue those who are drowning" 救度沉溺.

> Hence he transmitted and expounded the teachings and scriptures on precepts and regulations, thus initiating the conversion of humans and gods in the reality-realm, so that they would become beacons of wisdom for planting the fruits of good actions and cultivating beneficial karmic causes [of enlightenment] as well as vessels of compassion for ascending to Perfection and entering the Dao.

故傳演戒律經教、開化法界人天、為植福修因之慧炬、登真入道之慈航也。

Subsequent to this revelation, "generation after generation received it, master after master transmitted it, and some records are still found in the Daoist Canon (Daozang)" 代代相承、師師相授、道藏列欵有載矣.

After such an initial Golden Age, transmission was interrupted. In the words of the preface's author, this stage involved a tragic degeneration:

> Subsequently, because of the tragic incident of the Qin (Shaanxi) conflagrations, eight or nine out of every ten scriptures containing precepts and regulations were destroyed, and only one or two of the ordinances were preserved. Consequently, in recent times, the precept-method continuously degenerated until today when no more than one or two in one hundred million people are in possession of it.

後因秦火大變、道經戒律十損八九、科條門列止存一二。故此近代以來、戒法日廢、至於今日、間有得傳者、萬萬一二矣。

But fortunately not everything was lost. Signs of a third stage, regeneration, could be discerned and Wang is portrayed as the protagonist of this new era. "Wang" explains:

> Nonetheless, the Daoist Vinaya that has remained the same for ten thousand generations has not been lost. Today we have summoned and gathered you, the good people, in order to broadly explain the transformation from the mysterious origin and to increase the influence of the legacy of purity and clarity. Hence you can know that the time has come to accomplish this wondrous action and that the hopes of the future depend on today.

雖然萬代不磨之玄律、亦未嘗終於湮沒也。今感集眾善、茂闡玄元之化、益宏清靜之宗、可知時至之妙在斯一舉、將來之望在於今日也。

Following this pronouncement, "Wang" describes his mission as reformer and explains how he received this calling after the encounter with his master:

> Accordingly, I was called to devote myself to this enterprise. In 1628 I followed the cloud traces to Chu (Hubei) in order to visit the Perfected Zhao Fuyang of Jiugong Mountain. There I kindly received the method of precepts and obtained guidance concerning what is essential.

遂告余從事、余因崇禎初歲雲蹟於楚、謁九宮山復陽趙真人、親授戒法、得其領要。

On such a solid foundation, and after obtaining the transmission of the "precept-method" from his master, "Wang" goes on to present his "transmission" narrative marking the rebirth of the Daoist Vinaya 玄律 at the capital's Baiyun guan in 1656:

> Thus, in order to avoid the crime of overstepping my authority by reckless acts, on the fifteenth day of the third month of the *bingshen* year (1656) I lawfully established at Baiyun guan the ordination altar in order to transmit the precepts and proclaim the bowl [rite]. I offer my wishes to the present emperor for his long-lasting imperial way and pray that officials, scholars, and common people and their families be all blessed. In order for the time-honored tradition to continue, may the saints fulfill their original vow to save the world and ensure continuity by making us find companions of the Dao so that the genuine teachings may not be forgotten.

故不避僭妄之罪、按法於丙申歲三月望日、就白雲觀設立戒壇、傳戒演缽。上祝當今聖主帝道遐昌、下祈宰官士庶身家胥慶。接續先宗、啟至聖度世之本願、提續後進、開道流無妄之真風。

After vows for the auspicious beginning of the new era, "Wang" addresses the ordinands and encourages them to persist in their practice. The author ends his preface with a description of the prodigious benefits attained by those who follow his Vinaya path:

> If the ordinands can really temper themselves physically and spiritually, regard their lives as mere floating clouds and make the observation of precepts their top priority, they will bring to completion the great enterprise of birth-and-death and fully realize the genuine constancy of their nature and life. They should not swerve in their self-cultivation even when beset with such hardships as hunger, cold, wind, and heat. Nor should they waver in their purpose even when facing death and humiliation or when trapped in great difficulties. If they make great efforts to cultivate the real and genuine doctrine, their accumulated karma will naturally melt away, and every day they will make achievements.

入戒者果能磨勵身心、覷身世若浮雲之變、精勤戒行、以戒律為急務之修、了生死之大事、盡性命之真常。雖有饑寒風暑切身之苦、不易其操。雖有死生困辱臨難之變、不奪其志。實際真宗加功著力、業累自是冰消、功勳自是日就。

If you practice the precepts you will naturally penetrate to the heart of all transformations. If you grasp even half a sentence of the Vinaya, you will be able to appear and disappear in the world of Yin and Yang as well as hells and paradises, thus bringing to completion the family tradition of the ordinands. The sun and moon, stars and constellations are all the work of our own heart-mind, and [feats like] riding the luminosities to roam the void are not worthy of admiration. If these teachings spread forever and their legacy is transmitted without change, then not only will the laws of the reign be promoted but also the transfer of merits to the common people achieved.

一身戒行自然融通於變化之中、半句律言亦可出沒於陰陽之內、天堂地獄渾然成戒子之家風、日月星辰都是我心中之活計、駕景凌虛不為尚也。倘若教衍天長、宗傳地久、首則默佐於王綱、次則歸功於眾善也。

From this preface we can gather that its author—purportedly Wang—presents himself as the agent of regeneration. His narrative follows a tripartite pattern of "Golden Age," "degeneration," and "regeneration." After the initial "Golden Age" transmission by Xuhuang daozun—the central deity of the Yuqing 玉清 Heaven, better known as the Celestial Worthy of Original Commencement (Yuanshi tianzun 元始天尊)—the Vinaya teachings entered a period of degeneration. Just when the method of the precepts 戒法 is on the verge of disappearing after the loss of most of its scriptures, Wang enters the stage and assumes the all-important role of regenerator of the original pure doctrine.

This tripartite scheme in Wang's preface conforms exactly to "Ur-tradition" movements as defined and described by Urs App. Such movements legitimize a reform of religious doctrine based on the claim that they are the sole representatives of an "original" teaching that is on the verge of disappearing:

> The raison d'être of such movements is the revival of a purportedly most ancient, genuine, "original" teaching after a long period of degeneration. Hence their need to define an "original" teaching, establish a line of its transmission, identify stages and kinds of

degeneration, and present themselves as the agent of "regeneration" of the original "ancient" teaching.¹⁹²

In our particular case, the original "ancient" teaching is the Daoist Vinaya, namely, *qingdu yülü* 清都玉律. In the words of "Wang" this original, pure teaching had originally been transmitted in the Heavens by Xuhuang daozun. After a period of initial prosperity it entered a protracted degeneration process that continued until the time of Wang's regeneration of the original teaching through his compilation of scriptures and through his performance of the grand ordination at the Baiyun guan. This regenerative act marks the revival of Wang's "Ur-tradition," namely, the tradition that came to be known as Longmen lüzong 龍門律宗: the Longmen Vinaya tradition. However, in order to reinforce this new tradition, a reformer like "Wang" needed a corpus of texts attesting its purity and orthodoxy. For this reason the "conservative" narrative in this preface credits Wang Changyue 王常月 with the *Chuzhen jielü* 初真戒律 and associates it with his Baiyun guan ordination of 1656 in Beijing. Because of his renowned "Vinaya-circuits" in southern China, the tradition also attributed a text called *Longmen xinfa* 龍門心法 to Wang. It consists of sermons that Wang supposedly held on the occasion of the 1663 Nanjing ordination. But interestingly, both the *Chuzhen jielü* and the *Longmen xinfa* were published hundreds of years after Wang's death. This fact inevitably raises doubts about Wang's authorship of these texts.

It is also worthy of note that, like the *Chuzhen jielü*, the *Longmen xinfa* touts Wang's status as a crucial agent of regeneration. Both texts are thus vehicles of Wang's claim to have established the precept-altar at Baiyun guan after having received the Vinaya transmission from his master Zhao.¹⁹³ But in contrast to the *Chuzhen jielü*, the *Longmen xinfa* has Wang proclaim

---

¹⁹² Urs App, *The Birth of Orientalism* (Philadelphia: Pennsylvania University Press, 2010), pp. 255–256.

¹⁹³ In reality the name Zhao Fuyang 趙復陽 is mentioned only in the two Prefaces to the *Chuzhen jielü* 初真戒律 attributed to Wang Changyue (see above) and to Long Qiqian 龍起潛. In the Preface attributed to Long there is also the reference to Baiyun guan ordination and to Wang's relationship with the Qing emperor: "崑陽王老師得戒法于复陽趙真人、當世祖章皇帝時、于京都白雲觀設立戒壇、傳戒演鉢、一時授受弟子千有余人." In the *Longmen xinfa* and *Biyuan tanjing*, Wang Changyue's master is mentioned only in reference to the two places where Wang supposedly met him prior to receiving the transmission of the precepts. More on Wang's master in the JGXD and in Esposito, "The Longmen School and its Controversial History" {chapter 2 of *Facets of Qing Daoism*}.

the uninterrupted legacy of Qiu Chuji, thus establishing a link between his Vinaya teachings and Quanzhen. In a chapter of the *Longmen xinfa* titled "Chanjiao hongdao 闡教弘道 (Expanding the teachings and spreading the Way), "Wang" tells about the difficulties of spreading the Way because of the "degeneration" of the Daoist community of his time. It is in this context that he introduces himself once more as the agent of regeneration:

> My fellow practitioners, I am but an ordinary person without any ability to perform miracles. I only use common and everyday methods to cause people to awaken to the truth. However, there are some members of our community who drink wine, eat meat, and sell magic drawings while begging for alms. They do not understand the true meaning of clothing and food, not to mention the true meaning of birth-and-death. They are unable to draw respect from the people, nor are they capable of moving spirits and gods. They just idle away their time like tramps, eating food and wearing clothes for which they have not labored. They seem to be begging for alms, but actually they are creating karma. I hope you can spur yourselves on and make diligent efforts in order both to promote our teachings and to benefit sentient beings. You are supposed to live for others, not for your own benefit.
>
> 大眾、我貧道乃一介凡夫、不會神通、單以平常日用的工夫、教人開悟。不過是為道門中的人、飲酒食肉、賣訣化緣、連衣食二字、還不周全、安能明得生死。一則不能令人敬念、二則不能感動鬼神。游手好閒、就如流浪光棍、白口吃飯、白手著衣、名雖說隨緣、其實是作業。只得把自己的精神、奮發起來、為普度之計、上則興教相、下則利眾生。原系為人、不是為己。

After this admonition, "Wang" links his narrative of previous decline to that of the regeneration of an original teaching featuring himself as protagonist:

> Furthermore, it makes me think that the ruin of our tradition was due to the increasing number of devious-minded people compared to the upright ones in our community, which had caused people to disrespect the Way or even to disparage it. This was the reason why the teachings had not been revitalized.
>
> It also makes me think that from the Yuan dynasty, when the Patriarch Changchun [Qiu Chuji] talked about the precepts and revitalized Daoism, until today no less than four hundred years have passed during

which his precepts were no longer enacted. Thirty years ago, when I decided to visit Daoist masters, I met by divine grace [an enlightened] master in Wangwu Mountain and received the teachings in Jiugong Mountain. I maintained them in secret for more than twenty years. Then, through a stroke of good fortune, life became prosperous and I met the Qing emperor and his virtuous governors. Again, I enjoyed predestined relationships by meeting men of identical aspirations: the time was ripe and the opportunities arose for action, and following my installation of the ordination altar at the capital, eight years of intensive activities took place until today, meeting wide approval and the support of thousands of Perfected. Daoist priests and lay believers predestined for the Way all took refuge in the gate of precepts, meditation, and wisdom, thereby gaining direct access to the wondrous path of pure emptiness. I, a humble Daoist priest, have not made any conscious attempt or effort in this regard. I did, however, have a divine spark that, when employed sincerely and silently, moved Heaven and Earth and gave me the opportunity [of spreading the Way], ascending to the Dharma seat, and becoming a Vinaya master even though I felt unworthy of all this. With regard to preaching and spreading the doctrine far and wide: this has always been my wish. But I had to abide by the wishes of Heaven and wait for the proper time to carry them out.

又想教門裡的禍根、從本教中、匪品多、正人少。使人不敬道、招人來謗道、所以不能復興。又想長春祖師、自從元朝說戒興玄、到今四百年來、不行其戒。三十年前、發心參訪、天從其願、王屋逢師、九宮受法、密密行持、二十多年。天開道運、遭逢盛世、得遇清朝、上有聖君賢宰。又遇凤緣、得逢同志、凝真時至、機會當行、在京都開壇、至于今日雷鳴八載、風動千真。羽流道眾、居士善人、凡有道緣、莫不皈依戒定慧門、直入清虛之妙。而貧道何嘗有心去做、用力去為、不過是這個一點靈機、真誠默運、感動天恩、得其際遇、僭登法座、妄作律師而已。至於大闡教門、普宏道法、貧道素願也。須順天待運、時至則行。

As in the Preface to the *Chuzhen jielü* 初真戒律 that was analyzed above, Wang is here presented as the quintessential agent of regeneration who puts an end to the age of degeneration. In this case the degeneration phase gained clearer temporal definition as it is said to have begun after the prosperous

Chapter 1: The Invention of the Quanzhen Ur-Vinaya Tradition   105

time of Qiu Chuji. We have seen that in the Preface to the *Chuzhen jielü* the Golden Age period was not yet historically defined because it focused on the original, a-temporal transmission in Daoist Heavens. But here it is clearly situated in the period following Qiu Chuji's promulgation of the original teachings. While both texts speak of a period of degeneration, the *Longmen xinfa* specifies that it lasted four centuries (that is, from the Yuan dynasty to the Qing dynasty). "Wang" describes how he encountered, under the auspices of the Qing court, the kind of favorable conditions that allowed him to establish the precept altar at Baiyun guan which embodies his claim of re-establishing Qiu Chuji's Yuan-time legacy. Both texts agree on the date for the new beginning, namely, 1656. This date is based on "Wang's" claim that, after the first ordination at Baiyun guan, "eight years of intense activities have elapsed until today [i.e., 1663]" 至于今日雷鳴八載.

In a telling contrast to the Preface to the *Chuzhen jielü*, the "Wang" of the *Longmen xinfa* links his "Ur-tradition" to Quanzhen and presents his tradition as continuous with the teachings spread by the famous Jin / Yuan era Quanzhen leader Qiu Chuji during the "Quanzhen golden era." The version of the *Longmen xinfa* titled *Biyuan tanjing* 碧苑壇經, which was revised by the eleventh Longmen patriarch Min Yide (1748/58?–1836) at the end of the Jiaqing period, presents a similar scenario; but now "Wang" presents his "Ur-tradition" with even more specificity as linked with Longmen. Now the narrative features a Golden Age of Longmen beginning with Qiu Chuji; a degeneration period lasting four centuries; and Wang as the concrete, living regenerator of Longmen Vinaya. The *Biyuan tanjing* passage reads as follows:

> My Longmen [tradition] began during the Yuan dynasty with the Patriarch Qiu who made Daoism prosperous and missionized, and from then until today four hundred years have passed during which eminent masters were rare and men of integrity hard to meet. During this period of Daoism's degeneration, I did not expect that thirty years of maintaining the precepts, observing the codes and conforming to the rules while visiting places in search of genuine masters could provoke the divine grace of meeting an enlightened master in Wangwu and give me access to the teachings in Jiugong Mountain. Then more than twenty years elapsed until fortune opened up and I had the pleasure to encounter our present dynasty and flourishing times when retired officials appreciate the good, scholars and merchants devote themselves to charitable works, and men of

the same aspirations congregate. Because this was the right time for conversion and practice, I installed the altar at the capital to perform ordinations. Since then, eight years of intense activities have met with wide approval and gained the support of thousands of Perfected, of predestined clerics, and laymen who all took refuge in precepts and practiced meditation (*ding* 定), thus entering directly into the wondrous path of pure emptiness. I only employed sincerely and silently the divine spark in me, but my actions moved Heaven which provided me with the opportunity of ascending to the Dharma seat and becoming a Vinaya master, even though in fact I was unworthy of all this. As to preaching and spreading the doctrine far and wide, it has always been my wish.

我龍門乃始于元朝邱祖、興玄闡化、到今四百年來、高人罕覯、志士難逢。今我道末、不期于三十年心奉持戒、守律循規、參訪求眞、天從志願、王屋逢師、九宮受法、二十多年。天開道運、欣遇皇朝、得逢盛世、紳宦好善、士商樂施、同志有緣、皈修遇時、因在都中開壇設戒、寒暑八度、風動千眞、羽俗有緣、莫不皈依戒定、直入清虛妙道。貧道唯憑這一點靈機、眞誠默運、感動天恩、得眞際遇、僭登法座、妄作律師而已。至于大闡玄門、普宏道場、貧道之素願也。

These materials present an almost identical transmission narrative based on the tripartite schema of "Golden Age," degeneration," and "regeneration." The cited texts, attributed as they are to Wang Changyue, portray Wang in person as the agent of regeneration: it is Wang who is credited with the reinvigoration of the "Ur-Vinaya tradition" by the foundational act of establishing the precept-altar at Baiyun guan, and this act has a specific date: 1656. Furthermore, in the *Longmen xinfa* and *Biyuan tanjing*, Wang's "Ur-Vinaya tradition" assumes a specific historical and doctrinal identity: it is portrayed as the rebirth of the pure teaching of Qiu Chuji, the famous Quanzhen patriarch of the Yuan era and alleged founder of the Longmen lineage. Thus the Longmen tradition appears not only as deeply rooted in Qiu Chuji's "original" teachings but also as the sole heir of Wang, the quintessential regenerator of genuine ancient Daoism's "complete truth" (*quanzhen* 全真).

Chapter 2

The Three Stages of Precepts

The ordination system attributed to Wang Changyue 王常月 alias Wang Kunyang 王崑陽 is mainly explained in the *Chuzhen jielü* 初真戒律. Its presumed author Wang presents Daoist precepts as divided into three degrees or stages linked to three ranks of ordination: Initial Perfection precepts (*chuzhen jie* 初真戒) corresponding to the first rank of Master of Wondrous Practice (*miaoxing shi* 妙行師); Medium Ultimate precepts (*zhongzhen jie* 中極戒) corresponding to the rank of Master of Wondrous Virtue (*miaode shi* 妙德師);[194] and Celestial Immortals' precepts (*tianxian jie* 天仙戒) corresponding to the rank of Master of Wondrous Dao (*miaodao shi* 妙道師).[195] A reference to this last rank is also found in the *Longmen xinfa* 龍門心法 (Core Teachings of the Longmen).[196]

---

[194] An allusion to this rank is made at the end of the *Zhongji jie* 中極戒; see below the section "The 300 Medium Ultimate Precepts according to the *Zhongji jie*," p. 126 ff.

[195] "Those who receive the Precepts of the Celestial Immortality are called Masters of the Wondrous Dao. Those who receive the Precepts of the Medium Ultimate are called Masters of Wondrous Virtue. Those who receive the Precepts of the Initial Perfection are called Masters of Wondrous Activity. Those who receive the same precepts but belong to the younger generation are called 'same robes.' Those who receive the seat of honor are called 'earlier awakened masters.'" 受天仙戒者、稱妙道師。中極戒者、稱妙德師。初真戒者、稱妙行師。同戒晚輩者、稱同衣。上座稱先覺師。(*Chuzhen jielü*, 38a, CK 24: 10475).

[196] *Longmen xinfa*, chapter "智慧光明"(also contained in the *Biyuan tanjing* with slight modifications): "My fellow practitioners, what is wise, bright, glittering in the ultimate mystery, and shining upon the dharma-world is not beyond the *Yushu baojing* [Precious Scripture of the Jade Axis] revealed by the Heaven-Honored One. The jade axis is the genuine, incipient activating force in you. Those who want to recite it [*zhuanjing*, lit. to revolve the scripture] must first tap the genuine, incipient activating force, wherein lies wisdom, energy and brightness. With regard to the nurturing of the body of the Way without leaks and the cultivation of the dharma-body that never perishes, if you do not diligently turn the genuine, incipient activating force in you and secretly cultivate fortune and wisdom, I am afraid you will not be capable of hearing and seeing the receptacle of brightness, not to mention knowing the appearance of ghosts and gods, grasping the axis of creativity, participating in the nourishing and transforming process of Heaven and Earth, roaming with sun and moon, placing the dharma-world into a grain of millet, arranging things and events

The three stages of precepts are said to be conferred successively and include specific numbers of precepts to be observed. Subsequent ordination procedures were to take the *Chuzhen jielü* 初真戒律 as model but modified the gradual conferral of the precept series, the length of the ordination retreat (*rula* 入臘), the texts to be recited, etc. According to the *Chuzhen jielü*, the *chuzhen jie* or initial precepts are to be observed for 100 days before conferral of the intermediate precepts (*zhongji jie* 中極戒).[197] These intermediate precepts, in turn, must be observed for three years before conferral of the ultimate precepts, the *tianxian jie* 天仙戒.[198] But the more recent ordination procedures of the Tongzhi (1862–1874) and Guangxu eras (1875–1908) stipulate that the applicants can receive on the same day all three series of precepts with their associated ordination certificates.[199] Furthermore, while in the *Chuzhen jielü* the ordination retreat is said to last 100 days, the more recent ordination procedures shorten its length to 53 days.[200]

With regard to the recitation of texts, each series of precepts has its own specific scriptures listed in the *Chuzhen jielü*. This was adopted with few modifications in the more recent ordination procedures of the Tongzhi era. What is worthy of note is that, apart from a text attributed to Qiu Chuji—the *Qiuzu chanhui wen* 邱祖懺悔文 that is recorded in late Quanzhen monastic liturgy (*gongke* 功課)—the literature quoted in the *Chuzhen jielü*

---

before they appear or take place, being called 'Masters of the Wondrous Way,' and entering the realm of the Celestial Immortals." 大眾、智慧光明、晁朗太玄、照燭法界、豈能出天尊　玉樞寶經　之外哉。玉樞即大眾之真機。欲轉經者、先轉真機、則智能光明、在其中矣。至於養成無漏之道體、修真不壞之法身、若不勤轉真機、密修福慧、只恐光明藏、不能聞不能見也。安能知鬼神之情狀、握造化之樞機、參天地之化育、斡日月之運行、攝法界於黍米之中、定事物於未萌之始、稱妙道之師、進天仙之境耶。 For the other two ranks one finds only generic references to the term *miaoxing* 妙行 and no mention of *miaode* 妙德 or *Miaode shi* 妙德師. In the *Zhongji jie* 中極戒 one finds the title "Miaode zhenren" 妙德真人; see here below.

[197] More precisely, the text states that the applicant should practice the Refuge and the five precepts for 100 days before receiving the ten precepts. See here below.

[198] The text says: "已入鉢堂修煉身心、及行持中極戒、歷三年者、方受天仙戒。"(47a, CK 24: 10480). See also the discussion below in Chapter 4 of this part.

[199] Hackmann, *Die dreihundert Mönchsgebote des chinesischen Taoismus* (Amsterdam: Koninklijke Akademie van Wetenshapen, 1931) and Wang Ka 王卡 & Wang Guiping 汪桂平 eds., *Santong shiyi* 三洞拾遺 (Hefei 合肥: Huangshan shushe 黃山書社, 2005, 20 vols.), here vol. 11.

[200] Oyanagi 1934, p. 70.

does not show any particular connection with Quanzhen.²⁰¹ In fact, the majority of texts quoted in the *Chuzhen jielü* derive from early medieval Daoist literature. In what came to be known as the "Quanzhen ordination of the three altars," nothing appears to point to a specific "Quanzhen identity." As we are going to see, the same can be said regarding the precept-text used for the conferral of the Intermediate precepts, the *Zhongji jie*.

Another point worthy of note is that, apart from a few sections of the *Chuzhen jielü* dealing with the three series of precepts, the remaining sections reproduce texts from the Daoist Canon (*Daozang*) that have no particular link with Quanzhen and its identity. Indeed, the majority of such texts derive from the earlier liturgy of the Celestial Masters 天師道.²⁰²

Based on this earlier legacy, the *Chuzhen jielü* (in the section titled *sanyige* 三衣格) mentions different sets of precepts that come to be linked to the three stages—Chuzhen, Zhongji, and Tianxian—in the following manner:

> Those who have received the Ten Precepts of Initial Perfection, the Three Precepts, the Five, the Eight, and the Wondrous Precepts of Ninefold Perfection/Nine Perfected,²⁰³ wear the Devotion Robe of

---

²⁰¹ *Qingwei hongfan daomen gongke* 清微宏範道門功課, in *Zaotan gongke* 早壇功課, 10a (CK 23: 10218), and *Taishang xuanmen gongke jing* 太上玄門功課經 13a (CK 23: 10241).

²⁰² Apart from the section dedicated to the conferral of the precepts of the first stage (see here below p. 121 ff., "The Conferral of the Three Refuges, Five Precepts and Ten Precepts of Initial Perfection according to the *Chuzhen jielü*"), the section "Xuanmen chijie weiyi 玄門持戒威儀" (47a–57a) includes rules also found in earlier works like the *Zhengyi weiyi jing* 正一威儀經 (DZ 791) and the *Xuanmen shishi weiyi* 玄門十事威儀 (DZ 792). The section "Dizi fengshi kejie" 弟子奉師科戒 (54a–55b) reproduces with few variants the thirty-six rules of the *Sandong zhongjie wen* 三洞眾戒文 (DZ 178, 2b–4b)—here wrongly presented as thirty-nine items—and the "Jieyi sishiliu tiao" 戒衣四十六條 (56a–57a) from Zhang Wanfu's 張萬福 *Sandong fafu kejie wen* 三洞法服科戒文 (DZ 788, 7b–9b).

²⁰³ The *Sandong zhongjie wen* 三洞眾戒文 (DZ 178) includes the "Sangui jie" 三歸戒 (1.1a–2b) as well as *sanjie* 三戒, *wujie* 五戒, and *bajie* 八戒 (2.2a–4b). These sets of precepts were administered during the Tang era for the conferral of the Zhengyi rank of "Lusheng dizi" 籙生弟子 (Novices of the Register). See Kristofer Schipper, "Taoist Ordination Ranks in the Tunhuang Manuscripts," in *Religion und Philosophie in Ostasien*, eds. Gert Naudorf, Karl-Heinz Pohl and Hans-Hermann Schmidt (Würzburg: Königshausen & Neumann, 1985), pp. 127–48, here 120–130. Explanations about sets of five and eight precepts are also found in the *Yunji qiqian* 雲笈七籤 (j. 39 "Laojun shuo wujie 老君說五戒", and j. 40 "Shouchi bajie zhaiwen 受持八戒齋文"). *Jiuzhen miaojie* refers to *Taishang jiuzhen miaojie jinlu duming bazui miaojing* 太上九真妙戒金籙度命拔罪妙經 (DZ 181), a Lingbao text that proba-

Initial Perfection consisting of two hundred and forty patches,[204] three layers and ten pleats, a cloud-belt with two ends, a pure kerchief, and straw sandals. If they practice one thousand and two hundred good deeds and recite the *Qingjing jing*, *Datong jing*, and *Donggu jing*, they will attain the fruit of the Precepts of the Perfected.

領受初真十戒、三戒、五戒、八戒、九真妙戒者、身著初真信衣、計二百四十條、三台十襵、雲帶二拽、淨巾、芒鞋。行千二百善、持清靜經、大通經、洞古經、得真人戒果。

If they observe the previous precepts in their entirety, they will receive the Pure Precepts of the Medium Ultimate, or the Precepts for Maintaining the Body, or the Precepts of Wisdom, or the Precepts for Observing the Self, or the Precepts of the Wondrous Forest[205] wearing

---

bly stems from the Tang dynasty (*The Taoist Canon*, 543–44; trl. Kohn, *Supplement*, 144) and also used in the new liturgical school of the Song period, the Tianxin 天心正法新符籙派 (see *Yutang dafa* 玉堂大法, DZ 220, 20.10b–11, dated 1158). A set of nine precepts reserved to women under the name of *Nuzhen jiujie* is also mentioned at the end of the *Chuzhen jielü* 58a–b (CK 24: 10485). The Daoist Canon contains various sets of nine precepts associated with Lingbao (see for instance the *Duren jing* 度人經 [DZ 1] which at the end of its juan 4 mentions the *Lingbao jiujie* 靈寶九戒 after the *Jiuzhen miaojie* 九真妙戒). Furthermore, a list of the so-called *chuzhen jie* with nine precepts plus the formula of refuge is found in the *Jingming zongjiao lu* 淨明宗教錄 (Qingyunpu zangban 青雲譜藏版) 5.12–13.

[204] This robe was tailor-made on the model of the Buddhist monks' outer robe worn during alms rounds or when in presence of high officials; this is what the term "patchrobed monk," frequently encountered in Chan texts, refers to. See John Kieschnick, "The Symbolism of the Monk's Robe in China," *Asia Major* 12.1 (1999): 9–32, here 13.

[205] In the *Daozang* one finds "Ten Precepts and Fourteen Precepts of Self-Control 十戒十四持身戒" followed by the note: "Those who receive these precepts have the title of 'Disciples of Laozi's Green Thread and Gold Knob'" 受稱老子青絲金鈕弟子; see *Dongxuan lingbao sandong fengdao kejie yingshi* 洞玄靈寶三洞奉道科戒營始 j. 4.7a. This set of precepts is included in the *Dongxuan lingbao tianzun shuo shijie jing* 洞玄靈寶天尊說十戒經 DZ 459 (trl. Kohn, 2004a:184–186). During the Tang, the conferral of this set corresponded to the ordination for the rank of Qingxin dizi 清信弟子 or Disciples of Pure Faith, a very common ordination in those times. See Schipper, "Taoist Ordination Ranks in the Tunhuang Manuscripts," pp. 130, 135–137, and 138–39). *Zhihui jie* 智慧戒 might refer to "Zhihui shangpin dajie" 智慧上品大戒, the set of precepts of the *Taishang dongshen zhihui shangpin dajie* 太上洞玄靈寶智慧上品大戒經 (DZ 177 03 / 018; trl. Kohn, 2004a, 168–183) which was conferred for the middle stage of the Lingbao alliance 靈寶中盟 (see Schipper, "Taoist Ordination Ranks in the Tunhuang Manuscripts," p. 130) or to

the Pure Robe of Light Dust made of simple indigo cotton or pure three-layered silk, a cloud-belt, pure kerchief, and straw sandals. If they practice two thousand and four hundred good deeds and observe the great method of the Jade Emperor, they will attain the fruit of the Precepts of Earthly Immortals.

行持具足、受中極淨戒、或持身戒、或智慧戒、或觀身戒、或妙林戒、俱著輕塵淨衣、或用淺藍單布為之、或用純帛為之、亦三台、雲帶、淨巾、芒鞋。行二千四百善、持玉帝大法、得地仙戒果。

If they observe the above-mentioned precepts in their entirety, they will receive the Wondrous Precepts of the Great Virtue of the Celestial Immortals, after which they must put in practice the One hundred and eighty Esoteric Precepts to be Meticulously Observed 行一百八十細行密戒 or the Three Hundred Great Precepts.[206] If they practice

---

the *Taishang dongxuan lingbao zhihui benyuan dajie shangpin jing* 太上洞玄靈寶智慧本願大戒上品經 (DZ 344 04 / 012. p. 111; also found in the section "Dajie shangpin 大戒上品" in *Taishang jingjie* 太上經戒 DZ 787, 2b–12b 08 / 063). For other sets of "Zhihui jie" see also Min Zhiting, *Daojiao yifan*, 89–91. Furthermore, "Zhihui jie" and "Guanshen jie" might both refer to the *Shangqing dongzhen zhihui guanshen dajie wen* 上清洞真智慧觀身大戒文 (DZ 1364), see here below. *Miaolin jie* 妙林戒 should refer to the "27 precepts of the *Miaolin jing* 妙林經二十七戒" listed in *Taishang jingjie* 太上經戒 (DZ 787, 16–17b) and YJQQ j. 38 (cf. *Dacheng miaolin jing* 大乘妙林經, DZ 1398 j. zhong 05 / 024)

[206] Apart from the *Chuzhen jielü*, the only text that mentions the Precepts of the Celestial Immortals (*tianxian jie*) is the *Yuquan* 玉詮, a Qing spirit writing collection included in the old *Daozang jiyao* (see below). The reference to 180 precepts may refer to the well-known One-Hundred and Eighty Precepts of the Three Principles (in *Taishang dongxuan lingbao sanyuan pinjie gongde jingzhong jing* 太上洞玄靈寶三元品戒功德輕重經 DZ 456 03 / 043, 766) that in Tang medieval ordinations marks the third great stage of the Lingbao alliance 靈寶大盟 (Schipper, "Taoist Ordination Ranks in the Tunhuang Manuscripts," p. 131). Another well-known set of 180 precepts is found in the *Laojun yibai bashi jie* 老君一百八十戒 (section included in the *Taishang laojun jinglü* 太上老君經律 DZ 786, 4a–12b; *Yaoxiu keyi jielü chao* 要修科儀戒律鈔 DZ 463, 5.14a–19a; *Yunji qiqian* 雲笈七籤 DZ 1032, 39.1a–14b, etc; see here below) and was conferred to the Masters of the Zhengyi (Zhengyi daoshi). See Schipper, "Taoist Ordination Ranks in the Tunhuang Manuscripts," p. 130. As we shall see, the majority of the one-hundred and eighty precepts are also reproduced in the "Three hundred precepts for the contemplation of the Body of Sapientia (*Zhihui guanshen sanbai dajie* 智慧觀身三百大戒; see *Shangqing dongzhen zhihui guanshen dajie wen* 上清洞真智慧觀身大戒文, DZ 1364) conferred to the highest rank of the Masters of the Shangqing. See Schipper, "Taoist Ordination Ranks in the Tunhuang Manuscripts," p. 131. On the three hundred precepts, see

three thousand and six hundred good deeds and observe the *Daode zhenjing*, they will wear the Mist-Robe of the Celestial Immortality featuring a straight, open collar and sleeves of unjoined seams, a mist girdle with cloud-style borders, the Cap/Crown of the Perfect Form of the Five Peaks, and the Light Shoes of the Five Clouds[207]. If they observe these precepts completely they will attain the fruit of the Precepts of the Celestial Immortals.

行持具足、當受天仙大德妙戒、行一百八十細行密戒、或三百大戒。行三千六百善、叅道德真經、身著天仙霞衣、領用直開、袖不合縫、霞帶雲邊、戴五岳真形冠、著五雲輕履。行持具足、得天仙戒果。

From these passages we can gather that different sets of precepts are mentioned for the three stages of precepts. For some of them it is difficult to ascertain which sets are referred to. Generally speaking, one can see that, for the first or initial stage, the majority of the mentioned sets was already part of Tang-era ordination systems (*durenyi* 度人儀) for the lower ranks (novitiate). For the second or middle stage the text refers to progressive sets mostly related to the conferral of Lingbao ranks until the highest ones of Shangqing. Thus I argue that the *Chuzhen jielü* appears to rely on earlier systems of ordination that follow the general line of the seventh-century Lingbao *Qianzhen ke* 千真科: "People who leave their family can observe the three, five, nine, and ten precepts up to the three hundred great precepts" 出家之人、能持三戒、五戒、九戒、十戒、乃至三百大戒等.[208] At the same time, the *Chuzhen jielü* reduces the number of ranks (*fazhi* 法職) and related ordination procedures to three basic categories:

1) Chuzhen 初真—Master of Wondrous Practice 妙行師;
2) Zhongji 中極—Master of Wondrous Virtue 妙德師;
3) Tianxian 天仙—Master of Wondrous Dao 妙道師.

---

also the section "The 300 Medium Ultimate Precepts according to the *Zhongji jie*," p. 126 ff.

[207] Normally known as "cloud shoes" or "blue shoes," these are the boat-shaped shoes worn during Daoist ceremonies (see Yoshioka Yoshitoyo 吉岡義豊, *Dōkyō no jittai* 道教の實態).

[208] *Dongxuan lingbao qianzhen ke* 洞玄靈寶千真科 DZ 1410, 2b [42 / 004; Schipper and Verellen eds., *The Taoist Canon*, 576], also repeated in the *Yaoxiu keyi jielü chao* 要修科儀戒律鈔 DZ 463 j. 4.1a [42 / 019].

These three ranks come now to be associated with the practice of a specific number of good deeds (one thousand and two hundred for the first stage, one thousand and two hundred for the second stage, and three thousand and six hundred for the third stage) leading to three different attainments: Zhenren (*zhenren jiege* 真人戒果) for the first stage, Dixian (*dixian jiege* 地仙戒果) for the second stage, and Tianxian (*tianxian jiege* 天仙戒果) for the third and last stage.

In Daoist medieval ordinations (*durenyi* 度人儀 / *durenyili* 度人儀禮) the transmission of precepts with their related ranks are also associated with the conferral of scriptures, but here their number is rather limited: *Qingjing jing* 清靜經, *Datong jing* 大通經, and *Donggu jing* 洞古經 for the first stage; and an unspecified Great Law of the Jade Emperor (*yudi dafa* 玉帝大法) for the last stage. All of these scriptures lack a specific link with Quanzhen since they are meditative and philosophical texts that predate Quanzhen. They are "fundamental scriptures" (*benwen* 本文) conferred without commentary because they form part of the universal legacy of Daoism.[209] As with medieval ordinations, the transmission of scriptures is also associated with the conferral of Daoist regalia (robes, caps, shoes, etc.), but here it is also classified in three: three main robes and related accessories.[210] This

---

[209] It is interesting to see that the *Datong jing* and the *Donggu jing* were part of the printed materials transmitted on the occasion of the 1873 (同治十二年) ordination at Baiyun guan. They are included in the printed compilation titled *Shoujie bizhi* 守戒必持 received during the three-altar ordination of 1873 by a certain Wang Xinzhi 王信祉. It consists of the *Taishang ganying pian*, *Datong jing*, and *Dongu jing* along with ten poems composed by the Baiyun guan abbot Meng Yongcai 孟永才 (?–1881) and a copy of the *Dengzhen lu* 登真錄. See Wang Ka 王卡 and Wang Guiping 汪桂平 eds., *Sandong shiyi* 三洞拾遺, vol. 11, pp. 89–192, under the title *Taishang zhenchuan shoujie bichi* 太上真傳守戒必持. While some modern scholars tend to classify the *Datong jing* and the *Donggu jing* as "Quanzhen" (see for instance Goossaert, *The Taoist of Peking*, p. 155, note 69, who claims that "they were written in Quanzhen circles during the Yuan"), other scholars simply classify them as Daoist philosophical scriptures (see Schipper and Verellen, eds. *The Taoist Canon*). Some additional texts (such as the *Nanhua jing* 南華經, *Wenshi jing* 文始經, *Tanzi* 譚子, *Huangting jing* 黃庭經) are also mentioned in the *Chuzhen jielü* (38b) in relation to ordination training. Again, one does not find any scripture specifically linked to Quanzhen and its identity. The same applies to the *Sanguan jing* 三官經, the *Taishang ganying pian* 太上感應篇 for the conferral of the Chuzhen jie, and some additional scriptures for the conferral of the ultimate ordination of the Tianxian that are mentioned below.

[210] The *Chuzhen jielü*, in the section "Rujie yaogui 入戒要規," 38a–40a (CK 24: 10475–6), also lists a specific number of rules to be observed regarding personal

may have contributed to the formation of the expression "Three robes and one bowl" (*sanyi yibo* 三衣一缽).[211]

The tripartite division is also applied to the number of masters. As the *Chuzhen jielü* explains in its section titled "Basic Guidance for the Three Masters" ("Sanshi yuanshuo" 三師原說, 40a-b) three masters are involved:

1) The Principal master who transmits the precepts (*Chuanjie benshi* 傳戒本師);
2) The Confirmation master (*Zhengming dashi* 證明大師);
3) The Discipline master (*Jianjie dashi* 監戒大師).

These three types of master are described as follows:

> The primary master who transmits the precepts is the master of the great virtue who initiates conversion, having inherited the lineage of the Most High[Laozi] for proclaiming the teachings. If one has not received the Precepts of Celestial Immortality, one may not transmit these precepts. Each year, on the fifteenth day of the first lunar month, the fifteenth day of the seventh lunar month, and the fifteenth day of the tenth lunar month, the master after assembling the four ranks of the community [i.e., monks, nuns, laymen and laywomen] opens the altar and transmits the precepts. After the conferral and enactment of the precepts, the bowl-clepsydra ritual is performed for one hundred days.
>
> 傳戒本師、乃太上繼宗演教、接化大德之師。不受天仙戒者、不得傳戒。每於正月十五、七月十五、十月十五日、會集四眾、開壇傳戒。戒後行持、演鉢一百日。
>
> The great master who confirms illumination gives direction concerning the rules and regulations of conduct regarding scriptures, repentances, teachings and books. He trains and guides the ordinands concerning body and heart-mind, specifically with regard to regulating and

---

objects and paraphernalia that the applicants received, such as the bowl 鉢體, the staff 策杖, the discipline stick 戒尺, the pure water pitcher 淨水瓶, the certificate pouch 牒囊, etc. The rules also concern the monastic robes and attire.

[211] Yan Yonghe 閻永和, *Xuandu lütan chuanjie yinli guize* 玄都律壇傳戒引禮規則 (abbr. *Yinli guize* 引禮規則) (Chengdu: Qingyanggong publication) 47a, 51a, 54a. It is worthy of note that while for the first two stages the name of the related robes is the same: *xinyi* 信衣 (*chuzhen xinyi* 初真信衣) for the first stage and *jingyi* 淨衣 (*qingchen jingyi* 輕塵淨衣) for the second stage, two different names of robes—*dongyi* 洞衣 (*tianxian dongyi* 天仙洞衣) and *xiayi* 霞衣 (*tianxian xiayi* 天仙霞衣)—are given for the last stage. See *Chuzhen jielü* 39a, 41a, and 46a.

governing the seven emotions and six desires. If one has not received the Medium Ultimate Precepts, one may not hold this position.

證明大師、指授經懺教典威儀規範。調御戒子身心、制遣七情六慾。非受中極戒者、不得師之。

The great master inspecting the precepts supervises and examines those who have received the precepts and does not allow them to transgress the precepts or violate the statutes. If there is someone who is not compliant, he determines the severity of the offense and uses the discipline stick to mete out punishment and obtain repentance. If one has not received the Medium Ultimate Precepts, one may not hold this position either.

監戒大師、監察入戒者、不許犯戒違律。如有不法者、量律輕重、以戒尺責罰懺悔。非受中極戒者、亦不得師之。

As the *Chuzhen jielü* explains, the *Chuanjie benshi* 傳戒本師 (principal master transmitting the precepts) has the authority of opening the altar and administering the precepts (*kaitan chuanjie* 開壇傳戒), but from the adduced passage we can see that his transmission of precepts is still performed in the Lingbao traditional context of the Sanyuan zhai 三元齋 which "takes place every year on the fifteenth day of the first, seventh, and tenth month" 正月十五、七月十五、十月十五日. The transmission of precepts and related training were not yet linked to the two periods of autumn and/or spring as adopted in late Qing Quanzhen ordination procedures and related training at Baiyun guan.[212]

Finally, the tripartite division is also applied to the altars by which this system of Quanzhen ordination later came to be known: *santan dajie* 三壇大戒. Again, the tripartite division of the altar, or the mention of "three altars" in rituals, is not something new for Daoism. By contrast, the use of the expression "*santan dajie*" and the reference to a "Quanzhen *lütan* 全真律壇" do appear to be more recent creations.[213] Unfortunately, no explana-

---

[212] Oyanagi Shigeta 小柳司氣太, *Baiyun guan zhi* 白雲觀志, 70. See also Yan Yonghe, *Yinli guize*, 1a–b. For the Quanzhen training of one hundred days see note 237 below.

[213] See the ordination certificates corresponding to the conferral of the three series of precepts—Chuzhen jie, Zhongji jie, and Tianxian jie—in 1873 (Wang Ka and Wang Guiping 2005, vol. 11:91, 128, 140). See also the epitaph written by Peng Dingqiu 彭定求 (1645–1719) in honor of Zhan Tailin 詹太林 (1625–1712): "Zhan Weiyang lüshi taming 詹維陽律師塔銘" 10.15a, in the twelve-juan version of Peng Dingqiu's *Nanyun wengao* 南畇文稿, *Siku quanshu cunmu congshu* 四庫

tions are found in the texts attributed to Wang Changyue. According to the descriptions by Oyanagi Shigeta 小柳司氣太 of the ordinations performed at Baiyun guan in the 1930–40s, the conferral of the three series of precepts took place at three altars, but it apparently was still performed according to the earlier Lingbao tripartite system:

> The first altar was located in front of the Grand Hall where the declaration of the essentials took place.
>
> The second altar was the esoteric altar where during the night the declaration took place in secret. After passing through this ordination altar, the newly ordained were recognized as genuine and orthodox Daoist priests and received the four items: ordination robe, ordination certificate, tin bowl, and kneeling cloth (gui 規).
>
> At the third altar the declaration of the hundred-odd articles of the Quanzhen full/great ordination took place.
>
> 第一壇在大殿之前、宣示要目。第二壇為密壇。夜間人靜時 宣示之、不令外人知。過此壇後、新戒方為真正道士、發給戒衣、戒牒、錫缽、規之四種。第三壇宣示全真大戒、約一百餘條。[214]

全書存目叢書, 集部, vol. 246: 775–76). But given Tan's link with the Jingming *Tiezhu gong* 鐵柱宮, one wonders if the term Quanzhen here refers to the Quanzhen school 全真道／全真派 or rather to a generic *qingxiu daojiao* 清修道教, as Akzuki Kan'ei already pointed out in 1978. It is known that Jingming monastic establishments had a "Quanzhen tang" 全真堂 (Quanzhen hall) reserved for the ordained ascetic monks (see *Xiaoyaoshan wanshougong zhi* 7.11a, ZWDS 2:748, where this hall is said to have been built by Xiu Shoucheng 徐守誠 [1633–1692] and the Jingming master Zhou Defeng 周德鋒). The mention of *lütan* and *santan* is also found in the late stela of 1919, "Baiyun guan Chen Yukun fangzhang erci chuanjie beiji 白雲觀陳毓坤方丈二次傳戒碑記" (Oyanagi 小柳司氣太, *Baiyun guan zhi* 白雲觀志: 179–81, here 180).

[214] Oyanagi Shigeta 小柳司氣太, 白雲觀志, p. 71. A passage summarizing Oyanagi is also found in Yoshioka Yoshitoyo 吉岡義豐, *Dōkyō no jittai* 道教の実態 (Beijing: Xinmin yinshuguan 新民印書館, 1941), p. 404. Such a tripartite division of the altars reminds us of the Lingbao tripartite ordination: 1) the Initial Covenant (*chumeng* 初盟) was a rite for Rending the Tally (*fenquan* 分券), thus establishing the ordinand's official status with the gods; 2) the Middle Covenant (*zhongmeng* 中盟) was a performance of the Nocturnal Annunciation (*suqi* 宿啟), a declaration to the gods that was also an essential element of Lingbao *zhai* 齋; 3) the Grand Covenant (*dameng* 大盟) consisting of the conferral of the 180 precepts. See Charles Benn, "Ordination and Zhai rituals," in *Daoism Handbook*, ed. Livia Kohn (Leiden: Brill, 2000), p. 318. See also here below.

As I have emphasized in previous publications, the inspiration for the Daoist "three altars" in the *santan dajie* 三壇大戒 procedure apparently came from Buddhism and its ordination system, which was reformed by Chan masters around the end of the Ming.[215] In Buddhism such a system purportedly reproduced the three-tiered altar of ordination (see Fig. 12) mythically attributed to Shakyamuni and allegedly received through vision by Daoxuan 道宣 (596–667), the famous Tang Vinaya master.[216]

The Buddhist ritual comprised three different ordination procedures:

1. for novices (with the taking of the three refuges and 10 precepts);
2. the full ordination for Buddhist monks and nuns *bhikhsu /bhikshuni* (with the observance of all 250 precepts);
3. the Bodhisattva precepts for both Buddhist clergy and laity.

Instead of administering these three rites separately, the Triple Platform Ordination (Ch. *santan jiehui*, J. *sandan kaie* 三壇戒會) of the late Ming held novice initiation, full ordination, and bodhisattva ordination all together in one place and within a short span of time.[217]

---

[215] Monica Esposito. "Shindai dōkyō to mikkyō 清代道教と密教," pp. 292–93, 317–18, and 321–22 note 12 and 340, note 130 {revised English version in *Facets of Qing Daoism*, chapter 5, here pp. 242–246 and 291}, and "Shindai ni okeru Kingaisan Ryūmonha no seiritsu to Kinka shūshi 清代における金蓋山龍門派の成立と金華宗旨" {revised and enlarged English version here below, Part Four}.

[216] Funayama Tōru 船山徹, "Guṇavarman and Some of the Earliest Examples of Ordination Platforms (*jietan*) in China," Paper presented at the conference "Images, Relics and Legends: Formation and Transformation of Buddhist Sacred Sites" (University of British Columbia, October 15–16, 2004), and John R. McRae, "Daoxuan's Vision of Jetavana: The Ordination Platform Movement in Medieval Chinese Buddhism," in *Going Forth: Visions of Buddhist Vinaya*, ed. William M. Bodiford (Honolulu: University of Hawai'i Press, 2005), 68–100, in particular 79–84.

[217] Jiang Wu, *Enlightenment in Dispute. The Reinvention of Chan Buddhism in Seventeenth-Century China* (New York: Oxford University Press, 2008), p. 31.

Fig. 12: Three-tiered altar, *Shishi yuanliu yinghua shiji* 釋氏源流應化事蹟, 1486

Finally, with regard to the tripartite division of Daoist ordination that was allegedly established by Wang Changyue at Baiyun guan as the fruit of the Yuan Quanzhen legacy of the patriarch Qiu Chuji, I argue that this cannot be seen as a true innovation because earlier ordination procedures already followed a tripartite division (Lingbao chumen 靈寶初盟, zhongmeng 中盟, dameng 大盟; Sandong 三洞; Sanyuan 三元; Sanpin 三品; etc.).[218] An early Qing example of a tripartite ordination is also preserved in the Lingbao procedure recorded in the *Jingming zongjiao lu* 淨明宗教錄 where one finds the division into *Chuzhen jie* 初真戒, *Zhengzhen jie* 正真戒, and *Shangzhen jie* 上真戒.[219] The same holds true for the number of masters conferring the precepts. In medieval times, too, three kinds are mentioned; they were called Preceptors of Ordination (*dushi* 度師), Registration (*jishi* 籍師), and Scriptures (*jingshi* 經師).[220] On the basis of extant materials and appellations of participants we can nonetheless gather that in the late Qing the number of masters officiating at "santan dajie" procedures was higher than three.[221]

---

[218] Yan Yonghe 閻永和 (fl. 1891–1908) in his *Yinli guize* 引禮規則 (1a) also refers to the Sanyuan 三元 as the tripartite division of the ordination system: "With regard to the opening of an altar and the performance of the precepts, the enrolment and re-enrolment are slightly different in each place. Some have the Highest Prime, others the Middle Prime, and others the Lower Prime; yet all rely on the transmission of precepts according to the Sanyuan system" 夫開壇演戒、挂號轉單、各處稍異。或有上元、或有中元、或有下元、總依三元傳戒. On the Lingbao tripartite ordination see also above note 181. It seems quite clear that the earlier Lingbao system and the later system known as "santan dajie 三壇大戒" which was exported from Beijing's Baiyuan guan to Sichuan in 1883 by the master of Yan Yonghe, were both performed during the Guangxu era in the different Daoist public monasteries.

[219] These three sets are related to their respective precept-texts: *Taishang lingbao jingming chuzhen jiejing* 太上靈寶淨明初真戒經, *Taishang lingbao jingming zhengzhen jiejing* 太上靈寶淨明正真戒經, and *Taishang lingbao jingming shangzhen jiejing* 太上靈寶淨明上真戒經. See *Jingming zongjiao lu* (Qingyunpu zangban 青雲譜藏版), j. 5, pp. 9–22.

[220] See for instance Zhang Zehong 張澤洪, *Daojiao zhaijiao fuzhou yishi* 道教齋醮符咒儀式 (Chengdu: Bashu shushe, 1999), 239, and Charles Benn, "Daoist Ordinations and Zhai Rituals in Medieval China," 2000:309–339, here 328. For the Zhengyi transmission of ordination and conferral of the registers (正一傳度授籙儀式) one also finds three main masters: *dushi* 度師, *jiandushi* 監度師, and *baodushi* 保舉師. See Zhang Zehong 張澤洪, op. cit., p. 230.

[221] See for instance the list of masters in Igarashi, Kenryū 五十嵐賢隆, *Taiseikyū shi* 太清宮志 (Tokyo: Kokusho kankōkai 国書刊行会, 1938), pp. 110–112, and the ordination certificates collected by Hackmann in 1911 at the Shangqinggong 上清

To my knowledge, scholars have not yet discovered materials presenting the ordination procedures in vigor around the end of the Ming and the beginning of the Qing, which is the time when Wang Changyue supposedly reformed the Daoist ordination procedures and established the ordination altar at Baiyun guan. The known extant sources belong to the late Qing and Republican eras. It is on the basis of the latter that we can gather how late Qing reformers staged Wang's "tripartite ordination procedure" and how they connected it for the first time with the conferral of three related precept-texts. Despite a supposedly ancient tradition of "Quanzhen" ordination procedure initiated by patriarch Qiu Chuji, it was only then that Quanzhen first became equipped with its own three "precept-texts" 戒經. These three precept-texts—published for the first time in the old *Daozang jiyao* of the Jiaqing era (see Part Three)—came to represent, in the eyes and under the pens of the late Qing reformers, the "Quanzhen ordination of the three altars." Distributed to the applicants, these three precept-texts were now seen as an ancient, standardized Quanzhen ordination procedure. According to this projection on the past, this procedure had been established in 1656 at the Beijing Baiyun guan and had subsequently spread to all Quanzhen public monasteries. Thanks to these three texts, the standard set of precepts was eventually established:

- Three Refuges, Five Precepts, and Ten Precepts (according to the *Chuzhen jielü* 初真戒律);
- Three hundred Precepts (according to the *Zhongji jie* 中極戒);
- Ten Precepts (according to the *Tianxian dajie* 天仙大戒).

In the following, each of these three texts will be briefly examined with an eye on the claim that they form part of an ancient, standardized Quanzhen system of ordination with a continuous history reaching to the present time.

宮 of Laoshan (Shandong). See also Zhang Zehong 張澤洪, *Daojiao zhaijiao fuzhou yishi* 道教齋醮符咒儀式, 1999:246, and Fig. 13 here below (p. 130).

The Conferral of the Three Refuges, Five Precepts and Ten Precepts of Initial Perfection according to the *Chuzhen jielü* 初真戒律

In the *Chuzhen jielü* 初真戒律 the conferral of the precepts of Initial Perfection (*chuzhen jie*) comprises:

1) *The Three Refuges in Dao, Scriptures, and Masters* ("Sangui yijie 三皈依戒," 34a–b).
This reproduces the portion of the Refuge found in the early eighth-century Zhengyi ordination text by Zhang Wanfu 張萬福 (fl. 713), the *Sandong zhongjie wen* 三洞眾戒文 (DZ 178, 2a–b), with the addition of short annotations. Interestingly, these annotations (included below in parentheses and italics) are found in Qing scriptures of the old *Daozang jiyao* connected with Jiang Yuanting's[222] spirit writing altar.[223] Before taking the Refuge, the applicant is asked to submit a pledge to the disciplinary Celestial Lord Wang 都天糾察王天君, better known as Wang Lingguan 王靈官, a powerful exorcist deity associated with the Thunder rite (*shenxiao leifa* 神霄雷法) legacy who later became a protector of Daoist monasteries.[224] The passage of the *Chuzhen jielü* introducing the Three Refuges reads as follows:

> When first entering the Dharma-gate of the orthodox lineage of the Most High [Laozi], regardless of whether you come from Daoist clerical or lay background, you must honor and follow the highest golden rules and jade statutes as well as the *Precept texts of the Three Caverns*. You must also present offerings to the statues of the worthies of the great Dao and send a formal petition to the Celestial Lord

---

[222] Jiang Yuanting 蔣元庭 (alias Jiang Yupu 蔣予蒲, 1755–1819) was the main compiler of the old *Daozang jiyao* of the Jiaqing era. On this important figure and his spirit writing altar see below.

[223] *Xiantian doudi chiyan wushang xuangong lingmiao zhenjing shujie* 先天斗帝勅演無上玄功靈妙眞經疏解 (CK 7: 2867–79); *Chanfa daguan* 懺法大觀 (CK 21: 9219–9499); *Qingwei hongfan daomen gongke* 清微宏範道門功課 (CK 23: 10213–35). Later added in the 1906 *Chongkan Daozang jiyao* was the *Taishang sanyan cifu shezui jie'e xiaozai yansheng baoming miaojing* 太上三元賜福赦罪解厄消災延生保命妙經 (CK 23: 10252–57).

[224] *Daofa huiyuan* 道法會元, j. 241–243. For a short presentation of Wang Lingguan see the article by Paul Katz in *The Taoist Encyclopedia*, 2 vols., ed. Fabrizio Pregadio (London: Routledge, 2008), vol. 2, pp. 1013–14. See also Chapter 4 below on "The Manufacture of Quanzhen ordination," p. 155 ff. including note 282.

Wang, disciplinary supervisor of the various heavens, with the request to become a member of the community. Then you must take the precepts of the Three Refuges.

凡初入太上正宗法門、不問道俗、必先遵依太上金科玉律、三洞戒文、供養大道尊像、表通都天糾察王天君、請祈盟證、受三皈依戒。

First: I take refuge with my body in the supremely great Dao.

(Note: Through this you may be forever liberated from the cycle of transmigration; thus we refer to this as the Treasure of the Dao).

Second: I take refuge with my spirit in the venerable scriptures in thirty-six sections.

(Note: Through this you are able to hear the orthodox teachings; thus we refer to this as the Treasure of the Scriptures).

Third: I take refuge with my life-destiny in the great masters of dark mystery.

(Note: Through this you will not fall into heretical views, which is why we refer to this as the Treasure of the Masters).

第一皈。身太上無極大道(永脫輪迴、故曰道寶)。第二皈。神三十六部尊經(得聞正法、故曰經寶)。第三皈。命玄中大法師(不落邪見、故曰師寶)。

2) *The conferral of the Five Precepts ordained by the Most-High Lord Lao* 太上老君所命積功歸根五戒 (34b–35a).

This consists of the five lay precepts that have their origin in Buddhism but were adopted in Daoism:[225]

    1. Do not kill any living being.
    2. Do not partake of impure food or wine.
    3. Do not say "yes" and think "no."
    4. Do not rob and steal.
    5. Do not fornicate.

一者、不得殺生。二者、不得葷酒。三者、不得口是心非。四者、不得偷盜。五者、不得邪淫。

---

[225] See for instance *Zhaijie lu* 齋戒籙 (DZ 464), and *Taishang laojun jiejing* 太上老君戒經 (DZ 784, 6a–15a).

As explained in the *Chuzhen jielü* 初真戒律, after the taking of these five precepts, the applicant is asked to recite each morning and evening specific scriptures including the *Sanguan jing* 三官經[226] and the twelfth-century popular morality book (*shanshu* 善書) entitled *Taishang ganying pian* 太上感應篇, a text that is associated with the practice of self-examination:

> Once you have received the Five Precepts revealed by the Most High Lord Laozi, which enable you to accumulate merit and return to the Source, you must each morning and evening offer incense and recite the *Highest Perfect Scriptures of the Great Thearchs of the Three Primes, Three Ranks and Three Bureaus for protecting the community, assisting the people, extending life, and protecting life-destiny*. You should also recite the *Taishang ganying pian* 太上感應篇. As you recite this text each day, rectify your own body and heart-mind and examine whether you have committed any transgressions. With every sentence of your recitation of the scriptures, reflect and think: Can I properly receive this or not? Am I able to practice this or not?
>
> 既受太上老君所命、積功歸根五戒、每日早晨焚香誦太上三元三品三官大帝護國佑民延生保命真經。接念太上感應篇、逐日演誦、校正自己身心有無所犯。每誦經篇一句、則反思曰我能受得否、我能不行否。

Provided that one observes the Three Refuges and Five Precepts for one hundred days, one will be liberated from evil thoughts and attain internal purification. Then the applicant is ready to receive the Ten Precepts of Initial Perfection:

> If you are brave and committed in your efforts in this way, your words will show no discrepancy from your practice, you will not violate the Three Refuges or transgress the Five Precepts; and after one hundred days of assiduous training, evil thoughts will completely disappear and your organs and vessels will be purified. Then you may receive the Ten Precepts of Initial Perfection as revealed by the Celestial Worthy, the Sovereign of Emptiness.
>
> 如此勇往精進、言行不苟、三皈不犯、五戒無虞、煆煉百日、惡念盡消、器皿已淨。方許受虛皇天尊所命初真十戒。

---

[226] Also known as the *Taishang sanyuan cifu shezui jie'e xiaozai yansheng baoming miaojing* 太上三元賜福赦罪解厄消災延生保命妙經 (DZ 1442).

3) *The conferral of the Ten Precepts of Initial Perfection revealed by the Celestial Worthy, the Sovereign of Emptiness* 虛皇天尊所命初真十戒 (35a–36a).

This conferral consists of ten precepts derived from the Lingbao scripture *Xuhuang tianzun Chuzhen shijie wen* 皇天尊初真十戒文 (DZ 180) stripped of its commentaries.[227] While adding more prohibitions "do not... 不得," it combines prohibitive precepts with prescriptive ones introduced by "you must 當..."

1. Do not be disloyal and unfilial, malevolent and faithless. You must show the utmost allegiance to lord and family, and sincerity to the myriad beings.

第一戒者：不得不忠不孝、不仁不信。當盡節君親、推誠萬物。

2. Do not furtively steal from or harm others for your own gain. You must practice virtue without a show and indiscriminately aid living beings.

第二戒者：不得陰賊潛謀、害物利已。當行陰德、廣濟羣生。

3. Do not kill or harm any living being in order to satisfy your own appetites. You must show compassion and benevolence to all, even insects and vermin.

第三戒者：不得殺害含生、以充滋味。當行慈惠、以及昆虫。

4. Do not be lascivious and devious, defiling and disdaining the numinous energy. You must maintain true integrity and strive to be without shortcomings and offenses.

第四戒者：不得淫邪敗真、穢慢靈炁。當守真、操使無缺犯。

5. Do not harm others for your own profit, or spread discord in your family. You must through the Dao help others so that all nine generations live in harmony.

第五戒者：不得敗人成功、離人骨肉。當以道助物、令九族雍和。

6. Do not slander and defame the wise and good, or boast of your talents and elevate yourself. You must appreciate the beauty and

---

[227] This seventh- or eighth-century text is also contained in the old *Daozang jiyao* (KX 23: 10285–87).

goodness of others without being contentious about your own merit and ability.

第六戒者：不得譏毀賢良、露才揚己。當稱人之美善、不自伐其功能。

7. Do not drink wine and eat meat in violation of the prohibitions. You must maintain harmonious energy and character, and single-mindedly strive for purity and emptiness.

第七戒者：不得飲酒食肉、犯律違禁。當調和氣性、專務清虛。[228]

8. Do not be greedy and driven by endless desire, accumulating possessions without sharing with others. You must be frugal but show generosity to the poor and destitute.

第八戒者：不得貪求無厭、積財不散。當行節儉、惠卹貧窮。

9. Do not mingle with the foolish and live among the dregs of society. You must seek those who are better than yourself and stay with those who gather in purity and emptiness.

第九戒者：不得交游非賢、居處雜穢。當慕勝己、棲集清虛。

10. Do not speak or laugh lightly and promote what is not genuine. You must hold on to what is important and utter few words, making the Dao and virtue your main concern.

第十戒者：不得輕忽言笑、舉動非真。當持重寡辭、以道德為務。

The conferral of these initial ten precepts, which were given in early medieval Daoism to those who had just decided to leave their family, constitutes a preliminary stage which should be immediately followed by the second-stage precepts, i.e., the Three Hundred Precepts of the Medium Ultimate:

> Receiving the Ten Precepts of Perfection is already regarded as the fruit of the realization of Perfection. If one continues to progress and observe the precepts with enthusiasm and vigor without even the slightest transgression in word and deed, one will be soon allowed to receive the Three Hundred Medium Ultimate Precepts as revealed by the Most High Lord Laozi.

---

[228] In comparison with the *Xu huang tianzun chuzhen shijie wen* 虛皇天尊初真十戒文 (DZ 180, 5b), the seventh precept, as presented in the *Chuzhen jielü*, is a bit more rigid. On this see Yin Zhihua, "Qingdai Quanzhendao chuanjie chutan" (2010).

既受初真十戒、以證真人之果。更猛勇精進持守、言行毫無過犯、方許再受太上老君所命中極三百大戒。

The 300 Medium Ultimate Precepts of the *Zhongji jie* 中極戒

The anonymous text included in the old *Daozang jiyao* after the *Chuzhen jielü* 初真戒律 is entitled *Zhongji jie* 中極戒 and derives from the sixth-century *Shangqing dongzhen zhihui guanshen dajie wen* 上清洞真智慧觀身大戒文 (DZ 1364, 1a–b). In fact, the header includes the subtitle "Zhongji Shangqing dongzhen zhihui guanshen dajie jing" 中極上清洞真智慧觀身大戒經. Like the text DZ 1364, the *Zhongji jie* opens with an account of its revelation in the Heavens in form of "floating rays of light, diffused and overflowing, radiating through the great void" 流景散漫映煥太虛. After more than 3,000 kalpas 三千餘劫, its wondrous scripts were assembled by the Celestial King of the Original Commencement (Yuanshi tianwang 元始天王) and transmitted to the Most High Lord and Lofty Sage of the Dao (Taishang gaosheng daojun 太上高聖道君). After having been explained and recited in the halls of the Cavern of Perfection (Dongzhen zhi tang 洞真之堂) they ended up being transmitted to the Celestial Emperor of the Great Tenuity (Taiwei tiandi 太微天帝) and to the Celestial King, Lofty Immortal of Great Ultimate (Taiji gaoxian tianwang 太極高仙天王). When the Celestial Emperor received them, he composed an introductory hymn preceding the list of the three hundred precepts. It is known as the "Hymn to Wisdom" (Zhihui song 智慧頌) and consists of three stanzas that appear frequently in Daoist medieval texts and were recited during ordination ceremonies.[229] This poem also came to be recited during the late Qing Quanzhen ordination for the conferral of the Zhongji jie as performed at Chengdu's Erxian'an 二仙庵. This ceremony was reportedly staged in 1882 at the Baiyun guan according to the "santan dajie" procedure by abbot Gao Yunxi 高雲溪 (1841–1907) and is said to

---

[229] *Taishang lingbao zhihui guanshen jing* 太上靈寶智慧觀身經, DZ 350, 1b–2a; *Wushang biyao* 無上秘要, DZ 1138, 35.5a–b, 48.3a–b, 50.2b–3a; *Dongxuan lingbao sandong fengdao kejie yingshi* 洞玄靈寶三洞奉道科戒營始 DZ 1125, 6.10b; *Yaoxiu keyi jielü chao* 要修科儀戒律鈔 DZ 463, 5.23b–24a; *Lingbao lingjiao jidu jinshu* 靈寶領教濟度金書 DZ 466, 10.6b. It was also used during the Zhengyi Song-era ordination described in the *Taishang chujia chuandu yi* 太上出家傳度儀, DZ 1236. See also Kohn, *Cosmos and Community*, 202–4.

have been inherited by the Chengdu Erxian'an abbot Yan Yonghe 閻永和 (fl. 1891–1908) via his master Song Hui'an 宋慧安 (fl. 1884–94).[230]

The overall content of the three hundred precepts derives from DZ 1364 even if the sequence is no exact match especially in the first series of one hundred and eighty precepts. In particular, the Zhongji jie omitted precepts that are repeated to prevent others from committing the same fault, e.g., "Do not instruct anyone to... 道學不得教人做甚麼". For example, one begins with "Do not kill..." 第一戒者不得殺... ; but in contrast with DZ 1364 the Zhongji jie does not say "Do not instruct anyone to kill... ." The precepts are implicitly divided according to three categories that mirror the Three Primes (sanyuan 三元) division found in DZ 1364. They consist of:

1. One hundred and eighty prohibitive precepts (1–180) beginning with "you must not 不得." They were originally given to those under the supervision of the Lower Prime (xiayuan jiepin 下元戒品).
2. Thirty-six precepts including four prohibitive (181–184) and thirty-two prescriptive precepts (185–216) that suggest appropriate conduct: "When walking with others, always let them go in front 與人同行當讓人以前" (185). These precepts were originally given to those under the supervision of the Middle Prime (zhongyuan jiepin 中元戒品).
3. Eighty-four "commemorative" precepts (217–299) based on the cultivation of thought via different topics for mental concentration. They begin with the formula: "I must keep in mind" (dangnian 當念). Initially they deal with practical advice and the cultivation of good habits and intentions such as vegetarian food (217: "I must keep in mind to have vegetarian food as regular diet and be singularly committed to purity and frugality" 當念菜食爲常一志清儉) or altruism (218: "I must keep in mind to first save others before I save myself" 當念先度人後度己身). Precepts 267 to 300 concern Shangqing 上清 cosmic wanderings and visits to immortals and gods. This last series was originally given to the advanced disciples of Higher Prime (shangyuan jiepin 上元戒品).

---

[230] See Yan Yonghe 閻永和, Yinli guize 引禮規則), p. 1a, and 52b. For the recitation of the poem see also the Xuandu lütan weiyi jieke quanbu 玄都律壇威儀戒科全部 (Wang Ka 王卡 and Wang Guiping 汪桂平 eds., Sandong shiyi 三洞拾遺, 2005:11.84), but here it is mentioned in the context of the conferral of the Tianxian jie.

One finds variations and newly reformulated precepts especially among the first series of precepts (7,12–13, 20, 27, 35–36, 38, 40, 52–53, 56–57, 60, 64, 70, 72, etc.). More than half of these precepts are also found in the *Laojun yibai bashi jie* 老君一百八十戒.[231] The remaining one hundred and twenty precepts match with few exceptions those included in DZ 1364.[232]

The last part of DZ 1364 (17b–24b) is not reproduced in the *Zhongji jie*. It includes instead five secret invocations (*mizhu* 秘咒) for

(1) the Medium Ultimate Vestments 中極衣咒 referred to as "the scarlet robe of the precepts" 戒衣絳服;

(2) the Jade Tablet 玉簡咒 referred to as "the turquoise board and jade tablet" 碧笏玉簡;

(3) the Shoes and Kneeling Cloth (*gui*) 鞋規咒 referred to as "the ordination kneeling cloth and yellow altar-shoes" 戒規黃壇;

(4) the Kerchief and Headgear 巾冠咒 referred to as "the mysterious kerchief and starry headgear as the primordial garb of the head" 玄巾星冠爲首元服;

(5) the Submitted Registration 歸單咒 for "ascending to the seat of the Fivefold Radiance as the perfect king of the divine law" 升五明座爲眞法王.

Four of these five invocations concern the regalia—the cap or starry crown *xingguan* 星冠, the purple robe *jiangfu* 絳服, the court tablet *chaoban* 朝板 called *bijian* 碧簡, and the altar shoes *huangtan* 黃壇—which Daoists received during a ceremony modeled on the ancient Chinese ritual of the capping of young men as they came of age. The text of these four invocations derive from a poem titled *Wei tushu gei guanhe* 爲徒屬給冠褐 by Zhao Yizhen 趙宜真 (?–1382) that is used in the ordination ceremony of his disciples and is included in Zhao's *Yuanyangzi fayu* 原陽子法語 (DZ 1071, 2.3b–4a [下卷 27 / 043].[233]

---

[231] See the sections included in the *Taishang laojun jinglü* 太上老君經律 DZ 786, 4a–12b; *Yaoxiu keyi jielü chao* 要修科儀戒律鈔 DZ 463, 5.14a–19a; *Yunji qiqian* 雲笈七籤 DZ 1032, 39.1a–14b, etc.

[232] These exceptions are listed with some mistakes in Kohn, *Cosmos and Community*, 212–219.

[233] While Zhao Yizhen 趙宜真's poem begins with the starry crown *xingguan* 星冠, here the first invocation is related to the ordination robe *jiehe* 戒衣 (Zhao only writes of *jiangfu* 絳服). Apart from a few differences that are often found at the beginning of each invocation in the Zhongji jie (see for instance the modification of the poem to *huangtan* 黃壇, here used for *xie gui zhou* 鞋規咒), there is no reference in Zhao's poem to *gui dan zhou* 歸單咒, an invocation added in the Zhongji jie.

The recitation of these invocations is followed by the oath of maintaining the precepts with the submission of the pledge by the ordinand under his/her new title of "Perfected of Wondrous Virtue of the Gate of the Most High" 太上門下妙德眞人. The text ends with a prayer addressed to all spirits and protectors (諸大神王威神力士官將吏兵) supporting the ordinand in "upholding and perfecting the precepts and their practice" 護持保成戒行.

See also Kristofer Schipper, "Master Chao I-chen 趙宜真(?–1382) and the Ch'ing-wei 清微 School of Taoism," in *Dōkyō to shūkyō bunka* 道教と宗教文化 edited by Akizuki Kan'ei 秋月観英 (Tokyo: Hirakawa shuppansha 平川出版社, 1987), pp. 715–34, here 727.

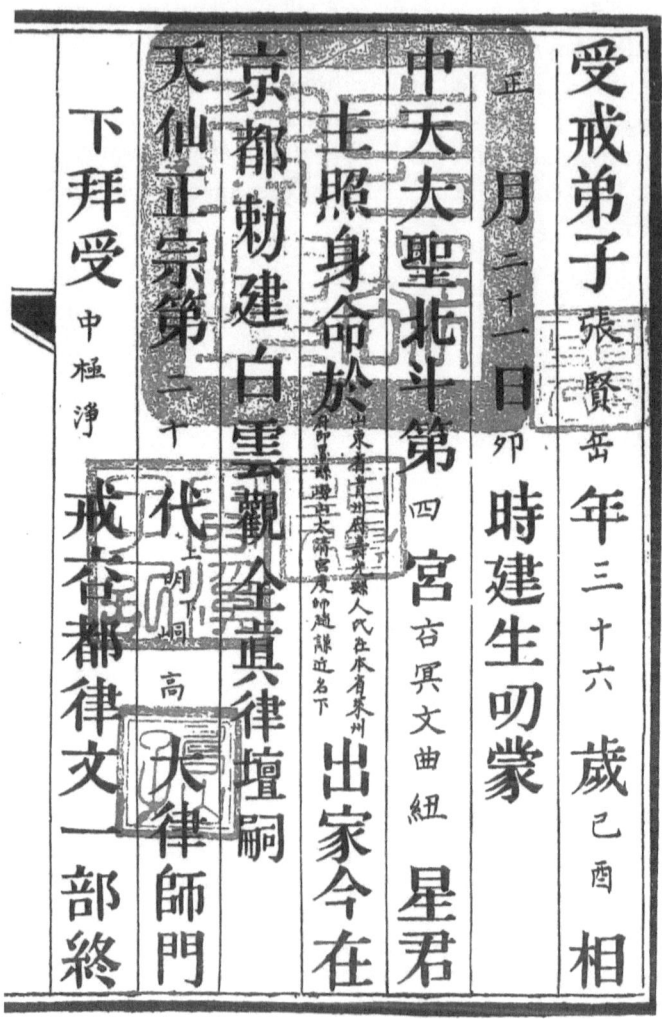

Fig. 13: Ordination certificate from Beijing's Baiyun guan (Hackmann 1931)[234]

---

[234] Hackmann's copy belongs to a certain Zhang Xianyue 張賢岳 (1849–?), a Daoist from the Shangqinggong 上清宮 of Laoshan 嶗山 (Shandong) who received the precepts of the Medium Ultimate in 1884 at Beijing's Baiyun guan from the 20th Longmen Great Vinaya master (*dalüshi* 大律師) Gao Mingdong 高明峒 (alias Gao Rendong 高仁峒, 1841–1907). Another copy of these medium ultimate precepts with the ordination certificate of a certain Wang Xinzhe 王信祉, who received the same precepts earlier in 1873 at Beijing Baiyun guan under the 18th Longmen Vinaya Master Meng Yongcai 孟永才, is reproduced in Wang Ka 王卡 and Wang Guiping 汪桂平 (2005:11.91).

Chapter 3

The Search for the Perfect Precepts

With regard to the ultimate stage, the Tianxian jie 天仙戒, we find only few indications in the *Chuzhen jielü* 初真戒律. Whereas for the previous two stages the *Chuzhen jielü* mentions different sets of precepts that must have been taken by the applicant,[235] for the last stage it only specifies: "If one observes the previous precepts in their entirety, one will receive the Wondrous Precepts of the Great Virtue of the Celestial Immortals, after which one must enact the One Hundred and Eighty Esoteric Precepts to be Meticulously Observed (一百八十細行密戒) or the Three Hundred Great Precepts (三百大戒). It also explains that this last series of precepts can only be administered three years after the conferral of the intermediate precepts (Zhongji jie 中極戒), and that only recipients of this ultimate level of Celestial Immortals' precepts are allowed to administer ordinations on a platform (*kaitan chuanjie* 開壇傳戒) in their quality as "Precept-transmitting Original Master" (*chuanjie benshi* 傳戒本師 or, as recorded in late Qing ordination certificates, as "Precept-transmitting Vinaya Master (*chuanjie lüshi* 傳戒律師).[236] The practice during the one-hundred-day ordination retreat (*rula* 入臘) consists mainly of the recitation of the *Daodejing* 道德經 and meditation.[237] As mentioned in the above-quoted

---

[235] 領受初真十戒、三戒、五戒、八戒、九真妙戒者、…行持具足、受中極淨戒、或持身戒、或智慧戒、或觀身戒、或妙林戒, etc.

[236] *Chuzhen jielü* 40a–b (CK 24: 10476); see also below. The title "Chuanjie lüshi," often figures in the ordination certificates; see for instance Oyanagi Shigeta 小柳司氣太, *Hakuunkan shi* 白雲觀志, p. 72.

[237] The *Chuzhen jielü* states: "Those who have entered the ordination-retreat and received the Precepts of the Celestial Immortals should recite the *Daodejing* for the overall period of 100 days. Between 11–1 p.m. they should practice quiet sitting and inner contemplation without being concerned with personal matters until they

passages of the *Chuzhen jielü*, the applicant for this last stage received a specific robe that in the text's different sections has two different names (see note 211 on p. 114).

Because of the lack of guidelines for the conferral of this last series of precepts of Celestial Immortals in the works attributed to Wang Changyue, posterity felt the need to create *ex novo* and via spirit writing a text for this purpose. Under the title "Integral Outline of the Great Precepts of the Celestial Immortals of the Three Altars 三壇圓滿天仙大戒略說" (abbreviated as *Tianxian dajie* 天仙大戒), this text was allegedly transmitted by Liu Shouyuan 柳守元, an immortal linked with the spirit writing altar of Jiang Jiang Yuanting 蔣元庭 (also called Jiang Yupu 蔣予蒲, 1755–1819), the main compiler of the old *Daozang jiyao* of the Jiaqing era.

The Ten-Precept Set in the Tianxian Dajie 天仙大戒

The text for the last stage of ordination, the *Tianxian dajie* 天仙大戒, has been studied by Mori Yuria 森由利亞.[238] One of the main aims of Mori's study was to show how the identity of the presumed author of this text, Liu Shouyuan, was linked to previous spirit writing groups involved in the compilation of the *Lüzu quanshu* 呂祖全書, and how a new identity was elaborated around the altar of Jiang Yuanting. Regarded as the second patriarch of the so-called Tianxian pai 天仙派, Liu Shouyuan inserted himself in the lineage of Lü Dongbin 呂洞賓 and not in the "Quanzhen Longmen" lineage of Wang Changyue. However, according to Mori, the creators of this text were conscious of the genealogical link with Quanzhen and presented the revelation of Lü Dongbin's Tianxian pai as the source of the Southern and Northern Lineages 南北宗 of Quanzhen. Mori emphasizes that, although this text is a fruit of Lü Dongbin's revelation at Jiang Yuanting's spirit writing altar rather than the product of Wang Changyue's legacy, it was created with the aim of accomplishing the Quanzhen ordina-

---

have accomplished the purification of the three activities [i.e., word, thought, and body]." 入臘領受天仙戒者、持道德經一百日。每於寅刻、信禮十方、共十拜、子午二時靜坐內觀、不關人事、致三業清靜。*Chuzhen jielü* 38a–b (CK 24: 10475). See also below.

[238] Mori Yuria 森由利亞, "Shinchō Zenshinkyō no denkai to Ryoso fukei shinkō: Tensen kai no seiritsu wo megutte 清朝全真教の伝戒と呂祖扶乩信仰：天仙戒の成立をめぐって," in *Ajia bunka no shisō to girei* アジア文化の思想と儀礼, edited by Fukui Fumimasa hakushi taishoku kinen ronshū kankōkai 福井文雅博士古稀・退職記念論集刊行会 (Tokyo: Shunjūsha 春秋社, 2005), pp. 441–61.

tion of the three altars of Wang Changyue. In fact, according to Mori, the three-altars ordination (*santan dajie* 三壇大戒) was originally introduced to Quanzhen Daoism by Wang Changyue.

Instead of associating this scripture with Quanzhen based on Lü Dongbin's presumed genealogical links with this school and regarding the Tianxian jie as the accomplishment of Wang Changyue's ordination of the three altars, I will here first summarize the structure and the content of this text. Leaving aside the supposed relationship between Quanzhen and Tianxian pai emphasized by Mori, I will focus on what for me represents the core of the scripture.[239]

The text begins with an announcement made by the alleged compiler of this scripture, the immortal Liu Shouyuan 柳守元:

> From my correct [teacher's] seat I declare: all of you disciples should know that after the *Chuzhen jielü* and the *Zhongji lingwen* there is a supreme and transcending dharma of the wondrous Daoist teachings called *Tianxian dajie*.
>
> 正座唱言：諸法子等、既初眞戒律、中極靈文、更須知有無上妙門飛昇寶筏曰天仙大戒.

After a few more lines of Liu's short preamble, the text reproduces the structure of a traditional Lingbao scripture, introducing the revelations of Yuanshi tianzun 元始天尊 at the request of a Perfected named Wujie 無戒:[240]

---

[239] In this article ("Shinchō Zenshinkyō no denkai," pp. 457–458), Mori emphasizes that the Tianxian pai in its transmission of the highest ordination of the Celestial Immortals (tianxian dajie) does not ignore the Quanzhen transmission of precepts and the figure of the Longmen patriarch Wang Changyue, yet does not include itself in this transmission. However, in a later article devoted to Quanzhen liturgy, Mori airs a different opinion. On p. 100 of "Shō Yoho no Ryoso fukei shinkō to Zenshinkyō 蔣予蒲の呂祖扶乩信仰と全真教"(in Horiike Nobuo 堀池信夫 and Sunayama Minoru 砂山稔, eds., *Dōkyō kenkyū no saisentan* 道教研究の最先端, Tokyo: Taiga shobō 大川書房, 2006) Mori states that Jiang Yuanting and his spirit-altar congregants wanted to be part of Quanzhen. He thus interprets Jiang Yuanting's work as the product of their will to be legitimized by Quanzhen.

[240] Inspired by Buddhist sutras, Lingbao scriptures are often built on revelations transmitted by Yuanshi tianzun 元始天尊, Taishang Daojun 太上道君, etc. during an assembly upon requests addressed to Perfected ones whose names are often indicative of the content or topic of the revealed teachings. See for instance the other Lingbao scripture (*Dongxuan lingbao sanyuan wuliangshou jing* 太上洞玄靈寶三元無量壽經, DZ 323) reproduced in the *Tianxian dajie* and mentioned here below.

The Great Precepts of the Ultimateless of the Celestial Immortals revealed by Yuanshi tianzun state: At the time when Yuanshi tianzun, sitting on the nine-lotus throne at the center of the Baohua forest, revealed the wondrous beginningless Way to all Celestial Worthies, to the Celestial assembly of all saints, and to all spirits of the Celestial Dragon, a Perfected among them by the name of Wujie rose from his seat and, after performing his prostrations holding the court tablet, knelt down and presented his request. The Celestial Worthy said: Ever since conversion began, this wondrous Way has not yet been heard. If you now listen to these sounds of mercy, you will become pure and clear from the bottom of your hearts and be greatly awakened. Though students of the Dao and observers of the precepts could learn of Chuzhen and Zhongji, they have not yet heard the *Tianxian dajie* explained. What hope had there been of being instructed in this method?

元始天尊說天仙無極大戒曰：爾時元始天尊在寶華林中、九蓮座上、與諸天尊、諸天聖眾、及諸天龍鬼神、說無始妙道時、座中有一真人、名曰無戒、從座中起、覿顙作禮執簡、長跪上白。天尊曰：自開化以來、未曾聞此妙道。今聆慈音、肺腑清涼、大生解悟。但學道之士、戒行修持、初真、中極皆有可聞、獨於天仙大戒曾未聞說。有何道法臻此地位惟望。

This passage emphasizes that, in contrast with the previous series of precepts (the *Chuzhen jie* and the *Zhongji jie*), the supreme precepts had hitherto not been communicated to the world. In reality, though, what is revealed in this text appears to be a compilation of earlier Daoist scriptures found in the *Daozang* that are associated with Lingbao.[241] Thus the *Tianxian dajie*

---

[241] The quoted passages derive from the following *Daozang* scriptures: *Wushang neibi zhenzang jing* 無上內秘真藏經 (DZ 4, 卷6.8b, 6.14a); *Taishang dongxuan lingbao yebao yinyuan jing* 洞玄靈寶業報因緣經 (DZ 336, 4.1a–b); *Taishang xuhuang tianzun sishijiu zhanjing* 太上虛皇四十九章經 (DZ 18, 1b–2a, 7a, 8b); *Taishang dongxuan lingbao yebao yinyuan jing* 洞玄靈寶業報因緣經 (DZ 336, 4.3b, 4.6a); *Dongxuan lingbao sanyuan wuliangshou jing* 太上洞玄靈寶三元無量壽經 (DZ 322 in its entirety, see here below); *Taishang shier shangpin feitian falun quanjie miaojing* 太上十二上品飛天法輪勸戒妙經 (DZ 182, 10b); *Dongxuan lingbao qianzhen ke* 洞玄靈寶千真科 (DZ 1410, 13a); *Dongxuan lingbao changye zhi fu jiuyou yukui mingzhen ke* 洞玄靈寶長夜之府九幽玉匱明真科 (DZ 1411, 4a); *Taishang lingbao yuanyang miaojing* 太上靈寶元陽妙經 (DZ 334, 6.5b); *Yuhuang benxing jijing* 玉皇本行集經 (DZ 10, 1.7b, 3.3b); *Huangjing jizhu* 皇經集註 (DZ 1440, 8.15a); *Sandong zhongjie wen* 三洞眾戒文 (DZ 178, 2.7b–9b); and *Taiwei lingshu ziwen*

does not seem to have a text of its own. Rather, it consists merely of excerpts culled from various texts. Furthermore, the selection of its different passages regarding earlier precepts is not simply the fruit of the alleged transmission of Yuanshi tianzun or the spirit writing revelation of Lü Dongbin via Liu Shouyuan. Interestingly, many passages were already recorded in the section "伍太一十九問" (Nineteen questions by Wu Taiyi) of Wu Shouyang 伍守陽 (1574–1644?)'s *Xianfo hezong yulu* 仙佛合宗語錄 (Recorded Sayings on the Merged Tradition of Buddhism and Daoism) that is included in the old *Daozang jiyao*.[242] I shall return to this topic later because of the important role of Wu Shouyang in establishing the "Immortals' precepts (*xianjie* 仙戒) and in promoting the creation of a reformed and public Daoist ordination system able to compete with Buddhism.

Though it is overall a patchwork of Lingbao textual excerpts, the *Tianxian dajie* reproduces one Lingbao text in its entirety: the *Dongxuan lingbao sanyuan wuliangshou jing* 太上洞玄靈寶三元無量壽經 (DZ 323 04 / 021).[243] This scripture consists of twenty-seven incommensurable (*wuliang* 無量) methods extending from "how to distance oneself from the body" 遠身行法 to "how to bear the unbearable" 忍不忍法. These methods were purportedly revealed by the Most High Lord Lao 太上道君 during a "great assembly" 大會 held in the Palace of the Three Primes 三元宮 at the request of a Perfected named Yike 儀可. According to the Most High, all these methods issue from the Dao (三界諸法皆從道生) and can be summarized as "practice of contemplative wisdom" (*xiu guanhui* 修觀慧). Each method has ten modalities: One gains distance from the body by means of 1) wisdom 智慧; 2) compassion 慈悲; 3) endurance 含忍; 4) good works 行功; 5) cultivation of the mind 修心; 6) good karmic deeds 善業; 7) assiduity 精進; 8) regulation of the body 飾身; 9) elimination of passions 遣情, and 10) universality of mind 普心. Incommensurable longevity (延無量壽筭) and incommensurable fields of merit (長無量福田) are among the blessings promised to those who recite, copy, and distribute this text.[244]

---

xianji zhenji shangjing 太微靈書紫文仙忌真記上經 (DZ 179, 1a-b, 2a-b, 4a).

[242] *Xianfo hezong yulu* 仙佛合宗語錄, CK 17:7494–96). It is also in this chapter that one finds the mention of the text titled *Taishang lingbao dacheng miaofa lianhua shenjing* 太上靈寶大乘妙法蓮華眞經.

[243] See the article on this scripture by John Lagerwey in Schipper and Verellen, eds., *The Taoist Canon*, vol. 1, 534–35.

[244] For the relation of these celestial virtues to the first six Buddhist *pāramitās* (perfections) see Kohn, *Cosmos and Community*, p. 111-2.

Such blessings are naturally transferred to adepts who, in preparation of the *Tianxian jie* ordination ceremony, were trained to recite this text over and over.[245] However, it is worthy of note that the core of the *Tianxian dajie* was yet to be revealed. After brief references to other sets of precepts including the list of the ten precepts of Fuyou dijun 孚佑帝君 (Lü Dongbin 呂洞賓) included in the old *Daozang jiyao*,[246] the compilers finally introduce the specific set of precepts chosen for this highest ordination ceremony:

> Presently Yuguang puzhao tianzun is asking all of you about the *Biyu zhengong dajie*. All you disciples who are listening to the rules regarding the taking of precepts should be determined and straightforward, well focused and devoted, persisting in One Truth, and resolute and firm in facing all doubts and difficulties.
>
> 今即玉光普照天尊、碧玉真宮大戒、問於汝等。諸法子聽受戒規、端在立志、志在精勤、一真不懈、志在堅確、萬有難惑。[247]

The *Biyu zhengong dajie* 碧玉真宮大戒 mentioned in this passage consists of a set of ten precepts allegedly revealed by Yuguang puzhao tianzun 玉光普照天尊, an avatar of Yuhuang dadi 玉皇大帝. As described in the

---

[245] As shown by Yan Yonghe 閻永和 in his *Yinli guize* 引禮規則 (pp. 56a–59a), the entire *Tianxian dajie* was recited during the ordination ceremonies held at Chengdu Erxian'an. As the *Xuandu lütan weiyi jieke quanbu* 玄都律壇威儀戒科全部 (Wang Ka 王卡 and Wang Guiping 汪桂平, 2005:11.43–44) informs us, the applicants were instructed to recite the list of precepts and the precept texts until they knew them by heart.

[246] *Fuyou dijun shijie gongguo ke* 孚佑帝君十戒功過格 (CK 23: 10309–39) presents the ten precepts in fully annotated and commented form. The Tianxian dajie (16a) concludes its presentation of precepts by stating: "The above-mentioned excerpts offer a rough presentation of the precepts. As to detailed explanations, there is no way to exhaust in words the *Tianxian dajie* even within the True Scripts of the Three Caverns" 以上數條。粗說戒相。若詳言之。三洞真文內。天仙大戒。窮劫說之亦不能盡。The Daozang includes a scripture titled *Jiao sandong zhenwen wufa zhengyi mengwei lu licheng yi* 醮三洞真文五法正一盟威籙立成儀 (DZ 1212), compiled by Zhang Wanfu 張萬福 (fl. 713), that features a list of all titles of the registers comprising virtually all initiation documents of the time; see Kristofer Schipper's abstract in *The Taoist Canon*, vol. 1, 460–61.

[247] A similar passage is found in the *Yuquan* 玉詮 (CK 17: 8975) where Wang Lingguan comments on these precepts: "本師言有志者、聽受戒規、選擇清修之子、便當立志、志在精勤、方始植得鳳根、不畏霜雪之壓覆。志在堅確、方始成得品行、不爲利欲所搖惑。"

Tianxian dajie, the ceremony of the conferral of the ten precepts takes place as follows :

> The Supreme Emperor says: "Those who take these precepts should not kill even the smallest living creature: this teaches you to develop a compassionate mind. A thousand precepts, ten thousand precepts are nothing other than the complete realization of this compassionate mind. How can all of you disciples become equipped with this mind? You must vow: Right from this moment and for innumerable world-ages until the end of the world, my compassionate mind will be totally without limits. Can you maintain this limitless mind?" All answer in unison: "I shall neither spare body nor life to constantly maintain this mind and carry out my practice according to the teachings."
>
> 上帝云：受戒者、不殺微命、是教爾等發慈憫心。千戒萬戒、無非圓滿這個慈憫心。諸法子何以具有此心？須要自今以始、迄無量劫、世界有盡、我此慈憫心量無盡。此無量心、能持否？眾白：盡形壽命、常持此心、依教奉行。

Each of the subsequent nine precepts follows the same pattern: the Supreme Emperor presents a particular precept and explains that it forms the essence of myriads of precepts, whereupon he asks the congregants if they are able to observe it; and all vow in unison that they will neither spare body nor life to observe it and practice in conformity with the teachings. Thus they must vow:

(1) not to kill even the smallest living creature, which teaches them to develop a compassionate mind; 不殺微命、是教爾等發慈憫心。

(2) not to give rise to lascivious thoughts, which teaches them to develop a pure mind; 不起淫意、是教爾等發潔白心。[248]

(3) not to harbor contentious thoughts, which teaches them to develop a forbearing mind; 不生諍念、是教爾等發忍辱心。

(4) not to steal anything, which teaches them to develop a clear and pure mind; 不盜一芥、是教爾等發明淨心。

(5) not to cheat, which teaches them to develop a genuine mind; 不欺一愚、是教爾等發真實心。

---

[248] The full text reads: 上帝云：受戒者、不起淫意、是教爾等發潔白心。千戒萬戒、無非圓滿這個潔白心。諸法子何以具有此心、須要自今以始、迄無量劫、世界有盡、我此潔白心量無盡。此無量心、能持否？眾白：盡形壽命、常持此心、依教奉行。The subsequent precepts follow exactly the same pattern.

(6) to make the utmost effort, which teaches them to develop the original mind; 敦行盡力、是教爾等發報本心。

(7) not to engage in vain talk, which teaches them to develop a sincere mind; 語言無妄、是教爾等發誠一心。

(8) not to be diverted by any ghosts, which teaches them to develop a steadfast mind; 千魔不轉、是教爾等發堅固心。

(9) to unbridle the power of intention, which teaches them to develop a broad mind; 宏發願力、是教爾等發廣大心。

(10) to aspire to sainthood, which teaches them to develop a progressive mind. 事聖不倦、是教爾等發精進心。

As we can see, all ordinands, after having received these ten precepts (each of which corresponds to the development of a specific virtuous state of mind), must repeat in unison the closing formula "I shall neither spare body nor life to constantly maintain this mind and carry out my practice according to the teachings" 盡形壽命、常持此心、依教奉行。[249]

This ultimate set of precepts is not found in the *Daozang* but is mentioned and recorded in the scriptures of the old *Daozang jiyao* in association with spirit writing.[250] This ceremony of the conferral of the ten precepts was in fact crucial for the foundation of the spirit writing altar of Yuguang puzhao tianzun 玉光普照天尊 whose key members were linked with the Zhengyi 正一 Xuanmiao guan 玄妙觀 of Suzhou.[251] This altar, known under the name of Yutan 玉壇 (Jade Altar), was located west of Tianxin Bridge 天心橋 in Sucheng 蘇城 (Suzhou).[252] Whereas Jiang Yuanting associated this

---

[249] This is also found in the late ordination text compiled by Yan Yonghe 閻永和, *Yinli guize* 引禮規則, section "Yingshi shuo Tianxian jie 迎師說天仙戒," 57a-b.

[250] The list is found in the *Yuquan* 玉詮 (1.6b; CK 20: 8973) and is also mentioned in the postface by Shang Kai 賞鍇 to the *Jingshi gongguoge* 警世功過格 (張 3, 86a; CK 23: 10353).

[251] *Chongyin Xuanmiao guan* 重印玄妙觀 (ZWDS 20: 481, 501). Jiang Yuanting and other congregants, too, wrote stele inscriptions for the Zhengyi Xuanmiao guan of Suzhou. See Esposito, "The Discovery of Jiang Yuanting's *Daozang jiyao* in Jiangnan," 87–92 (Chinese version, *Zongjiaoxue yanjiu* 宗教學研究 2010.3, p. 19; revised English version here below, Part Three, chapters 1 & 2).

[252] I follow here the location given by Peng Shaosheng in *Yutanji* 玉壇記 (*Yixing juji* 一行居集, j. 5, p. 24a (reproduction in 4 volumes of 1825 edition: Nanjing, Gujiu shudian 古舊書店, 1990). For a study on Peng Shaosheng and his involvement with spirit writing see Shi Huidou 釋慧鐸 (secular name: Lin Yiluan 林一鑾), *Peng Shaosheng (1740–1796) yu shendao shejiao zhi jiaoshe* 彭紹升 (1740–1796) 與神道設教之交涉 (The Involvement of Peng Shaosheng [1740–1796] in Supernatu-

altar with Peng Dingqiu 彭定求 (1645–1719),[253] Peng Shaosheng 彭紹升 (1740–1796)—the great-grandson of Peng Dingqiu—linked it instead to Jin Yuanding 金淵鼎 (?–1687) who became the Yutan 玉壇 altar's supervisor in 1683.[254] The elected adepts of this altar (ranked as disciples of the superior vehicle of Yuguang 玉光上乘弟子) were asked to observe the above-mentioned ten precepts as revealed by their principal master (*benshi* 本師) Yuguang puzhao tianzun 玉光普照天尊. The observance of these ten precepts formed part of their "Guitan guiyue 皈壇規約" (Pledge of Commitment to the Rules of the Altar), as preserved in the *Yuquan* 玉詮 version of the precepts published in the old *Daozang jiyao*. The list of these precepts is followed by a lengthy commentary, dated 1691, that is attributed to the Shenxiao protector Wang Shan 王善 (i.e., Wang Lingguan 王靈官). As Wang Lingguan explains: "Neither Chan Bodhisattva precepts nor Daoist Tianxian precepts go beyond the scope [of these ten precepts] 禪門之菩薩戒元門之天仙戒亦不出此範圍."[255]

---

ral Revelations) (Ph.D. thesis, Huafan University, Taipei 華梵大學東方人文思想研究所, 2009) and the same author's article about the Yutan altar of Suzhou and the role of *Yuquan* entitled "Qing chu Suzhou Yutan de jiangluan yinghua — yi 'Yuquan' wei zhongxin" 清初蘇州玉壇的降鸞應化 — 以 玉詮 為中心, *Journal of Religion and Culture of National Cheng Kung University* 成大宗教與文化學報 11 (2008): 90–124. For the association of this altar with Peng Dingqiu see note 326 below (pp. 186–187).

[253] In the *Yuquan yulu* 玉詮語錄, a component of the *Yulu daguan* 語錄大觀 (壁 3, 77a; CK 13:5753), Jiang Yuanting adds the following note: "What 'Jade Expositions' denote are teachings conveyed by Yuguang puzhao tianzun at his respective or principal altar of Peng Dingqiu in the Tianxin community of Sucheng, whence its title *Yuquan* 謹按玉詮乃蘇城天心里彭氏定求、本壇係玉光普照天尊開化、故名曰 玉詮. It is worthy of note that the passages of the *Yuquan yulu* (77a–88a; CK 13: 5753–5758) are also found in the *Yuquan* under the section revealed by Fuyou dijun 孚佑帝君 (1.99a–109a; CK 23: 9020–9025), albeit not in the same sequence. This indicates that the *Yuquan yulu* had been derived from the *Yuquan*. The *Yuquan yulu*, in its turn, stems from Shao Zhilin's *Lüzu quanshu* in 64 *juan* (here 44.46a–58b) under the title *Yuqingtan yulu* 玉清壇語錄, here a component of *yulu huicui* 語錄會粹.

[254] According to Peng Shaosheng's "*Yutanji* 玉壇記" (*Yixing juji* 一行居集, 5.24a) in 1683 the congregation of the Jade Altar chose a site west of Tianxin Bridge 天心橋 to set up a Public Altar (Gongtan 公壇) under the supervision of Jin Yuanding 金淵鼎 (d. 1687). A descendant of Luo Hongxian 羅洪先 (1504–1564) by the name of Luo Cheng 羅澄 is said to have been responsible for its establishment in the winter of 1674. The Jade Altar that Luo originally set up in his home featured an image of the Jade Emperor (Yuhuang 玉皇).

[255] *Yuquan* 玉詮 1.10a (CK 20: 8975).

Such an affirmation—put in the mouth of Wang Lingguan, the deity in charge of monitoring the ordinands (and guardian of all Daoist monasteries)—may help us understand why Jiang Yuanting and his altar congregants decided to integrate this set in the *Tianxian dajie* and decided to put it right at the core of their newly revealed ordination procedure. At the same time, the mention of "Tianxian jie 天仙戒" shows that *Yuquan*'s compilers were already aware of the existence of this kind of precepts which they regarded as counterpart to the Buddhist Bodhisattva precepts. Moreover, while the Bodhisattva precepts are mentioned in connection with the Chan school 禪門, the Tianxian jie are associated with Daoism under the generic appellation of Yuanmen 元門 (i.e., Xuanmen 玄門).[256] Unfortunately we do not know to which set of Tianxian jie *Yuquan*'s compilers refer; but it is quite obvious that such Tianxian jie predate the compilation of the *Tianxian dajie* where, by following the advice of Wang Lingguan, Jiang Yuanting and his congregants included this set from the Yutan.

After the conferral of the Yutan 玉壇's ten precepts, the ordinands received four Invocations in form of laissez-passer or pledges (*fujuan* 符券 or *fuxin* 符信) for realizing Celestial Immortality and its golden elixir, along with the recitation of four related scriptures that are reproduced in their entirety. The conferral of such "laissez-passer" reminds us of the *fujie* 符節 mentioned in the work of Wu Shouyang as an indispensable part of the orthodox transmission of the Lineage of the Immortals 仙宗 (which in the commentary added by Wu Shouxu 伍守虛 is referred to, more specifically, as "Longmen xianpai 龍門仙派") and a testimony of the complete transmission of the Great Dao of the Tianxian (天仙大道) as well as the inner and outer Golden Elixir (內外金丹). Such a *fujie* 符節 confers the permission to the adept to ascend to Heaven (*shengtian* 昇天), as it is "what is

---

[256] Xuanzong 玄宗 and Chanzong 禪宗 are juxtaposed in the spirit writing text revealed at Jiang Yuanting's altar; see the Preface to the *Xuanzong zhengzhi* 玄宗正旨 attributed to Liu Shouyuan, the alleged compiler of the *Tianxian dajie* (CK 8: 3045–57): 玄宗者天仙至道 …與禪宗實爲相近. Many central passages in the *Tianxian dajie* reproduce fundamental thoughts of this text, indicating that the *Tianxian dajie* was written in the circles of Jiang Yuanting. See also note 274 below (p. 149). For the term "Xuanmen" see also the passages of the *Tianxian dajie* associated with the revelation of Liu Shouyuan pointing at an idea of authentic and universal Daoist path, as well as the sections of the *Chuzhen jielü*. (In *Yuquan* 玄宗妙寶無極無涯粤自上帝授五老赤書則五老爲法寶大藏之宗; in *Zhenquan* 遇眞記然玄宗之所謂學天仙者非歟).

possessed by the disciples initiated by the Tianxian 此天仙度弟子之所有事者."[257]

In the *Tianxian dajie* these invocations or pledges and their laissez-passer refer concretely to:

1) The "Esoteric Invocation of the Celestial Emperor (Tianhuang mizhou) as laissez-passer for the realization of the Celestial Immortality" 天皇密咒以為天仙證果符券.[258] This invocation is accompanied by the recitation of the *Taishang changqing changjing zhenjing* 太上常清常靜真經 (corresponding to DZ 620).

---

[257] *Xianfo hezong yulu* 仙佛合宗語錄, 畢集3, 3.53b (CK 17: 7537). On the use of this term in Wu Shouyang's works for claiming his orthodox heritage from Qiu Chuji as expression of the *Tianxian dadao* 天仙大道 and his "Longmen" legacy different from that of Wang Changyue, see Monica Esposito, "The Longmen School and its Controversial History," pp. 656–660 {*Facets of Qing Daoism*, pp. 103–107}. On the meaning of *fujie*, see in particular p. 656, and p. 682 note 90 {*Facets of Qing Daoism*, p. 102 and note 90}. For a recent analysis of this term see the study by Paul van Enckevort, "Quanzhen and Longmen Identities in the Work of Wu Shouyang" (in Xun Liu and Vincent Goossaert, eds., *Quanzhen Daoism in Modern Chinese History and Society*. Berkeley: Institute of East Asian Studies, 2014).

[258] 天生雲龍、道本上昇、張烈正氣、麗於太清、輔弼正道、行於正平、六甲洞元、九天超形、福祿子孫、先行自真、次及人皇、人敬長生、六丁九炁、秘密真成、敬之終吉、昊天貴名、久之道妙、身體常充、聞此真句、與道合真。急急如元、始天尊律令。The text of this invocation (except for the last verse "急急如元始天尊律令," the substitution of the penultimate verse "與道合真" replacing "常任之清," and the character 充 in "身體常充" for 寧) is found at the beginning of the Southern Song scripture *Sanhuang neiwen yibi* 三皇內文遺祕 (DZ 856, 2a) under the title *Tianhuang neiwen shang* 天皇內文上. This scripture is associated with the *Sanhuang wen* 三皇文 legacy and the *Dongshen jing* 洞神經, a scripture quoted by Wu Shouyang (*Xianfo hezong yulu* 仙佛合宗語錄, 3.53a) in order to explain the meaning of *fujie* as "昇天券"(the same quotation is also found at the end of j. 2 of the *Yuanshi wuliang duren shangpin miaojing sizhu* 元始无量度人上品妙經四注 DZ 87 and in *Yuanshi wuliang duren shangpin miaojing neiyi* 元始無量度人上品妙經內義, DZ 90, j. 3). On the *Sanhuang wen*, see the entry by Yamada Toshiaki in *The Encyclopedia of Taoism*, ed. F. Pregadio (London: Routledge, 2008), pp. 837–39, here 838. On the *Sanhuang neiwen yibi* 三皇內文遺祕 see the article by Poul Andersen in *The Taoist Canon*, p. 977. An invocation with the similar name *Tianhuang xinzhou* 天皇心呪, written in pseudo-Sanskrit (唵毘盧喳浙唎吽摂唵天王伽梛霹靂摂), was recited at the Jingming 淨明 spirit writing altar of Taiyi 太乙法派 for the transmission of the Jinhua zongzhi 金華宗旨. See Monica Esposito, "Shindai ni okeru Kingaisan Ryūmonha no seiritsu to Kinka shūshi 清代における金蓋山龍門派の成立と金華宗旨" {revised and enlarged English version here below, Part Four}.

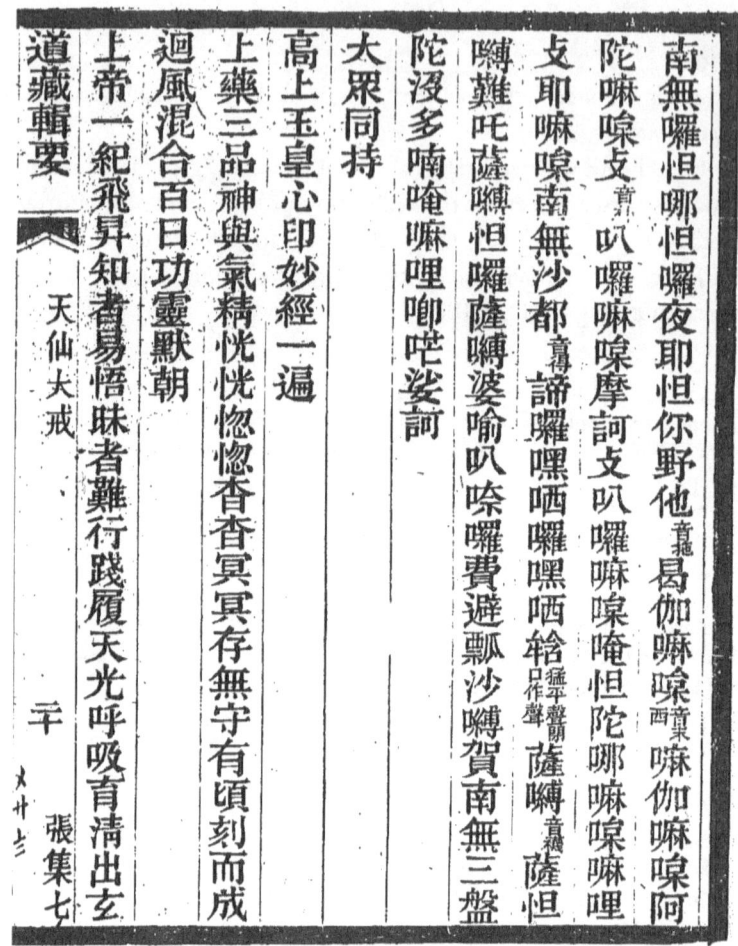

Fig. 14: From the Invocation of the Wondrous Spirit of the Northern Dipper (CK 24:10466)

2) The "Heart Invocation of the Wondrous Spirit of the Northern Dipper (Beidou xuanling xinzhou, i.e., Doumu 斗姥) as laissez-passer for the golden elixir of the Celestial Immortality" 北斗玄靈心咒以為天仙金丹符券.[259] This invocation, which abounds in variant characters (Fig. 14), is

---

[259] The same invocation is included in the *Tongcan jing* 同參經 (室集 3, chap. 31, 60b; CK 12: 5383–5415) under the title "Doumu xinzhou" 斗姥心咒, and also in the *Chanfa daguan* 懺法大觀 (柳集 3, 3.8a; CK 21:9314) under the label "dharani" 陀羅尼. These two scriptures are linked with the spirit writing altar of Jiang Yuanting. The *Tongcan jing* was originally derived from the *Cantong jing* 參同

accompanied by the recitation of the *Gaoshang Yuhuang xinyin miaojing* 高上玉皇心印妙經 (corresponding to DZ 13).

3) The "Heart Invocation of the Patriarch of the Dao (i.e., Lü Dongbin) for expelling ghosts (Daozu chumo xinzhou) as laissez-passer for the golden elixir of Celestial Immortality" 道祖除魔心咒以為天仙金丹符券.[260]

This invocation is accompanied by the recitation of the *Fuyou shangdi chunyang Lüzu tianshi xinjing* 孚佑上帝純陽呂祖天師心經 (a scripture attributed to Lü Dongbin 呂洞賓 and included in the old *Daozang jiyao*).[261]

4) The "Supreme Invocation of the Ultimateless of the Patriarch of the Dao (i.e., Lü Dongbin) as laissez-passer for the golden elixir of Celestial

---

經 included in Liu Tishu 劉體恕 ed, *Lüzu quanshu* 呂祖全書 in 32 juan. However, in its juan 18 one finds a different "Doumu xinzhou" 斗姥心咒 invocation (which is also reproduced in Shao Zhilin 邵志林 ed., *Lüzu quanshu* 呂祖全書 in 64 juan, here in juan 14). An invocation more similar to that included in Jiang Yuanting's works is found in Chen Mou 陳謀 ed., *Lüzu quanshu zongzheng* 呂祖全書宗正 (j. 7. 76a–b). The last two verses giving the name of Doumu as Marici (唵嘛哩啋𠱥娑訶) were recited, under the title of "Doumu xinzhou," at the Jingming spirit writing altar of Taiyi 太乙法派 for the transmission of the *Jinhua zongzhi* (Secret of the Goden Flower). On the different editions of the Lüzu quanshu and the ritual of transmission of the Jinhua zongzhi, see Monica Esposito, "Shindai ni okeru Kingaisan Ryūmonha no seiritsu to Kinka shūshi 清代における金蓋山龍門派の成立と金華宗旨" {see Part Four here below}.

[260] 三五雷霆、正一玄宗、道為法本、法滅魔情、內魔既蕩、外魔亡形、靈根合一、齋月會空、天罡在成、祖氣羅胸、默朝帝座、靜悟無生、至微至奧、無盡無窮、爽靈胎光、幽精黃庭、泥丸有電、遍照洪濛、一切魔魅、汞化塵風、九陽運化、永保離宮。吾奉純陽道祖、萬正紫極真人勅令。 This invocation is found in the *Jinyu baojing* 金玉寶經, a component of the *Wujing hebian* 五經合編 (室集 4, 28b–29a; CK 12: 5430-31) under the identical title of "chumo xinzhou 除魔心咒." The *Jinyu baojing* is a spirit writing scripture from the altar of Jiang Yuanting originally published in Jiang Yuanting's *Quanshu zhengzong* 全書正宗 (4.27a–47a).

[261] This scripture corresponds to the *Lüdi xinjing* 呂帝心經, which also forms part of the *Wujing hebian* 五經合編 (室集 4, 4a–5a; CK 12:5418–19). It was originally published in Shao Zhilin, *Lüzu quanshu* in 64 juan (j. 21.1a–2b) under the title *Fuyou dijun xinjing* 孚佑帝君心經 and later included in Jiang Yuanting, *Quanshu zhengzong* (4.1a–3a). The same scripture, under the title of "Fuyou shangdi Chunyang Lüzu tianshi xinjing 孚佑上帝純陽呂祖天師心經," is reproduced in the *Qingwei hongfan daomen gongke* 清微宏範道門功課 (張集 1, 8b–9b; CK 23: 10217) attributed to the same immortal Liu Shouyuan: it is part of a series of scriptures to be recited during the morning liturgy 早壇功課.

Immortality" 道祖無極上咒。以為天仙金丹符券。"[262] This invocation is accompanied by the recitation of the *Wuji zhidao chongxu taimiao jinyu xuanjing* 無極至道沖虛太妙金玉玄經 (a scripture attributed to Lü Dongbin and included in the old *Daozang jiyao*).[263]

While the first two scriptures—both recited in the Song Huanglu zhai 黃籙齋 (see *Lingbao wujing tigang* 靈寶五經提綱, DZ 529)—are respectively part of the Tang-era Lingbao 靈寶 and Song-era Qingwei 清微 legacies preserved in the *Daozang* (DZ 620 and DZ 13), the latter two scriptures are the fruit of Lü Dongbin's spirit writing revelations connected to his altar networks. With regard to the invocations it can be said that, apart from the first one found in a Southern Song (1127–79) text from the *Daozang* (*Sanhuang neiwen yibi* 三皇內文遺祕, DZ 856, 2a) linked to the earlier *Sanhuang wen* 三皇文 legacy, the remaining three invocations stem from scriptures connected with Jiang Yuanting's spirit writing altar.

Traces of a similar ritual consisting of the recitation of invocations and scriptures (*chisong yishi* 持誦儀式)[264] as well as the observance of codes and precepts (*jielü*) under the supervision of Tianjun 天君 (i.e., Wang Lingguan) are preserved in the famous *Secret of the Golden Flower* (*Jinhua zongzhi* 金華宗旨, see Part Four) under the name of "Jinhua keyi 金華科儀." Thanks to this we get an idea of the manner in which spirit writing groups elaborated their rituals of initiation at their spirit writing altars in Jiangnan at the beginning of the Qing era. During such a ceremony, the master of initiation (*dushi* 度師) conferred a lineage name (*faming* 法名) to his initiates while transmitting the history of the origins of his lineage (開宗闡教, 宗教源流), its founding patriarchs, a lineage poem 派詩, and so on.[265]

---

[262] 乾坤浩蕩、日月光盈、三台朗照、應地安貞、玉都師相、呂聖真君、大慈大憫、大德大仁、十方三界、六道四生、遇緣斯化、有感必靈、天神拱衛、威將隨行、大災急難、永化微塵、仙宗玄教、耀古騰今、太虛無極、聚象成形、口口存道、存道道存、存乎至道、慧炬常明、邪魔遠遁、災障無侵、修持匪懈、道果圓成。急急如天仙肇派、純陽道祖律令。This "supreme invocation" 無極上咒 is found in the *Chanfa daguan* 懺法大觀 (CK 21:9406–07) where it lacks the two last verses (急急如天仙肇派、純陽道祖律令).

[263] This text is also quoted in its entirety in the *Xuanzong zhengzhi* 玄宗正旨 (斗集4, 15a–b ; CK 8: 3053).

[264] For a detailed description of the ritual of recitation *chisong yishi* 持誦儀式 in relation to the *Taishang yuhuang benxin jing* 太上玉皇本行集經 see Yoshioka Yoshitoyo 吉岡義豐, *Dōkyō no jittai* 道教の実態, pp. 253–264.

[265] Monica Esposito, "Shindai ni okeru Kingaisan Ryūmonha no seiritsu to Kinka

Chapter 3: The Search for the Perfect Precepts   145

The *Tianxian dajie* and its last invocation, which portrays the Tianxian pai and its founding patriarch Lü Dongbin 呂洞賓[266] as representative of the Mysterious Doctrine of the Tradition of Immortals (*xianzong* 仙宗玄教), suggest that the ceremony for the conferral of the *Tianxian jie* follows a similar blueprint. The Master presiding over the ordination altar, here Liu Shouyuan, before conferring the Tianxian jie, re-enacts the history of its tradition of immortals 仙宗. From his seat of honor (*zhengzuo* 正座) he introduces, after Yuanshi tianzun's transmission, the Daoist pantheon and its related lineage by recounting, as is typical of a religious reformer, the three-stage-scenario of Golden Age, degeneration, and regeneration. He begins his discourse as follows:

> My disciples, what is it that you call "this affair"? This body and mind are not the [ordinary] body and mind, this Nature and Life are not the [ordinary] Nature and Life, this practice and merits are not the [ordinary] practice and merits. When words and discourses on the Way are cut off, one realizes by knowing perfect enlightenment that there is nothing to attain.
>
> 諸法子,你道這事是什麼事。是身心非身心、是性命非性命、是功修非功修。語言道斷、惟證乃知圓滿菩提、真無所得。

After this introduction, the immortal Liu Shouyan 柳守元 lays out his transmission and lineage scenario, beginning with the Golden Age (emphases are of course mine):

> Fortunately, the wondrous Way was transmitted continuously from Sanqing Daozu, Yudi zhizun, Five Ancient Lords (Wulao),[267] Four

---

shūshi 清代における金蓋山龍門派の成立と金華宗旨". As I emphasized in that study and in Part Four below, it is worthy of note that in an initiation ritual called "Jinhua keyi" that was performed in the Taiyi branch (Taiyi fapai 太乙法派), there were spirit writing lineages whose legacies are linked to Jingming and do not belong to Southern and Northern Lineages. Qiu Chuji is presented as Principal of the Quanzhen tradition 全真宗主, whereas Ma Danyang 馬丹陽 is called an attendant of Shenxiao 神霄侍宸. For the transmission of genealogical charts of masters received during Daoist clerical ordinations, see "Ti shoushou tu" 題授受圖 (*Yuanyang zi fayu* 原陽子法語, DZ 1071, 1.12a–b) and Kristofer Schipper, "Master Chao I-chen 趙宜真(?–1382) and the Ch'ing-wei 清微 School of Taoism," p. 727.

266 "急急如天仙肇派、純陽道祖律令."

267 The Five Ancient Lords (Wulao 五老), known from imperial ritual and from Han "weft texts" (weishu 緯書), control each of the five sections and ensure the safe passage of the texts' recipients through the calamities of the end-times, which are

Sovereigns (Siyu),²⁶⁸ Jiuji Shihua to the sages of the antiquity and the lofty Perfected. *The transmission of the wondrous Way began with Donghua shizu, Zhengyang dijun. Luckily, the transmission came down to Fuyou dijun, the First Patriarch of the Tianxian who opened the Southern and Northern Lineages.* The five Southern lineages manifested and once their spirits communicated with the Dao and its Virtue, they began to be actualized via an assiduous practice. The seven Northern lineages eliminated the worldly worries and cared for the day of attaining the Dao persisting in their intention from the beginning to the end without release. *In realizing their own final goal, each differed in being fast or slow, gradual or sudden but without need of creating divisions or distinguishing factions or currents.*

賴我三清道祖、玉帝至尊、五老四御、九極十華、以及古聖高真。遞傳妙道、肇啟我東華始祖、正陽帝師。幸逮天仙初祖孚佑帝君、得啟南北宗派、南五宗得顯、神通於德道之後、其始實刻苦功修、北七宗、打塵勞於成道之日、其志自始終無懈。成就歸宿、各有遲速、頓漸支流派演、無須別戶分門。

Then Liu turns to a description of the dire situation of the era and explains his own vocation and role in the Age of Degeneration (emphases are mine):

In these days many are those who become monks but few those who transcend the dust of the world. As for the prominent Daoist priests and lofty Daoist teachings, it is not only hard to have a look at their esoteric teachings, but also impossible to have a way of training. Our Fuyou dijun [Lü Dongbin], the First Patriarch, continuously following the edict of the Sanqing, saves this entire world showing mercy by thousands of means while guiding people in hundreds of directions. *Today he especially ordered me* [i.e., Liu Shouyuan] *to transmit and present in this world the esoteric teachings of the Tianxian dajie in order to establish the three altars and complete the merits.* All of you disciples, concentrate your spirit and listen attentively!

近來出家者多、出塵者少、煌煌羽士、巍巍玄門、非特奧秘難窺、亦且修持無路。我天仙初祖孚佑帝君、屢荷三清

---

graphically described. See Stephen Bokenkamp, "Wupian zhenwen." In *The Encyclopedia of Taoism*, ed. by F. Pregadio. London / New York: Routledge (2008), vol. 2: 1060–1062.

²⁶⁸ Four Sovereigns (siyu 四御), namely, Yuhuang 玉皇, Taihuang 太皇, Tianhuang 天皇, and Tuhuang 土皇.

法敕、普濟塵寰、千計垂慈、百方接引。今特命予、將天
仙大戒秘旨、傳示人間、以作三壇圓滿功德、諸法子一志
凝神諦聽。

Like the immortal Liu Shouyuan, the late Qing Quanzhen Longmen abbots (*fangzhang* 方丈) also re-actualized the history of their lineage during the performance of this highest ordination at their public altar of ordination (*jietan* 戒壇). At the image of their first Longmen Vinaya abbot at Baiyun guan, Wang Changyue, they introduced themselves as the direct heirs of Qiu Chuji within the so-called "orthodox lineage of celestial immortals" (*tianxian zhengmai* 天仙正脈)—a line purportedly transmitted without the slightest interruption from Qiu Chuji (Changchun) until the present:

> From our Ancestor [Qiu] Changchun, the heart-seal of the Celestial Immortals was secretly transmitted to the Perfected Zhao Jingxu [i.e., the first Longmen Vinaya patriarch], and after him it was reciprocally transmitted within the assembly of saints until today. (…) Today, the orthodox line of the Tianxian at the present altar is conferred upon you.
>
> 自我長春老祖以此天仙心印密傳盧靜趙真人、自此後聖眾相傳以及于今年。…今天仙正脈當壇付汝。[269]

The genealogy of these purported heirs of Qiu Chuji is recounted following the line of ancestral Longmen Vinaya patriarchs worshiped at the Beijing Baiyun guan Memorial Hall (*citang* 祠堂) and reaches from the first Longmen Vinaya patriarch Zhao Xujing 趙虛靜律師 (Zhao Daojian) until the present.[270] Such a religious pedigree, inscribed in the "dharma scrolls"

---

[269] See the *Xuandu lütan weiyi jieke quanbu* 玄都律壇威儀戒科全部 (Wang Ka 王卡 and Wang Guiping 汪桂平 2005:11.84). This manuscript, copied by Fang Yongqian 房永謙 in 1874 同治十三年, records the discourse that an abbot should pronounce at his altar of ordination (here at Beijing Baiyun guan) before the recitation of the *Tianxian dajie*. See also Yan Yonghe, *Yinli guize*, p. 54b. This ordination ritual clearly re-enacts the moment when the founding patriarch of the Longmen Vinaya Qiu Chuji allegedly transmitted the precept method to the first Longmen Vinaya Patriarch Zhao Xujing 趙虛靜 (alias Daojian 道堅). As recorded in the *Jingai xindeng* 金蓋心燈, this act was also staged during the transmission of the precept method 戒法 from the sixth Longmen Vinaya Patriarch Zhao Fuyang 趙復陽 (alias Zhensong 真嵩) to the seventh Longmen Vinaya patriarch Wang Changyue. See Monica Esposito, "The Longmen School and its Controversial History," pp. 628–29, 649, 653–54 {*Facets of Qing Daoism*, pp. 67–68, 93–94, 98–100}, and above notes 177 and 193.

[270] See the section "祖堂奉師法座" in the *Xuandu lütan weiyi jieke quanbu* 玄都律壇

法卷/法簡, was at the end of this ordination finally conferred upon the most qualified ordinands destined to become in their turn abbots with the power to re-enact at their own ordination altar this purportedly uninterrupted Longmen Vinaya legacy.²⁷¹

Fig. 15: Qiuzu dian 邱祖殿 (Hall of Patriarch Qiu Chuji) at Baiyun guan

Like initiates of spirit writing altars (*fuluantan* 扶鸞壇) who received a lineage name from their initiation master (*dushi* 度師), the ordinands at this highest ordination altar (*jietan* 戒壇) of the Tianxian also obtained a new lineage name that falls in line with their ordination master (*chuanjie lüshi* 傳戒律師).²⁷² Quanzhen Longmen Vinaya masters, in administering

---

威儀戒科全部 (Wang Ka 王卡 and Wang Guiping 汪桂平 eds., 2005:11.51–52). For a comparison of the "祖堂奉師法座" with the Ancestral Hall of the Baiyun guan see Oyanagi Shigeta 小柳司氣太, *Hakuunkan shi* 白雲觀志, pp. 31–34.

²⁷¹ Igarashi Kenryū 五十嵐賢隆, *Taiseikyū shi* 太清宮志, pp. 58–75. Yoshioka Yoshitoyo 吉岡義豊 (*Dōkyō no jittai* 道教の実態, p. 404) states that the *fajian* 法簡 were given to the first two adepts qualified to become abbots.

²⁷² See the first page of the *Tianxian dajie* text which records the ordination certifi-

the Tianxian precepts according to the *Tianxian dajie*, even took on the title "Generation so-and-so of the orthodox lineage of celestial immortals" (*tianxian zhengzong* 天仙正宗).273 In this creative manner the late Qing Longmen abbots (*Longmen fangzhang* 龍門方丈) inserted themselves into the ortodox blood-line of Celestial Immortals (*tianxian zhengmai* 天仙正脈), a lineage that corresponded for them to the Quanzhen Longmen Vinaya tradition 全真龍門律宗, that is, the "Ur-Vinaya" tradition of Qiu Chuji supposedly re-actualized by Wang Changyue in 1656 at the Baiyun guan ordination altar.

By contrast, in the eyes of the spirit writing immortal (*jixian* 乩仙) Liu Shouyuan who is said to have inherited the Tianxian lineage (*tianxian fapai* 天仙法派) from its founding patriarch Lü Dongbin 呂洞賓, his tradition is not a sectarian manifestation such as the "Quanzhen Longmen" but rather an expression of "Ur-Daoism," that is, the true bloodline of genuine Daoism.274 Hence Liu has his transmission narrative in the *Tianxian dajie* end in the august presence of three original masters: Lü Dongbin 呂洞賓 as the central master; Liu Haichan 劉海蟾 as the patriarch of the Southern

---

cate conferred in 1873 at Beijing Baiyun guan to Wang Xinzhi 王信祉. On that occasion, Wang's name was changed to Wang Yuanzhi 王元祉, which shows that he became the 19th-generation Longmen heir (the character 元 stands for 圓) according to the Longmen lineage poem. See Wang Ka 王卡 and Wang Guiping 汪桂平 2005:11.149. See also the ordination certificates reproduced in Hackmann's materials and Fig. 13 here above (p. 130).

273 Wang Ka 王卡 and Wang Guiping 汪桂平 eds., *Sandong shiyi* 三洞拾遺 vol. 11, p. 54, and Igarashi Kenryū 五十嵐賢隆, *Taiseikyū shi* 太清宮志, p. 121.

274 As Liu allegedly revealed in the closing formula (*shouzan* 收贊) of the morning service 早功課 of his *Qingwei hongfan daomen gongke* 清微宏範道門功課 (張集 1, 11a; CK 23: 10218), it is only thanks to the direct transmission of the Celestial Immortal Lineage—whose spirit writing altar, visited by all immortals and gods, "is full of auspices"—that "Quanzhen will enact its [orthodox] teaching and Zhengyi will perform the [correct] liturgy" (全真演教、正一垂科、天仙法派吉祥多). Jiang Yuanting and his congregants (i.e., the creators of the Tianxian dajie) wanted to re-establish an authentic Daoist path. This path was put under the supervision of the Tianxian lineage via its own patriarchal immortals who transcend both Quanzhen and Zhengyi. In their standardized view, Zhengyi was in charge of spreading the correct liturgy and Quanzhen of implementing the correct teaching. Of course it was up to Lü Dongbin to define, via Jiang Yuanting's spirit writing and the mediation of Liu Shouyuan, what "correct" or "orthodox" (*zheng* 正) truly means. See Monica Esposito (莫尼卡), "Yibu Quanzhen Daozang de faming: Daozang jiyao ji Qingdai Quanzhen rentong 一部全真道藏的發明：道藏輯要及清代全真認同," 317–19 {revised English version here below, Part Three, pp. 170–171}.

150 PART TWO: CREATION OF ORDINATION

Lineages; and Wang Chongyang 王重陽 as the patriarch of the Northern lineages. These three masters, who form part of the Lineage of Immortals (*xianzong* 仙宗) of Wu Shouyang,[275] are here called upon as witnesses approving the vows conferred to the new Tianxian ordinands and finally sealing the "three-altar ordination":

> All of you disciples, you should know that the Southern and Northern Lineages of our Daoist school all stem from the time when Chunyang miaodao da tianzun [i.e., Lü Dongbin 呂洞賓] opened the Tianxian fapai and transmitted widely. Today the right time has arrived for you to know that for the achievement of the three altars, the Lord Emperor Sustaining the Nine Heavens 九天扶正帝君 [i.e., Liu Haichan 劉海蟾] and the Celestial Worthy of Wondrous Transformations of Flying Rain 飛雨妙化天尊 [i.e., Wang Chongyang 王重陽][276] all came to assist Emperor Lü [Dongbin 呂洞賓] on his right and left, and to inform you about the profound fortune of previous world-ages (kalpas) and the light obstacles of the present one that enable your entry into the School of Mystery (Daoism).

> 諸法子、當如我道門、南北兩宗、皆由純陽妙道大天尊、垂慈開啟天仙法派、廣化普傳。今日時節因緣、三壇圓滿、當知九天扶正帝君、飛雨妙化天尊、皆來輔弼呂帝左右、證知爾等前劫福深、現生障淺、得入玄門。

This announcement is followed by a detailed description of the wondrous effects of this "entry into the School of Mystery" on the ordinands:

> Capable of transcending heaven due to the repeated recitation of the esoteric invocations and to another exposition of the Golden scriptures,

---

[275] Compare this passage with *Xianfo hezong yulu* 仙佛合宗語錄, 畢集 1, 1.85a and 1.108b (CK 17: 7445 and 7456). While Wu Shouyang's Xianzong 仙宗 claims to represent the Northern lineage (Beizong)—the authentic lineage of Qiu Chuji and Wang Chongyang—, Jiang Yuanting adopts a conciliatory view by presenting his Tianxian lineage as the source of Nanzong and Beizong which transcends all divisions and thus is capable of supervising the correct implementation of Daoist teachings in the world both for Quanzhen and Zhengyi. See also note 274 above.

[276] These two titles appear only in the spirit writing scriptures revealed at Jiang Yuanting's altar and are used for Liu Haichan 劉海蟾, the alleged founder of the Southern Lineage, and Wang Chongyang 王重陽, the alleged founder of the Northern Lineage; see *Qingwei hongfan daomen gongke* 清微宏範道門功課 (張 1, 29a–b; CK 23: 10227) attributed to Liu Shouyuan. See also the statement in the *Chanfa daguan* 懺法大觀 (柳 5, 5.66a; CK 21: 9423): "南宗啟教九天扶正帝君、北宗啟教飛雨妙化天尊."

all will respectfully implore our Chunyang Daozu Miaodao tianzun 純陽道祖妙道大天尊. In silence you will be accorded the numinous elixir that universally reveals the light of Wisdom, thus strengthening everybody's resolve to keep in mind the Way and stabilizing forever the true basis [of practice]. The virtue of the precepts is accomplished, the light of the precepts is bright and limpid, the substance of the precepts is clear and pure, the pearl of the precepts is perfectly round and bright, opening widely the unique rules established by Daoist schools that deserve the name of Quanzhen zhengjiao 全真正教 (Quanzhen orthodox teachings).

堪超碧落、所以重宣秘咒、兩啟金經、無非仰祈我純陽道祖妙道大天尊。默錫靈丹、普垂慧照、俾人人克堅道念、令個個永固真基。戒德完成、戒光明澈、戒體清淨、戒珠圓明、宏開道派宗風，足稱全真正教。

At this point the ordinands are asked to take refuge and recite the precious titles (大眾同聲宣揚寶誥) of the Tianxian pai's founding patriarch Lü Dongbin, their primal master of initiation, and this recitation concludes the ceremony.[277]

Thanks to the intervention of Lü Dongbin via the intermediary Liu Shouyuan, this ordination could be finally revealed to the world and an authentic monastic path for contemporary Daoist clergy could at last be restored. Because "in these days, those who become monks are many but those who transcend the dust of this world are few" 近來出家者多、出

---

[277] 玉清內相、金闕選仙、化身爲三教之師、掌法判五雷之令、黃粱夢覺、忘世上之功名、寶劍光騰、掃人間之妖怪、四生六道、有感必孚、三界十方、有求必應、黃鶴樓中留聖蹟、玉盧殿內煉丹砂、存芝像於山崖、顯仙踪於雲洞、闡法門之香火、作玄嗣之梯航、大聖大慈、大仁大孝、開山啟教、元應祖師、天雷上相、靈寶真人、純陽演正警化孚佑帝君興行妙道天尊. This was originally included in the *Lüzu quanshu* as one of the formulas of refuge (至心皈命禮) of the "Precious Announcements of Fuyou dijun" 孚佑帝君寶誥. These invocations contain not only the canonical titles of Lü Dongbin but also his attributes along with elements of his hagiography. They form part of the liturgy in honor of Lü Dongbin that many texts of the old *Daozang jiyao* also feature in abridged form. See for instance *Taiwei dijun sanbu bajing huiyuan jing* 太微帝君三部八景回元經 in *Yuanshi dadongyu jing* 元始大洞玉經 (CK 3: 1127-74); *Taishang ganyingpian fu chisong yize* 太上感應篇附持誦儀則 (*Taishang ganyingpian jianzhu* 太上感應篇箋註), CK 6: 2269; *Jiuhuang doulao jiesha yansheng zhenjing* 九皇斗姥說戒殺延生真經 (CK 7: 2898); *Fuyou dijun baogao* 孚佑帝君寶誥 (*Shiliupin jing* 十六品經), CK 12: 5294; *Chanfa daguan* 懺法大觀 (CK 21: 9441); *Qingwei hongfan daomen gongke* 清微宏範道門功課 (CK 23: 10227).

塵者少,²⁷⁸ Liu Shouyuan in his role as Lü Dongbin's envoy is put in charge of revealing, via spirit writing, the ideal and orthodox Daoist monastic path and its related liturgy. ²⁷⁹ It is only via the revelation of the second Tianxian Patriarch Liu Shouyuan that an ideal and universal "Quanzhen" could establish itself: one that truly "deserves the name of *Quanzhen zhengjiao* 足稱全真正教" (lit., "orthodox teaching of complete truth").

In comparison with the *Chuzhen jielü* and the *Zhongji jie*, which were still linked to Daoist clerical institutions, the *Tianxian dajie* is associated with lay spirit writing groups. The highest ordination of Celestial Immortals (Tianxian) that enabled access to the abbotship and to the title of "Vinaya master"—a title conferred upon the person with the exclusive power to establish an altar of ordination in the Quanzhen public monasteries—was, it turns out, in reality derived from an initiation ceremony (*kaidu* 開度) created and performed by lay members at spirit writing altars. These lay members were not at all associated with Quanzhen institutions but rather with Zhengyi 正一.

Finally, it is no cause of surprise that Jiang Yuanting 蔣元庭 (alias Jiang Yupu 蔣予蒲, 1755–1819) in his canon positioned this scripture before the two precept-texts *Chuzhen jielü* and *Zhongji jie*. In Jiang's eyes this scripture, reproducing as it does the ceremony of initiation for elite members at spirit writing altars, represented "the perfection of the three altars 三壇圓滿," the highest spiritual ordination comparable to the Bodhisattva precepts in Chan Buddhism. Despite a supposedly ancient tradition of "Quanzhen" ordination procedures performed by its patriarch Qiu Chuji in the Yuan era, Quanzhen late clerical institutions adopted such a spirit writing altar initiation procedure in order to ensure the legitimacy of their abbots in performing "Quanzhen ordinations" at Quanzhen public monasteries.

---

²⁷⁸ *Tianxian dajie*, 3b (CK 24: 10458).

²⁷⁹ Liu also authored a number of prefaces and postfaces included in the Daozang jiyao along with a scripture on monastic liturgy, the *Qingwei hongfan daomen gongke* 清微宏範道門功課 (CK 23: 10213–35).

Fig. 16: Ordination Platform (*jietan* 戒壇) at Beijing's Baiyun guan (Zhongguo daojiao xiehui, 1983)

Chapter 4

The Manufacture of Quanzhen Ordination

Our presentation of the content and analysis of the background of the three precept-texts clearly showed the lack of evidence for a "Quanzhen clerical identity" with regard to the three-stage ordination that was allegedly established by Wang Changyue at Beijing's Baiyun guan in 1656. The *Chuzhen jielü* 初真戒律 attributed to Wang Changyue appears to be a compilation of earlier Daoist texts (mostly from the early Heavenly Masters 天師道 and Lingbao 靈寶) intermingled with more innovative sections or passages that sometimes contain contradictory information. This suggests that the text was not the product of a single author. While some parts refer to an ordination system for all Daoist priests integrating earlier Daoist traditions and different sets of precepts (where the earlier Lingbao tripartite ordination is still central and the ceremony for the conferral of the precepts still takes place in the context of the Lingbao "sanyuan zhai" 靈寶三元齋), other parts standardize and simplify the procedure according to what later came to be known as "santan dajie" 三壇大戒. In the parts proposing standardized sets of precepts one also finds quotations from scriptures that originated after Wang's death and are apparently related to the spirit writing altar of Jiang Yuanting 蔣元庭 (1755–1819).

With regard to the *Zhongji jie* 中極戒 we have seen that it is mostly derived from the earlier Shangqing text (DZ 1364) with slight modifications in the formulation of some precepts, especially in the first series of one hundred and eighty precepts. The relatively innovative parts are found at the end of the text where one finds four invocations from the earlier work of Zhao Yizhen 趙宜真 (d. 1382) dealing with the ordination of his disciples—an ordination modeled on the capping rite which has nothing to do with Quanzhen or with its presumed special "guanjin keyi" 冠巾科儀

(see here below). Since this text is for the most part a recasting of the sixth-century *Shangqing dongzhen zhihui guanshen dajie wen* 上清洞真智慧觀身大戒文 (DZ 1364), it is difficult to establish its authorship. However, a new name in the final part ("Taishang menxia Miaode zhenren") appears to allude to Wang Changyue's legacy of the three new ranks and in particular to the title of "Miaode shi" 妙德師 (Master of Wondrous Virtue).

With regard to the *Tianxian dajie* 天仙大戒 we can say that this text is a product of spirit writing from the altar of Jiang Yuanting 蔣元庭 whose creative aspects we already analyzed.

Another topic of interest is the emergence in all of these materials of Shenxiao protector Wang Lingguan 王靈官, the deity in charge of monitoring the ordinands (and guardian of all Daoist monasteries), as the guiding spirit in matters of discipline and precepts for both Daoist laypersons and clergy. Such a role does not derive from Quanzhen but was originally connected with Shenxiao. Wang Lingguan's fame was probably enhanced due to the imperial support for his cult during the reign of Ming emperor Yongle 永樂 (re. 1402–24).[280] A study is yet to be made of the progressive rise of Wang Lingguan from the group of *lingguan* 靈官 (who had since the earlier Tang supervised ordination)[281] to the status of a distinct and anthropomorphic protector to whom initiates or ordinands would offer their vows.

At any rate, the overall aim of the *Chuzhen jielü*'s compilers, as formulated in its prefaces, is to establish Wang Changyue as the creator of this Daoist reform ordination in three stages with all its apparent innovations.[282]

---

[280] See the article by Zhang Guangbao 張廣保 in Xun Liu & Vincent Goossaert (eds), *Quanzhen Daoism in Modern Chinese History and Society*. Berkeley: Institute of East Asian Studies (2014).

[281] See *Chuanshou sandong jing jiefa lulüe shuo* 傳授三洞經戒法籙略說 (DZ 1241) juan 2, and Catherine Despeux, "L'ordination des femmes taoïstes sous les Tang," *Études chinoises* V, no. 1–2 (1986): 53–100, here 75–76.

[282] In this context it is of interest to consult the "Biography of the Vinaya master Huang Chongyang" 黃冲陽律師傳 in the *Jingai xindeng* 金蓋心燈 (2.30a–32b). As a disciple of Wang Changyue, Huang allegedly came to Beijing and received the three series of precepts: "一日、隋雲眾進演祇堂、王糾察現（即天王君、其諭文有都天糾察大靈官之號、故稱天糾察）." As we can see, Wang Lingguan is mentioned with the same title (都天糾察) as in the *Chuzhen jielü* (section 三皈依戒: "一、皈依道、經、師之三皈依"). The same title is also used at the spirit writing altar of Jiang Yuanting 蔣元庭 in his text *Qingwei hongfan daomen gongke* 清微宏範道門功課 (張集 1, 34a; CK 23: 10230). Other innovative parts of the *Chuzhen jielü* that are clearly associated with Wang Changyue are *Kunyang lüshi*

However, neither in the *Chuzhen jielü* nor in other texts attributed to Wang Changyue (such as the *Longmen xinfa* and *Biyuan tanjing*) do we find any mention of a division in three altars or use of the term "Santan dajie" for this ordination system.

With regard to the presumed Quanzhen clerical identity connected with this ordination system via its alleged creator "Wang," it is surprising that—apart from the *Qiuzu chanhui wen* 邱祖懺悔文 (a text recorded in the *Daozang jiyao* of the Jiaqing era and used in late Quanzhen monastic liturgy 功課)—one does not find any scripture specifically associated with Quanzhen. The same can be said for the set of precepts. Despite the fame and long-standing tradition of discipline attributed to Quanzhen and its patriarchs, no trace is found of the transmission of such sets of precepts in the early Quanzhen school.²⁸³ Texts with a Quanzhen connection are conspicuous for their absence; these include the *Chongyang lijiao shiwu lun* 重陽立教十五論 (DZ 1233 [26/021]) offering "Quanzhen" behavioral guidelines; Quanzhen texts such as the *Zhenxian zhizhi yulu* 真仙直指語錄 (DZ 1256 [27/003]) featuring the set of ten admonitions associated with Ma Danyang 馬丹陽 (1123–1183); or the *Xianle ji* 仙樂集 (DZ 1141 26 / 034) including the precepts associated with Liu Chuxuan 劉處玄 (1147–1203). Even more surprising is the fact that no mention or use is made of the famous *Pure Rules of Complete Perfection* (*Quanzhen qinggui* 全真清規, DZ 1235, 27 / 035). The only items that might remind of it are a reference in the *Chuzhen jielü* to a 100-day ordination period (*jieqi* 戒期) and the occurrence of expressions related to the monastic bowl 缽.

With regard to the training period, the *Chuzhen jielü* in its section "Rujie yaogui" 入戒要規 refers to it as *rula* 入臘. In contrast to the 14th-century *Quanzhen qinggui* 全真清規 (DZ 1235), the training focuses on the practice of precepts. Such training appears to have taken place *after* the conferral of the precepts and not before, as was the case in the late Qing adaptation of this ordination system. There, ordinands were asked to devote themselves to specific practices according to the series of precepts they had *already* received:

> Those who have entered the ordination-retreat and received the Precepts of the Celestial Immortality should recite the *Daodejing*

---

fuzhu jie 崑陽律師付囑偈 and the transmission of the Nine Precepts for Women *Nü zhen jiujie* 女眞九戒.

²⁸³ On these precepts see Louis Komjathy, *Cultivating Perfection: Mysticism and Self-transformation in Early Quanzhen Daoism* (Leiden: Brill, 2007), pp. 148–57.

for the total period of one hundred days. Each morning [between 3 and 5 a.m.] they should practice devotion and bow ten times in the ten directions. Between 11 a.m. and 1 p.m. they should practice quiet sitting and inner contemplation without being concerned with personal matters until they have accomplished the purification of the three activities [i.e, word, thought, and body].

入臘領受天仙戒者、持道德經一百日。每於寅刻、信禮十方、共十拜。子午二時靜坐內觀、不關人事、致三業清靜。

Those who have received the Precepts of the Medium Ultimate should every day between 9 and 11 a.m first offer obeisance at the feet of the Vinaya Master. After that they should rise to bow and recite the *Chaotian chan* 朝天懺 and the *Lingbao dachan* 靈寶大懺 for the overall period of one hundred days. Once the repentance recitations are completed they should practice cessation and stillness.

中極戒者、每日巳刻、先禮足律師。然後起拜朝天懺、併靈寶大懺、共一百日。懺畢止靜。

Those who have received the Precepts of the Initial Perfection should every day between 9 and 11 a.m. first offer obeisance at the feet of the Vinaya Master. After that they should rise to bow and recite the *Youzui fachan* 宥罪法懺 for the overall period of one hundred days. Once the repentance recitations are completed, they should practice cessation and stillness.

初真戒者、每日巳刻、先禮足律師。然後起拜宥罪法懺一百日、懺畢止靜已。

The training program does not contain any clear reference to a communal practice such as the *zuobo* 坐缽 described in the *Pure Rules*. Only the persons who have received the Tianxian jie are asked to focus on "quiet sitting and introspection 靜坐內觀"—Daoist meditative and individual practices predating Quanzhen—while the recipients of the *Chuzhen jie* or the *Zhongji jie* appear to be rather busy performing liturgical activities. "Once the repentance recitations are completed, they should practice cessation and stillness 懺畢止靜已."[284] There is, however, a passage in the section

---

[284] In its description of ordination training, the late manual *Xuandu lütan weiyi jieke quanbu* 玄都律壇威儀戒科全部 (Wang Ka 王卡 and Wang Guiping 汪桂平 eds., *Sandong shiyi* 三洞拾遺 11:44) refers, besides the daily liturgical training, also to meditation training with the use of incense sticks.

entitled 玄門持戒威儀 (47a) that appears to refer to a training period in the so-called Botang (Bowl Hall):

> Only those who have entered the Bowl Hall to cultivate mind and body and observed the Precepts of the Medium Ultimate for three years should receive the Precepts of the Celestial Immortals.
>
> 已入鉢堂修煉身心、及行持中極戒、歷三年者、方受天仙戒。

As is known, the Botang was a place associated with Quanzhen monastic institutions, and more specifically with the establishment of intensive communal meditation practice similar to what in Japanese Zen Buddhism is referred to as *sesshin* 摂心 in a meditation hall (*zendō* 禅堂). This communal meditation practice, which came to be central in the construction of "Quanzhen identity" during the Yuan, was performed in a hall at whose center a bowl used as a clepsydra was placed.[285] The Botang and its regulated practice, known as "*zuobo* 坐鉢," came to be progressively integrated in Daoist monastic practice also outside Quanzhen networks, and during the Ming it was also associated with Daoist monastic training supervised by Celestial Masters. In the end it came to be regarded as a Daoist patrimony of ascetic practices that was also widely adopted and promoted by schools such as Zhengyi, Jingming, etc.[286]

It is difficult to know to which extent the term "Botang" in the abovementioned passage of the *Chuzhen jielü* refers to the Quanzhen system as described in the *Pure Rules*. It is certainly legitimate to wonder if the term "Botang" might in the course of the time also have taken on other meanings. In this context it may be useful to draw attention to another term,

---

[285] See the study by Goossaert, "La creation du Taoïsme moderne, l'ordre Quanzhen," (PhD thesis, Paris: École Pratique des Hautes Études, Section des Sciences Religieuses, 1997), pp. 220–258, and Mori Yuria, "Mingdai Quanzhendao yu zuobo 明代全真道于坐鉢" in Quanzhendao yanjiu zhongxin 全真道研究中心 ed., *Quanzhen hongdao ji* 全真弘道集 (Hong Kong: Qingsong chubanshe, 2004), pp. 126–142. In Chan and Zen meditation halls, incense sticks were used for the same purpose (keeping time of periods of still meditation).

[286] On the integration of this Quanzhen communal practice inside Celestial Masters institutions see Esposito, "The Longmen and its Controversial History," pp. 627–28, 637–40 {*Facets of Qing Daoism*, pp. 63–65, 80–82}, and also here below note 287. An important section dealing with Botang and *zuobo* is found in the *Tianhuang zhidao taiqing yuce* 天皇至道太清玉冊 (DZ 1483), a work by the Ming Jingming 淨明 master Zhu Quan 朱權 (fl. 1444), the seventeenth son of Ming emperor Taizu (r. 1368–1398).

namely *yanbo* 演缽, which is used a few more times in the *Chuzhen jielü* and may help us understand the evolution of Botang and its role during the ordination period 戒期. In the preface attributed to Wang Changyue (who is referred to as "Chuanjie daoshi" 傳戒道士) that was quoted at the beginning of our Part Two, "Wang" uses the term "*yanbo* 演缽" precisely in the passage of his auto-proclamation as the person responsible for establishing the ordination altar at Baiyun guan in 1656:

> Thus, without evading the crime of overstepping my authority and recklessly acting, on the fifteenth day of the third month of the *bingshen* year [1656], I lawfully established at Baiyun guan the ordination altar in order to transmit the precepts and perform the bowl [rite].

> 故不避僭妄之罪、按法於丙申歲三月望日、就白雲觀設立戒壇、傳戒演缽。

The same expression is used in another Preface to the *Chuzhen jielü* (dated 1674) where it is attributed to Long Qiqian 龍起潛, the alleged disciple of Wang Changyue alias Kunyang who received Wang's precepts in Wudang-shan:

> Master Wang Kunyang, after having during the reign of Shizu [Shunzhi 順治, r. 1644–1661] Zhang Huangdi [Shizu's posthumous name] obtained the precept method from the Perfected Zhao Fuyang, established the ordination altar at Beijing Baiyun guan and transmitted the precepts while performing the bowl [rite], conferring it at once to more than a thousand people.

> 崑陽王老師得戒法于复陽趙真人、當世祖章皇帝時、于京都白雲觀設立戒壇、傳戒演鉢、一時授受弟子千有余人。

Finally, in the above-quoted section on the "Basic Guidance for the Three Masters" (*sanshi yuanshuo* 三師原說) of the *Chuzhen jielü*, it is specified with regard to the duties of the Principal Master who transmits the precepts (*chuanjie benshi* 傳戒本師) that "after the [conferral] of the precepts, the [rite] of performing the bowl should be carried out for one hundred days 戒後行持演缽一百日."

As we can see, the expression *yanbo* 演缽 in the *Chuzhen jielü* is associated with Wang Changyue and his ordination procedure at Baiyun guan, but also with its re-enactment by the man who, after having received the Tianxian jie and inherited the title of "Chuanjie benshi," had the authority of opening the altar and transmitting the precepts (though still in the traditional context of the Lingbao sanyuan zhai 靈寶三元齋). Interestingly,

Chapter 4: The Manufacture of Quanzhen Ordination   161

the expression "yanbo" came also to be employed by late Qing Quanzhen reformers. Min Yide 閔一得 (1748/58–1836), the Longmen reformer of Jingaishan, used this expression in his work while describing the ordination ceremony of Wang Changyue at the Baiyun guan:

> It was between the Shunzhi 順治 (1644–1661) and Kangxi 康熙 (1662–1722) eras that the Vinaya Patriarch [Wang Changyue] opened five times the Hall for Performing the Bowl [rite] and conveyed the Taishang sandajie 太上三大戒 (Three Great Precepts of the Highest Lord). The disciples numbered more than three thousand.[287]
>
> [王常月] 律祖於順治康熙間五開演鉢堂、付授太上三大戒。弟子三千餘人。

The expression *yanbo* 演鉢 is also used for the establishment of the Baiyun guan ordination ceremony in other Quanzhen public monasteries such as the public monastery of Zhangliang miao 張良廟 in Shaanxi Liuba 陝西留壩:[288]

---

[287] *Huangji xianjing* 皇極仙經 in ZWDS 10:381. The term *yanbo* 演鉢 is also used by Min Yide in his *Jingai xindeng* (6A.1a–b) in connection with Jizu daozhe 雞足道者, a legendary disciple of Wang Changyue who reportedly visited Baiyun guan at the time when Wang Changyue was performing his ordination ceremony: "In 1660 when he (Jizu daozhe) first came to the capital, he visited [the hall] of the performance of the bowl" 順治庚子始至京師、觀光演鉢. For more on this and on the use of this term in Min Yide's works see Monica Esposito, "Shindai dōkyō to mikkyō 清代道教と密教," pp. 314–318 {*Facets of Qing Daoism*, Chapter 5, pp. 285–291}. There are many passages containing this term in the *Jingai xindeng* but also in local gazetteers. It is also found, more clearly associated with the Botang and with Qiu Chuji, in the work of the Longmen reformer Zhou Tailang 周太朗 (*zi* Xuan[Yuan]zhen 玄真, 1628–?). Before explaining the pure rules (*qinggui* 清規) that he established at his Jingudong 金鼓洞 of Hangzhou, he said: "Formerly, [Qiu] Changchun performed the correct teachings of the Hall of the Bowl, giving priority to the rules" 昔長春演鉢堂正教、規模為先. See the *Jingudong zhi* 金鼓洞志 4.29a (ZWDS 20: 254). A similar passage is also recorded by Min Yide: "長春演鉢堂之教、規模為先"; see in *Qinggui xuanmiao quanzhen canfang* 清規玄妙全眞參訪 (section 清規榜 29b; ZWDS 10: 612). On the history of Zhou Tailang and the foundation of his tradition originally linked with the Longmen line which he, according to the *Jingai xindeng* (2.25a), is said to have unified in Jiangnan with the Vinaya 律 line, see Monica Esposito, "La Porte du Dragon," vol. 1, 117–118. This master also refers to a tripartite division of the ordination system, but under the name of "three ultimate precepts (*sanji jie* 三極戒)."

[288] *Liuba miao kaishan yuanliu* 留侯廟開山源流, quoted in the manuscript by Fan Guangchun 樊光春 (now published as "Urban Daoism, Commodity Markets, and Tourism. The Restoration of the Xian City God Temple." In David A. Palmer and

A group of Daoists was advised to come to Beijing Baiyun guan and asked to present the dharma scrolls before reaching the Zhangliang miao on the tenth month of the fifth year *binyin* of the Tongzhi era [1866]. There, on an auspicious [day] of the autumnal period of the *xuchen* year (1868), the transmission of the precepts and performance of the bowl [rite] took place as training of body and mind.

道眾勸往京都白雲觀、請來法卷、同治五年歲次丙寅十月至廟、戊辰秋期之吉、傳戒演缽煉磨身心也。

These passages suggest that the term "Botang 缽堂" in conjunction with the expression *yanbo* 演缽 seems to have acquired a different meaning in the minds of late Qing Quanzhen reformers. A clue is furnished by the *Yinli guize*. The Chengdu Erxian'an abbot Yan Yonghe uses the expression *yanbo* 演缽 in the context of a specific ritual originally performed at the Baiyun guan in 1882 during the ordination supervised by abbot Gao Yunxi 高雲溪 (1841–1907). This ritual mainly involves concrete explanations about the Eight Trigrams bowl received at the ordination altar, for example on how to handle it and how to use it in different circumstances. The ordinands are also taught to observe specific precepts and recite specific invocations—allegedly transmitted by Wang Changyue and included in the *Chuzhen jielü*—connected with the daily ceremonial meal 食齋 and its etiquette 飲食威儀, for instance "the Invocation for receiving food into the empty bowl" 空缽受食咒, "the Invocation for the Living" 出生咒, the "Invocation when eating" 食齋咒, etc.[289]

We can see that we are a bit far from the meaning of Botang 缽堂 connected with *zuobo* 坐缽 as described in the 14th-century *Quanzhen qinggui* 全真清規 (DZ 1235). At the same time, the description of the "yanbo ritual" 演缽法 may help us understand why the Botang Hall, which was reportedly rebuilt at Baiyun guan in the 1700s, was related to the refectory 齋堂 rather than the residence for wandering monks 雲水居 that was also used as a communal meditation hall.[290] Such understanding apparently

---

Xun Liu [eds.], *Daoism in the Twentieth Century. Between Eternity and Modernity*. Berkeley: University of California Press, 2012: 108–122).

[289] Yan Yonghe, "迎師演缽法," in *Yinli guize*, 60b–63a. The invocations and precepts are found in the *Chuzhen jielü*, 43a–44b (CK 23: 10478) and 50b (CK 23: 10481).

[290] See "Chongxiu Baiyun guan beiji" attributed to Wang Changyue but dated 1706 (?) where it is stated that a "bowl-hall" was built in 1440 in the Baiyun guan before it was rebuilt in 1706 (Oyanagi Shigeta, BYGZ 白雲觀志, pp. 141–142): "正統五年 [1440] 建造玉皇閣、長春殿、及道舍缽堂 ... 今上重建玉皇殿、... 並缽堂

continued at Baiyun guan; when its Daoist priests 道士 are asked today about the location of the Botang, they often point to the refectory.[291]

In the context of the ordination procedure attributed to Wang and explained in the *Chuzhen jielü*, it appears rather clear that the Botang 鉢堂 and the related expression *yanbo* 演鉢 acquired new liturgical connotations not present in the earlier Quanzhen Pure Rites (*Quanzhen qinggui*). These new connotations show the necessity of re-examining Quanzhen history and its sources from new angles. This term may be an example of the ease with which we modern Quanzhen scholars tend to read Quanzhen history in the way Quanzhen apologists want us to read it, namely, by embracing their view of Quanzhen as a unique Daoist monastic tradition transmitted in an uninterrupted way from the Yuan until today.

We often tend to succumb to this because of the reputation of Quanzhen in matters of strict discipline, *neidan*, monastic institutions, and ordination procedures. Based on this, we are seduced into believing in a stable Quanzhen clerical identity from the Yuan until the present time thanks to the uninterrupted transmission and preservation of Quanzhen ascetic methods of cultivation, Quanzhen lineages, Quanzhen monastic institutional systems (*shifang conglin zhidu* 十方叢林制度), and specific Quanzhen ordination procedures (*chuanjie yishi* 傳戒儀式). The singularity of Quanzhen tends to be increasingly emphasized in present-day scholarship both in connection with and opposition to Zhengyi. Contrasts between Quanzhen and Zhengyi are often summarized by the oppositon of a strictly celibate Quanzhen clergy to a usually (but not necessarily) married Zhengyi (more precisely, Qingwei Lingbao) clergy. The first (Quanzhen) are described as having "collective ordination training and ritual" and "the taking of pre-

---

廚庫..." Compare this also with the "Baiyun guan chongxiu ji" 白雲觀重修記 by Hu Ying 胡濙 (1375–1463): "正統五年 (1440) ... 營方丈道舍、廚庫鉢堂, 以展四方修真之士." (Oyanagi Shigeta, BYGZ 白雲觀志, pp. 124–128). For the southern heritage of the Bowl Hall in Jiangnan at the public Chongyang'an 十方大重陽庵 of Hangzhou, which was established under the supervision of the 38th-generation Heavenly Master Zhang Yucai 張羽材 (r. 1295–1316), see *Chongyang'an ji* 重陽庵集 (ZWDS 20: 416). It is worthy of note that the institution of the Botang is here attributed to Qiu Chuji in person who allegedly established a Botang for wandering monks 雲水鉢堂 that served for both meditation and the housing of monks on pilgrimage ("坐鉢招雲水四眾闡教於此") during the Ruiping 瑞平 era of the Song (1234–36)—even though we know that Qiu already died in 1227 (ZWDS 10: 422).

[291] This was reported by Goossaert in his "La création du Taoïsme moderne," p. 247.

cepts" (*shoujie* 受戒), whereas the second (Qingwei Lingbao) is said to have "individual ordination" and "the reception of registers" (*shoulu* 受籙).²⁹²

The clear-cut contrast between Quanzhen and Zhengyi as expressions of two opposing systems of ordination that entail the fundamental distinction between celibate monks and married priests—a distinction that, as we know, did not exist in medieval Daoism in whose establishments celibate monks and married priests happily cohabited²⁹³—facilitates acceptance of the stories told time and again by the Qing reformers of Quanzhen. Omnipresent not only on paper but even set in stone, these tales effectively lionize the great Quanzhen patriarch Qiu Chuji, portraying him as the founder of China's Quanzhen public monastic institutional system 十方叢林制度 and as the founding patriarch of the Quanzhen monastic ordination system that supposedly was purely and directly transmitted to his Longmen Vinaya heirs.²⁹⁴ Despite such seemingly solid evidence that is preserved and cherished at today's "Vatican of Daoism," Beijing's Baiyun guan, I have so far been unable to locate any source that proves the existence of a specific and singular "Quanzhen ordination system" established in the Yuan and transmitted without interruption until the present day.²⁹⁵

Probably conscious of the lack of solid evidence, Quanzhen Daoist reformers often evoke a "conflagration scenario" involving the loss of Quanzhen precept-texts along with a "degeneration scenario" concerning its precept-method 戒法, both of which are intimately connected with (and necessarily lead to) the heroic intervention of Wang Changyue. As explained above, in the preface to the *Chuzhen jielü* attributed to Wang Changyue,

---

²⁹² These characteristics are enounced not only by Goossaert ("The Quanzhen Clergy 1700–1950," 701, and *Taoists of Peking*, 35–6) but have become commonplace in modern studies on Quanzhen on Daoism in general.

²⁹³ Livia Kohn, *Monastic Life in Medieval Daoism* (Honolulu: University of Hawai'i Press, 2003), p. 40.

²⁹⁴ See for instance the stela recorded in Oyanagi, BYGZ 白雲觀志, pp. 149, 158, 174–75.

²⁹⁵ Goossaert claims that during the Ming period "the ascetic tradition lived on, and Quanzhen monastic institutions and a part of Quanzhen's ordination [受度儀式] and consecration procedures [受戒儀式] survived under the benevolent supervision of the Qingwei Lingbao 清微靈寶 Taoists ..." (*The Taoists of Peking*, p. 33). My examination of extant Quanzhen sources in the *Daozang* has not produced any evidence for Quanzhen ordination nor its consecration procedures (受戒儀式). The only procedure I am aware of is the "Zanpi cixu 簪披次序" described in the *Quanzhen qinggui* which, however, does not appear to be a specific "Quanzhen" procedure.

"Wang" makes mention of "the great accident of Shaanxi fires 秦火大變" that destroyed the majority of scriptures containing precepts and regulations, which led to the ensuing degeneration of the precept-method. Along the same line, the Quanzhen Longmen reformer of Jingaishan, Min Yide, deplores the lack of Qiu Chuji's precept-text for the performance of ordinations during his Jiaqing period along with the "burning" of it by previous generations of Jingaishan masters, which led to the disastrous loss of scrolls and codes (今嘉慶間所開演缽、邱祖戒本失傳⋯我山先輩、亦守戒焚之。書則錄本倖存、而卷律亡矣).[296] Interestingly, the recent Baiyun guan abbot Min Zhiting 閔智亭 (1924–2004) also refers to the loss of a text by Qiu Chuji that he considered important for the Quanzhen legacy with respect to ordinations. In his book on Daoist rules (*Daojiao yifan* 道教儀範, p. 256) he for the first time reveals the origin of the unique Quanzhen initiation ceremony known as *guanjin keyi* 冠巾科儀 and explains that it had been described in a book by Qiu Chuji. Like "Wang" in his preface, Min Zhiting also advances in his preface a "conflagration scenario" but clearly posits it at the end of the Ming (emphases in the following quotation are mine):

> After having attained the Dao, Patriarch Changchun (i.e., Qiu Chuji) traveled throughout the empire in order to explain and propagate Daoist standards, to perform rituals, and to open the altars by establishing seventy-two Public monasteries (*conglin*) and leaving behind thousands of his writings. There was nothing he did not do to make future students completely understand the realm of the Great Vehicle and achieve liberation from the sufferings of reincarnation. Furthermore, since he was afraid that those who renounce the world (*chujia*) had no points of reference and confuse Daoist rules (*xuangui*), thus much augmenting bad retributions, he left to posterity a book called *Zanguan keyi* 簪冠科儀 (the ceremony of the hairpin and robe) in order to initiate those who take refuge in the Gate of the Mystery and enable them to know the rites and injunctions as well as the esoterica and precepts. Thus posterity, when performing good and bad

---

[296] *Huangji xianjing* 皇極仙經, 38b, ZWDS 10:381. The entire passage reads: "律祖三傳而道遂絕、今嘉慶間所開演缽、邱祖戒本失傳。近所傳訪諸淨明宗教錄、與邱祖所傳、小同而大異也。我山先輩、亦守戒焚之。書則錄本倖存、而卷律亡矣。" I have analyzed this passage several times in the context of the legitimacy of Min Yide's Longmen Jingai local tradition. See for instance "La Porte du Dragon," vol. 1, pp. 217–221 and "Shindai dōkyō to mikkyō 清代道教と密教," p. 317 {*Facets of Qing Daoism*, Chapter 5, p. 290}.

deeds, could be investigated by the Celestial officers and be regularly checked and properly monitored. *The succeeding men of determination had [Qiu's book] circulate for a long time until the destruction by fire, during the chaos of the end of the Ming, of its printing-blocks that had been stored in Sichuan at the Zitonggong monastery.* For that reason it came about that of those who intended to enter the gates of Daoism's arcana, sons revered their fathers as teachers and wives their husbands as they sought to gradually enter the gate of Daoism's mysteries.

昔時長春祖師、成道之后、遍歷天下、闡揚道范、演禮開壇、設叢林七十二座、傳道指訣、垂訓文千有余言、無非使后學盡大乘之境、悉脫輪回之苦、又恐出家無考、紊亂玄規、更增罪孽、故留簪冠科儀一書、俾初皈玄門之人即能知禮知警、知奧知戒、嗣后有功有過、天曹有案、照年照月、稽察對號、后之志士、刊版流行已久、其版存於四川梓潼宮、后因明末世亂、將宮焚燒、其版迭滅、故后引人入門者無所皈依、以致苟圖道教度玄之輩、子拜父為師、妻拜夫為師、重重漸入玄門。

Despite the purported loss of Quanzhen precept-texts, the reputation of Quanzhen's ancient monastic tradition in matters of discipline, monastic institutions, training, and ordinations made modern scholars feel confident in equipping Quanzhen with a singular and unique initiation ceremony "of the capping and clothing 冠巾科儀" that stands in contrast with the Zhengyi initiation (*shoudu* 受度).[297] Based on the assumption of a continuous Quanzhen clerical identity established during the Yuan and transmitted until today, they are also contrasting the full-fledged Quanzhen collective ordination ceremony (*shoujie yishi* 受戒儀式) with Zhengyi's individual ordination ceremony (*shoulu yishi* 受籙儀式).[298] The presumed loss of Quanzhen materials (and the burning of its Daoist Canon in 1281) may have played their part; but to my knowledge the extant sources we still dispose of today, and the entirety of Quanzhen texts preserved in the Ming *Daozang*,

---

[297] As mentioned above, the *Quanzhen qinggui* contains a section referring to it and titled "簪披次序." The content of this capping rite (*guanjin* 冠巾) does not appear to be specifically "Quanzhen," as is the comparison with the earlier Song Lingbao *Taishang chujia chuandu yi* 太上出家傳度儀 (DZ 1236) shows. On differences and similarities between Quanzhen and Zhengyi initiations see Gossaert, *The Taoists of Peking*, 35–39, 102–104.

[298] See for instance Zhang Zehong 張澤洪, *Daojiao zhaijiao fuzhou yishi* 道教齋醮符咒儀, p. 241–248, and Goossaert, *The Taoists of Peking*, 28–39, 102–107

furnish no evidence for Quanzhen's singularity in the field of initiation and ordination procedures. It is thus legitimate to ask if such confidence might not be the product of modern projections based on the glorification of Quanzhen's past and constitutes one more fruit of the dream of a Golden Age that late Quanzhen reformers kept advocating in their works. Might it not be the consequence of a long-harbored aspiration by these reformers to equip Quanzhen with a time-honored uniqueness in such crucial matters as discipline, public monastic institutions, and public ordination procedures?

The view that Quanzhen had a unique system of initiation since the Yuan era and that this system was later re-established in form of a public ordination procedure, resembles our past understanding of Quanzhen as an ascetic movement exclusively devoted to alchemy, meditation, and monastic training that had no interest in such things as rituals, talismans, etc. This kind of understanding came to be increasingly challenged, and the study of Quanzhen's early history has begun to show that Quanzhen Daoists were from the outset not so different from other Daoist priests. Like all other Daoists they were involved in the celebration of Daoist *jiao* 醮, *zhai* 齋, exorcism, rain-rituals, and the like. However, in contrast to other Daoist schools such as Lingbao or new liturgical movements (*xin fulu pai* 新符籙派) of the Song period that produced monumental compendia of rituals, Quanzhen appears not to have produced its own ritual texts.[299] Does this mean that Quanzhen priests received the same liturgical training as all other Daoist priests during the Yuan? And how about the Ming? Were Quanzhen priests then equipped with a singular training that began with a unique "Quanzhen" initiation ceremony of capping and clothing (*guanjin keyi* 冠巾科儀) which evolved into a full-fledged Quanzhen ordination procedure that made Quanzhen priests so unique compared to Zhengyi priests?

---

[299] See for instance Bartholomew Tsui, *Taoist Tradition and Change: The Story of the Complete Perfection Sect in Hong Kong* (Hong Kong: Hong Kong Christian Study Center on Chinese Religion and Culture, 1991): 154. See also the recent study by Fang Ling 方玲, "Quanzhen Daoism and zhuyou 祝由 ritual medicine" in Xun Liu & Vincent Goossaert (eds.), *Quanzhen Daoism in Modern Chinese History and Society*. Berkeley: Institute of East Asian Studies, 2014). Like the previous studies by Liu Zhongyu 劉仲宇 ("On the Rituals of Quanzhen Daoism in its Early Stage 早期全真教儀式初探") and Zhang Zehong 張澤洪 ("On the Zhai-jiao Rituals of Quanzhen Daoism in Yuan Dynasty 金元全真教齋醮科儀初探" in *Daojia wenhua yanjiu* 道家文化研究 22 (2008):144–166 and 167–191), Fang Ling argues that scholars have too long regarded Quanzhen Daoists as pure world-denying self-cultivators rather than the Daoist priests that they really were.

Even if we were to accept such a narrative, we could not overlook the lack of evidence for Quanzhen's singularity in matters of discipline and ordination procedures. It does appear that it was only during the Qing that Quanzhen finally got equipped with its own precept-texts, a distinctive Quanzhen monastic liturgy, and a full-fledged Quanzhen ordination procedure, and that it was only then that Quanzhen found itself finally in a position to assert its singularity in matters of discipline and ordination procedures.

As the revelation via spirit-wiriting of the *Tianxian dajie* shows, the activities of spirit writing groups and previous reformers such as Wu Shouyang 伍守陽 (1574–1644?) were crucial for preparing the ground and establishing a Daoist threefold altar ordination (*santan dajie*) capable of competing with Buddhism and its ordination system. The work of Wu Shouyang—besides furnishing selected passages on Daoist Vinaya and precepts from the *Daozang* utilized by Jiang Yuanting 蔣元庭 (1755–1819) and his congregants for compiling their *Tianxian dajie*—shows in particular that, despite the presumed earlier Vinaya activities of Wang Changyue 王常月 (?–1680), Quanzhen was at that point in time not yet in charge of transmitting the precepts. As we can see in the passage cited below, Wu in fact highlights the necessity for Daoists to become able, just like the Buddhists, to transmit the precepts and to have precept-texts (*jiejing* 戒經) along with Vinaya masters (*lüshi* 律師)[300] capable of explaining their meaning:

> Although Buddhist monks (僧流) belong to an inferior kind, they all have people that are said to be eminent and intelligent who received the precepts (受戒) The Daoists (道流), too, have eminent and intelligent companions, but they do not have precepts (無戒) like the Buddhists. This is therefore where Daoists are inferior to Buddhists. Why is that? It is precisely because Buddhist monks have precept scriptures (戒經) which they distribute and circulate throughout the world, along with specialists called Vinaya masters (*lüshi* 律師) who exclusively study these texts. By lecturing on and clarifying the meaning of these precepts, the people hear about the precepts, which makes it easy to study and learn about them. With regard to those who drape the robes of ordained clerics and go begging, the common

---

[300] As is known, the mention of *lüshi* in Daoism is found in j.4 of *Tang liudian* 唐六典. I was unable to locate this term in other Daoist sources until the Qing. Despite this, scholars like Ding Peiren 丁培仁 confidently claim that *lüshi* existed since the Tang period and that Quanzhen masters became their heirs as transmitters of rules and precepts. See Ding Peiren, "Daojiao jielü shu kaoyao 道教戒律書考要," *Zongjiaoxue yanjiu* 宗教學研究, 第2期 (2006): 4–23, here p. 6 and p. 22, note 21.

people do not care whether they are genuine or fake: they call all of them "ordained monks" 戒僧 and generously donate to them. Those who profit from the precepts in this manner are numerous.

僧流、雖庸下之流、每有道高明受戒者；道流、每有高明之輩、同於庸下無戒；此便是道者不及僧者處。是何故？蓋僧有戒經、頒行於遍世界、專習戒經者、名曰律師；以講明律義、大眾便於聞戒、易於習學。及披戒衣求乞者、俗人不擇真偽、曰戒僧也、慨施之、以是借戒者多。

Wu then turns to the causes of this dire state of affairs:

> With regard to the precepts of the Immortals 仙戒, the celestial statutes and illustrious codes 天律明科 are also very numerous, and among the scriptures there are some on precepts that contain rules and admonitions 戒條戒語. These are all in the *Daozang*. [But] they are all secretly stored 秘藏 by temple managers 住持 who prevent them from being known and from being seen by those in the world who study the Dao 世界中學道者. There are also no Vinaya masters who transmit precepts 傳戒. Hence they make the whole world doubt that the Perfected have any precepts at all. Why would people then develop the aspiration to receive the precepts 發心受戒? And where can they manage to hear about the precepts? When the [Buddhist] beggars do not don their ceremonial robes, the common people do not esteem them as they would ordained Buddhist monks, and they give them no alms. Therefore, it is because begging for alms is easy that so many of those who renounce the world 出家者 become Buddhists 入佛教.[301]

> 至於仙戒、天律明科甚多；有全說之戒經、有諸經之內、皆有戒條戒語、俱在　道藏　內。盡用住持者秘藏、不令世界中學道者得知得見、又無律師傳戒。遂使遍世界人、疑為仙真無戒。彼何由以發心受戒？抑從何處得以聞戒？及至求乞者無戒衣可披、俗人亦不以如有戒之僧一樣視之而施。故出家者、以易化緣之故、入佛教者多矣。

As is known, Wu Shouyang 伍守陽 (ca. 1574–1644?) claimed to be the eighth-generation disciple of Qiu Chuji within a Longmen legacy defined as "Xianzong 仙宗" or "Longmen xianpai 龍門仙派"— a legacy that differs from the institutionalized version of the "Longmen zhengzong" that

---

[301] *Xianfo hezong yulu* 仙佛合宗語錄, 畢集1, 1.119b–120a (CK 17: 7462). On this passage see also Paul van Enckevort, "Quanzhen and Longmen Identities in the Work of Wu Shouyang."

allegedly was re-established in 1656 at the Baiyun guan under the guidance of Wang Changyue. Even if Min Yide in his *Jingai xindeng* presents Wu Shouyang as the direct disciple of Wang Changyue, there is evidence that Wu's Longmen xianpai 龍門仙派 was not linked with Wang Changyue's legacy. This Longmen xianpai genealogy is different from the "Longmen zhengzong" genealogy (also referred to as "Lüzong 律宗") celebrated at the Baiyun guan ancestral hall and re-enacted during the late Qing Quanzhen ordinations of the three altars. Despite this, Wu's work emphasized the late construction of a Quanzhen Ur-Vinaya tradition known as Longmen lüzong 龍門律宗 or Longmen zhengzong 龍門正宗. This is because Wu's work points out the need of creating an authentic Daoist public ordination system capable of competing with that established by Buddhists. In other words, we can say that Wu's earlier work helped Quanzhen Daoists to fabricate during the Qing their own full-fledged Quanzhen clerical identity in matters of dicipline and ordination procedures. At the same time it also gave voice to the aspirations of lay and Daoist clerics, religious movements, and schools such as the Jingming, Shenxiao, or Qingwei Lingbao that aspired to build a "lineage of Immortals" (*xianzong* 仙宗) representing an ideal and universal "Quanzhen Way of Heavenly Immortals" (Quanzhen xiandao 全真仙道): a Daoist vehicle of enlightenment for both laypeople and clerics that could hold its own—just like Chan 禪宗, the Chinese school of Buddhism, which had become dominant in the Song period based on its claim of being the sole true heir of "original Buddhism" and on its invented transmission lineage linking it to founder Buddha.

Wu's discourse can thus also be regarded as an extension of Liu Shouyuan's mission to establish an Ur-Daoism of the Celestial Immortals. However, in the eyes of the spirit writing altar of Jiang Yuanting 蔣元庭 and his congregants, their own Celestial Immortal lineage (Tianxian fapai 天仙法派) is the fruit of the integration of all authentic sects and lineages revealed by its founding patriarch Lü Dongbin. Lü Dongbin's spirit writing revelation—also referred to as the "esoteric teaching of the tradition of Immortals" (*xianzong xuanjiao* 仙宗玄教)—has the power of changing the present situation where "renouncers of the world are numerous, yet those able to leave its dust behind are few" 近來出家者多、出塵者少. In the eyes of the creators of the *Tianxian dajie* (Jiang Yuanting and his spirit-writing congregants), Ur-Daoism represents the orthodox path: a path in which Quanzhen had to take care of the correct teaching and Zhengyi of the correct liturgy—but under the benevolent supervision of the immortal

Lü Dongbin 呂洞賓 and his spirit writing altar of the Heavenly Immortals (Tianxian 天仙) who own the monopoly of determining what "correct" or "orthodox" means. When needed, the Tianxian pai's spirit writing altar could dispatch to the world its Celestial Immortals as communicators and agents of regeneration. In the eyes of the late Qing Quanzhen reformers, "Wang" had an analogous role for the institutionalization of the heirs of the "Orthodox Lineage of Celestial Immortals" (*Tianxian zhengmai* 天仙正脈) at the Quanzhen Longmen ordination altar at Baiyun guan.

Conclusion

Through the analysis of the three precept-texts that continue to be used in Quanzhen Daoism for conferring Quanzhen ordinations, I questioned in this second part the "organic" connection that tends to be accepted between the Quanzhen collective ordination procedure of the three altars (*santan dajie* 三壇大戒) and Quanzhen clerical identity. By showing early Lingbao origins and connections, I challenged current assumptions about Wang's alleged creation of the *santan dajie* and its direct connection to a purported early Quanzhen tradition of ordination procedures. It is clear to everyone that Daoism possesses a long tradition in matters of Vinaya and precepts, a tradition that was progressively systematized and codified during the Tang era within the earlier communities of the Way of Heavenly Masters (Tianshi dao 天師道) and attained its full expression in the monumental Lingbao liturgical compilations preserved in the *Daozang*. However, what appears new to me is the use made by the Qing reformers of this Vinaya heritage under the name of "Wang," and their apparent determination to establish a Quanzhen Ur-Vinaya tradition. This invented tradition took form in the so-called Longmen lüzong 龍門律宗: the Longmen orthodox lineage 龍門正宗 that was allegedly restored in 1656 by Wang Changyue at Beijing's Baiyun guan, home of the grave-sanctuary of the legendary founder of the Longmen pai 龍門派, Qiu Chuji 邱處機 (1148–1227).

The analysis of materials attributed to Wang Changyue sheds light on the mechanisms through which a universal history of "Quanzhen Longmen zhengzong" was fabricated and glorified at the Baiyun guan under the name of "Wang." To a critical observer, the works originally attributed to him show how this universal history was linked to the creation of a "Quanzhen clerical orthodoxy" (that came to be commemorated during the Qing at the Baiyun guan) by erasing the names of the true protagonists. It is the duty of scholars today to bring these protagonists and creative spirits to light and credit them with the merit they deserve through a sober look at Quanzhen history and the adoption of a new perspective free of Quanzhen institutional propaganda, pseudohistoricity, and fixed ideas of "Wang" as protagonist.

As I already emphasized in previous studies on Longmen,[302] it is difficult to pinpoint when the "Longmen school" arose. However, on the basis of the data presented in those studies, I was already able to detect an earlier participation of local movements not necessarily linked with Quanzhen as a school, but inspired by the icon of its saint Qiu Chuji. Their aim was to "re-establish" an authentic path within Daoism. In previous studies I referred to the end of the Ming because I based myself on the first occurrences of Longmen as "pai 派" (in the commentary by Wu Shouxu 伍守虛 to Wu Shouyang's 伍守陽 work and the *Guangyang zaji* 廣陽雜記 by Liu Xianting 劉獻廷); but I did leave open the possibility that nascent local groups inspired by Quanzhen ideals already existed in different places of China without laying claim to a specific "Longmen pai" identity. At the time, my conclusion had been that "behind the strident melody of Wang Changyue's lineage, one could already detect distinct echoes of Longmen of earlier periods and its caves on Huashan, Laoshan, Qingchengshan or Wudangshan."[303]

Today, thanks to the research conducted by Chinese scholars on newly discovered epigraphic materials, my first working hypothesis seems to be increasingly confirmed. According to recent studies there are traces of earlier Longmen local epicenters at the beginning of the Ming, and even around the end of the Yuan, that show no link with Wang Changyue's Longmen zhengzong. It still remains to be seen if such earlier and local movements refer to themselves as "Longmen pai" or simply associate themselves with a more general "Qiu Chuji legacy" that, as we know, came to be part of religious movements and Daoist schools (such as Jingming, Zhengyi, etc.) both inside and outside Quanzhen clerical networks.

---

[302] Esposito, "La Porte du Dragon," and "The Longmen School and its Controversial History during the Qing Dynasty" pp. 622, 631, 654–7, 671 {*Facets of Qing Daoism*, chapter 2, pp. 56, 70, 99–103, 125–126}.

[303] Esposito, The Longmen School and its Controversial History during the Qing Dynasty" p. 674 {*Facets of Qing Daoism*, chapter 2, pp. 128–129}.

I shall end this second part with some questions to today's Quanzhen scholars.³⁰⁴ Based on the materials attributed to Wang Changyue presented in this part, I ask:

1) Can we still agree with previous scholars and modern scholarship which accept Wang Changyue as the founder of the ordination of the three altars? Is it appropriate to regard him as the author of the three precept-texts? Can we still assume that he first compiled the *Chuzhen jielü* in 1656?

2) Must we regard the three-altar-ordination as a late-imperial invention? Or is this ordination the fruit of the continuity of older Daoist ordination procedures? Is there any solid evidence linking this ordination system to Quanzhen and to patriarch Qiu Chuji?

3) How should we interpret the ultimate ordination of the Celestial Immortals?

---

³⁰⁴ My thanks to Xun Liu for having presented a much less elaborate draft version of this part at the 2009 Shandong "International Seminar on Qiu Chuji and Quanzhen Taoist Sect, Commemorating the 780th Anniversary of the Death of Qiu Chuji" in my stead, and for having submitted these questions to the attention of its participants. Unfortunately they seem to have produced little feedback.

Part Three

CREATION OF CANON

Chapter 1

HISTORIES OF DAOISM'S ULTIMATE CANON

Subsequent to the Daoist Canon of the Ming period (*Zhengtong Daozang* 正統道藏, 1445), the *Daozang jiyao* 道藏輯要 or *Essentials of the Daoist Canon* is the most important collection of Daoist texts of the Qing dynasty (1644–1912). It is by far the largest anthology of premodern Daoism and thus an indispensable source for the study of Daoism in the Ming and Qing periods (fourteenth century to the turn of the twentieth century). Although it is chiefly derived from the Ming Daoist Canon, the *Daozang jiyao* contains numerous texts that are not included there.[300] It features texts on inner alchemy (*neidan* 內丹), cosmology, philosophy, ritual, and precepts; commentaries on Buddhist, Confucian and Daoist scriptures; hagiographic, topographic, and epigraphic works; and much more.

Despite its importance as the most valuable collection of Daoist literature of the late imperial period, and even though scholars make frequent use of its texts, the *Daozang jiyao* has hitherto not been the object of systematic study.[301] The genesis of this collection is still hardly explored, and neither are its history and its various editions, some of which are classified as

---

[300] See the following chapters of this part.

[301] With the support of the Chiang-Ching Kuo Foundation, an international research project on the *Daozang jiyao* began under my direction in July 2006 at Kyoto University's Institute for Research in Humanities (Jinbun Kagaku Kenkyūjo 人文科學研究所). It is important to note that, except for the studies on the history of this compilation by Mori Yuria 森由利亞 ("Dōzo shūyō to Shō Yobu no Ryoso fukei shinkō" 道藏輯要と蔣予蒲の呂祖扶乩信仰, *Tōhō shūkyō* 東方宗教 98, 2001: 33–52) and by Kim Yunsu 金侖壽 ("Dojang jipyo wa Jang Yoepo" 道藏輯要와 蔣予蒲, *Dogyo Munhwa Yoengu* 道教文化研究 17, 2002: 277–316), no systematic research had then been published on the various editions of the *Daozang jiyao*. My thanks to Mori Yuria for sending me a copy of Kim Yunsu's article and to Kim Jihyun 金志玹 for her help in translating parts of it.

"rare" in Chinese, Taiwanese, European and Japanese libraries. Before entering this *terra incognita*, it is important to briefly present the main scholarly views on the history of the *Daozang jiyao*'s compilation.

Fig. 17 : Precinct of Qingyanggong 青羊宮 Daoist temple in Chengdu where original *Daozang jiyao* printing plates are stored even today (M.E., 2009)

Fig. 18: *Daozang jiyao* printing blocks, Qingyanggong (M.E., 2006)

Chapter 1: Histories of Daoism's Ultimate Canon   179

Three Main Theories about the History of the Daozang Jiyao Canon

Theory 1: According to the most common account presented even in recent articles,³⁰² the *Daozang jiyao* exists in at least three different editions:
1. An original edition compiled around 1700 by Peng Dingqiu 彭定求 (1645–1719) containing 200 works, all extracted from the Ming Canon;³⁰³
2. A second expanded edition by Jiang Yuanting 蔣元庭 (i.e., Jiang Yupu 蔣予蒲, 1755–1819) from the Jiaqing era (1796–1820) that, in addition to Peng Dingqiu's edition, contains 79 texts which are not included in the Ming Daoist Canon;³⁰⁴

---

³⁰² The given account stems from the article of Zhao Zongcheng 趙宗誠, "Daozang jiyao de bianzuan yu zengbu" 道藏輯要的編纂與增補, *Sichuan wenwu* 四川文物 2 (1995): 27–31. A similar view by the same author is also included in Qing Xitai 卿希泰 (ed.), *Zhongguo daojiao shi* 中國道教史 (Chengdu: Sichuan renmin, 1996): vol. 4, 453–464. See also the Preface by Qing Xitai 卿希泰, "Chongkan Daozang jiyao (suoyinben) xu" 重刊道藏輯要（縮印本）序, in Chen Dali 陳大利 et al. (eds.), *Daozang jiyao* 道藏輯要, 10 vols. (Chengdu: Bashu shushe, 1995): vol. 1, 1–3, also published in *Zongjiaoxue yanjiu* 宗教學研究 31 (1996.2): 1–2. Ding Changchun 丁常春 and Li Hechun 李合春 in their recent works ("Chengdu Erxian'an lishi yange" 成都二仙菴歷史沿革, *Hongdao* 弘道 24, 2005.3: 92–97 and *Qingyanggong Erxian'an zhi* 青羊宮二仙庵誌, Chengdu: Sichuansheng xinwen, 2006, 188–194) give an overview of this Canon by basing themselves on Zhao Zongcheng's hypothesis included in Qing Xitai. My thanks to Yin Zhihua 尹志華 for having offered me a copy of Ding and Li's book as soon as it was published. Articles on the internet present a similar account; see for instance Li Gang 李剛, "Daozang jiyao" 道藏輯要, *Daojiao wenhua ziliaoku* 道教文化資料庫 (http://www.taoism.org.hk/taoist-scriptures/taoist-canon/pg4-1-4-3.htm), and Hong Baijian 洪百堅, "Daozang jiyao" 道藏輯要, *Daojiao xueshu zixun wangzhan* 道教學術資訊網站 (http://www.ctcwri.idv.tw/IndexD2/D2-13/066-127/13102/071-137/109.htm). Zhao Zongcheng's hypothesis has also been accepted by some Western scholars; see for instance Elena Valussi, "Peng Dingqiu," in Fabrizio Pregadio (ed.), *Encyclopedia of Taoism*, 2 vols. (London: Routledge, 2008): 2.784–85, and Vincent Goossaert, *The Taoists of Peking, 1800–1949* (Cambridge, Mass.: Harvard University Asia Center, 2007): 275.

³⁰³ For the attribution of the original edition of the *Daozang jiyao* to Peng Dingqiu see also Li Yangzheng 李養正, *Daojiao shouce* 道教手冊 (Zhengzhou: Zhongzhou guji, 1993): 358–359, and the entry "Daozang jiyao," in Ren Jiyu 任繼愈 (ed.), *Zongjiao dacidian* 宗教大詞典 (Shanghai: Shanghai cishu, 1981) in which (on p. 1064) Peng Dingqiu's original edition is said to contain 283 texts representing "the essence of the *Daozang*." See also the next footnote.

³⁰⁴ One finds a list of these supposedly 79 additional titles in Zhao Zongcheng ("*Daozang jiyao* de bianzuan yu zengbu," 27–29, also in Qing Xitai, ed., *Zhongguo dao-*

3. A re-edition of Jiang Yuanting's *Daozang jiyao* by He Longxiang 賀龍驤 and Peng Hanran 彭瀚然, published in 1906 at the Erxian'an 二仙菴 of Chengdu (Sichuan) under the title of *Chongkan Daozang jiyao* 重刊道藏輯要 or *New Edition of the Essentials of the Daoist Canon* that supposedly contains a total of 319 texts.[305]

Theory 2: In contrast to this account, Yoshioka Yoshitoyo 吉岡義豊 in 1955 was the first scholar to affirm in his *Dōkyō kyōten shiron* 道教經典史論 that there are only two editions of the *Daozang jiyao* (number 2 and number 3 of the first theory). The extant edition (number 2 of the list above) belonged to Jiang Yuanting and consisted of 173 works, all from the Ming Canon. Between 1821 and 1900, Jiang Yuanting's edition was engraved twice, and in the process 96 extra-canonical texts were added for a total of 269 texts. Eighteen more extracanonical works are said to have been added in the 1906 *Chongkan Daozang jiyao* edition, bringing the total to 287 works.[306] Based on Yoshioka's work, Liu Ts'un-yan 柳存仁 gave the same account and proclaimed the attribution of the original edition of the *Daozang jiyao* to Peng Dingqiu 彭定求 as historically unlikely.[307]

---

jiao shi, vol. 4, 455–458). They derive from a list of *Daozang jiyao* extra-canonical texts compiled by Weng Dujian 翁獨健 in his *Daozang zimu yinde* 道藏子目引得 (*Combined Indices to the Authors and Titles of Books in Two Collections of Taoist Literature*), Harvard-Yenching Institute Sinological Index Series, no. 25 (Beiping [Beijing]: Yenching University Library, 1935): 38–40. For more information about this list, see Monica Esposito 莫尼卡, "*Daozang jiyao* ji qi bianzuan de lishi—Shijie Qingdai *Daozang* suoshou daojing shumu wenti" 道藏輯要及其編纂的歷史—試解清代道藏所收道經書目問題, Paper presented at the First International Academic Symposium of Daoist Literature and its Path to Immortality (Gaoxiong, Zhongshan University, November 10–12, 2006.

[305] We find also mention of these three editions but with a different number of texts (173, 176 or 283 for Peng's edition, 270 for Jiang's edition, and 287 for He Longxiang's edition); see Ozaki Masaharu 尾崎正治, "*Dōzō shūyō*" 道藏輯要, in Noguchi Tetsuro 野口鐵郎 et al. (eds.), *Dōkyō jiten* 道教事典 (Tokyo: Hirakawa shuppansha, 1994): 456–457. See also the entry "Daozang jiyao" in Ren Jiyu 任繼愈 (ed.), *Zongjiao dacidian* 宗教大詞典, 1064.

[306] Yoshioka, Yoshitoyo 吉岡義豊, *Dōkyō kyōten shiron* 道教經典史論 (Tokyo: Dōkyō kankōkai, 1955): 175–176.

[307] Liu Ts'un-yan 柳存仁, "The Compilation and Historical Value of the Tao-tsang," in Donald D. Leslie, Colin Mackerras, and Wang Gungwu (eds.), *Essays on the Sources of Chinese History* (Canberra: Australian National University Press, 1973): 104–119, in particular 107–108. On Liu Ts'un-yan's argument based on the previous statements of Yoshioka, see also in chronological order: Wang Shiu-hon,

Theory 3: In 1996 Ding Peiren 丁培仁, after having consulted the exemplar of the *Daozang jiyao* stored at Sichuan Provincial Library (i.e., the version owned by Yan Yanfeng 嚴雁峰 that served as basis for the 1906 *Chongkan Daozang jiyao*), confirmed Jiang Yuanting 蔣元庭 (1755–1819) as editor.[308] The fact that this collection includes taboo characters of the Kangxi to Jiaqing eras (1662–1820) but not of the Daoguang era (1821–1850) indicates the time period when Jiang Yuanting apparently compiled the collection, and it supports his being the original editor. According to Ding, the *Daozang jiyao* consists of 204 canonical texts and 93 extra-canonical texts. This means that this collection, in Ding's view, contained a total of 297 texts. Seventeen additional works that do not stem from the Ming Daoist Canon are said to have been included in the new edition of the *Daozang jiyao* of 1906 entitled *Chongkan Daozang jiyao*, bringing the total to 314 works.

Which of these three current accounts is correct? Who was the original editor of the *Daozang jiyao*? How many times was this collection edited or reprinted? How many texts are really contained in it? How many of the *Daozang jiyao*'s texts are canonical (i.e., contained in the Ming Daoist Canon), and how many were newly added? And what is the number of texts added in the 1906 new *Chongkan Daozang jiyao* edition by He Longxiang 賀龍驤 and Peng Hanran 彭瀚然?

I have discussed some of the intricate problems related to the extant editions of the *Daozang jiyao* and *Chongkan Daozang jiyao* as well as the numbering of its canonical and extra-canonical texts in an article which shows that both the identification of editors and the number of editions proposed by the above-mentioned scholars are questionable.[309] Here I will concen-

---

Investigations into the Authenticity of the Chang San-Feng Ch'uan-Chi (Canberra: Australian National University Press, 1982): 3–7; Julian Pas, "Preface," in William Chen, *A Guide to Tao-tsang Chi Yao* (Stony Brook N.Y.: The Institute for Advanced Studies of World Religion, 1987): vii; Zhu Yueli 朱越利, *Daojing zonglun* 道經總論 (Shenyang: Liaoning jiaoyi, 1991): 328; Wang Ka 王卡, "Daozang jiyao," in Hu Fuchen 胡孚琛 (ed.), *Zhongguo daojiao dacidian* 中國道教大辭典 (Beijing: Zhongguo shehui kexue, 1995): 230; and Tian Chengyang 田誠陽, *Daojing zhishi baodian* 道經知識寶典 (Chengdu: Sichuan renmin, 1995): 109.

[308] Ding Peiren 丁培仁, *Daojiao dianji baiwen* 道教典籍百問 (Beijing: Jinri Zhongguo, 1996): 216–218.

[309] Monica Esposito 莫尼卡, "*Daozang jiyao* ji qi bianzuan de lishi." The questionable attribution of *Daozang jiyao*'s editorship relates exclusively to Theory 1.

trate on some central questions concerning the editorship and content of this collection.

In accord with Yoshioka, my study of the extant editions has confirmed that an "original edition" by Peng Dingqiu 彭定求 (number 1 of the list above) is a fiction and does not exist. The edition by Jiang Yuanting (number 2) forms the basis of all extant printed editions; it is relatively rare but forms the kernel of the *Chongkan Daozang jiyao* of 1906 (number 3).[310]

Why then does the name of Peng Dingqiu 彭定求 still figure in the heading of today's reprints of the *Chongkan Daozang jiyao* instead of the original editor Jiang Yuanting 蔣元庭? How did this mistake arise and why is it perpetuated until today? How can we prove that the *Daozang jiyao* was the work of Jiang Yuanting? Let us begin with the purported editor Peng Dingqiu.

The Wrong Attribution to Peng Dingqiu or Peng Wenqin

If one searches the internet databases of many libraries around the world for the *Daozang jiyao*, one often finds Peng Dingqiu 彭定求 or Peng Wenqin 彭文勤 listed as editor.[311] The name of Peng Wenqin also appears, for instance, in the reprints of the *Chongkan Daozang jiyao* published by the Kaozheng 考正 (Taipei, 1971) and Xinwenfeng 新文豐 (Taipei, 1977, 1983 and 1986) publishing houses.[312] How did this come about?

---

[310] See Monica Esposito, *La Porte du Dragon. L'école Longmen du Mont Jingai et ses pratiques alchimiques d'après le Daozang xubian (Suite au canon taoïste)*, 2 vols. (Ph.D. diss., Paris VII, 1993 / PDF 2012): vol. 1, 4, 158, 162–163; "Daoism in the Qing (1644–1911)," in Livia Kohn (ed.), *Daoism Handbook* (Leiden: Brill, 2000): 623–658, in particular 634–635 {*Facets of Qing Daoism*, chapter 1, in particular pp. 21–22}; and Esposito, "Daozang jiyao ji qi bianzuan de lishi" (2006). Ding Peiren 丁培仁 (*Daojiao dianji baiwen*), Mori Yuria 森由利亜 ("Dōzo shūyō to Shō Yobu no Ryoso fukei shinkō"), and Kim Yunsu 金侖壽 ("Dojang jipyo wa Jang Yoepo") also confirm that the *Daozang jiyao* is the fruit of Jiang Yuanting's editorship. See also the entry "Daozang jiyao," in Qing Xitai (ed.), *Zhongguo daojiao* 中國道教, 4 vols. (Shanghai: Zhishi, 1994), vol. 2, 32–33.

[311] See for instance Taiwan Opac (http://nbinet.ncl.edu.tw) or the National Library of China (http://www.nlc.gov.cn/en/collections/books.htm) where one finds for the editor of the *Daozang jiyao* the mention "(清)彭定求等編" as well as "彭文勤等纂輯 賀龍驤校勘." In the website of the Academia sinica library (http://las.sinica.edu.tw/) one now also finds the atrribution to Peng Yuanrui: "彭元瑞 (1731–1803) 纂輯". On the figure of Peng Yuanrui see here below.

[312] In the reprint of the *Chongkan Daozang jiyao* in ten volumes (Chen Dali et al. eds.,

In 1892, when Yan Yonghe 閻永和 became abbot of the Daoist monastery of Erxian'an 二仙菴 in Chengdu, he decided to reprint the *Daozang jiyao*. Unfortunately, as its printing blocks were already ruined, Yan had them newly engraved.[313] Thanks to the economic support and help of Peng Hanran 彭瀚然 and the participation of He Longxiang 賀龍驤 as collator, this new edition of the *Daozang jiyao* was prepared on the basis of a printed exemplar of Yan Yanfeng 嚴雁峰 stored in Sichuan.[314] According to He Longxiang, this exemplar was the work of Peng Dingqiu. Referring to its Table of Contents, He Longxiang says in his "Preface to the Detailed Table of Contents of the *Chongkan Daozang jiyao*" (Chongkan Daozang jiyao zimu chubian xu 重刊道藏輯要子目初編序, 1906, 20a):

> We express our gratitude to the Premier of our dynasty, Peng Dingqiu, who compiled the *Daozang jiyao*. Unfortunately, the table of contents of the original collection stops short of recording the number of fascicles and does not provide a detailed listing of their contents.
>
> 我朝彭定求相公、撰道藏輯要一書、為世稱快。惜原書總目、止載卷數、未列子目。[315]

Daozang jiyao), one finds an earlier introduction by Ren Jiyu 任繼愈 dated 1985 (issued for the new edition in 314 fascicles/32 cases of the *Chongkan Daozang jiyao* after the restoration of its printing blocks by the Bashu shushe publishing house) which does not mention anything about the editorship, and an introduction by Qing Xitai (1995) based on the account of the three editions (see above note 302). More on the 1906 *Chongkan Daozang jiyao* and its editions also in Monica Esposito, "*Daozang jiyao* ji qi bianzuan de lishi" (2006).

[313] Whereas Yan Yonghe and Peng Hanran in their Prefaces (respectively: "Chongkan Daozang jiyao yuanqi" 重刊道藏輯要緣起, 15a/4, and "Chongkan Daozang jiyao bianyan" 重刊道藏輯要弁言, 16a/3, in *Chongkan Daozang jiyao*, Taipei: Xinwenfeng, 1986, vol. 1: 44) mention that the printing blocks were already ruined, He Longxiang ("Jiaokan Daozang jiyao shuhou" 校勘道藏輯要書後, 17b/8–9, in CK 1, 45) tells us that they were stored in Beijing but eaten by worms. More on the destiny of the *Daozang jiyao* printing blocks here below. I shall refer for the *Chongkan Daozang jiyao* to the Xinwenfeng reprint of 1986 in 25 volumes. The references to the *Daozang jiyao* are also given according to the widely available Xinwenfeng reprint of the *Chongkan Daozang jiyao*.

[314] See the Preface by Yan Yonghe, "Chongkan Daozang jiyao yuanqi," 15a–b (CK 1, 44). However, He Longxiang in his Preface ("Jiaokan Daozang jiyao shuhou," 18a, in CK 1, 45) informs us that for the collation he also used two manuscript versions of the *Daozang jiyao* of two bibliophiles: He Qichong 何起重 and Qin Pengsheng 秦芃生. See Monica Esposito 莫尼卡, "*Daozang jiyao* ji qi bianzuan de lishi."

[315] CK 1, 46. He Longxiang refers here to the "Daozang jiyao zongmu" 道藏輯要總目, the Table of Contents included in the printed exemplar of Yan Yanfeng. More

With regard to the content of this collection, in the " Preface to the Catalogue of the Imperial Edition of the Daoist Canon" (Qinding Daozang quanshu zongmu xu 欽定道藏全書總目序, 1b), He Longxiang adds:

> As for the *Daozang jiyao* compiled by the Minister of State Peng Dingqiu, it is partly derived from the [Ming] imperial edition [of the Daoist Canon] and partly from bookshops' current editions. Although the content of these current editions was genuine and refined, they were not included in the Daoist Canon.
>
> 相國彭定求所編 道藏輯要、出於頒行本者半、出於坊間本者亦半。雖坊本亦皆純正精粹、然非道藏 所有。[316]

While He Longxiang twice mentions Peng Dingqiu as editor and refers to him by the titles of *xianggong* 相公 and *xiangguo* 相國, in the "Postscript to the Collation of the *Daozang jiyao*" (Jiaokan Daozang jiyao shuhou 校勘道藏輯要書後, 17b) dated 1906 he uses the same title *xiangguo*, but this time with the name of Peng Wenqin 彭文勤:

> When I heard that the Erxian'an was re-editing the *Daozang jiyao* of the Minister of State Peng Wenqin, my heart was full of admiration.
>
> 聞二仙菴重刊相國彭文勤 道藏輯要、心輒慕之。[317]

The biography of Peng Dingqiu 彭定求 (1645–1719) contains no mention of the title *xiangguo* or the name Wenqin 文勤.[318] Conversely, the posthumous name Wenqin appears in the biography of Peng Qifeng 彭啟豐 (1701–1784), the grandson of Peng Dingqiu, as well as in the biography of a certain Peng Yuanrui 彭元瑞 (1731–1803) from Nanchang 南昌 (Jiangxi) who obtained the *jinshi* degree in 1757.[319] In his recent postdoc-

---

on this below.

[316] CK 1, 303. See also Wang Shiu-hon, *Investigations into the Authenticity of the Chang San-Feng Ch'uan-Chi*, 3–4.

[317] CK 1, 45.

[318] For the biography of Peng Dingqiu see *Qingshi gao* 清史稿, j. 480 (repr. in 48 vols., Beijing: Zhonghua shuju, 1976–77): vol. 43, 13155, and Rufus O. Suter, "P'eng Ting-ch'iu," in Arthur W. Hummel (ed.), *Eminent Chinese of the Ch'ing Period* (Taipei: Ch'eng wen Publishing Company, 1970): 616–617. Regarding the problem of the official titles, Zhao Zongcheng also notices that the biographies of Peng Dingqiu do not contain any mention of the title *xiangguo* or the name Wenqin, and he wonders if He Longxiang mistakenly took the title *xiangguo* 相國 to mean *xianggong* 相公. See also Qing Xitai (ed.), *Zhongguo daojiao shi*, vol. 4, 459, note 1, and Kim Yunsu, "Dojang jipyo wa Jang Yoepo," 282–283.

[319] "彭啟豐 ... 諡文勤." See Dou Zhen 竇鎮 (ed.), *Guochao shuhuajia bilu* 國朝書畫

toral work devoted to the *Daozang jiyao*, Wan Dekai 万德凯 notes that in the two passages where He Longxiang mentions the name of Peng Dingqiu, his role is specified as *bian* 編 or *zhuan* 撰 (i.e., compiler: 彭定求所編道藏輯要; 彭定求相公、撰道藏輯要一書). But in the only passage where He Longxiang mentions the name of Peng Wenqin, he simply writes of "the *Daozang jiyao* of Peng Wenqin" 彭文勤道藏輯要. According to Wan this might point either to a mistake by He Longxiang in transcribing Peng's names or to a possible connection of a transmitted copy of the *Daozang jiyao* with Peng Wenqin.[320] If He Longxiang refers to Peng Qifeng as "Peng Wenqin," it is worthy of note that Peng Qifeng was the person who stored in his house an old version of Lü Dongbin's writings, the *Quanshu zongzheng* 全書宗正. As is stated in various prefaces included in the *Daozang jiyao*, this collection should be one of the sources that Jiang Yuanting used for his *Quanshu zhengzong* 全書正宗 —a work that, as we are going to see, was central for the compilation of Jiang Yuanting's *Daozang jiyao*.[321]

家筆錄 (Taipei: Wenshizhe chubanshe, 1971): j. 1, 55a; and Mori Yuria 森由利亞, "Chūkan *Dōzō shūyō* to Shinchō Shisen chiiki no shūkyō" 重刊道藏輯要と清朝四川地域の宗教, in Okazaki Yumi 岡崎由美 (ed.), *Chūgoku koseki ryūtsūgaku no kakuritsu: ryūtsū suru koseki, ryūtsū suru bunka* 中國古籍流通學の確立：流通する古籍・流通する文化 (Tokyo: Yūzan shuppan, 2007): 339-401, here 351. As for Peng Yuanrui, at the beginning of the Jiaqing era he was ordered to revise Gaozong's *Shilu* 高宗實錄. In his younger days, Peng Yuanrui and Jiang Shiquan 蔣士銓 were referred to as "The Two Celebrities of Jiangxi 江右兩名士." In 1789-91 Peng rose to the high rank of president of the Board of Civil Office. See *Qingshi gao*, j. 320 (vol. 36, 1769-1770), and Tu Lien-che, "Chiang Shih-ch'üan," in Arthur W. Hummel (ed.), *Eminent Chinese*, 141. According to Kim Yunsu ("Dojang jipyo wa Jang Yoepo" 道藏集要와 蔣予蒲, 282-83) and Wan Dekai 万德凯 ("*Daozang jiyao* yanjiu" 道藏輯要研究, Postdoctoral report, Sichuan University, summer 2007, 8-10), the title *xiangguo* and the posthumous name (*shihao* 諡號) Wenqin should refer to Peng Yuanrui. My thanks to Dr. Wan for sending me a copy of his work on July 15, 2007.

[320] See Wan Dekai "*Daozang jiyao* yanjiu," 8-10.

[321] See Monica Esposito, "The Different Versions of the *Secret of the Golden Flower* and Their Relationship with the Longmen School," *Transactions of the International Conference of Eastern Studies* XLIII (1998): 90-109, here 95, note 17, and 103-105; and of the same author "Shindai ni okeru Kingai-san no seiritsu to *Kinka shūshi*," 清代における金蓋山の成立と金華宗旨 in Kyōto Daigaku Jinbun Kagaku Kenkyūjo (ed.), *Chūgoku shūkyō bunken kenkyū* 中国宗教文献研究 (Kyoto: Rinsen shoten, 2007, 239-264; here 261-262). See also here below, Part Four.

In any case, it is difficult to know on which basis He Longxiang established Peng's editorship; but we cannot but remark that, like his grandson Peng Qifeng, Peng Dingqiu had clear links with Daoism.

Born in Changzhou 長洲 (today's Suzhou, Jiangsu) into a family of military background, Peng Dingqiu (zi: Qinzhi 勤止, Fanglian 訪濂; hao: Nanyun 南畇), after having obtained his jinshi degree in 1676 or 1686,[322] served as Senior Compiler (xiuzhuan 修撰) at the Hanlin Academy in Beijing. Under the guidance of Tang Bin 湯斌 (1627–1687) he was a scholar of Wang Yangming and at the same time a Daoist devotee.[323] In 1674 he participated in vegetarian activities with the literati You Tong 尤侗 (1618–1704, zi: Meian 梅庵) in his hometown and produced Daoist poems.[324] In the Daozang jiyao his name is associated not only with a new edition of a Daoist scripture entitled Zhenquan 真詮 but also, as manager of a spirit writing altar,[325] with the transmission of morality texts including those in honor of Wenchang 文昌, the god of literary pursuits.[326]

---

[322] Qingshi gao, j. 304 (vol. 35, 10503) and j. 480 (vol. 43, 13155), respectively; see Qing Xitai (ed.), Zhongguo daojiao shi, vol. 4, 454, note 1. In Yuquan yulu 玉詮語錄 78b/4 (CK 13, 5753), Peng Dingqiu is said to be the number one scholar in 1676.

[323] It is interesting to notice that the mother and the wife of Jiang Yuanting were also connected to Tang Bin as they were fifth-generation members of his family from Suizhou 睢州 (Henan). See Kim Yunsu, "Dojang jipyo wa Jang Yoepo," 291.

[324] One of the first activities he organized in his hometown was a vegetarian society modeled after the Doufu hui 豆腐會 (Association of Bean Curd Eaters) founded by Gao Panlong 高攀龍 (1562–1626); see Rufus O. Suter, "P'eng Ting-ch'iu," in Arthur W. Hummel (ed.), Eminent Chinese, 617, and L. Carrington Goodrich and Fang Chaoying (eds.), Dictionary of Ming Biography, 1368–1644 (New York: Columbia University, 1976): 701–710. For the Daoist poems included in Meian nianpu 梅庵年譜 see Kim Yunsu, "Dojang jipyo wa Jang Yoepo," 283.

[325] As is well-known, "spirit writing" (in Chinese referred to as fuji 扶乩 "wielding the stylus," fuluan 扶鸞 "wielding the phoenix," feiluan 飛鸞 "flying phoenix," jiangluan 降鸞 "descending phoenix," jiangbi 降筆 "descending brush," etc.) is one of the most common practices of divination which, during the Ming and Qing dynasties, was en vogue among high-ranking officials and literati as well as common people. Its popularity largely derived from the belief of literati and officials who often used it for asking about examinations and attaining official posts. During the time of civil service examinations in the Ming and Qing the practice was so widespread that spirit writing altars (jitan 乩壇; see below Fig. 26, p. 213) could be found in almost every prefecture and county. See David K. Jordan and Daniel Overmyer, The Flying Phoenix: Aspects of Chinese Sectarianism in Taiwan (Princeton: Princeton University Press, 1986): 40–41. See also below, note 384 (p. 213).

[326] Peng Dingqiu showed not only interest in Daoist self-cultivation practices (see his

It is thus plausible, as Kim Yunsu has suggested, that on the basis of these quotations referring to Peng Dingqiu and included in the *Daozang jiyao*, He Longxiang ended up wrongly attributing the entire compilation to Peng Dingqiu.³²⁷ We can call this a "wrong attribution" because a look at the content of the *Daozang jiyao* and its prefaces and postfaces allows the identification of many traces that were left by the collection's true editor. But before following and analyzing such traces we will examine an irrefutable proof of the *Daozang jiyao*'s true editorship that is contained in the work of Min Yide 閔一得.

The Discovery of Jiang Yuanting's Daozang jiyao in Jiangnan

Min Yide 閔一得 (1748/58?–1836) who, as we have seen, was an important figure in Qing dynasty Quanzhen Daoism, mentions the *Daozang jiyao* various times in his writings.³²⁸ As eleventh patriarch of the Longmen 龍門

Preface dated 1710 to the *Zhenquan* 真詮, in CK 21, 9159), but also in spirit writing activities. The introductory note of the *Yuquan yulu* 玉詮語錄 (CK 13, 5753) states that this scripture belongs to Peng's spirit writing altar named Yuquan 玉詮 which was located in Sucheng 蘇城 (Suzhou). Furthermore, in the Preface to the *Dongjing shidu* 洞經示讀 attributed (via spirit writing) to Wenchang dijun 文昌帝君 and dated 1728 (CK 3, 1174–1175), the name of Peng Dingqiu appears related to Wenchang's cult. With regard to this, Rufus O. Suter ("P'eng Ting-ch'iu," 617) documents that occasionally Peng lectured to his younger fellow-villagers at the local temple of the God of Literature (i.e., Wenchang).

327 As Kim Yunsu ("*Dojang jipyo wa Jang Yoepo*," 285–286) emphasizes, He Longxiang does not seem very reliable in his attributions of Daoist works. In the "Qinding Daozang quanshu zongmu" 欽定道藏全書總目, 14a (CK 1, 310), for instance, he attributed the *Xiuzhen shishu* 修真十書 to Shi Tai 石泰 (?–1158) when, as is well known, Shi Tai is only the author of the *Huanyuanpian* 還源篇. Again in the "Guochao fangke daoshu mulu" 國朝坊刻道書目錄, 14a–b (CK 1, 352), although it is said that the printing blocks of the *Daoyan wuzhong* 道言五種 were carved in the Xianfeng era (1854), He attributed this collection to the Song-era figure Weng Baoguang 翁葆光 (fl. 1173). But from the content of this collection one can easily gather that it was a compilation by Tao Susi 陶素耜 (fl. 1676), a Qing official close to Qiu Zhao'ao 仇兆鰲 (1638–1713) who was interested in Daoist inner alchemy.

328 On the life of this master and his work see Part One above and earlier descriptions in *La Porte du Dragon* and in my entry on "Min Yide" in Fabrizio Pregadio (ed.), *Encyclopedia of Taoism*, vol. 2: 747–748. Recently a number of Chinese articles devoted to this important figure have appeared in various Chinese journals. See for instance Wu Yakui 吳亞魁, "Jingaishan ren Min Yide zhuanlüe" 金蓋山人閔一得傳略, *Zongjiaoxue yanjiu* 宗教學研究 (2004.3): 139–148, and the articles issued in the *Zhongguo daojiao* 中國道教 journal available online: Xie Zhengqiang 謝正強,

lineage at Mount Jingai 金蓋 (Zhejiang), while collecting and editing texts on inner alchemy related to his own tradition, he was aware of Daoist works that circulated at that time in the Jiangnan area. Min Yide noted that for his own *Collection from the Ancient Hidden Pavilion of Books* (*Gu Shuyinlou cangshu* 古書隱樓藏書) he edited two texts from the *Daozang jiyao*: the *Yinfujing xuanjie* 陰符經玄解 and the *Jinhua zongzhi* 金華宗旨.

The first text was a commentary by Fan Yibin 范宜賓 (fl. 1722) that editor Jiang Yuanting, as he explains in his Postscript, inserted in the "*Daozang [jiyao].*"[329] Min Yide states in his Preface that he added his own commentary (*zhengyi* 正義) and thus named it *Yinfujing xuanjie zhengyi* 陰符經玄解正義 (Correct Interpretation on the Profound Meaning of the *Yinfu jing*). For his explanations he based himself on a number of exegeses to the *Yinfu jing*—some of which, like the commentary by the Ten Perfects and those by Zhang Guo 張果 and Wang Daoyuan 王道淵, were also included in the *Daozang jiyao*.[330] Like Jiang in his Postscript, Min in his Preface simply refers to the *Daozang jiyao* as *Daozang* 道藏 or Daoist Canon, but he also uses the abbreviation *Jiyao* 輯要.

The second text edited by Min Yide, as is clearly mentioned in its title inside Min's collection, was another work edited by Jiang Yuanting:

> *Lü zushi xiantian xuwu Taiyi Jinhua zongzhi* (The Essence of the Tradition of the Supreme One's Golden Flower of the Primordial

---

"Min Yide xiaokao erze" 閔一得小考二則, *Zhongguo daojiao* (2004.1; http://big5.chinataoism.org/content.php?cate_id=1077#78); Liu Huanling 劉煥玲, "Shixi Min Yide zhi Longmen Fangbian famen" 試析閔一得之龍門方便法門, *Zhongguo daojiao* (2005.5; http://big5.chinataoism.org/showtopic.php?id=9370), and Wang Zongyao 王宗耀, "Min Yide shennian kaoyi" 閔一得生年考疑, *Zhongguo daojiao* (2005.6). For a Japanese presentation of Min Yide's life and his relation with Tantrism see Monica Esposito (モニカ・エスポジト), "Shindai dōkyō to mikkyō: Ryūmon seijiku shinshū" 清代道教と密教―龍門西竺心宗, in Kunio Mugitani 麥谷邦夫 (ed.), *Sankyō kōshō ronsō* 三教交涉論叢 (Kyoto: Jinbun Kagaku Kenkyūjo, 2005): 287–338, in particular 294–306 {revised English version in *Facets of Qing Daoism*, chapter 5, in particular pp. 248–268}.

[329] CK 8, 3192. Here the editor Jiang Yuanting uses the word *Daozang* for the *Daozang jiyao* and signs his Postscript with his appellation Lifu shanren 立甫山人. See here below for other appellations of Jiang.

[330] See the Preface by Min Yide to the *Yinfujing zhengyi* in his *Gu Shuyinlou cangshu* reprinted in Hu Daojing 胡道靜 (ed.), *Zangwai daoshu* 藏外道書, 20 vols. (Chengdu: Bashu shushe, 1992): vol. 10, 296–297. Min Yide quotes here all the commentaries to the *Yinfujing* that were included in the *Daozang jiyao* just before the commentary by Fan Yibin. See CK 8, 3148–3184.

Void by Patriarch Lü [Dongbin]), edited by the Vice-minister Jiang Yuanting and revised by Min Yide from Mount Jingai.

呂祖師先天虛無太一金華宗旨、蔣侍郎元庭先生輯、金蓋山人閱一得訂政。³³¹

Min Yide informs us of its relation to the *Daozang jiyao* by saying:

> This scripture appeared in the *wuchen* year of the Kangxi era (1688) and was transmitted at the Lineage altar of the Lodge of the Dragon Peak on Mount Jingai where a sage of this mountain, Tao Shi'an, printed it. During the Jiaqing era (1796–1820) Vice-minister [Jiang] Yuanting obtained and copied a spurious version of it and inserted it in the *Daozang jiyao*.

是書出於康熙戊辰、金蓋龍嶠山房宗壇所傳、本山先哲陶石菴先生壽諸梓。嘉慶間、侍郎元庭先生得傳抄訛本、纂入 道藏輯要。³³²

Min Yide thus seems to have been quite familiar with the content of the *Daozang jiyao*, at least with regard to the texts he was interested in. According to him, this Daoist Canon of the Jiaqing era was the fruit of Jiang Yuanting's editorship. Furthermore, Min notes that Jiang edited another work devoted to the teachings of the Patriarch Lü Dongbin, the *Lüzu tianxian zhengzong neiji* 呂祖天仙正宗內集 (Inner Collection of the Orthodox Tradition of the Celestial Immortals of Patriarch Lü), which he strongly relied on for his exegesis of the *Lü zushi sanni yishi shuoshu* 呂祖師三尼醫世説述 (Explanations on the Three Sages's Doctrine of Healing the World by the Founding Patriarch Lü).³³³

---

³³¹ *Jinhua zongzhi*, 3a (*Zangwai daoshu*, vol. 10, 328).

³³² *Jinhua zongzhi*, 3a (*Zangwai daoshu*, vol. 10, 328).

³³³ See *Zangwai daoshu*, vol. 10, 354. For a partial translation and presentation of the *Lü zushi sanni yishi shuoshu* and its related texts belonging to the central cycle of Lü Dongbin's teachings associated with Mount Jingai's tradition of Healing the World (Yishi zong 醫世宗), see Monica Esposito, *La Porte du Dragon*, vol. 1, 246–279; "Longmen Taoism in Qing China," *Journal of Chinese Religions* 29 (2001): 191–231, in particular 213–221 {*Facets of Qing Daoism*, chapter 2, in particular pp. 179–183}; and "Shindai ni okeru Kingai-san no seiritsu to Kinka shūshi" 清代における金蓋山の成立と金華宗旨, in Tokio Takata 高田時雄 (ed.), *Chūgoku shūkyō bunken kenkyū kokusai shinpojiumu hōkokusho* 中国宗教文献研究国際シンポジウム報告書 (Kyoto: Jinbun Kagaku Kenkyūjo, 2004): 259–268, in particular 262–265 (also published in Kyōto Daigaku Jinbun Kagaku Kenkyūjo, ed., *Chūgoku shūkyō bunken kenkyū* 中国宗教文献研究, Kyoto: Rinsen shoten, 2007, 239–264, and revised and augmented in Part Four here below). See also Mori Yuria 森由利

As we are going to see, as an affiliate of Lü Dongbin's orthodox lineage of Celestial Immortals, Jiang also compiled a collection of texts better known as *Lüzu quanshu shiliu juan* 呂祖全書十六卷 (Complete Works of Patriarch Lü in 16 scrolls), or *Quanshu zhengzong* 全書正宗 (Complete Works of the Orthodox Lineage).[334] Various prefaces included in the *Daozang jiyao* refer to this collection.[335]

It is thus clear that Min Yide knew Jiang's work. More than that: he also met the man in 1817 when Jiang was in Hangzhou. In the "Biography of Muzhaigong" (Muzhaigong zhuan 牧齋公傳), commented by Min Yide in his *Jingai xindeng* 金蓋心燈 or *Lamp History of Mount Jingai*, Min mentions that Jiang Yuanting wrote for him an essay entitled "Min recovers the epitaph of his ancestor" (Minshi fude zumu ji 閔氏復得祖墓記) which describes Min's discovery in 1817 of the epitaph of his ancestor Muzhaigong and its restoration.[336] We can assume that they exchanged their views on alchemical practice and information about texts in circulation.[337]

亞 "Ryo Dōhin to Zenshin-kyō: Shinchō koshū Kingai-san no jirei o chūshin ni" 呂洞賓と全真教—清朝湖州金蓋山の事例を中心に, in Kikuchi Noritaka 野口鐵郎 (ed.), *Dōkyō no kamigami to kyōten* 道教の神々と経典 (Tokyo: Yūzan kaku, 1999): 242–264, in particular 250–260.

[334] It is under the title of *Lüzu quanshu shiliu juan* that Zhu Gui 朱珪 (1732–1806) in his Preface dated 1803 ("Quanshu zhengzong houxu" 全書正宗後序, j. 首, 1a, in Jiang Yuanting 蔣元庭 ed., *Quanshu zhengzong*, 16 juan, 1805) quotes this collection and states that it was compiled by the Chief Minister Jiang Yupu (Yuanting) 蔣太僕予蒲; see Monica Esposito, "The Different Versions of the *Secret of the Golden Flower* and Their Relationship with the Longmen School," 94–95, and 103–104 (for more recent information see Part Four here below). For a presentation of this collection, see Mori Yuria, "*Dōzo shūyō* to Shō Yobu no Ryoso fukei shinkō," 36–43, and here below.

[335] See for instance the Postfaces by Wu Fengzhou 吳鳳洲 and Jiang Yupu (i.e., Jiang Yuanting) to the *Shiliupinjing* 十六品經 (CK 12, 5340), and below note 343 (p. 193). See also the study of Kim Yunsu ("Dojang jipyo wa Jang Yoepo," 296–303) and his hypothesis that this collection was named *Lüzu quanshu zongzheng jicheng* 呂祖全書宗正集成.

[336] *Jingai xindeng* 金蓋心燈, j. 7, 17b/7–8, in Du Jiexiang 杜潔祥 (ed.), *Daojiao wenxian* 道教文獻, 20 vols. (Taipei: Danqing tushu youxian gongsi, 1983, vols. 10–11): vol. 11, 588; quoted in Kim Yunsu, "Dojang jipyo wa Jang Yoepo," 290.

[337] Min Yide, in the *Yin zhenren Donghua zhengmai huangji hepi zhengdao xianjing* 尹真人東華正脈皇極闔證道仙經 (*Zangwai daoshu*, vol. 10, 367–383), quotes for instance Jiang Yuanting's alchemical views by mentioning Jiang under his style name Nanqiaozi 南樵子. Min also shows his disagreement with Jiang's explanations about the commentary of the *Jinhua zongzhi* by labeling it "Central Lineage" or

According to Min Yide, during the period when Jiang Yuanting was in his region, Jiang learned about another edition of the *Jinhua zongzhi* which was different from the version that Jiang had already inserted in his *Daozang jiyao*. This newly discovered version was transmitted at Mount Jingai, the Daoist sanctuary where Min Yide lived at that time. Jiang is thus said to have taken the decision to substitute the spurious version in his *Daozang jiyao* with that of Mount Jingai; but "as the printing blocks [of the *Daozang jiyao*] were in his residence at the capital (i.e., Beijing), he sent them back to the south. Then he moved again up north and passed away at the capital 而板在京邸、及送板歸南、而先生又北上、卒於京."338

From the biography of Jiang Yuanting we know that in 1816 Jiang indeed moved to Hangzhou with his son for three years, that in 1819 he decided to return to Beijing in order to celebrate the 60th birthday of the Jiaqing emperor, and that he passed away soon afterwards.339

Concerning the printing blocks of the *Daozang jiyao* that were "sent back to the south," there is an interesting passage in Min Yide's preface to the *Yin zhenren Donghua zhengmai huangji hepi zhengdao xianjing* 尹真人東華正脈皇極闔闢證道仙經 (Immortal Scripture by the Perfected Yin Testifying to the Path of Opening and Closing the August Ultimate according to

---

Zhongzong 中宗; see Monica Esposito, *La Porte du Dragon*, vol. 1, 184–221, in particular 205–210; and "Il Segreto del Fiore d'Oro e la tradizione Longmen del Monte Jingai," in Piero Corradini (ed.), *Conoscenza e interpretazione della civiltà cinese* (Venice: Cafoscarina 1996): 151–169, in particular 163–169. See also Kim Yunsu, "*Dojang jipyo* wa Jang Yoepo," 306–312.

338 See the Introductory note by Min Yide to the *Jinhua zongzhi* (*Zangwai daoshu*, vol. 10, 328) whose initial part was already translated above. The entire passage in Chinese reads as follows: 是書出於康熙戊辰、金蓋龍嶠山房宗壇所傳、本山先哲陶石菴先生壽諸梓。嘉慶間、侍郎元庭先生得傳抄訛本、纂入道藏輯要 。後在浙省見本山梓本、議即改梓。而板在京邸、及送板歸南、而先生又北上、卒於京、事故中止。此未了要事、一得之心、不能刻忘也。今歲遊金陵、得世所傳膳本、亦與陶本不盡合、而較蔣本多收一二節、似又出自陶本者、各以私意增損、言人人殊、何以信後。茲一準陶本訂政之。

339 See the epitaph ("Muzhi ming" 墓誌銘) devoted to Jiang Yuanting under his original name Jiang Yupu and compiled by Hu Jing 胡敬 in the Appendix to *juan* 94 of the *Guochao qixian leizheng chubian* 國朝耆獻類徵初編 in 480 *juan* edited by Li Huan 李桓 between 1884 and 1890 (in Zhou Junfu 周駿富 ed., *Qingdai chuanji congkan* 清代傳記叢刊, Taipei: Mingwen shuju, 1985): 146.183–188, in particular 188. More on Jiang Yuanting in Mori Yuria, "*Dōzō shūyō* to Shō Yobu no Ryoso fukei shinkō," 36–37, and Kim Yunsu "*Dojang jipyo* wa Jang Yoepo," 290–295. See also here below. My thanks to Mori Yuria for sending me materials related to the biography of Jiang Yuanting.

the Orthodox Lineage of the Eastern Florescence) dated 1831. Min Yide informs us that the blocks were now stored in Suzhou. It was thanks to them that Min could easily revise the *Jinhua zongzhi* before publishing it in his *Gu Shuyinlou cangshu* or *Collection from the Ancient Hidden Pavilion of Books*:

> Fortunately the spurious copy of the *Hepi jing* was not yet included in the *Daozang [jiyao]*. By contrast, a spurious copy of the *Jinhua zongzhi* was inserted in the Canon. But since its printing blocks were in Suzhou, once I obtained them it was simple to amend this.
>
> 今幸 闔闢經 訛本、未纂入 道藏 。 金華宗旨 訛本、雖入藏、而板存姑蘇、取以重梓、亦自易易。 340

Fig. 19: Heavily used *Chongkan Daozang jiyao* printing blocks at Qingyanggong

It is thus clear that in Min Yide's times, Jiang Yuanting was not only known as the compiler of Lü Dongbin's works but above all as the editor of the *Daozang jiyao*. Jiang is said to have stored the printing blocks of the

---

340 *Zangwai daoshu*, vol. 10, 367. For an almost integral translation of this interesting preface see Monica Esposito, *La Porte du Dragon*, vol. 1, 185–188.

Daozang jiyao in his residence at the capital, but after having moved to Hangzhou in 1816 he wanted them to be transferred to Suzhou. We do not know why Jiang chose Suzhou, but it is of interest to note that in 1815 he was exactly in this town: in December of that year he was invited to write the text of a stele for the rebuilding of the Great Hall of Wenchang in the Xuanmiao guan 玄妙觀 of Suzhou.[341] Two of his friends, Song Rong 宋鎔 and the great-grandchild of Peng Dingqiu, Peng Xilian 彭希濂, who both were living in Suzhou, were charged with its calligraphy.[342] At any rate, during the Daoguang 道光 era (1821–1850) the printing blocks were apparently in Suzhou, the hometown of Peng Dingqiu, but we do not know what happened after that.[343]

Ding Fubao and his Index to Jiang Yuanting's Daozang jiyao

We have to wait until the beginning of the twentieth century to find again some traces of this Canon. In 1922 the bibliophile Ding Fubao 丁福保 (*hao*: Shouyi zi 守一子, 1874–1952), after having obtained a copy of the *Daozang jiyao*, compiled a catalogue entitled *Daozang jiyao zongmu* 道藏輯要總目 which he went on to publish in his *Daozang jinghua lu* 道藏精

---

[341] See Jiang Yuanting, "Chongxiu Yuanmiaoguan Wenchang dadian ji" 重修元妙觀文昌大殿記, in *Chongyin Xuanmiaoguan zhi* 重印玄妙觀志, j. 10, 12b–13a (*Zangwai daoshu*, vol. 20, 501–502); quoted in Kim Yunsu, "Dojang jipyo wa Jang Yoepo," 294.

[342] See Kim Yunsu, "Dojang jipyo wa Jang Yoepo," 292–293. Kim suggests (p. 306) that the *Daozang jiyao* printing blocks could have been stored in Song Rong's house.

[343] It is worthy of note that the grandson of Peng Dingqiu, Peng Qifeng 彭啟豐 (1701–1784) stored in his house an old version of Lü Dongbin's writings, the *Quanshu zongzheng* 全書宗正 which, as is stated in various prefaces included in the *Daozang jiyao*, should be one of the collections that Jiang used for his *Quanshu zhengzong*. The "Conventions" (*Fanli* 凡例) to Jiang's *Quanshu zhengzong* in fact state that "this collection stems from the revision of the [*Quanshu*] *zongzheng* on the basis of the [*Lüzu*] *quanshu* by Liu Tishu 劉體恕 in 32 scrolls and by Shao Zhilin 邵志琳 in 64 scrolls." 是集係就 宗正 原本重訂、恭檢 全書、劉體恕所刻三十二卷、邵志琳所刻六十四卷。In 1852 the printing-blocks of the *Quanshu zongzheng* were restored by Chen Mou 陳謀 and published under the title *Lüzu quanshu zongzheng* 呂祖全書宗正 in 18 *juan*. See Monica Esposito, "The Different Versions of the Secret of the Golden Flower and Their Relationship with the Longmen School," 95 note 17, and 103–105 and "Shindai ni okeru Kingai-san no seiritsu to *Kinka shūshi*," 261–262 (here below, Part Four, Tables 6 & 7, pp. 290–2).

華錄 or *Record of the Quintessence of the Daoist Canons*.[344] In the explanatory note to his catalogue, Ding records a very similar account of what Min Yide reported in 1834 in his introductory note to the *Jinhua zongzhi*:

> This book (i.e., the *Daozang jiyao*) was compiled by the Vice-minister Jiang Yuanting during the Jiaqing era (1796–1820) of the Qing dynasty. Its printing blocks were first kept at his residence at the capital (Beijing), and later he had them sent back south. Then he moved again to the north and passed away at the capital. Thus there are only a few copies in circulation outside.
>
> 是書清嘉慶間蔣元庭侍郎輯、板在京邸、及送板歸南、而先生又北上、卒於京、故外間傳本甚少。

From this passage it is clear that Ding Fubao read Min Yide's note.[345] This is also supported by the fact that some years later Ding published the work of Min Yide.[346]

In his catalogue to the *Daozang jiyao*, Ding based himself not only on the Table of Contents included in his copy entitled *Daozang jiyao zongmu* 道藏輯要總目 but also recorded details regarding the content of texts.[347]

---

[344] Shanghai: Yixue shuju, 1922 (repr. Hangzhou: Zhejiang guji chubanshe, 1989). For a short introduction to this collection including works both from the Ming Daoist Canon and the *Daozang jiyao*, see Judith Boltz, "Daozang jinghua lu," in Fabrizio Pregadio (ed.), *Encyclopedia of Taoism*, vol. 1: 340–341.

[345] This is evident from the comparison of this passage with Min's quotation cited above in note 338 (in particular its underlined part).

[346] This work is entitled *Daozang xubian* 道藏續編. As its title page shows, its first xylographic edition was prepared in 1834 on Mount Jingai (see Fig. 50, p. 296). It includes twenty-three texts forming the core of Min Yide's *Gu Shuyinlou cangshu* 古書隱樓藏書 opening with the *Jinhua zongzhi*. After having bought a copy of it, Ding Fubao made a reproduction using metallic type characters and in 1952 published it. Later reprints in smaller format appeared in 1989 (Beijing: Haiyang chubanshe) and 1993 (Beijing: Shumu wenxian chubanshe); see "Bianji shuoming" 編輯說明 as well as the explanation given by Shou Yizi (i.e., Ding Fubao) in *Daozang xubian* (Beijing: Haiyang chubanshe, 1989). On this collection see Monica Esposito, *La Porte du Dragon*, and Esposito, "Daozang xubian" in Fabrizio Pregadio (ed.), *Encyclopedia of Taoism*, vol. 1, 347–350.

[347] This can be proven by comparing the information given in Ding Fubao's catalogue about the titles of texts, number of fascicles, chapters, authors, etc., and also data contained in the Table of Contents ("Daozang jiyao zongmu") of Jiang Yuanting's *Daozang jiyao*. See Appendix 1 to Monica Esposito, "*Daozang jiyao* ji qi bianzuan de lishi" (2006). The "Daozang jiyao zongmu" originally included in Jiang Yuanting's *Daozang jiyao* was also reedited by He Longxiang under the title "Chongkan Daozang jiyao zongmu" (CK 1, 12–31).

Interestingly, Ding's copy included two supplementary texts that are not found in the 1906 new edition of the *Daozang jiyao*: the *Yuqing zanhua jiutian yanzheng xinyin jijing* 玉清贊化九天演政心印集經 and the *Yuqing zanhua jiutian yanzheng xinyin baochan* 玉清贊化九天演政心印寶懺. Both texts are related to the immortal Lü Dongbin who is called Yuqing zanhua 玉清贊化, a title that was conferred on him in 1800 "on account of the great veneration that he enjoyed among Daoist clergy and laymen."[348]

The first of these two texts was also known to Min Yide because Min quoted it in a passage of his *Lü zushi sanni yishi shuoshu* 呂祖師三尼醫世說述,[349] whereas the second text was commented upon by Min's master Shen Yibing 沈一炳 (1708–1786) who transmitted many texts to Min that then were included in his collection of Daoist scriptures.[350] It is thus quite possible that both texts belonging to Min Yide's tradition came to the attention of Jiang Yuanting during his stay in Hangzhou between 1816 and 1819. One may infer that these were the last texts to be added to the *Daozang jiyao*; and it is conceivable that they were included after the

---

[348] See the Preface by Xiao Lun 蕭掄 (dated 1817) to the *Jingai xindeng*, 1a/3–5 (in Du Jiexiang 杜潔祥 ed., *Daojiao wenxian* 道教文獻, vol. 10, 5) where it is said: "However, in these days nobody is more venerated among Daoist clergy and laymen than the Immortal Lü. Today at the end of the fifth year of the Emperor's [Jiaqing] reign (1800), because of his popular veneration, the four characters Yuqing zanhua 玉清贊化 have been conferred in order to worship him." 而近世道俗所尊奉者莫呂仙若。今天子御極之五年、因民情所信向、特錫「玉清贊化」四字、以褒崇之。

[349] See *Lü zushi sanni yishi shuoshu*, 1a/7–8 (*Zangwai daoshu*, vol. 10, 348) where Min Yide quotes a passage from the *Yuqing zanhua jiutian yanzheng xinyin jijing* 玉清贊化九天演政心印集經 (6a–b) which is found in some versions of the *Daozang jiyao* including the lodge Jiji 箕集 10 (see here below). This passage reads as follows: "The Xinyin jijing says: Qingni (Laozi) reaches the Center, Zhongni (Confucius) catches the Center and Moni (Śākyamuni) empties the Center. 心印集經曰：青尼致中、仲尼時中、牟尼空中." See Monica Esposito, *La Porte du Dragon* (1993), vol. 1, 254–255.

[350] The biography of this master is found in Min's *Jingai xindeng*. Shen Yibing's transmission is particularly related to the cycle of teachings on Celestial Immortality and the tradition of Healing the World (see above, note 333, pp. 189–190) as well as to inner alchemical practices devoted to women {see *Facets of Qing Daoism*, chapter 4}. For an introduction to this master and the transmission of his scriptures see Monica Esposito, *La Porte du Dragon* (1993) vol. 1, and "Longmen Taoism in Qing China," 213–221 {*Facets of Qing Daoism*, chapter 3, pp. 179–190}.

Daozang jiyao printing blocks had been relocated to Suzhou.[351] The discovery of a version of the *Daozang jiyao* that closely matches the description by Ding Fubao would confirm this scenario.

Two Kinds of Extant Editions of Jiang Yuanting's Daozang jiyao

In 1933 the famous French scholar Paul Pelliot (1878–1945) bought a copy of the *Daozang jiyao* collection in China and offered it to the Library of the Collège de France in Paris. In the early 1990s, while I was working on my Ph.D. thesis, I discovered this copy and, by comparing it with Ding Fubao's catalogue, realized that it was a copy of Jiang Yuanting's *Daozang jiyao*.[352] It listed the texts in the same sequence as Ding Fubao's catalogue and, exactly like Ding's catalogue this "Paris copy" included the two above-mentioned texts.[353]

In 1997, when I was invited for the first time to Japan, I was surprised to see that different versions of this Canon were stored in various libraries. In contrast with the Paris version they did not contain the two supplementary texts. Some years later, when I began working at the Institute for Research in Humanities (Jinbun Kagaku Kenkyūjo 人文科学研究所) at Kyoto University, I analyzed a copy stored at the institute's library (in the following called "Jinbun version") and found that the Paris version of the *Daozang jiyao* contained more texts than the version stored at my institute's library. Comparing its table of contents with that of Paris version, I saw that the latter lists two additional texts included in a supplementary lodge Jiji 箕集 10–11 (see Figs. 20 and 21).

Apart from this discrepancy, the tables of contents ("Daozang jiyao zongmu") of the Jinbun and Paris versions do not differ. It is clear that the two versions stem from the same printing blocks except for the following newly engraved parts of the Paris version: 1) its Table of Contents corresponding to folio 15a; and 2) the two additional texts themselves. Unfortunately

---

[351] According to Kim Yunsu ("Dojang jipyo wa Jang Yoepo," 299–300) it is possible that these two texts were added by Jiang Yuanting to his collections just after 1801.

[352] See Esposito, *La Porte di Dragon*, vol. 1, p. 4.

[353] Ding Fubao's catalogue presents for instance a different sequence of texts in comparison with Jiang Yuanting's Table of Contents ("Daozang jiyao zongmu"); and among other things, the Paris version (like Ding Fubao's catalogue) does not include a text entitled *Han Tianshi shijia* 漢天師世家. See Monica Esposito, "*Daozang jiyao* ji qi bianzuan de lishi."

Chapter 1: Histories of Daoism's Ultimate Canon   197

it is difficult to know when these newly engraved parts were added to the Canon; but on the basis of the link of its content to Min Yide's tradition one may infer that this happened after 1801, possibly during the sojourn of Jiang Yuanting in Hangzhou (1816–19) or maybe after 1819 when the printing blocks were moved to Suzhou.

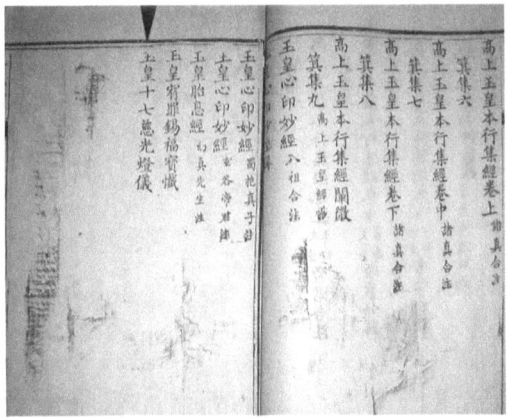

Fig. 20: *Daozang jiyao* Table of Contents (fol. 15a), Jinbun version; black triangle marker in top margin added (Photo M. Esposito, 2005)

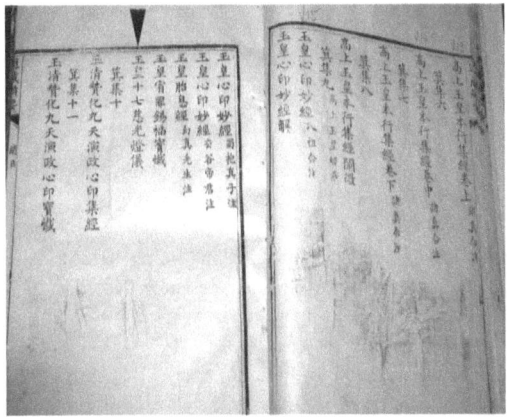

Fig. 21: *Daozang jiyao* Table of Contents (fol. 15a), Paris (Pelliot) version. Additional texts are on the left of the added black triangle marker (Photo M. Esposito, 2006)

Through the analysis of nine extant versions of Jiang Yuanting's Canon that I located at various libraries, I was able to distinguish two basic editions of the *Daozang jiyao*: an older one and a more recent one. I called them the "Jinbun edition" and the "Paris edition." Based on the included prefaces and postfaces, it appears that the Jinbun edition was finished between 1805–1806 and 1816. The Paris edition, by contrast, was probably completed after 1816.[354]

In the course of my subsequent examination of additional copies of this canon in different libraries, a clearer picture of the history, differences of content, and intentions of the canon's editors and compilers gradually emerged. These topics will be explored in the following chapters.

---

[354] In Jiang Yuanting's *Daozang jiyao* the most recent prefaces and postfaces are dated 1805 (see Postface to the *Yuanshi Dadong yujing* 元始大洞玉經 attributed to Liu Shouyuan 柳守元, in CK 3, 1173; Postface (attributed to Liu Shouyuan) to the *Gaoshang Yuhuang benxing jijing* 高上玉皇本行集經, in CK 7, 2585; Preface (attributed to Yuhuang shangdi 玉皇上帝) to the *Yuhuang benxing jijing chanwei* 玉皇本行集經闡微, in CK 7, 2743). There are also three Postfaces to the *Yuhuang benxing jijing chanwei* (CK 7, 2826–2829) that might be dated 1806. This means that the first edition was achieved after 1805 (or 1806) but before 1816 when Jiang moved to Hangzhou, because Min mentioned that the printing blocks were at that time already stored in Jiang's residence in Beijing. See also Mori Yuria, "Dōzō shūyō to Shō Yobu no Ryoso fukei shinkō," 48. According to Kim Yunsu ("Dojang jipyo wa Jang Yoepo," 294) one can assume that the *Daozang jiyao* was published before 1817.

{Editor's note: Shortly after the author's passing, members of the research team directed by her at Kyoto University's Institute of Humanistic Studies (Jinbun kagaku kenkyūjo 京都大學人文科學研究所) compiled the results of the team's research on the *Daozang jiyao* in a report for the Japan Society for the Promotion of Science (JSPS) which had supported Dr. Esposito's research project. This report, which has the number 20242001, concerns work in the years 2008–2011 and is entitled *Dōzō shuyō to meishin jidai no shūkyō bunka* 道藏輯要と明清時代の宗教文化, submitted by Prof. Kunio Mugitani 麥谷邦夫. Of particular interest for the different versions is the contribution by two members of the team, Tomoyuki Kakiuchi 垣内智之 and Noriko Ikehira 池平紀子, whom Dr. Esposito had tasked with research on *Daozang jiyao* versions stored in several Japanese libraries. Their report with the title *Dōzō shuyō hanpon kō* 道藏輯要版本考 (Considerations about *Daozang jiyao* versions) is found, along with its carefully documented tables and appendices, on pp. 271–442 of this JSPS research report.}

Fig. 22: Mr. Kakichi Uchida's old *Daozang jiyao* at Taiwan National Library, Taipei (Photo M. Esposito, 2006)

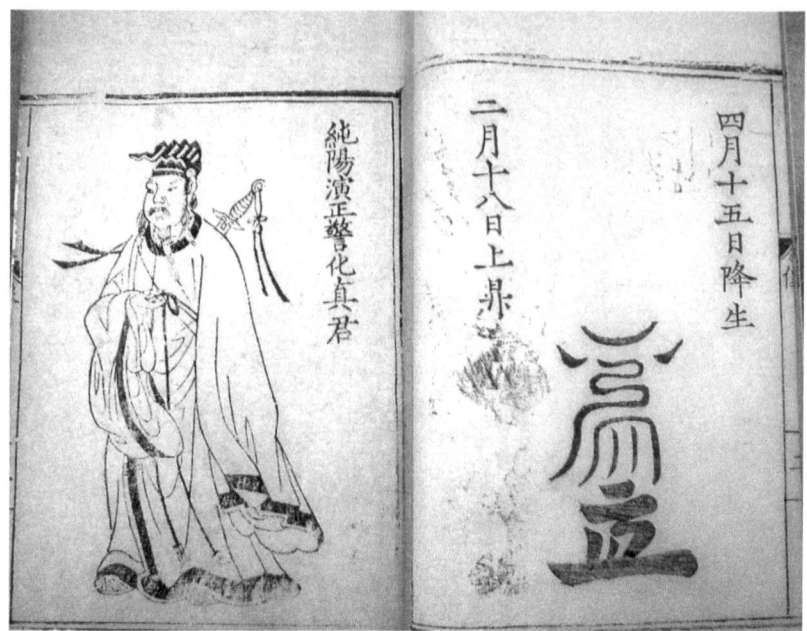

Fig. 23: Lü Dongbin in the old *Daozang jiyao* at Beijing University Library (Photo M. Esposito, 2006)

Chapter 2

Editor Jiang Yuanting's Work and Inspiration

As with the Ming Daoist Canon, some versions of the *Daozang jiyao* begin with the picture of the Sanqing 三清 (Three Pure Ones; see Fig. 44, p. 248) while others do not include it. Extant fascicles in the surveyed *Daozang jiyao* exemplars range from a minimum of 91 to a maximum of 280 depending of the binding and number of missing fascicles, texts, chapters, or folios.[355] The old Erxian'an and the new *Chongkan* edition (1906) of the *Daozang jiyao* feature the same number of lines per folio and characters per line (see Fig. 27).

The *Chongkan Daozang jiyao* and Jiang Yuanting's *Daozang jiyao*, in their most complete state, have the following overall content:

- Four **prefaces**, all except one (the one attributed to Guanyin 觀音) entitled "Daozang jiyao xu" 道藏輯要序: (1) Attributed to Lü Dongbin 呂洞賓; (2)Attributed to Guanyin 觀音; (3) Attributed to Zhongli Quan 鐘離權; (4) Attributed to Su Lang 蘇朗).[356]

---

[355] All extant versions of the *Daozang jiyao* have at least one or more missing texts and lack some chapters and folios. For instance the version stored at Taiwan National Library (see Fig. 22) lacks three entire fascicles. Even Yan Yanfeng's exemplar that was used as basis for the new edition of the *Chongkan Daozang jiyao* and was one of the most complete printed copies of Jiang Yuanting's *Daozang jiyao* (as He Longxiang informs us) does not contain the third fascicle of the lodge Bi 壁; see He Longxiang "Jiaokan Daozang jiyao shuhou," 18a/8–9 (CK 1, 45), and Esposito, "*Daozang jiyao* ji qi bianzuan de lishi" (2006).

[356] Except for the exemplar of Yan Yanfeng (used as basis for the new edition of 1906, the *Chongkan Daozang jiyao*) which, as Ding Peiren (*Daojiao dianji baiwen*, 217) states, contains four Prefaces, all versions of Jiang Yuanting's *Daozang jiyao* that I consulted include only one or two prefaces (those attributed to Su Lang and Zhongli Quan). In the *Chongkan Daozang jiyao*, three of the four prefaces feature the title

- **Conventions** or "Daozang jiyao Fanli" 道藏輯要凡列 in 12 items (1a–3a);

- **Table of Contents** titled "Daozang jiyao zongmu" 道藏輯要總目 (4a–44b);

- **Texts** divided into twenty-eight sections according to the names of the twenty-eight lunar lodges (ershiba xiu 二十八宿). Each section or lodge includes a varying number of subsections, between four and twelve, marked by numbers: ex. Jiaoji 角集 (1–7), Kangji 亢集 (1–7), Diji 氐集 (1–8), etc.[357]

The first six sections or lodges (角集 1–7 to 尾集 1–7) are modeled on the Three Caverns (sandong 三洞) of the Ming Daoist Canon including scriptures revealed by its Daoist Trinity: Yuanshi tianzun 元始天尊 with the *Duren jing* 度人經 placed as the opening text, Lingbao tianzun 靈寶天尊, and Daode tianzun 道德天尊. Sections 7 (箕集 1–9 / 箕集 10–11 only in Paris edition)[358] and 8 (斗集 1–11) are composed of texts attributed or related to Yuhuang, Huangdi (commentaries on the *Yinfu jing* 陰符經 and *Longhu jing* 龍虎經), and the Lords of the Five Dippers (*Wudou jing* 五斗經). Sections 9 (牛集 1–12) to 11 (虛集 1–11) include commentaries on philosophical Daoist works like *Zhuangzi* 莊子, *Liezi* 列子, *Wenzi* 文子, and commentaries on alchemical classics like *Cantongqi* 參同契 and *Ruyaojing* 入藥鏡. Section 12 (危集 1–7) is devoted to texts of the Zhong-Lü and Jingming traditions. Sections 13 (室集 1–7) and 14 (壁集 1–6) form the core of the *Daozang jiyao* including collections of texts attributed or related, via spirit writing, to the patriarch Lü Dongbin under his title Fuyou shangdi 孚佑上帝. Sections 15 (奎集 1–4) to 17 (胃集 1–11) include the texts of saints, patriarchs and masters of the Southern and Northern Lineages (with a prevalence of scriptures related to the Northern Lineage). Sections 18 (昴集 1–10) and 19 (畢集 1–6) are mainly devoted to texts on inner alchemy and attributed to authors from

---

"Daozang jiyao yuanxu" 道藏輯要原序. The Preface attributed to Guanyin is titled "Guanyin dashi bianyan" 觀音大士弁言. See CK 1, 6–10. See also Mori Yuria, "Dōzō shūyō to Shō Yobu no Ryoso fukei shinkō," 35–36.

[357] This division is based on the "old" Jiang Yuanting *Daozang jiyao* (Jinbun edition), its table of contents, and its interlinear commentary. On the content of the *Chongkan Daozang jiyao* see also Fabrizio Pregadio, "Daozang jiyao," in Fabrizio Pregadio (ed.), *Encyclopedia of Taoism*, vol. 1, 341–345.

[358] With the two supplementary texts related to Lü Dongbin as Yuqing zanhua 玉清贊化; see above note 48.

the Tang to Ming dynasties (section 19 contains the texts of Wu Shouyang 伍守陽, 1574–1644). Sections 20 (觜集 1–9) to 22 (井集 1–6) mainly include Daoist encyclopedic works like the *Zhengao* 真誥, *Daoshu* 道樞, and *Yunji qiqian* 雲笈七籤. Section 23 (鬼集 1–7) consists of more recent commentaries on inner alchemy such as the new edition of the *Zhenquan* 真詮 by Peng Dingqiu and the *Xinchuan shuzheng lu* 心傳述證錄 by Jiang Yuelun 蔣日綸 (1729–1803), the father of Jiang Yuanting. Sections 24 (柳集 (1–6) and 25 (星集 1–7)[359] contain litanies (*chan* 懺), Neoconfucian commentaries such as Zhuxi's 朱熹 *Taiji tushuo* 太極圖說, Shao Yong's 邵雍 *Huangji jingshi shu* 皇極經世書, hagiographies, and works related to Wenchang 文昌 and Guandi 關帝. Section 26 (張集 1–7) is mainly devoted to collections of monastic liturgy, rules and ethics. Finally, sections 27 (翼集 1–9) and 28 (軫集 1–6) contain biographical, epigraphical and topographical works.

 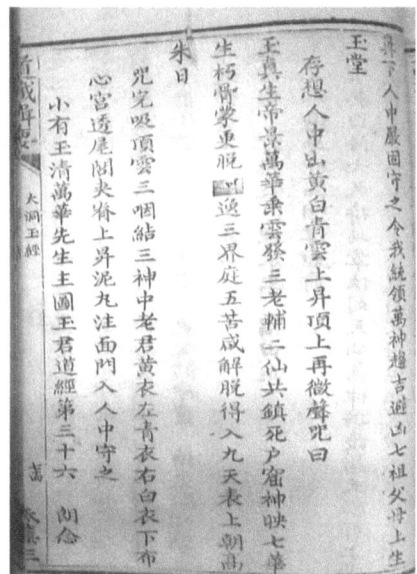

Fig. 24: Two major *Daozang jiyao* editions: Chongkan (1906; left) and Erxian'an exemplars (1805/6–1816; right) juxtaposed. Photographs by M. Esposito

---

[359] Although the tables of contents in the Jinbun and Paris editions of Jiang Yuanting's *Daozang jiyao* record the lodge Xingji 星集 8, in reality all consulted versions of this Canon stop at the lodge Xingji 7. See also Esposito, "*Daozang jiyao* ji qi bianzuan de lishi" (2006).

With regard to content, as the Preface attributed to Zhongli Quan 鐘離權 states, this collection represents "the quintessence of the Daoist Canon." By the order of the Immortal Lü Dongbin, the members of the so-called "Altar of the Source of Awakening" (Jueyuan 覺源) or "First Altar of Awakening" (Diyi Juetan 第一覺壇) directed by Jiang Yuanting,[360] were requested to compile and publish the *Daozang jiyao* in order "to collect the quintessence of the entire Canon and amend the omissions of the earlier [Ming] Canon 擷全藏之精華、補前藏之遺漏."[361] In contrast with the Ming Canon of 1445 and its precursors, which were all sponsored by the imperial court and are the outcome of a working relationship between church and state, the *Daozang jiyao* is the fruit of private initiative by high-ranking officials. In place of the emperors who, in all previous eras, had charged experts among the Daoist clergy with the compilation of Daoist canons, we are here faced with a legendary immortal (Lü Dongbin) who is said to have instructed his lay disciples via spirit writing to compile and publish a new Daoist canon under the editorial guidance of Jiang Yuanting 蔣元庭. Instead of the name Jiang Yuanting (used by Min Yide and Ding Fubao), this canon calls him Jiang Yupu 蔣予蒲 but also uses other appellations such as Mengyin 夢因, Huijue 惠覺, Guanghua dizi 廣化弟子 or Guanghuazi 廣化子, etc.

The Editor Jiang Yuanting 蔣元庭 alias Jiang Yupu 蔣予蒲

Jiang Yupu 蔣予蒲 (*zi*: Yuanting 元庭／沅庭, Nanqiao 南樵) was an elite official at the Qing court. Born in Suizhou 睢州 (Henan) in 1755 from a family of high-ranking officials, he obtained in 1781 the *jinshi* 進士 degree and progressed in his career, filling the post of Grand Secretariat Academician Reader-in-waiting (*Neige shidu xueshi* 內閣侍讀學士) in 1794 and of Chief Minister at the Court of the Imperial Stud (*Taipusi qing* 太僕寺卿) in 1802.[362] In 1806 he became Vice-director of the Ministry of Works

---

[360] This altar is mentioned in the *Daozang jiyao* with different names; see Mori Yuria, "Identity and Lineage—The *Taiyi jinhua zongzhi* and the Spirit writing Cult to Patriarch Lü in Qing China," in Livia Kohn and Harold Roth (eds.), *Daoist Identity* (Honolulu: University of Hawai'i Press, 2000): 165–184, in particular 174–175, and "Dōzō shūyō to Shō Yobu no Ryoso fukei shinkō," 38–41.

[361] See "Daozang jiyao yuanxu," attributed to Zhongli Quan (CK 1, 8).

[362] See the biography on Jiang Yupu / Yuanting, and his epitaph ("Muzhi ming") compiled by Hu Jing 胡敬 in Li Huan 李桓 (ed.), *Guochao qixian leizheng chubian*, j. 94

(*Gongbu youshilang* 工部右侍郎) before serving in 1808 at the Ministry of Revenue (*Hubu shilang* 戶部侍郎). Although involved in an official career, Jiang Yuanting also had religious aspirations. In 1795 he took the five lay precepts at the Guanghuisi 廣惠寺 from the Buddhist monk Mingxin 明心 and became a vegetarian.³⁶³ Jiang's master Mingxin, better known under his secular name Wang Shuxun 王樹勳, had become a monk at the same monastery in Beijing after having failed the official examination. Mingxin was known for spreading spirit writing practices among high officials. In the summer of 1792, Jiang and his Confucian father Jiang Yuelun 蔣曰綸 (1729–1803) often visited Mingxin's monastery and joined the Jueyuan 覺源 or Diyi juetan 第一覺壇, a spirit writing altar in honor of the immortal Lü Dongbin 呂洞賓.³⁶⁴ Jiang was known at this altar under the name

---

(Zhou Junfu ed., *Qingdai chuanji congkan*, 146.163 and 146). While in the biography 35b/10 (146.160) the year 1801 is mentioned, in the epitaph (146.185) one finds the date 1802.

³⁶³ See Jiang Yuanting's biography in Li Huan 李桓 (ed.), *Guochao qixian leizheng chubian*, j. 94, 37b (Zhou Junfu ed., *Qingdai chuanji congkan*, 146.160–163); Wang Xianqian 王先謙 (ed.), *Donghua xulu* 東華續錄 under "Jiaqing 39" 嘉慶三十九, 12a (in *Xuxiu Siku quanshu* 續修四庫全書, Shanghai: Shanghai guji, 1995): vol. 375, 163; and *Qing huidian shili* 清會典事例, j. 112 (Shibu 史部 96, Chufenli 處分例 35, "Sengdao dudie" 僧道度牒; in Academia Sinica electronic data, 448–1, 448–2). For the reference to Jiang Yuanting's vegetarianism taught by Mingxin (i.e., Wang Shuxun) see Chen Kangqi 陳康祺 (1840–?), *Langqian jiwen chubi erbi sanbi* 郎潛紀聞初筆二筆三筆, 2 vols., Sanbi 三筆 j. 1/34 ("Jiang Yupu jianli buming" 蔣予蒲見理不明, in *Qingdai shiliao biji congkan* 清代史料筆記叢刊, Beijing: Zhonghua shuju, 1984): vol. 2, 664.

³⁶⁴ See the Preface to *Chanfa daguan* 懺法大觀 by Jiang Yuelun, dated 1803 (CK 21, 9220), where it is reported that in the summer of 1792 Jiang Yuelun and his son Jiang Yuanting often visited Guanghuisi and were probably during that period introduced by Mingxin to spirit writing practice and its cults (cf. Kim Yunsu, "Dojang jipyo wa Jang Yoepo," 293). In this preface Jiang Yuelun, before introducing his visits with his son to the Buddhist monastery, says that before coming into contact with the monk Mingxin he ignored that the paths of Daoism and Buddhism were connected with his Confucian path (初不知仙佛之道與吾儒相通也). Via Mingxin, they experienced at Guanghuisi the practice of Nature and Life (*xingming zhi gong* 性命之功). The teachings transmitted by the monk Mingxin are clearly related to inner alchemical practice and linked to the important scripture *Jinhua zongzhi* 金華宗旨 which came to be known in the West as *The Secret of the Golden Flower* (see Part Four below). More particularly, in this preface Jiang Yuelun refers to the transmission of "the tenets of the Great Method of Celestial Immortals" (*Tianxian dafa zongzhi* 天仙大法宗旨) which do not rely on minor techniques like dietetics, operative alchemy, etc. These "tenets of the Great Method of Celestial Immortals" are at the center of the constitution of Jiang Yupu's altar and its "lineage of the Celes-

of Huijue 惠覺 or Guanghua dizi 廣化弟子, possibly in memory of his conversion at the Guanghui 廣惠 monastery under the Buddhist master Mingxin and of his association with the altar Juetan 覺壇.[365] Between 1803 and 1805, on the basis of previous anthologies attributed to the immortal Lü Dongbin entitled *Lüzu quanshu* 呂祖全書 (Complete Works of the Patriarch Lü),[366] Jiang with the help of his altar's companions compiled a new edition: the *Quanshu zhengzong* 全書正宗 (Complete Works of the Orthodox Lineage). As mentioned above this 16-*juan* collection was also known as *Lüzu quanshu*.[367] Except for a limited number of texts, most of its scriptures were also included in the central sections of the *Daozang jiyao*.[368]

tial Immortals" (Tianxianpai 天仙派) and also of the compilation of the *Daozang jiyao*. It is interesting to compare the view of this "Great Method" mentioned in this preface with the "Fanli" of the *Daozang jiyao* (in particular item 5) as well as the preface to the *Daozang jiyao* attributed to Zhongli Quan. As to Mingxin (original name: Wang Shuxun), after having failed the official examination, he became a monk at Beijing's Guanghuisi and was known for spreading spirit writing practice among high officials like Jiang Yuanting, Pang Shiguan 龐士冠, and others. Because of this Mingxin was later criticized and condemned to return to secular life. In 1815 he was accused of having obtained an official post by bribery and was finally sent to exile in Heilongjiang 黑龍江. Jiang Yuanting, Song Rong 宋鎔 and other disciples of Mingxin were obliged to resign. See Zhaolian 昭槤 (1776–1830), *Xiaoting zalu* 嘯亭雜錄, j. 8 on "Wang Shuxun" (in *Qingdai shiliao biji congkan* 清代史料筆記叢刊, Beijing: Zhonghua shuju, 1980): 236, and the biography of Shi Chengzao 石承藻 in *Qingshi gao*, j. 356 (vol. 37, 11319–11320).

[365] This has been suggested by Kim Yunsu ("*Dojang jipyo wa Jang Yoepo*," 295). It is interesting to note that even Min Yide in the notes to the *Jinhua zongzhi* mentions the monk Wang 王和尚 (i.e., Wang Shuxun) as master of Jiang Yuanting; see *Jinhua zongzhi* chap. 12, 31b/5 (*Zangwai daoshu*, vol. 10, 342).

[366] The first edition of the *Lüzu quanshu* in 32 scrolls was published by Liu Tishu 劉體恕 in 1744. In 1775 this edition was enlarged to 64 scrolls by Shao Zhilin 邵志琳. See also note 343, and below.

[367] See note 334 (p. 190). See also the preface attributed to Liu Shouyuan 柳守元 ("*Quanshu zhengzong zongxu*" 全書正宗總序, j. 首, 38b–39b in Jiang Yuanting ed., *Quanshu zhengzong*) where Huijue (Jiang Yuanting) is said to have been ordered to revise this collection with the help of his altar's companions.

[368] Except for the *Chanzong zhengzhi* 禪宗正旨, and the *Jingangjing zhu* 金剛經註 with its Appendix (*Xinjing zhu* 心經註), the remaining 17 texts were all included in the *Daozang jiyao*:

1. *Fuyou shangdi Chunyang Lüzu tianshi Shiliupin jing* 孚佑上帝純陽呂祖天師十六品經 (Section 13, lodge Shiji 室集 1, in CK 12, 5293-5340);

2. *Jinhua zongzhi* 金華宗旨 (Section 13, lodge Shiji 室集 2, in CK 12, 5349-5382);

Thanks to the *Quanshu zhengzong* and to its new revealed scriptures that are included in the *Daozang jiyao*, we can know more about Jiang Yuanting's religious beliefs, his involvement in spirit writing activities, and the foundation of his "orthodox lineage."

Jiang Yuanting's Spirit writing Altar: Beliefs and Aspirations

Like earlier spirit writing groups of literati, Jiang Yuanting and his companions—mostly elite officials involved in the compilation of the Imperial encyclopedia *Siku quanshu* 四庫全書[369]—had great interest in Daoist methods of self-cultivation, inner alchemy, and Daoist esoteric doctrines. In fact, among Ming and Qing literati the cult of immortals was very popu-

---

3. *Tongcan jing* 同參經 (Section 13, lodge Shiji 室集 3, in CK 12, 5383–5415);
4. *Wujing hebian* 五經合編 (Section 13, lodge Shiji 室集 4, in CK 12, 5417–5442);
5. *Lüdi wenji* 呂帝文集 (Section 13, lodge Shiji 室集 5, in CK 12, 5443–5507);
6. *Lüdi shiji* 呂帝詩集 (Section 13, lodge Shiji 室集 6–7, in CK 13, 5511–5622);
7. *Taishang Daodejing jie* 太上道德經解 (Section 5, lodge Xinji 心集 1, in CK 4, 1673–1726);
8. *Xiantian doudi chiyan wushang xuangong Lingmiao zhenjing* 先天斗帝敕演無上玄功靈妙真經 (Section 8, lodge Douji 斗集 1, in CK 7, 2867–2879);
9. *Yushu baojing* 玉樞寶經 (Section 8, lodge Douji 斗集 11, in CK 8, 3504–3512);
10. *Yishuo* 易說 (Section 14, lodge Biji 壁集 1–2, in CK 13, 5623–5714);
11. *Chuandaoji* 傳道集 (Section 12, lodge Weiji 危集 2, in CK 12, 5113–5142);
12. *Tianxian jindan xinfa* 天仙金丹心法 (Section 14, lodge Biji 壁集 6, in CK 13, 5859–5993);
13. *Xuanzong zhengzhi* 玄宗正旨 (Section 8, lodge Douji 斗集 4, in CK 8, 3045–3057);
14. *Shijie gongguoge* 十戒功過格 (Section 25, lodge Zhangji 張集 3, in CK 23, 10309–10339);
15. *Jingshi gongguoge* 警世功過格 (Section 25, lodge Zhangji 張集 3, in CK 23, 10339–10353);
16. *Shengji jiyao* 聖蹟紀要 (Section 14, lodge Biji 壁集 5, in CK 13, 5831–5857);
17. *Yulu daguan* 語錄大觀 (Section 14, lodge Biji 壁集 3, in CK 13, 5715–5778).

[369] Many of Jiang Yuanting's companions were elite officials mentioned in the *Siku quanshu zongmu* 四庫全書總目, j. 首. See also Mori Yuria "*Dōzō shūyō* to Shō Yobu no Ryoso fukei shinkō," 40–41, and Kim Yunsu, "*Dojang jipyo* wa Jang Yoepo," 291.

lar: Chen Tuan 陳摶, Lü Dongbin 呂洞賓, and Zhang Sanfeng 張三峰 were highly venerated for having realized the Dao thanks to inner alchemical practices. Regarded as a kind of idealized heroes, these immortals were often the protagonists of literary compositions produced via spirit writing that centered on their life, on biographical accounts and anecdotes, on the transmission of their esoteric teachings, moral injunctions, etc.[370]

Fig. 25: The dragon-headed tip of a spirit writing instrument, inspired fount of many texts in the *Daozang jiyao* canon (Photo Urs App, 1998)

While groups of devotees or spirit writing altars of private persons composing such scriptures existed just about everywhere, the community of Hansangong 涵三宮 (Palace Encompassing the Three) distinguished itself particularly in Lü Dongbin's cult. Established during the 18th century in the Hubei region as a special and independent sanctuary for receiving Lü Dongbin's teachings via spirit writing, this community was not only at the source of the first *Lüzu quanshu* 呂祖全書 but also of networks of Lü

---

[370] See Gōyama Kiwamu 合山究, "Min-Shin no bunjin to okaruto shumi" 明清の文人とオカルト趣味, in Arai Ken 荒井健 (ed.), *Chūka bunjin no seikatsu* 中華文人の生活 (Tokyo: Heibonsha, 1994): 469–502, and Shiga Ichiko 志賀市子, *Chūgoku no kokkurisan: Furan shinkō to kajin shakai* 中国のこっくりさん：扶鸞信仰と華人社会 (Tokyo: Taishūkan shoten, 2003): 124–125.

Dongbin's devotees spreading all over China. Before the foundation of independent temples for this purpose, spirit writing altars were often located in domestic residences. With the establishment of the Hansangong community thanks to the participation of functionaries of different Chinese provinces, an organization with its own regulations and practices was put in place, and members came to fulfill specified functions.³⁷¹ It is in this community that the project of composing the *opus magnum* of Lü Dongbin took shape.

In 1712 the Hansangong was the site where a group of texts central to the compilation of the *Lüzu quanshu* was produced, and in 1739 the *Cantong miaojing* 參同妙經 (Mysterious Scripture on the Equality of the Three [Teachings]) was completed.³⁷² In 1742 Liu Tishu 劉體恕 and Huang Chengshu 黃誠恕 gathered all scriptures which, as Huang put it, "could be called collecting contributions to the great completion of the Daoist Canon" 可謂集道藏之大成, and then published the *Lüzu quanshu* in 32 scrolls.³⁷³ Liu Tishu, who was also on the verge of publishing a compilation of spirit writing scriptures attributed to Wenchang, the *Wendi quanshu* 文帝全書 (Complete Writings of the Imperial Lord Wen, 1743), also gave the title *Quanshu* 全書 to Lü Dongbin's anthology.³⁷⁴

The community of Hansangong served as a model for Jiang Yuanting's spirit writing altar. For instance, the majority of Hansangong's scriptures was republished in a new Lü Dongbin anthology, the *Quanshu zhengzong* or *Complete Works of the Orthodox Lineage*. Moreover, Hansangong's so-

---

371 See the Preface by Huang Chengshu 黃誠恕 to the *Cantong miaojing* 參同妙經 ("Cantong miaojing xu," j. 16, 3a–4b) and to the *Sanpin jing* 三品經 ("Qingwei sanpinjing xu" 清微三品經序, j. 13, 3a–4b) in Liu Tishu 劉體恕 (ed.), *Lüzu quanshu* 呂祖全書. I have used the edition of 1868 (with a Preface added in 1879) in 33 juan (including the *Chanzong zhengzhi* 禪宗正指) from the woodblocks stored at the Xiangtan Chongshantang 湘潭崇善堂藏板. This edition is preserved at Kyoto University's Institute for Research in Humanities. See also Ma Xiaohong 馬曉宏, "*Daozang* deng zhuben suoshou Lü Dongbin shumu jianzhu" 道藏等諸本所收呂洞賓書目簡注, *Zhongguo daojiao* 中国道教 (1988.3): 34–37.

372 See "Lüzu quanshu Hansangong zayong xiaoxu" 呂祖全書涵三宮雜詠小序 j. 27, 1a) where the revelation of the *Sanpin jing* is said to have occurred in 1712, and that of the *Cantongjing* in 1730. Jiang Yuanting revised and published these two texts in his *Quanshu zhengzong*. The *Sanpin jing* has been included as part of the *Shiliupin jing* and positioned as opening text.

373 See the Preface by Huang Chengshu to the *Lüzu quanshu* ("Lüzu quanshu xu," 3a).

374 See the Postface by Huang Chengshu to the *Lüzu quanshu* ("Lüzu quanshu ba," j. 32, 9a).

called "great completion of the Daoist Canon" was in a sense incarnated in Jiang Yuanting's *Daozang jiyao*. After having compiled Patriarch Lü Dongbin's scriptures based on a previous *Lüzu quanshu* collection, Jiang Yuanting and his altar's companions decided to insert them in a new Daoist Canon that would pay the ultimate tribute to Lü Dongbin and his teachings by spreading them all across the country. In this way, texts representing at their origin beliefs and practices related to Lü Dongbin's communities could become part of larger Daoist lore under the umbrella of Jiang Yuanting's new orthodox lineage. In this respect, earlier beliefs and aspirations of the Hansangong community came also to be elaborated in a new key. An example of such elaboration is the transformation of Liu Qi 柳榮—the legendary disciple and assistant of Lü Dongbin in the *Lüzu quanshu* and in the late Quanzhen genealogic registers—into the prominent figure of Liu Shouyuan 柳守元.[375]

Among gods and immortals believed to descend at Jiang Yupu's altar, Liu Shouyuan plays a prominent role. As mediator between Lü Dongbin and his disciples, he not only assisted Jiang Yupu and his altar's companions in compiling the *Quanshu zhengzong* but also appears as the author of a number of prefaces and postfaces included in both of Jiang Yupu's compilations. Furthermore, Liu Shouyuan is also portrayed as author of a cycle of new scriptures that were included only in the *Daozang jiyao*.[376] If the ma-

---

[375] Liu Qi is, for instance, the purported author of a Postface to the *Sanpin jing* (*Lüzu quanshu*, j. 15, 21a). In the "Liu zhenjun gao" 柳真君誥, he is presented as the first disciple of Lü Dongbin 呂祖首座弟子 (*Lüzu gao* 呂祖誥, in *Lüzu quanshu*, j. 32, 6a). In the Longmen lineage of the Quanzhen tradition, Liu Qi is also mentioned as the first disciple of Chunyang dijun 純陽帝君 (i.e., Lü Dongbin); see "Daopu yuanliu tu" 道譜源流圖 in *Jingai xindeng*, 3a (vol. 10, 23). As Mori has emphasized, Jiang Yuanting in his *Quanshu zhengzong* and *Daozang jiyao* has published the same Postface to the *Sanpin jing* but under the name of Liu Shouyuan. See "Liu zushi sanpinjing houji" 柳祖師三品經後記, 87b/10 (CK 12, 5338–5339). For more information on this figure see Mori Yuria, "Shinchō Zenshin-kyō no denkai to Ryoso fukei shinkō" 清朝全真教の伝戒と呂祖扶乩信仰, in Fukui Fumimasa hakushi taishoku kinen ronshū kankōkai 福井文雅博士古稀・退職記念論集刊行会 (ed.), *Ajia bunka no shisō to girei* アジア文化の思想と儀礼 (Tokyo: Shunjūsha, 2005): 441–461, in particular 451–457.

[376] See *Santan yuanman Tianxian dajie lüeshuo* 三壇圓滿天仙大戒略說 (CK 24, 10457–10468) and *Qingwei hongfan daomen gongke* 清微宏範道門功課 (CK 23, 10213–10235). On these two scriptures see Mori Yuria, "Shinchō Zenshin-kyō no denkai to Ryoso fukei shinkō," and the same author's "Shō Yobu no Ryoso fukei shinkō to Zenshin-kyō" 蔣予蒲の呂祖扶乩信仰と全真教, in Horiike Nobuo 堀池信夫 and Sunayama Minoru 砂山稔 (eds.), *Dōkyō kenkyū no saisentan* 道教研究

jority of scriptures revealed at Jiang Yupu's spirit writing altar are the fruit of editorial recycling rather than literary creation, the scriptures attributed to Liu Shouyuan appear, by contrast, original. They shaped a new identity for the members of Jiang Yupu's altar. In this context the legendary holder and supervisor of Jiang Yupu's altar,[377] Liu Shouyuan, became recognized as the second patriarch of the orthodox lineage, the Tianxian pai 天仙派 or Celestial Immortals lineage, and was venerated as the successor of the founding patriarch Lü Dongbin.[378] This new lineage—created at Jiang Yupu's altar with its beliefs, aspirations, rules and commitments—became the driving force in the compilation of a new standardized Daoist Canon whose revelation lay in the magical hands of the founding patriarch Lü Dongbin.

The Central Role of Lü Dongbin and His Revelation

The central role of Lü Dongbin is clearly stated several times in the prefaces to the *Daozang jiyao* and its "Conventions" (*Fanli* 凡例). In item 2 of the Conventions, for instance, it is said that innumerable realized men and saints of the past and present all chose Lü Dongbin—here mentioned under his title Fuyou dishi 孚佑帝師 (Imperial Master, Savior of the Needy)—to guarantee the genuine transmission of the mysterious Dao. This choice is based not only on Lü Dongbin's traditional status as patriarch of the Southern and Northern lineages who, in handing down their sacred scriptures, is capable of explaining their mysterious meaning, but even more on his prowess as great savior capable of converting entire worlds.[379] In his role of savior, Lü Dongbin announced in front of Laozi his project of "compiling all cases [of scriptures] and harmonizing all together" into a single standardized

---

の最先端 (Tokyo: Taiga shobō, 2006): 82–108.

[377] From 1798 onward, Liu Shouyuan was admitted to Jiang Yupu's altar; see Mori Yuria, "Shinchō Zenshin-kyō no denkai to Ryoso fukei shinkō," 451.

[378] This is clearly stated in the Postface by Zhiqiu 志秋 (i.e., Fan Ao 范鏊, fl. 1780–1803) to the *Jinhua zongzhi* 金華宗旨, 4b/8 (CK 12, 5382) where Liu Shouyuan, under the title Hongjiao enshi 宏教恩師, is presented as second patriarch of the Tianxian pai.

[379] See item 2 of "Daozang jiyao Fanli" 道藏輯要凡例, 1a (expanded in 16 items in the *Chongkan Daozang jiyao* under the title "Chongkan Daozang jiyao Fanli shiliu ze" 重刊道藏輯要凡例十六則, 12a (vol. 1, 10). For a presentation of the Prefaces and Conventions to the *Daozang jiyao* see also Mori Yuria, "Dōzō shūyō to Shō Yobu no Ryoso fukei shinkō," 43–47.

compilation: the *Daozang jiyao*.[380] In authorizing this new Daoist Canon, Lü Dongbin realized the dream of generations of his devotees. This legendary Daoist immortal selected this Canon's texts carefully in order to "synthesize the true transmission of the alchemical path and to gather the essence of all scriptures 綜丹道之真傳、羅諸真之典要."[381] Always moved by great compassion he ordered "all disciples at the Altar of the Source of Awakening to compile the *Daozang jiyao*, to get rid of the false and return to the genuine, to delete the superfluous and arrive at the essential 命覺源諸子、編纂道藏輯要一書、棄偽而歸真、刪繁而就約 (...)."[382]

The divine revelation of the savior Lü Dongbin in itself is not so exceptional as one might think. As we know, the idea of divine revelation is central to many scriptures that are called "sacred" such as the Holy Bible or the Koran—both believed to be the word of God, and the latter dictated to the prophet Muhammad by the archangel Gabriel. Daoist canonical scriptures have a similar air of divine inspiration. The word of God himself or of angels, prophets, apostles, etc. ensured for the Abrahamic religions the legitimate nature of their sacred scriptures. Similarly, Daoist canonical scriptures carry the mark of legitimation by the Daoist trinity, the Sanqing, while Buddhist sutras are often portrayed as the words of Buddhism's founder Śākyamuni recorded by his immediate disciples ("Thus I have heard ...").

Like the previous Ming Daoist Canon, this newly standardized Canon of the Qing dynasty also bears the Sanqing's seal of approval. The image of this Daoist trinity is reproduced on the frontispiece of some of its versions (see Fig. 44, p. 248). But the entire compilation rests in the holy hands of the Daoist messenger Lü Dongbin. This immortal vows in front of the divine Laozi to carry out the project of compiling the "Essence of the Daoist Canon."[383] The *Daozang jiyao* is a beautiful example of a divine revelation in which central divinities, angels, or immortals effectuate the transmission of sacred scriptures and doctrines via chosen prophets, seers, and inspired mediums. Instead of dictating his message through dreams or visions, the

---

[380] See the Preface attributed to Lü Dongbin, "Daozang jiyao yuanxu," 4a (CK 1, 6). See also item 3 of "Daozang jiyao Fanli" 道藏輯要凡例, 1b (CK 1, 10).

[381] See the preface attributed to Su Lang, "Daozang jiyao yuanxu," 10b (*Chongkan Daozang jiyao*, vol, 1, 9).

[382] The entire Chinese passage reads as follows: 命覺源諸子、編纂 道藏輯要一書、棄偽而歸真、刪繁而就約；廣大精微、而天人之道備。 See the Preface attributed to Zhongli Quan, "Daozang jiyao yuanxu," 8a (CK 1, 8).

[383] See the Preface attributed to Lü Dongbin, "Daozang jiyao yuanxu," 4a (CK 1, 6).

immortal Lü Dongbin intervenes more spectacularly by guiding the writing instrument in the hands of devotees and by tracing his messages character by character on an altar covered with rice grains or sand (see Figs. 25, 26, 27).[384]

Fig. 26: Spirit writing altar (from *Dianshiji huabao* 點石齋畫報丙集, 1884). Two men hold the T-shaped writing instrument whose vertical tip traces Chinese characters on the altar table. The third deciphers the characters.

---

[384] In Chinese planchette or spirit writing, immortals, gods, well-known masters of the past, or cultural heroes are thought to descend into a spirit writing device which often is a T-shaped wooden device with a pointed protrusion on its long end (see Fig. 25, p. 208, and Fig. 27, p. 214). The handles are held by one or two persons above an altar table. As the device begins to "automatically" move, the protrusion at the long end of this device traces large characters on a tray covered with sand called *jipan* 乩盤 (planchette tray) or *shapan* 砂盤 (sand tray). In this way it can trace magical charms and predictions of the future, diagnose illnesses, issue moral exhortations, reveal examination questions, and convey all kinds of teachings (ranging from short phrases to voluminous texts) to the faithful gathered around the altar. For descriptions of different spirit writing devices, altar setups, and methods see David K. Jordan and Daniel Overmyer, *The Flying Phoenix*, 32–33, 38, 45, and *passim*. See also Gōyama Kiwamu, "Min Shin no bunjin to okaruto shumi," 469–502, and Shiga Ichiko, *Chūgoku no kokkurisan*, 2–12. On spirit writing see also here above note 325 (p. 186).

Fig. 27: "Flying Dragon" spirit writing instrument on sanded altar board (Hong Kong, Shang Sin Chun Daoist Temple, 1998; photo by Urs App)

Fig. 28: Author and editor of this book with a present-day spirit writing team (Hong Kong, Shang Sin Chun Daoist Temple, 1998)

This type of written divine communication via a special divinatory device was extremely popular in Qing times and offered a very effective way of reviving or creating a tradition through divine intervention. The entire project of collecting the scriptures and compiling a new, standardized edition of the Daoist Canon was thus intimately connected with and directed by a spirit writing altar, the altar of Jiang Yuanting. It was onto this altar that Lü Dongbin descended and gave precise orders to his disciples, instructing them to carry out his publication project in compliance with the divine Laozi and all saints and realized men.

A New Daoist Canon, Quintessence of the Genuine Path of Inner Alchemy

The criteria purportedly dictated by Lü Dongbin for achieving this compilation are laid out in the "Conventions" (*Fanli*) and prefaces of the *Daozang jiyao*. Here Lü Dongbin orders his disciples to select the essence of all scriptures by "synthesizing the true alchemical path." This synthesis of the "true alchemical path" forms the core of the *Daozang jiyao*, and the majority of the items in its "Conventions" deal with this task and its definition.

First of all it is important to understand the Daoist purport 道旨—the essence and goal of Daoist teaching—of what is called *dangong* 丹功, alchemical practice (item 4 of the Conventions). It is necessary to distinguish inner alchemy or *neidan* 內丹 from exterior practice or *waigong* 外功. "Inner alchemy can transcend the ordinary and enter the holy, while exterior practices can only chase away diseases and prolong life" 內丹可以超凡入聖、外功祗可卻病延年 (item 8). However, one must be capable of distinguishing those scriptures that, although they seem to deal with operative alchemy and use its terms and metaphors, "in reality are transmitting the secret of alchemical practice" 其實乃備傳丹功之秘. An example is the *Cantongqi* 參同契 which is said to represent "the heart transmission of the Patriarch Wei [Boyang] 魏伯陽"[385] (item 6).

It is thus necessary to discern ordinary practices from the Daoist goal: the attainment of true immortality (item 5). As the Preface attributed to Zhongli Quan 鍾離權 explains, practices like dietetics, gymnastics, breathing, operative alchemy, salivation techniques, spells, talismans, etc, represent the "small vehicle" and are far removed from the "genuine awakening" to the truth. If the previous Canon integrated such "small" practices, the

---

[385] *Weizu xinchuan* 魏祖心傳.

new Canon made the clear choice of omitting them in order to focus on the quintessence of Daoist teaching, the greatness of Dao. The motto thus was simplicity and purity, as opposed to complexity and adulteration.³⁸⁶ In this perspective, scriptures involving too much complexity like the *Daofa huiyuan* 道法會元, *Wushang biyao* 無上祕要, *Taiping jing* 太平經 or the *Lingbao lingjiao jidu jinshu* 靈寶領教濟度金書 were not included (item 9). The same holds true for specialized manuals on ritual or talismans (item 10).³⁸⁷ By contrast, alchemical scriptures like the *Lingbao bifa* 靈寶畢法 were preserved and appreciated for "their simple and unadorned words" 言皆平實, as was the *Huangting neiwaijing jing* 黃庭內外景經 that shares the same methods of eternal life (item 8).

A "puristic vision of *neidan*" is then at the basis of this new Canon whose aim it is to return to the essential purity of Daoism and "to amend the omissions of the earlier [Ming] Canon." Instead of voluminous and complex texts on rituals, specialized talismanic manuals, and books on physiological techniques and operative alchemy, the canonical choice ranges from texts on self-cultivation and soteriology, morality and ethics, precepts and discipline, to commentaries on Daoist philosophical and alchemical classics with their poems and songs.

In sum, the *Daozang jiyao* reflects an idealistic vision of Daoism that arose and spread among literati and spirit writing circles interested in self-cultivation who were caught up in moralistic and eschatological sentiments of sanctity and salvation. It pitted lay believers who, apart from their traditional Confucian background, had also Daoist and Buddhist knowledge as well as financial ability, against professional Daoists, priests, and specialists of ritual who had progressively lost their prestige at the imperial court. Finally this Canon mirrors, more specifically, the beliefs and aspirations of the members of the so-called Tianxian lineage (*Tianxianpai* 天仙派, allegedly founded by the patriarch Lü Dongbin 呂洞賓) and represents "the method

---

³⁸⁶ See the Preface attributed to Zhongli Quan, "Daozang jiyao yuanxu," 8a (*Chongkan Daozang jiyao*, vol 1, 8) and "Daozang jiyao Fanli," 12b–14a (item 3, item 5, and item 10; CK 1, 10–11).

³⁸⁷ This is only partly true because the *Daozang jiyao* also includes ritual texts and manuals of exorcism like the *Gaoshang shenxiao yuqing zhenwang zishu dafa* 高上神霄玉清真王紫書大法 (CK 8, 3253–3449). About this text originally included in the *Daozang* (DZ 1219) see Kristofer Schipper and Franciscus Verellen (eds.), *The Taoist Canon*, 3 vols. (Chicago & London: The University of Chicago Press, 2004): vol. 2, 1094–1095.

of the Golden Elixir 金丹之法,"³⁸⁸ which in the eyes of the reformers is the quintessence of orthodox Daoist teaching.

Unfortunately this great project did not bear the expected fruit. What was supposed to get recognized as the new Daoist Canon of the Qing dynasty became, after Jiang Yuanting's death, a rare text prized by collectors such as Ding Fubao. After its rediscovery at the end of the nineteenth century by the abbot of Erxian'an Yan Yonghe, it was completely dissociated from the community that had given birth to it: the Tianxian lineage and its manager Jiang Yupu. It was thanks to its emphasis on the purity of inner alchemy over ritual complexity that this Canon came to be appreciated by Yan Yonghe and his Daoist community who decided to have its printing blocks re-carved.³⁸⁹

But only after its 1906 publication as *Chongkan Daozang jiyao* with a wrong editor's name and newly added scriptures did it finally begin to live up to the original hopes and aspirations of Jiang Yuanting and his spirit writing congregation and assume the role of successor to the Ming Daoist Canon. Until the arrival of new orders from on high, the *Daozang jiyao* is destined the remain the ultimate Daoist Canon.

Unlike all previous Canons, the *Daozang jiyao* is a Canon that represents at its source the work and aspirations of laypeople. Profoundly inspired by the cult of Lü Dongbin, these laypeople were longing for the promotion and spreading of this cult and its associated practices and liturgy around the world. It was thanks to their altar and to their spirit writing practices, taught by a defrocked Buddhist monk, that their Canon happened to see the light of day.³⁹⁰

---

³⁸⁸ See the Postface by Xu Zhen 徐震 to the *Tianxian jindan xinfa* 天仙金丹心法, 78b (CK 13, 5933) and Mori Yuria "*Dōzō shūyō to Shō Yobu no Ryoso fukei shinkō*," 41–42.

³⁸⁹ As the abbot Yan Yonghe 閻永和 emphasized, the reason why the *Daozang jiyao* was reedited by his Quanzhen monastery Erxian'an in Chengdu (Sichuan) was the difficulty of finding *neidan* scriptures in Daoist networks—networks that conversely abounded in liturgical texts See the Preface by the abbot Yan Yonghe 閻永和, "Chongkan Daozang jiyao yuanqi" 重刊道藏輯要緣起, 15a (CK 1, 44).

³⁹⁰ I refer to Mingxin, Jiang Yupu's Buddhist master who was better known under his secular name Wang Shuxun; see above, notes 364 and 365 (pp. 205–206).

Fig. 29: The immortal Lü Dongbin 呂洞賓 who ordered the compilation of the *Daozang jiyao* canon and dictated several of its texts through spirit writing (*Jindan dayao* 金丹大要, CK 16).

Chapter 3

THE QING DAOIST CANON'S TWO MAIN EDITIONS

Though the "Essence of the Daoist Canon" (*Daozang jiyao* 道藏輯要) is the most important Daoist anthology of the Qing dynasty after the Ming Daoist Canon or *Daozang* 道藏 it has, as became clear in the previous chapters, not yet received due attention by scholars. One reason for this is that this large collection of around three hundred texts was regarded as a simple anthology derived from the *Daozang* stemming from the Jiaqing era (1796–1820). As its name "Essentials of the Daoist Canon" suggests, it includes numerous texts from the Ming Daoist Canon. However, it also features a conspicuous number of texts from other sources. Such texts, which can be classified as "extra-canonical texts," amount to about one third of the collection. However in terms of effective text volume (i.e., the number of Chinese characters), these added texts amount to about 40% of the whole and constitute an important corpus for the study of Daoism in the late imperial period.[390] The Canon's content covers a wide range of topics as it includes commentaries to Daoist and Neo-Confucian classics, Buddhism-inspired texts, inner alchemy, litanies, monastic and lay liturgies, moral instructions, epigraphy, and much else. Before investigating the Canon's connection with the Three Teachings in the next chapter, we need to examine in some more detail the history and differences of its two main editions: the "old" original edition of the early nineteenth century and the "new" *Chongkan* edition of the early twentieth century.

---

[390] The exact number of Chinese characters will be verified once the *Daozang jiyao* (old and new editions) is fully computerized in the context of the International Daozang jiyao project. More on this process of the *Daozang jiyao* in Christian Wittern, "Rebirth of the Daozang Jiyao—The never-ending Process of Creating a Digital Edition" (Paper presented at Cultural Crossing, University of Virginia, March 11–13, 2010, available at kanji.zinbun.kyoto-u.ac.jp/~wittern/data/cultural-crossings-wittern.pdf). The electronic texts of both editions will be made available on the project's web site (http://www.daozangjiyao.org).

As described above, a modern researcher is surprised to note that with regard to the *Daozang jiyao* there is not even agreement about editorship, the number of editions, the number of texts, and other basic facts. On the basis of research conducted in the framework of my International *Daozang jiyao* Project supported by Chiang-Ching Kuo Foundation (CCKF) and the Japan Society for the Promotion of Science (JSPS; see p. 198), we were able to conclusively establish the existence of only two basic editions of the *Daozang jiyao* collection:

1) the original or "old" *Daozang jiyao* of the Jiaqing 嘉慶 era (1796–1820)
2) the Erxian'an or "new" edition of the Guangxu era 光緒 (1875–1908) called *Chongkan Daozangjiyao* 重刊道藏輯要"

Fig. 30: *Hezhetu* from the old *Daozang jiyao* (j. 174.4a; Sichuan Provincial Library)

1. The early nineteenth-century Jiaqing edition ("old" DZJY)

The Jiaqing edition, here referred to as the "old" *Daozang jiyao*, was originally compiled under the supervision of a high-ranking official named Jiang Yupu 蔣予蒲 (style name: Yuanting 元庭, 1755–1819) during the Jiaqing 嘉慶 era (1796–1820). The analysis of the prefaces included in this edition shows that this collection was ascribed to the immortal Lü Dongbin 呂洞賓 and his revelations at the so-called Altar of the Source of Awakening (Jueyuantan 覺源壇), a spirit writing altar located in Beijing.[391] This altar was presided over by the elite official Jiang Yupu and his companions. It is noteworthy that most of these men were involved in work on the edition of the Qing imperial *Siku quanshu* 四庫全書. We have seen that Lü Dongbin is said to have ordered such an elite of disciples "to compile the *Daozang jiyao* in order to get rid of the false and return to the genuine, to delete the superfluous and arrive at the essential 命覺源諸子、編纂道藏輯要一書、棄偽而歸真,刪繁而就約 (...)," and thus "to collect the quintessence of the entire Canon and amend the omissions of the earlier [Ming] Canon 擷全藏之精華、補前藏之遺漏."[392]

Thus, for the first time in Daoist history, a Daoist Canon was created not as the result of a working relation between the Emperor and Daoist clergy but as product of a lay community under the divine guidance and inspiration of the immortal Lü Dongbin.[393] It was thus a lay community around high-ranking officials who, as members of a Lü Dongbin's spirit writing al-

---

[391] See p. 211 above. On the relation of Jiang Yupu's *Daozang jiyao* with spirit writing, see Ding Peiren 丁培仁, *Daojiao dianji baiwen* 道教典籍百問 (Beijing: Jinri Zhongguo, 1996): 216–218; Mori Yuria 森由利亜, "Dōzō shūyō to Shō Yobu no Ryoso fukei shinkō 道藏輯要と蔣予蒲の呂祖扶乩信仰," *Tōhō shūkyō* 東方宗教 98 (2001): 33–52; Kim Yunsu 金侖壽, "Dojang jipyo wa Jang Yoepo 道藏輯要와 蔣予蒲," *Dogyo Munhwa Yoengu* 道教文化研究 17 (2002): 277–316; and Monica Esposito, "Daoism in the Qing (1644–1911)," in *Daoism Handbook*, ed. Livia Kohn (Leiden: Brill, 2000), pp. 623–658, in particular pp. 634–635 {*Facets of Qing Daoism*, chapter 1, pp. 21–22} and our previous chapters here above.

[392] "Daozang jiyao yuanxu 道藏輯要原序," 8a, preface attributed to Zhongli Quan 鐘離權 (CK 1: 8).

[393] For an introduction to the history of the compilation of the Daoist Canons in China history see Kristofer Schipper, "General Introduction," in *The Taoist Canon*, ed. by Kristofer Schipper and Franciscus Verellen (Chicago: Chicago University Press, 2004), pp. 1–52, and Judith M. Boltz, "Daozang and subsidiary compilations," in *The Taoist Encyclopedia* ed. Fabrizio Pregadio, 2 vols. (London: Routledge, 2008), vol. 1, pp. 28–33.

tar, decided to compile and print a new Daoist Canon. As devotees of Lü Dongbin, they naturally placed the texts revealed by this immortal at the center of their collection. Representing at their origin beliefs and practices related to Lü Dongbin's communities, these texts thus became part of a larger Daoist "canonical" body.[394] The central position of these texts within the Canon (concretely embodied in their placement in the central Lunar Lodges Shi 室 and Bi 壁) reveals the basic purpose of the *Daozang jiyao* and its editors: to promulgate, via Lü Dongbin's spirit writing transmission, the quintessence of all authentic traditions and thus to establish the foundation for the restoration of "original Daoism."

With this goal in mind, Jiang Yupu and his congregants used new bibliographic categories and different classifications for scriptures while maintaining in their new Canon a basic structure still inspired by the earlier Ming Daoist Canon. Like the Ming Canon, the *Daozang jiyao* features initial sections with the Three Caverns and the scriptures revealed by the Daoist Trinity: Yuanshi tianzun 元始天尊, Lingbao tianzun 靈寶天尊, and Daode tianzun 道德天尊. Like the Ming Canon, the *Daozang jiyao* opens with the Lingbao duren jing 靈寶度人經, the scripture "spoken by the Yuanshi tianzun" 元始天尊所說經. And, again like the Ming Canon, it contains among the scriptures "spoken" by the Lingbao tianzun the *Dingguan jing* 定觀經 and also features among the texts "spoken" by the Daode tianzun 道德天尊 (Laozi) the *Daodejing* 道德經 and the *Riyong jing* 日用經.[395]

However, unlike the Ming Canon, the editors of the *Daozang jiyao* divided its scriptures into twenty-eight sections according to the names of the twenty-eight Lunar Lodges (ershiba xiu 二十八宿) and provided new bibliographic categories to some of its sections (including for instance a category for the *Huangting jing* 黃庭經, the *Yinfu jing* 陰符經, etc.).[396]

---

[394] For a list of these texts see note 368 above (pp. 206–207).

[395] Jiang Yupu (ed.), *Daozang jiyao zongmu* 道藏輯要總目, 4a–44b (Yan Yanfeng's copy stored at Sichuan Provincial Library, and its revised and enlarged edition in CK 1, pp. 12–34). For the Ming *Daozang* structure see Kristofer Schipper, "General Introduction," in *The Taoist Canon*, eds. K. Schipper and F. Verellen, p. 34. For the content and structure of the old *Daozang jiyao* see here above, chapters 1 and 2 of Part Three.

[396] Jiang Yupu (ed.), *Daozang jiyao zongmu*, 13a and 15b (also in *Chongkan Daozang jiyao*, 24a, 26b, vol. 1, pp. 16 and 17). More on the bibliographic categories of the *Daozang jiyao* in Monica Esposito, "Yibu Quanzhen Daozang de faming: Daozang jiyao ji Qingdai Quanzhen rentong 一部全真道藏的發明：道藏輯要及清代全真認同," in *Wendao Kunyushan* 問道昆崙山, ed. Zhao Weidong 趙衛東 (Jinan: Qilu, 2009), pp. 303–43, especially pp. 315–17, and the substantially enlarged

Furthermore, in conformity with other "canonical collections" that are by nature destined to be enlarged with new texts,[397] the *Daozang jiyao* was reprinted, revised and augmented many times over. In this way, different printed versions with a varying number of texts circulated in various regions of China. According to the analysis of fourteen copies stored in the libraries of China, Taiwan, Japan and France, it was possible to distinguish for the first time two main categories of the "old" Jiaqing edition.[398]

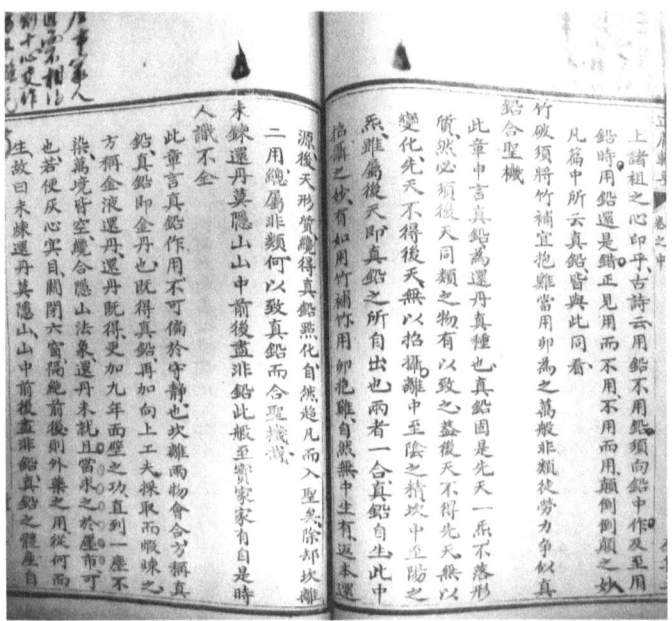

Fig. 31: Old *Daozang jiyao* (Yan Yanfeng's copy with his notes), Sichuan Provincial Library (photo M. Esposito, 2008)

English version, "The Invention of a Quanzhen Canon: The Wondrous Fate of the *Daozang jiyao*," in *Quanzhen Daoism in Modern Chinese Society*, eds. Xun Liu and Vincent Goossaert (Berkeley: Institute of East Asian Studies, 2014: 44–77). For the traditional categories used in previous *Daozang* compilations see Schipper, "General Introduction," in *The Taoist Canon*, pp. 1–52.

[397] This is also well illustrated in the history of the Korean Buddhist Canon. See Lewis Lancaster, "Introduction" to *The Korean Buddhist Canon: A Descriptive Catalog* (Berkeley: University of California Press 1979): ix–xvii.

[398] Among the list of fourteen copies, Ding Fubao's 丁福保 (*hao*: Shouyizi 守一子, 1874–1952) copy was inferred from the content recorded in his catalog published in 1922 in his *Daozang jinghua lu* 道藏精華錄 (Shanghai: Yixue shuju). On this list see Monica Esposito, "The Daozang Jiyao Project: Mutations of a Canon," pp. 131–133. {See also editor's note on p. 198 here above.}

The first category, "Old-1," includes the extant printed sets of the Jiaqing edition with a smaller number of texts. The second category, "Old-2," includes printed sets with a larger number of texts (along with the supplementary sections 10–11 of Lodge Ji 箕). On the basis of differences found in the number of texts, sequence of texts in the Lunar Lodges, revised passages, number of prefaces, etc., the "Old-1" category was divided into five provisional subcategories (a, b, c, d, e). Categories of the *Daozang jiyao*'s "old" edition can thus be represented in tabular form as follows:

Old-1	**a.** Tōyō Bunko 東洋文庫 Tokyo (218 fascicles).
	b. Osaka Prefecture Nakanoshima Library 大阪府立中之島図書館 (219 fascicles).
	c. Yan Yanfeng's 嚴雁峰 (1855–1918) copy stored at Sichuan Provincial Library (218 fascicles).
	d. Tōyō bunka kenkyūjo (Tōbunken, Tokyo) 東洋文化研究所 (200 fascicles).
	e. Tao Xiang's 陶湘 copy stored at the University of Kyoto, Institute for Research in Humanities 京都大學人文科學研究所 (268 fascicles) referred to as **"Jinbun version"** [similar to 1. Fang Gonghui's 方功惠 (1829–1897) copy stored at Beijing Academy of Social Science (190 fascicles); 2. Tokugawa Yorimichi's 德川賴倫 (1872–1925) fragmentary copy from his Private Collection "Nanki Bunko 南葵文庫," stored at the General Library of the University of Tokyo 東大総東大総合図書館 (230 fascicles)].
Old-2	Ke Fengshi's 柯逢時 (1844–1912) copy exported to France by Paul Pelliot (1878–1945) and stored at the Library of the Collège de France, Institut des Hautes Études Chinoises, referred to as **"Paris version"** [similar to 1. Zeng Zhao's 曾釗 (1793–1854) copy stored at Beijing Baiyun guan 白雲觀 (20 cases); 2. Li Shengfeng's 李盛鋒 fragmentary copy (including only 21 of the 28 Lunar Lodges) stored at Beijing University Library; 3. Shandong Normal University 山東師範大學 (180 fascicles); 4. Uchida Kakichi's 内田嘉吉 (1866–1933) fragmentary copy stored at the National Taiwan Library 國立中央圖書館臺灣分館 (211 fascicles); 5. Tokyo Diet Library 国立国会図書館 fragmentary copy (originally in 185 fascicles)].

Table 2: Two main categories and five subcategories of the old *Daozang jiyao*

Thanks to this provisional classification of printed sets of the old *Daozang jiyao* that are extant in the libraries of China, Taiwan, Japan, and France, it is possible to shed light on the revisions and modifications that the Canon underwent in the course of the nineteenth century until the turn of the twentieth century when Yan Yanfeng's copy (Old-1c), which circulated in Sichuan, served as the basis for the new Erxian'an 二仙菴 edition: the *Chongkan Daozang jiyao* 重刊道藏輯要 (published from 1906).

2. The early twentieth-century Erxian'an edition ("new" DZJY)

The Erxian'an edition, simply referred to as "new" *Daozang jiyao* or *Chongkan*, was originally prepared during the Guangxu era (1875–1908) by Yan Yonghe 閻永和 (style name: Shengjie 笙階, Daoist name: Yongyongzi 雝雝子, ?–1908/20?);[399] Peng Hanran 彭瀚然 (style name: Enpu 恩溥, fl. 1900–1908); and He Longxiang 賀龍驤 (style name: Jingxuan 靜軒, fl. 1891–1908), under the title *Chongkan Daozang jiyao* 重刊道藏輯要 (abbreviated *Chongkan* or CK).

The old *Daozang jiyao* would probably have become a rare collector's item if its reputation had not reached the ears of Yan Yonghe, a Daoist priest since he was ten years old, when he was on the verge of becoming abbot

---

[399] The date of death 1908 for the abbot Yan Yonghe is recorded in Zhang Yuanhe 張元和, "Chongyin *Daozang jiyao* jishi 重印道藏輯要紀實," *Zhongguo daojiao xiehui wang* 中國道教協會網 (www.taoist.org.cn/daojiaozazhi/zgdj1/87–3/20.htm); and Li Hechun 李合春 and Ding Changchun 丁常春 (eds.), *Qingyanggong Erxian'an zhi* 青羊宮二仙庵誌 (Chengdu: Sichuansheng Xinwen chubanju, 2006), pp. 20, and 97. However, as I have already noted ("Daozang jiyao ji qi bianzuan lishi," p. 14, note 30, and "Daozang Jiyao Project: Mutations of a Canon," pp. 109 and 117), it is interesting to see that in *Chongkan* printed sets produced after 1917 one finds the canonical text titled *Xiyi zhimi lun* 析疑指迷論 (DZ 276) with a colophon dated 1917 under the name of Yan Yonghe. This is one of the reasons why I prefer adding a question mark after the date of death of Yan Yonghe. Furthermore, one finds the name of Yan Yonghe and the date 1909 in some texts published in the *Zangwai daoshu* 藏外道書; see for instance vol. 13, p. 848. One even finds the year 1920 associated with Yan Yonghe in the *Yuqing Wenchang baochan* 玉清文昌寶懺 (My thanks to Dr. Yin Zhihua 尹志華 for sending me a copy of this text). See also Monica Esposito, "The Daozang jiyao Project and the Future of Daoist Studies," Paper presented at the International Conference "New Approaches to the Study of Daoism in Chinese Culture and Society," Chinese University of Hong Kong, 26–28 November 2009 (forthcoming in Lai Chi Tim & Cheung Neky Takching, *New Approaches to the Study of Daoism in Chinese Culture and Society*, Hong Kong: Chinese University Press).

of Chengdu's Erxian'an. Yan learned from the famous Hanlin official Wu Songsheng 伍崧生 (1829–1915), who was at that time heading the most prestigious academies of Chengdu, that the *Daozang jiyao* (i.e., Yan Yanfeng's copy, Old 1–c) is a precious Daoist repository and includes several rare commentaries on alchemical scriptures. In 1892, when Yan Yonghe became abbot, he expressed the wish to reprint the *Daozang jiyao*. Learning that its printing-blocks were ruined, he decided to have new printing blocks carved. However, the financial situation did not allow him to realize this project as soon as he would have wished. While in charge of the Bidongtang 碧洞堂 of the Erxian'an, Yan was very busy with restoring its different halls. But in 1900 Yan Yonghe's wish at last approached fulfillment when the Sichuan doctor Peng Hanran 彭瀚然 came to visit him in search of precious scriptures and commentaries.[400] Having heard about Yan Yonghe's project of reprinting the *Daozang jiyao*, Peng offered financial support and immediately set out to collect funds from friends and relatives in his hometown Xinjin 新津 (Sichuan). In 1903, the Sichuan native of Jingyan 井研 He Longxiang 賀龍驤 (provincial graduate 舉人 in 1821), who also heard about the *Daozang jiyao* project, visited Erxian'an and offered his help in cataloging, collating, and revising the old *Daozang jiyao* scriptures. It was thanks to these three persons—Yan Yonghe, Peng Hanran, and He Longxiang—that a new edition of the *Daozang jiyao* could be realized.[401]

In contrast with the old *Daozang jiyao*, the new *Chongkan* was produced on the basis of Sichuan local networks that provided both material resources and local craftsmen for the carving of its canonical blocks at Yuechi 岳池 in Sichuan.[402] The three editors, all from Sichuan, prepared their new edition on the basis of a printed Sichuan exemplar (Old–1c) from the private library of the Chengdu bibliophile Yan Yanfeng 嚴雁峰 (1855–1918).

---

[400] While the cyclic year *gengzi* 庚子 (1900) appears in both prefaces by Peng, the first preface ("Chongkan Daozang jiyao xu," 1a, CK 1: 5) mentions "the 24th year of Guangxu era 光緒" (1898) instead of 1900, which would be the 26th year of the Guangxu era.

[401] See the Prefaces by Peng Hanran, Yan Yonghe, and He Longxiang (CK 1: 5–6 and 44–46).

[402] It seems that in Yuechi County and the surrounding villages, printing block carving developed as a subsidiary handicraft during the eighteenth and nineteenth centuries; most of Yuechi's block cutters supplied commercial publishers in Chengdu and Chongqing. See Cynthia J. Brokaw, *Commerce in Culture: The Sibao Book Trade in the Qing and Republican Periods* (Cambridge, MA: Harvard University Press, 2007): 12–13.

Due to its fragmentary state, He Longxiang collated it with two manuscript copies obtained again in Sichuan from two bibliophiles from Chongqing: He Qichong 何起重 and Qin Pengsheng 秦芃生. It is thanks to the work of He Longxiang, who was assisted by two other Sichuanese proofreaders from Xinjin, Xiao Jichuan 蕭濟川 and Li Tingfu 李廷福,[403] that one of the most complete versions of the old *Daozang jiyao* is today available in form of the new *Chongkan* edition.

Due to the different backgrounds, motivations, and interests of its editors, the old and new *Daozang jiyao* inevitably have differences. While the old *Daozang jiyao* was the product of a lay spirit writing community of elite officials in Beijing devoted to the cult of Lü Dongbin, the *Chongkan* was the product of Sichuan networks that were supervised, as in the production of previous Daoist Canons, by clerical institutions. As a local and at the same time institutional enterprise, the production of the *Chongkan* blocks helped not only to raise the status of the newly restored Erxian'an public monastery of the Quanzhen Longmen branch along with the prestige of its new abbot Yan Yonghe but also, as we shall see, to "canonize" its local cults and liturgies. While the old *Daozang jiyao* was, as described in the preceding chapter, conceived as receptacle and vehicle for canonizing the spirit writing revelation of Lü Dongbin and its scriptures, the *Chongkan* now also served as repository for new texts circulating in Sichuan networks.[404]

Based on the different number of scriptures included in different extant sets of *Chongkan* reprints we can distinguish two main categories that I call New–1 and New–2. The first category (New–1) includes printed sets with fewer texts than the second category (New–2). The second category corresponds to *Chongkan* reprints produced by Bashu Publishing House

---

[403] Preface by He Longxiang, "Jiaokan Daozang jiyao shuhou 校勘道藏輯要書後," 18b/3–4 (CK 1: 45). In the Preface by Peng Hanran, "Chongkan Daozang jiyao bianyan 重刊道藏輯要弁言," 16a/7–8 (CK 1: 44) they are instead referred to by their alternative names: Xiao Zuozhou 蕭作舟 and Li Xiangting 李香亭. More on the collation work by He Longxiang on Yan Yanfeng's copy in Monica Esposito, "*Daozang jiyao* ji qi bianzuan," and "The Daozang jiyao Project: Mutations of a Canon."

[404] For a list of these texts see Monica Esposito, "The Daozang Jiyao Project: Mutations of a Canon," pp. 108–9, note 21, and here below. For a study of some of them see Mori Yuria, "Chūkan *Dōzō shūyō* to Shinchō Shisen chiiki no shūkyō 重刊道藏輯要と清朝四川地域の宗教," in *Chūgoku koseki ryūtsūgaku no kakuritsu: ryūtsū suru koseki, ryūtsū suru bunka* 中國古籍流通學の確立：流通する古籍・流通する文化, ed. Okazaki Yumi 岡崎由美 (Tokyo: Yūzan kaku shuppan, 2007), pp. 339–401.

after the restoration of the woodblocks at Chengdu's Qingyanggong in 1985.[405] Based on the study of several *Chongkan* sets stored in various libraries around the world, we were also able to identify for the first time three subcategories of the New–1 category (a, b, c). The *Chongkan* edition thus shows the following varieties:[406]

New-1	**a. Before 1917** without the *Xiyi zhimi lun* 析疑指迷論 (so far only one copy at Beijing University and one copy at the Beijing Academy of Social Science).
	b. After 1917 with the *Xiyi zhimi lun* (so far copies stored at Beijing Baiyun guan, Beijing University, Beijing Academy of Social Science, Shandong Normal University, Sichuan Provincial Library, Shanghai Library, Taiwan National Library, Chinese University of Hong Kong, Tenri University, Tsukuba University, Cambridge University Library—England).
	c. Photolithographic reprints by Kaozheng (1971) and Xinwenfeng (from 1977) based on a collation of New–1a and New–1b copies that lack Neo-Confucian texts (see also below, Table 4).
New-2	From 1985 on, Bashu reprints (245 fasc., 35 cases) include Lodge Shi 室 8 with the *Chunyang sanshu* 純陽三書, later also published by Jiangsu Guangling Guji 江蘇廣陵古籍 and the Qingyanggong (with some additional problems and misplaced folios);
	Bashu reduced format (10 vols.), 1995, also reprinted by Jilin Renmin (10 vols.) but with some additional mistakes.

Table 3: Main categories and subcategories of *Chongkan* and its reprints

---

[405] On this preliminary categorization see Monica Esposito, "*Daozang jiyao* ji qi bianzuan." More on the categories and subcategories of the *Chongkan* in Esposito, "The Daozang Jiyao Project: Mutations of a Canon." See also Table 4 below, pp. 242–3).

[406] My thanks to Professor Timothy Barrett for making me aware of the existence of the Cambridge copy of the Chongkan Daozang jiyao. I extend my gratitude to Dr. John Moffet, Librarian at East Asian History of Science Library—Needham Research Institute, and Dr. Charles Aylmer, Head of the Chinese Department of Cambridge University Library. Dr. Aylmer has kindly informed me about the content of the Cambridge copy that was acquired from Dr. Needham on May 1946. More information about this collection can be found at http://www.lib.cam.ac.uk/mulu/fb70302.html.

Chapter 3: The Qing Canon's Two Main Editions 229

Fig. 32: Printing bureau of the *Chongkan Daozang jiyao* canon at the Qingyanggong, Chengdu (photo M. Esposito, 2006)

Fig. 33: Newly printed fascicles of the *Chongkan Daozang jiyao* canon on sale at the Qingyanggong store in Chengdu (photo M. Esposito, 2006)

We will see in the following chapter (pp. 243 ff.) that there is in addition a group of eight texts listed in the "Chongkan Daozang jiyao xubian zimu" 重刊道藏輯要續編子目 that, if ever *Daozang jiyao* sets containing them were printed, would form a third Chongkan category. In order to get a clearer idea about some major differences between the "old" and "new" versions of this Daoist canon, I will in the next chapter focus on an aspect apt to highlight their different natures.

Chapter 4

THE THREE TEACHINGS IN THE NEW DAOZANG JIYAO CANON

Three-Teachings (*sanjiao* 三教) ideology was widespread in late imperial China. The contemporary Christian missionaries in China noted this in their works, too. During the Ming period the Jesuit Matteo Ricci (1522–1610) wrote (as reported by Nicolas Trigault): "Now, at this time the opinion held and approved by the wisest and best informed [Chinese] is that all of these three laws (i.e., religions) are united in one, and that they can and must all together be observed."[407] On the same line the Dominican Tommaso Maria Minorelli (1680—1733) observed that during the Qing "all Chinese without exception follow simultaneously the practice of the three sects."[408]

Three-Teachings ideology and practice shaped the daily life of late imperial literati and common people alike. Here I am not going to narrate the history of *sanjiao*, analyze its theory, ideology or worship, or translate the myriad formulas on the unity of the Three Teachings found in the *Daozang jiyao* or in Ming / Qing literati or popular works. [409] Instead I will in this and the following chapter address two main questions:

---

[407] "Or en ce temps cette-ci est l'opinion la plus recue & approuuee des plus sages & aduisez; que toutes ces trois loix sont vnies en vne, & qu'ensemble elles peuuent & doiuent toutes estre obseruees." *Du voyage de la Chine*, Book I, p. 188. The French version (Ricci 1616) is based on Nicolas Trigault's (1577–1628) Latin translation (1615) of Ricci's Italian manuscript (1609). For the original Italian, which was only published in the twentieth century, see Pasquale d'Elia (ed.), *Storia dell'introduzione del Cristianismo in Cina scritta dal Matteo Ricci*, Fonti Ricciane, Part I, Books 1–3 (Rome: La Libreria dello Stato, 1942), here Book 1, chap. 10, p. 132.

[408] "(...) tous les Chinois sans exception, depuis le prémier (sic) jusqu'au dernier, font profession de suivre en même temps les pratiques des trois sectes." See Tommaso Maria Minorelli, *Examen des faussetez sur les cultes chinois, Avancées par le Pere Joseph Jouvenci Jesuite, dans l'Histoire de la Compagnie de Jesus*, 1714, p. 60.

[409] For a study on the meaning of *sanjiao* in the late imperial period see for instance

1) Why did the *Chongkan* editors, in republishing the *Daozang jiyao* during the Guangxu era, feel the need to affirm the identity of this Canon as receptacle of the Three Teachings while the previous editors did not?

2) Why did the *Chongkan* editors include Three-Teachings materials at the beginning of their new edition while the previous editors did not?

In order to answer these questions we have to understand the different history of the two editions of the *Daozang jiyao* as well as the background and motivations of the editors who produced them. The study of these two editions and their history, discussed in the first chapters of Part Three, will be of help in finding answers. Some keys can also be gained by confronting the background of the old and new editions: while the old edition was the fruit of a lay community of high-ranking officials devoted to the cult of Lü Dongbin 呂洞賓, the new edition was the product of a clerical institution, the Erxian'an 二仙菴 of Chengdu. With the help of Sichuanese networks of devotees, this clerical institution tried to enhance its prestige via the publication of the new edition *Chongkan Daozang jiyao*.[410]

Having summarized the history of the two editions of the *Daozang jiyao*—old and new—and their different backgrounds, I will now put them face to face and try to understand their different nature with regard to the Three Teachings. In contrast to the old *Daozang jiyao*'s "Conventions" (*Fanli* 凡例) in fourteen items, the New *Chongkan* features enlarged Conventions in sixteen items. One item, the sixteenth and last one (see Fig. 34), mentions the Three Teachings in relation to this newly re-carved Canon and its status as a magnificent survey of the *Daozang*. It reads as follows:

> This [re-carved] Daoist Canon is the innermost teaching of Heaven and man, the heart-transmission of sages and deities. Though it serves as stepping stone to the gate of the Dao, in reality it sheds light on it in reciprocal compliance with the scriptures of the Confucian and Buddhist schools. May people with lofty ideals improve upon it and augment it by searching for scattered and lost books of ancient sages

---

Judith A. Berling, *The Syncretic Religion of Lin Chao-en* (New York: Columbia University, 1980), or Timothy Brook, "Rethinking Syncretism: The Unity of the Three Teachings." For a more recent study in Chinese on this topic see Tang Dachao 唐大潮, *Ming-Qing zhi ji daojiao "sanjiao heyi" sixiang lun* 明清之際道教"三教合一"思想論 (Beijing: Zongjiao wenhua chubanshe, 2000).

[410] Further information about these two editions and their history is found in Monica Esposito, "The Daozang Jiyao Project: Mutations of a Canon" (2009), and in "The Invention of a Quanzhen Canon: The Wondrous Fate of the *Daozang jiyao*" (2014).

Chapter 4: The Three Teachings in the New Daozang Jiyao Canon   233

so that it will become the great conspectus of the *Daozang*. This is our ardent hope.

道藏、係天人奧旨、聖神心傳。雖為道門之梯航、實與儒家、釋家之書互相發明。但願志士仁人能於先聖散帙遺編訪求、而增之、續之、以成道藏一大觀焉。斯誠幸甚。[411]

Furthermore, in its prefatory matter, the new edition or *Chongkan* added the famous 1733 edict of tolerance by the Qing Emperor Yongzheng 雍正 (r. 1723–35) along with Yongzheng's prefaces, all in vermilion ink, extracted from his recorded sayings *Yuxuan yulu* 御選語錄 (Imperial Selection of Recorded Sayings).[412] These materials are listed in a particular sequence.

---

[411] "Chongkan Daozang jiyao Fanli shiliuze," 14b (CK 1: 11).

[412] A presentation of this collection compiled by Yongzheng in 1733 is found in Jiang Wu, *Enlightenment in Dispute. The Reinvention of Chan Buddhism in Seventeenth-Century China* (New York: Oxford University Press, 2008):173–175. This collection is included in vol. 68, No. 1319 of the *Shinsan dai Nihon Zokuzōkyō* 新纂大日本續藏經 90 vols. (Tokyo: Kokusho Kankōkai, 1975–1989), abbreviated from now on as *Zokuzōkyō*. It is also available in electronic format (http://www.cbeta.org/result/X68/X68n1319.htm). In this *Imperial selection of the recorded sayings*, Yongzheng intended to select, according to his own standard, the writings of Chan masters along with works inspired by Chan without being constrained by Chan

Fig. 35: Yongzheng edict (1733) at the beginning of the *Chongkan* edition (1906)

The 1733 edict opens the collection and begins with the views of Emperor Yongzheng on the Three Teachings' purport of awakening "All-under-Heaven" whose "principles derive from the same source, and whose course runs parallel without conflicts" 理同出於一原、道並行而不悖 (see Fig. 35). It is an invitation to stop fighting for the preeminence of one teaching over the others. These assertions were made in the context of recognizing the legitimacy of Buddhism and Daoism and imposing conciliation by discouraging officials from sending memorials to the court asking for suppression.[413] By serving as the opening of the new sections of the *Chongkan*, this edict appears to function as an imperial talisman for the protection of this newly edited Qing Daoist Canon of the Guangxu era (1906).[414]

---

sectarian views.

[413] This was already pointed out by Timothy Brook in his "Rethinking Syncretism: The Unity of the Three Teachings and Their Joint Worship in Late-imperial China," *Journal of Chinese Religions* 21 (1993): 13–44, here pp. 23–24.

[414] It is worthy of note that this edict is also found in Confucian works, for instance as an appendix to Liu Mi 劉謐, *Sanjiao pingxin lun* 三教平心論 (Brook, "Rethinking Syncretism," p. 38, note 37) but also in Buddhist scriptures such as the *Shishanye daojing jiyao* 十善業道經節要 (Zokuzōkyō, vol. 39, No. 706, p. 260a [http://cbeta.bodhisutra.org/result/normal/X39/0706_001.htm]) which features an abridged version at its beginning, or in the *Bao'en lun* 報恩論 (Zokuzōkyō, vol. 62, No. 1205,

Chapter 4: The Three Teachings in the New Daozang Jiyao Canon   235

This opening is followed by Yongzheng's preface to his own recorded sayings titled *Yuanming jushi yulu* 圓明居士語錄 (Recorded Sayings of Layman Yuanming). Although the work itself consists mostly of Yongzheng's views about Chan Buddhist training and meditation (using the Buddhist sobriquet "Layman of Perfect Clarity 圓明居士" that Yongzheng gave to himself), the preface is portrayed as representative of the Confucian view, which was the official view of the Emperor himself (see Fig. 36 where the "elephant trunk" on the top left reads *Yuzhi Rujia yulu* 御製儒家語錄 and the small character *ru* 儒 is added after the title on the right).

This is followed by emperor Yongzheng's Preface to the Recorded Sayings of the Song-era Daoist master Zhang Boduan 張伯端 (987–1082). As we would expect, these sayings were also integrated in Yongzheng's *Yuxuan yulu* to represent the Daoist view (see Fig. 37 where the "elephant trunk" on the top left reads *Yuzhi Daojia yulu* 御製道家語錄, and the small character *dao* 道 is added after the title on the right).[415] Yongzheng appreciated Zhang's works, in particular his *Wuzhen pian* 悟真篇 (Awakening to Truth), as embodiment of the highest understanding of Chan teachings. As proof of his esteem, in the same year of 1733, the Emperor bestowed on Zhang the title Chanxian 禪仙 (Chan Immortal) and ordered the restoration of his Daoist abbey on Tongbai shan 桐柏山 (Tiantai, Zhejiang) under the name of Chongdaoguan 崇道觀.[416]

Regarding the Buddhist view, one finds Yongzheng's Preface to the recorded sayings of Zhuhong 袾宏 (see Fig. 38 where the "elephant trunk" on the top left reads *Yuzhi Shijia yulu* 御製釋家語錄, and the small char-

---

p. 717c, http://www.cbeta.org/result/normal/X62/1205_001.htm) as integral version. Even today, Chinese scholars or contemporary Buddhist masters use this 1733 Yongzheng edict for advocating ecumenical views free from sectarian considerations.

[415] The Preface to the *Yuxuan daci yuantong Chanxian Ziyang zhenren Zhang Pingshu* 御選大慈圓通禪仙紫陽眞人張平叔語錄 is included in j. 8 of the *Yuxuan yulu*. See *Zokuzōkyō*, vol. 68, No. 1319, p. 528b-c (http://www.cbeta.org/result/normal/X68/1319_008.htm).

[416] As we can see in the previous note, the new title Chanxian (Chan Immortal), with which Zhang was honored, figures in the title of his Recorded Sayings. On the Yongzheng edicts related to Zhang Boduan see Monica Esposito, "Shindai dōkyō to mikkyō: Ryūmon seijiku shinshū 清代道教と密教—龍門西竺派宗" in *Sankyō kōshō ronsō* 三教交涉論叢 (Interaction between the Three Teachings), ed. Kunio Mugitani 麥谷邦夫 (Kyoto: Jinbun Kagaku Kenkyūjo, 2005), pp. 289–338, here p. 300, and p. 327 note 46 {revised English version in *Facets of Qing Daoism*, chapter 5, pp. 258–261}.

acter *shi* 釋 is added after the title on the right).⁴¹⁷ Zhuhong (1533–1615) was the prominent Buddhist reformer of the late Ming dynasty known for his efforts to harmonize Chan and Pure Land and to integrate Chan, Vinaya, and Tantrism "in a broadly defined path of Pure Land."⁴¹⁸

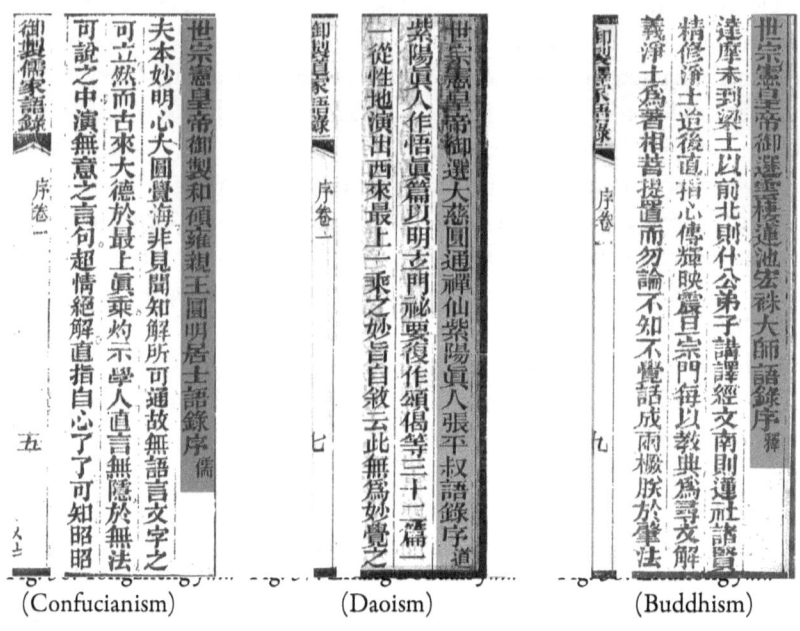

(Confucianism)   (Daoism)   (Buddhism)

The concluding part of Yongzheng's prefaces is devoted to the union of the Three Teachings. In the view of the *Chongkan* editors, this union is embodied in Yongzheng's preface for the establishment of his own religious congregation, "the Contemporary Dharma Assembly" (Dangjin fahui 當今法會). This was a group organized during the last years of the Yongzheng's reign at the imperial court in order to study and practice Chan Buddhism

---

⁴¹⁷ *Yuxuan Yunqi Lianchi Hong Zhu dashi yulu* 御選雲棲蓮池宏袾大師語錄 is included in j. 13 of the *Yuxuan yulu* under the title *Yuxuan Yunqi Lianchi Hong dashi yulu* 御選雲棲蓮池宏大師語錄. See *Zokuzōkyō*, vol. 68, No. 1319, p. 577b–c (http://www.cbeta.org/result/normal/X68/1319_013.htm).

⁴¹⁸ Chün-fang Yü, *The Renewal of Buddhism in China. Chu-hung and the Late Ming Synthesis* (New York: Columbia University Press, 1981), p. 5. Despite the critical opinion of Yongzheng regarding contemporary Chan masters, the Emperor praised Zhuhong for his "correct knowledge and views" and acknowledged him as a true Chan master. See Jiang Wu, *Enlightenment in Dispute*, p. 174.

Chapter 4: The Three Teachings in the New Daozang Jiyao Canon   237

and exchange views on it (Fig. 39; below the title one reads in small characters *ru shi dao* 儒釋道).⁴¹⁹ Appended to this preface is a list of the participants showing the involvement of exponents from all Three Teachings (Fig. 40). For the *ru* or Confucian side one finds the names of eight members: three princes (one of them being the future Qianlong emperor) and five high-ranking officials. For the *shi* or Buddhist side, the names of five Chan monks (three of them abbots of the Linji 臨濟 tradition) are listed, and for the *dao* or Daoist side a single name: the Celestial Master from Longhushan 龍虎山 (Jiangxi), Lou Jinyuan 婁近垣 (1689–1776).⁴²⁰

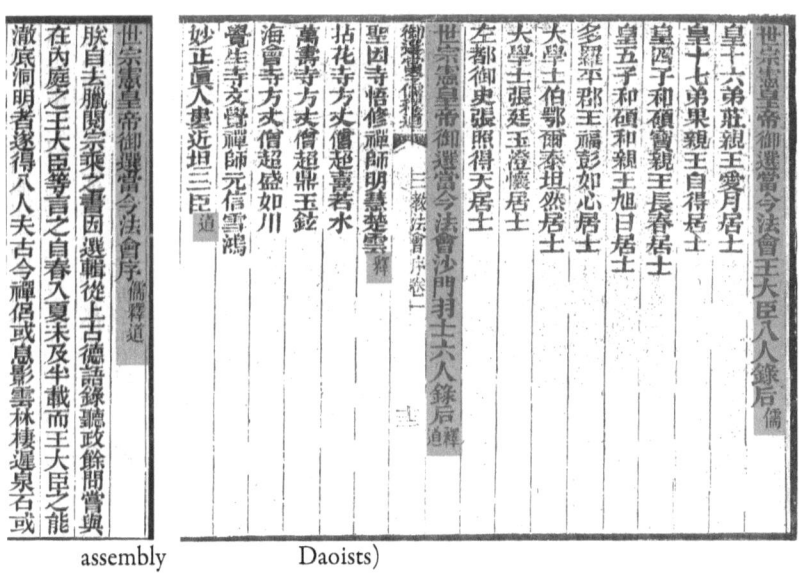

assembly   Daoists)

---

⁴¹⁹ Preface to the *Yuxuan Dangjin fahui* 御選當今法會 included in j. 19 of the *Yuxuan yulu* and found in the *Zokuzōkyō*, vol. 68, No. 1319, p. 722a–b (http://www.cbeta.org/result/normal/X68/1319_019.htm). For a presentation of the activities of this congregation see Jiang Wu, *Enlightenment in Dispute*, pp. 170–173.

⁴²⁰ For the identification of all these participants see Jiang Wu, *Enlightenment in Dispute*, pp. 171–172. For the relationship between Yongzheng and other Chan abbots linked to his court see Barend J. ter Haar, "Yongheng and His Buddhist Abbots," in *The People and the Dao. New Studies in Chinese Religions in Honor of Daniel L. Overmyer*, ed. Philip Clart and Paul Crowe (Nettetal: Steyler, 2009): 435–80. For the Celestial Master Lou Jinyuan and his relationship with Yongzheng, see the study by V. Goossaert, "Bureaucratic Charisma: The Zhang Heavenly Master Institution and Court Taoists in Late-Qing China," *Asia Major*, 3rd series 17. 2 (2004): 121–159.

An excerpt from another edict of Emperor Yongzheng serves as conclusion. It employs his favorite metaphor of the sun, moon, and polar star as an image for the relationship among the Three Teachings.[421] These three celestial bodies "share the quality of light yet retain their individuality. Likewise, the three teachings, though functioning differently, share the same substance."[422]

The vermilion-printed introductory section of the *Chongkan Daozang jiyao* containing Emperor Yongzheng's views on the Three Teachings (as seen by the new *Chongkan* editors) is followed by four prefaces by the new editors and a four-fascicle catalog, the "Chongkan *Daozang jiyao* zimu chubian 重刊道藏輯要子目初編." It provides a detailed table of contents of each text originally included in the old *Daozang jiyao*.[423] The last item at the end of its fourth *juan* is related to the Three Teachings: the Postface by editor He Longxiang 賀龍驤 (fl. 1891–1908). As collator of the *Chongkan*, He Longxiang aims at presenting Daoism along with Confucianism and Buddhism as a legitimate body of knowledge worthy of scholarly and intellectual reflection. He discusses this in two sections of his postface preceded by an introductory part titled "Sanjiao hezong qianshuo 三教合宗淺說" (Elementary Introduction to the Combined Doctrine of the Three Teachings). In it he applies Three Teachings rhetoric with the clear intention of promoting Daoist bibliographic science as a legitimate body of knowledge (Fig. 41).[424]

---

[421] It is an extract from the *Shangyu fulu* 上諭附錄 included in j. 12 of the *Yuxuan yulu* (*Zokuzōkyō*, vol. 68, No. 1319, p. 574a (http://www.cbeta.org/result/normal/X68/1319_012.htm).

[422] Jiang Wu, *Enlightenment in Dispute*, p. 175. He excerpts it from the *Jianmo bianyi lu* 揀魔辨異錄 (*Zokuzōkyō*, vol. 65, No. 1281, 193c–194a, here 194a/4–6) where the Yongzheng edict is also recorded.

[423] CK 1, pp. 48–214. For a list of the *Chongkan* materials including the various catalogs and prefaces as well as a comparison with the old *Daozang jiyao* see Monica Esposito, "The Daozang Jiyao Project: Mutations of a Canon," *Daoism: History, Religion and Society* 1 (2009): 95–153.

[424] Postface by He Longxiang to the "Chongkan Daozang jiyao zimu chubian 重刊道藏輯要子目初編," j. 4.101a–109a (CK 1: 210–214). He Longxiang's interest in cataloguing the scriptures of the old and new *Daozang jiyao* and presenting Daoism as a legitimate body of knowledge worthy of scholarly attention can also be observed in his prefaces, "Jiaokan Daozang jiyao shuhou" 校勘道藏輯要書後, 17a–19b, and "Chongkan Daozang jiyao zimu chubian xu" 重刊道藏輯要子目初編序, 20a–b (CK 1: 45–46). He Longxiang's views exemplify, among other things, the trend of evidential studies (*kaozheng* 考証) en vogue among the late Qing reformers

Chapter 4: The Three Teachings in the New Daozang Jiyao Canon 239

Fig. 41: Postface by He Longxiang with *sanjiao*-related parts highlighted

With regard to these new Three Teachings-related materials added in the *Chongkan* prefatory matter, we cannot but wonder if they are indicators of a new editorial policy. In comparison with the old *Daozang jiyao*, the new *Chongkan* proclaims allegiance to the flag of Three Teachings in a far more striking manner: Conventions, Yongzheng's edicts and prefaces, and He Longxiang's Postface (Figs. 32–41). What is the significance of such a

---

when Daoism began to be viewed as a legacy of Chinese culture, and when a new generation of scholars turned its attention to this legacy and the study of the Daoist Canon. See Xun Liu, *Daoist Modern Innovation, Lay Practice and the Community of Inner Alchemy in Republican Shanghai* (Cambridge, Mass.: Harvard University Press, 2009, p. 31) and the study by Benjamin Elman, *From Philosophy to Philology: Intellectual and Social Aspects of Change in Late Imperial China* (Cambridge, Mass.: Harvard University Press, 1984).

conspicuous display? Did the content of the new edition change so much with regard to the Three Teachings that the new editors felt compelled to put this on prominent display? Did the texts added by the new editors focus more on the Three Teachings than those included in the old edition?

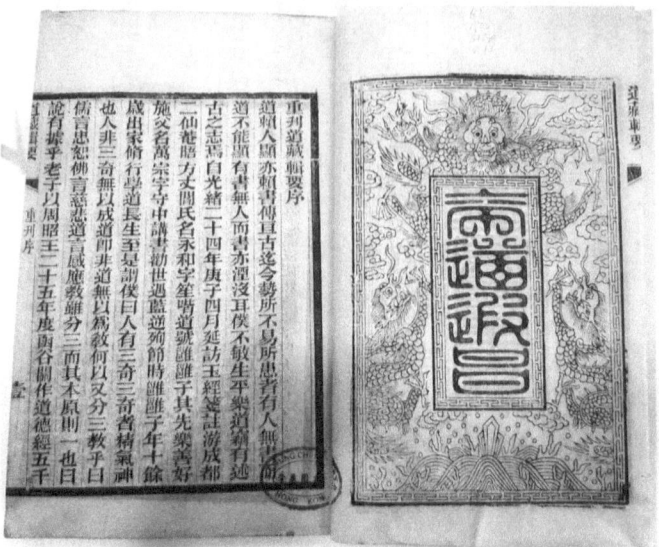

Fig. 42: Full-format print of the new *Chongkan Daozang jiyao* (Hong Kong)

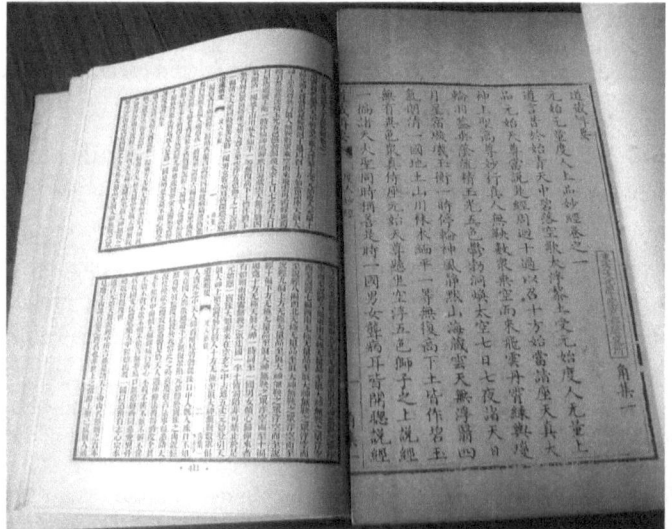

Fig. 43: Modern half-format print of new *Chongkan Daozang jiyao* (left) and old *Daozang jiyao* of Tōyō bunka kenkyūjo 東洋文化研究所 (right)

New Chongkan Scriptures and their Relation to the Three Teachings

Our analysis of the corpus of scriptures in these two *Daozang jiyao* editions shows that the scriptural core remained almost the same. The disposition of the texts in the twenty-eight Lunar Lodges is also almost identical except for the few sections containing supplementary texts that were added by the new editors. In order to find out if the changes with regard to the Three Teachings are due to the content of those supplementary scriptures, we need first to circumscribe the new textual corpus of the *Chongkan*. On the basis of Table 3 (p. 228), I shall list in Table 4 the titles of all additional texts in the *Chongkan* while indicating their location inside the collection (i.e., the Lunar Lodge preceded by the character *xu* 續 or other characters used in the printed sets of the *Chongkan*). Texts that deal with the Three Teachings are printed in bold type and marked by a dot (•); these include at least one or more occurrences of the term *sanjiao* (number given in parentheses).

Table 4 includes all *Chongkan* texts that were listed in the catalog titled "Chongkan Daozang jiyao xubian zimu 重刊道藏輯要續編子目." This catalog—first compiled (初編) by He Longxiang, revised (參訂) by Peng Hanran, and proofread (恭校) by Erxian'an abbot Yan Yonghe—provides a detailed list of the texts that were added or slated to be added to the *Chongkan*.[425] Some of these are also marked in the general index titled "Chongkan Daozang jiyao zongmu 重刊道藏輯要總目" with the character xu 續 (to be added). While some of these supplementary scriptures were inserted in the *Chongkan* printed sets New–1 and New–2 (see Table 3), others that were slated to be included form a new category that I shall call New–3. The texts of this new category, which feature in their header *Chongkan Daozang jiyao* (indicating the plan to include them in the Canon) are marked in this table by an asterisk.

---

[425] This catalog is presented as fifth *juan* in the prefatory matter (CK 1: 215–242). It is worthy of note that for the compilation of the fourth *juan* "Chongkan Daozang jiyao zimu chubian" 重刊道藏輯要子目初編, He Longxiang and Peng Hanran continued to have the same editorial role (respectively compiler and reviser), but the proofreading was performed by different clerics: Chen Wuyuan 陳悟元, prior of the Erxian'an for j. 2 (CK 1: 69–117), Wang Miaosheng 王妙生 (? 1953), supervisor of ordinands' protocol (Jiuyi 糾儀) of the Erxian'an for j. 3 (CK 1: 119–157), Yang Mingxing 楊明性, and rector (Daozhi 道值) of the Erxian'an for j. 4 (CK 1: 159–209). The abbot Yan was in charge of the proofreading only for j. 1 (CK 1: 48–68) and for the "Chongkan Daozang jiyao xubian zimu." He was, as we shall see, one of the central figures in selecting the new scriptures of the *Chongkan*.

NEW-1 **17/18 ADDI-TIONAL TEXTS**	**a. Before 1917: 17 additional texts** not counting the *Xiyi zhimi lun* 析疑指迷論: 1. • ***Guanyin dashi lianchuan jing*** 觀音大士蓮船經 續斗 1 (4 occurrences); 2. *Sun zhenren beiji qianjin yaofang* 孫真人備急千金要方 續虛 12. DZ 1163 (No occurrence); 3. *Lüzu benzhuan* 呂祖本傳 續室 1 (No occurrence); 4. *Dongyuan yulu* 東園語錄 續壁 7 - 又壁 7 (No occurrence); 5. *Taigong yinfu jing* 太公陰符經 又胃 2 (No occurrence); 6. • ***Wupian lingwen*** 五篇靈文 又胃 2 (1 occurrence); 7. • ***Zhang Sanfeng xiansheng quanji*** 張三丰先生全集 續畢 7–12 (42 occurrences); 8. *Sanbao wanling fachan* 三寶萬靈法懺 續柳 7–12 (No occurrence); 9. *Taishang lingbao chaotian xiezui fachan* 太上靈寶朝天謝罪法懺 續柳 13. DZ 189 (No occurrence); 10. • ***Wenchang dijun benzhuan*** 文昌帝君本傳 星 8 (1 occurrence); 11. • ***Wendi huashu*** 文帝化書 星 8. DZ 170 but with some differences (1 occurrence); 12. *Guansheng dijun benzhuan* 關聖帝君本傳 又星 9 (No occurrence); 13. • ***Taishang xuanmen gongke jing*** 太上玄門功課經 張 1 (2 occurrences); 14. *Taishang sanyuan cifu shezui jie'e xiaozai yansheng baoming miaojing* 太上三元賜福赦罪解厄消災延生保命妙經 張 1. DZ 1442 and DZ 71 (No occurrence); 15. *Erxian'an beiji* 二仙菴碑記 翼 1 (No occurrence); 16. • ***Qingyang gong beiji*** 青羊宮碑記 續翼 1 (1 occurrence); 17. *Qingcheng shan ji* 青城山記 [續]翼 10 (No occurrence);
	b. After 1917, one more additional text for a total of 18 18. *Xiyi zhimi lun* 析疑指迷論 奎 4. DZ 276 (No occurrence). This text, which includes a colophon dated 1917 mentioning Yan Yonghe, was not listed in any Indexes of the *Chongkan Daozang jiyao*.
	c. Photolithographic reprints by Kaozheng (1971) and **Xinwenfeng** (from **1977** on) include the above-mentioned **18 additional texts** but **lack 4 Neo-Confucian texts** included in the old edition of the *Daozang jiyao*: 1) *Taiji tu shuo* 太極圖說 星 7; 2) *Tongshu* 通書 星 7; 3) *Huangji jingshi shu* 皇極經世書 星 7; 4) *Jirang ji* 擊壤集 星 7.

Chapter 4: The Three Teachings in the New Daozang Jiyao Canon 243

New-2 (19 additional texts)	From 1985 on, **Bashu reprints** (245 fasc., 35 cases) include the above 18 texts with one additional text: • 19. *Chunyang sanshu* 純陽三書 室 8 (8 occurrences); **Bashu reduced format** (10 vols.) **1995**, also reprinted by Jilin Renmin (10 vols.) includes all of these **19 texts**.
New-3 (8 more texts, for a total of 27 texts)	**8 additional texts** listed in the "Chongkan Daozang jiyao xubian zimu" 重刊道藏輯要續編子目 (texts with CK header marked *): 張集1 續: 20. *Qingxuan jilian tieguan hushi* 青玄濟煉鐵貫斛食 (included in the *Guangcheng yizhi* 廣成儀制 under the title *Tieguan hushi quanji* 鐵鑽斛食全集, also reprinted in the *Zangwai daoshu* 藏外道書 vol. 14); 21. *Lingbao wenjian 靈寶文檢 (with the frontispiece "Guangxu bingwu Erxian'an cangban" 光緒丙午[1906]重刊二仙菴藏版 and the header *Chongkan Daozang jiyao*); 22. *Xinxiang miaoyu 心香妙語 (with the frontispiece "Guangxu bingwu Erxian'an cangban" 光緒丙午[1906]重刊二仙菴藏版 and the header *Chongkan Daozang jiyao*); 23. *Yayi ji 雅宜集 (with the frontispiece "Guangxu bingwu Erxian'an cangban" 光緒丙午[1906]重刊二仙菴藏版 and the header *Chongkan Daozang jiyao*); 翼集10 續: 24. *Taishang wuji dadao sanshiliu bu zunjing* 太上無極大道三十六部尊經 whose text corresponds to DZ 8 but with the commentaries attributed to Fuyou dijun 孚佑帝君 (i.e., Lü Dongbin 呂洞賓), which are not found in the *Daozang* (with the frontispiece "Guangxu bingwu Erxian'an cangban" 光緒丙午[1906]重刊二仙菴藏版); 25. **Taishang wuji dadao yanshou jifu xiaojie baochan* 太上無極大道延壽集福消切寶懺 (with the header *Chongkan Daozang jiyao*; also published in the *Guangcheng yizhi*); 26. *Taishang dongxuan lingbao yushu tiaoyuan yingxian xunjing* 太上洞玄靈寶玉樞調元應顯尊經. **Appended to the "Chongkan Daozang jiyao xubian zimu" as fifth juan:** 27. *Nüdan hebian* 女丹合編 (with the frontispiece "Guangxu bingwu Erxian'an cangban" 光緒丙午[1906]重刊二仙菴藏版 but published as independent Erxian'an collection).

Table 4: Main categories and subcategories of scriptures added in the *Chongkan Daozang jiyao* with number of Three Teachings occurrences

As indicated in Table 4, the eight additional texts included in the category "New–3" ended up being published as part of the *Guangcheng yizhi* 廣成儀制 and/or printed as independent texts.[426] I was unable to find *Chongkan* printed sets including the scriptures listed in New–3, and I ignore if such sets were ever produced at the Erxian'an.[427] What one can see is that all scriptures listed in the "Chongkan Daozang jiyao xubian zimu 重刊道藏輯要續編子目" are still printed at today's Chengdu Qingyanggong where the Erxian'an woodblocks were preserved and, after 1985, restored. As noted in the Table 2 in the category New–3, some of these texts were, as their header "*Chongkan Daozang jiyao*" shows, prepared to be included (texts 21–23 and 25, marked in Table 4 by asterisks.[428]

---

[426] For a study on the *Guangcheng yizhi* 廣成儀制 (compiled by Chen Fuhui 陳復慧, better known as Chen Zhongyuan 陳仲遠, 1734–1802) and a presentation of the *Lingbao wenjian*, *Xinxiang miaoyu*, and *Yayi ji* (texts 21–23 in Table 4) see respectively, Mori Yuria, "Shinchō shisen no Zenshinkyō to Tenshidō girei: Kōsei gisei taiseishō wo megutte 清朝四川の全真教と天師道儀禮：『廣成儀制』太清章をめぐって," in *Dōkyō no saishō girei no sisōshiteki kenkyū* 道教の齋法儀禮の思想史的研究, ed. Kobayashi Masayoshi 小林正美 (Tōkyō: Chisen shoin, 2006), pp. 137–84, and by the same author, "Chōkan Dōzō shūyō to Shinchō Shisen chiiki no shūkyō 重刊道藏輯要と清朝四川地域の宗教." As for the *Nudan hebian* (text 27 in Table 4) one finds its Table of Contents ("Nüdan hebian zongmu 女丹合編總目," 5.62a–b) with a preface written by He Longxiang in 1904 (5.57a–61b, CK 1: 243–45) and the detailed content of fifteen works in the fifth *juan* of "Chongkan Daozang jiyao xubian zimu" 重刊道藏輯要續編子目. This might suggest that the new Sichuanese editors planned to include this collection in the *Chongkan* but later decided to publish it as an independent collection. For a presentation of this collection see Elena Valussi, "Men and Women in He Longxiang's *Nüdan hebian*," *Nan Nü* 10 (2008): 247–78.

[427] It is nonetheless worth recalling that a set of "248 scrolls and 28 cases" was burned during a *zhai* organized at the Erxian'an, though we ignore to which category this set belongs; see here below.

[428] At present, text 26 (*Taishang dongxuan lingbao yushu tiaoyuan yingxian xunjing* 太上洞玄靈寶玉樞調元應顯尊經) is the only scripture I was unable to locate. Text 24 (*Taishang wuji dadao sanshiliu bu zunjing* 太上無極大道三十六部尊經) consists of an extra-canonical commentary attributed to Lü Dongbin. According to the "Chongkan Daozang jiyao xubian zimu" 重刊道藏輯要續編子目 (5.54a–56a, CK 1: 241–42) it features an introductory liturgical part which is published today at the Qingyanggong as an independent fascicle under the title *Taishang wuji dadao sanshiliubu zunjing qiqing keyi* 太上無極大道三十六部尊經啟請科儀 (in concertina format). The body of the text along with the commentary is being printed today as an independent three-fascicle text.

Among the nineteen texts included in the available printed sets of the *Chongkan* New–1 and New–2 categories, nine include the term *sanjiao* (in Table 4 set in bold and marked by a dot • . However, apart from many expected occurrences of this term in the *Zhang Sanfeng xiansheng quanji* 張三丰先生全集 (text 7)—a fruit of the Ming imperial cult to this immortal—the remaining eight feature only few occurrences: one (texts 6, 10, 16), two (text 13), four (text 1), and a maximum of eight (text 19). Interestingly enough, the majority of the supplementary texts concern liturgical and sectarian traditions of Sichuan. These local traditions focusing on services for the Sichuanese community appear removed from the Three Teachings universalism conveyed in the prefatory materials (see above Figs. 34–41). This universalism—expressed in formulas such as *sanjiao hezong* 三教合宗 (the Three Teachings share the same tradition) or *sanjiao chu wuyi zhi* 三教初無異旨 (the Three Teachings have originally no different intent)—is based on the ideal of unity of the Three Teachings whose principles are said to "derive from the same source and whose course runs parallel without conflicts" (see the header of Fig. 40 and the Yongzheng edict in Fig. 35). This ideal unity of the Three Teachings enunciated at the beginning of the *Chongkan* by the Yongzheng edict of tolerance relies on a common and shared content free from sectarian practices and beliefs. Opposing this idealized view in his Preface to the new edition, He Longxiang informs the readers that the abbot Yan Yonghe and Peng Hanran were ready to add liturgical manuscripts unrelated to the original canonical corpus of the old *Daozang jiyao*. He Longxiang puts this as follows:

> While reading again the collection [i.e., the *Chongkan Daozang jiyao*], I noticed that it included tens of scrolls of texts added so disorderly and confusedly that it was unsuitable for this collection to be titled 'Reprint' (*Chongkan*). I questioned Mr. Yan [Yonghe] and Mr. Peng [Hanran] about this and they answered me by saying: "Since the current situation is getting worse by the day, we should preserve the manuscripts while waiting for future editors. Indeed, we are afraid to 'lose pearls in the blue ocean'… ." Excellent, excellent![429]

---

[429] He Longxiang's Preface "Jiaokan Daozang jiyao shuhou 校勘道藏輯要書後," 18b (CK 1, p. 45). On the expression "losing pearls in the blue ocean" see Zhao Zongcheng, "*Daozang jiyao* de bianzuan," p. 30. More information about the meaning of this expression for the new Sichuanese editors is also found in Mori, "Chōkan Dōzō shūyō," pp. 356–8.

又閱輯中雜廁續本數十卷、似與重刊二字不符。質諸閻彭二公、謂:"因時事日非、聊存底稿、以俟選家。實恐珠遺滄海云云。"善哉、善哉。

These "lost pearls," added in a disorderly and confused manner to the body of the new Canon, correspond to complex liturgical texts strongly connected with Sichuanese local networks and cults. Rather than belonging to the canonical world of universalistic religions, their content appears closer to the domain of local religious activities dealing, more particularly, with specific ritual services for local communities. Therefore the new editors, in re-editing the old *Daozang jiyao*, took the opportunity to preserve their local scriptures which, in their eyes, were in danger of getting lost. One cannot ignore that local activities and cults were often regarded with suspicion by the government. Around the end of the Qing and during the Republican era when the *Chongkan* was published, spiritual and moral universalism was invoked as a sign of religious modernity by groups opposed to local cults labeled as "superstitious."[430] One of the aims of the Jiaqing-era editors of the old *Daozang jiyao* had been to preserve their own scriptures under the imperial protective talisman of the Yongzheng edict of tolerance, and to house them inside an imperially sanctioned, canonical body of scriptures. Whereas those first compilers had prepared their Jiaqing Canon in order to preserve and canonize the corpus of Lü Dongbin's inspired scriptures inside the orthodox quintessence of the Ming-era Daoist Canon, the new compilers wanted to produce a Canon for enhancing the prestige of their Erxian'an community and preserving at the same time their own scriptures. By adding them to the previous old *Daozang jiyao* corpus, they sought to legitimize these local and liturgical "lost pearls in the blue ocean 珠遺滄海" as part of a new Daoist Canon whose imperial preface in vermilion ink was to leave noone in doubt about its orthodoxy, legitimacy, and authenticity.

Finally, if we examine the overall content of the twenty-seven supplementary scriptures of the *Chongkan*, we can easily discover that the majority of them are not part of the Three Teachings ideology enunciated in the

---

[430] Claims of religious universalism were probably necessary also for the survival of the Erxian'an community and its Canon. On this see the works by Prasenjit Duara. "Knowledge and Power in the Discourse of Modernity: The Campaigns Against Popular Religion in Early Twentieth-Century China," *Journal of Asian Studies* 50.1 (1991): 67–83 and *Sovereignty and Authenticity: Manchukuo and the East Asian Modern* (Lanham: Rowman & Littlefield, 2003).

Chongkan prefatory matter. While some of these supplementary scriptures deal with Sichuanese yet universal gods like Wenchang (texts 10–11) and immortals like Zhang Sanfeng (7), others focus more specifically on local gods (1) and Sichuanese religious geography (15–18). But the majority is clearly devoted to liturgy (8–9, 13–14), and more particularly to Sichuanese liturgical and ritual traditions (20–23, 25–26). The latter focus on rituals of death adapted to the local society and known as Iron Bottle liturgy, ritual manuals, and documents to be used for lay communities dealing with the removal of the causes of misfortunes, the liberation of the souls of the dead, the pacification of residences or tombs, etc.[431]

Compared with the original corpus of the old *Daozang jiyao*, the content of these supplementary scriptures is no sufficient reason for changes regarding the perception of the Three Teachings. In fact, it is important to note that each section of the old *Daozang jiyao* already included scriptures referring to the Three Teachings. This can be easily verified by the fact that the term *sanjiao* 三教 (along with various formulas alluding to the unity of the Three Teachings) appears in each of its 28 Lunar Lodges. Interestingly, this term occurs more frequently in the scriptures attributed to Lü Dongbin which form the core of the new scriptural body of the old *Daozang jiyao* of the Jiaqing era.[432] The highest percentage of occurrences of the term *sanjiao* gave such texts a universal aura that was necessary for their final canonization. Even more interestingly, Lü Dongbin is in such a text called "Patriarch of the Three Teachings (Sanjiao Zongshi 三教宗師).[433] Thus, Three-Teaching ideology was already part of the old *Daozang jiyao*; however, as we shall see, proclaiming it was not a priority of its editors.

---

[431] An English presentation of these Sichuanese liturgical manuals by Mori Yuria ("Being Local Through Ritual: Quanzhen Appropriation of Zhengyi Liturgy in the *Chongkan Daozang jiyao*") is found in *Quanzhen Daoism in Modern Chinese Society and Culture, 1500–2010*, ed. by Xun Liu and Vincent Goossaert (Berkeley: Institute of East Asian Studies, 2014).

[432] The highest percentage of the occurrence of the term *sanjiao* is in fact found in the texts attributed to Lü Dongbin and included in Lodge Shi 室. Another important Lodge dealing with the term *sanjiao* is Lodge Wei 胃 that includes Quanzhen texts stemming from the Ming *Daozang*.

[433] See for instance the central scripture opening the Lodge Shi and titled *Shiliupin jing* 十六品經 2b/8, 2a/3, 70a/9 (CK 12: 5294, 5296, and 5330) and here below note 52.

Fig. 44: Frontispiece with the "Three Pure Ones" (Sanqing 三清) of the Tōyō bunko version of the *Daozang jiyao*

Chapter 5

Legitimacy and Canonization

If we cannot find an answer to our questions in the new corpus of *Chongkan* scriptures, we must search elsewhere. One avenue takes into consideration the social changes and transformations that the two editions mirror. They correspond to different periods and backgrounds of the editors as well as their different aims. Differences can be detected, as noted above, (1) in the last (sixteenth) item of the enlarged *Chongkan* Conventions that refers to the Three Teachings, (2) in the edicts and Prefaces by the Qing Emperor Yongzheng on the Three Teachings in vermilion ink, and (3) in the Postface by the editor He Longxiang (see above Figs. 34–41). But the different nature of these two editions is also strikingly apparent in the different frontispieces of the old and new *Daozang jiyao* (old *Daozang jiyao* in Fig. 44 and new *Chongkan Daozang jiyao* in Fig. 45).

Fig. 45: Frontispiece of the *Chongkan Daozang jiyao* (see pp. 257–259)

Whereas the old *Daozang jiyao*, like its precursor the Ming *Daozang*, opens with a frontispiece representing the Sanqing 三清 or Three Pure Ones, the new *Chongkan* reproduces two seals of the Dragon-clouds (*yunlong tu* 雲龍圖) featuring the characters "Huangtu gonggu 皇圖鞏固" and "Didao xiachang 帝道遐昌."⁴³⁴ As we shall see, these two different frontispieces embody the fundamental differences in the interpretative nature of orthodoxy of these two editions.

As mentioned above, the old *Daozang jiyao* adopts in its initial sections the structure of the Ming *Daozang* by opening with the scriptures revealed by the Daoist Trinity (Sanqing). Inside this seemingly traditional framework of the Sanqing revelation, the editors inserted a new model of revelation via spirit writing which determines the selection of the entire scriptural body of the old *Daozang jiyao*.⁴³⁵ This newly revealed "quintessence of the *Daozang*", after having been approved in the Daoist Heavens,⁴³⁶ was allegedly transmitted by the immortal Lü Dongbin to his direct disciples who all happened to be high-ranking officials at the Qing court.⁴³⁷ As far as I know, apart from the Buddhist monk known as Mingxin 明心 (secular name: Wang Shuxun 王樹勳) who was originally affiliated with the Beijing Bud-

---

⁴³⁴ Copies of well-preserved frontispieces of two fragmentary exemplars of the Ming *Daozang* are stored at the Bibliothèque nationale de France (Section of Oriental Manuscripts) in Paris (Chinois 9456, and Chinois 9547). My thanks to curator Nathalie Monnet for letting me consult and take photos of them. As for the frontispieces preserved in some extant copies of the old *Daozang jiyao*, see Esposito, "The Daozang Jiyao Project: Mutations of a Canon," p. 104, note 17.

⁴³⁵ I write of a "traditional framework of revelation" because many scriptures that are called "sacred," such as the Holy Bible or the Koran, rely on it. Revelation by God himself transmitted through angels, prophets, and inspired apostles ensured for the Abrahamic religions the legitimate nature of their sacred scriptures. Similarly, Daoist canonical scriptures carry the mark of legitimacy of the Daoist trinity, the Sanqing, while Buddhist sutras are often portrayed as the words of Buddhism's founder Śākyamuni. More on this on p. 212 above.

⁴³⁶ Lü Dongbin is portrayed as announcing, in front of the highest Daoist God Laozi (residing in the Shiqing Heaven 始青天), his project of "compiling all cases [of scriptures] and merging them into a single standardized compilation" 願以編輯諸函、折衷一是 which is the *Daozang jiyao*. See the Preface attributed to Lü Dongbin, "Daozang jiyao yuanxu," 4a (CK 1, p. 6). See also the Preface attributed to Su Lang 蘇朗, 10a–b (CK 1, p. 9).

⁴³⁷ As we know, many of them worked at the imperial literary enterprise of the *Siku quanshu* while others were involved in the waterways administration (*hechen* 河臣). More on this in Mori, "Chōkan Dōzō shūyō," and Esposito, "The Discovery of Jiang Yuanting's Daozang jiyao."

dhist monastery Guanghuisi 廣惠寺 but was later defrocked, no mention is made of clerical figures or clerical institutions involved in the compilation of the old *Daozang jiyao*.[438] Whereas previous Daoist Canons had been sponsored and commissioned by the imperial state as a result of a working relation between the Emperor and Daoist clerical elites, this Jiaqing-era Canon was sponsored by the Jueyuantan 覺源壇 (also named Diyi juetan 第一覺壇 or Juetan 覺壇), a lay spirit writing altar where elite officials gathered, summoned by the immortal Lü Dongbin who based on celestial mandate ordered via spirit writing the compilation of a new Canon. These two different modalities of canonization characterizing the Ming *Daozang* and the Qing *Daozang jiyao* can be schematized as follows:

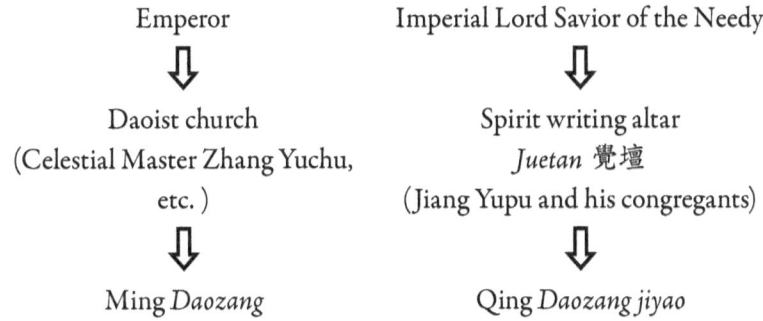

Fig. 46: Modalities of canonization of the Ming *Daozang* and Qing *Daozang jiyao*

---

[438] As mentioned above, Jiang Yupu's master Mingxin, better known under his secular name of Wang Shuxun 王樹勳, had become a monk at a Beijing Buddhist monastery after having failed the official examination. Mingxin was known for spreading spirit writing practices among high officials and for this reason was later condemned to return to secular life. In 1795 Jiang Yupu took the five lay precepts at Beijing's Guanghuisi 廣惠寺 from Mingxin and became a vegetarian. In 1815 Mingxin was indicted for having obtained an official post by bribery and was finally sent to exile in Heilongjiang 黑龍江. Jiang Yupu, Jin Guangti 金光悌 (alias Dagu 大固, 1747–1812), and other disciples of Mingxin linked with the Beijing Jueyuantan altar thereupon felt obliged to resign. Jiang Yupu was the object of an imperial decree accusing him of having become a "flawed official" (*dianguan* 玷官). For a different opinion about the involvement of Mingxin in the activities of the Jueyuantan altar see Mori, "Chōkan Dōzō shūyō," pp. 345–46.

Thus the legitimacy of the Qing Canon from the early nineteenth century—the old *Daozang jiyao*—is established and sanctioned for the first time in Daoist history not by the authority of an Emperor via Daoist clerical institutions but by the Imperial Lord, Savior of the Needy (Fuyou dijun 孚佑帝君) Lü Dongbin via divine revelation. As emphasized in the prefaces to the old *Daozang jiyao*, it is the immortal Lü Dongbin who, after having received the celestial mandate, authorized the publication of this Canon in order to preserve the spiritual inheritance of Daoism in the world. In his function as prime minister of the Heaven of Jade Purity (相玉清) and "on Heaven's behalf," Lü Dongbin "appeared throughout the world in order to spread salvation and to protect and sustain [the doctrine of] the Three Teachings" 代天宣化、變現十方、綱維三教. After having "gathered the canonical scriptural essence of all the Perfected by integrating the genuine transmission of the alchemical paths, he ordered his disciples of the First Awakening Altar (Diyi Juetan) to compile the *Daozang jiyao* and to have it carved in wood blocks. (...)" 綜丹道之真傳、羅諸真之典要、命第一覺壇諸弟子、編纂道藏輯要一書、付諸剞劂.[439]

As the fruit of Lü Dongbin's authoritative selection, this Canon is inevitably a receptacle of the Three Teachings, but proclaiming this is not part of its strategy. Rather, it pertains to the internal logic of Lü Dongbin's kingly

---

[439] The entire passage from the Preface to the old *Daozang jiyao* 道藏輯要原序 (attributed to Su Lang 蘇朗) reads as follows: "Our Imperial Lord, Savior of the Needy, as Prime Minister of the Heaven of Jade Purity, on Heaven's behalf appeared all over the world in order to spread salvation and to protect and sustain [the doctrine of] the Three Teachings. Each word and sentence he wrote is the secret doctrine of the Great Net Heaven (Daluo 大羅) and the mantras of the Mysterious abode (*xuanfu* 玄府). At this time, after having included what came early and what came late and penetrated the present and the past, he gathered the canonical scriptural essence of all the Perfected by integrating the genuine transmission of the alchemical paths and ordered the disciples at the First Awakening Altar to compile the *Daozang jiyao* and have it carved in wood blocks. From the [teachings of] the highest Primordial Heavenly Worthy [Yuanshi tianwang] to the [teachings of the] various Perfected and sages to the theories of the hundred schools and the explanations by various thinkers, [he ordered his disciples] to read [these works] widely and summarize them, culling their essence and discussing them in detail. 我孚佑帝君、相玉清、代天宣化、變現十方、綱維三教。凡所著述一字一言、胥玄府之總持、大羅之密諦。今乃囊括後先、條貫今始、綜丹道之真傳、羅諸真之典要、命第一覺壇諸弟子、編纂道藏輯要一書、付諸剞劂。上自元始天王、下逮諸真列聖、以及百家之論說、諸子之疏解、博觀而約取、擇之也精、語之也詳。(CK 1: 9–10).

rule and of his duties as Imperial Lord Savior of the Needy[440] as well as those of his officers.[441] For Jiang Yupu and his spirit writing altar's congregants, it is spiritual legitimacy that is of central importance. Caught up in moralistic and eschatological sentiments of sanctity and salvation, this Confucian elite at the service of their Imperial Lord is charged with the mission of "compiling the *Daozang jiyao* and having it carved in wood blocks" 編纂道藏輯要一書、付諸剞劂. It is their task and aim to establish themselves as the spiritual arm of the Emperor Savior of the Needy (Fuyou shangdi 孚佑上帝) so that, by way of their spirit writing altar, authentic Daoism can be once more revealed to the world.[442]

By contrast, the new *Chongkan* editors, who one century later were involved in republishing this Canon, appear to neglect such spiritual legitimacy ensured via spirit writing. As a project of the clerical institution Erxian'an, which was realized thanks to the help of Sichuanese local networks, the *Chongkan* inevitably displays a different strategy. It reflects the aim of ensuring institutional and temporal authority over Erxian'an's local community and its territorial cults. It is now up to the orthodox clergy to fulfill its duties in providing the appropriate religious content for its community based not on spirit writing but rather on its ability to communicate with the divine via the performance of correct rites.

In this context, it is interesting to see that the editorial board of the Erxian'an, while including the original prefaces of the old *Daozang jiyao*, ignore their underlying logic. The a-temporal revelation of Lü Dongbin's Canon, which was described in the undated prefaces of the old *Daozang jiyao* transmitted via spirit writing, is no more taken in consideration. In

---

[440] As a natural consequence of his functions of celestial emperor and universal savior, Lü Dongbin in fact is said "to protect and sustain the doctrine of the Three Teachings 綱維三教" and is, as noted above, in the central scripture authorized by him even called "Patriarch of the Three Teachings" 三教宗師.

[441] *Sanjiao* doctrine was part of the daily agenda of Jiang Yupu and his companions who were members of the Confucian elite employed in the imperial literary enterprise of the *Siku quanshu* and in the waterways administration (*hechen* 河臣). Beyond the above-quoted testimony of Christian missionaries (see p. 231), a recent study by Jeffrey Snyder-Reinke (*Dry Spells State Rainmaking and Local Governance in Late Imperial China*, Cambridge, Mass.: Harvard University Press, 2009) also emphasizes shared views on *sanjiao* among the local officers of the Qing dynasty.

[442] The new corpus of scriptures added to the old *Daozang jiyao* and attributed to Lü Dongbin often refers to him as Fuyou shangdi 孚佑上帝. See for instance the scriptures authorized by him that are placed at the center of the Canon (in the central Lodges Shi and Bi), *Chongkan Daozang jiyao*, vols. 12–13.

the words of the collator He Longxiang, the old *Daozang jiyao* is no longer a wondrously revealed Canon. It not only receives an editor in the flesh—Peng Dingqiu 彭定求 (1645–1719) and/or Peng Wenqin 彭文勤—but also a date of compilation pre-dated by about one century (1700 instead of 1800).[443] Although the old *Daozang jiyao* becomes, in the eyes of the twentieth-century *Chongkan* editors, a well-defined compilation in their spatio-temporal framework, no mention is ever made of the locus of its actual revelation: Beijing's Jueyuantan altar. The only person who refers to the previous compilers of the old *Daozang jiyao* under the generic appellation of "disciples below the altar of Fuyou dijun 孚佑帝君壇下弟子" is the Erxian'an abbot Yan Yonghe. But the name of their altar, "First Altar of Awakening" 第一覺壇 or "Source of Awakening" 覺源壇, goes unmentioned.[444] Did this name have a somehow uncomfortable ring for him and for his clerical institution? Should we see this from the perspective of a rejection of spirit-writing legitimacy by the "well-established" Erxian'an community?[445]

It is interesting to remember that the Celestial Master Zhang Yuchu, when he was in charge of collecting and classifying the scriptures for the Ming Daoist Canon, had dismissed the use of spirit writing and called it "a medium unfit for orthodox Daoists."[446] Thus, in contrast to the previous editors of the old *Daozang jiyao*, abbot Yan Yonghe who supervised

---

[443] See the presentation of the theory of three editions of the *Daozang jiyao* at the beginning of Part Three. This theory derived from He Longxiang's wrong attribution of the old *Daozang jiyao* to Peng Dingqiu and/or Peng Wenqing.

[444] It is worth noting that the reference to the previous compilers as "disciples below the altar of Fuyou dijun" does not appear in Yan Yonghe's prefaces to the *Chongkan* or inside that collection. It was only mentioned in the memorial compiled by the abbot Yan Yonghe. See here below.

[445] Rejecting spirit writing from the side of the Erxian'an editorial board may also had the meaning of protecting the community and its Canon from being accused of heterodoxy. We cannot ignore the fact that the original editor Jiang Yupu was labeled of "flawed official" for his involvement in a bribery with the Buddhist monk Mingxin. The latter was known for spreading spirit writing activities among elite officials (see above note 49).

[446] Introduction by K. Schipper to *The Taoist Canon*, p. 33. Yet this does not mean that Zhang Yuchu's selection of "canonical" scriptures did not include works written via spirit writing. See the recent study by Judith M. Boltz, "On the Legacy of Zigu and a Manual on Spirit Writing in Her Name," in *The People and the Dao. New Studies in Chinese Religions in Honor of Daniel L. Overmyer*, eds. Philippe Clart and Paul Crowe (Nettetal: Steyler, 2009), pp. 349–388.

the *Chongkan* enterprise, adopted the most suitable medium for orthodox Daoists. He organized a Great Yellow Register Retreat of the Universal Salvation of the Most High 太上黃籙度人大齋 at the Erxian'an in order to report to Heaven the completion of his important publishing project. On that occasion, a *Chongkan* set including various supplementary scriptures in "two hundred and forty eight scrolls and twenty-eight cases" was burned at the Doumu hall 斗姥殿 of the Chengdu Erxian'an "in order to repay the Sacred Grace, benefit the living and rescue the dead, and prolong forever the life of the country 酬答聖恩、利明濟幽、綿延國脈."[447] As abbot Yan Yonghe's "Memorial of the retreat-zhai, performed to present the newly-carved *Daozang jiyao* to Heaven by burning" composed for that occasion shows, both clerics and lay devotees were engaged. The clerics represent Daoist priests in charge of procuring salvation for the living and dead, for their local community, and for the entire country, whereas the lay people figure as contributors to the *Chongkan* publication:

> The disciples worshiping the Tao [like me, Yan Yonghe] led by their obligations [as Daoist priests], and the [laypersons] led by their commitment to [the publication of] the scriptures, have reprinted the *Daozang jiyao* in twenty-eight cases with various supplementary scriptures for a total of two hundred and forty eight scrolls. On this day, we burn and offer it in the hope of presenting it reverently to Holy inspection.
>
> 事緣奉道弟子某暨書緣人等, 重刊道藏輯要二十八函, 及續刻諸經, 共成二百四十八卷, 是日焚呈, 叩邀聖鑑。[448]

As a fruit of the collaboration between Daoist clergy and laypersons under the supervision of the Erxian'an, the *Chongkan Daozang jiyao* displays a mode of legitimacy that differs from that of the old *Daozang jiyao*. It can be schematized as follows:

---

[447] "Kanke Daozang jiyao fenshu chengtian xiuzhai shu 刊刻道藏輯要焚書呈天修齋疏" in *Erxian'an changzhu yingyong shiwen* 二仙菴常住應用時文, 18b–19b, here 19a–b (published under the title *Lingbao suishi wen* 靈寶歲時文 as a Qingyanggong publication). On this memorial compiled by Yan Yonghe see also Mori Yuria, "Chōkan Dōzō shūyō to Shinchō Shisen chiiki no shūkyō," pp. 352–353.

[448] *Erxian'an changzhu yingyong shiwen*, 19a–b. This passage was also presented in Mori, "Chōkan Dōzō shūyō," pp. 349–55.

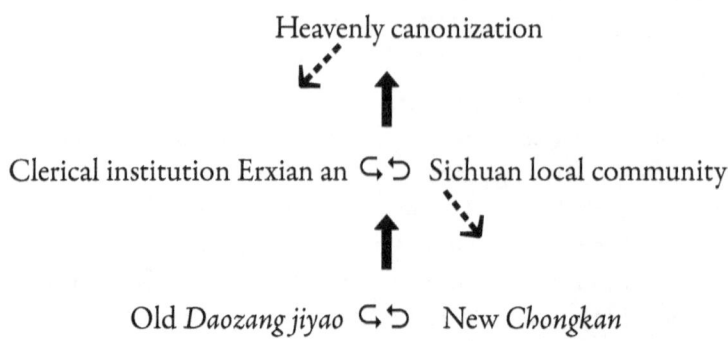

Fig. 47: Modality of Heavenly canonization of the new *Chongkan Daozang jiyao*

In the above graph we can see that, in contrast with the old *Daozang jiyao* (Fig. 46), the modality of canonization goes from bottom to top: from the old *Daozang jiyao* revealed on earth by an earthly compiler to its presentation to Heaven via the intermediacy of the Erxian'an clerical community in its new *Chongkan* format. Vertical circulations combine with horizontal fluxes of negotiation ⇆ between the clerical Erxian'an and its lay community in recreating and redefining the new content of the *Chongkan* and "presenting it reverently to Holy inspection" 叩邀聖鑑. Once this ritual for obtaining certification from Heaven is properly performed, it establishes authority and identification with authority.[449] Presenting itself as the spiritual arm of the imperial state, the Erxian'an community demonstrates by the correct performance of the rite its full devotion to orthodoxy and its acceptance of the primacy of the imperial order. Thus, it agrees to take its place in the system of the Three Teachings. Its heavenly approved Canon consequently displays imperial emblems such as the Yongzheng edicts on the Three Teachings in vermilion ink (exclusive to the Emperor), and it includes all other prefatory matter reproducing imperial rhetoric. Whereas in the old *Daozang jiyao* the Imperial Lord Savior of the Needy Lü Dongbin

---

[449] Stephan Feuchtwang, *The Imperial Metaphor* (London: Routledge, 1992), pp. 8–9. On the triangular structure (state, local elites, and clergy) that appears to exert influence on the Erxian'an and the publication of its Canon, see the recent article by Paul Katz (康豹), "Zhongguo dizhi wanqi yijiang shimiao yishi zai difang shehui de gongneng" 中國帝制晚期以降寺廟儀式在地方社會的功能, in Lin Fushi 林富士 (ed.), *Zhongguoshi xinlun—Zongjiaoshe fence* 中國史新論—宗教史分冊 (Taipei: Lianjing chuban gongsi, 2011), pp. 439–476.

was in charge of ensuring Three Teachings harmony in the world as part of his heavenly and kingly duties, in the *Chongkan* this harmony is ensured in the Qing Empire by the exemplary emperor on earth, Yongzheng (r. 1723–35).

As an imperially approved Daoist clerical institution, the Erxian'an also does not fail to display in its newly edited Canon the marks of its raised status and prestige. The important edicts granting the official gate plate (bian'e 匾額) for Erxian'an by Kangxi emperor in 1702 along with its imperial recognition as Daoist public monastery (*shifang conglin* 十方叢林) in 1849, one year before the end of the Daoguang 道光 reign, are of course included in the new scriptural body of the *Chongkan* (see above Table 4 on p. 242, text no. 15) and provide a historical dimension to the Erxian'an.[450] At the same time, in such an orthodox framework, scriptures dealing more specifically with Erxian'an local cults and liturgies could also be legitimized and promoted as part of this apparently imperially sanctioned Daoist Canon.

Finally it is evident that, in contrast with the old *Daozang jiyao*, the *Chongkan* displays a different kind of legitimacy. It reproduces Erxian'an institutional rhetoric and shows the will to legitimize a self-preserved and self-reproduced clerical authority over the local community that contributed to the completion of its *Chongkan* enterprise. In this light, the materials on the Three Teachings added in the Erxian'an newly edited Canon can be better understood. Thus it is not surprising that the Erxian'an, as a clerical institution, chose to engrave on the frontispiece of its newly edited Canon (see Fig. 45, p. 249) the two verses "Huangtu gonggu 皇圖鞏固 (Consolidation for the Imperial domain)" and "Didao xiachang 帝道遐昌 (Long-lasting prosperity to the Imperial way)." Like the Three Teachings-related materials, these two imperial seals are the emblems of imperial and clerical rhetoric. The Erxian'an decided to immortalize them on the frontispiece of its own Canon because they commemorate the enhanced prestige of its abbots in performing Quanzhen Daoist ordination and establishing the correct monastic liturgy for its clergy. In fact the two verses "Huangtu gonggu 皇圖鞏固" and "Didao xiachang 帝道遐昌" form part of a longer stanza to be intoned according to the *diaogua* 吊掛 melody by Quanzhen Daoist priests at the beginning of their daily morning liturgy. It reads as follows:

---

[450] *Erxian'an beiji* 二仙菴碑記 110b, 113a, 118b, 125a (for Kangxi), 120b, 126a (for Daoguang) in CK 24: 10556–57, 10560–61, and 10563–64.

上壇齊舉步虛聲、祝國迎祥竭寸誠。當日陳情金闕內、今朝香靄玉爐焚。

皇圖鞏固山河壯、帝道遐昌日月明。　萬民瞻仰堯舜日、歲稔豐登樂太平。 451

This stanza stems from the *Taishang xuanmen gongke jing* 太上玄門功課經, a text included in the newly added *Chongkan* corpus (see above Table 4 on p. 242, text no. 13) and created during the Qing for establishing the correct Quanzhen monastic liturgy. In Daoist circles it is believed that this stanza was originally a gatha of examination (*kaoji* 考偈) composed by the number-one future abbot on the occasion of the re-establishment of the "Quanzhen ordination" that was performed at the beginning of the Qing at the capital's public monastery Baiyun guan 白雲觀. Imitating the procedure of civil examinations, the Daoist ordinand who had written the best poem would be ranked first under the *tian* 天 character, the Daoist equivalent of the "Top graduate" (*zhuangyuan* 狀元) in the Confucian final examinations. We have seen in Part Two that tradition has Wang Changyue 王常月 (1594?–1680) alias Wang Kunyang 王崑陽, the first Quanzhen Longmen abbot who allegedly re-established such Quanzhen ordination, preside over the Baiyun guan altar. He was the one who purportedly gave to

---

451 *Taishang xuanmen gongke jing* 太上玄門功課經 2b (CK 23: 10236). Few occurrences of the two verses "Huangtu gonggu 皇圖鞏固" and "Didao xiachang 帝道遐昌" are also found, but not together, in the *Daozang* and *Daozang jiyao*, mainly in liturgical texts. For the expression "Huangtu gonggu 皇圖鞏固" see for instance the *Hong'en Lingji zhenjun qixie shejiao ke* 洪恩靈濟眞君祈謝設醮科 (DZ 473, in *Zhonghua Daozang* [ZHDZ] 31: 643c/4) and the *Jinlu dazhai suqi yi* 金籙大齋宿啓儀 (DZ 484 in ZHDZ 43: 14c/12). For "Didao xiachang 帝道遐昌" see the *Yulu sanri jiu chaoyi* 玉籙三日九朝儀 (DZ 505, section "Yulu dazhai diyi ri zaochao yi 玉籙大齋第一日早朝儀" in ZHDZ 43: 120c/3) and the dated Preface (1656) attributed to Wang Changyue of the *Chuzhen jielü* 初眞戒律 25b (CK 24: 10469). In the above-quoted memorial by Yan Yonghe (*Erxian'an changzhu yingyong shiwen*, 20b) we also find the verse "皇圖鞏固" followed by "國脈延長." It is worthy of mention that apart from the *Taishang xuanmen gongke jing* the only text reproducing the two verses "Huangtu gonggu 皇圖鞏固" and "Didao xiachang 帝道遐昌" together is the *Xuxian zhenlu ji* 徐仙眞錄集 j. 2 (DZ 1470 in ZHDZ 31: 799a/17–18). As is known, the latter was included in the supplement of the *Daozang* of 1607 and, as the title makes clear, it was a scripture related to the Lingjigong 靈濟宮 temple and the worship of the immortal Xu brothers under Imperial patronage; see the entry on this text by Yuan Bingling and Schipper in the *Taoist Canon*, vol. 2, p. 1212.

the ordinands the eight Chinese characters "上祝當今皇帝萬歲" which constitute the topic of the winning gatha of his future heir.[452]

The immortalization of the two verses from the poem of the number-one abbot on the *Chongkan* frontispiece thus appeared to serve as a reminder both of Erxian'an clerical legitimacy as a public monastery of the Quanzhen Longmen branch directly affiliated with Beijing's Baiyun guan, and of the supreme pedigree of Erxian'an abbot Yan Yonghe. If the state ensured control over society via the formation and education of its elites through official examinations on Confucian classics, the Erxian'an as religious institution was called to educate and regulate its clergy via the system of ordination performed by its abbots and its own Daoist Canon.[453] As a clerical institution it set up the proper liturgical framework to procure salvation for its community, its clergy, and the entire country, thus sharing the task and privilege of praying for the Emperor and supporting the state.

In face of such an overwhelming display of authority, one cannot but wonder if the will to orthodoxy, so strongly invoked in the *Chongkan Daozang jiyao*'s Three-Teachings rhetoric, is but an adoption of the imperial bureaucratic logic by a "Quanzhen" clerical institution (the Erxian'an).[454] Do the claims for religious universalism and tolerance, historically incarnated in the eyes of the *Chongkan* editors by Emperor Yongzheng, represent anything other than a strategy for protection, a means to attract or enhance

---

[452] On this event see Ren Zongquan 任宗權, *Daojiao jielü xue* 道教戒律學, 2 vols. (Beijing: Zongjiao wenhua chubanshe, 2007), vol. 2, pp. 625–26.

[453] It seems that the last Quanzhen ordination held before the takeover by the communist government took place here at the Erxian'an in 1947; see Lai Chi-tim, "Daoism in China Today, 1980–2002," *The China Quarterly* 2003, pp. 413–427, here p. 419, note 27.

[454] On the relationship between imperial bureaucratic logic and Zhengyi Daoist bureaucracy during the Qing see the article by Vincent Goossaert, "Bureaucratie, taxation et justice: Taoïsme et construction de l'État au Jiangnan (Chine), XVIIe–XIXe siècle," *Annales HHS* 4 (2010): 999–1027. It might be tempting to speculate that such a display of orthodoxy in the Chongkan would also be a symptom of a power vacuum foreboding the future disintegration of the Qing empire and its clerical institutions in the Republican and Communist states. As clerical institution, Erxian'an continued to perform ordinations until 1947 imitating the civil service examinations although the latter were already abolished in 1904 (that is, before the publication of the Chongkan). Although the Qing emperors did not convey any official request to the Daoist clergy regarding the compilation of a Daoist Canon during the Qing, the Erxian'an invested itself with such an authority and made use of the imperial memorials of Yongzheng.

imperial patronage? Is this wish for the "Long-lasting prosperity for the Imperial way" an ultimate appeal for state protection and an assertion of legitimacy both for the Erxian'an Daoist clerical institution and its newly edited Daoist Canon—or is it rather an expression of longing for a harmonious empire on earth in face of an uncertain present?[455] Is it an evocation of continuity with the past or a symptom of deperate nostalgy—a last Daoist prayer for a vanishing Empire, a last dream of power?

---

[455] This cannot but remind us of the frontispieces of the "precious scrolls": while the content of these books often dealt with the promise of a new world, the woodblock illustrations included a picture of a carved stele inscribed with the formulaic wish for imperial longevity. See Sawada Mizuhō 澤田瑞穂, Zōhō hōkan non kenkyū 増補寶卷の研究 (Tokyo: Kokusho Kankōkai, 1975), pp. 70–74, and Susan Naquin, *Peking and City Life 1400–1900* (Berkeley: University of California Press, 2000), p. 223. At the same time this was also, as noted above, the fruit of Erxian'an's offering of the Canon on the occasion of the Huanglu dazhai (Great Yellow Register Retreat) and a repayment for the emperor's grace.

Part Four

CREATION OF SALVATION

Fig. 48: Lü Dongbin 呂洞賓 in *Lüzu quanshu*, fascicle 33.

Chapter 1

THE SECRET OF THE GOLDEN FLOWER

The *Jinhua zongzhi* 金華宗旨 is a famous alchemical text attributed to the immortal Lü Dongbin 呂洞賓. Recently, an English translation has appeared in electronic format on the internet. The publisher presents this latest incarnation of our text as follows:

> This ancient esoteric treatise was transmitted orally for centuries before being recorded on a series of wooden tablets in the eighth century. It was recorded by a member of the Religion of Light, whose leader was the Daoist adept Lu Yen (also known as Lu Yen and Lu "Guest of the Cavern"). It is said that Lu Tzu became one of the Eight Immortals using these methods. The ideas have been traced back to Persia and the Zarathustra tradition and its roots in the Egyptian Hermetic tradition.[457]

Though this explanation is new, the English text now sold on the internet is merely an electronic version of the German sinologist Richard Wilhelm's pioneering translation into a Western language of a Chinese alchemical (*neidan* 內丹) text, the *Jinhua zongzhi* 金華宗旨. Wilhelm's translation was published in 1929 together with Carl Gustav Jung's psychological commentary under the title *Das Geheimnis der Goldenen Blüte: ein chinesisches Lebensbuch*.[458] What kind of text is this?

---

[457] See http://www.powells.com/cgi-bin/biblio?inkey=92-1932681787-0.

[458] The first edition was published in Munich (Dorn Verlag) in 1929. A new revised German edition with a new foreword by Jung (1875–1961) and his memorial address for Richard Wilhelm (1873–1930) was published in 1938 (Zürich: Rascher Verlag) and reprinted twice in 1944. The first English translation from the German, by C. F. Baynes, appeared in 1931 under the title *The Secret of the Golden*

The sales pitch on the Internet claims that it is an esoteric treatise associated with one of China's Eight Immortals, Lü Tsu (Patriarch Lü, i.e., Lü Dongbin 呂洞賓), the leader of a mysterious "Religion of Light" that is traced to "Persia and the Zarathustra tradition" and from there to the "Egyptian Hermetic tradition." That is quite a pedigree! Was this also Wilhelm's idea?

In his preface, Wilhelm tells us the story of this text as he saw it. He based his translation on a 1921 reprint of the *Jinhua zongzhi* 金華宗旨 by a certain Huizhenzi 慧真子 in Beijing. According to Wilhelm, the text's author Lü Dongbin was a man of the eighth century whom folklore later made into one of the Eight Immortals. Wilhelm claimed that Lü had been born around A.D. 796 and had founded the so-called Religion of the Golden Elixir (*jindan jiao* 金丹教). In Richard Wilhelm's eyes, this was an esoteric and secret religion from the Tang era that furnished a new interpretation of alchemy. He explains that in this new kind of alchemy the ingredients were no longer physical materials for fabricating the pill of immortality but had become symbols of a psychological process. This was one of the main reasons why C. G. Jung was so interested in this book as to write a commentary. Wilhelm portrayed this "new kind of alchemy" as syncretistic. Impressed by the Japanese Christian father Saeki's book entitled *The Nestorian Monument in China*,[459] Wilhelm saw a link between Lü Dongbin and Nestorian Christianity and associated Lü's teachings with the religion of light of Persia. This appears to be the basis for the outlandish claim quoted at the beginning of this chapter. Wilhelm's and C.G. Jung's German book was not only translated into English and other European languages but even into Chinese and Japanese (see Bibliography). Because Wilhelm had translated only the first eight chapters from a thirteen-chapter Chinese version published in 1921, readers got a false impression of the *Jinhua zongzhi*'s content and format. Wilhelm's conjectures about esoteric connections with secret societies and Nestorianism made things even more obscure but continue to this day to make the text very attractive for followers of Freemason orders, new religions, new-age movements, and the like. It is certain that the eclectic and esoteric nature of the *Jinhua zongzhi* has contributed to many speculations and misperceptions; but today we have a much better picture of the history and nature of this text. This will be the focus of the present chapter.

Flower: A Chinese Book of Life (London: Kegan Paul, Trench, Trubner and Co).

[459] Yoshiro Saeki (佐伯好郎, 1871–1965), *The Nestorian Monument in China*. London: Society for Promoting Christian Knowledge, 1916.

Chapter 1: The Secret of the Golden Flower: Content and Major Editions

It was in 1986 that I bought in Hong Kong a text of *the Golden Flower* included in the *Daozang jinghua* 道藏精華 collection.[460] One year later, I came across the same scripture in Paris at the Library of the Collège de France, this time as part of the *Daozang xubian* 道藏續編, a collection dating from 1834.[461] I was surprised to see that this version differed in some points from the one translated by Wilhelm. I continued to gather *Golden Flower* editions, and in 1997 I discovered one included in a so-called *Lüzu quanshu zongzheng* 呂祖全書宗正 at the Library of Ōtani University in Kyoto (see my photo in Fig. 49). In the same year I met a Japanese scholar, Mori Yuria, who to my great surprise was also interested in this text. We exchanged opinions on the obscure textual history of the *Golden Flower* while writing our articles. What follows presents the results of recent research.[462]

In the course of my studies I found out that the *Golden Flower* is a revealed text that forms part of a reformed liturgy associated with the Daoist Jingming 淨明 tradition. The revelation of the *Golden Flower* took place not in the eighth century, as Wilhelm believed, but in 1668 and 1692 among congregants of spirit writing altars located in Piling 毘陵 (Changzhou 常州, Jiangsu) who belonged to a so-called Taiyi lineage (Taiyi fapai 太乙法派). Under the guidance of Tu Yu'an 屠宇菴, a first compilation was achieved with the help of Zhang Shuang'an 張爽菴.[463] Different versions began circulating in Jiangnan among members of the elite and in spirit writ-

---

[460] *Longmen pai danfa yaojue Jindanfamai qinggui quanzhi hekan* 龍門派丹法訣要金丹法脈清規全指, in *Daozang jinhua* 8–1, ed. Xiao Tianshi 蕭天石, Taipei: Ziyou, 1982.

[461] See below.

[462] See in order of appearance: by Monica Esposito, "La Porte du Dragon" (esp. vol. 1, p. XX) (1993); "Il Segreto del Fiore d'Oro e la tradizione Longmen del Monte Jingai" (1996); "The Different Versions of the *Secret of the Golden Flower* and Their Relationship with the Longmen School," *Transactions of the International Conference of Eastern Studies* 43, 1998: 90–110; "Longmen pai yu *Jinhua zongzhi* banben laiyuan, Paper presented at the Research Meeting on Daoist Culture, Waseda University, Tokyo, 1998; "Longmen Taoism in Qing China: Doctrinal Ideal and Local Reality" JCR 29, 2001: 191–221 (esp. 203–207 and 213–221) {*Facets of Qing Daoism*, chapter 3, esp. pp. 165–171 and 179–190}. By Mori Yuria, "Taiitsu kinke shūshi no seiritsu to hensen," *Tōyō no shisō to shūkyō* 15, 1998: 43–64; "Ryo Dōhin to Zenshin kyō: Shinchō koshū kingai-san no jirei o chūshin ni," in *Kōza: Dōkyō*, ed. Sunayama Minoru, Ōzaki Masaharu, and Kikuchi Noritaka (Tokyo: Yūzan kaku, 1999); "Identity and Lineage," in *Daoist Identity* ed. by L. Kohn and H. Roth (Honolulu: University of Hawai'i Press, 2000): 165–184.

[463] This is well explained in the Prefaces to the earlier version. See below.

ing networks devoted to the cult of Lü Dongbin and to the collection of its scriptures. On the basis of a manuscript of a certain Wu 吳 from Suzhou, Shao Zhilin 邵志琳 (1748–1810) modified the format of the scripture htat had originally begun with liturgical instructions. Shao reduced it to thirteen chapters and published it in 1775 in his 64-*juan Lüzu quanshu* 呂祖全書 (Patriarch Lü [Dongbin]'s Collected Works). Another revised version based on Shao's version in thirteen chapters was published in a separate 18-*juan Lüzu quanshu* collection known as *Quanshu zongzheng* 全書宗正. It is on the basis of the latter version, revised again by Jiang Yuanting 蔣元庭 (1755–1819), that the text finally came to be published in the *Daozang jiyao*, the Daoist Canon of the Qing era whose origin and history was described in Part Three.

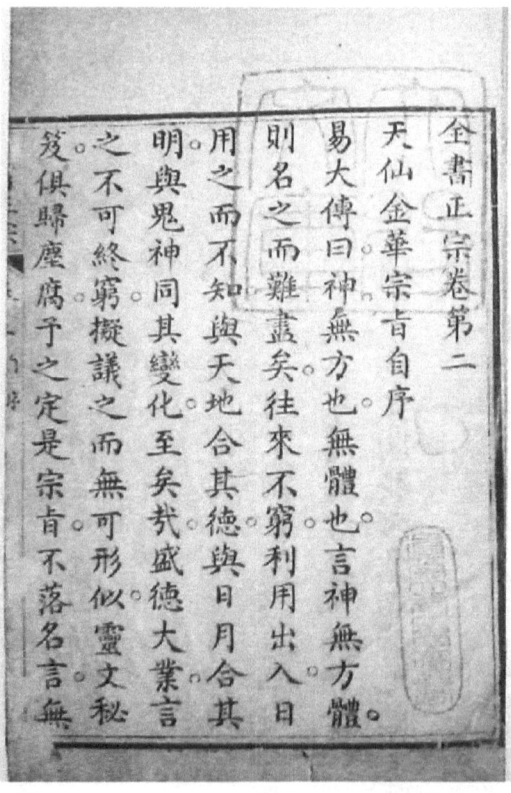

Fig. 49: Jiang Yuanting's edition of the "Golden Flower" (Ōtani University) in the *Quanshu zhengzong* 全書正宗 (see below under texts of Version 3)

Content of the Text

The complete text features thirteen chapters with an appended treatise titled *Jinhua zongzhi chanyou wenda* 金華宗旨闡幽問答 ("Questions and Answers for Clarifying Unclear Points on the Tenets of the Golden Flower"), which is seen as a complement to Lü Dongbin's revelation in form of a dialogue between the immortal and his disciples (see the postface by Qiu Tongxiao 邱通宵, fl. 1757). Traces of Jiang Yuanting 蔣元庭's reedition can be clearly detected in Jiang's two colophons (to the *Jinhua zongzhi* and *Jinhua chanyou wenda* 金華闡幽問答), in the Preface attributed to Liu Shouyuan 柳守元, and in the Postface by Zhiqiu 志秋 (i.e., Fan Ao 范鰲, fl. 1780–1803). The transmission of the *Golden Flower* is here associated with Jiang Yuanting's spirit writing altar in Beijing and its lineage of Celestial Immortals (Tianxian pai 天仙派), which recognizes the immortals Lü Dongbin and Liu Shouyuan respectively as founder and second patriarch. A Tianxian lineage poem in twenty-characters is also for the first time revealed and recorded in the Postface by Zhiqiu as proof of such legitimization. As a consequence even the title of the text changed. In the earlier version by Shao Zhilin 邵志琳 (1775), the title is *Xiantian xuwu Taiyi jinhua zongzhi* 先天虛無太乙金華宗旨 (Tenets of the Golden Flower of the Taiyi [lineage] of Pre-celestial Emptiness) in memory of the so-called Taiyi lineage associated with the Jingming tradition and the spirit writing altars in Piling. In Jiang Yuanting's version the title is changed into *Tianxian Taiyi jinhua zongzhi* 天仙太乙金華宗旨 (Tenets of the Golden Flower of the Supreme One of the Tianxian [lineage]), a title which emphasizes the role of Lü Dongbin as the founding patriarch of the Tianxian pai 天仙派 or Celestial Immortals lineage through which the genuine intent of this scripture could now be revealed (Section "Main Editions" below, Versions 3–4, and Table 5). The meaning of the new title, abbreviated in the heading of the *Daozang jiyao* (old and new edition) as *Jinhua zongzhi* 金華宗旨, is explained in its first chapter. The term *Taiyi* 太乙 or Supreme One refers to "what cannot be surpassed" (*wushang* 無上). In contrast to the variety of other alchemical teachings, the tenets or *zongzhi* 宗旨 it transmitted are unsurpassable because they are the direct instructions by the immortal Lü Dongbin concerning the practice of inner nature (*xinggong* 性功). In other words, these tenets point directly to the nature of mind which is symbolized by the golden flower (*jinhua* 金華), the light of self-enlightenment described as the "true pneuma of the Supreme One of the Celestial Immortals" 天仙太乙之真炁.[464] The term *jinhua* or golden flower is also presented as synonym of *jindan* 金丹 or golden elixir "whose spiritual transmutations are all guided by the mind" 神明變化、各師於心.

The central teaching is *huiguang* 回光 or "turning the light" using the method of reversal (*nifa* 逆法). It consists in reversing our ordinary view, our ordinary mind, and our ordinary perception. This lies at the core of the *Golden Flower* whose chapters are conceived as progressive stages for achieving that goal. Each chapter focuses on different aspects of the path of mind-and-body cultivation. These are presented via methods, explanations, and key terms from Daoism, Buddhism, and Confucianism. Passages from Daoist scriptures like the *Xinyin jing* 心印經 and the *Yinfu jing* 陰符經, but also from classics of medicine like the *Huangdi suwen* 黃帝素問 are explicitly quoted. Explanations on meditation phenomena and mental training are also taken from Buddhist popular scriptures such as the *Lengyan jing* 楞嚴經 or *Śūraṃgamasūtra*, Tiantai manuals of meditation like the *Xiao zhiguan* 小止觀 (Small manual of *śamatha-vipaśyanā*; referring to the *Zuochan fayao* 坐禪法要 T 1915), and Pure Land meditation sutras like the *Guan Wuliangshoufo jing* 觀無量壽佛經 (Sutra on Contemplating the Buddha of Immeasurable Life) or *Amitāyur-dhyāna-sūtra* (T 365). Metaphors from the *Yijing* 易經, expressions from *Zhuangzi*, *Daodejing*, and alchemical classics like the *Jindan sibaizi* 金丹四百字 and the *Wuzhen pian* 悟真篇 appear as part of a common background that even encompasses stories from Chan Kōan (*gong'an* 公案) collections.

The *Golden Flower*'s first chapter introduces the celestial mind (*tianxin* 天心) as a mind-to-mind transmission that was purportedly lost inside mainline Daoist schools like the Quanzhen 全真. Expressed in Chan terms as "a special transmission outside mainline teachings" (*jiaowai biechuan* 教外別傳), the revelation of the *Golden Flower* via spirit writing emphasizes, along the line of Chan Buddhism, sudden awakening (*dunwu* 頓悟) and unmediated mind-to-mind transmission (*yixin chuanxin* 以心傳心). Inspired by the Jingming patriarch Xu Xun 許遜 (trad. 239–374) and his wish of saving all beings, such revelation is at the basis of the establishment of religious associations (*fahui* 法會) recognizing Lü Dongbin as their

---

[464] All other versions of the *Golden Flower* (versions 1, 2, 5, 6; see below, section "Major Text Editions") have *xiantian* 先天 instead of Tianxian 天仙, that is, the "true pneuma of the Supreme One of the Former Heaven 先天太乙之真炁."

"master of initiation" (*dushi* 度師). The structure of the text itself mirrors this "master-disciple transmission": every chapter begins with the formula "Lüdi *yue* 呂帝曰" (Lü [Dongbin] says...), thus presenting teachings that were purportedly revealed at the spirit writing altar by Lü Dongbin—the Supreme Emperor Savior of the Needy (Fuyou shangdi 孚佑上帝)—to his disciples (*fazi* 法子, *zibei* 子輩).[465]

According to the *Golden Flower*'s second chapter, the practice begins with the experience of the subtle presence or awareness that distinguishes the original spirit from the conscious spirit. Original spirit (*yuanshen* 元神), the essence of the celestial mind, is associated with the higher soul (*hun* 魂) which sees the world from the celestial perspective, free of all ego-restrictions. Conscious spirit (*shishen* 識神), the essence of the ordinary mind, is associated with the lower soul (*po* 魄) which apprehends the world via its visceral emotions. Such different views generated by the ego and the non-self are experienced via the method of turning the light—the theme of chapter three—which is a term attributed to Guanyin zi 關尹子, the Guardian of the Pass.[466] This method is introduced via the key passage of the *Yinfu jing* 陰符經: "The Mechanism is in the eyes 機在目." The eyes are the means for perceiving the moment when "heaven is open, earth is broad, and all things are just as they are" 天空地闊萬法如如. This kind of openness of vision can be achieved by focusing on the Center (*yuanzhong* 緣中), the space or interstice between the arising and ceasing of every thought.[467] Such awareness can be realized via the Tiantai practice of *zhiguan* 止觀 (*samatha-vipaśyanā*) but also via the Chan examination of the source of thought. Suggestions on how to practice are then given in Chapter four which explains the method of attuning breath and mind. More technical advice, methods,

---

[465] This holds true for the old *Daozang jiyao*. In the *Chongkan Daozang jiyao* the first chapter opens with the formula "Lüzu yue 呂祖曰," whereas the remaining twelve chapters open with "Lüdi yue 呂帝曰." See below under versions 3 & 4, p. 284 ff.

[466] The term *huiguang* 回光 (turning the light), which abounds in Chan Buddhist literature (also in expressions such as *huiguang fanzhao* 回光返照, *huiguang neizhao* 回光內照) is here attributed to Yin Xi 尹喜, probably referring to the occurrence of this term in the *Wenshi zhenjing* 文始真經 (譬如兩目、能見天地萬物、暫時回光、一時不見), JY 134, Nüji 女集 1, j. xia.9a.

[467] This Buddhist term *yuanzhong* 緣中, a well-known occurrence of which is found in the *Sanfa dulun* 三法度論 (T 1506, vol. 25.20a6) is also put in parallel with the Daoist term "Yellow Center" (*zhonghuang* 中黃). See the commentaries by Min Yide 閔一得 (version 4, DZXB vol. 1.5b) and by Zhanran Hui 湛然慧 (Version 6c, 1921, p. 11) to the *Golden Flower* (see below).

and explanations about different levels of body and mind experiences as well as dangers that can arise during practice are presented in Chapters six and seven. As these two chapters emphasize, the doctrine revealed here goes beyond Chan teachings because psycho-physiological experiences (like hearing sounds, feeling of body lightness, floating upward, visualization experiences, etc.) are taken into consideration and verified. The text alludes to critiques that were often addressed to Chan practitioners, accusing them of neglecting body practices and sensorial experiences while focusing on the void of mind. Chan practitioners were said to lose mindfulness and fall into indifferent emptiness (*wankong* 頑空) or a dead void (*sixu* 死虛).

At the outset it is important to engage in early morning séances of meditation as long as awareness is present without fixing any span of time for this practice (Chap. 4). Gradually, meditation should be integrated in life through maintenance of mindfulness while managing affairs (Chap. 7). Then the text presents a synthesis of the teachings of its previous chapters in the form of verses on "The Secret of Freedom" (*Xiaoyao jue* 逍遙訣) attributed to Yuqing 玉清, the highest god of the Daoist Trinity (Chap. 8). The key formula is "doing without doing" or "acting without striving" (*wuwei er wei* 無為而為). The text's previous chapters dealing with specific methods for controlling mind and body are interpreted as first steps for controlling the inside from the outside. This refers, in more alchemical terms, to the practice of the first two lower passes of "refining the essence in pneuma and pneuma into spirit," which allows seeing mind and body not as solid entities but as a single conglomerate of increasingly subtle, changing forces. The aim is to transcend this in order to penetrate to the "upper pass," i.e. the superior stage where one abides in the center and controls the outside. This becomes possible after having established the foundation during one hundred days (*bairi liji* 百日立基)—the theme of Chapter nine—which is a symbolic expression for indicating a period of time of special effort needed to acquire power. As explained in Chapter ten, the aim is to arrive at the stage of observing the world without observer. Such a stage can be achieved via the exercise of the eight attributions (*bahuan* 八還) from the *Śūraṃgamasūtra* where even the subtle presence of the observer which marked the starting point of practice (Chap. 2) is eliminated.[468] The goal is seeing without any

---

[468] This exercise of meditation aiming at seeing the essence of the genuine mind is explained in this sutra (*Lengyan jing* 楞嚴經 T 945, vol. 19.106a–111b). It is designed to reach the essence of consciousness via a process of elimination going from 1. "The light returns to the sun 明還日輪" to 8. "Clear light returns to clarity 清明還霽."

trace of the person who watches, "like a mirror that reflects the light without any intention of reflecting it 如鏡之無心而照也." The duality of "duality and non-duality," which was experienced in the course of practice by establishing a new dimension of awareness via a detached observer, must be overcome. The "centered" and detached observer —symbolized in alchemical terms by the interaction of water and fire, yin and yang, inner nature (*xing* 性) and vital force (*ming* 命), body and mind, spirit (*shen* 神) and pneuma (*qi* 氣)— must be finally transcended (Chap. 11). "Whether it is dragon and tiger today, water and fire tomorrow: in the end they all turn into illusions" 若今日龍虎明日水火終成妄想. The aim is spontaneous meditation happening at each instant: water and fire—symbols of all duality, polarity, or dichotomy—disappear because the perceiver who knows what water and fire are, is no longer there: there is no more trace of the meditator. The alchemical process—that is, the entire process of mind and body cultivation—becomes spontaneous like cycles in nature that take place without any intervention. "When the *huozi* 活子 [active midnight]—i.e., action not generated by the ordinary impulsion under desire and attachment—appears at any moment, the *zhengzi* 正子 (true midnight) is finally reached." The text ends with a "Song to inspire the world" 勸世歌 (Chap. 13). It lays out in verse the stages of practice and the ultimate goal where the mind is liberated, cosmic space silent, and every sign and form has vanished.

Attached to Chapter thirteen as part of the scripture, the *Jinhua zongzhi chanyou wenda* 金華宗旨闡幽問答 offers questions and answers on important points of *Golden Flower* practice. This dialogue, which provides interpretations about different passages on body and mind cultivation from the three teachings (more centered on moral cultivation than on technical advices), probably has its origin in spirit writing séances when adepts asked for more clarification.

The practitioner, by reducing progressively the contents of consciousness, reaches its essence, "mirror-like awareness."

Major Text Editions

At present we know of six major different versions of the *Secret of the Golden Flower*:

1. The Shao Zhilin 邵志琳 version

Xiantian xuwu taiyi jinhua zongzhi 先天虛無太乙金華宗旨 (Tenet of the Supreme One Golden Flower Lineage, from the Emptiness of Former Heaven). In the forty-ninth scroll of the *Lüzu quanshu* 呂祖全書 (The Complete Works of the Patriarch Lü Dongbin) edited by Shao Zhilin 邵志琳 (1748–1810), 1775, 64 scrolls.

2. The Chen Mou 陳謀 version

Xiantian xuwu taiyi jinhua zongzhi 先天虛無太乙金華宗旨 (Tenet of the Supreme One Golden Flower Lineage, from the Emptiness of Former Heaven). In the tenth scroll of the *Lüzu quanshu zongzheng* 呂祖全書宗正 (The Orthodoxy of the Lineage of the Patriarch Lü's Complete Works), edited by Chen Mou 陳謀, 1852, 18 scrolls [based on the original version of Peng Qifeng 彭啟豐 (1701–1784) titled *Quanshu zongzheng* in 18 scrolls].

3. The Jiang Yuanting 蔣元庭 version

Fuyou shangdi tianxian jinhua zongzhi 孚佑上帝天仙金華宗旨 (Tenet of the Golden Flower by the Celestial Immortal Lineage of the Supreme Emperor and Sincere Protector [Lü Dongbin]; abbr. *Tianxian jinhua zongzhi* 天仙金華宗旨). In the second scroll of the *Quanshu zhengzong* 全書正宗 (The Complete Collection of the Orthodox Lineage, also known as *Lüzu quanshu* 呂祖全書 in 16 scrolls), edited by Jiang Yuanting 蔣元庭 (alias: Yupu 予蒲, 1756–1819), 1803, 16 scrolls.

4. The *Daozang jiyao* versions

Jinhua zongzhi 金華宗旨 (Quintessential Tenet of the Golden Flower). In the *Daozang jiyao* 道藏輯要 (*shiji* 室集 2), compiled by Jiang Yuanting 蔣元庭 (1755–1819) ca. 1796–1819, and in the *Chongkan Daozang jiyao*, edited by He Longxiang 賀龍驤 and Peng

Hanran 彭瀚然 under the supervision of the Abbot Yan Yonghe 閻永和 at the Erxian an 二仙菴 of Chengdu, 1906.[469]

5. The Min Yide version

Lü zushi xiantian xuwu taiyi jinhua zongzhi 呂祖師先天虛無太一金華宗旨 (Quintessential Tenet of the Patriarch Lü on the Supreme One Golden Flower, Emptiness of Former Heaven). In the first volume of the *Daozang xubian* 道藏續編 (Supplement to the Daoist Canon) edited by Min Yide 閔一得 (alias: Xiaogen 小艮, 1758–1836), 1834, 4 vols.

6. Post-1900 versions

After 1900 we find several editions and reprints mainly based on the 13 chapter-version 1 (but with some variants). One of these versions was used for Wilhelm's translation; see next chapter.

In all of these editions, the text of the *Golden Flower* is attributed to the immortal Lü Dongbin and portrayed as the fruit of spirit writing séances. Except for the editions of Min Yide (1834) and Zhanran Huizhenzi (1921, 1927), the text features 13 chapters without commentary. In the first three editions of our list, the text of the *Golden Flower* is inserted in *Lüzu quanshu* collections. The edition of the *Lüzu quanshu* which includes for the first time the *Golden Flower* is that by Shao Zhilin 邵志琳 dated 1775.[470]

---

[469] Both editions add, after the title *Jinhua zongzhi*, *Fuyou Shangdi Chunyang Lüzu Tianshi zhu* 孚佑上帝純陽呂祖天師著 (written by the Celestial Master Patriarch Lü, Pure Yang, Supreme Emperor and Sincere Protector), but in the Index of Jiang Yuanting's edition of the *Daozang jiyao* (found in the *Daozang jinghua lu* 道藏精華錄) we find Tianxian 天仙 instead of Tianshi 天師. The only difference between these two editions regarding the Golden Flower text is that the expression Lüdi 呂帝 that introduces the teaching given by the immortal in the Jiang Yuanting edition has (only in the first chapter) been substituted by Lüzu 呂祖 in the *Chongkan Daozang jiyao*. On the different editions of the *Daozang jiyao* see Mori Yuria 森由利亜 "Dōzō shūyō to Shō Yofu no Ryoso fuki shinkō" 道藏輯要と蒋予蒲の呂祖扶乩信仰, *Tōhō shūkyō* 東方宗教 98 (2001): 33–53. I have used Jiang Yuanting's edition of the *Daozang jiyao*, stored at the Library of the Collège de France in Paris, and the *Chongkan Daozang jiyao* version published by Taipei: Xinwenfeng, 1977 (vol. 12, pp. 5349–5361).

[470] Shao Zhilin's edition is generally based on a *Lüzu quanshu* version in 32 scrolls compiled by Liu Tishu 劉體恕 in 1744 which did not yet include the *Golden Flower*. For a presentation of the various editions of the *Lüzu quanshu* see my eponymous entry in F. Pregadio (ed.), *The Encyclopedia of Taoism*, vol. 1: 726–728.

Version 1. Shao Zhilin's edition and the Taiyi Lineage

As the compiler Shao Zhilin 邵志琳 (1748–1810) explains in his foreword to the *Golden Flower*, the text stems from a manuscript of a certain Wu from Suzhou. It purportedly was initially connected with the oral transmission that Xu Xun 許遜, the founder of the Jingming dao 淨明道, received from Douzhong Xiaoti Wang 斗中孝悌王, the Respected King of Filial Piety from the Dipper.[471] In 1688 the immortal Lü Dongbin, in the company of the two well-known Quanzhen Perfected Qiu Chuji 邱處機 and Tan Chuduan 譚處端, descended on the altar of Bailong jingshe 白龍精舍 in Piling 毘陵 (Changzhou, Jiangsu 江蘇) in order to reveal the Quintessential Tenet 宗旨. Seven people belonging to the Jingming tradition, among them Pan Qiande 潘乾德, received it.[472] Later in 1692, because the first seven predestined recipients of the transmission had already passed away or were scattered, the transmission of the Jingming Tenet was once more performed for seven other members. This time it was revealed at another altar of Piling, the Gu Hongmeige 古紅梅閣 (Old Red Plum Hall).[473] After having recorded it, Tu Yu'an 屠乾元 (alias Yu'an 宇菴) entrusted Zhang Kanzhen 張坎真 with revising and editing it as a book.[474]

---

[471] This deity is said to have two brothers, Xiaoxian Wang 孝仙王 (the sun) and Xiaoming Wang 孝明王 (the moon) who revealed Daoist cosmology to Langong; see K. Schipper, "Taoist Ritual and Local Cults" in M. Strickmann (ed.), *Tantric and Taoist Studies* (Bruxelles: Institut Belge des Hautes Etudes, 1985), p. 819.

[472] See also the preface by Pan Qiande who confirms this ("Pan Yian Taiyi jinhua zongzhi yuanxu" 9a–10a). For more information on this first revelation see also the prefaces by the other disciples (see Table 5, pp. 290–1), and the study by Mori Yuria, "*Taiitsu kinke shūshi* no seiritsu to hensen," pp. 45–51. In the prefaces by Zhuang Xing'an 莊惺菴 (14a–15a, in part. 14a) and Tu Yu'an 屠宇菴 (15b–17 a, in part. 16a), it is said that around 1666 the first seven recipients gathered at the spirit writing altar of Zhou Yehe 周埜鶴 in Piling. Mori guessed that this spirit writing altar was probably the Bailong jingshe; see Mori Yuria, "Identity and Lineage," p. 167.

[473] A Hongmeige located at Piling is mentioned in the biography of Xie Ningsu (JGXD 3.3a/2–3), one of the seven members receiving the text of the *Golden Flower* at Mount Jingai (see below). This temple is associated with the generation of Zhang Ziyang 張紫陽, Xue Daoguang 薛道光 and Chen Shangyang 陳上陽 associated with the Southern Lineage and its union with the Northern Lineage through Chen Shangyang.

[474] In the Preface by Tu Yu'an, Tu explains how he was admitted among the disciples of the spirit writing altar. He first received a text, the *Jingming zhongxiao lu* 淨明忠孝

Chapter 1: The Secret of the Golden Flower: Content and Major Editions   275

The resulting book included the recorded transmission by the Patriarch Lü, forewords by immortals and gods, as well as prefaces by the disciples who received it.

From this first part of Shao Zhilin's foreword we know that the text was the fruit of an oral transmission that the Jingming founder Xu Xun 許遜 (trad. 239–374) revealed via spirit writing to Jingming members through the intermediary of Lü Dongbin, Qiu Chuji and Tan Chuduan 譚處端. The scripture was accomplished in its written form only after the second revelation thanks to Tu Yu'an 屠宇菴 and Zhang Kanzhen 張坎真.[475] It was transmitted to disciples who were all affiliated with the Jingming whose genealogy "does not reside in the Northern and Southern Lineages" (皆係淨明法派、不在南北兩宗).

In the second part of his foreword, Shao Zhilin explains the compiling arrangement of the scripture.[476] Originally, the text of the *Golden Flower* edited by Zhang Kanzhen featured 20 chapters. Zhang's arrangement was based on the diachronic sequence in which Tan Chuduan 譚處端, Lü Dongbin, and Qiu Chuji had allegedly descended on the spirit writing altar of Piling. According to this sequence, the scripture began with the revelations by Tan Chuduan about the origin and development of the *Golden Flower*. Despite its title of *zongzhi* 宗旨, the Quintessential Tenet by Lü Dongbin came only in second place before the instructions by Qiu Chuji on the practice of precepts and their respect. Worrying that such an arrangement could mislead readers about the content of the scripture and might lead to their misunderstanding it as "Liturgy of the Golden Flower" 金華科儀, Shao Zhilin modified the format and reduced the text to 13 chapters (that is, to the Tenet by the immortal Lü Dongbin). The revelations by Tan and Qiu were added at the end as appendices. This means that the arrangement in 13 chapters, which characterizes all extant editions of the *Golden Flower* scripture, is the result of the compiling intervention by Shao Zhilin.[477] Based on Shao's foreword and table of contents 目錄 of the *Golden Flower*, the

---

錄, and after that the initiation directly from the immortal Lü via spirit writing; see Mori, "Identity and Lineage"169.

[475] See Mori Yuria "Identity and Lineage" (pp. 167–168) where some passages from the preface by Pan Qiande 潘乾德 are translated. Mori mentions that the text was gradually compiled over a period of months during which disciples repeatedly questioned Lü Dongbin for clarifications.

[476] See also the Conventions (*Fanli*) of his edition.

[477] See Mori "Identity and Lineage" and Esposito "Jinhua zongzhi banben".

20-chapter original text by Zhang was originally to include the following items:

> Chapters 1-5: The Instructions by Perfected Tan in five parts
> 譚真人垂示五則
>
> Chapters 6-18: The Doctrinal Tenet by Patriarch Lü Dongbin
> 太乙金華宗旨
>
> Chapters 19-20: The Instructions by Perfected Qiu Chuji in two parts
> 邱真人垂示二則

Although the index features the Instructions by Tan in five parts (譚真人垂示五則), we find in the text only four parts. They are:

> (a) *Kaizong chanjiao* 開宗闡教 (Clear Teachings on the Foundation of our Tradition);
> (b) *Jingming yuanliu* 淨明源流 (Origin and Development of the Jingming);
> (c) *Taiyi fapai* 太乙法派 (Taiyi Lineage);
> (d) *Jielü* 戒律 (Precepts and Codes).[478]

In the first part (*Kaizong chanjiao* 開宗闡教), Tan recalls that the transmission of the *Golden Flower* started with Xu Xun 許遜 via Lü Dongbin who founded this tradition 開宗闡教.

> The Perfected [Tan] said: According to the Perfected Lord Xuyang and the Saint Ancestor Chunyang, I accepted the endorsement from the Celestial Emperor to be in charge of this new post and heeded the order of the Perfected Lord to propagate the Daoist methods and teach the correct people. [I did so] not only for the Buddhist and Daoist clergy but first of all for saints and virtuous men who assist the secular world. For this reason I along with the Saint Ancestor transmit in particular the *Zongzhi* and gather the men of letters as the ridge pole of the Great Dao. Each generation should do its best to assume the charge and honestly shoulder it without abandoning hope.
>
> 真人曰:吾承旌陽真君、純陽聖祖保奏於天帝、新任此職、上奉真君命、闡揚道法、教育正人。不特為出世之仙佛、且先為輔世之聖賢、故吾同聖祖、特傳宗旨、收拾文人、為大道棟梁。子輩各宜一力擔當、實心肩荷。毋甘自棄。

---

[478] Unfortunately, we do not know if the content of the instructions by Tan and Qiu that is now found in the Appendix to the *Golden Flower* is the same as it was in the original scripture by Zhang Kanzhen or was already modified by Shao Zhilin.

Chapter 1: The Secret of the Golden Flower: Content and Major Editions

In the second part (*Jingming yuanliu* 淨明源流), Tan provides a description of the origin and development of such teachings in the context of the history of the Jingming. As is well known, this ritual and local tradition from Nanchang 南昌 (Jiangxi 江西), which was known during the Tang as Xiaodao 孝道, was allegedly founded in the Jin dynasty by Xu Xun 許遜 and connected with the Lingbao liturgy.[479] Enjoying imperial patronage, it became one of the most important traditions of the Song and Yuan under the name of Jingming zhongxiao dao 淨明忠孝道 in the wake of its patriarch Liu Yu 劉玉 (Yuzhenzi 玉真子 1257–1310) and his successor Huang Yuanji 黃元吉 (Zhonghuang 中黃, 1270–1325).[480] Hence Tan Chuduan 譚處端 reports:

> After seven more generations, Masters Yuzhen and Zhonghuang succeeded to [Xu Xun's] lineage. Today, as its transmission is again lost, we have brought it forth thanks to the *Tenet [of the Golden Flower]*.[481]

> 再七代、有玉真、中黃兩先生繼之。今又失其傳、故吾特為演出、即宗旨是也。

The quintessential doctrine of the Golden Flower was revealed for no other reason than to revive the lost tradition of the Jingming. Tan goes on to explain in his third part on the Taiyi lineage (*Taiyi fapai* 太乙法派) that a new lineage was formed:

> The Perfected [Tan Chuduan] said: "In the transmission of the Taiyi Jinhua 太乙金華 there is another lineage whose Patriarch Saint Chunyang [i.e., Lü Dongbin] is the Great Daoist Founding Master of the first generation. This is the main guiding principle within the Three Teachings, the genuine backbone among Immortals and

---

[479] The late Tang Daoist Du Guangting 杜光庭 (850–933) asserted that the ritual of Xiaodao was little different from that of the Lingbao tradition. See Richard Shek, "Daoism and Orthodoxy. The Loyal and Filial Sect," in Liu Kwang-Ching & R. Shek (eds.), *Heterodoxy in Late Imperial China* (Honolulu: University of Hawai'i Press, 2004): 146. On this issue see also K. Schipper, "Taoist Ritual and Local Cults." In M. Strickmann (ed.), *Tantric and Taoist Studies* (Bruxelles: Institut Belge des Hautes Études, 1985): 828.

[480] See Richard Shek, "Daoism and Orthodoxy," pp. 150–154, and the fundamental study on this tradition by Akizuki Kan'ei 秋月觀暎 (1978).

[481] "Jingming yuanliu" (LZQS 49.25b/3–4). See also Mori "Identity and Lineage," p. 169.

Buddhas. Each disciple at this altar [has a lineage name] in accord with the sequence of Qian, Kan, Gen, Zhen, Xun, Li, Kun and Dui. [482]

真人曰： 金華太乙之傳、另有宗派、以純陽聖祖為第一代開宗大道師。 此三教中大綱領、仙釋中真骨髓也。在壇弟子、俱依乾坎艮震、巽離坤兌為次。

The disciples who received such teachings were given a religious name taken from the Eight Trigrams. The "*Houtian* 後天 sequence" of the trigrams determined the generational sequence of the disciples. For instance the first disciples who received the *Golden Flower* had in their name the character Qian 乾 (as in Tu Qianyuan 屠乾元) as a sign that they belong to the first generation. The second generation's names feature Kan 坎 (as in Zhang Kanzhen 張坎真), and so on. Members initiated to the Taiyi lineage had to respect a specific discipline whose rules are succinctly presented in the fourth part of Tan's reports (*jielü* 戒律). Furthermore, in the instructions by Qiu Chuji in two parts (a. *xingchi* 行持; b. *shouji* 授記), a specific liturgy for these members is provided. It consists of collective recitations of morality texts centered on the accumulation of merits such as the *Taishang ganying hongwen* 太上感應鴻文, daily invocations of *Doumu xinzhou* 斗母心咒 and *Tianhuang xinzhou* 天皇心咒, as well as recitation of deity names such as *Tianzun baohao* 天尊寶號, *Jiufo baohao* 九佛寶號, and *Tianjun baohao* 天君寶號.[483]

In concluding the presentation of this earliest edition of the *Golden Flower* by Shao Zhilin, I would like to once more draw attention to the fact that the teachings of the *Golden Flower* were originally transmitted to members affiliated with the Jingming 淨明 movement. As the editor Shao Zhilin underlines in his foreword, this Jingming affiliation "does not reside in the Northern and Southern Lineages" （皆係淨明法派、不在南北兩宗）.

---

[482] See "Taiyi fapai" (LZQS 49.26b–27a). See also Mori "Identity and Lineage," p. 170 and Esposito "The Different Versions," pp. 101–102. The *Houtian* 後天 sequence marks the moment of the creation of the world in contrast with the *Xiantian* 先天 sequence or chaotic phase to which the patriarch Lü Dongbin belongs. As is known, the two sequences are used in the *neidan* 內丹 process. Tu Yu'an in his preface alludes to the revelation of the trigrams by Fuxi 伏羲 before the apparition of writing. It is worth mentioning that all prefaces of the Golden Flower refer to the principle of *Yi* 易 of the *Yijing*. On the role of the *Yijing* as a "medium" or "shaman" see Willard J. Peterson, "Making Connections: Commentary on the Attached Verbalizations of the *Book of Changes*," *Harvard Journal of Asiatic Studies*, 42.2 (1982): 67–116 (especially 107, 108).

[483] "Xingchi" 行持 (LZQS 49.27b–29b).

We also know that recipients of the transmission established a new lineage, the Taiyi lineage (Taiyi fapai 太乙法派). The origins of this new lineage go back to the Jingming and to the cult of its patriarch Xu Xun. But in this new lineage the founding patriarch is Lü Dongbin. Before receiving the tenet 宗旨, the altar disciples 壇弟子 were given a religious name. They then received instructions by the immortals Tan and Qiu about religious training and liturgy. The editor Shao Zhilin calls this specific liturgy *Jinhua keyi* 金華科儀. It is clear that the intent of Shao Zhilin is to present the scripture of the *Golden Flower* as *the* essential Daoist tenet, a tenet conveyed by Lü Dongbin that is free from sectarian and liturgical practices. As we are going to see, Shao Zhilin was not the only editor who had such a goal in mind.

> Version 1 summary
>
> *Xiantian xuwu Taiyi jinhua zongzhi* 先天虛無太乙金華宗旨 in Shao Zhilin's 邵志琳 (1748–1810), *Lüzu quanshu* 呂祖全書, abbr. LZQS, 64 *juan* (Wulin [Hangzhou] *kanben* 武林刊本, 1775) stemming from a manuscript of a certain Wu 吳 from Sumen 蘇門 (Suzhou, Jiangsu). It features:
>
> A) 15 Prefaces;
> B) 13-chapter text body;
> C) 2 Appendices;
> D) 1 Postface (see Table 5).
>
> In the opening preface by Shao Zhilin, the editor presents the history of this scripture as associated with the Jingming tradition and with the establishment of its Taiyi lineage 太乙法派 "transcending the Southern and Northern traditions" 不在南北兩宗. The congregants, who received this transmission in 1668 and 1692 at the spirit writing altars in Piling 毘陵 (Changzhou, Jiangsu), were also given an initiation name taken from the *houtian* 後天 sequence of the eight trigrams determining the generational sequence of the disciples. For instance, the first disciples who received the *Golden Flower* had in their name the character Qian 乾 (as in Tu Qianyuan 屠乾元, alias Tu Yu'an 屠宇菴) as a sign that they belong to the first generation. The second generation's name features Kan 坎 (as in Zhang Kanzhen 張坎真, alias Zhang Shuang'an 張爽菴). Among the remaining fourteen Prefaces, seven were written by the spirit

writing congregants of the first and second generation under the character Qian and Kan (see Table 5, p. 290).

According to Shao Zhilin 邵志琳, the original version by Tu Qianyuan 屠乾元 and Zhang Shuang'an 張爽菴 consisted of twenty chapters including

a) The Instructions by the Perfected Tan [Chuduan] in five items 譚真人垂示五則;

b) the text of the *Golden Flower* revealed by Lü Dongbin; and

c) "The Instructions by the Perfected Qiu [Chuji] in two items" 邱真人垂示二則.

Worrying that such an arrangement might mislead readers about the content of the scripture by seeing it as "Liturgy of the Golden Flower" *Jinhua keyi* 金華科儀, Shao modified the format and reduced the text into thirteen chapters (that is, to the tenets by the immortal Lü Dongbin) followed by the instructions of Tan and Qiu as Appendices (see Table 5). Thus the thirteen-chapter format, which is found in all the other editions, is due to Shao's editorial intervention.

Version 2: Chen Mou's edition and the Jinhua Lineage

The expurgation of sectarian and liturgical content combined with the local spirit writing altars of Piling continues in the *Lüzu quanshu zongzheng* 呂祖全書宗正 by Chen Mou 陳謀. This edition is still extant in Japan at the Ōtani Library of Kyoto (see Fig. 49, p. 266). It was restored by Chen Mou in 1852 with the help of associations and local temples devoted to Lü Dongbin.[484] It (or possibly just its preface?) was engraved by a certain Gu Qingya 顧晴崖 from Jiangning 江寧 and stems from a previous *Quanshu zongzheng* 全書宗正 in 18 scrolls by the Qing scholar Peng Qifeng 彭啟豐 (1701–1784) which circulated in Jiangsu.[485] The printing blocks were safe-

---

[484] In his "Xiubu Quanshu ji" 修補全書記, Chen Mou recounts the history of the printing blocks of this edition and how he finally restored them thanks to the financial help of Lü Dongbin's networks.

[485] See *Fanli*, 1.1a–b and "Xiubu Quanshu ji" 修補全書記 by Chen Mou (QSZZ 1.1a). Peng Qifeng 彭啟豐 (1701–1784), nephew/son? of Peng Dingqiu (cf. Ma Xiaohong, 1988, p. 36; see also Hummel, *Eminent Chinese of the Ch'ing Period*, and Zhang Huijian 張慧劍 ed., *Ming-Qing Jiangsu wenren nianbiao* 明清江蘇文人年

guarded by high-ranking officials who worshiped Lü Dongbin. Although it was published in 1852, the *Quanshu zongzheng* was already known in 1747 when a member of the Hanlin academy was charged by two high-ranking officials to engrave it. This explains why the 1803 edition by Jiang Yuanting is said to be based on it and why I have listed it after Chen's (see below).

In Chen's edition, the *Golden Flower* does not include the prefaces of the Jingming-Taiyi disciples who received the transmission at the spirit writing altars of Piling. The only exception is Tu Yu'an's preface. However, all references to Lü's revelations at Piling's altars and the time of such revelations have been eliminated. Furthermore, the "Jingming affiliation" 淨明嗣派 of the members has been changed into "Jinhua affiliation" 金華嗣派, and Tu Yu'an's original signature of *Jingming sipai dizi* 淨明嗣派弟子 (disciple of the inherited Jingming Lineage) has been substituted by *Jinhua sipai dizi* 金華嗣派弟子 (disciple of the inherited Jinhua lineage). The prefaces written by various immortals have been preserved, but all references to the Jingming affiliation and to the two local spirit writing altars of Piling were eliminated.[486]

The explanation about the origin of the so-called Taiyi Jinhua Lineage was summarized in Chen Mou's edition. The Appendix includes only two parts of Tan's instructions: "Kaizong chanjiao" 開宗闡教 (Clear Teachings on the Foundation of our Tradition), and "Taiyi Jinhua yuanliu" 太乙金華源流. After having mentioned the loss of the Jingming transmission, Tan's records simply add that "in 1668 Lü Dongbin revealed the Tenet and changed its name into *Taiyi Jinhua* 太乙金華." The history of the foundation of the Taiyi Jinhua lineage by Lü Dongbin as Founding Patriarch and the names conferred to his disciples were completely eliminated along with all references to the liturgy practiced by this lineage. But, in contrast to Shao's edition, Chen Mou's *Fanli* mentions that the transmission of the Taiyi Jinhua lineage stems from the Dipper Palace (*dougong* 斗宮) and is as-

---

表, Shanghai: Shanghai guji chubanshe 海古籍出版社, 1986), was a scholar from Changzhou who took part in Shao Zhilin's compilation of 1775; see Preface by Peng Qifeng and Preface by Wang Lüjie in Shao's *Lüzu quanshu*. Chen Mou in his "Xiubu Quanshu ji" (1857, 1.1a) also notes that before him a certain Qiu Tongxiao 邱通宵 who took part in the compilation of the *Jinhua chanyou* 金華闡幽 (see here below) wanted to print around 1757 the *Lüzu quanshu* on the basis of Peng Qifeng's copy. Peng Qifeng was also the editor of other works such as the *Lichao shengxian mingru renwu quantu* 歷朝聖賢名儒人物全圖 and *Zhiting xiansheng ji* 芝庭先生集.

[486] On this issue see Mori Yuria, "Identity and Lineage," 173.

sociated not only with the scripture of the *Golden Flower* as "separate transmission of the Dipper outside the established teachings" (金華宗旨乃斗中教外別傳) but also with a group of texts titled *Zhongxiao zhugao* (太乙金華法派傳自斗宮、原本忠孝、立言正大。劉邵本所刊忠孝諸誥). These texts are found in Liu Tishu and Shao Zhilin editions of the *Lüzu quanshu*, but there they lack any reference to such affiliation. Thus, in Chen Mou's edition the so-called Taiyi Jinhua lineage is said to be originally related to the transmission of "zhongxiao 忠孝" texts, and its affiliation with the Jingming seems to be overshadowed. The label "Jingming" 淨明 was in fact substituted by "Taiyi Jinhua" 太乙金華. This lineage is not further explained and there is no lineage poem, no liturgy, and above all no specific location: all references to the Piling altars and to the time of such revelations were eliminated, and so were the other prefaces by members of the the Piling altar.[487]

Finally, Chen Mou's edition includes after the 13- chapter *Golden Flower* a different text called *Jinhua chanyou* 金華闡幽. In its hitherto unpublished 1757 preface by Qiu Tongxiao 邱通宵, the *Jinhua chanyou* is presented as a scripture that originated with the revelation of the *Golden Flower* and serves to explain its secrets. It consists of questions and answers that disciples posed to the Immortal Lü Dongbin in order to get his explanations about obscure doctrinal points connected with the practice of the *Golden Flower*. This was probably the fruit of the protracted spirit writing communication that had been described by the first seven members of the Piling altar in their now eliminated prefaces. The nucleus of this text might have been formed during the first revelations of Lü Dongbin which supposedly occurred in 1668; but this requires more investigation.[488]

---

[487] This sounds quite strange from the part of someone like Peng Qifeng who came precisely from Changzhou, that is, the place where these altars wer located.

[488] In the preface by Pan Yi'an who describes how the members gathering at the altar of Zhou Yehe in Piling received the revelation, it is mentioned that the teachings by Lü Dongbin were compiled for days and months (Shao's *Lüzu quanshu* 49. Pref. 9a partly translated in Mori 'Identity and Lineage," 167). As Mori remarks (*ibid.*, 167–168), the compilation of the *Jinhua zongzhi* began as a record of questions and answers between the immortal and his disciples. This recorded dialogue might be just the text of the *Jinhua chanyou* 金華闡幽 which is now included in Chen Mou's edition.

Version 2 summary

Xiantian xuwu Taiyi jinhua zongzhi in *Lüzu quanshu zongzheng* 呂祖全書宗正, abbr. LZZZ, 18 *juan*, a revised and abridged collection based on the two earlier *Lüzu quanshu* 呂祖全書 by Liu Tishu 劉體恕 in 32 *juan* (1744), and by Shao Zhilin in 64 *juan* (1775). In 1852 Chen Mou 陳謀, after having restored its wood blocks, published this collection. He informs us that it was based on an ancient version of Peng Qifeng 彭啟豐 (1701–1784) from Changzhou 長洲 (Jiangsu). This version was already in circulation among elite officials since 1747 and was allegedly carved in 1757. Except for Tu Yu'an's 屠宇菴 preface, version 2 does not include any preface of the other spirit writing congregants. It now features:

A) 9 Prefaces (among which eight from version 1 and a new one by [Qiu] Tongxiao 邱通宵, who is associated with the inclusion of the *Jinhua chanyou wenda* 金華闡幽問答 [marked in grey in Table 5]);

B) 13-chapter text body (an abridged version slightly modified from version 1 including parts from its first Appendix), followed by the newly added *Jinhua chanyou wenda*.

Thus the text presents interesting modifications in content and structure; all previous references to the local altars of Piling are expurgated and there are no more Appendices and Postfaces. Instead of the Jingming Taiyi 淨明太乙 lineage one finds mention of the Taiyi Jinhua lineage (Taiyi Jinhua fapai 太乙金華法派), abbreviated as Jinhua 金華, but no further references to the conferral of initiation names and to the liturgy practiced by this lineage.

Chen Mou's collection is still extant at Bejing National Library (Guojia tushuguan 國家圖書館), Taiwan University Library (Guoli Taiwan daxue tushuguan 國立台灣大學圖書館), and Ōtani University 大谷大學 (Kyoto, Japan).

Versions 3 & 4: Jiang Yuanting's editions and the Tianxian 天仙 Lineage

The third and fourth editions of the *Golden Flower* form part of two collections, the *Quanshu zhengzong* 全書正宗 and the *Daozang jiyao* 道藏輯要, which were both edited by the same man, Jiang Yuanting 蔣元庭 (alias: Yupu 予蒲, 1756–1819). As Jiang explains in his conventions (*Fanli* 凡列), the *Quanshu zhengzong* stems from the revision of the *Lüzu quanshu zongzheng* on the basis of the *Lüzu quanshu* by Liu Tishu 劉體恕 in 32 scrolls and by Shao Zhilin in 64 scrolls (是集係就宗正原本重訂、恭檢全書、劉體恕所刻三十二卷、邵志琳所刻六十四卷). In the same Conventions (*Fanli*), referring specifically to the *Golden Flower*, Jiang Yuanting states:

> In the line of the "separate transmission outside the teachings," the *Jinhua zongzhi* belongs to the Tianxian Lineage. It is not a scripture exclusively of the Jingming like the *[Jingming] zongjiao lu* and others. Apprentices who do not reform themselves completely and do not thoroughly attain the Samadhi of the Golden Elixir will never be able to understand the secret of this scripture.
>
> 金華宗旨、後教外別傳、天仙的派、非僅淨明之道、如宗教錄等書也。學者非伐毛洗髓、深得金丹三昧者、未必能知此書之妙也。

In comparison with the first two editions, the third and fourth editions go one step further: they introduce a new lineage 法派, that is, the Tianxian pai 天仙派. The connection between this lineage and the *Golden Flower* scripture is explained as follows:

> The expression "Golden Flower" (*jinhua*) is firmly established in relation to the wondrous teaching of the Dao, but only few people can acquire the tenet of this tradition. This will never be clarified without the transmission of the Tianxian. There is no one who can throw light on this wonderful scripture except for the Daoist of the Tianxian [i.e., Lü Dongbin].[489]
>
> 金華之關於道妙者固鉅、而深得宗旨則為尤鮮。此非天仙之傳不足以明之、更非天仙道祖不克以示茲妙典也。

---

[489] *Quanshu zhengzong* 全書正宗, 2.67a. See also the translation by Mori, "Identity and Lineage," p. 174.

As a consequence, in these third and fourth editions by Jiang Yuanting even the title of the text undergoes a change: it is now called *Tianxian Jinhua zongzhi* 天仙金華宗旨, that is, the "Tenet of the Golden Flower tradition of the Tianxian [lineage]". This new title underlines the fact that Lü Dongbin is now not only the founding patriarch of the newly established Tianxian lineage but also the only being able to disclose its tenet to disciples. More information on this lineage is provided in the postface 後跋 to the *Golden Flower* that was authored by Zhiqiu 志秋, a disciple of Jiang Yuanting:

> I think that when Lord Fuyou [Lü Dongbin] named the Tianxian lineage, a phrase of the verse must have been transmitted. When I asked Huijie (Jiang Yuanting) about this he told me respectfully: "Once I heard that there was a verse composed of twenty characters that goes: "Tranquilly without any being (*jiran wu yiwu*), marvelously unified with the Former heaven (*miao he yu xiantian*), the Original Yang will return to its original position (*yuanyang fu benwei*) when in solitude you will pace the Jade Capital as an immortal (*dubu Yujing xian*)."
>
> 因思孚佑帝君名天仙派、必有留傳字句。詢之惠覺、蒙敬述云：昔聞有二十子曰：寂然無一物、妙合於先天、元陽復本位、獨步玉京仙。

This refers to the four verses composing the twenty-character lineage poem (*paishi* 派詩) of the Tianxian lineage 天仙派. The poem is followed by the instruction given to the postface's author Zhiqiu:

> He also told me: "(...) Our Lord Fuyou [Lüzu, i.e. Lü Dongbin] is the Founding Patriarch of the Tianxian Lineage, and Hongjiao enshi [Liu Shouyuan] is its second patriarch. You must remember this with respect."[490]
>
> 并告小子志秋曰：(...) 我孚佑帝師天仙之始祖也、宏教恩師天仙之二祖也。子其敬誌之。

As we can see, the editor Jiang Yuanting (here named Huijue) is connected with the Tianxian lineage.[491] He is the person who transmits to his disciple

---

[490] This passage from "Tianxian jinhua zongzhi houba" 天仙金華宗旨後跋 in *Quanshu zhengzong* 全書正宗 (2.67b–68a) has already been translated by Mori in "Identity and Lineage," pp. 173–74.

[491] In fact, as a disciple of the Tianxian lineage, Jiang Yuanting adds a final note at the end of chapter 13 of the *Golden Flower* by saying: 僅按此經乃性命兼修、天仙

Zhiqiu the lineage poem of the Tianxian. This lineage worships Lüzu (Patriarch Lü, i.e. Lü Dongbin) as founding patriarch and Liu Shouyuan as second patriarch.[492] We have seen that the editor Jiang was a high-ranking government official who established in Beijing a spirit writing altar known as Jueyuan tan 覺源壇 or Diyi kaihua tan 第一開化壇. This altar is at the source of the compilation of the *Quanshu zhengzong* 全書正宗 and also of the *Daozang jiyao* 道藏輯要, the Daoist Canon of the Qing dynasty whose history and role was described in Part Three.[493] The establishment of the altar and its activity in producing and spreading religious texts and teachings via spirit writing lies at the core of many Daoist movements during the Qing era. This phenomenon is still alive today in Hong Kong and Taiwan.[494]

Now, regarding Jiang Yuanting's altar, we know that his religious association was recognized at the Quanzhen public monastery of Beijing, the Baiyun guan. In fact the Tianxian lineage evoked in the cited poem is listed in the *Zhuzhen zongpai zongbu* 諸真宗派總簿 (Comprehensive Register of

之的傳也。(...) 孚佑帝師大佈慈悲、普施法力、將天仙妙道、於此處拈出。(...) 宗正本係仍屠子之舊。今 宗正本詳為釐定、歸入集中。以質後之天仙嗣派者、廣化弟子惠覺謹誌。

"This scripture, which explains the joint cultivation of Nature and Vital Force, represents the transmission of the Tianxian [Lineage]. The Master Emperor Sincere Protector [Fuyou dishi, i.e., Lü Dongbin], by spreading widely his compassion and universally carrying out the dharma power (supernatural power), has here picked up the wondrous Dao of the Tianxian. (...) In the [*Quanshu*] *zongzheng* edition, this scripture stems from the ancient version of the disciple Tu [Yu'an]. Today, after having collated and arranged in detail the content of the [*Quanshu*] *zongzheng* edition, I inserted it in this collection. Sincerely recorded by Huijue, disciple of the Broad Mission, heir of the Tianxian Lineage."

[492] Liu Shouyuan was a legendary immortal who authored important texts in the *Daozang jiyao* that are related to Longmen ordinations and Quanzhen liturgy in general. In particular, his name is connected with a text conveying the content of the ultimate stage of ordination, the *Tianxian dajie* (see Part Two). One wonders if the label Tianxian, as used by Jiang Yuanting for his lineage instead of the Chunyang label (i.e., the name of the lineage recorded at Baiyun guan), was chosen in order to show that this Tianxian is at the core of the ordination procedure that is said to have been re-established by Longmen patriarch Wang Changyue. See Part Two above.

[493] On the establishment of this altar and the link with the *Daozang jiyao*, see Mori Yuria, "Identity" pp. 172–175, and "Dōzō shūyō to Shō Yofu no Ryoso fuki shinkō" 道藏輯要と蔣予蒲の呂祖扶乩信仰 *Tōhō shūkyō* 2001, pp. 33–52).

[494] I refer the reader to the works by Shiga Ichiko (2003) and Philippe Clart on the religious organizations centered on spirit writing and the worship of deities in Hong Kong and Taiwan respectively.

All Genuine Lineages and Traditions). This is a document stored at the Baiyun guan that was copied in 1927 by the Japanese scholar Oyanagi Shigeta 小柳司氣太 and published his study on the Baiyun guan (ch. *Baiyun guan zhi* or jap. *Hakuunkan shi* 白雲觀志, p. 96).[495] Instead of being connected with the Tianxian lineage, this poem is listed under the Chunyang Lineage which is one of the Lineages of Lü Dongbin recognized by the Baiyun guan and its Quanzhen-affiliated public monasteries.[496]

Before returning to the role of the Baiyun guan during the Qing, I shall summarize some important points about these first four editions:

1. The *Golden Flower* was originally said to be the fruit of a spirit writing revelation that took place in 1668 at the altar of Piling in Jiangsu among Taiyi Jinhua 太乙金華 members.

2. In 1692, after a second spirit writing revelation, it was recorded by Tu Qianyuan and compiled by Zhang Kanzhen. At this point it consisted of twenty chapters.

3. In 1755, through the editorial intervention by Shao Zhilin, the *Golden Flower* was reduced to thirteen chapters conveying only the essential tenet 宗旨 revealed by Lü Dongbin. In this form the text circulated among high officials who worshiped this immortal and regarded the cult of Lü Dongbin as the core of Daoism. Editors such as Shao Zhilin and Chen Mou are likely to have held such opinions.

4. In 1803, Jiang Yuanting combined the cult of the immortal Lü Dongbin with the establishment of a recognized Quanzhen spirit writing altar belonging to the Tianxian Lineage.

---

[495] See BYGZ, pp. 91–121, in particular p. 96. A similar list was published under the name of *Zongpai bie* by Igarashi Kenryū in *Dōkyō sōrin taiseikyū shi* 道教叢林太清宮志 (pp. 77–108), his monograph on the Quanzhen public Taiqing monastery in Shenyang (Liaoning). See also the *Daotong yuanliu* and the *Xuanmen bidu*. Vincent Goossaert (2004, p. 731) also mentions an additional list included in the manuscript, *Nanmo daopai zongbu*.

[496] See also Igarashi, *Taiseikyū shi*, p. 91. This lineage is followed by other lineages allegedly founded by Lü Dongbin under the name of Tianxian. However, their lineage poems are different from the Chunyang lineage. The reference to the Tianxian lineage instead of Chunyang Lineage may point to a direct connection with the ordination program first established at the Baiyun guan whose ultimate stage involved the so-called Great Tianxian Precepts (see Part Two above). Liu Shouyuan, the second patrarch of this lineage after Lü Dongbin, authored a text in the *Daozang jiyao* which was transmitted for this last stage of precepts under the title of *Sanyuan tianjie*.

5. The Tianxian lineage appropriated the *Golden Flower* and changed its original name.

6. This move was designed to give equal authority to receive and spread the revealed scripture.

The claims of Jiang, the editor of the third and fourth edition, shows traces of an ongoing competition between, on one hand, Tianxian adepts who are recognized as "orthodox members of the Quanzhen community," and on the other Taiyi Jinhua 太乙金華 adepts affiliated with the Jingming. The latter's genealogy is presented as transcending the "Southern and Northern Lineages" of the Quanzhen. As editor Jiang Yuanting suggests, the *Golden Flower* is a scripture of the Taiyi Jinhua tradition and was originally included among Jingming texts like the *Jingming zongjiao lu*.[497] These texts were exclusively associated with the Jingming and its branches. It is against such claims that the Tianxian lineage apparently revolted.

> **VERSION 3 SUMMARY**
>
> *Fuyou shangdi Tianxian jinhua zongzhi* 孚佑上帝天仙金華宗旨 in Jiang Yuanting 蔣元庭 (1755–1819), *Quanshu zongzheng* 全書正宗, abbr. QSZZ, 16 *juan* (1803–1805), stored in Japan at Ōtani University (Kyoto). It features:
>
> A) 2 Prefaces (8 items);
> B) 13 chapter-text (based on version 2) with an added colophon by Jiang Yuanting (marked in grey in Table 5);
> C) Appendix containing *Jinhua chanyou wenda* 金華闡幽問答 with an added colophon by Jiang Yuanting (marked in grey in Table 5);
> D) 3 Postfaces (among which the first two stem from the last two prefaces [8–9] of version 2, along with new parts marked in grey in Table 5).

---

[497] This text was also included in the *Daozang jiyao* and one wonders whether the content of this scripture is the same as that here mentioned. As we will see below, this scripture played a role in the transmission of precepts being substituted with the scripture of precepts by Qiu Chuji. As Jiang Yuanting suggests it was recognized as exclusive property of the Jingming tradition. In the preface by Tu Yu'an, Tu explains how he was admitted to the spirit writing altar of Piling. In that case, he first received a so-called *Jingming zhongxiao lu* scripture. This title may refer to the most important Jingming scripture, that is, the *Jingming zhongxiao quanshu* dated 1327.

Chapter 1: The Secret of the Golden Flower: Content and Major Editions

Version 3 is now associated with the Tianxian lineage. It was also published in another collection titled *Lüzu shanding quanshu* 呂祖刪定全書 (Yihaitang *kanben* 藝海堂刊本) in 12 *juan* also associated with Jiang Yuanting's altar of the Tianxian lineage (Beijing), under the supervision of a certain Fayin 法因. Stored at the Diet Library of Tokyo (Kokkai toshokan 國會圖書館), this collection is also mentioned in Zhang Zhizhe 張志哲 ed. (*Daojiao wenhua cidian* 道教文化辭典. Nanjing: Jiangsu guji, 1994), p. 414.

Version 4 summary

Fuyou shangdi Tianxian jinhua zongzhi 孚佑上帝天仙金華宗旨 is the title given in the Table of Contents of Jiang Yuanting's *Daozang jiyao* (i.e., the "old" *Daozang jiyao*) abbr. YP[JY] (1805–1816), while *Jinhua zongzhi* 金華宗旨 is the title in the heading inside the collection.

Like version 3, version 4 includes the *Jinhua chanyou wenda* 金華闡幽問答 but also contains revisions such as modifications in the order of its prefaces. It features:

A) 3 Prefaces (8 items);
B) 13 chapter-text (based on version 3) with the *Jinhua chanyou wenda*;
D) 3 Postfaces (see Table 5).

Version 4 was later inserted in the *Chongkan Daozang jiyao* (i.e., the "new" *Daozang jiyao* of 1906). At the beginning of Chapter 1, this text employs instead of the formula "Lüdi *yue* 呂帝曰" (found in versions 1, 2, 5, and 6) the phrase "Lüzu *yue* 呂祖曰."

The following two tables (nos. 5 & 6) present an overview of the titles, overall arrangement of parts, and various kinds of changes in the four *Golden Flower* versions discussed so far.

ED	1. SHAO ZHILIN 邵志琳 EDITION LÜZU QUANSHU 呂祖全書 1775	2. CHEN MOU 陳謀 EDITION LÜZU QUANSHU ZONGZHENG 呂祖全書宗正 1852
A	(序1) Shao Zhilin 邵志琳 (1775) **Table of Contents** (序2) Xiaoti Wang 孝悌王 (1692) (序3) Xu Jingyang 許旌陽 (1692) (序4) Fuyou dijun 孚佑帝君 (1692) (序5) Zhang Sanfeng 張三丰 (1692) (序6) Qiu Changchun 邱長春 (1692) (序7) Tan Changzhen 譚長真 (1692) (序8) Wang Tianjun 王天君 (1692) (序9) Pan Yi'an 潘易菴 (乾德) (1692) (序10) Liu Du'an 劉度菴 (乾善) (1692) (序11) Xu Sheng'an 許深菴 (乾亨) (1692) (序12) Gu Danchu 顧旦初 (日融) (1695) (序13) Zhuang Xing'an 莊惺菴 (乾微) (1693) (序14) Tu Yu'an 屠宇菴 (乾元) (1692) (序15) Zhang Shuang'an 張爽菴 (坎真) (1692)	(序1) Xiaoti Wang (1692) (序2) Xu Jingyang (1692) (序3) Fuyou dijun (1692) (序4) Zhang Sanfeng (1692) (序5) Qiu Changchun (1692) (序6) Tan Changzhen (1692) (序7) Wang Tianjun (1692) (序8) Tu Yu'an (金華嗣派弟子) (no date/place) (序9) [Qiu] Tongxiao 通宵 (fl. 1757) **Table of Contents**
B	**TEXT** (j. 49) *Xiantian xuwu Taiyi jinhua zongzhi* 先天虛無太乙金華宗旨 (13 chapters)	**TEXT** (j. 10–11) j. 10: *Xiantian xuwu Taiyi jinhua zongzhi* (13 chapters) **Instructions by Tan** (神霄待宸譚長真真人宗旨垂示 (a) 開宗闡教; (b) 太乙金華源流 as supplementary part after chapter 13 j. 11: *Jinhua chanyou wenda* 金華闡幽問答
C	**APPENDICES** (附1) **Instructions by Tan in 5 items** (譚真人垂示五則 (a) 開宗闡教; (b) 淨明源流; (c) 太乙法派; (d) 戒律) (附2) **Instructions by Qiu in 2 items** (邱真人垂示二則: (a) 行持; (b) 授記)	
D	**POSTFACES** (跋) Zhang Shuang'an 張爽菴 (1692)	

Table 5: Contents and arrangement of the first four versions of the *Golden Flower* text

Chapter 1: The Secret of the Golden Flower: Content and Major Editions

3. JIANG YUANTING 蔣元庭 1 QUANSHU ZHENGZONG 全書正宗 1803–1805	4. JIANG YUANTING 蔣元庭 2 DAOZANG JIYAO 道藏輯要 1805–1816
(序1) a. Lü Dongbin (天仙金華宗旨自序) b. Liu Shouyuan 柳守元 (序2) *Liesheng baoxun tici* 列聖寶訓題辭 　[(a) Xiaoti Wang 孝悌王 　(b) Xu Jingyang 許旌陽 　(c) Zhang Sanfeng 張三丰 　(d) Qiu Changchun 邱長春 　(e) Tan Changzhen 譚長真 　(f) Wang Tianjun 王天君] **Table of Contents**	(序1) *Jinhua zongzhi bianyan* 　金華宗旨弁言 　[(a) Xiaoti Wang 　(b) Xu Jingyang 　(c) Zhang Sanfeng 　(d) Qiu Changchun 　(e) Tan Changzhen 　(f) Wang Tianjun] (序2) Lü Dongbin (金華宗旨自序) **Table of Contents** (序3) Liu Shouyuan (金華宗旨題詞)
TEXT (j. 2) *Fuyou Shangdi Tianxian Jinhua zongzhi* 孚佑上帝天仙金華宗 (13 chapters) with the colophon by Huijue 惠覺 [i.e., Jiang Yupu] (天仙嗣派廣化子惠覺)	**TEXT** (室 2) *Jinhua zongzhi* 金華宗旨 (孚佑上帝純陽呂祖天師著) with the colophon by Huijue 惠覺 *Jinhua chanyou wenda* 金華闡幽問答 with the colophon by Huijue 惠覺
APPENDIX (附) *Jinhua chanyou wenda* 金華闡幽問答 with the colophon by Huijue 惠覺	
POSTFACES (跋1) [Qiu] Tongxiao 邱通宵 (跋2) Tu Yu'an 屠宇菴 　(with postscript by Enhong 恩洪) (跋3) Zhiqiu 志秋	**POSTFACES** (跋1) [Qiu] Tongxiao 邱通宵 (跋2) Tu Yu'an 屠宇菴 　(with postscript by Enhong 恩洪) (跋3) Zhiqiu 志秋

Table 5 (cont.): Newly added elements in the second and third editions are highlighted

292　PART FOUR: CREATION OF SALVATION

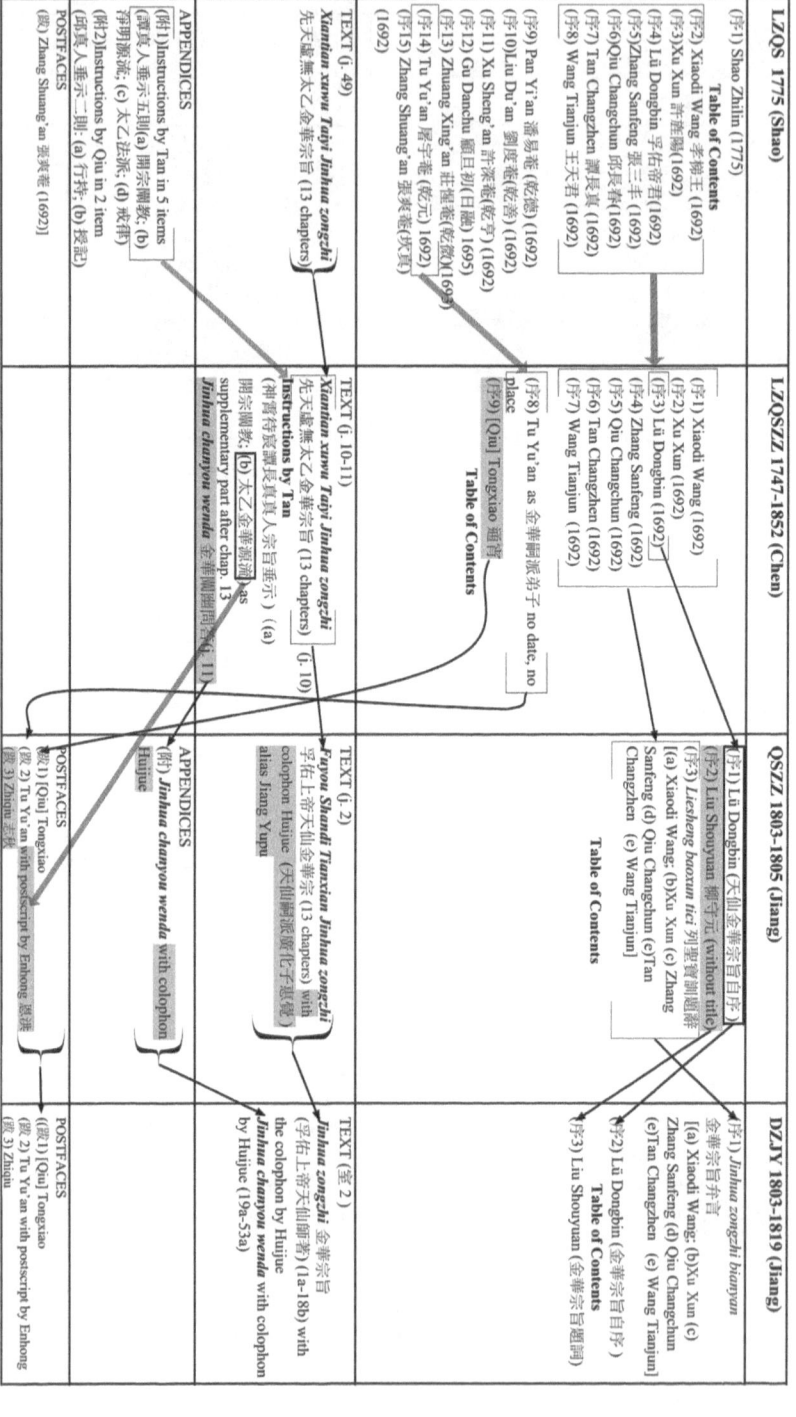

Table 6: Changes in the first four *Golden Flower* versions from 1775 to 1852. Additions in grey highlight, displacements (some with changes) by arrows

Chapter 2

The Golden Flower's Longmen Transplant (Version 5)

With our fifth text of the *Golden Flower*, the edition by Min Yide 閔一得 (1748/58–1836), a Longmen Patriarch of the eleventh generation,[498] the *Golden Flower* enters into the Longmen 龍門 network. In order to appreciate this process we have to recall what Longmen represented during the Qing dynasty. Longmen was the most important Daoist tradition affiliated with the Quanzhen during the late Imperial Period. In Buddhism, the Chan lineage of Linji dominated numerically and institutionally because of its monopoly of the ordination procedure. In Daoism the same can be said about Longmen. This is expressed in the following statement in the *Changchun daojiao yuanliu* 長春道教源流:

> What is commonly called "Longmen" and "Linji" each has half of the empire. The Longmen branch is to Daoism what the Linji tradition is to Buddhism.
>
> 世稱龍門、臨濟半天下。謂釋之臨濟宗、道之龍門派也。[499]

Analogous to "Linji" in Buddhism, "Longmen" was a kind of common label for the orthodox Daoist clergy from the Qing era until the present. Entering into a Daoist community meant to receive the Longmen ordination which, besides conferring a lineage name, included specific religious training and liturgy. All of this was offered by Longmen abbots presiding over Daoist public monasteries. As explained in the Introduction, the most

---

[498] As mentioned especially in the Introduction and Part One above, Min Yide is the author of extremely important works for the creation of Longmen history: the *Jingai xindeng* 金蓋心燈 (JGXD), *Gu Shuyinlou cangshu* 古書隱樓藏書 (YLCS), and *Daozang xubian* 道藏續編 (DZXB).

[499] This is a work by Chen Minggui 陳明珪 (1823–1881), a Quanzhen Daoist.

important of these institutions was and still is today what I have called modern "Daoism's Vatican": the Baiyun guan in China's capital Beijing. This is the sanctuary housing the grave of the Quanzhen Perfected Qiu Chuji 邱處機 (1148–1227), the mythical founder of the Longmen. Also in the Baiyun guan is the Memorial Hall (*citang* 祠堂) of Wang Changyue 王常月 (?–1680), the legendary promoter of the Longmen during the Qing dynasty. Recognized as the seventh Longmen patriarch in a wonderfully fictitious genealogy, Wang Changyue had become the central figure in the foundation myth of the Longmen.

Under the auspices of the Kangxi emperor, Wang was said to have reformed the ordination procedure before transmitting it to the whole of China. The system of ordinations, "re-established" by Wang under the Longmen label, was allegedly staged for the first time at Beijing's Baiyun guan in 1656 (see Part Two). This is said to have happened in the so-called "Hall of the Bowl" (*Botang* 缽堂, which may be a counterpart of the Buddhist "ordinands' hall") and lasted no less than one hundred days. During this period of collective seclusion the ordinands attended lectures, were trained in liturgy, and underwent severe ascetic practice.[500] Modeled on the Buddhist monastic ordination, this Daoist ordination is known—as we have seen in Part Two—as "the Great Precepts of the Threefold Altar" (*santan dajie* 三壇大戒). It included the Initial Precepts (*chuzhen jie* 初真戒), the Intermediate Precepts (*zhongji jie* 中極戒), and the Great Precepts of the Celestial Immortals (*tianxian dajie* 天仙大戒). Only recipients of the Great Precepts of the Celestial Immortals were in a position to ordain others.[501] Starting with Wang Changyue, the abbotship of the Baiyun guan in Beijing was thus held by Longmen-ordained masters—a fact that proved crucial for the legitimization of Longmen and its spread throughout China.

Let us now return to the fifth edition of the *Golden Flower* by Min Yide 閔一得 (1758–1836) that forms part of his *Daozang xubian* 道藏續編 (Supplementary Collection of the Daoist Canon) published in 1834. Min Yide linked this text to Patriarch Wang Changyue, which is how his edition gained legitimacy. In his preface to the *Golden Flower*, Min Yide presents a

---

[500] See *Chuzhen jielü* (attributed to Wang Changyue) in DZJY 24, p. 40b–41a. See also BYGZ, p. 35, 70–73, 141–142 and 162–63,

[501] In the *Chuzhen jielü* (DZJY 24, p. 40b) it is clearly stated that "those who do not receive the precepts of the Celestial Immortals cannot ordain others" 不受天仙戒者不得傳戒. See Part Two above.

brand-new history of revelation. Interestingly, Min's Preface is the only one included in this edition, and there we read:

> The Daoist Patriarch, Sovereign Sincere Protector, Celestial Venerable Promoter of the Mysterious Dao [i.e., Lü Dongbin], whose will it is to liberate all beings and whose bosom carries the comprehensive wish of healing the world, after having experimented the mysterious significance of the ten characters *Xian tian xu wu tai yi jin hua zong zhi* [Tenet of the Supreme One Golden Flower, Emptiness and Non-being of the Former Heaven], wrote this 13-chapter scripture in order to establish it for posterity as "the blueprint of healing the world."[502] The text was thus established and the teachings received: the mysterious tenet of the Celestial Venerable [Lü Dongbin]. (...) This scripture—the Tenet of Dao—is the fruit of the enlightenment first realized by Fuyou dijun [i.e., Lü Dongbin] who, after having transformed the four elements yet prior to healing the world, composed three poems under the title *Zhijiao zongzhi* [Tenet of the tradition of Ultimate Teaching]. During the Song and the Yuan these poems circulated already in printed form, the second of them being the *Xiaoyao jue* [The Key to Freedom] that is now included in this scripture. This scripture appeared in the year *wuchen* of the Kangxi era (1688) and was divulgated at the Hermitage of the Dragon Peak (Longjiao shanfang) of Mt. Jingai to none other than Tao Jing'an, Huang Yinzhen, Sheng Qingya, Zhu Jiuhuan, the venerable Min Xuesuo, Tao Shi'an, and Xie Ningsu, who all are well-known literati with a gift for healing the world.
>
> 道祖孚右帝君、興行妙道天尊、志在普度、懷有醫世鴻願、乃體『先天虛無太一金華宗旨』十字玄義、著書十有三章、以作後學醫世張本。文由是成、教有是授、天尊玄旨蓋如此。(...) 是書道旨、孚右帝君初證道果、四大已化、未及醫世、乃著詩三章、題曰『至教宗旨』。宋元之際、業已梓布、其次章、即是書「逍遙訣」也。是書出於康熙戊辰歲、演成於金蓋龍嶠山房、實為陶靖菴、黃隱真、盛

---

[502] This scripture is also put in relation with another scripture, namely the *Donghua zhengmai huangji hepi zhengdao xianjing* which is seen as a complementary scripture; they are both "blueprints for healing the world by cultivating Nature and Vital Force. Indeed, devotion to heal the world is the mysterious practice of Nature and Vital Force. (... 『東華正脈皇極闔闢證道仙經』、與此書相為表裡、修其性命、定為醫世張本、從事醫世、實即性命玄功。...)

青崖、朱九還、閔雪簑翁、陶石菴、謝凝素、諸名宿、皆醫世之材。(...)

According to Min Yide, the *Golden Flower* thus stems from the immortal Lü Dongbin. The nucleus of the *Golden Flower* forms part of the *Zhijiao zongzhi* 至教宗旨, the Tenet of our Tradition of the Ultimate Teaching represented in Lü Dongbin's poems of enlightenment. These poems are said to have been transmitted in printed form during the Song and Yuan eras. The second of these poems, The Key to Freedom (*Xiaoyao jue* 逍遙訣), is included in chapter eight of the *Golden Flower*.

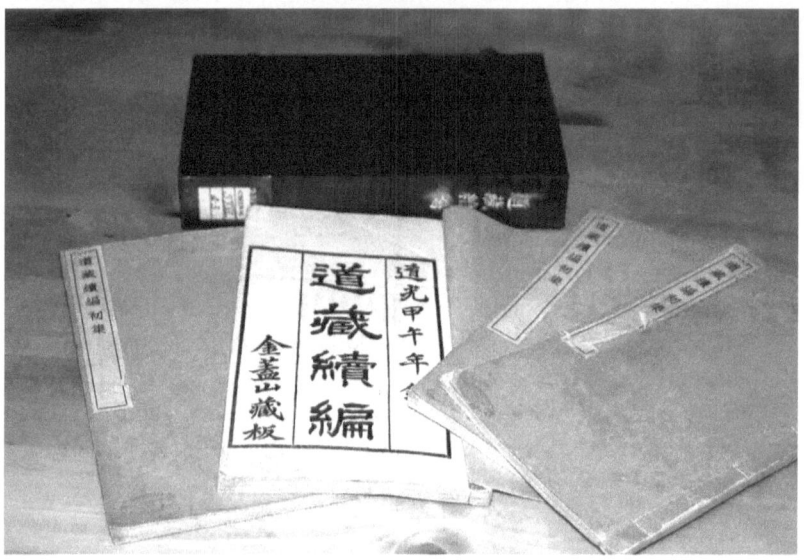

Fig. 50: Min Yide's *Daozang xubian* (Supplementary Collection to the Daoist Canon) which contains version five of the *Secret of the Golden Flower*

Compared with the other editions, Min Yide's preface thus presents a rather different scenario for the genesis of the *Golden Flower*. According to Min Yide this text was revealed in 1688 as "the blueprint for healing the world" at the Longjiao hermitage of Mt. Jingai (a small mountain in Zhejiang in today's outskirts of Huzhou) to seven "people endowed with the capacity for healing the world" 皆醫世之材. Instead of the seven adepts of the Jingming, Min Yide claims that it was revealed to seven Longmen masters of Mount Jingai. They are: 1. Longmen patriarchs of the eighth generation Tao Jing'an 陶靖菴 (1616–1673), Huang Yinzhen 黃隱真 (1595–1673), and Sheng Qingya 盛青崖 (fl. 1647); 2. their contemporaries Zhu Jiuhuan 朱九還 and Min Xuesuo 閔雪簑 (fl. 1669) who are not listed among Longmen patriarchs; and 3. Longmen patriarchs of the ninth generation Tao Shi'an 陶石菴 (?–1692) and Xie Ningsu 謝凝素 (fl. 1652). Furthermore, according to Min Yide, the revelation did not take place at the local altar of Piling in Jiangsu but rather at the local altar of the Longqiao-hermitage tradition of Mt. Jingai 金蓋龍嶠山房宗壇所傳.

Fig. 51: The Daoist temple complex on Mt. Jingai where Min Yide created history

THE ALTAR OF MOUNT JINGAI LINEAGE AND ITS TRADITION

The biographies of the seven Longmen masters indicate that only Tao Shi'an and Xie Ningsu were alive in 1688 when the scripture was purportedly revealed. The first in the list, Tao Jing'an 陶靖菴 (1616–1673), is the most important figure because he is recognized as master of Mt. Jingai's Tradition (金蓋之宗師) and as purported founder of its spirit writing altar where—at least according to Min Yide—the scripture of the *Golden Flower* had been revealed.[503] Tao is a semi-legendary figure with a double identity:

---

[503] Tao Jing'an is the founder of the Yunchao branch of Mount Jingai (金蓋山雲巢支派); see "Longmen pai zhengzong liuchuan zhipai tu," JGXD 1b. Yunchao 雲巢 is

under the name of Shen Hao 沈浩 he is known as a loyalist of the late Ming, and under the name of Tao Ran 陶然 as a Daoist hermit who withdrew to Mount Jingai at the beginning of the Qing.[504] Thanks to this affiliation, the altar of Mount Jingai can be regarded as one of the first sanctuaries dedicated to the cult of Lü Dongbin in the Longmen network of the Jiangnan region. This altar was allegedly inherited by Tao and his companion-in-practice Huang Yinzhen 黃隱真. Additional active participants were Zhu Jiuhuan 朱九還 and Min Xuesuo 閔雪簑. In 1673, after the death of masters Tao Jing'an and Huang Yinzhen, the altar was inherited by Tao Shi'an 陶石菴 (?–1692), the nephew of Tao Jing'an who purportedly received his uncle's secret manuscripts including the *Golden Flower*. In a Note of Introduction to the *Golden Flower*, Min Yide confirms this by stating:

> "This scripture appeared in the *wuchen* year of the Kangxi era [1688] and was transmitted at the altar of the Longqiao hermitage Lineage of Mt. Jingai where Tao Shi'an, the sage of this mountain, had it engraved."[505]

是書出於康熙戊辰、金蓋龍嶠山房宗壇所傳、本山先哲陶石菴先生壽諸梓。

In the biography of Tao Shi'an 陶石菴, the tradition of this altar is described as follows:

> (...) it goes back to the Lineage of Lü [Dongbin] and Wei [Zhengjie] which was not substituted by the Vinaya tradition of Qiu [Chuji] and Wang [Changyue].

上承呂衛之宗、不替邱王律派。[506]

This indicates that the local tradition of Mount Jingai stems from the worship of Lü Dongbin and Wei Zhengjie 衛正節, a local figure con-

---

the name of the temple where Min Yide lived.

[504] See Tao's biography in JGXD 2.9a–22b.

[505] *Shouzi* (*shou* has the meaning of carving, engraving in order to preserve something for a long time 鐫刻、鐫鏤。謂使之長遠留存). The expression *shou zhuzi* is found in Wang Shouren 王守仁 of the Ming (*Chuanxiu lu* 傳習錄 j. xia): 眾皆憚於翻錄、乃謀而壽諸梓; cf. HY 2-1201. In the Preface of the *Sanni yishi shuoshu* 呂祖師三尼醫世說述序 (2b3,15), it is said that Tao copied this text 其一為吾山石菴律師手錄於龍嶠山房.

[506] See JGXD 3.10a/1–2. Wei Zhengjie is a Confucian who allegedly withdrew to Mt. Jingai during the Song dynasty and founded its Shuyinlou library, that is the scriptural sanctuary of this mountain from which important collections of books were later published by Min Yide, for example the so-called *Gu Shuyinlou cangshu*.

nected with Mt. Jingai. Wei was virtuous Confucian who had withdrawn to this mountain at the end of the Song era and founded its library. By affirming that it does not want to replace the Vinaya tradition of Qiu Chuji and Wang Changyue, this local community pledged allegiance to the flag of the mythical founder and ideal promoter of the Longmen at the Baiyun guan of Beijing. This means that it agreed, as I explained at length in my 1993 Ph.D. thesis and subsequent articles, to put its local cults under the Longmen umbrella.

The Lineage for Healing the World

Furthermore, the editor Min Yide associates the *Golden Flower* of Mt. Jingai with the term *yishi* 醫世 (healing the world), calling the text itself a "precaution to heal the world" (*yishi zhangben* 醫世張本) and its recipients "means for healing the world" (*yishi zhi cai* 醫世之材). *Yishi* 醫世 is a counterpart of more common expressions such as *jishi* 濟世 (do good to all) or *dushi* 度世 (be delivered from the world, become an immortal). This term *yishi* is very important because it marks a new lineage and a new soteriological tradition within the Longmen tradition. According to the earliest edition by Shao Zhilin, the Taiyi lineage 太乙法派 had been created for the transmission of the *Golden Flower* at the Piling altars in order to revive the lost transmission of Jingming. But in this fifth edition by Min Yide, a new tradition, namely the Yishi zong 醫世宗, takes its place at Mt. Jingai within the orthodox Longmen tradition. More information on the Yishi zong 醫世宗 is contained in a commentary by Min Yide:

> The Lineage for Healing the World is the secret inside the pillow (*zhenmi*) of the Vinaya Lineage. (…) Those who do not believe this principle are asked to read the *Biyuan tanjing* (Platform Sutra of the Jade Garden) and receive the master's instructions. I [Min Yide] sincerely added this comment.
>
> 醫世一宗、律宗之枕祕。... 如或不信此理、請讀碧苑壇經、得承師訓。謹補述之。

The so-called "Healing-the-World tradition" (*yishi zong* 醫世宗) thus connects Mount Jingai's esoteric tradition within the orthodox Longmen Vinaya tradition 龍門正統律宗—a tradition that was allegedly re-established by Wang Changyue—with Wang's teachings (included in the *Biyuan tanjing*). These teachings stipulate that a disciple must submit to the guidance of a master if he cannot penetrate the esoteric meaning. As explained in Part Two, the *Biyuan tanjing* 碧苑壇經 (Platform Sutra of the Jade Garden) is said to be a record of Wang Changyue's discourses pronounced in 1663 at the ordination platform (*jietan* 戒壇) at the Biyuan monastery 碧苑觀 in Nanjing.

Now, in order to legitimize this new local tradition and to present the *Golden Flower* as its core, Min Yide recounts the following anecdote:

> The text of my mountain [i.e., Tao's text] here records the profound discourse by the Vinaya Patriarch Wang Changyue. It was in the autumn of the *wuchen* year of the Kangxi era [1688] that the Vinaya Patriarch came down from the North to the South and stayed in Hangzhou at the Zongyang gong. [Tao] Jing'an and [Huang] Yinzhen went to visit him and presented him with this scripture. The Vinaya Patriarch solemnly bowed, and after having read it said: "The mind-to-mind transmission of the Supreme One [Laozi] is fully expressed in this scripture. This is the method for the perfect practice in this world, and the achievement of the practice of saving the world [*shushi* 淑世 = *jishi* 濟世] is also found in the prediction that one cannot have a biased view. (...) You must not be modest or arrogant, the great practice [i.e., high morality and conduct] awaits you." So I order you, my fellows, to remember this, and to this end I am transmitting the printing blocks [of the *Golden Flower*] to posterity. May the disciples of the younger generation make efforts! Sincerely stated by [Shen] Taiding [Tao Shi'an 陶石庵, ?–1692].
>
> 山本此下、載有王崑陽律祖玄論。時為康熙戊辰秋、律祖自北南來、館於杭城宗陽宮。靖庵、隱真往謁、呈上此書。律師鄭重其儀、拜而閱之曰："太上心傳、備於此矣。是乃即世圓行之功法、而淑世功驗亦於此卜、不可偏在一身看。.....二三子毋自歉、亦毋自恃、大行正有待也。"乃命小子識之。今故附梓於後、後學者勉之、太定謹白。

Starting with the purported date of this meeting, it is obvious that we are dealing here with fiction. Tao Jing'an and Huang Yinzhen were both dead in 1688 when this encounter is said to have taken place, as was the Patriarch of Vinaya Wang Changyue. But this legend disseminated by Min Yide points to three major issues:

1. 1688 is the date when, according to Min Yide, the *Golden Flower* was revealed the Jingai altar and when Tao and Huang, the two main "managers" of the Jingai spirit writing altar, presented it to Wang Changyue;

2. Wang Changyue, the promoter of the Longmen ordinations, identified this scripture as the direct transmission of Laozi;

3. Through this act of legitimization by the seal of Wang Changyue, the *Golden Flower* was recognized as the essential mind-to-mind transmission for the universal salvation that is now safeguarded by Mt. Jingai's patriarchs.

This last issue has important implications for the members of the local community of Mount Jingai because it links the *Golden Flower* to a whole cycle of other texts which form the basis of a new ordination procedure established at Mount Jingai for Wang Changyue's successors. The following anecdote by Min Yide expresses this strategy:

> It was between the Shunzhi 順治 (1644–1661) and Kangxi 康熙 (1662–1722) eras that the Patriarch of Vinaya (Wang Changyue) performed ordinations five times at the Hall of the Bowl 五開演 缽堂 and conveyed the Three Great Precepts of the Highest Lord (*Taishang sandajie* 太上三大戒). The disciples numbered more than three thousand. The transmission of the precepts, the robe and the bowl 傳戒衣缽 included the *Lüzu yishi shuoshu* 呂祖醫世說述 (Explanations of the Three Sages' Doctrine for Healing the World by Patriarch Lü) of which more than 3,000 copies were obtained by the ordinands. Was it not a great performance of the true Tao? The Ordination Hall of the Vinaya Patriarch 律祖戒堂 was opened at the capital's Baiyun guan 京邸白雲觀. At that time Buddhist and Daoist ordinations needed to be authorized by imperial edict and could not take place in private. What was transmitted included the code 律, the scriptures 書, and the handbooks 手卷 in which the order of generations of the patriarchs and their lineage starting from the Supreme One is laid down. The precept-gathas [i.e., lineage poems] were in five, seven or four-character verses, to be handed down without fail.

> 律祖於順治康熙間五開演缽堂、付授太上三大戒。弟子三千餘人。傳戒衣缽、有呂祖醫世說述、則得受者有三千餘部。豈非真道之大行乎。況律祖戒堂、開在京邸白雲觀。爾時佛道兩宗傳戒、非奉旨不得私開。其所傳、有律、有書、有手卷。卷中載歷祖支派、自太上而下。所傳戒偈、或五言、或七言、或四言、累代相承無缺。

But three generations after Wang Changyue, that way [of precept transmission] no longer existed. Nowadays, in the Jiaqing era 嘉慶 (1796–1820), when an ordination is held, the text of precepts by

Patriarch Qiu [Chuji] 邱祖戒本 is no longer transmitted. What in recent times gets transmitted is the *Jingming zongjiao lu* 淨明宗教錄, a text that is quite different from the transmission by Patriarch Qiu. Previous masters from my own mountain [of Jingai], while maintaining the rules, had burned this [transmitted text by Patriarch Qiu], and though some writings survived in transcribed copies, the scrolls and code 卷律 were lost.

(...) 律祖三傳而道遂絕。今嘉慶間所開演缽、邱祖戒本失傳。近所傳訪諸淨明宗教錄、與邱祖所傳、小同而大異也。我山先輩、亦守戒焚之、書則錄本倖存、而卷律亡矣。

Thanks to the "*Yishi* scriptures" preserved at Mount Jingai, the patriarchs of this mountain now became the legitimate heirs of the Longmen orthodox Vinaya tradition, the very tradition that was allegedly re-established by patriarch Wang Changyue during the Shunzhi and Kangxi eras at the capital's Baiyun guan. Thanks in particular to the *Lüzu yishi shuoshu*, another scripture revealed at Mt. Jingai and printed (like the *Golden Flower*) by Tao Shi'an, Jingai patriarchs were allowed to perform ordinations. The *Lüzu yishi shuoshu* was designed to bring back the Golden Age when the genuine transmission of the precepts of Laozi was conveyed at the Baiyun guan. Through the repetition of that ideal act in Wang Changyue's re-establishment of ordinations at the Quanzhen public monastery in the capital, Jingai patriarchs could now legitimize their own transmission. However, for the Mt. Jingai patriarchs, the ordination occurred no longer at the ordination altars (*jietan* 戒壇) of a public monastery because, as Min Yide emphasizes, that kind of transmission of precepts lacked authenticity since the genuine book of precepts by Qiu Chuji had been substituted by ordinary texts such as the *Jingming zongjiao lu*. By contrast, it is at the spirit writing altar 扶乩壇 of Mount Jingai that genuine scriptures such as the *Lüzu yishi shuoshu* and the *Jinhua zongzhi* allowed recovering the one and only true ordination, namely, the "mind-transmission of the Supreme One" 太上心傳, Laozi. Thanks to the establishment of a line of Yishi Patriarchs (the Lineage for Healing the World 醫世宗) belonging to the esoteric transmission 律宗之枕秘 within the Longmen orthodox Vinaya tradition of Qiu Chuji and Wang Changyue, this direct transmission of precepts was now taking place thanks to Lü Dongbin and his wonderful power to express the will and doctrine of the Supreme One by means of guiding the hands of spirit writing attendants and tracing Chinese characters on the altar plate. It is in this line of ideal patriarchs of past and present that the *Golden Flower* now found its place at the altar of Mt. Jingai.

> **VERSION 5 SUMMARY**
>
> *Lüzu shi Xiantian xuwu Taiyi jinhua zongzhi* 呂祖師先天虛無太一金華宗旨 (1831) in Min Yide's 閔一得 (1748/58?-1836) *Daozang xubian* 道藏續編, abbr. DZXB, and *Gu Shuyinlou cangshu* 古書隱樓藏書, abbr. YLCS, (1834-1904).
>
> Version 5 is based on the *Daozang jiyao*'s version (4) but features important revisions and neither includes the *Jinhua chanyou wenda* nor any previous prefaces. Associated with the Longmen lineage (Longmen pai 龍門派), it provides annotations by Min Yide along with comments attributed to Longmen masters as product of a purported compilation by Tao Shi'an 陶石菴 (?-1692) on the basis of a spirit writing revelation by Lü Dongbin in 1688 at the Longqiao 龍嶠 hermitage of Jingaishan 金蓋山 (Huzhou 湖州, Zhejiang). Apart from Tao's compilation, Min also mentions a Jinling 金陵 (Nanjing) manuscript (close to version 1), a version by Zhu Gui 朱珪 (1732-1806), and another by Qian Baofu 錢寶甫 (1791-1827).

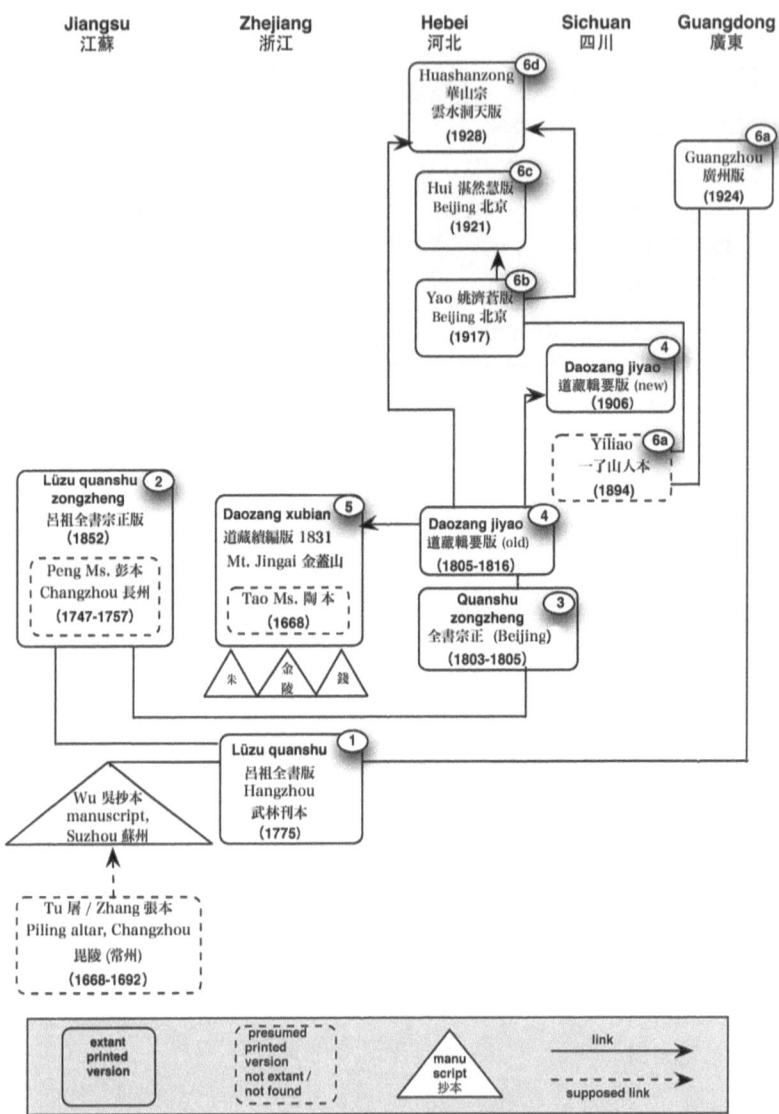

Fig. 52: Overview of the textual history of *Secret of the Golden Flower* in China

Chapter 3

The Golden Flower in the Twentieth Century

Many versions of the *Golden Flower* circulated in China from the eighteenth century onward. We have seen in the previous chapter that the *Daozang jiyao* version (number 4 in our list of major editions) was based on the *Quanshu zhengzong* 全書正宗 (Orthodox Tradition of the Complete Writings of Patriarch Lü [Dongbin]) (version 3), an earlier collection also published by Jiang Yuanting 蔣元庭 that appeared between 1803 and 1805. Jiang's version 3 is in turn based on a revised version of the *Golden Flower* that had appeared as part of the *Lüzu quanshu zongzheng* (version 2) collection, also called *Quanshu zongzheng*. There were thus at least five extant printed editions before the turn of the twentieth century, and in the twentieth century the *Golden Flower* editions and eventually translations into other languages proliferated to such an extent that they are difficult to cover in their entirety. In this final chapter I will first focus on early twentieth-century Chinese editions and then describe the seeds of the *Golden Flower* in the West.

The German translation of the *Golden Flower* by the sinologist Richard Wilhelm was based on a book by a certain Zhanran Huizhenzi 湛然慧真子 published in the early twentieth century under the title *Changshenshu Xumingfang hekan* 長生術續命方合刊 (Joint Edition of the 'Art of Long Life' and the 'Method for Increasing Vital Force').[507] It was in turn based on a book previously published by Yao Jicang 姚濟蒼 (alias Hedaozi 合道子) under the title *Changsheng shu* 長生術 (The Art of Longevity)—a new

---

[507] In the foreword by Salome Wilhelm to the new revised 1957 German translation of Wilhelm, the Chinese editor is mentioned under the name of Hui-chen-tzu (i.e., Huizhenzi 慧真子). His Chinese publication dates back to 1921, but in the Introduction on the "Origin of the book" R. Wilhelm mentions 1920.

title for the *Golden Flower*. Yao explains in his preface that he discovered this scripture in the Liulichang antiquity dealer's lane of Beijing, and that he decided to have seventy copies printed for free distribution. This Liulichang book contained only one preface by a certain Yiliao shanren 一了山人 and was published in 1894. Conscious of the existence of other prefaces, Yao decided to question the immortal Lü Dongbin directly. On an evening in the year 1917, he and his friend Long Xianfa organized a spirit writing séance. This took place at the private altar situated in the house of Long Xiangfa in Beijing. Lü Dongbin descended and revealed that the scripture was in fact initially compiled in 1403, but that it was completed only in 1663 (both dates predate the first revelation at the Piling altar in 1668). Lü Dongbin also prognosticated the future discovery of the original prefaces. Indeed, shortly afterwards Yao Jicang found the "missing prefaces" thanks to a man called Tong Chenghe 佟成和 who was the manager of a spirit writing altar in the Lüweng guguan of Huangliaomeng village in Hebei, and this finally enabled Yao in 1917 to have the *Golden Flower* text, now christened *Changsheng shu* 長生術 (The Art of Longevity), published with its newly revealed prefaces.

In 1921 Zhanran Huizhenzi published a thousand copies of a new edition of the *Golden Flower* containing not only the time-honored text but also his hitherto unpublished commentary and the text of the *Huimingjing* 慧命經 which he renamed *Changshengshu Xumingfang hekan*. On the basis of the prefaces (see Fig. 52 and version 6 summary below) we can deduce that there were at least two editions predating Zhanran Huizhenzi's publication: (1) the edition by Yiliao shanren 一了山人 (1894) and (2) the above-mentioned book by Yao Jicang 姚濟蒼 alias Hedaozi 合道子 (1917). Zhanran Huizhenzi's book shows that the scripture of the *Golden Flower* continued to be transmitted among spirit writing networks worshiping Lü Dongbin and other immortals. Content as well as format of the *Golden Flower* text are very close to the editions of Chen Mou and Jiang Yuanting. In contrast with the latter, the more recent publications of the *Golden Flower* by Yao Jicang and Zhanran Huizhenzi feature less literary prefaces. This may indicate that the *Golden Flower* continued to circulate among spirit writing groups less close to high-ranking officials or literati who had been the main supporters of its previous publications. Unbeknownst to Zhanran Huizhenzi, the seeds of his *Golden Flower* text and commentary were soon to be carried to the West where they soon sprouted new blossoms.

Version 6 Summary (Turn of the Twentieth Century)

6a) *Taiyi jinhua zongzhi* 太乙金華宗旨 (Canton reprint [Guangzhou 廣州: Wenkuige 文魁閣] of 1924, published without prefaces but with an abridged version of the *Jinhua chanyou* 金華闡幽 in Xiao Tianshi 蕭天石 ed. (*Daozang jinghua* 道藏精華 13-3. Taipei: Ziyou chubanshe 自由出版社, 1989). It was first published in Canton. In 1887 Zhou Weixin 周維新, after having obtained it from a certain Liaoxu daoren 了虛道人 brought it back to Chengdu and gave it to Yiliao shanren 一了山人, who reprinted it.

6b) *Taiyi jinhua zongzhi* 太乙金華宗旨, edited and reprinted by Yao Jicang 姚濟蒼 (alias: Hedao zi 合道子) in 1917 (Beijing: Tongshan zongshe 同善總社) on the basis of a book Yao bought in the Liulichang, the famous street of antiquities dealers of Beijing. The Liulichang book (stemming from version 6a) originally included only a preface by Yiliao shanren 一了山人 (1894). After a spirit writing revelation at a private altar in Beijing, Yao Jicang completed it with ten prefaces (corresponding to the nine prefaces and two appendices found in version 2; see Table 5) that he obtained from a certain Tong Chenghe 佟成和. Yao's edition is stored at Beijing National Library and Okayama University 岡山大學 (Japan). It was reprinted in 1918 in the *Zhongxue cantong* 中學參同 (Hechuan 合川: Huishantang 會善堂) as Appendix with the *Wuxing qiongyuan* 悟性窮原 (compiled by Hanguzi 涵穀子), and again in 1924 (Beijing: Tianhuaguan 天華館). The 1918 and 1924 reprints are both stored at Beijing National Library.

6c) *Changsheng shu* 長生術 [The Art of Long Life], in *Changsheng shu Xuming fang hekan* 長生術續命方合刊 [Joint edition of the 'Art of Long Life' and the 'Method for Increasing the Vital Force'] edited and printed in 1921 by Zhanran Hui zhenzi 湛然慧真子 along with the *Huiming jing* 慧命經 (titled *Xuming fang*). It is based on version 6b but includes Zhanran Hui's commentary on the *Golden Flower* (titled *Changsheng shu*). The 1921 edition of Zhanran Hui is stored at the Needham Research Institute (Cambridge, England). A microfilm (1996) is also available at Taiwan National Qinghua University Library (Guoli Qinghua daxue tushuguan 國立清華大學圖書館).

6d) *Taiyi jinhua zongzhi* 太乙金華宗旨, published in the three-volume *Daojing miji* 道經秘集 compilation by a Beijing spirit writing association known as Huashanzong Yunshui dongtian 華山宗雲水洞天 (Beijing: Zhonghua yinshuaju 中華印刷局, 1928). The *Golden Flower* is divided into two parts (*shang, xia*):

1 (上). 13 chapter-text based on Yao's edition (version 6b with revisions from version 4, in particular for chap. 3) with a final part allegedly revealed by Lü Dongbin in 1927 at the Beijing Dongyun Tianhetan 洞雲天鶴壇;

2. (下) *Jinhua chanyou* 金華闡幽, based on version 4 (with its postfaces). It ends with a Postface attributed to Tong Wuxuan 佟悟玄 (1928) as founding patriarch of the Yinxian sipai 隱仙嗣派 of the Mt. Hua tradition (Huashan zong 華山宗). The collection is stored at Beijing National Library and Japan's Okayama University. Also published by Wang Ka 王卡 et al. ed. (*Sandong shiyi* 三洞拾遺, 20 vols. Hefei 合肥: Huangshan shushe 黃山書社, 2005, vol. 1) and by Hu Daojing 胡道靜 et al. ed. (*Zangwai daoshu* 藏外道書, 36 vols. Chengdu: Bashu shushe 巴蜀書社, 1992-94).

The Golden Flower in the West

Richard Wilhelm's German translation of the *Golden Flower* marks the beginning of Western study of this kind of "inner alchemy" texts.[508] With regard to the propagation of the *Secret of the Golden Flower*, it is interesting to note that the majority of translations published in many languages all over the world rely on Wilhelm's translation.[509] We have seen that the text Wilhelm based his translation on was the *Changsheng shu* 長生術 [The Art of Long Life] contained in *Changsheng shu Xuming fang hekan* 長生術續命方合刊 [Joint Edition of 'The Art of Long Life' and 'The Method for Increasing the Vital Force'], a book edited and printed in 1921 and 1927 by Zhanran Huizhen zi 湛然慧真子 that included the editor's commentary on the *Golden Flower*.

Since Wilhelm translated only eight chapters and omitted parts of the original Chinese text without mentioning this fact, the reader got a false

---

[508] The revised and augmented 1957 German edition of Wilhelm's *Das Geheimnis der goldenen Blüte* that was published in Zürich includes a foreword by Salome Wilhelm and a partial translation of the *Huiming jing* 慧命經 (*Book of Wisdom and Life*)—a text authored by the Chan Buddhist monk Liu Huayang 柳華陽 (1735–1799)—by L. C. Lo, the secretary of the China Institute of Frankfurt am Main who was a collaborator of Richard Wilhelm. After having been revised by Wilhelm, this translation was thus among the earliest inner alchemy texts from China published in a Western language. It first appeared in the German review *Chinesische Blätter für Wissenschaft und Kunst* (Darmstadt 1926, pp. 104–114) and was joined to *Das Geheimnis der goldenen Blüte* in the 1957 edition of Wilhelm & Jung. The English translation of this German re-edition appeared in 1962 (New York: Harcourt Brace Jovanovich) and was reprinted multiple times by different publishing houses. Joseph Needham (see below) quotes, for example, reprints of 1965, 1967, and 1969. A recent English reprint is dated 1999 (London: Routledge). On Liu Huayang see the article by Farzeen Baldrian-Hussein in the *Encyclopedia of Taoism*, edited by Fabrizio Pregadio. For a presentation of the *Huiming jing*, see J. Needham, "The Secret of the Golden Flower unveiled," in J. Needham and Lu Gwei-djen, *Science and Civilization in China*, vol. V: 5, Cambridge: Cambridge University Press, 1983:252–257, and my entry "Huiming jing" in F. Pregadio (ed.), *The Encyclopedia of Taoism*, vol. 1: 520–521.

[509] The French translations by Liou Tse Houa (Paris: Librairie de Médicis, 1969) and by Pierre Grison (Paris: Editions traditionnelles, 1986) were both based on Wilhelm's translation. The same is true for the 1981 Italian translation by Augusto Vitale and Maria Anna Massimello (Torino: Boringhieri). These are translations that I personally consulted. In the French translation by Pierre Grison, the author quotes another partial translation, probably also based on Wilhelm, by André Préau entitled *La Fleur d'Or et le Taoïsme sans Tao* (Paris, 1931).

impression of the scripture's content and format.[510] Wilhelm's suppositions on esoteric connections with secret societies and Nestorianism made things even more obscure. The immortal Lü Dongbin (alias Lü Yan or Lüzu), the alleged author of the *Secret of the Golden Flower* and so-called "founder of the Religion of the Golden Elixir of Life" (Jindan jiao 金丹教), thus came to be associated with such trends.[511] Such associations had the effect of making the text more attractive for followers of Freemason orders, new religions, and various kinds of so-called new-age movements.

In spite of some misunderstanding and wrong ideas that still surround the *Secret of the Golden Flower*, it was natural that many people showed interest in such a pioneering enterprise; indeed, this was the first time that a text of Chinese alchemy was made accessible to Westerners in translation.[512] Even the Chinese and Japanese who could have had easier access to original Chinese editions of the text, translated the book by Wilhelm and Jung in their respective languages.[513]

---

[510] Due to some omitted sentences, for instance in the first chapter, and the translation of only eight chapters it is easy to identify renderings based on Wilhelm even when the editor or translator chooses not to mention this.

[511] See the Introduction by Wilhelm (English translation, Arkana reprint 1984, p. 5) where he also mentions that 1,500 adepts of this religion were killed in 1891 by the Manchu government. This account and, as mentioned above, the connection between Lü Dongbin and Nestorianism are based on the work by P. Y. Saeki, *The Nestorian Monument in China* (London: Society for Promoting Christian Knowledge, 1916, p. 53–61). Furthermore, in Carl Jung's autobiography (Memories, Dreams, Reflections, pp. 373–377), Jung wrote a section about his friend Wilhelm and said in its relevant part, "In China he had the good fortune to meet a sage of the old school whom the revolution had driven out of the interior. This sage, Lau Nai Suan, introduced him to Chinese yoga philosophy and the psychology of the Yijing. To the collaboration of these two men we owe the edition of the I Ching with its excellent commentary." Quoted in http://en.wikipedia.org/wiki/The_Secret_of_the_Golden_Flower#cite_note-1. See also Richard Noll, *The Jung Cult: Origins of a Charismatic Movement* (Princeton University Press, 1994).

[512] See for instance the Introduction by Jung on "Why Europeans have difficulty in understanding the East" (Arkana reprint 1984, pp. 81–86).

[513] The Japanese translation by Sadakata Akio 湯浅泰雄 and Yuasa Yasuo 定方昭夫 was made from the 1973 fifth German reprint of the Wilhelm and Jung edition and was first published in 1980 by the Jinbun shoin 人文書院 (Kyoto) under the title *Ōgon no hana no himitsu* 黄金の華の秘密 (reprint in 2004). The Chinese translation by Tongxian 通仙 was based on the 1962 English edition and was published by the Xinhua shudian 新華書店 (Beijing) in 1993 under the title *Jinhua yangsheng mizhi yu fenxi xinlixue* 金華養生秘旨与分析心理學.

In 1967 Miyuki Mokusen 目幸黙僊, a Japanese scholar, presented a diploma thesis at the C.G. Jung-Institute in Zürich entitled *The Secret of the Golden Flower, Studies and Translation*. As he could directly rely on the Chinese text of the *Golden Flower* which Wilhelm had used and consult previous Chinese works on alchemy, he made a more precise translation of the entire text in 13 chapters along with the Chinese commentary by Zhanran Huizhenzi. His thesis was later translated into German and published in book form under the title *Das Kreisen des Lichtes, Die Erfahrung der Goldenen Blüte* (Otto Wilhelm Barth Verlag, 1972). As Mokusen explains in his introduction, his aim was to explain the content of this text by situating it in a larger and historical context linked with "philosophical and religious Daoism" and the birth of inner alchemy (*neidan*) in China.[514] Consequently he did not lose one word about the textual history of the *Secret of the Golden Flower* and the Chinese edition on which his translation was based.[515] After Miyuki, some sinophiles or sinologists voiced some vague opinions. For instance, Alan W. Watts pointed out that the text dates back to the Ming or to the Qing dynasties,[516] and Anna Seidel suggested that it stems from a mediumistic Daoist sect of Lü Dongbin which was popular in Hubei after 1700.[517]

In 1986, Joseph Needham devoted a chapter to this text in volume 5 (part V) "Alchemy and Chemistry" of his *Science and Civilisation*. He began his presentation with the title "The Secret of the Golden Flower unveiled." Conscious of the mystery surrounding its textual history, he tried to understand

---

[514] In the Introduction to his thesis (p. 1), Mokusen explains its twofold purpose: "To understand the world of meditation in the Taoist tradition, which is called the Inner Elixir (*nei-tan* 內丹) presented in the *Secret of the Golden Flower* (*T'ai I Chin Hua Tsung Chih*, 太乙金華宗旨) via the Analytical Psychology of Carl Gustav Jung, and to understand Jung's psychology via the Taoist world."

[515] It is only mentioned in the Bibliography under the title *Ch'ang Sheng Shu* (長生術, Art of Prolongation of Life), or *Tai I Chin Hua Tsung Chi* (太乙金華宗旨, The Secret of the Golden Flower of the Great One), annotated by Tan Jan-Hui Chen Tzu (corrected by pencil in Chan Jan-Hui Chen Tzu, 湛然慧真子), Pei Ching, 1921. I am very grateful to Professor Miyuki Mokusen for having sent me a copy of his thesis.

[516] See Alan W. Watts, *The Way of Zen* (London: Thames & Hudson, 1957): note 45.

[517] Anna Seidel, "A Taoist Immortal of the Ming Dynasty; Chang San-Feng." In W. T. de Bary ed., *Self and Society in Ming Thought*. New York: Columbia University Press, 1970, p. 483. See also her *Taoismus, die inoffizielle Hochreligion Chinas* (Tokyo: OAG Aktuell, 1990, p. 41) where she mentions Wilhelm's lack of *neidan* knowledge following Needham's criticism (see below).

the *Golden Flower* in the context of Ming and Qing alchemical literature. He emphasized the difficulties Wilhelm had in dealing with the Chinese *neidan* tradition and the "mysticisation" of Wilhelm's interpretations due to the lack of such background knowledge. While appreciating the pioneering character of Wilhelm's translation, Needham showed that Wilhelm and Jung, in trying to emphasize common points of East and West, made facile equations and used questionable equivalents for Chinese alchemical terms. For example, distinctively European concepts such as *logos* were used for *xin* 心 (heart-mind) and *eros* for *shen* 腎 (kidney, sexuality), while *ying'er* 嬰兒 (infant) was translated as *puer aeternus* (the infant Christ who must be born in us).

The next translation of the *Secret of the Golden Flower* appeared in 1991. This time the translator Thomas Cleary used a different edition of the Chinese text, namely that from the *Daozang jiyao* 道藏輯要.[518] Calling it a "canonical version" but providing no further details, Cleary focused on translating the text and adding his personal commentary.[519] He repeatedly criticizes Wilhelm's misunderstandings and emphasized Chan Buddhist elements in the *Secret of the Golden Flower*. He did not mention that Wilhelm had used a different edition which, in contrast with his "canonical" one, featured a commentary and variants. Thus the textual history of the *Secret of the Golden Flower* remained in the dark.

A history of the propagation of the *Secret of the Golden Flower* in the West and its reception still waits to be written. It is certain that the eclectic and esoteric nature of the text has contributed to many speculations. Though some of them are completely misguided, it must be said that the complex textual origin of the *Secret of the Golden Flower* and the obscure conditions under which it came to light are not simple issues to deal with. As we saw, various Daoist lineages, whose origins are often elusive, appropriated the text and presented themselves as the genuine recipients of its transmission.

---

[518] See the short annotated Golden Flower bibliography below.

[519] See *The Secret of the Golden Flower: the Classic Chinese Book of Life*, translated, with introduction, notes, and commentary, by Thomas Cleary (San Francisco: Harper San Francisco, 1991).

Short annotated Golden Flower Bibliography

Translations

Wilhelm, Richard (trans.). *Das Geheimnis der Goldenen Blüte: ein chinesisches Lebensbuch*, with the commentary of Carl Gustav Jung. Munich: Dorn Verlag, 1929.

Wilhelm's translation is based on Zhanran Hui's edition (1921, 6c) but provides only a partial translation of eight chapters. A new revised German edition with a new foreword by Jung and his memorial address for Richard Wilhelm (died in 1930) was published in 1938 (Zürich: Rascher Verlag) and reprinted twice in 1944.

• The first English translation from the German by C. F. Baynes appeared in 1931 under the title *The Secret of the Golden Flower: A Chinese Book of Life* (London: Kegan Paul, Trench, Trubner and Co.) and was reprinted many times. The majority of translations in Western languages are based on Wilhelm's, even though the translators do not often mention this. If the translation consists of only eight chapters it tends to be based on Wilhelm.

• The first Japanese translation from the 1938 German edition was made by Motoyama Hiroshi 本山博 in 1964 (with revisions based on Motoyama's consultation of version 4 from the *Chongkan Daozang jiyao* and version 5 published in Xiao Tianshi 蕭天石 ed. *Daozang jinghua* 8-1) under the title *Taiitsu kinka shūshi: dōkyō chōjo yōjō hō* 太乙金華宗旨：道教長壽養生法 (Tokyo: Shūkyō shinrigaku kenkyūjo 宗教心理學研究所). It includes only the translation of eight chapters. Another translation was made by Sadakata Akio 湯浅泰雄 and Yuasa Yasuo 定方昭夫 from the 1973 fifth German reprint of Wilhelm and Jung's book but with a full 13 chapter-text translation including the *Huiming jing*. It was first published in 1980 under the title *Ōgon no hana no himitsu* 黄金の華の秘密 (Kyoto: Jinbun shoin 人文書院; reprint 2004).

• The Chinese translation by Tongxian 通仙 was based on the 1962 English reprint and was published in 1993 under the title *Jinhua yangsheng mizhi yu fenxi xinlixue* 金華養生秘旨與分析心理學 (Beijing: Xinhua shudian 新華書店). Another Chinese translation was published in 1994 by Wang Kuipu 王魁溥, based on the previous Japanese translation by Yuasa and Sadakata, under the title *Chunyang Lüzu gongli gongfa quanshi: Taiyi Jinhua zongzhi jinyi* 純陽呂祖功理功法詮釋: 太乙金華宗旨今譯 (Beijing: Waiwen chubanshe 外文出版社). Several Chinese translations of the *Golden Flower* are also listed on the Internet but their source is often not specified.

Miyuki Mokusen 目幸黙僊. *The Secret of the Golden Flower, Studies and Translation*. Diploma thesis at the C.G. Jung-Institute, Zürich, 1967. (Published in German as *Das Kreisen des Lichtes, Die Erfahrung der Goldenen Blüte*. Munich: Otto Wilhelm Barth Verlag, 1972).

The author relied on the Chinese text of the *Golden Flower* used by Wilhelm but translated and annotated the entire text in thirteen chapters along with the Chinese commentary by Zhanran Hui. No information is provided about the textual history of the *Secret of the Golden Flower* nor about the Chinese edition on which the translation is based.

Cleary, Thomas (trans.). *The Secret of the Golden Flower: The Classic Chinese Book of Life*. San Francisco, CA: Harper San Francisco, 1991.

Based on the *Chongkan Daozang jiyao* version (4), this translation includes personal comments and annotations by Cleary.

Feng Guanghong 馮廣宏 (trans.) *Taiyi jinhua zongzhi jinyi* 太乙金華宗旨今譯. Chengdu: Sichuan Kexue jishu chubanshe, 1995).

The annotated translation into modern Chinese by Feng Guanghong is based on Min Yide's version included in *Daozang xubian* (version 5) and on Jiang Yuanting's version in the *Chongkan Daozang jiyao* (version 4). It includes annotations based on the comparison between Min's version (5), the *Chongkan* version (4), Yao Jicang's version (6b), and Zhanran Hui's version (6c).

Du Zong 杜琮 and Zhang Chaozhong 張超中 (trans.). *Huangting jing jinyi Taiyi jinhua zongzhi jinyi* 黃庭經今譯・太乙金華宗旨今譯. Beijing: Zhongguo Shehui Kexueyuan chubanshe 中國社會科學院出版社, 1996.

The annotated translation in modern Chinese by Zhang Chaozhong is based on Min Yide's text edition in the *Daozang xubian* (version 5) but does not include Min Yide's comments.

Studies

Esposito, Monica. "Il Segreto del Fiore d'Oro e la tradizione Longmen del Monte Jingai." In *Conoscenza e interpretazione della civiltà cinese*, ed. Piero Corradini, 151–169. Venezia: Cafoscarina, 1996.

———. "The Different Versions of the *Secret of the Golden Flower* and Their Relationship with the Longmen School." *Transactions of the International Conference of Eastern Studies* 43 (1998): 90–109.

———. "Shindai ni okeru Kingai-san Ryūmon-ha no seiritsu to *Kinka shūshi* 清代における金蓋山龍門派の設立と『金華宗旨』" [The *Secret of the Golden Flower* and the establishment of the Longmen tradition at Mt. Jingai during the Qing dynasty]. In *Chūgoku shūkyō bunken kenkyū* 中国宗教文献研究 [Religions in Chinese Script: Perspectives for Textual Research], ed. Kyōto Daigaku Jinbun Kagaku Kenkyūjo 京都大学人文科学研究所, 239–264. Kyoto: Rinsen shoten 臨川書店, 2007.

———. "Taiyi jinhua zongzhi 太一金華宗旨." In *The Encyclopedia of Taoism*, ed. Fabrizio Pregadio, vol. 2: 961–962. London: Routledge, 2008.

Mori Yuria 森由利亞. "*Taiitsu kinka shūshi* no seiritsu to hensen 『太乙金華宗旨』の成立と変遷" [The compilation of the *Taiyi jinhua zongzhi* and its transformations]. *Tōyō no shisō to shūkyō* 東洋の思想と宗教 15 (1998): 43–64.

———. "Identity and Lineage: The *Taiyi jinhua zongzhi* and the Spirit writing Cult to Patriarch Lü in Qing China." In *Daoist Identity: History, Lineage, and Ritual*, eds. Livia Kohn and Harold D. Roth, 168–187. Honolulu: University of Hawaii Press, 2002.

Needham, Joseph. "The Secret of the Golden Flower unveiled." In *Science and Civilisation in China*, ed. Joseph Needham (with the participation of Lu Gwei-Djen), vol. V, part 5, 243–257. Cambridge: Cambridge University Press, 1983.

Bibliography

Primary Sources

(for the list of abbreviations see pp. IV–V)

Baiyun guan Chen Yukun fangzhang erci chuanjie beiji 白雲觀陳毓坤方丈二次傳戒碑記. 1919. Stele; Baiyun guan zhi 白雲觀志, pp. 179–81.

Baiyun guan juanchan beiji 白雲觀捐產碑記. 1811. Stele; Baiyun guan zhi 白雲觀志, p. 145.

Baiyun guan zhi (*Hakuunkan shi*) 白雲觀志 (Gazetteer of the Abbey of White Clouds) by Oyanagi Shigeta 小柳司氣太. Tokyo: Tōhō bunka gakuin Tōkyō kenkyūjo, 1934. Abbreviated as BYGZ.

Baiyun xianbiao 白雲仙表 (A Chart of the Immortals of Baiyun Abbey). 1848. Meng Huoyi 孟豁一. ZWDS 31: 373 ff. Abbreviated as *Immortals' Chart* or BYXB.

Biyuan tanjing 碧苑壇經 (Platform Sūtra of the Jade Garden). Transmitted by Wang Changyue 王常月 alias Wang Kunyang 王崑陽 (?–1680), compiled by Shi Shouping 施守平 and revised by Min Yide. YLCS edition, reprinted in ZWDS 藏外道書 10: 158–217.

Bojian lu 缽鑑錄 (apparently referring to the *Bojian* [Examination of the Bowl], a putative work attributed to Wang Changyue 王常月 alias Wang Kunyang 王崑陽 [?–1680]).

Cantong jing 參同經 (Scripture on the Equality of the Three [Teachings]). Included in Liu Tishu 劉體恕 ed., *Lüzu quanshu* 呂祖全書 in 32 juan.

Chanfa daguan 懺法大觀. CK 21:9219–9499.

Changchun daojiao yuanliu 長春道教源流 (Origins and Development of the Daoist Teachings of [Qiu] Changchun). 1879. Abbreviated as DJYL.

Changchun zhenren xiyouji 長春真人西遊記 (Record of the Journey to the West of the Perfected [Qiu] Changchun). 1228. Li Zhichang 李志常 (1193–1256). DZ 1429, fasc. 1056.

Chongkan Daozang jiyao 重刊道藏輯要 (Reedition of the Essence of the Daoist Canon). 1906. Chengdu: Erxian an 二仙庵. Reprint in 25 vols., Taipei: Kaozheng, 1971 (Reprint edition abbreviated as CK).

Chongkan Jingai xindeng xu 重刊金蓋心燈序 (Preface to the Reedition of *Jingai xindeng* 金蓋心燈 [Transmission of the Heart-Lamp from Mount Jingai]). Shen Bingcheng 沈秉成 (ZWDS 31:158).

Chongyang lijiao shiwu lun 重陽立教十五論 (Fifteen Lessons by [Wang] Chongyang to establish his Doctrine). Wang Zhe 王嚞 (1113–1170). DZ 1233.

Chongyang'an ji 重陽庵集 (Collection from the Abode of [Wang] Chongyang). Wang Zhe 王嚞 (1113–1170). ZWDS 20.

Chongyin Xuanmiaoguan zhi 重印玄妙觀志 (Reedited Gazetteer of the Xuanmiao guan [of Suzhou]). ZWDS 20.

Chuandaoji 傳道集 (Collection on Transmitting the Dao). Section 12, lodge Weiji 危集 2; CK12: 5113–5142.

Chuzhen jielü 初真戒律 (Code of Precepts of Initial Perfection). CK 24: 10469–87.

Dacheng miaolin jing 大乘妙林經 (Marvelous Forest of the Great Vehicle). DZ 1398, fasc. 1049.

Daode zhenjing sanjie 道德真經三解 (A Threefold Explication of the *Daodejing*). 1298. Deng Qi 鄧錡. DZ 687, fasc. 370–71.

Daofa huiyuan, 道法會元 (Collected Sources on Daoist Ritual). 1356. DZ 1220, fasc. 884–941.

Daojiao shi ziliao 道教史資料 (Materials for the History of Daoism). Shanghai: Guji chubanshe, 1991.

Daopu yuanliu tu 道譜源流圖 (a commented Daoist lineage chart compiled by Lü Yunyin 呂雲隱, fl. 1710).

Daotong yuanliu zhi 道統源流志 (Gazetteer on the Origins and Development of Orthodox Daoism). 1929, Wuxi: Zhonghua yinshuju. Abbreviated as *Gazetteer of Daoist Origins* or DTYL.

Daozang jinghua lu 道藏精華錄 (Record of Quintessence of the Daoist Canon). By Ding Fubao 丁福保. Shanghai: Yixue shuju, 1922. Abbreviated as DZJHL.

Daozang 道藏 (text numbers according to Kristofer Schipper and Franciscus Verellen, eds., *The Taoist Canon*, Chicago: Chicago University Press, 2004. Abbreviated as DZ.

Daozang xubian 道藏續編 (Supplementary Collection of the Daoist Canon), 4 vols., by Min Yide 閔一得(1758–1836). Wuxing: Jingai cangban, 1834. Photolithographic edition by Ding Fubao 丁福保. Shanghai: Yixue shuju. Reprint Beijing: Haiyang 1989. Abbreviated as DZXB.

Dongxuan lingbao changye zhi fu jiuyou yukui mingzhen ke 洞玄靈寶長夜之府九幽玉匱明眞科 (Liturgy of the Sworn Alliance with the Zhenren, Kept in the Jade Chest of the Nine Realms of Darkness in the Department of the Long Night [the regions of death and damnation]). DZ 1411 (fasc. 1052).

Dongxuan lingbao qianzhen ke 洞玄靈寶千真科 (Code of the Thousand Real Men, from the Dongxuan Lingbao Canon). DZ 1410 (fasc. 1052).

Dongxuan lingbao sandong fengdao kejie yingshi 洞玄靈寶三洞奉道科戒營始 (Regulations for the Practice of Daoism in Accordance with the Scriptures of the Three Caverns, a Dongxuan Lingbao Canon). DZ 1125, fasc. 760–1.

Dongyuan yulu 東園語錄 (Recorded Sayings of Dongyuan). Attributed to Lü Quanyang 呂全陽. CK 13:5935–79.

Fahai yizhu 法海遺珠 (Bequeathed Pearls from the Sea of Ritual). 1344. DZ 1166, fasc. 825–33.

Fuyou dijun baogao 孚佑帝君寶誥 (Precious Declaration by Lord Fuyou [Lü Dongbin]). CK 12: 5293 ff.

Fuyou dijun shijie gongguo ke 孚佑帝君十戒功過格 (Ledger of Merit and Demerit of Lord Fuyou's [i.e., Lü Dongbin's] Ten Commandments). CK 23: 10309–39.

Fuyou dijun xinjing 孚佑帝君心經 (Heart Scripture of Lord Fuyou [Lü Dongbin]). CK 12: 5418–19.

Fuyou shangdi Shiliupinjing 孚佑上帝十六品經 (Book of Supreme Lord Fuyou's [Lü Dongbin's] in Sixteen Articles). Section 13, lodge Shiji 室集 1, CK 12: 5293–5340.

Fuyou shangdi Chunyang Lüzu tianshi xinjing 孚佑上帝純陽呂祖天師心經 (also called *Lüdi xinjing* 呂帝心經 or Heart Scripture of Lord Lü [Dongbin]). Reproduced in the *Qingwei hongfan daomen gongke* 清微宏範道門功課, CK 23: 10213–35.

Gaoshang shenxiao yuqing zhenwang zishu dafa 高上神霄玉清真王紫書大法. CK 8: 3253–3449.

Gu Shuyinlou cangshu 古書隱樓藏書 (Collection from the Ancient Hidden Pavilion of Books). 14 vols., by Min Yide. Wuxing: Jingai Chunyang gong cangban, 1904. Reprint in ZWDS 10:150–721. Abbreviated as YLCS.

Guangyang zaji 廣陽雜記 (Miscellaneous Records of Guangyang). Liu Xianting 劉獻廷. Beijing: Zhonghua shuju, 1957.

Hakuunkan shi (Baiyun guan zhi) 白雲觀志 (Gazetteer of the Abbey of White Clouds) by Oyanagi Shigeta 小柳司氣太. Tokyo: Tōhō bunka gakuin Tōkyō kenkyūjo 東方文化學院東京研究所, 1934.

Han Tianshi shijia 漢天師世家 (Hereditary House of the Heavenly Master of the Han Dynasty). DZ 1463, fasc. 1066.

Huangji hepi xianjing 皇極闔闢仙經. Abbr. for *Yin zhenren Donghua zhengmai huangji hepi zhengdao xianjing* 尹真人東華正脈皇極闔闢證道仙經 (Immortal Scripture by the Perfected Yin Testifying to the Path of Opening and Closing the August Ultimate According to the Orthodox Lineage of the Eastern Florescence). ZWDS 10: 367–383.

Huangji xianjing 皇極仙經 (Book of Supreme Principles of the Immortals). YLCS, in ZWDS 10:381.

Huangjing jizhu 皇經集註 (Collected Commentaries to the Noble Scripture). DZ 1440, fasc. 1060–62.

Huayue zhi 華嶽志 (Gazetteer of the Peak of Hua). Compiled by Li Rong 李榕 (fl. 1821). Edited by Yang Xiwu 楊翼武 (fl. 1831). ZWDS 20: 3–185.

Jiao sandong zhenwen wufa zhengyi mengwei lu licheng yi 醮三洞真文五法正一盟威錄立成儀 (Complete Ritual for Offering to the Gods of Registers of the Three Caverns, the Five Methods, and the One and Orthodox Covenant). DZ 1212, fasc. 878.

Jingai xindeng 金蓋心燈 (Mind-Lamp of Mount Jingai). Huzhou 湖州, Zhejiang: Gu Shuyinlou cangshu 古書隱樓藏書 of Mt. Jingai 金蓋山. 1821. Re-edition of 1876: Wuxing, Yunchao: Gu Shuyinlou cangban. ZWDS 31. Abbreviated as *Mind-Lamp* or JGXD.

Jingshi gongguoge 警世功過格 (Exhortation about Ledgers of Merit and Demerit). Section 25, lodge Zhangji 張集 3, CK 23: 10339–53.

Jingudong zhi 金鼓洞志 (Gazetteer of the Jingu Grotto). 1807. Zhu Wenzao 朱文藻 (1736–1806). ZWDS 20: 189–299.

Jinhua zongzhi 金華宗旨 (The Secret of the Golden Flower). Edited by Jiang Yuanting 蔣元庭 (1755–1819) and revised by Min Yide 閔一得 (1758–1836). Section 13, lodge Shiji 室集 2, CK 12: 5349–82.

Jinlian zhengzong ji 金蓮正宗記 (Record of the Orthodox Lineage of the Golden Lotus). 1241. Qin Zhian 秦志安 (1188–1244). DZ 173, fasc. 75–76.

Jinlian zhengzong xianyuan xiangzhuan 金蓮正宗仙源像傳 (Illustrated Hagiographies of the Immortal Origins of the Orthodox Lineage of the Golden Lotus). 1326. Liu Tiansu 劉天素 and Xie Xichan 謝西蟾. DZ 174, fasc. 76.

Jiuhuang doulao jiesha yansheng zhenjing 九皇斗姥說戒殺延生眞經. CK 7: 2879–99.

Lingbao lingjiao jidu jinshu 靈寶領教濟度金書 (Golden Book of Salvation according to the Lingbao Tradition). DZ 466, fasc. 208–263.

Lingbao wujing tigang 靈寶五經提綱 (Summary of Five Lingbao Scriptures). DZ 529, fasc. 295.

Lishi zhenxian tidao tongjian 歷世真仙體道通鑒 (Comprehensive Mirror of the Perfected and Immortals who embodied the Dao through the Ages). Zhao Daoyi 趙道一 (late 13th c.). DZ 296, fasc. 138–48.

Longmen chuanjie puxi 龍門傳戒譜系 (Genealogy of Longmen's Transmission of Commandments). Also known as *Taishang lümai Longmen zhengzong* 太上律脈龍門正宗). 1919. Hand-scroll manuscript conserved at Baiyun guan. Abbreviated as TSLM.

Longmen xinfa 龍門心法 (Core Teachings of the Longmen). 1663. Transmitted by Wang Changyue 王常月 alias Wang Kunyang 王崑陽 (?–1680), and compiled by Zhan Tailin 詹太林 and Tang Qingshan 唐清善. ZWDS 6: 727–785.

Longmen zhengzong jueyun benzhi daotong xinchuan 龍門正宗覺雲本支道統薪傳 (Uninterrupted Transmission of the Orthodox Teaching in the Right Lineage of the Longmen Jueyun Branch). 1927. Lu Yongming 陸永銘. ZWDS 31: 427–446.

Longmen zhengzong liuchuan zhipai tu 龍門正宗流傳支派圖 (Diagram of Schools and Transmission Branches of the Orthodox Longmen Tradition). JGXD 1a.

Lüdi shiji 呂帝詩集 (Collected Poems of Lord Lü [Dongbin]). Section 13, lodge Shiji 室集 6–7, in CK 13: 5511–5622.

Lüdi wenji 呂帝文集 (Collected Texts of Lord Lü [Dongbin]). Section 13, lodge Shiji 室集 5, in CK 12: 5443–5507.

Lüdi xinjing 呂帝心經 (Heart Scripture of Lord Lü [Dongbin]), also called *Fuyou shangdi Chunyang Lüzu tianshi xinjing* 孚佑上帝純陽呂祖天師心經. Reproduced in the *Qingwei hongfan daomen gongke* 清微宏範道門功課. Lodge 張集 1, 8b–9b, CK 23: 10213–35.

Lushan Taiping xingguo gong Caifang zhenjun shishi 廬山太平興國宮訪真君事實 (Veritable Facts concerrning the True Lord Investigator of the Taiping Xingguo Temple on Mount Lu). DZ 1286, fasc. 1006–7.

Lüzu quanshu 呂祖全書 (Collected Works of Patriarch Lü). 1868 (with a Preface added in 1879). 33 juan, from the woodblocks stored at the Xiangtan Chongshantang 湘潭崇善堂 (Library of Kyoto University's Institute for Research in Humanities).

Lüzu quanshu zongzheng 呂祖全書宗正 (Orthodoxy of the Tradition of the Complete Writings of Ancestor Lü [Dongbin]). Ed. by Chen Mou 陳謀. 1852.

Qinghe miaodao guanghua guanghua zhenren Yin zongshi beiming 清和妙道廣化真人尹宗師碑銘. Stone inscription of 1264 in *Ganshui xianyuan lu* 甘水仙源錄 j. 3 (ZHDZ 47:136a).

Qingwei hongfan daomen gongke 清微宏範道門功課 (CK 23: 10213–35).

Qiongguan Bai zhenren ji 瓊琯白真人集 (Anthology of Perfected Bai of Haiqiong). CK 14: 6195–6366.

Qizhen nianpu 七真年譜 (Chronological Biographies of the Seven Zhenren). DZ 175, fasc. 76.

Quanzhen diwu dai zongshi Changchun yandao zhujiao zhenren neizhuan 全真第五代宗師長春演道主教真人內傳 (Stele of 1281). *Daojia jinshi lüe* 道家金石略, ed. by Chen Yuan 陳垣 and Chen Zhichao 陳智超. Beijing: Wenwu chubanshe, 1988: 634–37.

Quanzhen qinggui 全真清規 (Pure Rules of the Quanzhen School). Compiled by Lu Daohe 陸道和; 14th century. DZ 1235, fasc. 989.

Rixia jiuwen kao 日下舊聞考 (Investigation of Peking's Antiquities). 1774/1882. SKQS vols. 497–99.

Sandong shiyi 三洞拾遺. Hefei: Huangshan shushe 黃山書社, 2005.

Sandong zhongjie wen 三洞眾戒文 (Comprehensive Prescriptions of the Three Caverns). DZ 178, fasc. 77.

Sanhuang neiwen yibi 三皇內文遺祕 (Transmitted Secrets of the Inner Writs of the Three Sovereigns). DZ 856, fasc. 575.

Santan yuanman Tianxian dajie lüeshuo 三壇圓滿天仙大戒略說 (CK 24: 10457–68).

Shangqing dongzhen zhihui guanshen dajie wen 上清洞真智慧觀身大戒文 (Great Rules of Wisdom in Self-Examination). DZ 1364, fasc. 1039.

Shangyang zi jindan dayao 上陽子金丹大要 (Great Essentials on the Golden Elixir of Shangyang zi). Chen Zhixu 陳致虛 (1298–after 1335). DZ 1067, fasc. 736–38.

Shengji jiyao 聖蹟紀要 (Essential Chronicle of the Saint's Traces). CK 13: 5831–5857).

Shenxianzhuan 神仙傳 (Biographies of Divine Immortals). Longwei bishu 龍威秘書 edition 1794.

Shijie gongguoge 十戒功過格 (Ten-Precept Ledgers of Merit and Demerit). CK 23: 10309–39).

Shinsan dai Nihon Zokuzōkyō 新纂大日本續藏經. 90 vols. Tokyo: Kokusho Kankōkai, 1975–1989.

Shishi yuanliu yinghua shiji 釋氏源流應化事蹟 (History of the Life of Śākya, his Conversions, and other Events). 1425.

Siku quanshu [文淵閣]四庫全書 (Complete Texts in Four Repositories, 1773–1782), 1500 vols. by Yong Rong 永瑢 et al. Edited by Zhu Jianmin 朱建民. Taipei: Shangwu yinshuguan, 1986. Abbreviated as SKQS.

Taishang Daodejingjie 太上道德經解 (The Supreme Daodejing Explained). CK 4: 1673–1726.

Taishang dongxuan lingbao sanyuan pinjie gongde jingzhong jing 太上洞玄靈寶三元品戒功德輕重經 (Scripture of Great and Minor Merits, and the Classified Rules of the Three Principles). DZ 456, fasc. 202.

Taishang dongxuan lingbao sanyuan wuliang shou jing 太上洞玄靈寶三元無量壽經 (Marvelous Scripture of the Karmic Retribution of the Merit of the Ten Epithets, from the Dongxuan Lingbao Canon). DZ 323, fasc. 176.

Taishang dongxuan lingbao yebao yinyuan jing 太上洞玄靈寶業報因緣經 (Scripture of the Most High from the Dongxuan Lingbao Canon Regarding Retribution and Karmic Causes). DZ 336, fasc. 174–5.

Taishang dongxuan lingbao zhihui benyuan dajie shangpin 太上洞玄靈寶智慧本願大戒上品經 (Lingbao Scripture on the Great Superior Rules and Original Vows of Wisdom). DZ 344, fasc. 177.

Taishang ganyingpian jianzhu 太上感應篇箋註. CK 6:2267-98.

Taishang jingjie 太上經戒 (Canonical Commandments of the Most High). DZ 787, fasc. 562.

Taishang jingming zongjiao lu 太上淨明宗教錄. Zhu Daolang 朱道朗 et al. Nanchang: Qingyun pu (early Qing); reprint Nanchang: Xishan Wanshou gong / Nanchang Wanshou gong, 2005.

Taishang jiuzhen miaojie jinlu duming bazui miaojing 太上九真妙戒金籙度命拔罪妙經 (Book of the Golden Register for the Redemption of Sins and for Salvation, [Including] the Marvelous Commandmens of the Nine Zhenren). DZ 181, fasc. 77.

Taishang laojun jiejing 太上老君戒經 (Commandments of the Most High Lord Lao). DZ 784, fasc. 562.

Taishang laojun jinglü 太上老君經律 (Canonical Rules of the Most High Lord Lao). DZ 786, fasc. 562.

Taishang lingbao jingming chuzhen jiejing 太上靈寶淨明初真戒經 (Scripture of the Most High from the Lingbao Canon on Jingming's Initial Genuine Rules). In *Taishang jingming zongjiao lu* 太上淨明宗教錄.

Taishang lingbao jingming shangzhen jiejing 太上靈寶淨明上真戒經 (Scripture of the Most High from the Lingbao Canon on Jingming's Superior Genuine Rules). In *Taishang jingming zongjiao lu* 太上淨明宗教錄.

Taishang lingbao jingming zhengzhen jiejing 太上靈寶淨明正真戒經 (Scripture of the Most High from the Lingbao Canon on Jingming's Orthodox Genuine Rules). In *Taishang jingming zongjiao lu* 太上淨明宗教錄.

Taishang lingbao yuanyang miaojing 太上靈寶元陽妙經 (Marvelous Scripture of Primordial Yang). DZ 334, fasc. 168-9.

Taishang lingbao zhihui guanshen jing 太上靈寶智慧觀身經 (Lingbao Scripture on Wisdom and the Contemplation of the Body). DZ 350, fasc. 177.

Taishang lümai Longmen zhengzong 太上律脈龍門正宗. 1919. Handscroll manuscript conserved at Baiyun guan; also known as *Longmen chuanjie puxi* 龍門傳戒譜系. Abbreviated as TSLM.

Taishang sanyuan cifu shezui jie'e xiaozai yansheng baoming miaojing 太上三元賜福赦罪解厄消災延生保命妙經 (Most High Marvelous Life-Protecting Scripture of the Three Principles Granting Happiness, forgiving Sins, and Averting Disasters). DZ 1442, fasc. 1063.

Taishang shier shangpin feitian falun quanjie miaojing 太上十二上品飛天法輪勸戒妙經 (Scripture of the Twelve Superior Rules of Admonition of the Wheel of the Law of the Flying Devas). DZ 182, fasc. 77.

Taishang xuhuang tianzun sishijiu zhanjing 太上虛皇四十九章經 (Scripture of the Most High Heavenly Worthy of Vacuity in Forty-nine Sections). DZ 18, fasc. 25.

Taishang zhenchuan shoujie bichi 太上真傳守戒必持. *Sandong shiyi* 三洞拾遺, vol. 11: 89–192.

Taishō shinshū daizōkyō 大正新修大藏經, 85 vols., edited by J. Takakusu and K. Watanabe. Tokyo: Taishō issaikyō kankōkai, 1924–32. Abbreviated as T.

Taiwei lingshu ziwen xianji zhenji shangjing 太微靈書紫文仙忌真記上經 (True Record of Interdictions [to be Observed by] the Immortals). DZ 179, fasc. 77.

Ti'an nianpu 惕盦年譜. Yangzhou, 1877.

Tianhuang zhidao taiqing yuce 天皇至道太清玉冊 (Most Pure and Precious Books on the Supreme Tao of August Heaven). DZ 1483, fasc. 1109–11.

Tiantan Wangwu shan shengji ji 天壇王屋山聖迹記 (Account of the Sacred Vestiges of the Altar of Heaven on Wangwu Shan). DZ 969, fasc. 610; ZHDZ vol. 48.

Tianxian jindan xinfa 天仙金丹心法 (Core Teachings of Heavenly Immortals on the Golden Elixir). CK 13:5859–5993.

Tianxian zhengli qianshuo 天仙正理淺說 (Simple explanations of the Correct Principles of Celestial Immortality). Wu Shouyang 伍守陽 (1574–1634). CK 17: 7597–7619.

Tianxian zhengli zhilun 天仙正理直論 (Forthright Discourses on the Correct Principles of Celestial Immortality). 1639. Wu Shouyang 伍守陽. CK 17: 7541–95.

Tongcanjing 同參經 (CK 12:5383–5415).

Wenyuan ge Siku quanshu 文淵閣四庫全書 (Complete Texts in Four Repositories, 1773–1782), 1500 vols. by Yong Rong 永瑢 et al. Edited by Zhu Jianmin 朱建民. Taipei: Shangwu yinshuguan, 1986. Abbreviated as SKQS.

Wudang fudi zongzhen ji 武當富地總真集 (Collection of the Assembled Perfected of Mount Wudang). 1291. Compiled by Liu Daoming 劉道明. DZ 962, fasc. 609.

Wuji zhidao chongxu taimiao jinyu xuanjing 無極至道沖虛太妙金玉玄經 (scripture attributed to Lü Dongbin included in the old *Daozang jiyao*).

Wujing hebian 五經合編 (Convergence of the Five Classics). CK 12: 5417–5442.

Wushang biyao 無上秘要 (The Essence of the Supreme Secrets). DZ 1138, fasc. 768–779.

Wushang neibi zhenzang jing 無上內秘眞藏經 (Supreme Esoteric Writ of the True Reservoir). DZ 4, fasc. 14–15.

Xianfo hezong yulu 仙佛合宗語錄 (Recorded Sayings on the Merged Tradition of Buddhism and Daoism). Wu Shouyang, annotated by Wu Shouxu 伍守虛. CK 17: 7403–7540.

Xianle ji 仙樂集 (Pleasure of the Immortals). DZ 1141, fasc. 786.

Xiantian doudi chiyan wushang xuangong Lingmiao zhenjing 先天斗帝敕演無上玄功靈妙真經 (CK 7: 2867–79).

Xiyou ji 西游記 (Journey to the West). See *Changchun zhenren xiyouji* 長春真人西遊記.

Xu huang tianzun chuzhen shijie wen 虛皇天尊初真十戒文 (DZ 180).

Xuandu lütan chuanjie yinli guize 玄都律壇傳戒引禮規則 (abbr. *Yinli guize* 引禮規則). Chengdu: Qingyanggong.

Xuandu lütan weiyi jieke quanbu 玄都律壇威儀戒科全部 (Wang Ka 王卡 and Wang Guiping 汪桂平 eds., *Sandong shiyi* 三洞拾遺 11). 1874.

Xuanfeng qinghui tu 玄風慶會圖 (Felicitous Meetings with the Mysterious School, with Illustrations). 1305. Nara: Tenri Library, 1981; reprint of the Hanfenlou edition, 1925.

Xuanjiao da gong'an 玄教大公案 (Great Cases in the Teachings of the Mysteries). 1324. Wang Zhidao 王志道. DZ 1065, fasc. 734.

Xuanzong zhengzhi 玄宗正旨 (The Correct Meaning of the School of Mysteries). CK 8: 3045–57).

Xujing xiansheng neizhuan 虛靜先生內傳 (The Esoteric Transmission of Master Xujing). *Jingai xindeng*, ZWDS 31.

Yaoxiu keyi jielü chao 要修科儀戒律鈔 (Summary of Important Ceremonies, Rules, and Codices to be Practiced). DZ 463, fasc. 204–207.

Yin zhenren Donghua zhengmai huangji hepi zhengdao xianjing 尹真人東華正脈皇極闔闢證道仙經 (Immortal Scripture by the Perfected Yin Testifying to the Path of Opening and Closing the August Ultimate according to the Orthodox Lineage of the Eastern Florescence) dated 1831. Attributed to Yin Pengtou 尹蓬頭, edited by Min Yide. 1831. ZWDS 10:367–383.

Yishuo 易說 (Explanations on the Yijing). CK 13: 5623–5714.

Yuanshi dadongyu jing 元始大洞玉經. CK 3: 1127–74.

Yuanshi wuliang duren shangpin miaojing sizhu 元始無量度人上品妙經四注 (Four Commentaries on the Book of Salvation). DZ 87.

Yuanshi wuliang duren shangpin miaojing neiyi 元始無量度人上品妙經內義 (Esoteric Interpretation of the Book of Salvation). DZ 90, fasc. 43–44.

Yuanyang zi fayu 原陽子法語 (Religious Discourses by Master Original Yang). DZ 1071, fasc. 738.

Yuhuang benxing jijing 玉皇本行集經 (Collected Scriptures of the Founding Acts by the Jade Emperor). DZ 10, fasc. 23–24.

Yulu daguan 語錄大觀 (Grand Survey of Recorded Sayings). CK 13: 5715–78).

Yunji qiqian 雲笈七籤 (Cloudy Bookcase with Seven Labels). DZ 1032, fasc. 677–702.

Yuquan 玉詮. CK 20:8971–21:9158.

Yuquan yulu 玉詮語錄 (a component of the *Yulu daguan* 語錄大觀). CK 13: 5753–58.

Yushu baojing 玉樞寶經. CK 8:3 504–12.

Zangwai daoshu 藏外道書 (Daoist Texts not included in the Daoist Canon). Edited by Hu Daojing 胡道靜 et al. Chengdu: Bashu shushe, 1992 (vols. 1–20); 1994 (vols. 21–36). Abbreviated as ZWDS.

Zhaijie lu 齋戒錄 (Registers of Rules for Fasting). DZ 464, fasc. 207.

Zhan Weiyang lüshi taming 詹維陽律師塔銘, in *Nanyun wengao* 南昀文稿. 1726. SKQS 246: 775–6.

Zhang tidian shouzang ji 張提點壽藏記. Stele erected in 1320.

Zhao Xujing lüshi zhuan 趙虛靜律師傳 (Biography of the Vinaya Patriarch Zhao Xujing). 1821 (reprint 1873/1876; JGXD 1.1a–2b).

Zhenping xianzhi 鎮平縣志 (Gazetteer of Zhenping County). 1876.

Zhenxian zhizhi yulu 真仙直指語錄 (Recorded Discourses and Forthright Instructions of the Zhenren and Immortals). DZ 1256, fasc. 998.

Zhonghua Daozang 中華道藏 (China's Daoist Canon). 49 vols. Beijing: Huaxia, 2004. Abbreviated as ZHDZ.

Zhongji jie 中極戒 (Medium Ultimate Precepts). CK 24:10487–96.

Zhongnan shan zuting xianzhen neizhuan 終南山祖庭仙真內傳 (Inner Biographies of the Immortals and Perfected at [Wang Chongyang's] Ancestral Hall in Zhongnan Mountains). Li Daoqian 李道謙 (1219-1296). DZ 955, fasc. 604.

Secondary Sources

Akizuki, Kan'ei 秋月觀暎. 1978. *Chūgoku kinsei dōkyō no keisei: Jōmyōdō no kisoteki kenkyū* 中國近世道教の形成：浄明道の基礎的研究. Tokyo: Sōbunsha.

Andersen, Poul. 2004. Sanhuang neiwen yibi 三皇內文遺祕. In *The Taoist Canon*, edited by K. Schipper and Verellen Franciscus. Chicago & London: The University of Chicago Press: vol. 1, 977.

Andersen, Poul, and Florian Reiter. 2005. *Scriptures, Schools and Forms of Practices in Daoism: A Berlin Symposium*. Wiesbaden: Harrassowitz.

App, Urs. 2010. *The Birth of Orientalism*. Philadelphia: University of Pennsylvania Press.

Baldrian-Hussein, Farzeen. 2008. Liu Huayang. In *The Encyclopedia of Taoism*, edited by F. Pregadio. London / New York: Routledge. Vol. 1: 688–689.

Baynes, C. F. (tr.). 1931. *The Secret of the Golden Flower: A Chinese Book of Life*. London: Kegan Paul, Trench, Trubner and Co.

Benn, Charles. 2000. Daoist Ordination and Zhai rituals. In *Daoism Handbook*, edited by L. Kohn. Leiden: Brill: 309–339.

Berling, Judith A. 1980. *The Syncretic Religion of Lin Chao-en*. New York: Columbia University.

Billeter, Jean François. 2004. *Leçons sur le Tchouang-tseu*. Paris: Allia.

———. 2004. *Études sur Tchouang-tseu*. Paris: Allia.

Bodiford, William M. 2006. Remembering Dōgen: Eiheiji and Dōgen Hagiography. *Journal of Japanese Studies* 32.1:1–21.

Bokenkamp, Stephen. 2008. Wupian zhenwen. In *The Encyclopedia of Taoism*, edited by F. Pregadio. London / New York: Routledge. Vol. 2: 1060–1062.

Boltz, Judith M. 1987. *A Survey of Taoist Literature*. Berkeley: Institute of East Asian Studies University of California.

———. 2008. Daozang jinghua lu. In *The Encyclopedia of Taoism*, edited by F. Pregadio. London / New York: Routledge. Vol. 2: 340–341.

———. 2008. Daozang and subsidiary compilations. In *The Encyclopedia of Taoism*, edited by F. Pregadio. London: Routledge. Vol. 1: 28–33.

———. 2009. On the Legacy of Zigu and a Manual on Spirit writing in Her Name. In *The People and the Dao. New Studies in Chinese Religions in Honor of Daniel L. Overmyer*, edited by P. Clart and P. Crowe. Nettetal: Steyler: 349–388.

Bretschneider, Emil. 1888. *Si Yu Ki: Travels to the West of K'iu Ch'ang Ch'un. Medieval Researches from Eastern Asiatic Sources* London: Kegan Paul, Trench, Trubner & Co. Reprint: Routledge, 2000.

Brinker, Helmut, and Hiroshi Kanazawa. 1996. *Zen Masters of Meditation in Images and Writings*. Zürich: Artibus Asia Publishers, Supplementum 40.

Brokaw, Cynthia J. 2007. *Commerce in Culture: The Sibao Book Trade in the Qing and Republican Periods*. Cambridge, MA: Harvard University Press.

Brook, Timothy. 1993. Rethinking Syncretism: The Unity of the Three Teachings and Their Joint Worship in Late-imperial China. *Journal of Chinese Religions* 21:13–44.

———. 1997. At the Margin of Public Authority: The Ming State and Buddhism. In *Culture & State in Chinese History*, edited by T. H. Huters, B. R. Wong and P. Yu. Stanford, CA: Stanford University Press: 161–181.

Chen, Bing 陳兵. 1988. Qingdai Quanzhen dao Longmen pai de zhongxing 清代全真道龍門派的中興. *Shijie zongjiao yanjiu* 世界宗教研究 2:84–96.

Chen, Kangqi 陳康祺 1984. Langqian jiwen chubi erbi sanbi 郎潛紀聞初筆二筆三筆. In *Qingdai shiliao biji congkan* 清代史料筆記叢刊. Beijing: Zhonghua shuju.

Chen, William. 1987. *A Guide to Tao-tsang Chi Yao*. Stony Brook N.Y.: The Institute for Advanced Studies of World Religion.

Chen, Yuan 陳垣 and Chen, Zhichao 陳智超. 1988. *Daojia jinshi lüe* 道家金石略, ed. by. Beijing: Wenwu chubanshe.

Cleary, Thomas (tr.). 1991. *The Secret of the Golden Flower: The Classic Chinese Book of Life*. San Francisco: Harper San Francisco.

D'Elia, Pasquale M. (ed.). 1942. *Storia dell'introduzione del Cristianesimo in Cina* (Fonti Ricciane, Part I, Books 1-3). Rome: La Libreria dello Stato.

Despeux, Catherine. 1986. L'ordination des femmes taoïstes sous les Tang. *Études chinoises* V (no. 1–2): 53–100.

———. 1988. *La moelle du phénix rouge: santé et longue vie dans la Chine du XVIe siècle*. Paris: Guy Trédaniel.

Ding, Changchun 丁常春. 2005. Chengdu Erxian'an lishi yange 成都二仙菴歷史沿革. *Hongdao* 弘道 24 (2005.3): 92–97.

Ding, Fubao 丁福保. 1922. *Daozang jinghua lu* 道藏精華錄 (*Record of Quintessence of the Daoist Canon*). 2 vols. Shanghai: Yixue shuju.

Ding, Fubao 丁福保 (ed.). 1952. *Daozang xubian chuji* 道藏續編初集. Shanghai: Yixue shuju.

Ding, Peiren 丁培仁. 1996. *Daojiao dianji baiwen* 道教典籍百問. Beijing: Jinri Zhongguo.

———. 2006. Daojiao jielü shu kaoyao 道教戒律書考要. *Zongjiaoxue yanjiu* 宗教學研究 2: 4–23.

———. 2008. Jingai xindeng juan yi zhiyi 金蓋心燈卷一質疑 [Questions on the first juan of the Jingai xindeng]. *Daojia wenhua yanjiu* 道家文化研究 23: 411–29.

Dou, Zhen 竇鎮 (ed.). 1971. *Guochao shuhuajia bilu* 國朝書畫家筆錄. Taipei: Wenshizhe chubanshe.

Du, Jiexiang 杜潔祥 (ed.). 1983. *Daojiao wenxian* 道教文獻. 20 vols. Taipei: Danqing tushu youxian gongsi.

Du, Zong 杜琮, and Zhang Chaozhong 張超中. 1996. *Huangting jing jinyi Taiyi jinhua zongzhi jinyi* 黃庭經今譯・太乙金華宗旨今譯. Beijing: Zhongguo Shehui Kexueyuan chubanshe 中國社會科學院出版社.

Duara, Prasenjit. 1991. Knowledge and Power in the Discourse of Modernity: The Campaigns Against Popular Religion in Early Twentieth-Century China. *Journal of Asian Studies* 50.1: 67–83.

———. 2003. *Sovereignty and Authenticity: Manchukuo and the East Asian Modern*. Lanham: Rowman & Littlefield.

Elman, Benjamin A. 1984. *From Philosophy to Philology: Intellectual and Social Aspects of Change in Late Imperial China*. Cambridge, Mass.: Harvard University Press.

———. 1997. The Formation of 'Dao Learning' as Imperial Ideology During the Early Ming Dynasty. In *Culture & State in Chinese History*, edited by T. H. Huters, B. R. Wong and P. Yu. Stanford, CA: Stanford University Press: 58–82.

Eskildsen, Stephen. 2004. *The Teachings and Practices of the Early Quanzhen Taoist Masters*. Albany: State University of New York Press.

Esposito, Monica (莫尼卡). 1993. *La Porte du Dragon—L'école Longmen du Mont Jin'gai et ses pratiques alchimiques d'après le Daozang xubian*. Paris: Université Paris VII Ph.D. thesis. PDF edition containing the author's notes and corrections: UniversityMedia, 2012 (available at www.universitymedia.org).

———. 1995. *Il Qigong—La nuova scuola taoista delle cinque respirazioni*. Padova: Muzzio.

———. 1996. Il Segreto del Fiore d'Oro e la tradizione Longmen del Monte Jingai. In *Conoscenza e interpretazione della civiltà cinese*, edited by P. Corradini. Venice: Ca' Foscarina: 151–169.

———. 1997. *L'alchimia del soffio: la pratica della visione interiore nell'alchimia taoista*. Rome: Astrolabio / Ubaldini.

———. 1998. The Different Versions of the Secret of the Golden Flower and Their Relationship with the Longmen School. *Transactions of the International Conference of Eastern Studies* 43: 90–109.

———. 2000. Daoism in the Qing (1644–1911). In *Daoism Handbook*, edited by L. Kohn. Leiden: Brill: 623–658. Corrected and augmented edition in Esposito 2014c, *Facets of Qing Daoism*, chapter 1.

———. 2001. Longmen Taoism in Qing China: Doctrinal Ideal and Local Reality. *Journal of Chinese Religions* 29:192–231. Corrected and augmented edition in Esposito 2014c, *Facets of Qing Daoism*, chapter 3.

———. 2004a. The Longmen School and its Controversial History during the Qing Dynasty. In *Religion and Chinese Society*, edited by J. Lagerwey. Hong Kong / Paris: Chinese University Press and EFEO: 621–698. Revised and augmented edition in Esposito 2014c, *Facets of Qing Daoism*, chapter 2.

———. 2004b. Shindai ni okeru Kingai-san no seiritsu to Kinka shūshi 清代における金蓋山の成立と金華宗旨 (The Secret of the Golden Flower and the Establishment of the Longmen Tradition at Mount Jingai during the Qing Dynasty). In *Chūgoku shūkyō bunken kenkyū kokusai shinpojiumu hōkokusho* 中国宗教文献研究国際シンポジ

ウム報告書, edited by T. Takata 高田時雄. Kyoto: Jinbun Kagaku Kenkyūjo: 259–268. Revised and augmented English version in Esposito, *Creative Daoism*, Part 4.

———. 2004c. Gyakuten shita zō—jotan no shintai kan 逆転した像－女丹の身体觀. In Sakade Yoshinobu sensei taikyū kinen ronshū kankō kai 坂祥伸先生退休記念論集刊行会 (ed.), *Chūgoku shisō ni okeru shintai, shizen, shinkō* 中国思想における身体．自然．信仰 [Body, nature, and religious beliefs in Chinese thought] (A volume dedicated to Professor Yoshinobu Sakade), 113–129. Tokyo: Tōhō shoten 東方書店. Revised and augmented English version in Esposito 2014c, *Facets of Qing Daoism*, chapter 4.

———. 2005. Shindai dōkyō to mikkyō: Ryūmon seijiku shinshū 清代道教と密教—龍門西竺心宗 (An Example of Daoist and Tantric Interaction during the Qing Dynasty: The Longmen Heart Lineage of Western India). In *Sankyō kōshō ronsō* 三教交渉論叢, edited by K. Mugitani 麥谷邦夫. Kyoto: Kyōto Daigaku Jinbun Kagaku Kenkyūjo 京都大学人文科学研究所: 287–338. Revised and augmented English version in Esposito 2014c, *Facets of Qing Daoism*, chapter 5.

———. 2006. Daozang jiyao ji qi bianzuan de lishi—Shijie Qingdai Daozang suoshou daojing shumu wenti 道藏輯要及其編纂的歷史—試解清代道藏所收道經書目問題 (The History of the Compilation of the *Daozang jiyao*—Solving its Numbering Problem). In *First International Academic Symposium of Taoist Literature and its Path to Immortality* 第一屆道教仙道文化國際學術研討會. Gaoxiong, Zhongshan University, November 10–12, 2006.

———. 2007a. Shindai ni okeru Kingai-san Ryūmon-ha no seiritsu to Kinka shūshi 清代における金蓋山龍門派の設立と『金華宗旨』 [The Secret of the Golden Flower and the establishment of the Longmen tradition at Mt. Jingai during the Qing dynasty] (revised version). In *Chūgoku shūkyō bunken kenkyū* 中国宗教文献研究, edited by Kyōto Daigaku Jinbun Kagaku Kenkyūjo 京都大学人文科学研究所. Kyoto: Rinsen shoten 臨川書店: 239–264. Revised and augmented English version in Esposito, *Creative Daoism*, Part 4.

———. 2007b. The Discovery of Jiang Yuanting's *Daozang jiyao* in Jiangnan: A Presentation of the Daoist Canon of the Qing Dynasty. In *Kōnan dōkyō no kenkyū* 江南道教の研究, edited by K. Mugitani 麥谷邦夫. Kyoto: Jinbun Kagaku Kenkyūjo: 79–110. Revised and augmented version in Esposito, *Creative Daoism*, Part 3.

———. 2008a. Taiyi jinhua zongzhi 太一金華宗旨. In *The Encyclopedia of Taoism*, edited by F. Pregadio. London / New York: Routledge. Vol. 2: 961–962.

———. 2008b. Min Yide. In *The Encyclopedia of Taoism*, edited by F. Pregadio. London / New York: Routledge. Vol 2: 747–748.

———. 2008c. Daozang xubian. In *The Encyclopedia of Taoism*, edited by F. Pregadio. London / New York: Routledge. Vol 1: 347–350.

———. 2008d. Lüzu quanshu. In *The Encyclopedia of Taoism*, edited by F. Pregadio. London / New York: Routledge. Vol 1: 726–728.

———. 2008e. Huiming jing. In *The Encyclopedia of Taoism*, edited by F. Pregadio. London / New York: Routledge. Vol 1: 520–521.

———. 2008f. rDzogs chen in China: From Chan to Tibetan Tantrism in Fahai Lama's (1921–1991) footsteps. In Monica Esposito (ed.), *Images of Tibet in the 19th and 20th Centuries*, Paris: École française d'Extrême-Orient, Collection Thématique no. 22, vol. 2, 473–548 (revised and augmented edition in Monica Esposito, 2013a. *The Zen of Tantra*. Wil / Paris: UniversityMedia).

———. 2009a. Yibu Quanzhen Daozang de faming: *Daozang jiyao* ji Qingdai Quanzhen rentong 一部全真道藏的發明：道藏輯要及清代全真認同. In *Wendao Kunyushan* 問道昆崙山, edited by Zhao Weidong 趙衛東. Jinan: Qilu shushe: 303–343. Revised and augmented English version in Goossaert, Vincent, and Xun Liu (eds.). *Quanzhen Daoism in Modern Chinese History and Society*. Berkeley: Institute of East Asian Studies; see 2014b.

———. 2009b. The Daozang Jiyao Project: Mutations of a Canon. *Daoism: Religion, History and Society* 1: 95–153.

———. 2009c. The Daozang jiyao Project and the Future of Daoist Studies. In *International Conference "New Approaches to the Study of Daoism in Chinese Culture and Society"*, Chinese University of Hong Kong, 26–28 November 2009 (Forthcoming in Lai Chi Tim & Cheung Neky Tak-ching, *New Approaches to the Study of Daoism in Chinese Culture and Society*, Hong Kong: Chinese University Press).

———. 2010a. Qingdai Quanzhen jiao zhi chonggou: Min Yide ji qi jianli Longmen zhengtong de yiyuan 清代全真教之重構：閔一得及其建立龍門正統得意願. Paper presented at the International Quanzhen conference 探古監今 – 全真道的昨天,今天與明天. Hong Kong, January 6–8, 2010.

———. 2010b. Qingdai Daozang—Jiangnan Jiang Yuanting ben *Daozang jiyao* zhi yanjiu 清代道藏—江南蔣元庭本道藏輯要之研. In *Zongjiaoxue yanjiu* 宗教學研究 (2010.3): 17–27 (Chinese translation of Esposito 2007b). Revised and augmented English version in Esposito, *Creative Daoism*, Part 3, chapters 1 and 2.

———. 2011a. Shindai dōkyō ni okeru sankyō no hōko to shite no Dōzō shuyō—Zaike shinto to seishokusha no ken'i no taiji 清代における三教の寶庫としての《道藏輯要》—在家信徒と聖職の權威の對峙. [*Daozang jiyao*: The Last Qing Daoist Canon as Receptacle of the Three Teachings: Lay and Clerical Authorities Face to Face], in Kunio Mugitani 麥谷邦夫, *Sankyō kōshō ronsō zokuhen* 三教交涉論叢續編, Kyoto: Kyoto daigaku jinbun kagaku kenkyūjo: 431–469. Revised English version in Esposito, *Creative Daoism*, Part 3, chapters 3–5.

———. 2011b. Qingdai quanzhen santan dajie yishi de chuangli 清代全真三壇大戒儀式的創立 [The Creation of the Quanzhen Ordination of the Threefold Altars in Qing Daoism], in Zhao Weidong 趙衛東 (ed.), *Quanzhendao yanjiu* 全真道研究 II, Jinan: Qilu shushe, 204–220. See the substantially augmented argument in Esposito, *Creative Daoism*, Part 2.

———. 2013a. *The Zen of Tantra*. Wil / Paris: UniversityMedia.

———. 2013b. *Creative Daoism*. Wil / Paris: UniversityMedia.

———. 2014a. *Facets of Qing Daoism*. Wil / Paris: UniversityMedia.

———. 2014b. The Invention of a Quanzhen Canon: The Wondrous Fate of the Daozang jiyao. In Goossaert, Vincent, and Xun Liu (eds.), *Quanzhen Daoism in Modern Chinese History and Society*. Berkeley: Institute of East Asian Studies. Berkeley: Institute of East Asian Studies: 44–77.

Fan, Guangchun 樊光春. 2012. Urban Daoism, Commodity Markets, and Tourism. The Restoration of the Xian City God Temple. In: Palmer, David A., and Xun Liu (eds.), *Daoism in the Twentieth Century. Between Eternity and Modernity*. Berkeley: University of California Press: 108–122.

Fang, Ling 方玲. 2014. Quanzhen Daoism and Zhuyou 祝由 Ritual Medicine. In Goossaert, Vincent, and Xun Liu (eds.). *Quanzhen Daoism in Modern Chinese History and Society*. Berkeley: Institute of East Asian Studies.

Feng, Guanghong 馮廣宏 (tr.). 1995. *Taiyi jinhua zongzhi jinyi* 太乙金華宗旨今譯. Chengdu: Sichuan Kexue jishu chubanshe.

Feuchtwang, Stephan. 1992. *The Imperial Metaphor*. London: Routledge.

Fo Kuang shan. 1989. *The Sixth Patriarch Platform Sūtra in Religious and Cultural Perspective*. Taichong: Fo Kuang shan.

Foulk, Griffith T. 1998. The Ch'an Tsung in Medieval China: School, Lineage, or What? *The Pacific World*, New Series No. 8: 18–31.

Funayama, Tōru 船山徹. 2004. Guṇavarman and Some of the Earliest Examples of Ordination Platforms (jietan) in China. In *Images, Relics and Legends: Formation and Transformation of Buddhist Sacred Sites*. University of British Columbia, October 15–16, 2004.

Funayama, Tōru 船山徹, and Yoshikawa Tadao 吉川忠夫 (tr.). 2009–2010. *Kōsōden* 高僧伝. 4 vols. Tokyo: Iwanami bunko.

Goodrich, L. Carrington, and Chaoying (eds.) Fang. 1976. *Dictionary of Ming Biography, 1368–1644*. New York: Columbia University.

Goossaert, Vincent. 1997. *La création du Taoïsme moderne—l'ordre Quanzhen*. Paris: École Pratique des Hautes Études, Section des Sciences Religieuses (Ph.D. thesis).

———. 2004. Bureaucratic Charisma: The Zhang Heavenly Master Institution and Court Taoists in Late-Qing China. *Asia Major* 3rd series 17.2:121–159.

———. 2007. *The Taoists of Peking, 1800–1949*. Cambridge (Mass.): Harvard University Press.

———. 2010. Bureaucracie, taxation et justice: Taoïsme et construction de l'État au Jiangnan (Chine), XVIIe–XIXe siècle. *Annales HHS* 4: 999–1027.

Goossaert, Vincent, and Xun Liu (eds.). 2014. *Quanzhen Daoism in Modern Chinese History and Society*. Berkeley: Institute of East Asian Studies.

Gōyama, Kiwamu 合山究. 1994. Min-Shin no bunjin to okaruto shumi 明清の文人とオカルト趣味. In *Chūka bunjin no seikatsu* 中華文人の生活, edited by K. 荒. Arai. Tokyo: Heibonsha: 469–502.

Groner, Paul. 1989. The Ordination Ritual in the Platform Sūtra within the context of the East Asian Buddhist Vinaya Tradition. In *The Sixth Patriarch Platform Sūtra in Religious and Cultural Perspective*. Taichong: Fo Kuang shan: 220–250.

Hackmann, Heinrich. 1920. Die Mönchsregeln des Klostertaoismus. *Ostasiatische Zeitschrift* 8:141–170.

———. 1931. *Die dreihundert Mönchsgebote des chinesischen Taoismus*. Amsterdam: Koninklijke Akademie van Wetenshapen.

Henderson, John. 1998. *The Construction of Orthodoxy and Heresy: Neo-Confucian, Islamic, Jewish, and early Christian patterns*. New York: University of State Press.

Hobsbawn, Eric. 1983. Introduction: Inventing Traditions. In *The Invention of Tradition*, edited by E. Hobsbawn and T. Ranger. Cambridge: Cambridge University Press: 1–14.

Hong, Baijian 洪百堅. n.d. Daozang jiyao 道藏輯要. *Daojiao xueshu zixun wangzhan* 道教學術資訊網站, http://www.ctcwri.idv.tw/IndexD2/D2-13/066-127/13102/071-137/109.htm.

Hummel, Arthur (ed.). 1943–44. *Eminent Chinese of the Ch'ing Period (1644–1912)*. 2 vols. Washington, DC: U.S. Government Printing Office.

Igarashi, Kenryū 五十嵐賢隆. 1938. *Dōkyō sōrin taiseikyū shi* 道教叢林太清宮志. Tokyo: Kokusho kankōkai 国書刊行会.

Ishida, Kenji 石田憲司. 1992. Mingdai Dōkyō shijō no Zenshin to Seii 明代道教史上の全真と正一 Taiwan no shūkyō to Chūgoku. In *Taiwan no shūkyō to Chūgoku bunka* 台湾の宗教と中国文化, edited by T. Sakai. 酒井忠夫. Tokyo: Fukyūsha: 145–185.

Kakiuchi, Tomoyuki 垣内智之 and Noriko Ikehira 池平紀子. 2011. *Dōzō shuyō hanpon kō* 道蔵輯要版本考 (Considerations about Daozang jiyao versions). In Kunio Mugitani 麥谷邦夫 (ed.), *Dōzō shuyō to meishin jidai no shūkyō bunka* 道蔵輯要と明清時代の宗教文化 (The *Daozang jiyao* and the religious culture of the Ming and Qing eras). Kyoto: Kyoto University Institute for Humanistic Studies (Jinbun kagaku kenkyūjo), JSPS research report no. 20242001: 271–442.

Jordan, David K., and Daniel Overmyer. 1986. *The Flying Phoenix: Aspects of Chinese Sectarianism in Taiwan*. Princeton: Princeton University Press.

Jorgensen, John. 2005. *Inventing Hui-neng, the Sixth Patriarch. Hagiography and Biography in Early Ch'an*. Leiden / Boston: Brill.

Katz, Paul. 2001. Writing History, Creating Identity: A Case Study of Xuanfeng qinghui tu. *Journal of Chinese Religions* 29:161–189.

———. 2008. Wang lingguan (Numinous Officer Wang 王靈官) or Marshal Wang (Wang Yuanshuai 王元帥). In *The Encyclopedia of Taoism*, edited by F. Pregadio. London: Routledge. Vol. 2: 1013–1014.

———. 2011. Zhongguo dizhi wanqi yijiang shimiao yishi zai difang shehui de gongneng 中國帝制晚期以降寺廟儀式在地方社會的功能. In *Zhongguoshi xinlun—Zongjiaoshe fence* 中國史新論—宗教史分冊, edited by Lin Fushi 林富士. Taipei: Lianjing chuban gongsi: 439–476.

Kieschnick, John. 1997. *The Eminent Monk Buddhist Ideals in Medieval Chinese Hagiography*. Honolulu: University of Hawai'i.

———. 1999. The Symbolism of the Monk's Robe in China. *Asia Major* 12 (1):9–32

Kim, Yunsu 金侖壽. 2002. Dojang jipyo wa Jang Yoepo 道藏輯要와 蔣予蒲. *Dogyo Munhwa Yoengu* 道教文化研究 17:277–316.

Kohn, Livia. 2003a. Monastic Rules in Quanzhen Daoism: As Collected by Heinrich Hackmann. *Monumenta Serica 51* 51:367–397.

———. 2003b. *Monastic Life in Medieval Daoism*. Honolulu: University of Hawai'i Press.

———. 2004a. *Cosmos and Community*. Cambridge, MA: Three Pines Press.

———. 2004b. Translation of the Zhongji jie based on Hackmann's work in the Supplement to Cosmos and Community (electronic publication, 2004).

———. 2008. *Chinese Healing Exercises. The Tradition of Daoyin*. Honolulu: University of Hawai'i Press.

Kohn, Livia, and Harold D. Roth. 2000. *Daoist Identity*. Honolulu: University of Hawai'i Press.

Kohn, Livia (ed.). 2000. *Daoism Handbook*. Leiden: Brill.

Komjathy, Louis. 2002. *Title Index to Daoist Collections*. Magdalena, NM: Three Pines Press.

———. 2007. *Cultivating Perfection: Mysticism and Self-transformation in Early Quanzhen Daoism*. Leiden: Brill.

Lagerwey, John. 2004. Abstract on the Dongxuan lingbao sanyuan wuliangshou jing 太上洞玄靈寶三元無量壽經 (DZ 323). In *The Taoist Canon*, edited by K. Schipper and Verellen Franciscus (eds.). Chicago: Chicago University Press. Vol. 1: 534–535.

Lai, Chi-tim. 2003. Daoism in China Today, 1980–2002. *The China Quarterly* 174: 413–427.

Lancaster, Lewis. 1979. Introduction. In *The Korean Buddhist Canon: a Descriptive Catalog*. Berkeley: University of California Press: ix–xvii.

Li, Gang 李剛. "Daozang jiyao 道藏輯要." *Daojiao wenhua ziliaoku* 道教文化資料庫, http://www.taoism.org.hk/taoist-scriptures/taoist-canon/pg4-1-4-3.htm.

Li, Hechun 李合春, and Ding Changchun 丁常春. 2006. *Qingyanggong Erxian'an zhi* 青羊宮二仙菴誌. Chengdu: Sichuansheng Xinwen chubanju.

Li, Yangzheng 李養正. 1993. *Daojiao shouce* 道教手冊. Zhengzhou: Zhongzhou guji.

———. (ed.). 2000. *Dangdai daojiao* 當代道教 Beijing: Dongfang chubanshe 東方出版社.

———. 2003. *Xinbian Beijing Baiyun guan zhi* 新編北京白雲觀志. Beijing: Zongjiao wenhua chubanshe.

Liu, Houhu 劉厚祜. 1980. Baiyun guan yu daojiao 白雲觀與道教. *Dao xiehui kan* 道協會刊 6 (1980/11): 16–41.

Liu, Huanling 劉煥玲. 2005. Shixi Min Yide zhi Longmen Fangbian famen 試析閔一得之龍門方便法門. *Zhongguo daojiao* (2005.5), http://big5.chinataoism.org/showtopic.php?id=9370.

Liu, Tishu 劉體恕 (ed.). 1868. *Lüzu quanshu* 呂祖全書. Edition of 1868 (with a Preface added in 1879) in 33 juan (including the Chanzong zhengzhi 禪宗正指) from the woodblocks stored at the Xiangtan Chongshantang 湘潭崇善堂藏板 (Library of Kyoto University's Institute for Research in Humanities).

Liu Ts'un-yan 柳存仁. 1973. The Compilation and Historical Value of the Tao-tsang. In *Essays on the Sources of Chinese History*, edited by D. D. Leslie, C. M. Mackerras and G. Wang. Canberra: Australian National University Press: 104–119.

Liu, Xun. 2004. Visualizing Perfection: Daoist Paintings of Our Lady, Court Patronage, and Elite Female Piety in the Late Qing. *Harvard Journal of Asiatic Studies* 64.1: 57–115.

———. 2006. General Zhang buries the bones: early Qing reconstruction and Quanzhen Daoist collaboration in mid-seventeenth century Nanyang. *Late Imperial China* 27.2 (Dec. 2006): 67–98.

———. 2009. *Daoist Modern Innovation, Lay Practice and the Community of Inner Alchemy in Republican Shanghai.* Cambridge, Mass.: Harvard University Press.

Liu, Xun and Vincent Goossaert (eds.). 2014. *Quanzhen Daoism in Modern Chinese History and Society.* Berkeley: Institute of East Asian Studies.

Liu, Zhongyu 劉仲宇. 2008. On the Rituals of Quanzhen Daoism in its Early Stage 早期全真教仪式初探. *Daojia wenhua yanjiu* 道家文化研究 23: 144–166.

Ma, Xiaohong 馬曉宏. 1988. Daozang deng zhuben suoshou Lü Dongbin shumu jianzhu 道藏等诸本所收吕洞宾书目简注. *Zhongguo daojiao* 中国道教 1988.3: 34–37.

Marsone, Pierre. 1999. Le Baiyun guan de Pékin: épigraphie et histoire. *Sanjiao wenxian* 3: 73–113.

McRae, John R. 2005. Daoxuan's Vision of Jetavana: The Ordination Platform Movement in Medieval Chinese Buddhism. In *Going Forth: Visions of Buddhist Vinaya*, edited by W. M. Bodiford. Honolulu: University of Hawai'i Press: 68–100.

Min, Zhiting 閔智亭. 1990. *Daojiao yifan* 道教儀範. Beijing: Zhongguo daojiao xueyuan.

Minorelli, Tommaso Maria, and Charles Maigrot. 1714. *Examen des faussetez sur les cultes chinois, Avancées par le Pere Joseph Jouvenci Jesuite, dans l'Histoire de la Compagnie de Jesus.* Paris.

Miura, Kunio 三浦邦夫. 1989. The Revival of Qi: Qigong in Contemporary China. In *Taoist Meditation and Longevity Techniques*, edited by L. Kohn. Ann Arbor: The University of Michigan: 331–362.

Miura, Shūichi 三浦秀一. 1992. Gendai shisō kenkyū josetsu: Zenshin dōshi Ri Dōken no dōkō o shujiku ni 元代思想研究序說—全真道士李道謙の動向を主軸に" [A preliminary study of Yuan thought, based on the stance of the Quanzhen master Li Daoqian]. *Shūkan tōyōgaku* 集刊東洋學 67: 66–84.

Miyuki, Mokusen 目幸黙僊. 1967. *The Secret of the Golden Flower, Studies and Translation.* Zürich: C.G. Jung-Institute (Diploma thesis).

———. 1972. *Kreisen des Lichtes. Die Erfahrung der Goldenen Blüte.* München: Otto Wilhelm Barth Verlag.

Mori, Yuria 森由利亞. 1998. Taiitsu kinka shūshi no seiritsu to hensen 太乙金華宗旨の成立と変遷. *Tōyō no shisō to shūkyō* 東洋の思想と宗教 15: 43–64.

———. 1999. Ryo Dōhin to Zenshin-kyō: Shinchō koshū Kingai-san no jirei o chūshin ni 呂洞賓と全真教—清朝湖州金蓋山の事例を中心に. In *Dōkyō no kamigami to kyōten* 道教の神々と経典, edited by Kikuchi Noritaka 野口鐵郎. Tokyo: Yūzan kaku: 242–264.

———. 2000. Identity and Lineage—The Taiyi jinhua zongzhi and the Spirit writing Cult to Patriarch Lü in Qing China. In *Daoist Identity*, edited by L. Kohn and H. D. Roth. Honolulu: University of Hawai'i Press: 165–184.

———. 2001. Dōzo shūyō to Shō Yobu no Ryoso fukei shinkō 道蔵輯要と蔣予蒲の呂祖扶乩信仰. *Tōhō shūkyō* 東方宗教 98:33–52.

———. 2002. Identity and Lineage: The Taiyi jinhua zongzhi and the Spirit writing Cult to Patriarch Lü in Qing China. In *Daoist Identity: History, Lineage, and Ritual*, edited by L. Kohn and H. D. Roth. Honolulu: University of Hawai'i Press: 168–187.

———. 2004. Mingdai Quanzhendao yu zuobo 明代全真道于坐缽." In *Quanzhen hongdao ji* 全真弘道集, edited by Quanzhendao yanjiu zhongxin 全真道研究中心. Hong Kong: Qingsong 青松 chubanshe: 126–142.

———. 2005. Shinchō Zenshinkyō no denkai to Ryoso fukei shinkō: Tensen kai no seiritsu wo megutte 清朝全真教の伝戒と呂祖扶乩信仰：天仙戒の成立をめぐって. In *Ajia bunka no shisō to girei* アジア文化の思想と儀礼, edited by Fukui Fumimasa hakushi taishoku kinen ronshū kankōkai 福井文雅博士古稀・退職記念論集刊行会. Tokyo: Shunjūsha 春秋社: 441–461.

———. 2006. Shō Yoho no Ryoso fukei shinkō to Zenshinkyō 蔣予蒲の呂祖扶乩信仰と全真教. In *Dōkyō kenkyū no saisentan* 道教研究の最先端, edited by Horiike Nobuo 堀池信夫 and Sunayama Minoru 砂山稔. Tokyo: Taiga shobō 大川書房.

———. 2006. Shinchō shisen no Zenshinkyō to Tenshidō girei: Kōsei gisei taiseishō wo megutte 清朝四川の全真教と天師道儀禮：『廣成儀制』太清章をめぐって. In *Dōkyō no saishō girei no sisōshiteki kenkyū* 道教の齋法儀禮の思想史的研究, edited by Kobayashi Masayoshi 小林正美. Tokyo: Chisen shoin: 137–84.

———. 2007. Chōkan Dōzō shūyō to Shinchō Shisen chiiki no shūkyō 重刊道藏輯要と清朝四川地域の宗教. In *Chūgoku koseki ryūtsūgaku no kakuritsu: ryūtsū suru koseki, ryūtsū suru bunka* 中國古籍流通學の確立：流通する古籍・流通する文化, edited by Okazaki Yumi 岡崎由美. Tokyo: Yūzankaku shuppan: 339–401.

Motoyama, Hiroshi 本山博. 1964. *Taiitsu kinka shūshi: dōkyō chōjo yōjō hō* 太乙金華宗旨：道教長壽養生法. Tokyo: Shūkyō shinrigaku kenkyūjo 宗教心理學研究所.

Mugitani, Kunio 麥谷邦夫 (ed.). 2011. *Dōzō shūyō to meishin jidai no shūkyō bunka* 道藏輯要と明清時代の宗教文化 (The *Daozang jiyao* and the religious culture of the Ming and Qing eras). Kyoto: Kyoto University Institute for Humanistic Studies (Jinbun kagaku kenkyūjo), Research report no. 20242001 for the Japan Society for the Promotion of Science (JSPS).

Naquin, Susan. 2000. *Peking and City Life 1400–1900*. Berkeley: University of California Press.

Needham, Joseph. 1983. The Secret of the Golden Flower unveiled. In *Science and Civilisation in China*, edited by J. Needham and G.-D. Lu. Cambridge: Cambridge University Press: Vol. V, part 5, 243–257.

Oyanagi, Shigeta 小柳司気太. 1934. *Hakuunkan shi* 白雲觀志. Tokyo: Tōhō bunka gakuin Tōkyō kenkyūsho 東方文化學院東京研究所.

Ozaki, Masaharu 尾崎正治. 1994. Dōzo shūyō 道藏輯要. In *Dōkyō jiten* 道教事典, edited by Noguchi Tetsurō 野口鐵郎 et al. Tokyo: Hirakawa shuppansha: 456–457.

Palmer, David A. 2007. *Qigong Fever: Body, Science, and Utopia in China*. New York: Columbia University Press.

Palmer, David A., and Xun Liu (eds.). 2012. *Daoism in the Twentieth Century. Between Eternity and Modernity*. Berkeley: University of California Press.

Peterson, Willard J. 1982. Making Connections: Commentary on the Attached Verbalizations of the Book of Changes. *Harvard Journal of Asiatic Studies* 42.2: 67–116.

Pregadio, Fabrizio (ed.). 2008. *The Encyclopedia of Taoism*. 2 vols. London / New York: Routledge.

Pregadio, Fabrizio. 2008. Daozang jiyao. In *The Encyclopedia of Taoism*, edited by F. Pregadio. London: Routledge. Vol. 1: 341–345.

Qing, Xitai 卿希泰. 1995. Chongkan Daozang jiyao (suoyinben) xu" 重刊道藏輯要（縮印本）序. In *Daozang jiyao* 道藏輯要. Chengdu: Bashu shushe: 1–3.

———. 1996. Chongkan Daozang jiyao (suoyinben) xu" 重刊道藏輯要（縮印本）序. *Zongjiaoxue yanjiu* 宗教學研究 31: 1–2.

———. 1996. *Zhongguo daojiao shi* 中國道教史. 4 vols. Chengdu: Sichuan renmin.

Ray, Reginald. 1994. *Buddhist Saints in India: A Study in Buddhist Values & Orientations*. Oxford: Oxford University Press.

Reiter, Florian. 2004. Lijiao shiwu lun (DZ 1233). In *The Taoist Canon*, edited by K. Schipper and F. Verellen. Chicago: The University of Chicago Press. Vol. 2: 1170.

Ren, Jiyu 任繼愈 (ed.). 1981. *Zongjiao dacidian* 宗教大詞典. Shanghai: Shanghai cishu.

———. 2001. *Zhongguo daojiao shi* 中國道教史. 2 vols. Beijing: Zhongguo Shehui kexue chubanshe.

Ren, Zongquan 任宗權. 2007. *Daojiao jielü xue* 道教戒律學. 2 vols. Beijing: Zongjiao wenhua chubanshe.

Ricci, Matteo. 1615. *De Christiana expeditione apud Sinas suscepta ab societate Jesu ex P. Matthaei Ricci eiusdem societatis commentariis*. Edited by N. Trigault. Agustae Vindecorum (Augsburg): C. Mangium.

———. 1616. *Histoire de l'expedition chrestienne au royaume de la Chine*. Edited by N. Trigault. Lyon: Horace Cardon.

Sadakata, Akio 湯浅泰雄, and Yuasa Yasuo 定方昭夫. 1980. *Ōgon no hana no himitsu* 黄金の華の秘密. Kyoto: Jinbun shoin 人文書院.

Sawada, Mizuhō 澤田瑞穂. 1975. *Zōhō hōkan non kenkyū* 増補寶卷の研究. Tokyo: Kokusho Kankōkai.

Schipper, Kristofer. 1985. Taoist Ordination Ranks in the Tunhuang Manuscripts. In *Religion und Philosophie in Ostasien*, edited by G. Naudorf, K.-H. Pohl and H.-H. Schmidt. Würzburg: Königshausen & Neumann: 127–148.

———. 1985. Taoist Ritual and Local Cults. In Michel Strickmann ed., *Tantric and Taoist Studies*. Bruxelles: Institut Belge des Hautes Études: 812–834.

———. 1987. Master Chao I-chen and the Ch'ing-wei School of Taoism. In *Dōkyō to shūkyō bunka* 道教と宗教文化, edited by Akizuki Kan'ei 秋月観英. Tokyo: Hirakawa: 715–734.

———. 1995. *Concordance du Tao-tsang (references to Zhengtong daozang* 正統道藏, *Taoist Canon of the Zhengtong era)*. Paris: Ecole Française d'Extrême-Orient.

Schipper, Kristofer, and Franciscus Verellen (eds.). 2004. *The Taoist Canon*. 3 vols. Chicago & London: The University of Chicago Press.

Seidel, Anna. 1970. A Taoist Immortal of the Ming Dynasty; Chang San-Feng. In *Self and Society in Ming Thought*, edited by W. T. de Bary. New York: Columbia University Press: 483–531.

———. 1990. *Taoismus: die inoffizielle Hochreligion Chinas*. Tokyo: Deutsche Gesellschaft für Natur- und Völkerkunde Ostasiens.

Shek, Richard. 2004. Daoism and Orthodoxy. The Loyal and Filial Sect. In *Heterodoxy in late Imperial China*, edited by R. Shek and K.-C. Liu. Honolulu: University of Hawai'i Press: 139–171.

Shi, Huidou 釋慧鐸 (secular name: Lin Yiluan 林一鑾). 2008. "Qing chu Suzhou Yutan de jiangluan yinghua — yi 'Yuquan' wei zhongxin" 清初蘇州玉壇的降鸞應化 — 以 玉詮 為中心. *Journal of Religion and Culture of National Cheng Kung University* 成大宗教與文化學報 11 (2008): 90–124.

———. 2009. *Peng Shaosheng (1740–1796) yu shendao shejiao zhi jiaoshe* 彭紹升(1740–1796) 與神道設教之交涉 (The Involvement of Peng Shaosheng (1740–1796) in Supernatural Revelations). Ph.D. thesis, Huafan University, Taipei 華梵大學東方人文思想研究所.

Shiga, Ichiko 志賀市子. 2003. *Chūgoku no kokkurisan: furan shinkō to kajin shakai* 中国のこっくりさん：扶鸞信仰と華人社会. Tokyo: Taishūkan shoten.

Shinohara, Kōichi. 1994. Passages and Transmission in Tianhuang Daowu's Biographies. In *Other Selves: Autobiography and Biography in Cross-Cultural Perspective*, edited by P. Granoff and K. Shinohara. Oakville: Mosaic Press: 132–149.

Snyder-Reinke, Jeffrey. 2009. *Dry Spells State Rainmaking and Local Governance in Late Imperial China*. Cambridge, Mass.: Harvard University Press.

Strickmann, Michel (ed.). 1985. *Tantric and Taoist Studies*. Bruxelles: Institut Belge des Hautes Études.

Suter, Rufus O. 1970. P'eng Ting-ch'iu. In *Eminent Chinese of the Ch'ing Period*, edited by A. W. Hummel. Taipei: Ch'eng wen Publishing Company: 616–617.

Tang, Dachao 唐大潮. 2000. *Ming-Qing zhi ji daojiao "sanjiao heyi" sixiang lun* 明清之際道教"三教合一"思想論. Beijing: Zongjiao wenhua chubanshe.

ter Haar, Barend. *Qigong movements* n.d. Available at http://website.leidenuniv.nl/~haarbjter/chinPRCbib.html.

———. *Falun Gong*. n.d. Available at http://website.leidenuniv.nl/~haarbjter/falun.htm.

———. 2009. Yongheng and His Buddhist Abbots. In *The People and the Dao. New Studies in Chinese Religions in Honor of Daniel L. Overmyer*, edited by P. Clart and Crowe Paul. Nettetal: Steyler: 435–480.

Tongxian 通仙. 1993. *Jinhua yangsheng mizhi yu fenxi xinlixue* 金華養生秘旨与分析心理學. Beijing: Xinhua shudian 新華書店.

Tsui, Bartholomew. 1991. *Taoist Tradition and Change: The Story of the Complete Perfection Sect in Hong Kong*. Hong Kong: Hong Kong Christian Study Center on Chinese Religion and Culture.

Valussi, Elena. 2008. Peng Dingqiu. In *The Encyclopedia of Taoism*, edited by F. Pregadio. London / New York: Routledge: 784–785.

———. 2008. Men and Women in He Longxiang's Nüdan hebian. *Nan Nü* 10:247–278.

Van Enckevort, Paul. 2014. Quanzhen and Longmen Identities in the Work of Wu Shouyang. In Goossaert, Vincent, and Xun Liu (eds.). *Quanzhen Daoism in Modern Chinese History and Society*. Berkeley: Institute of East Asian Studies. Berkeley: Institute of East Asian Studies.

Waley, Arthur. 1931. *Travels of an Alchemist: The Journey of the Taoist Ch'ang-ch'un to the Hindukush at the Summons of Chingiz Khan*. London: George Routledge & Sons, Ltd.

Wan, Dekai 万德凯. 2007. Daozang jiyao yanjiu 道藏辑要研究. In *Postdoctoral report*. Sichuan University, Summer 2007.

Wang, Jianchuan 王見川. 2005. Longhu shan Zhang Tianshi yu Huangdi

龍虎山張天師與皇帝. *Daotong zhi mei* 道統之美 3 (2005/11):84–109.

Wang, Kuipu 王魁溥. 1994. *Chunyang Lüzu gongli gongfa quanshi: Taiyi Jinhua zongzhi jinyi* 純陽呂祖功理功法詮釋: 太乙金華宗旨今譯. Beijing: Waiwen chubanshe 外文出版社.

Wang, Ka 王卡. 1995. Daozang jiyao. In *Zhongguo daojiao dacidian* 中國道教大辭典, edited by Fuchen Hu 胡孚琛. Beijing: Zhongguo shehui kexue.

Wang, Ka 王卡, and Wang Guiping 汪桂平. 2005. *Sandong shiyi* 三洞拾遺. 20 vols. Vol. 11. Hefei: Huangshan shushe 黃山書社.

Wang, Richard G. 2009. Ming Princes and Daoist Ritual. *T'oung Pao* 95: 51–119.

Wang, Shiu-hon. 1982. *Investigations into the Authenticity of the Chang San-Feng Ch'uan-Chi*. Canberra: Australian National University Press.

Wang, Zhizhong 王志忠. 2000. *Ming-Qing Quanzhen daojiao lungao* 明清全真道教論稿. Chengdu: Bashu shushe.

Wang, Zongyao 王宗耀. 2005. Min Yide shengnian kaoyi 閔一得生年考疑. *Zongguo daojiao* 中國道教 no. 5 (6): 46–47.

Wang, Zongyu 王宗昱. 2005. Historical Materials for the Quanzhen Daoism in the Wuxing Area. In *Scriptures, Schools and Forms of Practices in Daoism: A Berlin Symposium*, edited by P. Andersen and F. Reiter. Wiesbaden: Harrassowitz: 215–232.

———. 2006. Quanzhen jiao de rujiao chengfen 全真教的儒教成份. *Wenshi zhishi* 文史知識 12.

Watson, Burton. 1968. *The Complete Works of Chuang Tzu*. New York: Columbia University Press.

Watts, Alan. 1957. *The Way of Zen*. London: Thames & Hudson.

Weinstein, Stanley. 1989. The Schools of Chinese Buddhism. In *Buddhism and Asian History*, edited by Joseph M. Kitagawa. New York: Macmillan / London: Collier Macmillan: 257–267.

Welter, Albert. 1988. The Contextual Study of Chinese Buddhist Biographies: the Example of Yung-Ming Yen-Shou (904–975). In *Monks and Magicians: Religious Biographies in Asia*, edited by P. Granoff and K. Shinohara. Oakville: Mosaic Press: 247–68.

Weng, Dujian 翁獨健 1935. *Daozang zimu yinde* 道藏子目引得 (*Combined Indices to the Authors and Titles of Books in Two Collections of Daoist Literature*), Harvard-Yenching Institute Sinological Index Series no. 25. Beiping [Beijing]: Yenching University Library.

Wilhelm, Richard. 1929. *Das Geheimnis der Goldenen Blüte: ein chinesisches Lebensbuch. Mit dem Kommentar von C. G. Jung.* Munich: Dorn Verlag.

Wittern, Christian. 2010. Rebirth of the Daozang Jiyao—The never-ending Process of Creating a Digital Edition. In *Cultural Crossing*. University of Virginia, March 11–13, 2010.

Wu, Jiang. 2008. *Enlightenment in Dispute. The Reinvention of Chan Buddhism in Seventeenth-Century China.* Oxford / New York: Oxford University Press.

Wu, Yakui 吳亞魁. 2004. Jingaishan ren Min Yide zhuanlüe" 金蓋山人閔一得傳略. *Zongjiaoxue yanjiu* 宗教學研究 2004.3:139–148.

———. 2006. *Jiangnan Quanzhen daojiao* 江南全真道教. Hong Kong Zhonghua shuju 中華書局.

Xie, Zhengqiang 謝正強. 2004. Min Yide xiaogao erze 閔一得小考二則. *Zongguo daojiao* 中國道教 2004 (1):46–47.

Yamada, Toshiaki. 2008. Sanhuang wen. In *The Encyclopedia of Taoism*, edited by F. Pregadio. London: Routledge. Vol. 2: 837–839.

Yampolsky, Philip B. 1967. *The Platform Sutra of the Sixth Patriarch.* New York: Columbia University Press.

Yan, Yonghe 閻永和, Peng Hanran 彭瀚然, and He Longxiang 賀龍驤. 1906. *Chongkan Daozang jiyao* 重刊道藏輯要 (*Reedited Essence of the Daoist Canon*). 25 vols. Chengdu: Erxian an 二仙庵.

Yanagida, Seizan 柳田聖山. 2000. *Shoki zenshū shisho no kenkyū* 初級禪宗史書の研究. Vol. 6, *Yanagida Seizan shū* 柳田聖山集. Kyoto: Hōzōkan 法藏館.

———. 2001. *Zenbunken no kenkyū (jō)* 禪文獻の研究(上). Vol. 2, *Yanagida Seizan shū* 柳田聖山集. Kyoto: Hōzōkan 法藏館.

Yang, Haiying 楊海英. 2008. Qing qianqi de daojiao yu gongting 清前期的道教與宮廷. *Daojia wenhua yanjiu* 道家文化研究 23:365–410.

Yao, Tao-chung. 2000. Quanzhen: Complete Perfection. In *Daoism Handbook*, edited by L. Kohn. Leiden: Brill: 567–593.

Yin, Zhihua 尹志華. 2007. Wang Changyue chuanjie de xushu lishi 王常

月傳戒的敘述歷史. *Daojiao wenhua yanjiu zhongxin tongxun* 道教文化研究中心通訊 8: 1–2.

———. 2008. Qing tongzhi shiernian Beijing Baiyun guan chuanjie kaoshu (shang) 清同治十二年北京白雲觀傳戒考述(上). *Sanqin daojiao* 三秦道教 46: 31–34.

———. 2008. Qing tongzhi shiernian Beijing Baiyun guan chuanjie kaoshu (xia) 清同治十二年北京白雲觀傳戒考述(下). *Sanqin daojiao* 三秦道教 47: 34–37.

———. 2009. Beijing Baiyun guan zang Longmen chuanjie puxi chutan 北京白雲觀藏龍門傳戒譜系初探. *Shijie zongjiao yanjiu* 世界宗教研究 2: 72–82.

———. 2010. Qingdai Quanzhendao chuanjie chutan 清代全真道傳戒初探. Paper presented at the International Quanzhen Conference 探古監今 – 全真道的昨天,今天與明天. Hong Kong, January 6–8, 2010.

Yoshioka, Yoshitoyo 吉岡義豐. 1941. *Dōkyō no jittai* 道教の実態. Beijing: Xinmin yinshuguan 新民印書館.

———. 1955. *Dōkyō kyōten shiron* 道教經典史論. Tokyo: Dōkyō kankōkai.

Yü, Chün-fang. 1981. *The Renewal of Buddhism in China. Chu-hung and the Late Ming Synthesis*. New York: Columbia Univesity Press.

Zhang, Guangbao 張廣保. 2008. Jinyuan shiji Quanzhen jiaozu ting yanjiu" [The Quanzhen Patriarchal Halls during the Jin-Yuan period]. In *Daojia wenhua yanjiu 23*, edited by G. Chen: 52–143.

———. 2011. Mingdai Quanzhenjiao de zongxi fenhua yu paizi pude xingcheng 明代全真教的宗系分化與派字譜的形成. In Zhao Weidong 趙衛東 (ed.), *Quanzhen yanjiu* 全真研究(第1輯). Shizhong (Jinan): Qilu Press 齊魯书社.

———. 2014. Quanzhen Daoist Studies in China (1879–2007). In Goossaert, Vincent, and Xun Liu (eds.). *Quanzhen Daoism in Modern Chinese History and Society*. Berkeley: Institute of East Asian Studies. Berkeley: Institute of East Asian Studies.

Zhang, Yuanhe 張元和. Chongyin Daozang jiyao jishi 重印道藏輯要紀實. *Zhongguo daojiao xiewei wang* 中國道教協會網. Available at www.taoist.org.cn/daojiaozazhi/zgdj1/87-3/20.htm.

Zhang, Zehong 張澤洪. 1999. *Daojiao zhaijiao fuzhou yishi* 道教齋醮符咒儀式. Chengdu: Bashu shushe.

———. 2008. Jin Yuan Quanzhen jiao zhaijiao keyi chutan 金元全真教齋醮科儀初探. *Daojia wenhua yanjiu* 道家文化研究 23: 167–191.

Zhao, Zongcheng 趙宗誠. 1995. Daozang jiyao de bianzuan yu zengbu 道藏輯要的編纂與增補. *Sichuan wenwu* 四川文物 2: 27–31.

Zhongguo daojiao xiehui yanjiushi 中國道教協會研究室 (ed.). *Daojiao shi ziliao* 道教史資料. Shanghai: Guji chubanshe.

Zhou, Junfu 周駿富 (ed.). 1985. *Qingdai chuanji congkan* 清代傳記叢刊. Taipei: Mingwen shuju.

Zhu, Yueli 朱越利. 1991. *Daojing zonglun* 道經總論. Shenyang: Liaoning jiaoyi.

List of Publications by Monica Esposito

MONOGRAPHS

1987 *La pratica del Qigong in Cina. Introduzione ad una scuola contemporanea e ai suoi testi (con una traduzione del Wuxi chanwei, breve studio sulle cinque respirazioni)* [Qigong Practice in China. Introduction to a Contemporary School and its Texts (with a translation of the *Wuxi chanwei*, Succinct Presentation of the Five Respirations)]. M.A. thesis. Venice: Università degli Studi di Venezia, Facoltà di Lingue e Letterature Straniere.

1993 *La Porte du Dragon. L'école Longmen du Mont Jin'gai et ses pratiques alchimiques d'après le Daozang xubian (Suite au Canon Taoïste)* [The Dragon Gate. The Longmen School of Mt. Jingai and its Alchemical Practices according to the *Daozang xubian* (Supplementary Collection of the Daoist Canon)]. Ph. D. thesis (under the direction of Isabelle Robinet). Paris: University of Paris VII. (For emended PDF version of 2012 see here below)

1995 *Il Qigong, la nuova scuola taoista delle cinque respirazioni* [Qigong, the New Daoist School of Five Breaths]. Padova: Muzzio. ISBN 978-8-876694-74-5

1997 *L'alchimia del soffio: La pratica della visione interiore nell'alchimia taoista* [The Alchemy of Breath: The Practice of Inner Vision in Daoist Alchemy]. Rome: Astrolabio–Ubaldini. ISBN 978-8-834012-30-7

2012 *La Porte du Dragon—L'école Longmen du Mont Jin'gai et ses pratiques alchimiques d'après le Daozang xubian (Suite au canon taoïste)*. 2 vols. Ph. D. thesis, University Paris VII, 1993. Indexed PDF version with emendations and handwritten comments by the author and with English bookmarks for all chapters and subsections: Rorschach / Kyoto: UniversityMedia, 2012. Free download of both volumes at the address www.universitymedia.org/Esposito_PhD.html

Vol. 1: ISBN 978-3-906000-15-2, PDF, 86 MB

Vol. 2: ISBN 978-3-906000-16-9, PDF, 54 MB

2013 *Creative Daoism*. Wil / Paris: UniversityMedia. ISBN 978-3-906000-04-6 (hardcover)

2013 *The Zen of Tantra*. Wil / Paris: UniversityMedia. ISBN 978-3-906000-25-1

2014 *Facets of Qing Daoism*. Wil / Paris: UniversityMedia. ISBN 978-3-906000-06-0 (hardcover)

2016 *Creative Daoism*. Wil / Paris: UniversityMedia. ISBN 978-3-906000-05-3 (paperback)

2016 *Facets of Qing Daoism*. Wil / Paris: UniversityMedia. ISBN 978-3-906000-07-7 (paperback)

Editions

1998 Editor in chief of all articles on Chinese religion (Daoism) and Inner Alchemy (Daoism) in Jean Servier (ed.), *Dictionnaire critique de l'ésotérisme* [Critical Dictionary of Esoterism]. Paris: Presses Universitaires de France.

2004 (In collaboration with Hubert Durt). Special volume of *Cahiers d'Extrême-Asie* (no. 14) in memory of Isabelle Robinet: Pensée taoïste, alchimie et cosmologie [Daoist Thought, Alchemy and Cosmology].

2006~ Guidelines for project collaborators and edition of articles submitted by specialists for the *International Daozang jiyao Project*, founded and directed by Monica Esposito.

2008 *Images of Tibet in the 19th and 20th Centuries* (2 volumes). Collection "Études thématiques" (no 22). Paris: École française d'Extrême-Orient.

Articles

1988 Review of "Shen Hongxun, Taiji wuxigong–La pratica delle cinque respirazioni del Polo Supremo" [Taiji wuxigong–The Practice of the Five Breaths of the Supreme Ultimate] publ. Shanghai: Taiji wuxigong yanjiuhui, 1986. In *Biologica* (Journal of the philosophy department, Università Ca'Foscari, Venice), 1/1988, pp. 225-226.

1992 "Il Daozang xubian, raccolta di testi alchemici della scuola Longmen" [The Daozang xubian, a Collection of Alchemical Texts of the Longmen School]. Venice: *Annali dell'Istituto Universitario Orientale*, LII / 4, pp. 429-449.

1993 "Journey to the Temple of the Celestial-Eye", in David W. Reed (ed.), *Spirit of Enterprise, The 1993 Rolex Awards*. Bern: Buri, pp. 275-277.

1995 "Il Ritorno alle fonti– per la costituzione di un dizionario di alchimia interiore all'epoca Ming e Qing" [Return to the Sources. Preparation of a Dictionary of Inner Alchemy of the Ming and Qing]. In Maurizio Scarpari (ed.), *Le fonti per lo studio della civiltà cinese* [Sources for the Study of Chinese Civilization]. Venice: Libreria Editrice Cafoscarina, pp. 101-117.

1996 "Il Segreto del Fiore d'Oro e la tradizione Longmen del Monte Jin'gai" [The Secret of the Golden Flower and the Longmen Tradition of Mt. Jin'gai]. In Piero Corradini (ed.), *Conoscenza e interpretazione della civiltà cinese* [Knowledge and Interpretation of Chinese Civilization]. Venice: Libreria Editrice Cafoscarina, pp. 151-169.

1998   (In collaboration with Chen Yaoting 陳耀庭) "Yidali daojiao de yanjiu 意大利道教的研究" [Research on Daoism in Italy]. *Dangdai zongjiao yanjiu* 當代宗教研究 No. 1, pp. 44-48.

1998   A dozen articles in the *Dictionnaire critique de l'ésotérisme* [Critical Dictionary of Esoterism], ed. by Jean Servier (Paris: Presses Universitaires de France): "Absorption des effluves cosmiques" [Absorption of Cosmic Essences], pp. 5-6; "Alchimie féminine" [Feminine Alchemy], pp. 51-52; "Alchimie intérieure" [Inner Alchemy] (in collaboration with Isabelle Robinet), pp. 55-58; "Art de l'alcôve" [Arts of the Bedroom], pp. 58-60; "Corps subtil" [Subtle Body], pp. 343-345; "Daoyin" [Daoyin Gymnastics], pp. 365-367; "Délivrance du cadavre" [Deliverance of the corpse], pp. 377-378; "Exorcisme" [Exorcism], pp. 500-502; "Géographie sacrée" [Sacred Geography], pp. 532-534; "Immortalité et Taoïsme" [Immortality and Daoism], pp. 642-645; "Souffle et respiration embryonnaire" [Breath and embryonic respiration], pp. 1216-1218; "Tao" [Dao], pp. 1262-1263.

1998   "Longmen pai yu *Jinhua zongzhi* banben laiyuan" 龍門派與金華宗旨版本來源 [The Longmen School and the Origin of the Different Editions of the *Secret of the Golden Flower*]. Paper presented at the Dōkyō bunka kenkyūkai 道教文化研究会 at Waseda University, Tokyo (March 1998).

1998   "The different versions of the Secret of the Golden Flower and their relationship with the Longmen school." *Transactions of the International Conference of Eastern Studies*, XLIII, pp. 90-109.

1998   "Italia no kangaku to dōkyō kenkyū" イタリアの漢学と道教研究 [Italian Sinology and Daoist Studies], in Nakamura Shōhachi 中村璋八 (ed.), *Chūgokujin to dōkyō* 中国人と道教. Tokyo: Kyūko shoin 汲古書院, pp. 83-104.

1998   (In collaboration with Jean-Luc Achard) "Una tradizione di rDzogs-chen in Cina. Una nota sul Monastero delle Montagne dell'Occhio Celeste" [A Tradition of rDzogs chen in China: A Note on the Celestial Eye Monastery]. *Asiatica Venetiana* 3, pp. 221-224.

1999   "Orakel in China" [Oracles in China]. In A. Langer and A. Lutz (eds.), Orakel – Der Blick in die Zukunft [Oracles—Visions of the Future]. Zürich: Museum Rietberg, pp. 304-314.

2000   "Daoism in the Qing (1644-1911)", in L. Kohn (ed.), *Daoism Handbook*. Leiden: Brill, pp. 623-658. (Revised edition: Chapter 1 of M. Esposito, *Facets of Qing Daoism*. Wil / Paris: UniversityMedia, 2014, pp. 5-53).

2001   "Longmen Taoism in Qing China–Doctrinal Ideal and Local Reality", *Journal of Chinese Religions* 29 (special volume on Quanzhen edited by Vincent Goossaert and Paul Katz), pp. 191-231. (Revised and enlarged edition: Chapter 3 of M. Esposito, *Facets of Qing Daoism*. Wil / Paris: UniversityMedia, 2014, pp. 143-221).

2001 "In Memoriam Isabelle Robinet (1932-2000) –A Thematic and Annotated Bibliography". *Monumenta Serica* XLIX, pp. 595-624.

2001 Articles on Daoism and Inner Alchemy in *Le grand dictionnaire Ricci de la langue chinoise* (six volumes). Paris: Desclée de Brouwer.

2004 "The Longmen School and its Controversial History during the Qing Dynasty." In John Lagerwey (ed.), *Religion and Chinese Society: The Transformation of a Field*, pp. 621–698. Hong Kong: École française d'Extrême-Orient & Chinese University of Hong Kong. (Revised edition: Chapter 2 of *Facets of Qing Daoism*. Wil / Paris: UniversityMedia, 2014, pp. 55-142).

2004 "A Thematic and Annotated Bibliography of Isabelle Robinet (revised and enlarged edition)". *Cahiers d'Extrême-Asie* 14, pp. 1-42.

2004 "Sun-worship in China–The Roots of Shangqing Taoist Practices of Light". *Cahiers d'Extrême-Asie* 14, pp. 345-402.

2004 "Gyakuten shita zō—Jotan no shintai kan" 逆転した像–女丹の身体觀 [The Inverted Mirror: The Vision of the Body in Feminine Inner Alchemy], tr. by Umekawa Sumiyo 梅川純代. In Sakade Yoshinobu sensei taikyū kinen ronshū kankō kai 坂祥伸先生退休記念論集刊行会 (ed.), *Chūgoku shisō ni okeru shintai, shizen, shinkō* 中国思想における身体・自然・信仰 [Body, Nature, and Faith in Chinese Thought]. Tokyo: Tōhō shoten 東方書店, pp. 113-129. (English version entitled "Beheading the Red Dragon: The Heart of Feminine Inner Alchemy" in Chapter 4 of M. Esposito, *Facets of Qing Daoism*. Wil / Paris: UniversityMedia, 2014, pp. 223-237).

2004 "Shindai ni okeru Kingai-zan no seiritsu to Kinka shūshi" 清代における金蓋山龍門派の成立と『金華宗旨』 [The Secret of the Golden Flower and the Establishment of the Longmen Tradition on Mt. Jingai in the Qing Era], in Takata Tokio 高田時雄 (ed.), *Chūgoku shūkyō bunken kenkyū kokusai shinpojiumu hōkokusho* 中国宗教文献研究国際シンポジウム報告書. Kyoto: Kyoto daigaku Jinbun kagaku kenkyūjo 京都大学人文科学研究所, pp. 259-268. (See below for the annotated version of 2007 and for the enlarged English version in Part IV of M. Esposito, *Creative Daoism*).

2005 "Shindai dōkyō to mikkyō: Ryūmon seijiku shinshū" 清代道教と密教：龍門西竺心宗 [An Example of Daoist and Tantric Interaction during the Qing: The Tantric Lineage of Xizhu xinzong]. In Mugitani Kunio 麦谷邦夫 (ed.), *Sankyō kōshō ronsō* 三教交渉論叢 [Studies on the Interaction between the Three Teachings]. Kyoto: Kyoto daigaku Jinbun kagaku kenkyūjo 京都大学人文科学研究所, pp. 287-338. (Revised English version in Chapter 5 of M. Esposito, *Facets of Qing Daoism*. Wil / Paris: UniversityMedia, 2014, pp. 239-304).

2007 "Shindai ni okeru Kingai-zan no seiritsu to Kinka shūshi" 清代における金蓋山龍門派の成立と『金華宗旨』 [The Secret of the Golden Flower and the Establishment of the Longmen Tradition on Mt. Jingai in the Qing Era], in Kyoto: Kyoto daigaku Jinbun kagaku kenkyūjo 京都大学人文科學研究所 (ed.), *Chūgoku shūkyō bunken kenkyū* 中国宗教文献研究, Kyoto: Rinsen shoten 臨川書店, pp. 239-264. (Enlarged and revised English version in Part IV of Monica Esposito, *Creative Daoism*. Wil / Paris: UniversityMedia, 2013, pp. 263-315).

2007 "The Discovery of Jiang Yuanting's Daozang jiyao in Jiangnan—A Presentation of the Daoist Canon of the Qing Dynasty", in Mugitani Kunio 麦谷邦夫 (ed.), *Kōnan dōkyō no kenkyū* 江南道教の研究 [Research on Jiangnan Daoism]. Kyoto: Kyoto daigaku Jinbun kagaku kenkyūjo 京都大学人文科學研究所, p. 79-110. Chinese translation published in *Xueshu Zhongguo* 學術中國, 2007.11, pp. 25-48. (Revised and augmented version in Part III of Monica Esposito, *Creative Daoism*. Wil / Paris: UniversityMedia, 2013).

2008 Twenty-one articles for *The Encyclopedia of Taoism* (edited by Fabrizio Pregadio), London, Routledge. 1. Collected Works of the Perfected Lü of Pure Yang (Chunyang Lü zhenren wenji 純陽呂真人文集) (vol. 1, p. 280-281); 2. "exteriorization of the spirits"; "egress of the Spirit" (chushen 出神) in inner alchemy (vol. 1, p. 282-284); 3. Sequel to the Taoist Canon (Daozang xubian 道藏續編) (vol. 1, p. 347-350); 4. Mother of the Dipper (Doumu 斗母 / 斗姆) (vol.1, p. 382-383); 5. Spirit of the Valley (gushen 谷神) (vol. 1, p. 466); 6. Scripture of Wisdom and Life (Huiming jing 慧命經) (vol. 1, p. 520-521); 7. "fire times"; fire phasing (huohou 火候) in inner alchemy (vol.1, p. 530-531); 8. Gate of the Dragon (Longmen 龍門) (vol. 1, p. 704-706); 9. Complete Writings of Ancestor Lü [Dongbin] (Lüzu quanshu 呂祖全書) (vol. 1, p. 726-728); 10. Min Yide 閔一得 (vol. 2, p. 747-748); 11. Gate of the Vital Force (mingmen 命門) (vol. 2, p. 750); 12. Bathing; ablutions (muyu 沐浴) in inner alchemy (vol. 2, p. 753-754); 13. Muddy Pellet (niwan 泥丸) (vol. 2, p. 775-777); 14. Inner alchemy for women (nüdan 女丹) (vol. 2, p. 778-780); 15. Three Passes (sanguan 三關) (vol. 2, p. 835-836); 16. Joint cultivation (shuangxiu 雙修) (vol. 2, p. 906-907); 17. The Ultimate Purport of the Golden Flower of the Great One (Taiyi jinhua zongzhi 太一金華宗旨) (vol. 2, p. 961-962); 18. Heart of Heaven; Celestial Heart (tianxin 天心) (vol. 2, p. 988); 19. Wang Changyue 王常月 (vol. 2, p. 1008-1010); 20. Mysterious Pass (xuanguan 玄關) (vol. 2, p. 1131-2); 21. Intention (yi 意) (vol. 2, p. 1158-9)

2008 "rDzogs chen in China: From Chan to Tibetan Tantrism in Fahai Lama's (1921-1991) footsteps", in Monica Esposito (ed.), *Images of Tibet in the 19th and 20th Centuries*. Collection Thématiques no 22, Paris: École française d'Extrême-Orient, vol. 2, p. 473-548. (Revised and augmented version in Monica Esposito, *The Zen of Tantra*. Wil / Paris: UniversityMedia, 2013).

2009 "Yibu Quanzhen Daozang de faming: *Daozang jiyao* ji Qingdai Quanzhen rentong 一部全真道藏的發明：道藏輯要及清代全真認同 [The Invention of a Quanzhen Canon: The Daozang Jiyao and Qing-era Quanzhen Identity]. In *Wendao Kunyushan* 問道昆嵛山, edited by Zhao Weidong 趙衛東. Jinan: Qilu shushe: 303–343. (Revised and much augmented English version in Xun Liu and Vincent Goossaert [eds.]. *Quanzhen Daoism in Modern Chinese History and Society*. Berkeley: Institute of East Asian Studies, 2014, pp. 44-77).

2009 "The Daozang Jiyao Project: Mutation of a Canon". *Daoism: Religion, History and Society*, 2009.1, pp. 95-153.

2010 "Qingdai daozang—Jiangnan Jiang Yuanting ben Daozang jiyao zhi yanjiu 清代道藏—江南蔣元庭本《道藏輯要》之研究 [The Daoist Canon of the Qing — A Study of the Daozang jiyao version by Jiang Yuanting]. *Zongjiao xue yanjiu* 宗教學研究 3, pp. 17-27.

2011 "Shindai dōkyō ni okeru sankyō no hōko to shite no Dōzō shuyō—Zaike shinto to seishokusha no ken'i no taiji 清代における三教の寶庫としての《道藏輯要》—在家信徒と聖職の權威の對峙." [Daozang jiyao – The Last Qing Daoist Canon as Receptacle of the Three Teachings: Lay and Clerical Authorities Face to Face], in Kunio Mugitani 麥谷邦夫, *Sankyō kōshō ronsō zokuhen* 三教交涉論叢續編. Kyoto: Kyoto daigaku jinbun kagaku kenkyūjo, pp. 431–469. Revised English version in Monica Esposito, *Creative Daoism*, Part 3, chapters 3–5 (pp. 219-260).

2011 "Qingdai quanzhen santan dajie yishi de chuangli" 清代全真三壇大戒儀式的創立, Zhao Weidong 趙衛東 (ed.)., *Quanzhendao yanjiu* 全真道研究 II. Jinan: Qilu shushe, pp. 204-220. (See the substantially augmented argument in Monica Esposito, *Creative Daoism*. Wil / Paris: UniversityMedia, 2013, pp. 91-173).

2014 "The Invention of a Quanzhen Canon: The Wondrous Fate of the *Daozang jiyao*." In Xun Liu and Vincent Goossaert (eds.), *Quanzhen Daoism in Modern Chinese History and Society*. Berkeley: Institute of East Asian Studies, pp. 44-77.

Forthcoming: "The Daozang Jiyao and the Future of Daoist Studies", in Lai Chi Tim and Cheung Neky Tak-ching (eds.), *New Approaches to the Study of Daoism in Chinese Culture and Society*. Hong Kong: Chinese University Press.

Translations

1991 (from French) Catherine Despeux, *Le immortali dell' antica Cina. Taoismo e Alchimia femminile*. Rome: Ubaldini.

2008 (from Japanese) Onoda Shunzō 小野田俊藏, "The Meiji Suppression of Buddhism and Its Impact on the Spirit of Exploration and Academism of Buddhist Monks", in *Images of Tibet in the 19th and 20th Centuries*, collection "Études thématiques" no 22. Paris: École française d'Extrême-Orient, vol. 2, pp. 225-242.

2008 (from Chinese) Chen Bing 陳兵, "The Tantric Revival and Its Reception in Modern China", in *Images of Tibet in the 19th and 20th Centuries*, collection "Études thématiques" no 22. Paris: École française d'Extrême-Orient, vol. 2, pp. 387-427.

Conference Papers

2002 "A Sino-Tibetan Tradition in China at the Southern Celestial Eye Mountains: A First Comparison between Great Perfection (rDzogs chen) and Taoist Techniques of Light." Paper presented at the Conference "Tantra and Daoism: The Globalization of Religion and its Experience." Boston University, April 19-21, 2002.

2003 "How Neidan has developed: A View on Inner Alchemy in Late Imperial China." Paper presented at the conference "The Roots of Taoist Inner Alchemy", Stanford University, May 30-31, 2003. (The distributed list of texts contained in the *Daozang xubian* forms in revised and completed form the Appendix to Chapter 3 in M. Esposito, *Facets of Qing Daoism*. Wil / Paris: UniversityMedia, pp. 191-211).

2006 "Daozang jiyao yanjiu jihua-Cong zhushushi bianmu dao shuweihua diancang." 道藏輯要研究計畫—從註疏式編目到數位化典藏 [The Daozang Jiyao Research Project—From an Annotated Catalog to the Digitization of its Scriptures]. Paper presented at the Conference of Exchange of Experiences in the Work of Digitizing Religious Scriptures 數位寶典—宗教文獻數位化工作經驗交流會, Academia Sinica Institute of History and Philology, March 7, 2006.

2006 "Daozang jiyao ji qi bianzuan de lishi—Shijie Qingdai Daozang suoshou daojing shumu wenti 道藏輯要及其編纂的歷史—試解清代道藏所收道經書目問題" [The History of the Compilation of the *Daozang jiyao*—Solving its Numbering Problem]. Paper presented at the *First International Academic Symposium of Taoist Literature and its Path to Immortality* 第一屆道教仙道文化國際學術研討會. Gaoxiong, Zhongshan University, November 10–12, 2006.

2008 "Yibu Quanzhen Daozang de faming: Daozang jiyao ji Qingdai Quanzhen rentong" 一部全真道藏的发明：道藏辑要及清代全真认同. Paper presented at the Quanzhen conference in Shandong Moping, October 9-12, 2008.

2009 "The Daozang Jiyao and the Future of Daoist Studies." Paper presented at the international conference "New Approaches to the Study of Daoism in Chinese Culture and Society", Chinese University of Hong Kong, November 26-28, 2008.

2010 "Qingdai Quanzhen jiao zhi chonggou: Min Yide ji qi jianli Longmen zhengtong de yiyuan" 清代全真教之重構：閔一得及其建立龍門正統的意願 [The Reinvention of Quanzhen during the Qing Dynasty: Min Yide and his Will to Orthodoxy]. Paper presented at the International Quanzhen conference 探古監今－全真道的昨天,今天與明天, Hong Kong, January 6-8, 2010.

Documentaries

1993 Journey to the Temple of the Celestial-Eye Mountains. 10-minute video, Rolex Awards for Enterprise, Selected Projects.

1995 Voyage dans le Khams et l'Amdo méridionale [Voyage in the Khams and Southern Amdo]. 10-minute video, CNRS European Project.

2000 (In collaboration with Urs App) *Oracles in China*. 11-minute video for the millennial "Oracle" exhibition at the Museum Rietberg, Zürich.

2000 (In collaboration with Urs App) *Oracles in Japan*. 10-minute video for the millennial "Oracle" exhibition at the Museum Rietberg, Zürich.

2000 (In collaboration with Urs App) *Dangki: Chinese Oracle Kids*. 11-minute video for the millennial "Oracle" exhibition at the Museum Rietberg, Zürich.

2001 (In collaboration with Urs App) *Dangki – Les chamanes de la Chine* [Dangki: Shamans of China]. 51-minute video, broadcast in 2001 and 2002 on the France 2 TV channel.

2002 (In collaboration with Urs App) *On the Way to Tōhaku's Pine Forest*. 20-minute video for the exposition on the art of painter Hasegawa Tōhaku at the Museum Rietberg, Zürich.

2003 (In collaboration with Urs App) *Der Teebesen* [Chasen—The Tea Whisk]. 20-minute video shown at the "Bamboo" exposition in the Ethnological Museum of Zurich University (2003), at the Völkerkundemuseum München (2006), and at the Ethnological Museum of Zurich University (2014-2015).

Index

A

Akizuki, Kan'ei 秋月觀暎 11, 129, 277
alchemy 2, 7, 9, 43, 46, 54, 82, 167, 177, 187, 188, 190, 195, 202, 203, 205, 207, 208, 212, 215, 216, 217, 219, 226, 252, 263, 264, 267, 268, 270, 271, 309, 310, 311, 312
    alchemical practice (dangong 丹功) 190, 205, 215
    alchemical process 271
    Daozang jiyao and the true alchemical path 215–216
    inner alchemy (neidan 內丹) 2, 163, 177, 187, 188, 202, 207, 215–217, 219, 263, 278, 309, 311, 312
    outer alchemical practice (waigong 外功) 215
altar 12, 30, 38, 47, 79, 81, 91, 93, 97, 100, 102, 104–106, 109, 113–121, 128, 132, 133, 138–152, 155–157, 160, 162, 165, 168, 170, 171, 173, 186, 187, 189, 204–206, 208–211, 213, 215, 217, 221, 251, 253, 254, 258, 265, 267, 269, 274, 275, 278–283, 286–289, 297–300, 302, 303, 306, 307
App, Urs XI, 101, 102
asceticism 9, 33, 35, 58, 59, 64, 116, 159, 163, 164, 167, 294

B

bahuan 八還 (eight attributions) 270
Bai Huizhi 白慧直 (d. 1740) 86
Bailong jingshe 白龍精舍 (Piling 毘陵, Changzhou in Jiangsu) 274
Baiyun guan 白雲觀 (White Cloud Abbey) 4, 6–12, 17–23, 29, 30, 33–35, 38, 41, 47, 52, 53, 58, 61, 67– 73, 75, 77–79, 81, 83–88, 91–96, 98, 100, 102, 105, 106, 113, 115, 116, 119, 120, 126, 130, 147–149, 153, 155, 160–165, 170–172, 224, 228, 258, 259, 286, 287, 294, 299, 301, 302, 317, 320, 321, 325
    as modern Daoism's Vatican 4–13, 294
    construction and restoration 10–11
    erected on "Longmen founder" Qiu Chuji's grave 8
    Memorial Hall (citang 祠堂) 61, 93, 147, 294
Baiyun guan chongxiu ji 白雲觀重修記 11, 163
Baiyun guan zhi 白雲觀志 (jap. Hakuunkan shi; Gazetteer of the Abbey of the White Clouds) by Oyanagi Shigeta (1934) 4, 6, 8, 10, 11, 41, 61, 70, 72, 77, 83, 91, 92, 115, 116, 131, 148, 162, 163, 287, 294, 317, 321

Baiyun xianbiao 白雲仙表 (Chart of the Immortals of the White Clouds) 6, 17, 19, 21, 23, 24, 25, 26, 37, 60, 61, 63–65, 67, 69, 73, 317
Baldrian-Hussein, Farzeen 309
Bao Kun 鮑錕 (fl. 1814) 6, 12, 18, 29, 49, 51, 60
Bao Tingbo 鮑廷博 (1728-1814) 6, 12, 18, 29, 49, 51, 54, 60, 72
Bao'en lun 報恩論 235
Baohua forest 寶華林 134
Barrett, Thomas 228
Barzaghi, Iris XI
Baynes, C.F. 263, 313
Beijing 4, 6, 8–10, 12, 21, 23, 24, 26, 28, 33, 34, 41, 67, 69, 71, 75, 77, 78, 80, 83, 85, 86, 91, 102, 119, 120, 130, 147, 148, 153, 155, 156, 160, 162, 164, 171, 183, 186, 191, 198, 200, 205, 206, 221, 224, 227, 228, 250, 251, 254, 259, 264, 267, 286, 289, 294, 299, 306–308
Benn, Charles 116, 119
Berling, Judith 232
Bible 212, 250
   New Testament 88
Billeter, Jean François 55
Biyu zhengong dajie 碧玉真宮大戒 136
Biyuan guan 碧苑觀 (Biyuan monastery, Nanjing) 300
Biyuan tanjing 碧苑壇經 (Platform Sūtra of the Jade Garden) 58, 61, 72, 78, 83, 91, 102, 105, 106, 107, 157, 299, 300, 317
Bodhidharma 菩提達摩 (ch. Puti damo, jap. Bodai daruma) 3, 43, 45
Bodhisattva, Bodhisattva precepts 3, 117, 139, 140, 152
Bodiford, William M. 8, 117
Bojian 鉢鑑 (Examination of the Bowl; attributed to Wang Changyue) 12, 18, 21, 54, 58, 60, 61, 63, 65, 69, 317
Bokenkamp, R. Stephen 145
Boltz, Judith 9, 10, 194, 221, 254
Botang 鉢堂 (Hall of the Bowl) 8, 159, 160, 161, 162, 163, 294
Bretschneider, Emil 23, 27
Brokaw, Cynthia 226
Brook, Timothy 53, 181, 232, 234
Buddha 34, 170, 268
Buddhism, Buddhist 2, 5, 6, 34, 46, 47, 53, 57–59, 88, 110, 117, 122, 133, 135, 140, 152, 159, 168, 169, 170, 177, 205, 206, 212, , 216, 217, 219, 223, 233, 234–238, 250, 251, 254, 268, 293, 294, 301, 309, 312
   Linji 臨濟 (jap. Rinzai) lineage 237, 293 (*see* also Chan Buddhism)
   ordination procedures 117
   Buddhist Canon 223
   Buddhist sutras and Lingbao scriptures 133

C

Cantong jing 參同經 142, 317
Cantong miaojing 參同妙經 209
Cantongqi 參同契 82, 202, 215
Cao Changhua 曹常化 (1562-1622) 16
Celestial Masters (*see also* Zhengyi 正一) 4, 50, 109, 159
Central Asia 9, 22
Cha Fugong 查復功 (fourteenth Longmen generation) 39
Chan 禪 Buddhism 5, 6, 46, 53, 56, 88, 93, 117, 139, 140, 152, 159, 170, 233, 235–237, 268–270, 293, 309
    as inspiration for Longmen symbols of transmission 41
Chanfa daguan 懺法大觀 121, 142, 144, 150, 151, 205, 317
Chang Guang 常光 (Huashan line) 16
Changchun daojiao yuanliu 長春道教源流 (Origins and development of the Taoist Teachings of [Qiu] Changchun) 19, 50, 61, 62, 69, 293, 317
Changchun gong 長春宮 (Palace of Perennial Spring) 10
Changchun zhenren xiyou ji 長春真人西遊記 (Record of the Journey to the West by the Perfected Changchun) 9, 19, 22, 26, 317, 326
Changde 常德 (Hunan) 71
Changshengshu 長生術 (The Art of Longevity) 305–307, 309
Changshenshu Xumingfang hekan 長生術續命方合刊 (Joint Edition of 'The Art of Long Life' & 'The Method for Increasing Vital Force') 305–9
Chanzong zhengzhi 禪宗正旨 206, 209
Chaotian chan 朝天懺 158
Chen Bing 陳兵 91
Chen Dali 陳大利 179, 182
Chen Minggui 陳銘珪 (1824-1881) 19, 27, 34, 50, 61, 293
Chen Mou 陳謀 143, 193, 272, 280, 281, 282, 283, 287, 306, 322
Chen Shangyang 陳上陽 274
Chen Ting 陳鼎 (1650–?) 73, 75, 76, 77, 80
Chen Tongwei 陳通微 (fl. 1387; second generation Longmen Vinaya line) 16, 44, 48, 48–51, 51
Chen Tuan 陳摶 (ca. 906-989) 208
Chen Wuyuan 陳悟元 241
Chen Zhongyuan 陳仲遠 (1734-1802) 244
Cheng Xiangyan 程香岩 (fl. 1737-68) 86
Chengdu 84, 86, 126, 127, 136, 162, 178, 180, 183, 217, 226, 228, 229, 232, 244, 255, 273, 307, 308
Chiang-Ching Kuo Foundation 177, 220

Chinggis Khan 9, 22
Chion-in 知恩院 (Pure Land temple in Kyoto) 8
Chongkan Daozang jiyao xubian zimu 重刊道藏輯要續編子目 230, 241, 243, 244
Chongkan Daozang jiyao zimu chubian 重刊道藏輯要子目初編 97, 183, 238, 241
Chongyang'an 重陽庵 (Hangzhou) 163, 318
Chongyang'an ji 重陽庵集 163, 318
Chongyin Xuanmiao guan 重印玄妙觀 138
Chuandaoji 傳道集 207, 318
chuanjie 傳戒 (transmission of precepts) 30, 52
chuanjie benshi 傳戒本師 (principal precept-transmitting master) 114, 115, 131, 160
chuanjie lüshi 傳戒律師 (ordination master) 131, 148
Chuanshou sandong jing jiefa lulüe shuo 傳授三洞經戒法籙略說 156
Chunyang sanshu 純陽三書 228, 243
chuzhen jie 初真戒 (precepts of intial perfection) 12, 22, 41, 75, 94, 107, 110, 121, 294
Chuzhen jielü 初真戒律 (Precepts of Initial Perfection, attr. Wang Changyue) 37, 38, 46, 59, 61, 62, 65, 66, 76, 77, 91, 92, 94, 96–98, 102, 104, 105, 107–115, 120–123, 125, 126, 131–133, 140, 152, 155–157, 159, 160, 162–164, 173, 258, 294, 318
    aim of establishing Wang Changyue as ordination reformer 156
    not product of a single author 155
chuzhen xinyi 初真信衣 114
citang 祠堂 (memorial hall) 93, 147, 294
Clart, Philippe 237, 254, 286
Cleary, Thomas 312, 314
clepsydra 114, 159
clergy 53, 65, 117, 151, 156, 163, 195, 204, 221, 253, 255, 256, 257, 259, 276, 293
compassion 98, 124, 135, 212, 286
conflagration scenario 164, 165
Confucianism 2, 4, 7, 53, 54, 56, 59, 79, 82, 177, 205, 216, 219, 232, 234–238, 242, 253, 258, 259, 268, 298, 299
Confucius 195
cosmology 7, 177, 274
Cui Yangtou 崔羊頭 (Zhao Daojian's teacher) 24

D

Da Chongguang 笪重光 (1623-1692) 76
Dacheng miaolin jing 大乘妙林經 111, 318
Daode tianzun 道德天尊 202, 222
Daodejing 道德經 31, 48, 49, 56, 64, 112, 131, 157, 222, 268, 318, 323
Daodejing jie (太上)道德經解 207
Daofa huiyuan 道法會元 121, 216, 318
Daoguang 道光 (emperor / reign 1820-1850) 181, 193, 257
Daoist Canon of Ming era 23, 79, 166, 177, 179–181, 194, 201, 202, 204, 212, 216, 217, 219, 221, 222, 246, 247, 250, 251, 254
    and the Daozang jiyao 177
Daoist gymnastics 2, 3, 215
Daoist trinity (Sanqing 三清) 145, 146, 201, 202, 212, 222, 248, 250, 270
Daojiao wenxian 道教文獻 190, 195
Daojing miji 道經秘集 308
Daolu si 道錄司 (Central Daoist Registry) 11
Daopu yuanliu tu 道譜源流圖 (Map of the Origins and Development of Taoist Genealogical Registers) 18, 20, 21, 22, 82, 210, 318
daoqi 道器 (vessel of the Tao) 43
Daoshu 道樞 203
Daotong yuanliu zhi 道統源流志 (Gazetteer on the Origins and Development of Orthodox Taoism) 6, 19, 22, 27, 34, 38, 41, 49, 52, 61, 65, 72, 73, 76, 287, 318
Daoyan wuzhong 道言五種 187
Daozang jinghua lu 道藏精華錄 (Record of Quintessence of the Taoist Canon) 193, 194, 223, 265, 273, 307, 313, 318
Daozang jiyao 道藏輯要 (Essence of the Daoist Canon) 12, 13, 20, 22, 23, 91, 94, 96, 97, 111, 120, 121, 124, 126, 132, 135, 136, 138, 139, 143, 144, 149, 151, 152, 157, 177–260, 266, 267, 269, 272, 273, 284, 286–289, 303, 305, 312, 313, 314, 318, 319
    and the Ming Daoist Canon 177
    and the true alchemical path 215–216
    as fruit of private initiative of high-ranking officials 204
    as source for Ming and Qing Daoism 177
    central role of Lü Dongbin, spirit writing 211
    earlier research 177
    Fanli 凡列 (conventions) 193, 202, 206, 211, 212, 215, 216, 232, 233, 275, 280, 281, 284
    four prefaces 201
    international research project directed by Monica Esposito XI, 177, 198
    largest anthology of premodern Daoism, importance as source 177

list of texts added to various Chongkan Daozang jiyao editions 242–243
overall content of Daozang jiyao collection 201–203
overview of content of 28 lunar lodges (ershiba xiu 二十八宿) 202–203
previous theories about its history 179–181
twenty-eight lunar lodges (ershiba xiu 二十八宿) 202

Daozang jiyao zongmu 道藏輯要總目 (Comprehensive Table of Contents of the Daozang jiyao) 97, 183, 184, 187, 193, 194, 196, 202, 207, 222, 241, 244

Daozang xubian 道藏續編 (Supplementary Collection of the Daoist Canon) 1, 20, 62, 182, 194, 265, 269, 273, 293, 294, 296, 303, 314, 319

Daozu 道祖 (Ancestor of the Dao, i.e. Laozi) 143, 145, 150

Datong jing 大通經 110, 113

de Bary, William Theodore 311

degeneration 99, 101, 102, 103, 104, 105, 106, 145, 164, 165

degeneration scenario 164

deities 232, 286

Deng Xiaoping 鄧小平 1

Dengzhen lu 登真錄 113

Despeux, Catherine 3, 156

dhyāna (ding 定, concentration) 268

Dianying ji 顛影集 82

Ding Changchun 丁常春 179, 225

Ding Fubao 丁福保 (1874-1952) 193, 194, 196, 204, 217, 223, 318, 319

Ding Peiren 丁培仁 24, 25, 29, 32, 41, 44, 168, 181, 182, 201, 221

Dingguan jing 定觀經 222

divination 28, 186, 215

dixian jiege 地仙戒果 113

Diyi juetan 第一覺壇 (First Altar of Awakening) 204, 205, 251

Donggu jing 洞古經 110, 113

Donghua zhengmai huangji hepi zhengdao xianjing 東華正脈皇極闔闢證道仙經 295

Dongjing shidu 洞經示讀 187

Dongshen jing 洞神經 141

Dongxuan lingbao changye zhi fu jiuyou yukui mingzhen ke 洞玄靈寶長夜之府九幽玉匱明真科 134, 319

Dongxuan lingbao qianzhen ke 洞玄靈寶千真科 112, 134, 319

Dongxuan lingbao sandong fengdao kejie yingshi 洞玄靈寶三洞奉道科戒營始 110, 126, 319

Dongxuan lingbao sanyuan wuliangshou jing (太上)洞玄靈寶三元無量壽經 133–135

Dongxuan lingbao tianzun shuo shijie jing 洞玄靈寶天尊說十戒經 110

dongyi 洞衣 114
Dongyuan yulu 東原語錄 (Recorded Sayings of Dongyuan) 54, 242, 319
Dongyun Tianhetan 洞雲天鶴壇 308
Doufu hui 豆腐會 (Association of Bean Curd Eaters) 186
dougong 斗宮 (Dipper palace) 281
Doumu 斗母 (Mother of Dipper; Mārīcī) 68, 142, 143, 255, 278
Doumu xinzhou 斗母心咒 142, 143, 278
Douzhong Xiaoti Wang 斗中孝悌王 (Respected King of Filial Piety from the Dipper) 274
Du Guangting 杜光庭 (850-933) 277
Du Zong 杜琮 314
Duara, Prasenjit 246
dunwu 頓悟 (sudden awakening) 268
Duren jing 度人經 110, 202
durenyili 度人儀禮 112, 113
dushi 度師 (initiation master) 119, 144, 148, 269, 299

E

Eight Immortals 263, 264
eight trigrams (bagua 八卦) 162, 278, 279
Eight Trigrams bowl 162
elite 18, 56, 59, 83, 152, 204, 207, 221, 227, 251, 253, 254, 265, 283
elixir 11, 140, 142, 143, 151, 217, 264, 268, 284, 310, 311, 323, 325 (see also Golden Elixir, jindan)
Elman, Benjamin A. 54, 239
Enckevort, Paul van 141, 169
Enhong 恩洪 291–292
Erxian'an beiji 二仙菴碑記 242, 257
Erxian'an changzhu yingyong shiwen 二仙菴常住應用時文 255, 258
Erxian'an 二仙庵 (Hermitage of the Two Immortals) 96, 97, 126, 127, 136, 162, 179, 180, 183, 184, 201, 203, 217, 220, 225, 226, 227, 232, 241, 242, 243, 244, 246, 253, 254, 255, 256, 257, 258, 259, 260
Eskildsen, Stephen 25
Esposito, Carlo XI
Esposito-Pozza, Adriana XI
ethics 7, 203, 216
examinations 54, 79, 186, 206, 213, 251, 258, 259
exorcism 48, 121, 167, 216

F

Fahai yizhu 法海遺珠 319
Fan Ao 范鏊 (fl. 1780-1803) 211
Fan Taiqing 范太清 60, 61
Fan Yibin 范宜賓 (fl. 1722) 188
Fang Ling 方玲 167
fangzhang 方丈 (abbot, abbot's quarters) 147
fashi 法師 34
fasting 328
feiluan 飛鸞 (the flying phoenix [in spirit writing]) 186
Feng Guanghong 馮廣宏 314
Feuchtwang, Stephan 256
filial piety 53, 59, 75
Five Dippers (wudou 五斗) 202
Five Precepts (wujie 五戒) 109, 120–123
Five Precepts ordained by the Most-High Lord Lao 太上老君所命積功歸根五戒 122–123
fly-whisk 55, 56
fortune 43, 76, 105, 107, 150, 310
Foulk, Theodore Griffith 5
founders' gravesites and religious headquarters 8
freemasonry 264, 310
fu yibo 付衣鉢 (transmission of robe and bowl). *See* robe and bowl transmission
fuji 扶乩 lit. supporting the spirit writing instrument) 186 (*see* spirit writing)
fujie 符節 140
fujuan 符券 (laissez-passer, pledge) 140
fuluan 扶鸞 (supporting the phoenix [in spirit writing]) 186
fuluantan 扶鸞壇 (spirit-writing altar) 148
Funayama, Tōru 59, 117
fuxin 符信 (laissez-passer, pledge) 140
Fuyang dedao ji 復陽得道記 60
Fuyou dijun shijie gongguo ke 孚佑帝君十戒功過格 136, 319
Fuyou dijun xinjing 孚佑帝君心經 143, 319
Fuyou dijun 孚佑帝君 (=Lü Dongbin 呂洞賓, q.v.) 136, 139, 143, 146, 151, 243, 254, 290–292, 295, 319
Fuyou shangdi 孚佑上帝 (=Lü Dongbin 呂洞賓, q.v.) 143, 202, 206, 253, 269, 272, 288, 289, 319, 322
Fuyou shangdi Chunyang Lüzu tianshi Shiliupin jing 孚佑上帝純陽呂祖天師十六品經 206

Fuyou shangdi Chunyang Lüzu tianshi xinjing 孚佑上帝純陽呂祖天師心經 143, 319, 322

Fuyou shangdi Tianxian Jinhua zongzhi 孚佑上帝天仙金華宗旨 291–292

G

Ganfa 紺髮 73
Ganshui xianyuan lu 甘水仙源錄 25, 30, 31, 34, 322
Gansu province 24
Gao Mingdong 高明峒 (alias Gao Rendong 高仁峒, 1841–1907) 130
Gao Panlong 高攀龍 (1562–1626) 186
Gao Rendong 高仁峒. *See* Gao Mingdong
Gao Yunxi 高雲溪 (1841–1907) 126, 162
Gaoseng zhuan 高僧傳 (Biographies of the Eminent Monks) 59
Gaoshang shenxiao yuqing zhenwang zishu dafa 高上神霄玉清真王紫書大法 216, 319
Gaoshang Yuhuang benxing jijing 高上玉皇本行集經 198
Ge Hong 葛洪 (283-343) 57
genealogical chart 22
genealogy 6, 12, 22, 93, 147, 170, 275, 288, 294
Golden Age 9, 99, 101, 105, 106, 145, 167, 302
Golden Age / degeneration / regeneration narrative 98–106
golden elixir (jindan 金丹) 11, 140, 142–3, 217, 264, 268, 284, 310, 323, 325
Golden Flower. *See* Jinhua zongzhi
gong'an 公案 (jap. kōan) 268
good deeds 110–113
Goossaert, Vincent X, 4, 12, 23, 31, 42, 65, 94, 96, 97, 113, 159, 163, 164, 179, 223, 237, 247, 259, 287
government 8, 11, 53, 246, 259, 310
Gōyama, Kiwamu 208, 213
Granoff, Phyllis 59
Grison, Pierre 309
Gu Danchu 顧旦初 290–292
Gu Hongmeige 古紅梅閣 (Old Red Plum Hall) 274
Gu Qingya 顧晴崖 280
Gu shuyinlou cangshu 古書隱樓藏書 (Collection from the Ancient Hidden Pavilion of Books) 5, 61, 62, 65, 91, 188, 192, 194, 293, 298, 303, 317, 320
Guan Wuliangshoufo jing 觀無量壽佛經 (Sutra on Contemplating the Buddha of Immeasurable Life; Amitāyur-dhyāna-sūtra) 268

Guandi 關帝 203
Guangcheng yizhi 廣成儀制 (Ritual Systematization of Master Guangcheng) 80, 243, 244
Guanghuisi 廣惠寺 205, 206, 251
Guangxu 光緒 (emperor / reign 1875-1908) 108, 119, 220, 225, 226, 232, 234, 243
Guangyang zaji 廣陽雜記 (Miscellaneous Records of Guangyang) 41, 172, 320
guanjin keyi 冠巾科儀 155, 165, 167
Guanshan 冠山 (Mt. Guan, Suzhou) 72, 77
    Guanshan Lüyuan 冠山律院
Guansheng dijun benzhuan 關聖帝君本傳 242
Guanyin 201, 202, 242
Guanyin dashi lianchuan jing 觀音大士蓮船經 242
Guanyin zi 關尹子 (Guardian of the Pass) 269
Guitan guiyue 皈壇規約 (Pledge of Commitment to the Rules of the Altar) 139
Guizhou 71
Guo Shouzhen 郭守真 (1606-1708) 69
Guochao fangke daoshu mulu 國朝坊刻道書目錄 187
Guochao qixian leizheng chubian 國朝耆獻類徵初編 191, 204, 205

H

Hachiya, Kunio 蜂屋邦夫 24, 31
Hackmann, Heinrich 95, 96, 108, 119, 130, 149
Hakuunkan shi 白雲觀志 (ch. Baiyunguan zhi; Gazetteer of the Abbey of the White Clouds) by Oyanagi Shigeta (1934) 4, 6, 8, 10, 11, 41, 61, 70, 72, 77, 83, 91, 92, 115, 116, 131, 148, 162, 163, 287, 294, 317, 321
Han Jichou 韓箕疇 62
Han Tianshi shijia 漢天師世家 196, 320
Hanguzi 涵穀子 307
Hangzhou 33, 54, 72, 92, 161, 163, 190, 191, 193, 194, 195, 197, 198, 279, 300
    Chongyang'an 重陽庵 163, 318
    Jingudong 金鼓洞 20, 23, 161, 320
Hanlin academy 翰林院 186, 226, 281
Hansangong 涵三宮 (Palace Encompassing the Three) 208, 209, 210
He Longxiang 賀龍驤 180, 181, 183, 184, 185, 186, 187, 194, 201, 225, 226, 227, 238, 239, 241, 244, 245, 249, 254, 272
He Qichong 何起重 183, 227
healing 62, 295, 296, 299

Heavenly Masters' Dao (tianshi dao 天師道) 155, 171
Hedaozi 合道子 (Yao Jicang 姚濟蒼) 305, 306
Henan province 20, 26, 28, 43, 58, 64, 186, 204
hermeticism 263, 264
heterodoxy 66, 74, 254
Hobsbawn, Eric 3
Hōnen 法然 (1133-1212) 8
Honganji 本願寺 (headquarters of Reformed Pure Land Buddhism in Kyoto, Japan) 8
Hong Baijian 洪百堅 179
Hong Kong XI, 77, 93, 167, 214, 225, 228, 240, 265, 286
Hongwu edict (1394) 53
houtian 後天 (after heaven) 279
Hu Jing 胡敬 191, 204
Hu Ying 胡濙 (1375-1463) 10, 11, 163
Huang Chengshu 黃誠恕 209
Huang Chongyang 黃沖陽 47, 71, 72, 75, 76, 156
Huang Shouyuan 黃守元 (1585-1673; Longmen Doctrinal line, eighth generation) 16
Huang Shouzhong 黃守中 (Yedaposhe) 72
Huang Yinzhen 黃隱真 (1595-1673) 72, 295, 297, 298, 300
Huang Yuanji 黃元吉 (1270-1325) 277
Huangdi 黃帝 (Yellow Emperor) 48, 160, 202, 268
Huangdi suwen 黃帝素問 268
Huangji jingshi shu 皇極經世書 203, 242
Huangji xianjing 皇極仙經 161, 165, 320
Huangjing jizhu 皇經集註 134, 320
Huangting jing 黃庭經 113, 222, 314
Huanyuanpian 還源篇 187
Huashan 華山 (Mt. Hua, Shaanxi province) 16, 44, 48, 67, 172, 308
  Longmen Huashan 華山 line 16
Huashanzong Yunshui dongtian 華山宗雲水洞天 308
Huating 華亭 (Gansu) 24
Huayue zhi 華嶽志 (Gazetteer of Sacred Mount Hua) 320
Hubei 湖北 province 57, 59, 66, 71, 75, 79, 86, 99, 208, 311
huiguang 回光 (turning the light) 268, 269
Huijue 惠覺 (= Jiang Yuanting, q.v.) 291–292
Huike 慧可 (second Chinese Chan patriarch) 43, 45
Huiming jing 慧命經 (Book of Wisdom and Life) 307, 309, 313

Huizhenzi 慧真子 264, 273, 305, 306, 311
Huju shan 虎踞山 75
Hummel, Arthur W. 280
Hunan province 71, 73

I

Igarashi, Kenryū 五十嵐賢隆 6, 73, 74, 77, 81, 84, 92, 119, 148, 149, 287
Ikehira, Noriko 池平紀子 198
illness 62
immortal 24, 62, 73, 132, 133, 143, 145, 147, 149, 170, 195, 204, 205, 206, 212, 213, 221, 222, 245, 250, 251, 252, 258, 263, 267, 273, 274, 275, 280, 282, 285, 286, 287, 296, 299, 306, 310
immortality 12, 40, 46, 57, 59, 94, 107, 112, 114, 140, 141, 142, 143, 157, 180, 195, 215, 264, 325
imperial patronage 260, 277
imperial ritual (li 禮) 145
initial precepts of perfection (*see* chuzhen jie 初真戒)
inner alchemy (neidan 內丹; *see also under* alchemy) 2, 163, 177, 187, 188, 202, 207, 215–217, 219, 263, 278, 309, 311, 312
intermediate precepts (*see* zhongji jie 中極戒)
Ishida, Kenji 石田憲司 10, 11

J

Jiang Shanxin 姜善信 (fl. 1260-1283; Huashan line) 16
Jiang Shiquan 蔣士銓 185
Jiang Yihe 蔣一鶴 84
Jiang Yuanting 蔣元庭 (=Jiang Yupu 蔣予蒲, 1755-1819) 121, 132, 133, 138–140, 142–144, 149, 150, 152, 155, 156, 168, 170, 179, 180–182, 185–198, 201–211, 215, 217, 221, 222, 250, 251, 253, 254, 266, 267, 272, 273, 281, 284–289, 305, 306, 321
    biography 204–207
    Guanghua dizi 廣化弟子 204, 206
    Guanghuazi 廣化子 204
    Huijue 惠覺 204, 206
    Mengyin 夢因 204
Jiang Yuelun 蔣曰綸 (1729-1803) 203, 205
Jiang Yupu 蔣予蒲 (1755-1819) *see* Jiang Yuanting
jiangluan 降鸞 (descent of the phoenix [in spirit writing]) 186
Jiangnan 江南 1, 5, 6, 7, 70, 72, 76, 81, 82, 83, 84, 138, 144, 161, 163, 187, 188, 259, 265, 298

Jiangning 江寧 75, 280
Jiangsu province 57, 74, 80, 81, 86, 92, 186, 228, 265, 274, 279, 280, 283, 287, 289, 297
Jiangxi province 79, 184, 185, 237, 277
jianjie dashi 監戒大師 (discipline master) 114
Jianmo bianyi lu 揀魔辨異錄 238
Jiao sandong zhenwen wufa zhengyi mengwei lu licheng yi 醮三洞真文五法正一盟威錄立成儀 136, 320
jiaowai biechuan 教外別傳 (special transmission outside mainline teachings) 268, 282
Jiaqing 嘉慶 (emperor / reign 1796-1820) 20, 85, 87, 97, 105, 120, 121, 132, 157, 165, 179, 181, 185, 189, 191, 194, 195, 205, 219, 220, 221, 223, 224, 246, 251, 301
jiefa koujue 戒法口訣 (secret oral transmission of precepts) 22, 37
jiefa 戒法 (method of precepts) 20, 57
jieqi 戒期 (ordination period) 157
jietan 戒壇 (ordination platform) 91, 117, 147, 148, 153, 300, 302
Jin Guangti 金光悌 (alias Dagu 大固, 1747-1812) 251
Jin Yuanding 金淵鼎 (d. 1687) 139
Jin Zhenchang 靳貞常 (Huashan line) 16
jindan 金丹 (Golden Elixir) 11, 140, 142–3, 207, 217, 264, 268, 284, 310, 323, 325
jindan jiao 金丹教 264
Jindan sibaizi 金丹四百字 (Four Hundred Words on the Golden Elixir) 268
Jingai shan (Mt. Jingai) 金蓋山 (Huzhou, Zhejiang province) 5, 6, 17, 20, 21, 36, 37, 38, 44, 46, 72, 91, 161, 165, 187–191, 194, 274, 295–299, 301–303, 315, 318, 320
  Longqiao 窿蹺 hermitage 297, 298, 303
  spirit writing altar 297–299
  Yunchao 雲巢 ("Cloud's nest") temple 297, 320
Jingai xindeng 金蓋心燈 (Mind-Lamp of Mount Jingai) 5–8, 11, 12, 17–26, 28–34, 36–38, 40–44, 46–50, 54–65, 67, 69, 70–73, 75–77, 79, 82–85, 91–94, 102, 147, 156, 161, 170, 190, 195, 210, 274, 293, 297, 298, 320
  and Min Yide's creation of a transmission history 5–8
  and subsequent sources on Longmen lineage 5–7
  and the invention of a universal Longmen orthodox history 93
  as fundamental source for earlier history of Longmen 38
  as important source for Ming and Qing Daoism 5–7
Jingai xindeng zhengkao wenxian lu 金蓋心燈徵考文獻錄 (Index of works used for the compilation of the Transmission of the Mind-Lamp from Mount Jingai) 6, 18, 60
Jingai yunjian 金蓋雲笈 (Cloudy Satchel of Jingai) 60

Jingangjing zhu 金剛經註 (Commentary on the Diamond Sutra) 206
Jingkou 京口 (today's Zhenjiang 鎮江, Jiangsu) 81
Jingming 淨明 (Pure Brightness) School 3, 11, 81, 110, 116, 119, 141, 143, 145, 159, 170, 172, 202, 265, 267, 268, 274, 275, 276, 277, 278, 279, 281–284, 288, 296, 299, 302, 324
Jingming zhongxiao dao 淨明忠孝道 11, 277
Jingming zongjiao lu 淨明宗教錄 3, 110, 119, 288, 302
Jingshi gongguoge 警世功過格 138, 207, 320
Jingudong zhi 金鼓洞志 (Gazetteer of the Jingudong) 20, 23, 161, 320
jingxu wuwei 清虛無為 37
jingyi 淨衣 3, 114
Jinhua chanyou 金華闡幽 267, 281–283, 288, 289, 303, 307, 308
Jinhua chanyou wenda 金華闡幽問答 267, 283, 288–292, 303
Jinhua keyi 金華科儀 (liturgy of the Golden Flower) 144, 279, 280
Jinhua zongzhi 金華宗旨 (Secret of the Golden Flower) X, 13, 141, 143, 144, 185, 188–194, 205, 206, 211, 263–315, 321
  bibliography, annotated 313–315
  content of text 267–271
  survey of different editions 272–273
  Version 1: Shao Zhilin. Xiantian xuwu taiyi jinhua zongzhi 先天虛無太乙金華宗旨 (Tenet of the Supreme One Golden Flower Lineage, from the Emptiness of Former Heaven) 272, 274–279
  Version 2: Chen Mou. Xiantian xuwu taiyi jinhua zongzhi 先天虛無太乙金華宗旨 (Tenet of the Supreme One Golden Flower Lineage, from the Emptiness of Former Heaven) 272, 280–282
  Version 3: Jiang Yuanting, Lüzu quanshu. Fuyou shangdi tianxian jinhua zongzhi 孚佑上帝天仙金華宗旨 (Tenet of the Golden Flower by the Celestial Immortal Lineage of the Supreme Emperor and Sincere Protector [Lü Dongbin]) 272–273, 284–289
  Version 4: Jiang Yuanting, Daozang jiyao. Jinhua zongzhi 金華宗旨 (Quintessential Tenet of the Golden Flower) 272–273, 284–289
  Version 5: Min Yide, Lü zushi xiantian xuwu taiyi jinhua zongzhi 呂祖師先天虛無太一金華宗旨 (Quintessential Tenet of the Patriarch Lü on the Supreme One Golden Flower, Emptiness of Former Heaven) 273, 293–303
  Versions after 1900 273, 305–307
  Versions in the West 309–312
Jinhua zongzhi bianyan 金華宗旨弁言 291–292
Jinlian zhengzong ji 金蓮正宗記 (Account of the Orthodox Lineage of the Golden Lotus) 321
Jinlian zhengzong xianyuan xiangzhuan 金蓮正宗仙源像傳 (Illustrated Biographies of the Immortal Origins of the Orthodox Lineage of the Golden Lotus) 24, 25, 321

jinshi 進士 degree 18, 30, 44, 184, 186, 204, 322
Jinyu baojing 金玉寶經 143
jipan 乩盤 (spirit writing tray; planchette) 213
Jirang ji 擊壤集 242
jitan 乩壇 (spirit writing altar, q.v.) 186
Jiugong shan 九宮山 (mountain in Hubei) 59, 65, 66, 99, 104, 105
Jiuhuang doulao jiesha yansheng zhenjing 九皇斗姥說戒殺延生眞經 151, 321
Jiuzhen miaojie 九真妙戒 109, 110
jixian 乩仙 (spirit-writing immortal) 149
Jizhou 濟州, Shengshou gong 聖壽宮 44
Jizu daozhe 雞足道者 (Daoist of Chicken Foot Mountain) 72, 161
Jōdo Shinshū (Reformed Pure Land denomination of Japanese Buddhism) 8
Jōdoshū 净土宗 (Pure Land denomination of Japanese Buddhism) 8
Jordan, David K. 186, 213
Jorgensen, John 53, 84
juetan 覺壇 (see Jueyuantan)
jueyuan 覺源 (see Jueyuantan)
Jueyuantan 覺源壇 ([Spirit-writing] Altar of the Source of Awakening) 204, 205, 221, 251, 254, 286
Jung, Carl Gustav (1875-1961) 263, 264, 309, 310, 311, 312, 313, 314
Juqu 句曲 (today's Jurong 句容, Jiangsu) 81

K

kaidu 開度 (initiation ceremony) 152
Kaifeng 43
Kakiuchi, Tomoyuki 垣内智之 198
Kangxi 康熙 (emperor / reign 1662-1722) 17, 20, 42, 72, 76, 161, 181, 189, 257, 294, 295, 298, 300, 301, 302
karma 100, 103
Katz, Paul 33, 47, 121, 256
Ke Fengshi 柯逢時 (1844-1912) 224
Kieschnick, John 58, 59, 110
Kim, Jihyun 金志玹 177
Kim, Yunsu 金侖壽 177, 182, 184, 185, 186, 187, 190, 191, 193, 196, 198, 205, 206, 207, 221
Kōan (ch. gong'an 公案) 268
Kohn, Livia 3, 96, 110, 126, 128, 135, 164
Komjathy, Louis 157

Koran 212, 250
Kublai Khan (emperor Shizu 世祖, r. 1260-1293) 22, 25, 29, 30, 39, 40, 41, 66, 69, 160
Kunyang lüshi fuzhu jie 崑陽律師付囑偈 156
Kunyang Wang zhenren daoxing bei 崑陽王真人道行碑 (Stele on the Virtuous Behavior of the Perfected Wang Kunyang) 60

L

Lagerwey, John 92, 135
Lai, Chi-tim XI, 95, 259
laissez-passer (fujuan 符券 / fuxin 符信) 140, 141, 142, 143
Lamp histories 5, 6
lamp of mind (xindeng 心燈) 17, 20, 21, 28
Lancaster, Lewis 223
Lao-tse. *See* Laozi
Laojun yibai bashi jie 老君一百八十戒 111, 128
Laoshan 嶗山 (Mt. Lao) 16, 49, 50, 96, 120, 130, 172
Laozi 老子 5, 20, 37, 47, 87, 110, 114, 121, 122, 123, 125, 133, 135, 195, 211, 212, 215, 250, 300, 301, 302
lay precepts 122, 205, 251
leifa 雷法 (thunder rites) 121
Lengyan jing 楞嚴經 (Śūraṃgamasūtra) 268, 270
Li Daoqian 李道謙 (1219-1296) 19, 20, 23, 24, 25, 26, 27, 28, 29, 30, 31, 32, 33, 34, 37, 328
Li Gang 李剛 179
Li Hechun 李合春 179, 225
Li Huan 李桓 191, 204, 205
Li Lian 李濂 64
Li Lingyang 李靈陽 25
Li Qingao 李慶翱 29
Li Rong 李榕 320
Li Shengfeng 李盛鋒 224
Li Tingfu 李廷福 227
Li Xiangting 李香亭 227
Li Yangzheng 李養正 83, 92, 95, 179
Li Zhenyuan 李眞元 (1525-1573?; Wudangshan line) 16
Li Zhichang 李志常 (disciple of Qiu Chuji) 19, 22, 23, 24, 25, 26, 27, 28, 30, 33, 34, 37, 317
Liaoxu daoren 了虛道人 307

Liaoyang dian wenda bian 寥陽殿問答編 (Questions and Answers from the Liaoyang Hall) 62
Lichao shengxian mingru renwu quantu 歷朝聖賢名儒人物全圖 281
Liesheng baoxun tici 列聖寶訓題辭 291-292
Liezi 列子 202
lineage name (paiming 派名 or ming 名) 20
lineage poem 22, 41, 39-42, 144, 149, 267, 282, 285-287, 301
Lin Yiluan 林一鑾 (Shi Huidou 釋慧鐸) 138
Lingbao 靈寶 49, 52, 93, 109-112, 115, 116, 119, 124, 126, 133-135, 144, 155, 158, 160, 163, 164, 166, 167, 170, 171, 202, 216, 222, 243, 244, 255, 277
    Lingbao scriptures inspired by Buddhist sutras 133
    Lingbao tripartite ordination 119
Lingbao bifa 靈寶畢法 216
Lingbao dachan 靈寶大懺 158
Lingbao jiujie 靈寶九戒 110
Lingbao lingjiao jidu jinshu 靈寶領教濟度金書 126, 216, 321
Lingbao sanyuan zhai 靈寶三元齋 155, 160
Lingbao suishi wen 靈寶歲時文 255
Lingbao tianzun 靈寶天尊 202, 222
Lingbao wenjian 靈寶文檢 243, 244
lingguan 靈官 47, 156
Lingyougong 靈祐宮 69, 80, 83
Liou, Tse Houa 309
literati 30, 73, 186, 207, 216, 231, 295, 306
liturgy 7, 12, 54, 91, 108, 109, 133, 143, 149, 151, 152, 157, 168, 170, 203, 217, 247, 257, 258, 265, 277, 278, 279, 281, 282, 283, 286, 293, 294
Liu Changsheng 劉長生 (1147-1203) 25
Liu Chengyin 劉誠印 (?-1894) 61
Liu Chuxuan 劉處玄 (1147-1203) 157
Liu Du'an 劉度菴 290
Liu Haichan 劉海蟾 149, 150
Liu Huanling 劉煥玲 188
Liu Huayang 柳華陽 (1735-1799) 309
Liu Mi 劉謐 234
Liu Qi 柳棨 210
Liu Shouyuan 柳守元 97, 132, 133, 135, 140, 143, 145-147, 149-152, 170, 198, 206, 210, 211, 267, 285-287, 291-292
Liu Tishu 劉體恕 143, 193, 206, 209, 273, 282, 283, 284, 317

Liu Ts'un-yan 劉存仁 180
Liu Xianting 劉獻廷 41, 172, 320
Liu Xun 18, 23, 29, 173, 223, 239, 247
Liu Yu 劉玉 (founder of Jingming school) 277
Liu Yuanran 劉淵然 (1351-1432; Qingwei master) 11
Liu Zhongyu 劉仲宇 167
Liuba 留壩 (Shaanxi) 161–162
    Zhangliang miao 張良廟 161–162
Liuba miao kaishan yuanliu 留侯廟開山源流 161
liutong 六通 (six divine or magical powers) 58
Liuxi waizhuan 留溪外傳 (Unofficial Biographies from Liuxi) 73
local cults 227, 246, 257, 299
local deities 247
Lo, L.C. (collaborator of Richard Wilhelm) 309
Long Qiqian 龍起潛 (disciple of Wang Changyue) 76, 92, 102, 160
Longhu jing 龍虎經 202
Longhu mountain 龍虎山 in Jiangxi 48
Longmen 龍門 (Dragon Gate) *passim*
    and Baiyun guan 4–12
    and public ordinations 56
    beginning of modern popularity in 1980s 1–2
    establishment of orthodox patriarchal lineage, genealogy 6–12
    lineage poem 22, 41, 39–42, 149, 267, 282, 285–287, 301
    Longmen lüzong 龍門律宗 (Longmen Vinaya tradition) 92, 98, 102, 170, 171; *see also* lüshi
    Longmen orthodox line 龍門正宗 16, 38
    Longmen is to Daoism what the Linji tradition is to Buddhism 293
    Vinaya line masters 律師 16–18, 20, 22, 34, 42, 43, 48, 50–88, 115, 131, 148, 156, 168
    Longmen xianpai 龍門仙派 140, 169, 170
    Longmen zhengzong 龍門正宗 (Longmen orthodox lineage) 6, 13, 16, 17, 19, 20, 23, 38, 39, 43, 44, 46, 51, 52, 61, 70, 73, 85, 92, 169, 170–172, 321, 325
    Longmen zuting 龍門祖庭 (Longmen patriarchal garden) 93
    Mind-Lamp of Mt. Jingai as fundamental source for early Longmen history 38
    Mount Longmen 21, 35, 41
    orthodox transmission (zhengzong liuchuan 正宗流傳) 23, 297, 321
    provenience of term 8
    Taishang lümai Longmen zhengzong 太上律脈龍門正宗 (1919) 6, 19–21, 38, 43, 44, 46, 49, 51, 52, 54–59, 61, 63–65, 67–69, 73–77, 79–81, 84, 85, 92, 321, 324, 325
    Taishang zhengzong 太上正宗 (orthodox lineage of the Most High) 46
    will to orthodoxy 93, 259

Longmen chuanjie puxi 龍門傳戒譜系 6, 17, 19, 21, 37, 321, 325
Longmen xinfa 龍門心法 (Core Teachings of the Longmen, attr. Wang Changyue) 58, 61, 78, 80, 82–84, 92, 102, 103, 105–107, 157, 321
Longmen zhengzong fajuan 龍門正宗法卷 (Longmen orthodox Dharma scrolls) 77
Longmen zhengzong Jueyun benzhi daotong xinchuan 龍門正宗覺雲本支道統薪傳 6, 17, 19, 20, 21, 22, 38, 39, 61, 62, 63, 69
Longzhou 隴州 prefecture (Shaanxi province) 8
Lou Jinyuan 婁近垣 (1689-1776) 237
Lu Yongming 陸永銘 61, 321
Lu Yongzhi 陸永銘 19, 38
Lü Dongbin 呂洞賓 X, 3, 5, 13, 87, 132, 133, 135, 136, 143–145, 149–152, 170, 171, 185, 189, 190, 192, 193, 195, 200–202, 204–206, 208–213, 215–218, 221, 222, 227, 232, 243, 244, 246, 247, 250–253, 256, 263, 264, 266–269, 272–282, 284–287, 290–292, 295, 296, 298, 301–303, 305, 306, 308, 310, 311, 315, 319, 321, 322, 326
  central role in the Daozang jiyao 211–214
  Chunyang Daozu Miaodao tianzun 純陽道祖妙道大天尊 150
  Chunyang dijun 純陽帝君 210
  Fuyou dijun 孚佑帝君 136, 139, 143, 146, 151, 243, 252, 254, 295, 319
  Fuyou dishi 孚佑帝師 211, 286
  Fuyou shangdi 孚佑上帝 143, 202, 206, 253, 269, 272, 288, 289, 319, 322
  Lü zushi sanni yishi shuoshu 呂祖師三尼醫世說述 (Explanations on the Three Sages's Doctrine of Healing the World by the Founding Patriarch Lü) 189, 195, 301, 302
  Lüdi shiji 呂帝詩集 207, 321
  Lüdi wenji 呂帝文集 207, 322
  Lüdi xinjing 呂帝心經 143, 319, 322
  Lüzu benzhuan 呂祖本傳 242
  Lüzu quanshu 呂祖全書 (Patriarch Lü [Dongbin]'s Collected Works) 132, 139, 143, 151, 190, 193, 206, 208, 209, 210, 265, 266, 272, 273, 279, 280, 281, 282, 283, 284, 305, 317, 322
  Lüzu quanshu shiliu juan 呂祖全書十六卷 (Complete Works of Patriarch Lü in 16 scrolls) 190
  Lüzu quanshu zongzheng 呂祖全書宗正 (Orthodoxy of the Tradition of the Complete Writings of Ancestor Lü [Dongbin]; Chen Mou ed.) 185, 193, 266, 272, 280, 281, 288, 305
  Lüzu quanshu zongzheng jicheng 呂祖全書宗正集成 190
  Lüzu Tianxian zhengzong neiji 呂祖天仙正宗內集 (Inner Collection of the Orthodox Tradition of the Celestial Immortals of Patriarch Lü) 189
  Quanshu zhengzong 全書正宗 (Complete Works of the Orthodox Lineage; Jiang Yuanting ed.) 143, 185, 190, 193, 206, 207, 209, 210, 266, 272, 280, 281, 284, 285, 286, 288, 305
  Yuqing zanhua 玉清贊化 195, 202

Lü Quanyang 呂全陽 54, 319
Lü Yunyin 呂雲隱 (fl. 1710; eighth-generation Longmen Vinaya master) 18, 60, 61, 63, 69, 72, 318
Lu'an 潞安 (Shanxi) 60, 61, 62
Lulongsai 廬龍塞 (today's Xifengkou 喜峰口, Hebei) 80
Luo Hongxian 羅洪先 (1504-1564) 139
Luoyang 43
Lusheng dizi 籙生弟子 (Novices of the Register) 109
lüshi 律師 (Vinaya masters / lineage) 16–18, 20, 22, 34, 42, 43, 48, 50–88, 115, 131, 148, 156, 168
Lüzong 律宗 (Vinaya line; *see* under Longmen)

M

Ma Danyang 馬丹陽 (1123-1183; one of the Seven Perfected of Quanzhen) 20, 24, 31, 145, 157
Ma Xiaohong 馬曉宏 209, 280
Ma Zhenyi 馬眞一 (Huashan line) 16
magic 58, 103
Manchu 18, 310
mantras 252
Maoshan 茅山 (mountain in Jiangsu province) 57, 76, 79, 80, 81, 82, 84
Maoshan zhi 茅山志 (Gazetteer of Maoshan) 76
Marici 嘛哩唧 143
Marsone, Pierre 10, 11, 29, 61
martial arts 2
Massimello, Maria Anna 309
McRae, John R. 117
medicine 167, 268
meditation 2, 31, 58, 59, 82, 104, 106, 113, 131, 135, 158, 159, 162, 163, 167, 235, 268, 270, 271, 311
meditation hall 159, 162
mediums 212
Meian nianpu 梅庵年譜 186
Meng Yongcai 孟永才 (d. 1881) 18, 19, 113, 130
Miaodao shi 妙道師 (Master of Wondrous Dao) 107, 112
Miaode shi 妙德師 (Master of Wondrous Virtue) 107, 108, 112, 156
Miaolin jing 妙林經 111
Miaoxing shi 妙行師 (Master of Wondrous Practice) 107, 112
Min Xuesuo 閔雪簑 (fl. 1669) 295, 297, 298
Min Yide 閔一得 (1748/58-1836) XVIII, 1, 4, 5, 7, 8, 12, 17, 18, 20–22, 28,

31, 36–39, 44, 46, 47, 49, 51, 52, 60–62, 65, 72, 78, 83, 84, 91, 93, 105, 161, 165, 170, 187–192, 194, 195, 197, 204, 206, 269, 273, 293, 294, 296–303, 314, 317, 319–321, 327

Min Zhiting 閔智亭 (1924-2004) 92, 96, 111, 165, 281

mind-to-mind transmission (yixin chuanxin 以心傳心) 22, 268, 300, 301

Ming dynasty 3, 5, 10, 11, 42, 48–50, 52–54, 63, 69, 71, 73, 91, 117, 120, 156, 159, 164–167, 172, 177, 186, 203, 207, 231, 236, 245, 298, 311, 312

Mingxin 明心 (Wang Shuxun 王樹勳) 205, 206, 217, 250, 251, 254

Minorelli, Tommaso Maria (1680—1733) 231

Miura, Kunio 三浦邦夫 3, 29

Miyuki, Mokusen 目幸黙僊 311, 314

mizhu 秘咒 (secret invocations) 128

monasticism 7, 11, 12, 59, 65, 91, 96, 108, 114, 116, 151, 152, 157, 159, 163, 164, 166–168, 203, 219, 257, 258, 294

moon 38, 75, 101, 107, 238, 274

morality 62, 208, 213, 219, 246, 271

morality texts 123, 186, 278

Mori, Yuria 森由利亞 132, 133, 159, 177, 182, 185, 189–191, 198, 202, 204, 207, 210, 211, 217, 221, 227, 244, 245, 247, 250, 251, 255, 265, 273–275, 277, 278, 281, 282, 284, 285, 286, 315

Motoyama, Hiroshi 本山博 313

Mu Qingfeng 穆清風 81, 84

Mu Yufang 穆玉房 (fl. 1709) 86

Mugitani, Kunio 麥谷邦夫 XI, 93, 188, 198

N

Nanchang 南昌 79, 81, 184, 277, 324

Nanjing 南京 61, 70, 75, 76, 77, 78, 79, 80, 83, 84, 86, 92, 102, 289, 300, 303
    Biyuan guan 碧苑觀 (Biyuan monastery) 300
    Yinxian'an 隱仙庵 70, 75–78, 80, 86

Nanyun wengao 南畇文稿 79, 115, 328

Naquin, Susan 260

Needham, Joseph 228, 309, 311, 312, 315

neidan 內丹 (inner alchemy; see also under alchemy) 2, 163, 177, 187, 188, 202, 207, 215–217, 219, 263, 278, 309, 311, 312

Neo-Confucianism 4, 66, 203, 219, 228, 242

Nestorianism 264, 310

nifa 逆法 (method of reversal) 268

non-duality 271

Nüdan hebian 女丹合編 243, 244

Nü zhen jiujie 女眞九戒 157

O

officials 1, 2, 30, 54, 56, 80, 83, 100, 105, 110, 186, 204–207, 221, 227, 232, 234, 237, 250, 251, 254, 281, 283, 287, 306
ordinands 95, 100, 101, 114, 138, 140, 148, 150, 151, 156, 157, 162, 241, 259, 294, 301
ordination 4, 6–8, 11–13, 53, 56, 67, 69, 72, 75, 76, 78, 79, 80, 81, 83–87, 88, 92–98, 100, 102, 104–113, 115–117, 119–121, 126, 128, 130–133, 135, 136, 138, 140, 145, 147–152, 155–158, 160–168, 170, 171, 173, 257–259, 286, 287, 293, 294, 300–302
    ordination of three altars. *See* santan dajie 三壇大戒 (Great ordination of threefold altars)
    tripartite division in Daoism 119
    Triple Platform Ordination (ch. Santan jiehui, J. sandan kaie 三壇戒會) 117
ordination altar 100, 104, 116, 120, 145, 148, 149, 160, 162, 171
ordination certificates 95, 96, 108, 115, 116, 119, 130, 131, 148, 149
ordination platform 56, 67, 79, 84, 131, 300
orthodoxy 3, 4, 8, 11, 13, 39, 53, 93, 102, 172, 246, 250, 256, 259
Ōtani University 大谷大学 library (Kyoto) 266, 280, 283, 288
Overmyer, Daniel L. 186, 213, 254
Oyanagi, Shigeta 小柳司氣太 4, 6, 8, 41, 70, 72, 77, 79, 83, 91, 108, 115, 116, 131, 148, 162, 163, 164, 287, 317, 320
Ozaki, Masaharu 尾崎正治 180

P

paishi 派詩 (lineage verse; *see also* lineage poem) 285
Palmer, David 2
Pan Qiande 潘乾德 274, 275
Pan Yi'an 潘易菴 290–292
Pang Shiguan 龐士冠 206
Panxi 磻溪 (Shaanxi) 21
pāramitās (Buddhist perfections) 135
Pas, Julian 181
Pelliot, Paul (1878-1945) 196, 197, 224
Peng Dingqiu 彭定求 (1645-1719) 53, 79, 81, 82, 84, 115, 139, 179, 180, 182–187, 193, 203, 254, 280
    career and role in compilation of Daozang jiyao 186–187
Peng Hanran 彭瀚然 180, 181, 183, 225, 226, 227, 241, 245, 272
Peng Qifeng 彭啟豐 (1701-1784) 184, 185, 186, 193, 272, 280, 281, 282, 283
Peng Shaosheng 彭紹升 (1740-96) 138, 139

Peng Wenqin 彭文勤 182, 184, 185, 254
Peng Xilian 彭希濂 193
Peng Yuanrui 彭元瑞 (1731-1803) 182, 184, 185
Perfected Yin (Yin zhenren 尹真人) 191, 320, 327
piety 53, 59, 75
Piling 毘陵 (Changzhou 常州, Jiangsu) 265, 267, 274, 275, 279, 280, 281, 282, 283, 287, 288, 297, 299, 306
planchette 213 (*see also* spirit writing)
possession 99
precept-altar. *See* jietan 戒壇
precepts 8, 12, 22, 30, 37–41, 46–49, 52, 53, 55, 61–64, 66–69, 71, 72, 75, 76, 79, 85, 91–140, 144, 149, 151, 152, 155–162, 164, 165, 168, 169, 171, 177, 205, 216, 251, 275, 276, 287, 288, 294, 301, 302
    standard set of the late Qing 120
precept-texts (jiejing 戒經) 47, 63, 69, 92, 94–98, 119, 120, 152, 155, 164, 166, 168, 171, 173
Precious scrolls 260
Pregadio, Fabrizio 202
prohibitions 124, 125
propaganda 172
Pure Land Buddhism 236, 268
purification 123, 132, 158

Q

Qi Zhicheng 祁志誠 (1219-1293) 30
Qian Baofu 錢寶甫 (1791-1827) 303
Qian Daxin 錢大昕 (1728-1804) 23
Qianfa 鉗髮 73
Qianlong 乾隆 (emperor, re. 1736-1795) 72, 237
Qianshan Wulonggong 千山五龍宮 (Liaoning) 95
Qianyuanguan 乾元觀 (Yugang, Maoshan) 79, 81, 82, 84
Qiaoyang 樵陽 62
qigong 氣功, qigong fever 氣功熱 2, 3
Qin Pengsheng 秦芃生 183, 227
Qinding Daozang quanshu zongmu 欽定道藏全書總目 184, 187
Qing Xitai 卿希泰 58, 72, 79, 179, 183
qingchen jingyi 輕塵淨衣 114
Qingcheng shan 青城山 (mountain in Sichuan) 49, 51, 55, 58, 60, 95, 242
Qingcheng shan ji 青城山記 242
Qinggui xuanmiao quanzhen canfang 清規玄妙全眞參訪 161

Qingjing jing 清靜經 82, 110, 113
qingjing ziran 清靜自然 (pure quiescence and natural spontaneity) 21, 37
Qingshi gao 情史稿 (Draft History of the Qing) 18, 184, 185, 186, 206
Qingwei 情微 11, 109, 121, 143, 144, 149, 151, 152, 156, 163, 164, 170, 209, 210
Qingwei hongfan daomen gongke 清微宏範道門功課 109, 121, 143, 149-152, 156, 210
Qingwei Lingbao 清微靈寶 163, 164, 170
Qingwei sanpinjing xu 清微三品經序 209
qingxu ziran 清虛自然 (pure emptiness and natural spontaneity) 21, 37
Qingxuan jilian tieguan hushi 青玄濟煉鐵貫斛食 243
Qingyang gong 青羊宮 (Black Sheep Temple, Chengdu) 114, 178, 179, 192, 225, 228, 229, 242, 244, 255, 326
Qingyang gong beiji 青羊宮碑記 242
Qingyang gong Erxian'an zhi 青羊宮二仙庵誌 179, 225
Qiu Changchun 邱長春 (= Qiu Chuji)
Qiu Chuji 邱處機 (1148-1227) 3, 8, 9-12, 16-18, 20-35, 38-40, 44, 46, 50, 52, 53, 67, 82, 87, 88, 91-94, 103, 105, 106, 108, 119, 120, 141, 145, 147-150, 152, 161, 163-165, 169, 171-173, 274,-276, 278, 288, 290-292, 294, 299, 302
Qiu Tongxiao 邱通宵, fl. 1757) 267, 281, 282, 290-292
Qiu Zhao'ao 仇兆鰲 (1638-1713) 187
Qiuzu chanhui wen 邱祖懺悔文 108, 157
Qixia 棲霞 (Shandong) 25
Qiyan sanshi yun 七言三十韻 64
Quanshu zhengzong 全書正宗 (Jiang Yuanting ed.) 143, 185, 190, 193, 206, 207, 209, 210, 266, 272, 280, 281, 284, 285, 286, 288, 305
Quanshu zongzheng 全書宗正 (Chen Mou ed.) 185, 193, 266, 272, 280, 281, 288, 305
Quanzhen 全真 (Complete Perfection) 1, 5, 8-12, 20, 23-31, 34, 39-42, 46, 49, 50, 53, 58, 65, 79, 81, 85, 87, 91-98, 103, 105, 106, 108, 109, 113, 115, 116, 119-121, 126, 132, 133, 141, 145, 147-152, 155-159, 161-173, 187, 210, 217, 222, 223, 227, 247, 257-259, 268, 274, 286-288, 293, 294, 302
    association with Baiyun guan 9-11
    Northern tradition 11, 53
    Quanzhen identity 12, 98, 109, 159
    Quanzhen "innovation" and "conservation" narratives 94
    Quanzhen Longmen orthodox lineage 全真教龍門正宗 and key figure Wang Changyue 93
    Quanzhen ordination altar (Quanzhen lütan 全真律壇) 79, 115

Quanzhen ordination, genesis of 155–170
Quanzhen precepts and Golden Age / degeneration / regeneration narrative 98–106
Quanzhen Ur-Vinaya tradition (Longmen lüzong 龍門律宗) 91, 98, 106, 149, 170, 171
Quanzhen zhengjiao 全真正教 (Quanzhen orthodox teachings) 151, 152
Quanzhen qinggui 全真清規 157, 158, 159, 162, 163, 164, 166, 322
Quanzhen's Seven Perfected (qizhen 七真) 8, 9, 20
  and Longmen patriarchs 8–9
  and Zhao Daojian 20
Queen Mother of the West (Xiwang mu 西王母) 64
quietude 21, 75

R

Ray, Reginald 34
regalia 56, 113, 114, 128
regeneration 99, 101, 102, 103, 104, 106, 145, 171
Reiter, Florian 5, 65
relics 34
religious associations 268, 286
Ren Jiyu 任繼愈 179, 180, 183
Ren Zongquan 任宗權 92, 259
revelation 37, 47, 80, 99, 107, 12–126, 132–136, 139, 140, 149, 150–152, 168, 170, 202, 207, 209, 211, 212, 222, 227, 250, 252–254, 256, 265, 267–270, 274, 275, 277, 278, 280–282, 287, 288, 295–297, 300, 302, 303, 306–308
Ricci, Matteo (1522–1610) 231
ritual 27, 30, 48, 49, 53, 56, 64, 67, 87, 88, 91, 114–117, 128, 143–145, 147, 162, 163, 165, 167, 177, 216, 217, 246, 247, 253, 256, 274, 277, 315
Riyong jing 日用經 222
robe and bowl transmission 22, 41, 43, 46, 56, 67, 301
Robinet, Isabelle XI
Ruan Dacheng 阮大鋮 (1587–1646) 79
rula 入臘 (ordination retreat) 108, 131, 157
Ruyaojing 入藥鏡 202

S

Sadakata, Akio 湯浅泰雄 310, 313
Saeki, Yoshiro 佐伯好郎 (1871-1965) 264, 310
Sairam (Sailan) 塞藍 26
Śākyamuni 195, 212, 250

Samarkand 25, 27, 34
Sanbao wanling fachan 三寶萬靈法懺 242
sandajie 三大戒 161, 301
sandong 三洞 (Three Caverns) 202
Sandong fafu kejie wen 三洞法服科戒文 109
Sandong zhongjie wen 三洞眾戒文 109, 121, 134, 322
Sanfa dulun 三法度論 269
Sanguan jing 三官經 113, 123
sangui yijie 三皈依戒 (three refuges: Dao, scriptures, master) 121–122
Sanhuang neiwen yibi 三皇內文遺祕 141, 144, 323
Sanhuang wen 三皇文 141, 144
sanji jie 三極戒 (three ultimate precepts) 161
sanjiao 三教 *see* Three Teachings
sanjiao chu wuyi zhi 三教初無異旨 245
sanjiao heyi 三教合一 (unity of the Three Teachings) 232
sanjiao hezong 三教合宗 245
Sanjiao pingxin lun 三教平心論 234
sanni 三尼 (Three Sages: Confucius, Laozi, Buddha) 189, 195
sanni yishi 三尼醫世 (the Three Sages' [Doctrine of] Healing the World) 189, 195
Sanni yishi shuoshu 三尼醫世說述 298
Sanpin jing 三品經 209, 210
Sanqing 三清 (Three Pure Ones) 145, 146, 201, 202, 212, 222, 248, 250, 270
Sanshan guan lu 三山館錄 62
santan dajie 三壇大戒 (great ordination of threefold altars) 7, 12, 94, 96, 97, 115, 117, 119, 126, 133, 155, 157, 168, 171, 294
    first publication in early 19th century 97
    problematic attribution to Wang Changyue 96–97
Santan yuanman Tianxian dajie lüeshuo 三壇圓滿天仙大戒略說 97, 210, 323
sanyi yibo 三衣一鉢 (three robes and one bowl) 114
Sanyuan 三元 (Three Primes) 119, 127
    and tripartite Daoist ordination 119
Sawada, Mizuho 260
Schipper, Kristofer 11, 109, 110, 111, 129, 136, 145, 221, 222, 223, 254, 258, 274, 277
Secret of the Golden Flower (*see* Jinhua zongzhi 金華宗旨)
sectarian groups and activities 31, 38, 149, 234, 235, 245, 279, 280
Seidel, Anna 311
self-cultivation 7, 49, 56, 74, 100, 186, 207, 216

Shaanxi province 8, 21, 44, 48–51, 86, 99, 161, 165
Shandong province 25, 30, 48, 50, 57, 120, 130, 173, 224, 228
Shang Kai 賞鍇 138
Shang Sin Chun temple (Hong Kong) 214
Shangqing 上清 111, 112, 126, 127, 155, 156, 323
Shangqing dongzhen zhihui guanshen dajie wen 上清洞真智慧觀身大戒文 111, 126, 156, 323
Shangqinggong 上清宮 (Laoshan, Shandong) 119, 130
Shangyang zi jindan dayao 上陽子金丹大要 323
shanshu 善書 (morality books) 123, 186, 278
Shanxi province 48, 49, 58, 60, 61
Shao Shoushan 邵守善 72
Shao Yong 邵雍 (1011-1077) 203
Shao Zhilin 邵志林 (1748-1810) 139, 143, 193, 206, 266, 267, 272–276, 278–284, 287, 290–292, 299
shapan 砂盤 (spirit writing tray; planchette) 213
Shek, Richard 11, 277
Shen Bingcheng 沈秉成 5
Shen Changjing 沈常靜 (1523-1633; Longmen Doctrinal line, seventh generation) 16
Shen Jingyuan 沈靜圓 (fl. 1448; fifth generation Longmen orthodox line; doctrinal line) 16, 52
Shen Yibing 沈一炳 (1708-1786), 11th-generation Longmen patriarch 195
Shen Yicheng 沈一誠 84
Sheng Qingxin 盛清新 84
Sheng Qingya 盛青崖 (fl. 1647) 295, 297
Shengji jiyao 聖蹟紀要 207, 323
Shengshou gong 聖壽宮 (Jizhou 濟州) 44
Shenxiao 神霄 legacy 121, 139, 145, 156, 170
shenxiao leifa 神霄雷法 (thunder rite) 121
Shi Chengzao 石承藻 206
Shi Huidou 釋慧鐸 (Lin Yiluan 林一鑾) 138
Shi Shouping 施守平 317
Shi Tai 石泰 (d. 1158) 187
Shi Zhijing 史志經 (1205-?; second-generation disciple of Qiu Chuji) 33
shifang conglin 十方叢林 (public monasteries) 163, 257
Shiga, Ichiko 志賀市子 208, 213, 286
Shijie gongguoge 十戒功過格 207, 323
Shiliupin jing 十六品經 151, 247

Shinohara, Kōichi 59
Shinran 親鸞 (1173-1263) 8
Shishanye daojing jiyao 十善業道經節要 234
Shishi yuanliu yinghua shiji 釋氏源流應化事蹟 118, 323
Shizu 世祖 (first Yuan emperor Kublai Khan, r. 1260–1293) 22, 25, 29, 30, 39, 40, 41, 66
Shizu 世祖 (first Qing emperor Shunzhi 順治, r. 1644–1661) 69, 160, 161, 301
Shoujie bizhi 守戒必持 113
shoujie 受戒 (taking the precepts; *see also* precepts, ordination) 164, 166, 325
shoulu 受籙 (receiving registers, ordination) 72, 164, 166
Shunzhi 順治 (first Qing emperor Shizu 世祖, re. 1644-1661) 69, 160, 161, 301
Sichuan province 49–51, 55, 58, 81, 84, 86, 95, 119, 166, 179–181, 183, 185, 217, 220, 222–228, 232, 244–247, 253, 256, 314
Siku quanshu 四庫全書 79, 115, 205, 207, 221, 250, 253, 323, 326
Sima Chengzhen 司馬承禎 3
siyu 四御 (Four Sovereigns) 146
Snyder-Reinke, Jeffrey 253
Song Hui'an 宋慧安 (fl. 1884-1894) 127
Song Rong 宋鎔 193, 206
spirit writing, or planchette writing 111, 121, 132, 135, 138, 140–145, 148–150, 152, 155, 156, 168, 170, 171, 186, 187, 202, 204–209, 211, 213–217, 221, 222, 227, 250, 251, 253, 254, 265, 267–269, 271, 273–275, 279–283, 286–288, 297, 300, 302, 303, 306–308, 315
    and inspired writing in different religions 212
    and role of Lü Dongbin in Daozang jiyao canon 211–214
    feiluan 飛鸞 (flying phoenix) 186
    fuji 扶乩 (wielding the stylus) 186
    fuluan 扶鸞 (wielding the phoenix) 186
    fuluantan 扶鸞壇 (spirit-writing altar) 148
    jiangbi 降筆 (descending brush) 186
    jiangluan 降鸞 (descending phoenix) 139, 186
    jitan 乩壇 (spirit writing altar) 186
    shapan 砂盤 (spirit writing tray; planchette) 213
spirit writing altar 121, 132, 138, 141–144, 148, 149, 152, 155, 156, 170, 171, 186, 187, 205, 208, 209, 211, 215, 221, 251, 253, 265, 267, 269, 274, 275, 279, 280, 281, 286–288, 297, 300, 302, 306
Su Lang 蘇朗 201, 212, 250, 252
Suizhou 睢州 (Henan) 186, 204
Sun Xi 孫錫 28

Sun Xuanqing 孫玄清 (1497-1563; Laoshan line) 16, 49, 50
Sun Yuyang 孫玉陽 (eighth Longmen patriarch) 82
Sun zhenren beiji qianjin yaofang 孫真人備急千金要方 242
Śūraṃgamasūtra. *See* Lengyan jing 楞嚴經
Suter, Rufus O. 184, 186, 187
Suzhou 蘇州 2, 72, 76, 79, 81, 138, 139, 186, 187, 192, 193, 196, 197, 266, 274, 279, 318
syncretism 232, 234, 264

T

taboo character 17, 42
Taigong yinfu jing 太公陰符經 242
Taihegong 太和宮 (Yunnan) 72, 77
Taihetang 太和堂 (Wudangshan) 77, 86
Taiji gaoxian tianwang 太極高仙天王 126
Taiji gong 太極宮 30
Taiji tu 太極圖 (Chart of the Great Ultimate) 242
Taiji tu shuo 太極圖說 242
taijiquan 太極拳 (T'ai-chi) XI, 2
Taiping jing 太平經 216
Taiqing gong 太清宮 (Longmen abbey in Shenyang 沈陽, Liaoning) 69
Taiseikyū shi 太清宮志 (ch. Taiqing gong zhi; Gazetteer of the Taiqing gong) 73, 74, 77, 92, 119, 148, 149
Taishang chujia chuandu yi 太上出家傳度儀 126, 166
Taishang Daodejing jie 太上道德經解 207
Taishang Daojun 太上道君 133, 135
Taishang dongshen zhihui shangpin dajie jing 太上洞玄靈寶智慧上品大戒經 110
Taishang dongxuan lingbao sanyuan pinjie gongde jingzhong jing 太上洞玄靈寶三元品戒功德輕重經 111, 323
Taishang dongxuan lingbao yebao yinyuan jing 洞玄靈寶業報因緣經 134, 323
Taishang dongxuan lingbao yushu tiaoyuan yingxian xunjing 太上洞玄靈寶玉樞調元應顯尊經 243, 244
Taishang dongxuan lingbao zhihui benyuan dajie shangpin 太上洞玄靈寶智慧本願大戒上品經 111, 323
Taishang ganying hongwen 太上感應鴻文 278
Taishang ganying pian 太上感應篇 113, 123
Taishang ganying pian fu chisong yize 太上感應篇附持誦儀則 151

Taishang ganying pian jianzhu 太上感應篇箋註 151, 324
Taishang gaosheng daojun 太上高聖道君 126
Taishang jingjie 太上經戒 111, 324
Taishang jiuzhen miaojie jinlu duming bazui miaojing 太上九真妙戒金籙度命拔罪妙經 109, 324
Taishang laojun jinglü 太上老君經律 111, 128, 324
Taishang lingbao chaotian xiezui fachan 太上靈寶朝天謝罪法懺 242
Taishang lingbao dacheng miaofa lianhua shenjing 太上靈寶大乘妙法蓮華真經 135
Taishang lingbao jingming chuzhen jiejing 太上靈寶淨明初真戒經 119, 324
Taishang lingbao jingming shangzhen jiejing 太上靈寶淨明上真戒經 119, 324
Taishang lingbao jingming zhengzhen jiejing 太上靈寶淨明正真戒經 119, 324
Taishang lingbao yuanyang miaojing 太上靈寶元陽妙經 134, 324
Taishang lingbao zhihui guanshen jing 太上靈寶智慧觀身經 126, 324
Taishang lümai Longmen zhengzong 太上律脈龍門正宗 (1919) 6, 19–21, 38, 43, 44, 46, 49, 51, 52, 54–59, 61, 63–65, 67–69, 73–77, 79–81, 84, 85, 92, 321, 324, 325
Taishang qingjing lübao 太上清靜律寶 37
Taishang sandajie 太上三大戒 (Three Great Precepts of the Highest Lord) 161, 301
Taishang sanyuan cifu shezui jie'e xiaozai yansheng baoming miaojing 太上三元賜福赦罪解厄消災延生保命妙經 123, 242
Taishang shier shangpin feitian falun quanjie miaojing 太上十二上品飛天法輪勸戒妙經 134, 325
Taishang wuji dadao sanshiliu bu zunjing 太上無極大道三十六部尊經 243, 244
Taishang wuji dadao sanshiliubu zunjing qiqing keyi 太上無極大道三十六部尊經啟請科儀 244
Taishang xuanmen gongke jing 太上玄門功課經 109, 242, 258
Taishang xuhuang tianzun sishijiu zhanjing 太上虛皇四十九章經 134, 325
Taishang yuhuang benxin jing 太上玉皇本行集經 144
Taishang zhenchuan shoujie bichi 太上真傳守戒必持 113, 325
Taishang zhenmai 太上真脈 (Genuine lineage of the Most High) 44, 46
Taiwei dijun sanbu bajing huiyuan jing 太微帝君三部八景回元經 151
Taiwei lingshu ziwen xianji zhenji shangjing 太微靈書紫文仙忌真記上經 134, 325

Taiwei tiandi 太微天帝 126
Taiyi fapai 太乙法派 (Taiyi branch) 144, 265, 267, 276–279
Taiyi jinhua lineage (Taiyi Jinhua fapai 太乙金華法派) 281–283, 288, 283, 299
Taiyi jinhua zongzhi 太乙金華宗旨 (Secret of the Golden Flower; *see also* Jinhua zongzhi) 204, 263–315
Taizu 太祖 (emperor, r. 1368-1394) 53
talismans 167, 215, 216
Tan Changzhen 譚長真 290
Tan Chuduan 譚處端 274, 275, 277
Tan Shoucheng 譚守誠 (?-1689?; eighth Longmen Vinaya patriarch) 70, 71, 71–78, 72, 79, 83, 86
Tang Bin 湯斌 (1627-1687) 186
Tang Chuyang 唐初陽 (successor of ninth Longmen patriarch Zhan Tailin) 81, 84
Tang Dachao 唐大潮 232
Tang liudian 唐六典 35, 168
Tantrism 188, 236
Tanzhou 檀州 (Miyun district, Beijing) 23, 24, 26
Tanzi 譚子 113
Tao Hongjing 陶宏景 81
Tao Jing'an 陶靖菴 (1616-1673; founder of Mt. Jingai Yunchao branch) 60, 72, 295, 297, 298, 300
Tao Shi'an 陶石庵 (?-1692) 60, 62, 189, 295, 297, 298, 302, 303
Tao Susi 陶素耜 (fl. 1676) 187
ten precepts of Initial Perfection 109, 123, 124, 125
three hundred precepts of the Medium Ultimate 125–128
three refuges 47, 109, 117, 120, 121, 122, 123
Three Teachings (sanjiao 三教: Confucianism, Buddhism, Daoism) 59, 65, 219, 231–260, 271
three-stage ordination 69, 155
Tian Chengyang 田誠陽 181
Tianchang guan 天常觀 (Abbey of Celestial Endurance, Beijing) 10, 30
Tianhuang neiwen shang 天皇内文上 141
Tianhuang xinzhou 天皇心咒 141, 278
Tianhuang zhidao taiqing yuce 天皇至道太清玉冊 159, 325
Tiantai shan 天台山 (mountain in Zhejiang province) 54, 55, 57, 59, 235, 268, 269
Tiantan Wangwu shan shengji ji 天壇王屋山聖迹記 64, 325

Tianxian dadao 天仙大道 (Great Way of Heavenly Immortals) 141
Tianxian dafa zongzhi 天仙大法宗旨 (Tenets of the Great Method of Celestial Immortals) 205
tianxian dajie 天仙大戒 (Great Precepts of Celestial Immortals) 12, 22, 94, 96, 97, 107, 108, 111, 115, 120, 127, 131–152, 156, 158, 160. 168, 170, 210, 286, 294, 323
    as product of Jiang Yuanting's spirit writing altar 156
tianxian jiege 天仙戒果 113
Tianxian jindan xinfa 天仙金丹心法 207, 217, 325
Tianxian pai 天仙派, Tianxian fapai 天仙法派 (Tianxian lineage) 132, 133, 145, 149–151, 170, 171, 206, 211, 216, 217, 267, 285, 286, 288, 289
Tianxian Taiyi jinhua zongzhi 天仙太乙金華宗旨 (Tenets of the Golden Flower of the Supreme One of the Tianxian [lineage]) 267
tianxian xiayi 天仙霞衣 114
Tianxian zhengli 天仙正理 (Proper Principles of Celestial Immortality), by Wu Shouyang 325
tianxian zhengmai 天仙正脈 (orthodox lineage of celestial immortals) 147, 149, 171
tianxin 天心 (celestial heart/mind) 110, 138, 139, 268
Tiaoxi 苕溪 (Zhejiang) 54
Tiezhugong 鐵柱宮 (Nanchang, Jiangxi) 79, 81
Tong Chenghe 佟成和 306, 307
Tong Wuxuan 佟悟玄 308
Tongbai shan 桐柏山 (mountain in Tiantai, Zhejiang) 57, 235
Tongcan jing 同參經 142, 207
Tongshu 通書 242
Tongxian 通仙 310, 313
Tongzhi 同治 (emperor / reign 1861-1875) 108, 162
Trigault, Nicolas (1577-1628) 231
Tsui, Bartholomew P. M. 167
Tu Qianyuan 屠乾元 278–280, 287
Tu Yu'an 屠宇菴 265, 274, 275, 278, 279, 281, 283, 286, 288, 290–292

U

Uchida Kakichi 內田嘉吉 (1866-1933) 199, 224
Ur-Daoism 122, 149, 170
Ur-tradition 101, 102, 105

V

Valussi, Elena 179, 244
Vatican 1, 4, 5, 8, 88, 164, 294
vegetarian 127, 186, 205, 251
vegetarian society 186
vinaya 7, 16, 18, 20, 22, 26–28, 34, 35, 37–40, 43, 44, 46–48, 50–57, 60, 62, 63, 67, 69–72, 75–88, 91–94, 98, 99, 100–106, 117, 130, 131, 147–149, 152, 156, 158, 161, 164, 168–171, 236, 298–302, 328
Vinaya transmission 47, 52, 53, 67, 69, 70, 77, 102
Vinaya line masters 律師 16–18, 20, 22, 34, 42, 43, 48, 50–88, 115, 131, 148, 156, 168
Vitale, Augusto 309

W

Waley, Arthur 9, 23, 27, 28, 30, 34
Wan Dekai 万德凱 185
Wang Changyue 王常月 (Wang Kunyang 王崑陽, ?-1680) 6,–8, 11, 12, 16, 18, 37, 38, 46, 47, 52, 53, 55, 56, 58–72, 74, 76, 77, 80, 83–86, 88, 91–94, 96–98, 102, 106, 107, 116, 119, 120, 132, 133, 141, 147, 149, 155–157, 160–162, 164, 165, 168, 170–173, 258, 286, 294, 298–302, 317
    and aim of Chuzhen jielü's preface authors 156
    and Longmen, Baiyun guan 11–12
    and the myth of Quanzhen reestablishment 91–93
    as alleged author of Quanzhen precept texts 94–96
    as great "Longmen restorer" 11–13
    as key figure of foundation myth of the Quanzhen Longmen orthodox lineage 93
    as pivotal figure in Longmen foundation myth 12
    as promoter of Quanzhen vinaya renaissance of Qing 91
    portrayed as agent of regeneration 102–110
    Vinaya-tours 92
Wang Chongyang 王重陽 24, 25, 65, 149, 150, 328
Wang Daoyuan 王道淵 188
Wang Ka 王卡 181
Wang Kuipu 王魁溥 314
Wang Kunyang 王崑陽. See Wang Changyue 王常月
Wang Kunyang lüshi zhuan (Biography of Vinaya Master Wang Changyue) 王崑陽律師傳 60
Wang Lingguan 王靈官 (Numinous Officer Wang) 47 121, 136, 139, 140, 144, 156

Wang Miaosheng 王妙生 241
Wang Qingzheng 王清正 (fl. 1651; Huashan line) 16
Wang Quechen 王卻塵 (fl. 1728-30) 86
Wang Shan 王善 (= Wang Lingguan 王靈官, q. v.) 139
Wang Shiu-hon 180, 184
Wang Shuxun 王樹勳 (also called Mingxin 明心) 205–6, 217, 250, 251, 254
Wang Tianjun 王天君 290–292
Wang Xinzhi 王信祉 113, 148
Wang Yangming 王陽明 186
Wang Yuanshuai 王元帥 (Marshal Wang) 47
Wang Yuanzhi 王元祉 149
Wang Zhizhong 王志忠 28, 58
Wang Zongyao 王宗耀 1, 188
Wang Zongyu 王宗昱 34
Wang, Richard G. 64
Wangmu dong 王母洞 (Wangwu shan, Henan) 64
Wangwu shan 王屋山 (mountain in Henan province) 57–59, 63, 64, 69, 104, 105, 325
Wanyan Chongshi 完顏崇實 (1820–1876) 17–19, 60
Watson, Burton 55
Wei tushu gei guanhe 為徒屬給冠褐 128
Wei Zhending 衛眞定 (Longmen doctrinal line) 16
Wei Zhengjie 衛正節 298, 299
Weinstein, Stanley 5
weishu 緯書 (weft texts) 145
Weituo 韋駝 (jap. Ida; guardian deity of Buddhist monasteries and their kitchens) 47
weiyishi 威儀師 34
Welter, Albert 59
Wenchang dijun benzhuan 文昌帝君本傳 242
Wenchang 文昌 (divinity of literature) 186, 187, 193, 203, 209, 225, 242, 247
Wendi huashu 文帝化書 242
Weng Baoguang 翁葆光 (fl. 1173) 187
Wenshi jing 文始經 113
Wenshi zhenjing 文始真經 269
Wenzi 文子 202
Wilhelm, Richard (1873-1930) 263–265, 305, 309–313
Wilhelm, Salome 305, 309
William Chen 181
Wittern, Christian XI, 219

Wofo si 臥佛寺 (Monastery of the Reclining Buddha, Beijing) 34
Wu Fengzhou 吳鳳洲 190
Wu Jiang 117, 233, 236, 237, 238
Wu Lianyuan 吳聯元 29
Wu Shouxu 伍守虛 16, 140, 172, 326
Wu Shouyang 伍守陽 (1574-1644?) 16, 41, 69, 135, 140, 141, 150, 168, 169, 170, 172, 203, 325, 326
Wu Songsheng 伍崧生 (1829–1915) 226
Wu Taiyi 吳太一 77, 135
Wu Yakui 吳亞魁 1, 187
Wuchang 武昌 (Hubei) 71
Wudang shan 武當山 (Mt. Wudang) 16, 57, 70, 74–77, 86, 92, 160, 172, 326
    Taihetang 太和堂 77, 86
    Wudangshan 武當山 line 16
Wudou jing 五斗經 202
Wuhuashan 五華山 34
Wujie 無戒 (name of Perfected) 133, 134
Wujing hebian 五經合編 143, 207, 326
Wulao 五老 (Five Ancient Lords) 145
Wuling 武陵 (Hangzhou) 71
Wupian lingwen 五篇靈文 242
Wushang biyao 無上祕要 126, 216, 326
Wushang neibi zhenzang jing 無上內秘真藏經 134, 326
wushu 武術 (martial arts) 2
wuwei er wei 無為而為 (doing without doing / acting without striving) 270
Wuxing qiongyuan 悟性窮原 307
Wuzhen pian 悟真篇 235, 268

X

Xianfeng 咸豐 (emperor, re. 1850-1861) 187
Xianfo hezong yulu 仙佛合宗語錄 (Recorded Sayings on the Common Tradition of Daoism and Buddhism) 135, 141, 150, 169, 326
xianjie 仙戒 (Immortals' precepts) 135
Xianle ji 仙樂集 157, 326
xiantian 先天 (before Heaven) 188, 268, 273, 285
Xiantian doudi chiyan wushang xuangong lingmiao zhenjing 先天斗帝敕演無上玄功靈妙真經 207, 326
Xiantian doudi chiyan wushang xuangong lingmiao zhenjing shujie 先天斗帝敕演無上玄功靈妙真經疏解 121

Xiantian xuwu Taiyi jinhua zongzhi 先天虛無太乙金華宗旨 (Tenets of the Golden Flower of the Taiyi [lineage] of Pre-celestial Emptiness) 267, 279, 283, 290–292, 303
xianzong 仙宗 (tradition of Immortals) 140, 145, 150, 169, 170
xianzong xuanjiao 仙宗玄教 (esoteric teaching of the tradition of Immortals) 170
Xiao Jichuan 蕭濟川 227
Xiao Lun 蕭掄 195
Xiao Tianshi 蕭天石 265, 307, 313
Xiao zhiguan 小止觀 (Small manual of śamatha-vipaśyanā) 268
Xiao Zuozhou 蕭作舟 227
Xiaodao 孝道 277
Xiaoti Wang 孝悌王 290–292
Xiaoyao jue 逍遙訣 (The Key to Freedom) 270, 295, 296
xiayi 霞衣 114
Xie Ningsu 謝凝素 (fl. 1652) 274, 295, 297
Xie Zhengqiang 謝正強 1, 187
Xifengkou 喜峰口 (Hebei) 80
xinchuan 心傳 (mind-to-mind transmission) 17, 19, 20, 38, 39, 215, 321
Xinchuan shuzheng lu 心傳述證錄 203
xinggong 性功 (practice of inner nature) 267
Xinjing zhu 心經註 206
Xinxiang miaoyu 心香妙語 243, 244
Xinye 新野 (Hebei) 20
xinyi 信衣 114
xinyin 心印 (seal of mind) 22, 41, 68, 74, 76, 85, 143, 195
Xinyin jing 心印經 82, 268
Xishan 西山 (mountain in Jiangxi province) 324
xiu guanhui 修觀慧 (practice of contemplative wisdom) 135
Xiu Shoucheng 徐守誠 (1633–1692) 116
Xiubu Quanshu ji 修補全書記 280
Xiuzhen biannan 修真辯難 (Debate on the Cultivation of Perfection) by Liu Yiming 劉一明 20
Xiuzhen shishu 修真十書 (Ten Books on the Cultivation of Perfection) 187
Xiwang mu 西王母 (Queen Mother of the West) 64
Xiyi zhimi lun 析疑指迷論 225, 228, 242
Xiyou ji 西游記 (Journey to the West) 25, 27, 28, 30, 33, 34, 326
Xu huang tianzun chuzhen shijie wen 虛皇天尊初真十戒文 125, 326
Xu Jingyang 許旌陽 290–292

Xu Sheng'an 許深菴 290–292
Xu Xun 許遜 (trad. 239-374) 3, 81, 268, 274, 275, 276, 277, 279
Xu Ziyuan 徐紫垣 (1630–1719) 60
Xuandu lütan chuanjie yinli guize 玄都律壇傳戒引禮規則 114, 326
Xuandu lütan weiyi 玄都律壇威儀戒 6, 77, 85, 127, 136, 147, 326
Xuanfeng qinghui tu 玄風慶會圖 or Felicitous Meetings with the Mysterious School, with Illustrations (1305) 31, 32, 33, 326
Xuanjiao da gong'an 玄教大公案 326
xuanmen 玄門 (mysterious teaching) 17, 242, 258
Xuanmen shishi weiyi 玄門十事威儀 109
Xuanmiao guan 玄妙觀 (Suzhou) 138, 193, 318
Xuanzong zhengzhi 玄宗正旨 144, 207, 327
Xuanzong 玄宗 140
Xue Daoguang 薛道光 274
Xuhuang tianzun Chuzhen shijie wen 皇天尊初真十戒文 124
Xujing xiansheng neizhuan 虛靜先生內傳 (Inner Biography of Master Zhao Xujing) 32, 327

Y

Yamada, Toshiaki 山田利明 141
Yanagida, Seizan 柳田聖山 5
yanbo 演缽 160–163
Yang Haiying 楊海英 69, 80
Yang Mingxing 楊明性 241
Yang Shen'an 揚慎菴 12, 18
yangsheng 養生 310
Yang Weikun 揚維崑 5
Yan Hui 顏回 55
Yan Liuqian 嚴六謙 19, 38, 61, 73
Yan Yanfeng 嚴雁峰 (1855-1918) 181, 183, 201, 222, 223, 224, 225, 226, 227
Yan Yonghe 閻永和 (fl. 1891-1908) 114, 115, 119, 127, 136, 138, 147, 162, 183, 217, 225, 226, 227, 241, 242, 245, 254, 255, 258, 259, 273
Yao Jicang 姚濟蒼 (alias Hedaozi 合道子) 305, 306, 306–308, 307, 314
Yao Tao-chung 10
Yaoxiu keyi jielü chao 要修科儀戒律鈔 111, 112, 126, 128, 327
Yayi ji 雅宜集 243, 244
Yedaposhe (Huang Shouzhong 黃守中) 72
Yi Gou 弋毅 25
Yijing 易經 268, 278, 310

Yiliao shanren 一了山人 306, 307
Yilin 逸林 12, 18, 21, 22, 41
yin and yang 陰陽 271
Yin Pengtou 尹蓬頭 327
Yin Xi 尹喜 (guardian of the pass) 269
Yin zhenren Donghua zhengmai huangji hepi zhengdao xianjing 尹真人東華正脈皇極闔闢證道仙經 62, 190–192, 320, 327
Yin Zhihua 尹志華 8, 18, 19, 30, 70, 77, 92, 125, 179, 225
Yin Zhiping 尹志平 (1169-1251; disciple of Qiu Chuji) 10, 25, 26, 28, 34
Yinfujing 陰符經 (Scripture on Joining with Obscurity) by Li Quan 李筌 188, 202, 222, 268, 269
Yinfujing xuanjie zhengyi 陰符經玄解正義 (Correct Interpretation of the Profound Meaning of the Yinfujing) 188
Yinli guize 引禮規則 114, 115, 119, 127, 136, 138, 147, 162, 326
Yinxian sipai 隱仙嗣派 308
Yinxian'an 隱仙庵 (Nanjing) 70, 75–78, 80, 86
yishi zhangben 醫世張本 299
Yishi zong 醫世宗 (Tradition of Healing the World) 189, 299
yishi 醫世 (healing the world) 120, 144, 163, 166, 189, 195, 256, 298, 299, 301, 302
Yishuo 易說 207, 327
yixin chuanxin 以心傳心 (mind-to-mind transmission) 22, 268, 300, 301
Yixing juji 一行居集 138, 139
yoga 2, 310
Yongle 永樂 (Ming emperor, re. 1402-1424) 54, 156
Yongming Yanshou 永明延壽 (904-975) 59
Yongzheng 雍正 (emperor, re. 1722-1735) 233, 234, 235, 236, 237, 238, 239, 245, 246, 249, 256, 257, 259
Yongzheng emperor's tolerance edict 233–234
Yoshioka, Yoshitoyo 40, 47, 112, 116, 144, 148, 180, 182
You Tong 尤侗 (1618-1704) 186
Youzui fachan 宥罪法懺 158
Yü, Chün-fang 236
Yuan dynasty (1281-1367) 9, 10, 44, 51, 52, 66, 87, 93, 103, 105
Yuan Jiuyang 袁九陽 (fl. 1728) 86
Yuanmen 元門 (= Xuanmen 玄門) 140
yuanqi 元氣 (original Qi) 183, 217
yuanshen 元神 (original spirit) 269
Yuanshi 元史 (History of the Yuan) 9, 28, 31

Yuanshi dadongyu jing 元始大洞玉經 151, 198, 327
Yuanshi tianwang 元始天王 126, 252
Yuanshi tianzun 元始天尊 (Celestial Worthy of Original Commencement) 101, 133–135, 145, 202, 222
Yuanshi wuliang duren shangpin miaojing neiyi 元始無量度人上品妙經內義 141
Yuanshi wuliang duren shangpin miaojing sizhu 元始无量度人上品妙經四注 141, 327
Yuanyangzi fayu 原陽子法語 128, 145, 327
yuanzhong 緣中 (focusing on the center) 269
Yuasa, Yasuo 定方昭夫 310, 313
yudi dafa 玉帝大法 (Great Law of the Jade Emperor) 113
Yugang 鬱岡 79, 81, 82
Yuguang puzhao tianzun 玉光普照天尊 136, 138, 139
Yuhang 餘杭 (modern Hangzhou) 54
Yuhuang benxing jijing 玉皇本行集經 134, 198, 327
Yuhuang benxing jijing chanwei 玉皇本行集經闡微 198
Yuhuang dadi 玉皇大帝 136
Yuhuang shangdi 玉皇上帝 198, 202
yulu 語錄 (Recorded Sayings) 54, 76, 135, 139, 141, 150, 157, 169, 186, 187, 233, 235–238, 242, 319, 326–328
Yulu daguan 語錄大觀 139, 207, 327
Yunji qiqian 雲笈七籤 (Seven Tablets in a Cloudy Satchel) 109, 111, 128, 203, 327
Yunnan 雲南 71, 72, 77
Yuqing Wenchang baochan 玉清文昌寶懺 225
Yuqing zanhua jiutian yanzheng xinyin baochan 玉清贊化九天演政心印寶懺 195
Yuqing zanhua jiutian yanzheng xinyin jijing 玉清贊化九天演政心印集經 195
Yuqingtan yulu 玉清壇語錄 139
Yuquan yulu 玉詮語錄 139, 186, 187, 327
Yuquan 玉詮 111, 136, 138, 139, 140, 186, 187, 327
Yushu baojing 玉樞寶經 107, 207, 327
Yutan 玉壇 (Jade Altar, Suzhou) 138, 139, 140
Yutang dafa 玉堂大法 110
Yutanji 玉壇記 138, 139
Yuxuan Dangjin fahui 御選當今法會 237

Yuxuan yulu 御選語錄 (Imperially Selected Recorded Sayings) 233, 235, 236, 237, 238

Yuxuan Yunqi Lianchi Hong Zhu dashi yulu 御選雲棲蓮池宏袾大師語錄 236

Z

Zangwai daoshu 藏外道書 (Daoist scriptures not contained in the Daoist Canon) 5, 91, 188–193, 195, 206, 225, 243, 327

Zarathustra 263, 264

Zeng Zhao 曾釗 (1793-1854) 20, 224

Zhan Shouchun 詹守椿 72, 79

Zhan Tailin 詹太林 (1625-1712) 70, 75, 77, 78, 79–86, 115, 321

Zhan Yiyang 詹怡陽 69, 83

Zhang Bizhi lüshi zhuan 張碧芝律師傳 43

Zhang Boduan 張佰端 (ca. 983-ca. 1082) 235, 236

Zhang Chaozhong 張超中 314

Zhang Dechun 張德純 (fl.1312-1367; Longmen Vinaya line, second generation) 16, 22, 26, 28, 37, 43–47, 94

Zhang Guangbao 23, 34, 41, 156

Zhang Guo 張果 188

Zhang Hongren 張洪仁 (1624-1667; 53rd Celestial Master) 69, 80

Zhang Huisheng 張慧生 (?-1840) 85, 86

Zhang Jingding 張靜定 (fl. 1450; fifth generation Longmen Vinaya line) 16, 51, 52, 54–57

Zhang Jingxu 張靜虛 (1432?- ?; Wudangshan line) 16

Zhang Kanzhen 張坎真 274–276, 278, 279, 287

Zhang Langran 張朗然 (?-1807?) 85, 86

Zhang Mayi 張麻衣 62–64

Zhang Sanfeng 張三丰 3, 208, 242, 245, 247, 290–292

Zhang Sanfeng xiansheng quanji 張三丰先生全集 242, 245

Zhang Shuang'an 張爽菴 265, 279, 280, 290–292

Zhang Wanfu 張萬福 (fl. 713) 109, 121, 136

Zhang Wuwo lüshi zhuan 張無我律師傳 54

Zhang Xianyue 張賢岳 (1849–?) 130

Zhang Yuanhe 張元和 225

Zhang Yucai 張羽材 (Celestial Master, r. 1295–1316) 163

Zhang Yuchu 張宇初 (43rd Celestial Master) 11, 251, 254

Zhang Zehong 張澤洪 119, 120, 166, 167

Zhang Ziyang 張紫陽 274

Zhangliang miao 張良廟 (Liuba 留壩, Shaanxi) 161–162
Zhanran Hui 湛然慧 (Zhanran Huizhen zi 湛然慧真子) 269, 307, 309, 313, 314
Zhao Daojian 趙道堅 (1163-1221; Longmen Vinaya line, first generation) 8, 16–18, 20–23, 26, 29, 32, 34, 37, 39, 43, 50, 85, 147
 and Longmen generational poem 39–42
 biographical sources 17–19
 nineteenth-century biographies 20–26
Zhao Fuyang 趙復陽 57, 63, 66, 82, 99, 102, 147, 160
Zhao Fuyang lüshi zhuan 趙復陽律師傳 57
Zhao Xujing lüshi zhuan 趙虛靜律師傳 17, 18, 20, 42, 328
Zhao Yizhen 趙宜真 (d. 1382) 11, 128, 155
Zhao Zhensong 趙真嵩 (fl. 1522/1628?; Longmen Vinaya line, sixth generation) 16, 57–60, 62, 63
Zhao Zongcheng 趙宗誠 179, 184, 245
Zhaolian 昭槤 (1776-1830) 206
Zhejiang 5, 54, 55, 57, 58, 71, 72, 76, 92, 188, 194, 235, 296, 303, 320
Zhengao 真誥 80, 203
Zhengming dashi 證明大師 (confirmation master) 114
Zhengyi weiyi jing 正一威儀經 109
Zhengyi 正一 (Orthodox Unity) 2, 4, 10, 11, 48, 49, 109, 111, 119, 121, 126, 138, 149, 150, 152, 159, 163, 164, 166, 167, 170, 172, 259
Zhenping xianzhi 鎮平縣志 (Gazetteer of Zhenping county; 1876) 29, 328
Zhenquan 真詮 140, 186, 187, 203
zhenren jiege 真人戒果 113
Zhenxian zhizhi yulu 真仙直指語錄 157, 328
zhiguan 止觀 (śamatha-vipaśyanā) 268, 269
Zhihui guanshen sanbai dajie 智慧觀身三百大戒 111
Zhihui jie 智慧戒 110, 111
Zhihui song 智慧頌 (Hymn to wisdom) 126
Zhijiao zongzhi 至教宗旨 (Tenet of the Tradition of Ultimate Teaching) 295, 296
Zhiqiu 志秋 (i.e., Fan Ao 范鏊, fl. 1780-1803) 211, 267, 285, 291–292
zhonghuang 中黃 (Yellow Center) 269
Zhongji jie 中極戒 (intermediate precepts) 12, 22, 41, 94–97, 107–117, 120, 126–128, 131, 134, 152, 155, 158, 294, 328
 and the Shangqing dongzhen zhihui guanshen dajie wen 上清洞真智慧觀身大戒文 155–156
Zhongji Shangqing dongzhen zhihui guanshen dajie jing 中極上清洞真智慧觀身大戒經 126

Zhongli Quan 鍾離權 201, 204, 206, 212, 215, 216, 221
Zhongnan shan Zuting xianzhen neizhuan 終南山祖庭仙真內傳 (Inner biographies of the immortals and perfected of the Ancestral Court in the Zhongnan mountains) 19, 23, 34
Zhongxue cantong 中學參同 307
Zhou Defeng 周德鋒 116
Zhou Tailang 周太朗 (1628-1711; united Longmen Doctrinal & Vinaya lines) 16, 161
Zhou Weixin 周維新 307
Zhou Xuanpu 周玄朴 (fl. 1450?; fourth generation Longmen Vinaya line) 16, 49, 50, 50–53, 55
Zhu Gui 朱珪 (1732-1806) 190, 303
Zhu Jiuhuan 朱九還 295, 297, 298
Zhu Quan 朱權 (fl. 1444) 159
Zhu Taihe 朱太和 (1562-1622) 16
Zhu Wenzao 朱文藻 320
Zhu Yicun 朱彝尊 (1629–1709) 30
Zhu Yueli 朱越利 181
Zhu Ziming 朱自明 (fl. 1714) 86
Zhuang Xing'an 莊惺菴 290–292
Zhuangzi 莊子 20, 55, 56, 202, 268
    Commentary Nanhua jingzhu 南華經注 (by Lou Jinyuan) 64, 113
Zhuhong 袾宏 (1533–1615) 235, 236
Zhuxi 朱熹 (1130-1200) 203
Zhuzhen zongpai zongbu 諸真宗派總簿 (Comprehensive Register of all Genuine Lineages) 286
Ziqi 子綦 55
ziran 自然 (self-so) 21, 37
Zitonggong 梓潼宮 (Chengdu) 84, 86, 166
zongshi 宗師 (doctrinal master) 19, 20, 23–25, 30, 82, 322
Zongyang gong 宗陽宮 (Hangzhou) 300
Zou Qingru 鄒清如 84
zuobo 坐缽 (collective meditation) 158, 159, 162
Zuochan fayao 坐禪法要 268
zuting 祖庭 (ancestral hall) 27, 31, 77, 78, 93, 328

Other Books by Monica Esposito

Facets of Qing Daoism
Wil / Paris: UniversityMedia, 2014. 387 p. ISBN 978-3-906000-06-0 (hardcover)
Wil / Paris: UniversityMedia, 2016. 403 p. ISBN 978-3-906000-07-7 (paperback)

This volume contains five major articles by Monica Esposito and a bibliography of all her publications.
The first three articles are revised / augmented versions of "Daoism in the Qing" (2000), "The Longmen School and its Controversial History"(2004), and "Longmen Daoism in Qing China: Doctrinal and Local Reality" (2001, with hitherto unpublished appendix).
The fourth and fifth articles, "The Inverted Mirror: The Vision of Body in Feminine Inner Alchemy" (2004) and "An Example of Daoist and Tantric Interaction during the Qing Dynasty: The Longmen Xizhu Xinzong" (2005) have hitherto only been available in Japanese. Dr Esposito's revised English manuscripts are here published for the first time.

The Zen of Tantra
Wil / Paris: UniversityMedia, 2013. 179 p. ISBN 978-3-906000-25-1 (paperback)

Tibetan Buddhism has a long history in China. Various forms of it were practiced and promoted since the Yuan dynasty (1271-1368), and during the Qing dynasty (1644-1911) it was at times even China's state religion. But the teachings and practices of Tibetan Buddhism known as Great Perfection (Dzogs chen) are only now becoming more widely known. On a journey to an old Daoist site on the Celestial Eye mountains (Mt. Tianmu, Zhejiang) in 1988, Dr Esposito discovered a thriving community of Buddhist nuns in a monastery founded and headed by the Chan (Chinese Zen) and Dzogs chen master Fahai Lama (1920-1991). In documenting this man's life and teachings as well as daily life at his monastery in text and photographs, this book offers a unique glimpse into the reception of Tibetan Buddhist teachings in a nunnery in modern Communist China.

La Porte du Dragon—L'école Longmen du Mont Jin'gai et ses pratiques alchimiques d'après le Daozang xubian

Vol. 1: ISBN 978-3-906000-15-2, PDF. Free download at www.universitymedia.org
Vol. 2: ISBN 978-3-906000-16-9, PDF. Free download at www.universitymedia.org

Monica Esposito's hitherto unpublished two-volume Ph.D. thesis (Université Paris VII, 1993). Searchable PDF format with embedded index and English bookmarks. Includes the original text as well as the author's handwritten corrections and notes.

www.ingramcontent.com/pod-product-compliance
Lightning Source LLC
Chambersburg PA
CBHW031411230426
43668CB00007B/273